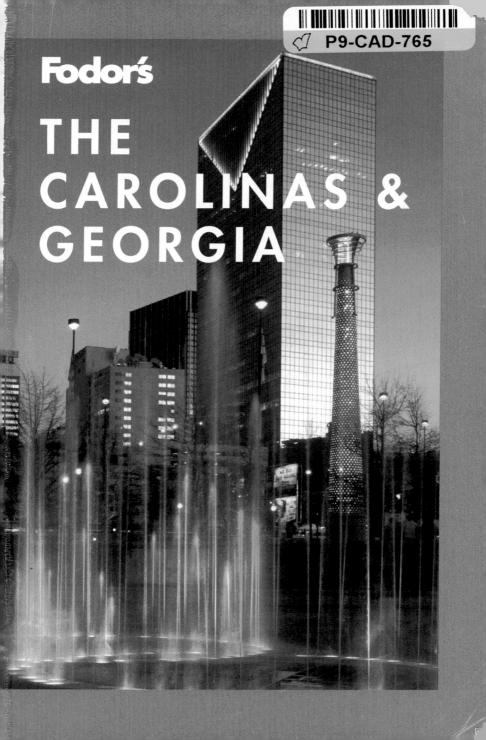

P9-CAD-765

Fodor's

THE
CAROLINAS &
GEORGIA

WELCOME TO THE CAROLINAS & GEORGIA

The Carolinas and Georgia unite the best of the Old South's charms with the New South's cosmopolitan verve. Tour antebellum mansions in Charleston or stroll beneath the Spanish moss-draped live oaks of Savannah. Experience the buzz of Atlanta's nightlife or the roar of Charlotte's Motor Speedway. Outside the cities, secluded barrier islands and the Great Smoky Mountains provide plenty of outdoor recreation, while Hilton Head Island's exclusive resorts make the perfect retreat. Wherever you go, expect a friendly "hey y'all," excellent barbecue, and many glasses of sweet tea.

TOP REASONS TO GO

★ **Southern Food:** Fried chicken, barbecue, shrimp and grits, plus fresh takes on tradition.

★ **Glorious Beaches:** From family-friendly Myrtle Beach to the serene Outer Banks.

★ **Hip Small Towns:** Asheville, Raleigh, Durham, Chapel Hill, Athens, and more.

★ **History:** From plantation homes and Civil War battlefields to Dr. King's legacy.

★ **Outdoors:** Hiking, biking, fishing, scenic drives, and lovely gardens to explore.

★ **Southern Culture:** Slow down and sit a spell—Southern hospitality is infectious.

Fodor's THE CAROLINAS & GEORGIA

Editorial: Douglas Stallings, *Editorial Director*; Salwa Jabado and Margaret Kelly, *Senior Editors*; Alexis Kelly, Jacinta O'Halloran, and Amanda Sadlowski, *Editors*; Teddy Minford, *Associate Editor*; Rachael Roth, *Content Manager*

Design: Tina Malaney, *Associate Art Director*

Photography: Jennifer Arnow, *Senior Photo Editor*

Maps: Rebecca Baer, *Senior Map Editor*; Mark Stroud (Moon Street Cartography) and David Lindroth, *Cartographers*

Production: Jennifer DePrima, *Editorial Production Manager*; Carrie Parker, *Senior Production Editor*; Elyse Rozelle, *Production Editor*; David Satz, *Director of Content Production*

Business & Operations: Chuck Hoover, *Chief Marketing Officer*; Joy Lai, *Vice President and General Manager*; Stephen Horowitz, *Head of Business Development and Partnerships*

Public Relations: Joe Ewaskiw, *Manager*

Writers: Michele Foust, Chanté LeGon, Stratton Lawrence, Sally Mahan, Rachel Quartarone, Summer Teal Simpson Hitch, Lan Sluder, Kristen Wile

Editors: Amanda Sadlowski, Alexis Kelly, Jacinta O'Halloran

Production Editor: Carrie Parker

Production Design: Liliana Guia

Copyright © 2018 by Fodor's Travel, a division of Internet Brands, Inc.

Fodor's is a registered trademark of Internet Brands, Inc. All rights reserved. Published in the United States by Fodor's Travel, a division of Internet Brands, Inc. No maps, illustrations, or other portions of this book may be reproduced in any form without written permission from the publisher.

22nd Edition

ISBN 978-0-14-754696-8

ISSN 1525–5832

All details in this book are based on information supplied to us at press time. Always confirm information when it matters, especially if you're making a detour to visit a specific place. Fodor's expressly disclaims any liability, loss, or risk, personal or otherwise, that is incurred as a consequence of the use of any of the contents of this book.

PRINTED IN THE UNITED STATES OF AMERICA

10 9 8 7 6 5 4 3 2 1

CONTENTS

Fodor's Features

MAPS

ABOUT THIS GUIDE

Fodor's Recommendations

Everything in this guide is worth doing—we don't cover what isn't—but exceptional sights, hotels, and restaurants are recognized with additional accolades. Fodor's Choice★ indicates our top recommendations. Care to nominate a new place? Visit Fodors.com/contact-us.

Trip Costs

We list prices wherever possible to help you budget well. Hotel and restaurant price categories from **$** to **$$$$** are noted alongside each recommendation. For hotels, we include the lowest cost of a standard double room in high season. For restaurants, we cite the average price of a main course at dinner or, if dinner isn't served, at lunch. For attractions, we always list adult admission fees; discounts are usually available for children, students, and senior citizens.

Hotels

Our local writers vet every hotel to recommend the best overnights in each price category, from budget to expensive. Unless otherwise specified, you can expect private bath, phone, and TV in your room. For expanded hotel reviews visit Fodors.com.

Top Picks		Hotels & Restaurants	
★ Fodor'sChoice		🖅	Hotel
		⬎	Number of rooms
Listings		🍽	Meal plans
✉	Address	✕	Restaurant
✉	Branch address	⚓	Reservations
☎	Telephone	🏛	Dress code
🖶	Fax	▭	No credit cards
⊕	Website	$	Price
✉	E-mail		
🎫	Admission fee	**Other**	
⊙	Open/closed times	⇨	See also
Ⓜ	Subway	☞	Take note
⊹	Directions or Map coordinates	🏌	Golf facilities

Restaurants

Unless we state otherwise, restaurants are open for lunch and dinner daily. We mention dress code only when there's a specific requirement and reservations only when they're essential or not accepted.

Credit Cards

The hotels and restaurants in this guide typically accept credit cards. If not, we'll say so.

EUGENE FODOR

Hungarian-born Eugene Fodor (1905–91) began his travel career as an interpreter on a French cruise ship. The experience inspired him to write *On the Continent* (1936), the first guidebook to receive annual updates and discuss a country's way of life as well as its sights. Fodor later joined the U.S. Army and worked for the OSS in World War II. After the war, he kept up his intelligence work while expanding his guidebook series. During the Cold War, many guides were written by fellow agents who understood the value of insider information. Today's guides continue Fodor's legacy by providing travelers with timely coverage, insider tips, and cultural context.

EXPERIENCE
THE CAROLINAS
AND GEORGIA

THE CAROLINAS AND GEORGIA TODAY

The People

No matter who you meet in the Carolinas and Georgia, expect them to be friendly. Folks in this part of the Southeast like to say hello—or rather hey and how y'all doing. Such openness dates back to 18th- and 19th-century plantation days when scattered neighbors in remote, rural areas had only each other to depend on.

But migrations from the Northeast and Midwest in the late 20th century dramatically changed the region's agrarian lifestyle. Coastal and metropolitan areas boomed. The mild climate and reasonable cost of living attracted businesses while retirees and vacationers came seeking leisure, especially golf resorts and seaside and mountain homes. New job opportunities brought people from all over the country and world, allowing diversity to flourish. The region's cities host some of America's best-known colleges, including Duke University in Durham, North Carolina; Emory University in Atlanta, Georgia; and Clemson University in Clemson, South Carolina. Needless to say, college sports rivalries run deep for citizens of this region.

Economy

It used to be that nearly everyone in the Carolinas and Georgia had agricultural ties. Colonists planted the first crops for sustenance, but by the mid-1800s the region's economy depended on cotton and tobacco, and slave labor worked large plantations. Civil War ravages and subsequent Reconstruction forced economic diversity.

Agriculture still characterizes the region—Georgia produces nearly half of America's peanuts and is the nation's leading poultry-producing state—but much larger employers in the region now are government, technology, transportation, retail, manufacturing, education, healthcare, and tourism.

The region also has a number of U.S. military bases. Among them is the country's largest: Fort Bragg in North Carolina, with nearly 54,000 troops. Marine Corps bases like Camp Lejeune, the nation's largest amphibious training base, employ thousands of troops and civilians in North Carolina's coastal plain. Georgia hosts Fort Benning Army base, with more than 27,000 troops. South Carolina houses military complexes, too, most famously the Marine recruit base Parris Island.

Other government employers like the Centers for Disease Control and Prevention in Atlanta help cushion the region from economic downturns. Georgia also ranks high in aerospace exports and is the headquarters of 18 Fortune 500 companies. The state's numerous corporate headquarters include Coca-Cola, UPS, and Delta Airlines in Atlanta. North Carolina's Piedmont is a research and science hub, and Charlotte is a major U.S. banking center. South Carolina claims BMW's only American assembly plant; Michelin's American headquarters; and Boeing South Carolina's assembly plants, as well as research, design, and engineering facilities. Tourism and service industries are important sectors throughout the area too.

Sports

During one week each spring, work slows a bit in many Georgia and Carolinas locations—and bosses don't mind one bit because everyone is drawn to the college basketball craze. This is Atlantic Coast Conference (ACC) country, and when the mighty league hosts its annual March college basketball tournament, fans here have many teams to cheer. Schools in these three states make up nearly half of the ACC's 15 members. North Carolina alone owns the powerhouse UNC Tar Heels (the 2017 NCAA champions), Duke Blue Devils, and Wake Forest Demon Deacons.

The region is represented in the Southern, Southeastern, and Big South conferences, too, and basketball isn't the only hot game. College football is just as significant.

Professional sports are dearly loved too. Tailgaters root for the National Football League's Atlanta Falcons and Carolina Panthers. Mild winters don't deter hockey madness in Raleigh, North Carolina, home to the Carolina Hurricanes, while baseball fans have the Atlanta Braves and hoops-lovers cheer for the National Basketball Association's Atlanta Hawks and Charlotte Hornets.

NASCAR races were born on North Carolina's mountain roads, where drivers ran bootleg whiskey during prohibition. The first NASCAR "strictly stock" car race took place in 1949 in Charlotte. Today, the region boasts major NASCAR tracks Charlotte Motor Speedway in Concord, North Carolina; Atlanta Motor Speedway in Atlanta, Georgia; and Darlington Raceway in Darlington, South Carolina. Charlotte's 150,000-square-foot NASCAR Hall of Fame features 18 historic cars.

Golf lovers relish the region's hundreds of courses, some of the world's most challenging. Pinehurst in North Carolina has staged more golf championships than any other American golf resort and hosted the 2014 U.S. Open and U.S. Women's Open (the U.S. Open is scheduled to return there in 2024). The Masters Golf Tournament is played annually in Augusta, Georgia.

Cuisine

Early explorers arriving in what would become the Carolinas and Georgia found Native Americans eating corn, beans, pecans, and seafood. These humble foods, combined with imported ingredients, shaped the regional cuisine and inspired cooks to create distinctive local fare.

Soul food and Southern cooking can be found throughout the area, but Georgia's rich African American culture may lay claim to fried chicken. Slaves brought deep-fat frying to the area, along with many favorites like candied yams and stewed collards with cornbread. African and Caribbean influences also season Lowcountry cuisine, associated mainly with South Carolina's shore but stretching south to Savannah, Georgia, and north to Wilmington, North Carolina. Bountiful seafood and coastal rice plantations provided ingredients for famous dishes like shrimp and grits, she-crab soup, and the rice-and-black-eyed-pea dish named hoppin' John.

Barbecue debates rage in North Carolina. Westerners prefer tomato-based sauce while Easterners want vinegar-based sauce. Everyone agrees on one thing: barbecue means pork butts, pork shoulders, or whole hogs roasted slowly over a wood or charcoal fire and then shredded or "pulled" after cooking.

Each state also claims popular foodstuffs. Coca-Cola was invented in Georgia, Pepsi in North Carolina, and Firefly Iced Tea Vodka in South Carolina. North Carolina is also home to Cheerwine and Krispy Kreme.

WHAT'S WHERE

The following numbers refer to chapters in the book.

2 The North Carolina Coast. Nothing in the region compares with the Outer Banks. This thin band of barrier islands with wind-twisted oaks and gnarled pines has some of the East Coast's best beaches.

3 Central North Carolina. The New South comes alive in three major metropolitan centers: Charlotte; the Triangle, which consists of Raleigh, Durham, and Chapel Hill; and the Triad, which consists of Greensboro, Winston-Salem, and High Point. Shopping, dining, and nightlife abound. Sports get top billing here, from college football games to NASCAR races.

4 Asheville and the North Carolina Mountains. Western North Carolina is home to more than 1 million acres of stupendous vertical scenery. In addition to opportunities for outdoor adventures, visitors find edgy art galleries and sophisticated eateries in Asheville. The nation's largest privately owned residence, the Biltmore Estate, sits nearby and welcomes tourists.

5 Great Smoky Mountains National Park. Eleven million visitors annually can't be wrong; while the Smokies is the most visited of the national parks, there is more than enough beauty and deserted woodland for peaceful communion with nature.

6 Myrtle Beach, SC, and the Grand Strand. South Carolina's Grand Strand, a 60-mile-long expanse of white, sandy beach, offers varied pleasures: the quiet refuge of Pawleys Island and its sometimes shabby, often elegant summer homes; Brookgreen Gardens, with its magnificent sculptures and landscaped grounds; dozens of golf courses; and the bustle of Myrtle Beach.

7 Charleston, SC. Charleston anchors the Lowcountry in high style. The city's past, dating to 1670, is evident in cobblestone streets, antebellum mansions and plantations, and Gullah accents. It also hosts the renowned Spoleto performing arts festival. Lately, Charleston has garnered a reputation as a foodie hub. The city is home to award-winning chefs, top-rated restaurants, and a celebrated food and wine festival.

8 Hilton Head, SC, and the Lowcountry. The coastal lowlands feature picturesque landscapes of coastal forests and wide-open marshes, undisturbed beaches, and quaint fishing villages. Hilton Head Island is home to 25 world-class golf courses and even more resorts, hotels, and top restaurants.

1

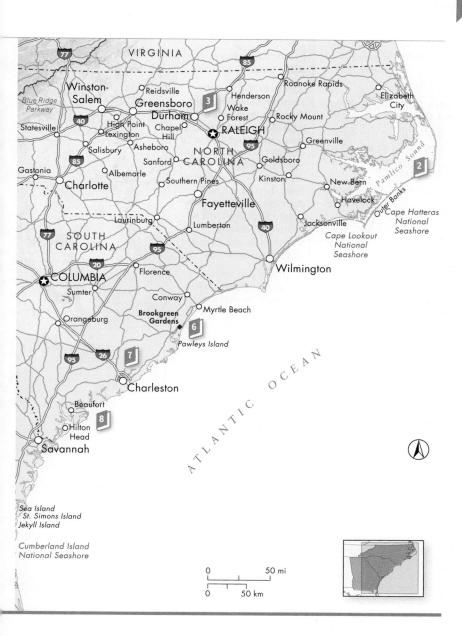

VIRGINIA

77

85

Winston-Salem
Reidsville
Greensboro
Durham
3
Henderson
Roanoke Rapids
Wake Forest
Elizabeth City

Blue Ridge Parkway
40
High Point
Lexington
Chapel Hill
RALEIGH
Rocky Mount

Statesville
Salisbury
Asheboro
95
Greenville

NORTH CAROLINA

85
Albemarle
Sanford
Goldsboro
Pamlico Sound
2

Gastonia

Charlotte
Southern Pines
Kinston
New Bern
Outer Banks

Fayetteville
Havelock

Laurinburg
Lumberton
40
Jacksonville
Cape Hatteras National Seashore

77
SOUTH CAROLINA
95
Cape Lookout National Seashore

20
COLUMBIA
Florence
Wilmington

Sumter
Conway

Orangeburg
Brookgreen Gardens
Myrtle Beach

95
26
7
6
Pawleys Island

Charleston
ATLANTIC OCEAN

Beaufort

8
Hilton Head

Savannah

Sea Island
St. Simons Island
Jekyll Island

Cumberland Island National Seashore

0   50 mi

0   50 km

WHAT'S WHERE

9 The Midlands and the Upstate, SC. Radiating out from Columbia, South Carolina's engaging capital, the area's small towns have their claims to fame: Aiken is a national equestrian center; Camden is the place to go for well-priced antiques; Abbeville is steeped in Civil War history.

10 Savannah, GA. Georgia's oldest and grandest city, Savannah is known for its elegant mansions, Spanish moss, and summer heat. It has more than 1,200 restored or reconstructed buildings dating from 1733.

11 Georgia's Coastal Isles and the Okefenokee. Stretching south from Savannah, Georgia's coastal isles are "almost Florida" but more appealing. The Cumberland Island National Seashore—with more than 120 wild horses—and the wild and mysterious Okefenokee Swamp (home to alligators, bears, and more) are must-sees. Upscale visitors favor Sea Island, while St. Simons Island and Jekyll Island have something for everyone.

12 Southwest Georgia. The serenity of this quiet corner of Georgia has been thoroughly enjoyed by two U.S. presidents. Franklin Delano Roosevelt had a summer home, the Little White House, in Warm Springs. Jimmy Carter, a Plains native, returned there to begin work as one of America's most active former presidents.

13 Atlanta, GA. Georgia Aquarium, World of Coca-Cola, High Museum of Art, great shopping, and restaurants keep visitors busy in the capital of the New South. The Martin Luther King Jr. National Historic Site and the National Center for Civil and Human Rights bring to life Atlanta's racially divided past and its ties to the civil rights movement, as well as human rights efforts worldwide.

14 Central and North Georgia. Stretching from Augusta to Macon, Central Georgia lies at the heart of the Old South. White-column mansions and shady verandas evoke a romanticized past. The pace picks up in Athens, home to the University of Georgia. Near Dahlonega, site of America's first gold rush, vineyards now produce new "gold" for the region. In the northwest, walk the hallowed ground of Chickamauga, the site of one of the Civil War's bloodiest battles.

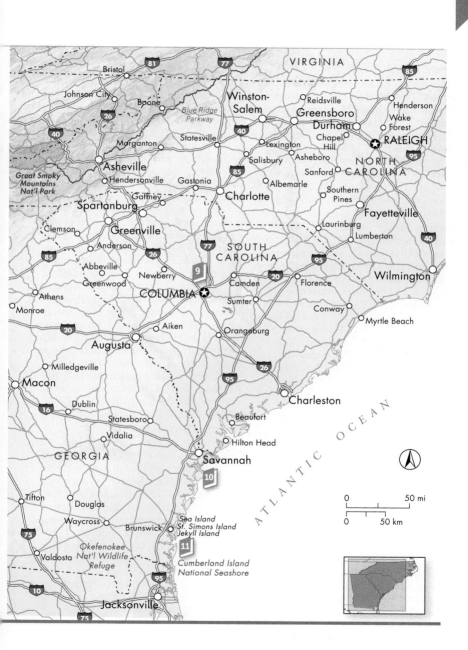

CAROLINAS AND GEORGIA PLANNER

When to Go

Spring is the best time to see the Carolinas and Georgia in bloom. Fall can bring spectacular foliage in the mountains and stunning coastal sunsets. Spring and fall daytime temperatures are delightful; bring a jacket for cool nights. Summer is hot and humid, especially along the coast. In winter, mild weather is punctuated by brief bouts of cold. Short afternoon thunderstorms are common in spring and summer.

Getting Here

Due to the sheer number of flights into Hartsfield-Jackson Atlanta International Airport (ATL), it's often the most logical, if hectic, choice for the region's south end. Flying here means navigating a crowded airport and Atlanta's notorious traffic snarls. If you are staying in Atlanta, especially in Downtown, Midtown, or Buckhead, consider taking the MARTA train from the airport to your hotel. Charlotte Douglas International Airport (CLT) in North Carolina is a good option for travelers heading to both Carolinas. Raleigh-Durham International Airport (RDU) is in the heart of the state, making it convenient for North Carolina's eastern and central areas. Asheville Regional Airport (AVL) provides access to the mountains and adjoining areas. Piedmont Triad International Airport (GSO) serves Greensboro, Winston-Salem, and High Point. For links to these airports, the airlines that serve them, and more, go to ⊕ *www. airlineandairportlinks.com.*

Getting Around

Driving is the best way to get around this part of the country, although there is bus and train service between major cities. Once in the region, major highways—such as Interstates 75, 85, 20, 40, and 95—lead to major cities and many other destinations. For beachgoers, the route to hit is U.S. Highway 17, which hugs the coast of the Carolinas to Savannah, Georgia. In the mid-Carolinas, Interstates 40 and 77 are important connectors. Especially around big cities such as Charlotte and Atlanta, plan your trips to avoid rush hours. If staying in town, check with your hosts for expected road conditions, even on the weekends, when concerts, ball games, and special events can delay traffic. In Georgia, the Department of Transportation's Georgia Navigator (⊕ *www.georgia-navigator.com*) provides real-time traffic data, including trip times and construction and accident information on major highways statewide. Myrtle Beach, South Carolina, is likely to feel the effects of travelers jamming in on Highway 17 during holiday weekends. Sports fans rush into college towns such as Clemson, South Carolina; Athens, Georgia; Chapel Hill and Raleigh, North Carolina; and Atlanta, Georgia, during big game days. Come equipped with GPS or maps.

Beat the Heat

Southerners like to say, "It's not the heat, it's the humidity." From late June to September's end, high temperatures and humidity can take your breath away. Don't let the weather dampen your fun. Plan plenty of indoor, air-conditioned breaks. Be prepared, too, by packing hats, sunblock, water bottles, UVB-blocker sunglasses, and lots of light-color and lightweight clothing. And remember, summer heat and moisture means mosquitoes, too—carry insect repellent or wear clothing that will protect you from bites, especially at dusk.

Festivals

Celebrate Southern culture at festivals that happen throughout the year. Join North Carolina's great barbecue debate in October by sampling western-style pork barbecue with tomato-based sauce at **Lexington's Barbecue Festival.** In April (sometimes late March) head to the coast for eastern-style 'cue with vinegar-based sauce at the **Newport Pig Cookin' Contest** in Newport, North Carolina. During Macon, Georgia's **International Cherry Blossom Festival** in March, the city's more than 300,000 cherry trees glow pink and white. Beaufort, South Carolina's **Gullah Festival** on the May weekend before Memorial Day highlights fine arts, customs, language, and dress of Lowcountry African Americans. Find out more about the region's festivals at ⊕ *www.southfest.com.*

Visitor Information

Whether you want to attend a festival, take a winery tour, hike a mountain trail, explore the many Civil War sites that dot the Carolinas and Georgia, or just laze on the beach and contemplate your sandy toes, state tourism agencies are available to help plan your vacation.

Georgia Tourism. ☎ *800/847–4842* ⊕ *www. exploregeorgia.org.*

North Carolina Division of Tourism. ☎ *800/847–4862* ⊕ *www.visitnc.com.*

South Carolina Department of Parks, Recreation, and Tourism. ☎ *866/224–9339* ⊕ *www.discoversouthcarolina.com.*

Food and Drink

Sweet tea, made by dissolving cupfuls of sugar in hot orange pekoe tea and then adding ice, is the aptly named universal beverage of the South. Half-and-half simply means half sweet tea, half unsweet.

Many Southern restaurants offer **meat-and-three** menus: your choice of a meat or seafood main accompanied by three sides.

Whenever possible, order **biscuits,** so light they seem as if they could float on air. Smother them with butter and molasses or sausage gravy.

Boiled peanuts, found at roadside stands and country stores, are nothing like their roasted Virginia cousins. The texture is akin to boiled beans. The peanuts are served hot or cold, salty and wet, many times packed in their juice.

NORTH CAROLINA TOP ATTRACTIONS

Cape Hatteras National Seashore

(A) The mighty Atlantic Ocean meeting a 70-mile ribbon of sand composes one of America's most beautiful beaches. Find some of the country's best fishing, surfing, and seaside strolling, not to mention maritime history. Three lighthouses mark the coast, including the Cape Hatteras Lighthouse, the nation's tallest brick beacon, and Ocracoke Lighthouse, the second-oldest operating U.S. lighthouse.

Airlie Gardens, Wilmington

(B) Southern hospitality and flowery scents fill this 67-acre garden dating to1886. A wealthy industrialist's wife planted it to accommodate her many guests and lavish parties. The estate features more than 75,000 azalea cultivars, along with dozens of camellias and magnolias framing two freshwater lakes. The massive circa-1545 Airlie oak tree anchors it all.

North Carolina Museum of Art, Raleigh

(C) Thirty works by French sculptor Auguste Rodin are among the 300-plus European and American artworks, making this museum the leading repository of Rodin's work from Philadelphia to the West Coast. It also houses one of only two American general art museum collections of Jewish ceremonial art. Touring exhibitions have ranged from Michelangelo Merisi da Caravaggio's dramatic realism to Norman Rockwell's feel-good Americana.

Duke Chapel, Durham

(D) Stone piers, pointed arches, and flying buttresses delight architectural history buffs, but this medieval-looking Duke University centerpiece is more modern than it looks. The neo-Gothic chapel was built in the 1930s using 17 shades of stone from a nearby quarry, and the bell tower rises 210 feet.

Old Salem Museum and Gardens, Winston-Salem

(E) One of the nation's most well-documented colonial sites comes to life at a 100-acre complex of heirloom gardens and 82 original and reconstructed buildings. Costumed interpreters and craftsmen demonstrate daily life at this former backcountry trading center founded in 1766. Learn about Moravian settlers and then head to the shops for samples of their superthin spice cookies.

Biltmore Estate, Asheville

(F) Much of America's largest privately owned home and its gardens are open to the public. The French Renaissance château was built in the 1890s. Exquisite art and antiques that the Vanderbilts collected fill the home's 250 rooms. Frederick Law Olmsted, designer of New York's Central Park, landscaped the original 125,000-acre estate, now 8,000 acres, 75 acres of which are formal gardens.

Blue Ridge Parkway

(G) Connecting the Great Smoky Mountains in North Carolina and Shenandoah National Park in Virginia, the parkway is among America's most scenic roadways. Relax and enjoy the view on the meandering 469-mile road, 252 miles of which are in North Carolina. You can stop at 215 scenic overlooks on the parkway.

Levine Museum of the New South, Charlotte

(H) Study central North Carolina's difficult Reconstruction era to flourishing modern times. The 8,000-square-foot Cotton Fields to Skyscrapers interactive exhibit brings visitors into a one-room tenant house and one of the South's first African American hospitals. The museum also hosts historic Charlotte walking tours in May.

SOUTH CAROLINA
TOP ATTRACTIONS

Brookgreen Gardens, Murrells Inlet
This idyllic public sculpture garden—America's oldest—showcases 1,400 pieces of American sculpture in outstanding outdoor garden galleries. Daniel Chester French, Frederic Remington, and Anna Hyatt Huntington pieces are on display. Plus, the Lowcountry Zoo is kid-friendly.

Spoleto Festival USA, Charleston
(A) Elegant Charleston becomes an entertainment paradise for more than two weeks each May and June. Dance, opera, theater, and music events—from symphony to rap—have been filling churches, auditoriums, and open-air sites since the festival's 1977 debut.

Broadway Grand Prix Family Race Park, Myrtle Beach
(B) Experience high-speed thrills in NASCAR replica cars you get to drive. Choose from seven tracks, some slick, some winding, some with high banking. Even kids

get to take the wheel. When everyone's done driving, mini-golf, bumper cars, and carnival rides supply the fun.

Old Slave Mart Museum, Charleston
(C) Likely South Carolina's only existing slave market building on one of the city's last cobblestone streets, the circa-1859 structure offers a poignant look at a horrific part of U.S. history. The complex includes a kitchen, a morgue, and the jail where slaves were held before public auctions. A museum recounts the lives of people who passed through the market.

Battery Park, Charleston
(D) This promenade affords lovely Charleston Harbor views, the city's most beautiful historic mansions, White Point Gardens' massive live oaks, and views of Fort Sumter, where the Civil War's first shot was fired. Along the way you'll also see the Civil War prison Castle Pinckney, the Revolutionary War's Fort Moultrie, and the World War II aircraft carrier USS *Yorktown*.

Middleton Place, Charleston

(E) America's oldest landscaped garden, begun in 1741, is a fairy-tale setting where peacocks roam acres of camellias, magnolias, azaleas, and roses. Swans glide on pools, and terraced lawns overlook butterfly-wing-shape lakes. The Civil War claimed the main mansion, but gentleman guest quarters contain some of the Middletons' original furnishings. Garden wine tastings and a fine Lowcountry restaurant add contemporary panache.

St. Helena Island

(F) The heart of Gullah culture is a starting point for anyone interested in Lowcountry history. Penn Center, the South's first school for freed slaves, today is a museum that explains the area's past. Residents here still speak their native tongue and use hand-tied nets to harvest shrimp.

Congaree Swamp National Park, Hopkins

(G) High bluffs border this 22,200-acre South Carolina park. Some of the oldest and largest trees in the southeastern United States fill America's biggest, old-growth, bottomland hardwood forest. Miles of hiking and canoe trails ensure views of varied wildlife, even wild boar. Primitive camping is available, and naturalists lead evening tours into the dark, creepy forest.

Riverbanks Zoo and Garden, Columbia

(H) Siberian tigers, siamang apes, lemurs, giraffes, koalas, and zebras are among more than 2,000 animals that roam natural habitats. More than 4,200 native and exotic species fill five separate gardens, including one dedicated to old roses. See Civil War ruins here, too.

GEORGIA
TOP ATTRACTIONS

The Georgia Aquarium, Atlanta

(A) Breathtaking beluga whales and whale sharks, the largest fish on the planet, reside at the largest aquarium in the Western Hemisphere. Pass through the 100-foot-long underwater tunnel to see thousands of saltwater creatures, from sharks to manta rays. The 10-million-gallon aquarium, home to more aquatic life than any other aquarium, also has sea lions, otters, penguins, and a coral reef with tropical fish.

MLK National Historic District, Atlanta

(B) Make a pilgrimage to Atlanta's Sweet Auburn neighborhood to learn about Dr. Martin Luther King Jr.'s role in the civil rights movement. King's tomb and that of his wife, Coretta Scott King, are here, as well as a number of Dr. King's personal effects. Take a guided tour of the modest home where King was born, and then visit Ebenezer Baptist Church, where members of the King family preached for three generations.

Chickamauga and Chattanooga National Military Park

(C) Nine thousand acres of preserved and enhanced battlefields honor upward of 34,000 Union and Confederate soldiers killed or injured here in one of the Civil War's bloodiest conflicts. More than 1,400 monuments and historical markers chronicle the September 1863 battles.

Cumberland Island

The largest of Georgia's coastal islands remains a mostly unspoiled wonderland of beaches, lakes, ponds, and maritime forest. Wild horses roam the shore. Stroll sand roads and foot trails in the shade of live oaks.

City Squares and Forsyth Park, Savannah

(D) Twenty-two beautifully landscaped public squares, some with fancy fountains, monuments, and shady resting areas, have historical significance. Five of them lead down Savannah's central

Bull Street to magnificent Forsyth Park. Thirty acres include a showy 1858 fountain, Civil and Spanish-American war memorials, a fragrant garden for the blind, and a grand, tree-shaded pedestrian boulevard.

Owens-Thomas House and Museum, Savannah

(E) Considered *the* historic home to see in Savannah, Owens is among the country's finest examples of English Regency architecture. Curving walls, Greek-inspired ornamental molding, half-moon arches, stained glass, and a second-floor, hardwood bridge that spans the stairwell thrill history buffs. Rare, urban slave quarters on the property contain original furnishings and slave-made haint-blue paint, a color folklore claims wards off evil spirits.

Amicalola Falls State Park and Lodge, Dawsonville

(F) The Southeastern United States' tallest waterfall cascades down 729 feet of massive rock steps, which, in the fall, are surrounded by a rainbow display of changing leaf colors. View the beauty from a heart-pumping foot trail or over a relaxing buffet brunch at the park's Maple Restaurant.

Okefenokee National Wildlife Refuge

(G) The famous Okefenokee Swamp is just a small part of this 730-square-mile rugged landscape containing one of the world's largest intact freshwater wetlands. Alligators, otters, bald eagles, and black bears populate the complex's varied landscapes, including bogs where the earth quivers like gelatin.

TOP EXPERIENCES

Eat your way through Charleston

Charleston, South Carolina, has quickly become one of America's foodie hot spots over the past few years. Plan delicious experiences around March's **Charleston Wine + Food Festival,** where more than 20,000 participants, 300 chefs, and 140 beverage pros gather to celebrate Charleston cuisine and watch James Beard Award-winning Charleston chefs, like Sean Brock and Mike Lata, show off their skills. Top-ranked restaurants offer special deals during **Restaurant Week** in the fall. Autumn also brings the **Taste of Charleston** food-sampling fair, while winter means the **Lowcountry Oyster Festival.**

Learn secrets from the vintners

On Georgia's Dahlonega Wine Trail or on tours through the north Georgia wine country, oenophiles savor award-winning wines, walk among the vineyards, admire outstanding views, and hear vintners tell secrets about the grapes. Information flows as easily as fine wines from winemakers such as John Ezzard at **Tiger Mountain Vineyards,** near Clayton. Georgia is home to a total of 55 wineries, with 25 of those located in the north.

Hit a hole in one like a pro

The Southeast is known for outstanding golf courses. While no one but members can play the **Augusta National Golf Course,** longtime home of the Masters Tournament, the hundreds of courses in the region provide ample opportunities to get in some practice. Masters Tournament tickets are rarely available, but Augusta National offers a limited number of Practice Rounds ground passes and Daily Tournament ground passes (these are offered a year in advance and by online application only).

Swim or dive with the fishes

Make a splash at the **Georgia Aquarium,** where you may pay for a swim or dive in the Ocean Voyager's 6.3-million-gallon tank. You'll cavort with whale sharks, manta rays, schools of tarpon, cownose rays, and many more ocean creatures.

Touch the clouds

By car or by trail, check out the clouds and gorgeous scenery at the tip-tops of North and South Carolina and Georgia. Taking top honors is **Mt. Mitchell,** near Burnsville, North Carolina, the highest point east of the Mississippi at 6,684 feet. **Sassafras Mountain,** with an elevation of 3,533 feet, is located in northwestern South Carolina. In Georgia, **Brasstown Bald** near Hiawassee claims the honor at 4,784 feet.

Live like royalty for a day

Tour the luxurious **Biltmore Estate** château and grounds, taste the estate-made wine, and enjoy a meal at one of the estate's restaurants. You can even stay the night on the 8,000-acre property at the **Inn on Biltmore Estate.** A visit during the holiday season means sparkling Biltmore decorations, special events, and live music. Another memorable North Carolina splurge is spending the night at the legendary **Omni Grove Park Inn** in Asheville and enjoying a fine dinner, drinks, and music in front of the massive fireplace in the lobby. Wake up to pampering at the more than 43,000-square-foot spa, featuring swimming and mineral pools, waterfalls, and hot tubs. It's been named one of the country's finest spas.

Take a hike—all the way to Maine

The **Appalachian National Scenic Trail** begins at Springer Mountain in Georgia and meanders more than 2,189 miles north to Maine. Walkers, day hikers, or backpackers can catch portions of the trail in parks and at highways that cross it. Hiking is especially spectacular in the spring, when wildflowers bloom, and fall, when the leaves paint the mountains red, orange, and yellow. If you're just looking for a great photo op featuring a massive AT-engraved rock, head to Dicks Creek Gap, on U.S. 76 near Clayton, Georgia.

Drive like a speed demon

Richard Petty Driving Experience participants can drive a 600-horsepower, NASCAR race car at high speeds around the Charlotte Motor Speedway track in Concord, North Carolina, or they can choose to go along for a ride with an instructor at speeds as high as 165 mph. Laps allowed 'round the track range from 3 to 50, depending on the package selected. The adventure is a hands-on, inside look at the sport from the driver's perspective. For many fans, it's a lifelong dream fulfilled. Reservations are required for driving; ride-alongs are available on a first-come, first-served basis. Ride-along participants may be as young as age six, but they must be accompanied by a parent or legal guardian if younger than 18. Drivers must be at least 16 and have a valid driver's license.

Chill out at the beach

If your preferred beach experience means shag music, tacky T-shirts, and water parks, you'll find all in ample supply at South Carolina's **Myrtle Beach**. Prefer quiet days spent contemplating one of the most beautiful shorelines, looking for dolphins, and shell collecting? Head instead to Georgia's **Jekyll Island**. The Carolinas–Georgia coast has universal appeal. Treat yourself to a truly Southern experience and rent a cottage—or grand home—right on the shore for a vacation retreat.

Go on a shopping spree

Southerners know how to look gorgeous in the most humid weather and to dress their homes to dispense the grandest Southern hospitality. That takes great shopping experience and demand for quality. Check out upscale **King Street** in Charleston for Palm Avenue Lilly Pulitzer, kate spade new york, and antiques and specialty shops aplenty. Atlanta's **Phipps Plaza** and **Lenox Square** are quintessential shopping destinations. **Concord Mills** in Concord, North Carolina, near Charlotte, keeps shoppers more than satisfied with Bass Pro Shops Outdoor World, Polo Ralph Lauren Factory Store, Bose Factory Outlet, VANS outlet, Coach, and Brooks Brothers. **North Georgia Premium Outlets** offers Restoration Hardware, Ann Taylor, Burberry, Armani, and many more.

Explore historic plantations

While the Yankees occupied the small mill town of Roswell, Georgia, in 1864 and burned its cotton and woolen mills, they spared its antebellum mansions, mill workers' homes, and churches on their trek toward the Battle of Atlanta. Today visitors tour a 640-acre historic district. Highlights are three historic homes open daily: **Bulloch Hall**, where Teddy Roosevelt's mother was married; **Barrington Hall**, a stunning Greek Revival home; and the **Archibald Smith Plantation**, once part of a 300-acre cotton farm. Catch weekend ghost tours featuring tales of haunted houses.

IF YOU LIKE

Southern Dining

Although Southerners still thrive on meat-and-three menus, cooking with fresh regional foods and herbs has also caught on in the South.

Bacchanalia, Georgia. Summerland Farm grows organic herbs and produce for use in Anne Quatrano and Clifford Harrison's award-winning Atlanta restaurant.

Elizabeth on 37th, Georgia. On your way into the Greek Revival mansion that houses this Savannah restaurant, you might see the staff snipping herbs that flavor remarkable dishes.

Empire State South, Georgia. In Atlanta, James Beard Award–winning celebrity chef Hugh Acheson puts fresh twists on Southern classics at Empire State South, as well as 5&10, located in Athens.

Lantern, North Carolina. Chapel Hill is home to lauded Lantern, where James Beard Best Chef Southeast Andrea Reusing uses North Carolina ingredients in Asian dishes.

McCrady's, McCrady's Tavern, and Husk, South Carolina. Charleston has become a foodie hub and chef Sean Brock leads the pack with New South cuisine focused on local foods at his restaurant, McCrady's, which offers a tasting menu only, and McCrady's Tavern, which serves lunch, dinner, and weekend brunch. At Husk, Brock features heirloom products and crafts menus throughout each day, depending on what local purveyors bring to his kitchen.

Poole's Diner, North Carolina. Yet another James Beard Award winner, Ashley Christensen, serves seasonally changing menus in a retro-chic setting at this downtown Raleigh restaurant.

Golf

The Carolinas' and Georgia's mild climate allows play all year, and the scenery is as good as the game. Courses abound, but the chance to play top links during high seasons—spring and fall—can be a bigger challenge than getting a hole in one. Resorts and country clubs offer first-choice tee times to guests. If any times are left open, it is possible to get reservations.

Harbour Town Golf Links, South Carolina. In the shadow of the Harbor Town Lighthouse, this course on Hilton Head Island is devilishly difficult. Although deceptively short by today's standards, this top course leaves no room for error.

Kiawah Island Golf Resort's Ocean Course, South Carolina. All 18 holes offer sea views. The greens wind through salt marshes and seaside forests filled with wildlife, including the occasional alligator. This has one of the most dramatic last holes in golf.

Pine Lakes Country Club, South Carolina. Often called the "granddaddy of golf," this has long been a landmark in Myrtle Beach. The clubhouse, resembling an antebellum mansion, was built in 1927.

Pinehurst, North Carolina. Golf legend Bobby Jones called this course "the St. Andrews of United States golf." As the site of more championships than any other golf resort in the country, the resort is consistently ranked among the best in the world. Among its nine courses, the Donald Ross–designed Number Two is considered the masterpiece.

Grand Gardens

The temperate climate in the Carolinas and Georgia, combined with the region's huge diversity of flora, makes this area a draw for garden lovers.

Biltmore Estate, North Carolina. The castle-like grandeur of America's largest privately owned residence has gorgeous grounds designed by Frederick Law Olmsted of New York City's Central Park fame.

Callaway Gardens, Georgia. This superb landscape is part of a resort, but that shouldn't dissuade a visit to this spot in Pine Mountain, Georgia. Its **Overlook Azalea Garden** has some 700 varieties of azaleas, and the **Callaway Brothers Azalea Bowl** has 3,400 native and hybrid azalea plants that should not to be missed in the spring.

Magnolia Plantation and Gardens, South Carolina. One of America's oldest gardens, first planted in the mid-1680s, includes the **Audubon Swamp Garden** traversed with boardwalks and bridges over waters that host, yes, alligators.

Middleton Place, South Carolina. Henry Middleton, First Continental Congress president, began these lush, semitropical gardens in 1741. Restoration of the gardens began during World War I. Today they are among the most beautiful in the world, ablaze with camellias, azaleas, roses, and magnolias.

Civil War History

The Civil War forever changed the South. In the region's many museums, period furnishings offer glimpses into antebellum life, heart-wrenching letters tell of the war's toll on families rich and poor, and photographs show the horror suffered by slaves.

The Atlanta History Center, Georgia. While Atlanta has few preserved battlefields, it boasts one of the largest Civil War artifact and document collections in the world. The center has more than 7,500 original artifacts, with 1,500 on display. They range from weapons and documents to the steam engine *Texas.* The museum is currently in the process of restoring *The Battle of Atlanta,* a massive, 360-degree painting of the Civil War battle, painted in 1886.

Chickamauga and Chattanooga National Military Park and Visitor Center, Georgia. The site of one of the Civil War's worst conflicts, Chickamauga battlefield saw around 34,000 soldiers killed or injured during a three-day struggle in September 1863. North Georgia offers a glimpse into the strategies used by both sides during the campaign. Visitors can take a 7-mile driving tour to see many of the 1,400 monuments and historical markers and take ranger-guided tours during the summer.

Fort Sumter, South Carolina. Although it was built to protect Charleston after the War of 1812, the fort became a symbol of Southern resistance after it hosted the Civil War's first battle. The first shots were fired here on April 12, 1861.

Beaches

From North Carolina's Cape Hatteras to Georgia's Cumberland Island National Seashore, the Carolinas and Georgia have some of the East Coast's best sand and sea. Much of the coastline is preserved, meaning you can still see wild dunes and historic lighthouses between bustling boardwalks and cottage-lined shores.

Cape Hatteras National Seashore, North Carolina. Seventy miles of protected beach stretch from the town of Nags Head to Ocracoke Inlet. See wild dunes, experience some of the country's best fishing, and climb Cape Hatteras Lighthouse, America's tallest brick lighthouse.

Hilton Head Island, South Carolina. World-class golf, tony homes, stylish stores, and hot restaurants may be the markers on this famous island, but it also hosts quiet places to sit by the sea and a network of hiking and biking trails.

Kure Beach and Carolina Beach, North Carolina. Fishing, family fun, and old-fashioned pleasures characterize these two communities on a ribbon of sand named Pleasure Island. The area has the oldest fishing pier on the Atlantic coast, a charter fishing fleet, and carnival rides. The North Carolina Aquarium at Fort Fisher has a 235,000-gallon saltwater tank full of sharks, stingrays, and other fish, all next door to the Civil War–era Fort Fisher State Historic Site.

Sapelo Island, Georgia. Wild, uncrowded beaches keep local traditions alive in this quiet place accessible only by ferry. Listen for locals' native Geechee dialect, a blend of English and West African languages, as you watch crafters make their famous sweetgrass baskets.

Hiking

Load a backpack and head along a challenging mountain trail, take a leisurely walk around a lake, or bang out an urban concrete route. Hiking doesn't always require working up a sweat in the Carolinas and Georgia, but paths always lead to enchanting places.

Asheville Urban Trail, North Carolina. The 1.7-mile walk in this city rewards urban hikers with architecture, historic sites, and restaurants. Pass the Basilica of St. Lawrence, designed by the same architect who drew Biltmore Estate.

Atlanta Beltline, Georgia. The Beltline is a 22-mile urban trail in the making (currently scheduled for full completion in 2030). The popular sections already open include an urban farm and public art displays.

Sesquicentennial State Park, South Carolina. A 30-acre lake centers this park near downtown Columbia, making for a great afternoon of exploring miles of trails with a picnic basket in tow.

Springer Mountain, Georgia. The more than 2,100-mile Appalachian Trail begins here, a few miles north of Amicalola Falls, the tallest cascading waterfall east of the Mississippi River. Ambitious hikers set aside months to hike the entire Appalachian Trail, but you can choose sections for hikes as short as a couple of hours.

Three Waterfalls Loop, North Carolina. This 2.4-mile hike in Great Smoky Mountains National Park has three lovely waterfalls. Don't forget lunch and a bathing suit. There are a picnic area and swimming opportunities along the way.

SOUTHERN SOUNDS

Trace bluegrass, blues, and gospel to the Carolinas and Georgia. Each distinctive genre was nurtured and passed to future generations in the region's homes, churches, and social clubs.

Old-time and Bluegrass

Ballads, fiddles, and pluck-string instruments are well known throughout the region thanks to Africans and Scotch-Irish immigrants in Appalachia. North Carolina's continuing old-time music tradition influenced bluegrass and country. Top performers Doc Watson, Del McCoury, and the famous Earl Scruggs, known for his revolutionary three-finger banjo-plucking style, all were born in North Carolina. The state is a hotbed of music festivals, including late April's famous **MerleFest**, in Wilkesboro, where players gather to honor bluegrass and Appalachian music. **Folkmoot USA** brings folk music and dance to Waynesville during the last two weeks of July.

Gospel to Rhythm and Blues

Spirituals that slaves in the South sang enriched gospel's signature repetitive lyrics and simple tunes, creating soulful songs that define the gospel genre. Georgia natives James Brown and Little Richard fused gospel with blues and boogie-woogie to create soul music and rhythm and blues. In the 1960s, Georgia's Gladys Knight and Otis Redding added strong emotion to their songs, bringing rhythm and blues to the mainstream.

Beach Music

Blues, jazz, big-band swing, R&B, doo-wop, boogie, rockabilly, and old-time rock and roll make up the Carolinas' easygoing Beach Music. Legendary bands like the Tams, the Embers, and Band of Oz supply the sound's shuffle-foot "shag" dance done to titles like "Summertime's Calling Me" and "Under the Boardwalk." Myrtle Beach radio station 94.9 FM plays all Beach Music, and it lists live music shows and other events at its website ⊕ *www.949thesurf.com,* but many stations from North Carolina south to Georgia broadcast Beach Music. Each November, North Myrtle Beach hosts the Carolina **Beach Music Awards,** when bands perform at famous clubs like **Fat Harold's.**

New South Sounds

To find today's Southern sounds, all you have to do is look to the college towns in the Carolinas and Georgia. Athens, Georgia; Chapel Hill, North Carolina; and Columbia, South Carolina, host clubs where Hootie and the Blowfish, Ben Folds Five, R.E.M., and the B-52s got their start. In more recent years, the Avett Brothers formed their punk/bluegrass band in Charlotte, North Carolina. Over the past decade, Atlanta has become the defining center for hip-hop, crunk, and trap music, with Outkast, Lil Jon, Ciara, Ludacris, 2 Chainz, Migos, and Gucci Mane (among many others) all getting their start in the city.

GREAT ITINERARIES

ASHEVILLE AND THE GREAT SMOKY MOUNTAINS

The soft mountain peaks, blue fog, and fall leaves of the Great Smoky Mountains have long inspired painters, writers, and musicians. Art-centric Asheville edges this great American landscape and makes the perfect launch pad for mountain touring. Pack your hiking boots to see the natural beauty up close.

Day 1: Downtown Asheville

Drive into **Asheville** or land at pleasant **Asheville Regional Airport**, one of the South's best small airports, and rent a car. Stay downtown at **Haywood Park Hotel**—the expansive suites are close to the action. Hip Asheville is a center of North Carolina's craft beer and local food movements, so lunch at lively **Lexington Avenue Brewery**, better known as LAB. Pair a beer flight with small plates like green chili pork nachos and mussels fra diavolo in the historic building that was once the city's oldest store. Hit the sidewalks for a look at Asheville's art scene; watch glass artists work and patiently explain their craft at Lexington Glassworks, which also hosts a monthly concert series. Check out incredible architecture at the elaborate bricked and polychrome-tiled **Basilica of St. Lawrence** and **Black Mountain College Museum + Arts Center**. The legendary college nurtured maverick 20th-century artists. Alternately, kick around the architectural wonder that is **Grove Arcade Public Market,** built in 1929. Armies of stone gargoyles guard numerous locally owned stores and restaurants. Make advance reservations for a dinner of extraordinary tapas at **Cúrate,** the hottest restaurant in town, which is partially owned by chef Felix Meana, formerly of the famed elBulli restaurant on the Costa Brava of Spain. Or, if you're craving a meat-and-three Southern meal made with quality local ingredients, head to **Early Girl Eatery.** An early dinner allows time for a show at **Asheville Community Theater,** which stages productions year-round.

Day 2: Great Smoky Mountains
(1½ hours by car)

Rise early to visit one of Asheville's more than 50 tailgate markets, including **Asheville City Market**. Stock up on locally made foods for the ride to **Great Smoky Mountains National Park**. Interstate 40 heading west is the quickest route out of Asheville. Take the highway to U.S. 19, which links to the spectacular **Blue Ridge Parkway** just west of Maggie Valley. The parkway leads into Great Smoky Mountains National Park. At the park entrance, stop by **Oconaluftee Visitor Center** for maps and information. Spend the day exploring by vehicle and by foot. **Newfound Gap Road** (U.S. 441) is one of the park's most scenic drives and leads to **Clingmans Dome Trail**. This moderately difficult 1-mile trail ends at a 54-foot-tall observation tower affording amazing mountain views from the highest point in the Smoky Mountains. The round-trip hike takes about an hour, a nice warm-up before a picnic lunch and then another hike along **Trillium Gap Trail to Grotto Falls.** The 1.3-mile, moderately difficult hike ends at the 30-foot-high falls, the only falls in the park that you can walk behind. Stick around the park for sunset views at **Chimney Tops Overlook.** Camp at the park or depart for two luxurious nights at nearby **Omni Grove Park Inn.** The grand hotel, built in 1913 with locally mined

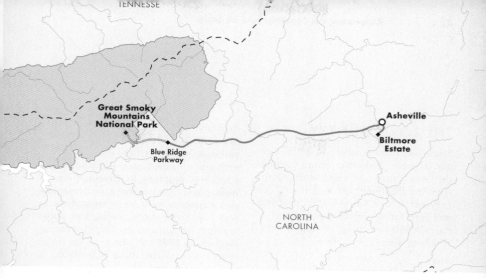

stone, is home to the world's largest collection of Arts and Crafts furniture. The 43,000-square-foot spa offers massages, skin-care treatments, indoor lap pools, outdoor whirlpools, and a subterranean sanctuary to ease tired hiking muscles.

Day 3: Biltmore Estate
(15 minutes by car from Asheville)

Stick around Omni Grove Park Inn for a sunrise breakfast. If the weather is warm, book a day of kayaking, canoeing, or white-water rafting at the Nantahala Outdoor Center, the nation's largest outdoor recreation company. The center also offers mountain biking, hiking, climbing, fishing, and horseback riding adventures in the Blue Ridge and Great Smoky mountains.

If the weather is chilly, set off instead for a morning tour of **Biltmore Estate**, America's largest privately owned home. Built in the 1890s as George Vanderbilt's private residence, this castle of sorts has 250 rooms, including its own bowling alley, and 75 acres of gardens and grounds. Be sure to visit the complex's state-of-the-art winery and tasting rooms. Dine at Village Social Bistro or Cedric's Tavern for lunch.

Spend the late afternoon at the **North Carolina Arboretum**, created by Fredrick Law Olmsted, designer of New York City's Central Park, and part of the original Biltmore Estate. See 65 acres of cultivated gardens and a bonsai exhibit of native trees. You can also explore a 10-mile network of trails.

Biltmore Village boasts many fine eateries, including **Corner Kitchen**. The renovated Victorian cottage has a fireplace in one dining room. The restaurant serves American classics with a twist like pecan-crusted mountain trout with bourbon sauce or Jamaican jerk smoked chicken breast over black beans.

Day 4: Head Home

If you're flying out of Asheville, enjoy breakfast at Omni Grove Park Inn, where window-lined dining rooms provide fantastic views. If you're driving home, check out early and head to downtown Asheville's funky **Tupelo Honey Café** for down-home Southern cooking with an uptown twist. Think house-cured pork belly, goat-cheese grits, and caramelized sweet-onion sauce. Don't forget a souvenir: a slice of Tupelo Honey Café brown-butter pecan pie to go.

THE LOWCOUNTRY

Stretching from genteel Savannah, Georgia, to lively Charleston, South Carolina, the Lowcountry serves up history, culture, stunning coastlines, urban flair, and culinary adventures. Unspoiled natural areas and captivating seaside communities dot the easy 150-mile drive between these two Southern hospitality centers.

Days 1 and 2: Savannah

Drive into **Savannah** or arrive by plane at **Savannah/Hilton Head International Airport** and rent a car. Immerse yourself in the feel of old Savannah with a stay at the elegant but inviting **Foley House Inn,** where you'll be treated to complimentary breakfast, afternoon tea, and evening wine and hors d'oeuvres.

Once refreshed, spend a few leisurely hours strolling Bull Street. Enjoy beautifully landscaped squares and the **Green-Meldrim House,** a Gothic Revival mansion that was General Sherman's headquarters when the Union Army occupied Savannah, then head on to **Forsyth Park.** Massive, moss-draped oaks line wide park lanes leading to war memorials, an old fort, and a magnificent fountain.

For dinner, head to the historic (and supposedly haunted) Olde Pink House in Planters Inn, where you can enjoy cocktails and classic Southern cuisine like fried chicken, mac and cheese, and shrimp and grits.

Savannah's various tours offer fun and easy overviews of the city's rich history. On Day 2, step back in time on a morning horse-drawn history tour with **Carriage Tours of Savannah.** The 50-minute journey winds through the historic district as drivers narrate. Afterward, set out on foot for the **Owens-Thomas House and Museum,** one of America's finest examples of English Regency architecture. Grab lunch at **Angel's BBQ,** a favorite for brisket, pork barbecue, and stewed collard greens laced with peanut butter, a top seller. Spend the afternoon shopping at **Riverfront/Factors Walk,** where a network of iron crosswalks and stairways leads to renovated warehouses hosting shops, cafés, and pubs. Splurge for dinner at award-winning **Elizabeth on 37th;** call ahead to see if the seven-course tasting menu is available.

Day 3: Hilton Head Island
(1 hour by car from Savannah)

Hilton Head Island beaches span 12 miles, offering respite after busy Savannah. **Burkes Beach,** mid-island, is a quiet place to stroll or sunbathe before being pampered at **Spa Montage at Palmetto Bluff,** a 13,000-square-foot full-service spa and hair salon. Soak up more island beauty at **Old Fort Pub.** Tucked under an umbrella of old oaks hung with Spanish moss, the restaurant has near-panoramic views of stunning sunsets and sweeping marshlands, not to mention an impressive wine list and a tasting menu. Classic she-crab soup might share space with prime pork chop with whipped potatoes, French beans, baby apples, onions, ginger, and hard cider sauce. The **Jazz Corner** serves a musical nightcap.

Day 4: St. Helena Island
(1 hour by car from Hilton Head Island)

The Lowcountry is rooted in Gullah culture. The Gullah people, descendants of 18th-century slaves, maintain their dialect and heritage, much of it centered on **St. Helena Island,** where Gullahs still catch shrimp with hand-tied nets. **Penn Center,** the first school for freed slaves, is official Gullah headquarters and part of the Penn School Historic District, which includes old burial grounds and Gantt Cottage,

where Martin Luther King Jr. stayed. At **York W. Bailey Museum**, request to see Gullah indigo stamping, wood-burning art, and sweetgrass basket-making demonstrations. **Gullah Grub** restaurant features authentic Lowcountry cooking.

Days 5 and 6: Charleston
(2½ hours by car from Hilton Head Island)
Charleston's status as the South's foodie capital gives the city a delicious layer of appeal atop all the art, architecture, history, and natural beauty there. Arrive in time for freshly made breakfast crepes and cold-pressed coffee at **Queen Street Grocery**. Walking **Charleston's Historic District** is a great way to see key landmarks such as the 1752 **St. Michael's Episcopal Church**, the city's oldest surviving church, and a National Historic Landmark. For lunch, take a seat at the **Slightly North of Broad** chef's table, which overlooks the kitchen, giving you a view of all that goes into your meal preparation at the lively Lowcountry bistro.

No culinary tour of Charleston is complete without visiting James Beard Award–winning chef Sean Brock's **McCrady's**, **McCrady's Tavern**, and **Husk** restaurants. Book a tasting-menu dinner at McCrady's and lunch the next day at Husk or McCrady's Tavern (which is also open for dinner). All three spots highlight new Southern cooking and local ingredients. Husk also has a reputation for cool cocktails and an amazing weekend brunch. The historic Charleston Light Dragoon's Punch recipe blends California brandy, Jamaican rum, peach brandy, black tea, lemon juice, and raw sugar.

With a Husk lunch reservation secured, spend Day 6 working up an appetite by touring Charleston's magnificent plantations. **Magnolia Plantation Gardens** has a huge array of blooming plants on more than 70 acres of gardens and a rebuilt 19th-century plantation house. **Drayton Hall**, where building began in 1738, is a National Trust Heritage site and the only plantation on the road that is a complete original (the rest were burned during the Civil War). Stunning **Middleton Place** has terraced lawns, butterfly-shaped lakes, and, for dinner, Lowcountry specialties at Middleton Place Restaurant.

After dinner, toast this grande dame of Southern cities at the swanky outdoor Pavilion Bar atop **Market Pavilion Hotel**. Terrific views and creative cocktails make this Charleston's best rooftop bar.

Day 7: Fuel Up for Takeoff
Have breakfast of house-made sausage with fresh ginger pumpkin bread at homespun **Hominy Grill** before catching a flight or driving home.

ATLANTA

Traditional but always forward-looking Atlanta earns its place as the New South's capital. A city that began as a railroad terminus in 1837 grew to become Georgia's cosmopolitan center. Old-school Southern hospitality meets business and industry here. The world's busiest airport and a clean, safe, aboveground rail line called MARTA make Atlanta an easy weekend getaway.

Day 1: Arrive in Atlanta

Landing early at **Hartsfield-Jackson Atlanta International Airport** means plenty of time to dive into Atlanta's thrilling urban scene. Sleek glass, steel, and stone towers and grand city views at **Omni Hotel at CNN Center** set the mood and are close to public transportation. Start with a 50-minute, behind-the-scenes tour of **CNN Center,** but make sure to get reservations at least 24 hours in advance. Next stop: **Georgia Aquarium.** That this landlocked city is home to the largest aquarium in the Western Hemisphere (10 million gallons of water) is testimony to Atlanta's progressive attitude. Take the MARTA metro to Midtown for a contemporary Southern lunch at **JCT Kitchen & Bar.** Billed as a "farmstead bistro" with Southern flair, JCT is the place for deviled eggs with country ham, pimento cheese with serrano chilies, shrimp and grits, and chicken and dumplings. Don't leave Midtown without checking the evening lineup at the **Fox Theatre.** The vintage movie palace built in 1929 is worth seeing for its Moorish-Egyptian style alone. The ceiling has moving clouds and twinkling stars. These days, it's a venue for dance, concerts, musicals, and film festivals. Head back to the hotel to ready for a night on the town, whether it's a Fox Theatre show or one of Midtown's hot clubs. In Midtown, on Crescent Avenue, you'll find **Opera,** a hopping theaterlike dance club with balcony VIP boxes and personal cocktail service. Don your fancy garb here; there's a strict dress code.

Day 2: Art and History
(15 minutes by subway)

Stick around the hotel for breakfast, and then head to the **National Center for Civil and Human Rights** nearby to begin a day of civil-rights-themed touring. It's as notable for its modern architecture as it is for its impressive galleries, one housing some of civil rights leader Dr. Martin Luther King Jr.'s personal papers and effects, and others devoted to human rights campaigns worldwide. Next find your way to Atlanta's **Sweet Auburn** district to tour the area where King was born, raised, and later returned, making Atlanta a center for social change. Sign up early in the day for a guided tour of the **Martin Luther King Jr. National Historic Site and Birth Home,** as a limited number of visitors are allowed to visit the home daily. Nearby **Ebenezer Baptist Church** is where King was baptized and later preached alongside his father. Pay tribute to King and his compatriots at the **King Center,** which houses the Eternal Flame and the Kings' final resting place. Note the inscription on King's white marble tomb: "Free at last, free at last, thank God almighty I'm free at last." Have a late lunch at **Sweet Auburn Curb Market,** named for the days when whites were allowed to sell their goods inside while African Americans had to sell theirs along the curb. Cafés, meats, and fresh produce fill the market.

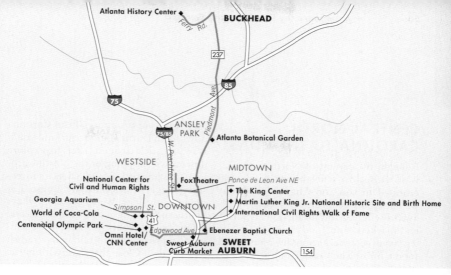

After lunch, make your way to fashionable **Buckhead**. With its history museums, cool shopping, and hot restaurants, the neighborhood is a perfect example of Atlanta's Old South/New South blend. While in Buckhead, visit the **Atlanta History Center,** which focuses on Atlanta, the South, and the Civil War. Its 9,200-square-foot Civil War gallery displays 1,500 of the center's 7,500 war artifacts. Items are as large as a railroad engine and as small as a button. The Kenan Research Center there, offering historical documents, is also open to the public. A period farm and a 1928 mansion are on the 33-acre complex too. Stick around Buckhead for shopping and dinner. Hip **Eclipse di Luna** is a fun place for a glass of wine and shared tapas like duck empanadas, although you may want to hoard your own paella.

Day 3: Brunch and Stroll
(15 minutes by subway)

Rise early for a walk on **Beltline Trail,** which will eventually be a 22-mile loop around Atlanta's urban center. Parks, an urban farm, and public art are located on the portions of the trail that are already opened (the rest are expected to be complete by 2030). Breakfast is at **Flying Biscuit,** an easy mark for tall, pillowy biscuits with cranberry-apple butter or full-on grilled flatiron steak and eggs. Choosing the Midtown location will put you near **Ponce City Market,** a retail, entertainment, and residential complex inside the historic Sears & Roebuck Co. building. At 2.1 million square feet, it's the largest brick structure in the South. Some of the city's top chefs offer meals in the Central Food Hall. The complex continues to add high-end retailers and features Skyline Park, a rooftop arcade of vintage games and a spot for great city views. Nearby, the 30-acre **Atlanta Botanical Garden,** inside Piedmont Park, boasts the nation's largest orchid center, conservation gardens, a Japanese garden, a hardwood forest with a canopy walkway, and an interactive kids garden. Stroll-and-stop options are plenty at **Centennial Olympic Park,** where you'll find the College Football Hall of Fame and its massive wall holding the helmets of 700 teams. Before departing the Centennial Olympic Park area, stop by **World of Coca-Cola,** a shrine to the famous soda corporation based in Atlanta. Sample more than 100 Coke beverages sold around the world, see more than a century's worth of marketing, and, of course, buy a refrigerator magnet to take home.

CENTRAL NORTH CAROLINA TO THE COAST

Raleigh, the capital of North Carolina, is so close to its neighboring Triangle cities—Durham and Chapel Hill—that traveling between cities is easy. With award-winning restaurants, great farmers' markets, and food tours, these cities have become nationally recognized foodie hubs. The Outer Banks, home to some of the nation's best beaches and lighthouses, is a four-hour drive away.

Day 1: Downtown Raleigh

Fly into no-fuss **RDU International Airport**, not far from downtown Raleigh, and rent a car or cruise in driving your own vehicle. Stay at centrally located **Raleigh Marriott City Center**, walking distance from sights, shopping, and the city's best restaurants. Before you head out, book a Durham Afternoon Tasting Tour with Taste Carolina for Day 2 of your trip. The company stages gourmet foodie tours throughout the Triangle, but this one blends local history and farm-to-table restaurants. That done, take a walk to get your bearings, starting with a local beer and vegan wings at **Remedy Diner**. Fortified, stroll **City Market's** cluster of shops, galleries, and restaurants on cobblestone streets. You're bound to find a place for dinner.

Day 2: Downtown Raleigh to Durham
(30 minutes by car)

After an early breakfast at the hotel, drive to Durham and spend some time marveling at Duke Chapel's 210-foot-tall Gothic-style bell tower and the intricate woodwork inside the chapel, which dates to 1930. The cathedral is on the grounds of Duke University and close to Sarah P. Duke Gardens' 55 enchanting acres.

Lunch is your afternoon Taste Carolina downtown Durham food tour, and you'll want to stick around after to explore downtown shopping or the North Carolina Museum of Life and Science's three-story Magic Wings Butterfly House. For dinner, consider **Watts Grocery**, where Southern cooking meets French finesse. Think grilled trout over field peas, scallion, and rice hoppin' John with a radish fennel salad. Close the night with music at the various bars at the **American Tobacco Historic District.**

Day 3: Downtown Raleigh to Chapel Hill
(40 minutes by car)

Check out of your hotel and plan to spend the night at Chapel Hill's **Fearrington House Inn**. Accommodations and the Fearrington Village Center, totaling 100 acres, sit on a former dairy farm. The Fearrington House restaurant here is one of the country's best, and it was doing farm-to-table cooking years before it was cool. Challenge your foodie sensibilities with the likes of venison with quince and rutabaga. You could book spa services and relax the entire day here or take the 20-minute drive into Chapel Hill to visit **Morehead Planetarium and Science Center**, one of America's largest planetariums. More than 60 NASA astronauts trained here in celestial navigation.

Day 4: Chapel Hill to the Outer Banks
(4 hours by car)

Get an early start for the drive to the **Outer Banks**. Book the centrally located **First Colony Inn** at Nags Head. Spend your first day chilling at **Coquina Beach**, which locals consider the OBX's nicest beach. Fish, take a long walk, and hunt for shells before dinner at **Basnight's Lone**

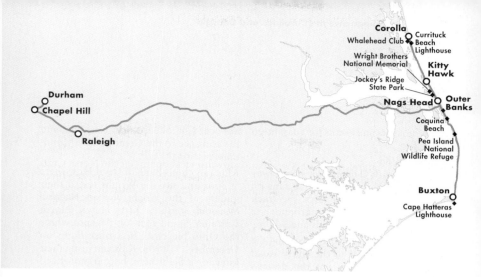

Cedar Café. The huge, lively restaurant with waterfront views has its own herb garden and a specials menu that lists the name of fishermen who supplied the day's catch.

Day 5: Nags Head to Buxton
(1 hour by car)

Grab a hearty breakfast at local favorite **Sam & Omie's,** open since 1937 and still serving salty country ham steaks with eggs. Today's mission is climbing the 210-foot-tall **Cape Hatteras Lighthouse,** the nation's tallest brick lighthouse. On the way, driving across the 5,800-acre **Pea Island National Wildlife Refuge,** watch for some of the more than 365 birds that have been spotted in the refuge. Plan dinner at **Breakwater,** famous for its potato-chip-crusted Fat Daddy crab cakes with creole mustard sauce.

Day 6: Nags Head to Kitty Hawk
(40 minutes by car)

Book your last two nights at ocean-front **The Sanderling Resort.** On the way there, stop for a tour of **Wright Brothers National Memorial** in Kill Devil Hills, where America's first powered flight took place. Nearby, hike **Jockey's Ridge State Park,** home to the East Coast's tallest sand dunes, 80 to 100 feet high, depending on which way the wind blows the sand. Visitors can also stroll on a 384-foot boardwalk. Grab lunch or an early dinner at **Outer Banks Brewing Station,** where a wind turbine partially powers the brewery. The brewery regularly stages live music if you're ready for a night on the town.

Day 7: Corolla
(20 minutes by car)

Corolla is home to the impressive red-brick **Currituck Beach Lighthouse,** which you may climb, and the historic **Whalehead Club,** a former luxury home and hunting lodge built between 1922 and 1925. Both spots are open for touring and the pair stand on beautifully landscaped grounds perfect for a day of strolling. Stop at a grocery store on the way for lunchtime picnic provisions. Back at the resort, spend the late afternoon lazing on the beach or relaxing at the Spa at Sanderling. Then dine at **Kimball's Kitchen** for a perfect end to your vacation week before driving home or flying out of Norfolk International airport two hours north in Virginia.

WITH KIDS

Try these sights and events for guaranteed family fun.

Wet and Wild

NASCAR's slick **Charlotte Motor Speedway** in Concord holds up to 89,000 fans on race days. On non–race days, racetrack tours—including a drive around the track—are available for kids and adults. Get a look at 18 stock cars spanning the history of NASCAR in the Glory Road "ICONS" exhibit, or get the driver's experience by sitting inside a racing simulator that provides virtual laps around a speedway at the **NASCAR Hall of Fame** in Charlotte.

Atlanta's **Georgia Aquarium** is the largest in the Western Hemisphere, with sea creatures in 10 million gallons of water. Special programs are aimed at toddlers, and families with kids can take a behind-the-scenes tour to learn about all the aquarium's animals and the care they receive.

Riverbanks Zoo and Garden in Columbia, South Carolina, supplies grounds for exotic animals like Siberian tigers, siamang apes, lemurs, and giraffes. More than 2,000 animals occupy natural habitats, while 4,200 native and exotic plant species fill gardens. Civil War ruins dot the landscape, too.

Embrace History

Take a self-guided tour or follow guides in native costume at the **Oconaluftee Indian Village,** which tracks back more than 250 years with demonstrations of weaving, hunting techniques, and canoe construction. The nearby **Museum of the Cherokee Indian** contains artifacts and displays that cover 11,000 years. Nature walks, dance programs, and traditional Cherokee dinners are available, in addition to museum tours. Both the village and the museum are near Cherokee, North Carolina, and the entrance to the Great Smoky Mountains National Park.

Kids can climb Big Kill Devil Hill where Wilbur and Orville Wright tested their gliders at the **Wright Brothers National Memorial,** south of Kitty Hawk, North Carolina. Stand right on the spot where the Ohio bicyclists first took flight on December 17, 1903. Kids can bring their kites for a flight here, but no motorized aircraft are allowed.

Hands-on Adventures

Along the way to major attractions, take side trips to spots guaranteed to please. **EdVenture Children's Museum** in Columbia, South Carolina, is nothing but hands-on fun, from science experiments to climbing in a 24-foot fire truck and manning the siren.

Myrtle Beach is awash with activities guaranteed to bring smiles—and squeals—from the more than 35 rides at **Family Kingdom Amusement Park** to **Myrtle Waves,** South Carolina's largest water park, and many colorful and putt-putt golf courses.

Meet Big Bird, Kermit the Frog, and Miss Piggy at Atlanta's **Center for Puppetry Arts,** which houses the largest Jim Henson display in the world. The collection includes more than 500 puppets and artifacts donated by the Henson family. Another centerpiece at the attraction is a large global collection, with puppets dating back to the 1500s. The exhibits feature hands-on learning; live puppet performances are held daily; and kids even have a chance to make their own puppets.

THE NORTH CAROLINA COAST

WELCOME TO
THE NORTH CAROLINA COAST

TOP REASONS TO GO

★ **Water, water everywhere:** Surfers delight in Cape Hatteras's formidable waves. Kayakers and boaters prefer the Crystal Coast's sleepy estuaries. Beach strollers love Ocracoke's remote, unspoiled shore.

★ **Pirate lore and hidden booty:** The Graveyard of the Atlantic is littered with shipwrecks to dive. See artifacts from Blackbeard's flagship *Queen Anne's Revenge* at Beaufort's North Carolina Maritime Museum.

★ **Lighting the darkness:** North Carolina has seven lighthouses, each with its own personality; a few, you can climb to the top.

★ **The Lost Colony:** In a mystery for the ages, 117 settlers disappeared without a trace. Their story is presented both in historical context and dramatic entertainment in Manteo.

★ **Fresh seafood:** Prepared practically every way possible—fried, grilled, steamed, stuffed, blackened, or raw—the bounty of the ocean is available all along the coast.

1 The Outer Banks. Long stretches of wild beach are intermingled with small, lively towns on this ribbon of sand. The north end is a tourist mecca of shops, resorts, restaurants, beach cottages, and historic sites. Quieter villages and open, undeveloped beaches mark the south end, where travelers often hear nothing but surf and shorebirds. With just one two-lane road stretching the length of the Outer Banks, locals refer to mile markers instead of street numbers when giving directions.

2 Cape Hatteras National Seashore. With challenging waves, myriad fish, and the impressive Cape Hatteras lighthouse anchoring the south end, this part of the Outer Banks is a surfer's playground, an angler's dream, and a history buff's treasure.

3 The Crystal Coast and New Bern. History here ranges from historical colonial sites to the birthplace of Pepsi, while extensive stretches of ocean, sound, and rivers please boaters, anglers, watersports lovers, and those who just want to relax on a big Southern porch with a glass of sweet tea.

Winton
Ahoskie
13
Windsor
Williamston
64
← TO RALEIGH
Greenville
Washington
11
17
304
Vanceboro
Kinston
70
New Bern
70
Pollocksville
258
Richlands
17
TO RALEIGH
Jacksonville
Swansboro
24
58
172
421
Burgaw
Atkinson
40
○ N. Topsail Beach
Surf City
Poplar Grove 17
TOPSAIL ISLAND
Historic Plantation
Topsail Beach
4
Bolton
Wilmington
Wrightsville Beach
211
Airlie Gardens
Brunswick Town
Myrtle Grove
State Historic Site
Carolina Beach
130
Shallotte 17
Kure Beach
Caswell
Fort Fisher State Historic Site
Beach ○ Southport
Sunset
Oak Island
Bald Head Lighthouse
Beach
Lighthouse
CAPE FEAR COAST

2

VIRGINIA

17
Sunbury   South   168   Barco   Carova
         Mills   Corolla
158   Merchants   Currituck
      Millpond   158   Lighthouse
      State Park
32   Elizabeth   12
           City
      Hertford   Duck
                          1
                    Kitty Hawk   Kill Devil Hills
17   Edenton   Wright Brothers   Jockey's Ridge
                  National Memorial   State Park
     Albemarle Sound   64   Nags Head
                          Manteo   Bodie Island
Plymouth   Lake   Mann's   Lighthouse
           Phelps Harbor   Coquina
           94   Beach
Dismal   ROANOKE
Swamp   ISLAND   12
32   Neur   Lake   Rodanthe
      Lake Mattamuskeet Waves
264 Pantego   264   Salvo   Cape
     Belhaven   Engelhard   Hatteras
Bath   HATTERAS   National
      Swanquarter   ISLAND   Seashore
                                  Avon
Aurora   Frisco 12 Buxton
                  Hatteras
Bayboro Mesic   Ocracoke   Cape Hatteras
                 Lighthouse   Lighthouse
         Ocracoke 12 OCRACOKE
55   Ferry   ISLAND
306   Oriental   Portsmouth Village
                      PORTSMOUTH
Minnesott Atlantic   ISLAND
Beach   12
Morehead CORE BANKS Cape Lookout
City   70   National Seashore
     Beaufort
Atlantic   HARKERS ISLAND
Beach
  3   Cape Lookout
Fort Macon Lighthouse
State Park

ATLANTIC   OCEAN

Pamlico Sound
Pamlico River

0   20 mi
0   20 km

Your first decision is whether to choose one destination for thorough exploration or to sweep the entire coast in five to six days, which is more doable in spring or fall when traffic is lighter. Arrival options include driving here from nearby locales or flying into airports at Wilmington or New Bern, North Carolina; Myrtle Beach, South Carolina; or Norfolk, Virginia; then renting a car. A vehicle is essential for navigating the coast here, as little public transportation is available. State-operated vehicle ferries and smaller private ferries provide essential links between islands and offer enjoyable alternatives to land routes. Boat touring is another option. Dozens of marinas line the shore, and the Intracoastal Waterway runs the length of the North Carolina coast.

4 **Wilmington and the Cape Fear Coast.** Part cosmopolitan, part old-fashioned Southern charm, the Cape Fear region has attracted people from all over the world since the early 1500s, when explorers first arrived. You can still cast a line off an old wooden pier or spend the day roaming art galleries and wine bars.

NORTH CAROLINA BEACHES

"Endless beaches" is hardly an overstatement when it comes to North Carolina's coast. White or khaki sands and pristine seas are common themes from the north end's Outer Banks to the Central Coast's unspoiled Cape Lookout and the cottage-lined southern shores.

(above) All kids need is a pail and a shovel to enjoy a day at Wrightsville Beach. (lower right) The Cape Fear Kite Festival features large show kites. (upper right) Surfers gather near piers where sandbars create better waves.

Barrier islands and rambling shores comprise more than 300 miles of coastline, where you can explore lighthouses, aquariums, museums, woodlands, and historic sites galore. Playtime means golf, carnival rides, fishing, and water sports. The 100-mile-long Outer Banks region ranges from the north end's quiet Corolla, where wild horses roam, to shopping and nightlife in Nags Head, to untouched beaches of the Hatteras National Seashore on the far south end. The Crystal Coast beams with the historical maritime town of Beaufort and the artsy made-for-movies town of Southport. Wilmington's eclectic downtown—including more than 200 blocks of historic district—gives the Cape Fear region an urban beat.

HANG TEN

You can hardly walk a North Carolina beach without encountering a surfer. The Outer Banks (especially Cape Hatteras), Wrightsville Beach, and Ocean Isle are surfing hot spots, especially near piers and jetties. It's best to take a class rather than try to teach yourself to surf. Check out the local surf shop for information on classes.

2

NORTH CAROLINA'S BEST BEACHES

NAGS HEAD

Couples, families, and friends all find options along **Nags Head,** where 11 miles of beaches include many with lifeguards. Plenty of accommodations—vacation homes, hotels, and cozy inns—line the shore, and getting onto the beach is no problem. There are 41 public access points, many with wheelchair access, so you're always within a short driving distance.

CAPE HATTERAS NATIONAL SEASHORE

Long stretches of unspoiled beaches hidden behind tall dunes, interspersed with small villages, along this 60-mile geographical treasure provide opportunities for shelling, surfing, birding, fishing, camping, lighthouse exploring, or simply getting lost in thought. The park's undeveloped **Coquina Beach** and **Ocracoke Island beaches** are considered by locals to be the Outer Banks' loveliest shorelines.

CAPE LOOKOUT NATIONAL SEASHORE

Exchange real-world stress for the magical wonderlands of this 56-mile stretch extending from the historic Portsmouth Island village to **Shackleford Banks,** where wild horses roam. The 28,400 acres of uninhabited land and marsh include remote, sandy islands linked to the mainland by nothing more than private ferries. You can climb an old lighthouse, see historic buildings in abandoned fishing villages, set up camp, stay in an old-timey cabin, or keep a (discreet) lookout for loggerhead sea turtles nesting at night.

WRIGHTSVILLE BEACH

Quiet and moderately upscale, with longtime family homes and striking contemporary cottages jamming the lifeguard-protected shore, **Wrightsville Beach** is a perfect family or couple's retreat. The white-sand beaches are sports lovers' favorites. Surfers, kayakers, paddleboarders, and bodyboarders dig Wrightsville's tasty waves while anglers love its concrete fishing pier. College kids fill downtown clubs at night. Arrive early, as parking spaces fill up quickly.

KURE AND CAROLINA BEACHES

Aptly named, **Pleasure Island** offers all sorts of fun for families and singles. On the south end kids will love the **Kure Beach** aquarium, while history buffs can discover a Civil War fort. Beaches are wide, with plenty of room for fishing and surfing. There's even an old wooden pier. Head north to **Carolina Beach** for charter-boat fishing excursions and the nostalgic charm of an old-fashioned, somewhat funky, boardwalk with arcades, carnival rides, candy, and ice cream.

Updated by
Lan Sluder

Three hundred miles of breathtaking barrier islands and mainland beaches make North Carolina's coastline a beach lover's dream. White sands and pristine waters, lighthouses, and a plethora of vacation homes mark the shore. Athletes and anglers; history buffs and gallery hoppers; singles, couples, and families of every configuration find plenty to do here, but snoozing along the quiet shore is just as appealing.

Distinctive port cities dot broad rivers that lead inland from the sounds. You'll find American Revolution and Civil War battle sites, elegant golf links and kitschy putt-putt courses, upscale boutiques and big-box surf shops. Aquariums, fishing charters, and museum outreach programs put you up close and personal with the seashore critters. North Carolina's small towns (mostly of 1,000 to 3,000 people) offer their own special brand of genuine warmth and hospitality.

The coast is divided into three broad sections that include islands, shoreline, and coastal plains: the Outer Banks (Corolla south through Ocracoke, including Roanoke Island), the Crystal Coast (Core and Bogue Banks, Beaufort, Southport, Morehead City, and the inland river cities of New Bern and Edenton), and the greater Cape Fear region (Wrightsville Beach south through Wilmington to the Brunswick Isles). The Outer Banks are visible from space: the thin, delicate white tracings are barrier islands that form a buffer between the Atlantic Ocean and the mainland.

Although other states' coasts have wall-to-wall hotels and condominiums, much of North Carolina's coast belongs to the North Carolina Division of Parks and Recreation and the U.S. National Park Service. This arrangement keeps large chunks of the coast accessible to the public for exploration, athletic activities, picnicking, and camping. Still, property values have skyrocketed as summer residents' dream houses continually replace generations-old beach cottages.

Some of the coast either closes or operates on reduced hours during midwinter, which makes the colder season a special time to escape both crowds and peak prices but still enjoy seafood, beaches, and museums. Whether you're seeking peace or adventure, or a combination of both, you can find it on the coast.

PLANNING

WHEN TO GO

North Carolina's coast shines in spring (March to May) and fall (September and October), when the weather is most temperate and the water reasonably warm. Traveling during these times means you can avoid long lines and higher prices associated with the peak summer tourist season.

PLANNING YOUR TIME

The North Carolina coast is a string of beach and inland towns, each with its own character. Pick one and plan day trips from there. Boisterous Nags Head and sophisticated Wilmington provide dining, shopping, and nightlife, but they are only short drives from lovely gardens, quiet beaches, dense woodlands, and historic landmarks. Front-porch friendly Beaufort is a brief, private ferry ride away from barrier islands where wild horses roam. Southport is a living backdrop for movie filming. Just an hour inland are New Bern's charming downtown and historic Tryon Palace and gardens, and nearby Edenton's outstanding collection of colonial structures. In summer, secondary roads and some major highways are lined by fresh-seafood vendors and colorful produce stands.

GETTING HERE AND AROUND

AIR TRAVEL

The closest large, commercial airports to the Outer Banks are Norfolk International in Virginia, a two-hour drive, and Raleigh-Durham International Airport, a four-hour drive. Norfolk International is served by American, Delta, Southwest, and United; Raleigh-Durham International has service by nine airlines, including Air Canada, Alaska, Allegiant, American, Delta, Frontier, Jet Blue, Southwest, and United. Coastal Carolina Regional Airport in New Bern has connector flights, charter service, and car rentals available. Wilmington International Airport serves the Cape Fear Coast.

Barrier Island Aviation provides charter service between the Dare County Regional Airport and major cities along the East Coast. American and Delta fly into Coastal Carolina Regional Airport in New Bern as well as Wilmington International Airport.

Air Contacts Barrier Island Aviation. ✉ 407 Airport Rd., Manteo ☎ 252/473–4247 ⊕ www.barrierislandaviation.com. **Coastal Carolina Regional Airport.** ✉ 200 Terminal Dr., New Bern ☎ 252/638–8591 ⊕ www.newbernairport.com. **Dare County Regional Airport.** ✉ 410 Airport Rd., Manteo ☎ 252/475–5570 ⊕ www.darenc.com/departments/airport. **Norfolk International.** ✉ 2200 Norview Ave., Norfolk ☎ 757/857–3351 ⊕ www.norfolkairport.com. **Raleigh-Durham International Airport.** ✉ 2400 John Brantley Blvd., Morrisville ☎ 919/840–2123 ⊕ www.rdu.com. **Wilmington International Airport.** ✉ 1740 Airport Blvd., Wilmington ☎ 910/341–4125 ⊕ www.flyilm.com.

CAR TRAVEL

Getting around the Outer Banks is a snap because there's only one road—NC Route 12. Sometimes, though, traffic can make that one road a route of pure frustration, especially on a rainy midsummer day when everyone is looking for something to do besides sunbathing. Low-lying areas of the highway are also prone to flooding. ■TIP➜ Two major bridge construction projects are underway on NC 12: Herbert C. Bonner Bridge over Oregon Inlet and the Rodanthe Bridge. Occasional traffic delays may occur.

Highways into the other areas along the coast—U.S. 158 into Kitty Hawk and Nags Head; U.S. 64 around Nags Head and Manteo; Interstate 40, which can take you from Wilmington all the way to Las Vegas or California if you desire, or Raleigh if you're catching a plane; and U.S. 17, which services Wilmington and New Bern—usually run smoothly during all but weekday rush hours and the busiest days of the high summer season.

Driving on the beaches is allowed in designated areas only, and permits are usually required. The most notable ORV (off-road vehicle) driving area is north of Corolla where NC Route 12 pavement ends. Continuing on the beach where NC Route 12 ends, by 4WD vehicle only, brings you to the village of Carova, where there are rental cottages and wild ponies and a few year-round residents. Other popular seasonal ORV areas include Hatteras and Ocracoke islands in the Cape Hatteras National Seashore; advance permits are required. A 10-day permit is $50. Visit ⊕ *www.outerbanks.com/driving-on-the-beach.html* for more information. The 25 mph on-the-beach speed limit is strictly enforced, and pedestrians always have the right-of-way. Driving on sand can be tricky, so be careful to lower the air pressure in your tires. Locals are happy to instruct.

FERRY TRAVEL

The state-run car ferry system operates 22 ferries on seven regular routes over five bodies of water: Currituck and Pamlico sounds and the Cape Fear, Neuse, and Pamlico rivers. Emergency routes are also provided when storms damage the main coastal highways. The North Carolina Department of Transportation's ferry information line and website have full details. ■TIP➜ There's a charge for most ferries, but the Hatteras-Ocracoke ferry is free.

Ferry Contacts North Carolina Department of Transportation Ferry Division. ☎ 800/293–3779 ⊕ www.ncdot.gov/ferry.

TAXI TRAVEL

Island Limousine, headquartered in Nags Head, serves the entire area, including Norfolk International Airport, although its main service area is the Outer Banks. Getting to the airport in a van costs about $160 from Nags Head. Uber and Lyft also are options for getting around the Outer Banks, and for transportation to and from airports and ferries.

Taxi Contacts Island Limousine. ✉ 6933 S Croatan Hwy., Nags Head ☎ 252/441–5466 ⊕ www.islandlimo.com.

RESTAURANTS

Seafood houses and many restaurants sell each day's local catch: tuna, wahoo, mahimahi, mackerel, sand dabs, scallops, shrimp, or blue crabs. Raw bars serve oysters and clams on the half shell. For years, the Coast has been a magnet for highly trained chefs, and emerging talents are constantly raising the bar with creative preparations and diversified menu options. Seafood dishes—broiled, fried, grilled, or steamed—are listed alongside globally inspired entrées fusing Asian, European, and Latin flavors with traditional Southern ingredients such as black-eyed peas. On the negative side, restaurants in beach areas often close in winter and may have to hire new chefs and staff for the high season, leading to quality that can vary from year to year.

Expect up to hour-long waits, sometimes longer, at many restaurants during summer and festival periods. Many places don't accept reservations. Restaurant hours are frequently reduced in winter, and some restaurants in remote beach communities close for several months. Casual dress is acceptable in most restaurants. *Dining reviews have been shortened. For full information, visit Fodors.com.*

HOTELS

Most visitors to the Outer Banks and other beach areas rent vacation homes instead of motels or hotels. Thousands of rental properties are available. Small beach cottages can be had, but increasingly so-called sand castles—large multistory homes with every imaginable amenity (private pools, movie theaters, elevators, etc.)—suit families and large groups. These can cost up to $15,000 a week or more in summer, but prices off-season often are slashed by 75% or more. Motels and hotels clustered along the coast are usually the more affordable way to go for couples or small families.

Throughout the coast, you have a choice of cottages, condos, and waterfront resorts. Chain hotels have a presence here, but you can also stay at a surprising number of small, family-run lodgings. You might also consider selecting from a variety of bed-and-breakfasts, usually owned and managed by resident hosts. Always ask about special packages (price breaks on multiple-night stays) and off-season rates. Most hotels, inns, and B&Bs on the coast offer free parking on their property. A few have street parking only, but you can expect not to pay parking fees even at the priciest hotels. *Hotel reviews have been shortened. For full information, visit Fodors.com.*

WHAT IT COSTS				
	$	**$$**	**$$$**	**$$$$**
Restaurants	under $15	$15–$19	$20–$24	over $24
Hotels	under $150	$150–$200	$201–$250	over $250

Restaurant prices are the average cost of a main course at dinner or, if dinner is not served, at lunch. Hotel prices are the lowest cost of a standard double room in high season.

VISITOR INFORMATION
Contacts National Park Service–Cape Hatteras National Seashore. ✉ *1401 National Park Dr., Manteo* ☎ *252/475–9000 park information for Hatteras National Seashore* ⊕ *www.nps.gov/caha.*

THE OUTER BANKS

North Carolina's Outer Banks stretch from the Virginia state line south to Cape Lookout. Think of the OBX (shorthand used on popular bumper stickers) as a series of stepping-stones in the Atlantic Ocean. Throughout history, the treacherous waters surrounding these islands have been the nemesis of shipping, earning them the collective nickname "Graveyard of the Atlantic." A network of lighthouses and lifesaving stations, which grew around the need to protect seagoing craft, attracts curious travelers, just as the many submerged wrecks attract scuba divers. The islands' coves and inlets, which sheltered pirates—the notorious Blackbeard lived and died here—now give refuge to anglers, sunbathers, and bird-watchers.

The main Outer Banks region is divided into four sections: the Northern Beaches, followed by Roanoke Island, Hatteras Island, and then Ocracoke Island. For many years the Outer Banks remained isolated, with only a few hardy commercial fishing families. Today, the islands are linked by bridges and ferries, and much of the area is included in the Cape Hatteras and Cape Lookout national seashores. The largest towns are also the most colorfully named: Kitty Hawk, Kill Devil Hills, Nags Head, and Manteo. Vacation rentals here are omnipresent—thousands of weekly rental cottages line the Outer Banks.

You can travel the region from the south end by taking a car ferry from either Cedar Island or Swan Quarter to Ocracoke Island, then another from Ocracoke Island to Hatteras Island. Starting from the north, driving the 120-mile stretch of Route 12 from Corolla to Ocracoke—including an hour on the free ferry from Hatteras village to Ocracoke Island—can be managed in a long day, but be sure to start early in the morning and allow plenty of extra time in summer to accommodate heavy traffic and ferry waiting times. If you end up with extra time, there are plenty of undeveloped beaches, historic lighthouses, and interesting beach communities to explore along the way. Mile markers (MM) indicate addresses all along the Outer Banks.

Sudden squalls frequently blow up on the Outer Banks in summer, and the Atlantic hurricane season runs from June 1 to November 30. Be aware that during major storms and hurricanes, evacuations are mandatory and roads and bridges become clogged with traffic following the blue-and-white evacuation-route signs (for current emergency weather information, see ⊕ *www.ncdot.gov*).

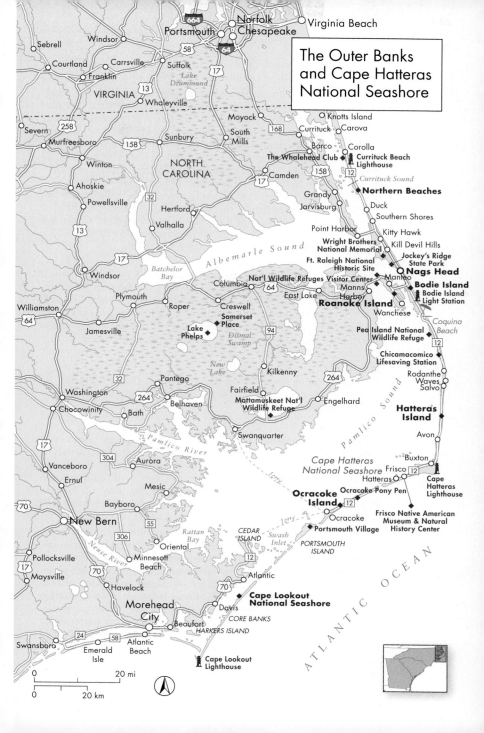

The Outer Banks and Cape Hatteras National Seashore

NORTHERN BEACHES

Corolla: 91 miles south of Norfolk, VA; 230 miles east of Raleigh. Duck: 16 miles south of Corolla. Kitty Hawk: 9 miles south of Duck.

The small northern beach settlements of Corolla and Duck are largely seasonal, residential enclaves full of summer rental homes and condominiums. Drive slowly in Corolla, where freely wandering, federally protected wild horses always have the right-of-way. The tony village of Duck has expensive homes and is dotted with upscale restaurants and shops. Kitty Hawk and contiguous Kill Devil Hills, with a combined population of about 10,000 residents, has fewer rental accommodations, but more chain retail. The towns' respective roles in the drama of the first powered flight occasionally create some confusion. When arriving at the Outer Banks, the Wright brothers first stayed in the then-remote fishing village of Kitty Hawk, but their flight took place some 4 miles south on Kill Devil Hills, a gargantuan sand dune where the Wright Brothers National Memorial now stands.

GETTING HERE AND AROUND

Most people drive to the northern beaches via U.S. 17, 64, and 264, which all link to the local U.S. 158 and NC Route 12. The main route from Norfolk, Virginia, is U.S. 158. Some commercial and charter flights are available from nearby airports. Plan your time wisely, however, as heavy traffic can lead to long travel delays in summer. Marked paths and wide shoulders accommodate bikers and walkers along some main roads. Guided tours are available, too. Still, a car is essential for getting around on your own time.

ESSENTIALS

Visitor Information Aycock Brown Welcome Center. ⊠ *5230 N. Croatan Hwy., MM 1, Kitty Hawk* ☎ *252/261–4644* ⊕ *www.outerbanks.com/aycock-brown-welcome-center.html.*

EXPLORING

FAMILY
Fodor'sChoice
★

Currituck Beach Lighthouse. The 1875 lighthouse was built from nearly 1 million bricks, which remained unpainted. Except in high winds or thunderstorms, or during winter when the lighthouse is closed, you can climb 220 steps to the top of the northernmost lighthouse on the Outer Banks. ⊠ *1101 Corolla Village Rd., off Rte. 12, Corolla* ☎ *252/453–4939* ⊕ *www.currituckbeachlight.com* ⛴ *Lighthouse $10 (cash or check only); grounds free* ☉ *Closed late Nov.–mid-Mar.*

The Whalehead Club. This 21,000-square-foot monument to gracious living was built in the 1920s as the private residence of a northern couple attracted by the area's reputation for waterfowl hunting (the home was given its current name by the second owner). After having been abandoned, sold, and vandalized, it was renovated and opened for tours in 2002. Inside the ornamental Art Nouveau structure, a floral motif is evident in Tiffany lamps with flower detailing and mahogany woodwork carved with water lilies. The home is on 39 waterfront acres inside Currituck Heritage Park and is now listed on the National Register of Historic Places. ⊠ *Currituck Heritage Park, 1100 Club Rd., off Rte. 12, Corolla* ☎ *252/453–9040* ⊕ *www.visitcurrituck.com/things-to-do/attractions/whalehead-in-historic-corolla* ⛴ *$7; ghost tour $15* ☉ *Closed Sun.*

First in Flight

December 17, 1903, was a cold and windy day on the Outer Banks, but Wilbur and Orville Wright took little notice. The slightly built brothers from Ohio were undertaking an excellent adventure. With Orville at the controls, Wilbur running alongside, and the men of the nearby Lifesaving Service stations acting as ground crew, the fragile *Wright Flyer* lifted off from the Kill Devil Hills dune near Kitty Hawk and flew 120 feet in 12 seconds.

Outer Banker John Daniels photographed the instant the world forever changed: a heavier-than-air machine was used to achieve controlled, sustained flight with a pilot aboard. To prove they were not accidental aviators, the Wrights took two flights each that day, and in Wilbur's second attempt, he flew 852 feet in 59 seconds.

Others were attempting—and dying in the attempt of—powered flight as the Wright brothers opened their Dayton bicycle-repair shop in 1892. Using information on aerodynamics from the Smithsonian Institution and observation of birds in flight, they began experimenting with a box kite roughly shaped like a biplane and a makeshift wind tunnel. Strong, steady winds drew them to the then-remote Outer Banks, where they could test their next phase, manned glider flights, in privacy. In time, by adding power to the three-axis control they had developed, they eventually solved the problems of mechanical flight, lift, and propulsion that had vexed scientists for hundreds of years.

Their success is honored at the Wright Brothers National Memorial in Kill Devil Hills, where the museum is undergoing a major renovation through 2018, and by the North Carolina boast emblazoned on millions of license plates: "First in Flight."

FAMILY
Fodor's Choice
★

Wright Brothers National Memorial. One of the most popular photo sites on the Outer Banks, 5 miles south of Kitty Hawk, this 60-foot granite airplane's tail stands as a tribute to Wilbur and Orville Wright, two bicycle mechanics from Ohio who took to the air here on December 17, 1903. A sculptured replica of their *Wright Flyer* helps you to experience the historic day humans first made powered flight. Informative talks by National Park Service rangers also help bring the event to life. ■ TIP→ The main museum, visitor center, and exhibits are undergoing a total restoration and are not expected to reopen until late 2018. However, visitors can still tour the Memorial high atop a hill and also see the Wright Flyer sculpture. There is a temporary welcome center with an information desk and a few exhibits. ✉ *1000 N. Croatan Hwy., off U.S. 158 at MM 7.5, Kill Devil Hills* ☎ *252/473–2111* ⊕ *www.nps. gov/wrbr* ☜ *$7 (free for National Park pass holders)*.

WHERE TO EAT

$$$$
MODERN
AMERICAN

✕ **AQUA Restaurant.** This beautifully located restaurant offers creative takes on locally sourced seafood and other dishes; there's seating at a waterside patio for great sunset views, at the bar (live music some nights), or in the main dining area. You can also get a massage at AQUA Spa upstairs or relax with a craft cocktail at the restaurant's popular afternoon happy hour. **Known for:** waterfront dining on Currituck Sound; fresh, locally caught seafood. $ *Average main: $26* ⌧ *1174 Duck Rd., Duck* ☎ *252/261–9700* ⊕ *www.aquaobx.com* ⊗ *Usually closed Mon. and Tues. Jan.–early Mar.; check ahead as dates vary.*

$$$$
AMERICAN
Fodor's Choice
★

✕ **Blue Point Bar & Grill.** The Outer Banks' first farm-to-table restaurant, this upscale foodie haven marries Southern roots with contemporary flair and Currituck Sound views. During its nearly three decades of existence, Blue Point has had several incarnations, but one thing that hasn't changed is the owners' commitment to a sustainable menu sourced as locally as possible, with seafood, beef, and other dishes prepared to highlight their texture and flavor. **Known for:** locally sourced seafood and other dishes; sunset views over Currituck Sound. $ *Average main: $32* ⌧ *1240 Duck Rd., Duck* ☎ *252/261–8090* ⊕ *www.thebluepoint. com* ⊗ *Closed Mon.*

$
BAKERY
FAMILY

✕ **Duck Donuts.** Morning traffic in Duck includes the sidewalks, filled with walkers, joggers, runners, and bicyclers—many of whom will be carrying bags, boxes, or buckets of Duck Donuts. Each doughnut starts with a coating—traditional favorites like vanilla and chocolate, or more daring varieties like lemon, peanut butter, and maple; then, you pile on toppings like shredded coconut, chopped peanuts, or even bacon. **Known for:** deliciously different doughnuts. $ *Average main: $3* ⌧ *1190 Duck Rd., Duck* ☎ *252/480–3304* ⊕ *www. duckdonuts.com.*

$$$$
AMERICAN

✕ **Urban Kitchen.** Don't be fooled by its strip mall location and low-frills decor: here you'll get farm-fresh, creatively constructed dishes served in generous portions. The menu changes frequently, but you can always expect interesting versions of seafood, beef, pork, and other standards. **Known for:** innovative seafood and other dishes for foodies; minimalist decor. $ *Average main: $25* ⌧ *603-B Currituck Clubhouse Dr., Corolla* ☎ *252/453–4453* ⊕ *www.urbankitchenobx.com* ⊗ *Closed days vary monthly. No lunch.*

WHERE TO STAY

$$$$
HOTEL
FAMILY

🏨 **Hampton Inn & Suites Outer Banks.** If you need a family-friendly motel with a range of amenities or simply want a no-surprises oceanfront property with plenty of extras, this hotel fits the bill. **Pros:** convenient location near attractions; free Wi-Fi throughout the hotel; free self-parking; fitness and business centers. **Cons:** pets not allowed; fitness center may be crowded during early-morning hours. $ *Rooms from: $304* ⌧ *333 Audubon Dr., Corolla* ☎ *252/453–6565* ⊕ *hamptoninn3. hilton.com* ⤳ *123 rooms* ⦿ *Breakfast.*

$$$$
HOTEL
FAMILY

🏨 **Hilton Garden Inn.** Opened in 2006, with some renovations in 2017, this beachside resort is one of the largest of the chain properties on the Outer Banks. **Pros:** full-service beachfront resort with all amenities; spacious rooms; convenient location next to Kitty Hawk Pier. **Cons:** beach is fairly narrow in this area; breakfast is an additional charge if you're not a Hilton Gold and Diamond member. $ *Rooms from: $325* ⌧ *5353 N. Virginia Dare Trail, Kitty Hawk* ☎ *252/261–1290, 855/618–4697 toll-free reservations* ⊕ *www.hiltongardeninn3.hilton. com* ⤳ *180 rooms* ⦿ *No meals.*

$$$$ RESORT FAMILY Fodor's Choice ★ 🏨 **Sanderling Resort.** Drenched in decades of tradition, this luxury resort comprising three multistory buildings and five large rental homes spreads over 16 quiet acres of ocean-to-sound property, 5 miles north of Duck and 10 miles south of Corolla. **Pros:** on-site spa; private balconies with hammock chairs; there is an adults-only pool; oversized bathrooms. **Cons:** limited elevator access in some buildings; DVD players and microwaves must be requested at the front desk. [$] *Rooms from: $395* ✉ *1461 Duck Rd., Duck* ☎ *252/261–4111, 855/412–7866 toll-free reservations, 877/650–4812* 🌐 *www.sanderling-resort.com* 🛏 *96 rooms, 5 vacation homes* 🍴 *Breakfast.*

$$$ HOTEL 🏨 **Shutters on the Banks.** This oceanfront, family-owned hotel is a bargain-hunter's dream (at least by Outer Banks standards), with spacious rooms updated in 2016, and a generous package of amenities. **Pros:** on the beach and near attractions; less expensive than some of the chain motels; some rooms have full kitchens. **Cons:** not all rooms face the ocean; outside entrances to rooms; noise levels during high season can be intrusive. [$] *Rooms from: $229* ✉ *405 S. Virginia Dare Trail, Kill Devil Hills* ☎ *252/441–5581, 800/848–3728* 🌐 *www.shuttersonthebanks.com* 🛏 *86 rooms* 🍴 *Breakfast.*

SPORTS AND THE OUTDOORS

GOLF

Currituck Club. Rolling fairways with bent-grass greens and a sweeping view of Currituck Sound characterize this 18-hole semiprivate championship course designed by Rees Jones. Anchoring the Currituck Club resort community, the course also serves as an Audubon Society Cooperative Sanctuary, which makes it an environmental host for a variety of wildlife. During summer, the club's PGA professionals schedule instructional clinics for adults and juniors of all skill levels. Additionally, Currituck's popular practice facility comprises an 8,000-square-foot putting green and bunker, plus a driving range. Family members of golfers who rent Currituck accommodations have access to beaches, lighted tennis courts, a fitness center, five swimming pools, biking and walking trails, and a valet trolley service. ✉ *619 Currituck Clubhouse Dr., Currituck* ☎ *252/453–9400* 🌐 *www.currituckclubobx.org* 🎟 *$60–$165 for 18 holes, $35–$85 for 9 holes, including cart (discounts for club guests and renters)* 🏌 *18 holes, 6885 yards, par 72; pro shop, putting green, lessons.*

Sea Scape Golf Links. Winds from the nearby ocean and sound make this short links course an unexpected challenge, while sand dunes and a maritime forest provide a serene setting. The course, which opened in 1965, was designed by Art Wall, a Masters champion. It's kept in good condition and features some tricky par 3s and dogleg par 4s. It offers a satisfying round to all levels of ability. ✉ *300 Eckner St., Kitty Hawk* ☎ *252/261–2158* 🌐 *www.seascapegolf.com* 🎟 *18 holes $50–$115, 9 holes $34–$50, depending on day and time* 🏌 *18 holes, 6231 yards, par 70; pro shop.*

NAGS HEAD

9 miles south of Kitty Hawk.

It's widely accepted that Nags Head got its name because pirates once tied lanterns around the necks of their horses to lure merchant ships onto the shoals, where they would be wrecked and pilfered for profit. Dubious citizenry aside, Nags Head was established in the 1830s and has become an iconic North Carolina tourist haven.

The town—one of the largest on the Outer Banks even though it has fewer than 3,000 residents—lies between the Atlantic Ocean and Pamlico Sound, along and between U.S. 158 ("the bypass") and Route 12 ("the beach road" or Virginia Dare Trail). Both roads are congested in the high season, and the entire area is commercialized. Many lodgings, whether they're dated cottages, shingled older houses, or sprawling new homes with plenty of bells and whistles, are available through the area's plentiful vacation rentals. Numerous restaurants, motels, hotels, shops, and entertainment opportunities keep the town hopping day and night.

Nags Head has 11 miles of beach with 41 public access points from Route 12, some with paved parking, many with wheelchair access, and some with restrooms and showers. ■TIP➜ **It's easy to overlook the flagpoles stationed along many area beaches; but if there's a red flag flying from one of them, it means the water is too rough even for wading. These are not suggestions—ignoring them is dangerous and carries hefty fines.**

GETTING HERE AND AROUND

From the east, arrive by car on U.S. 64 or from the north, on U.S. 17 and U.S. 158. Although many people cycle and walk on designated paths, most exploring requires a car.

ESSENTIALS

Visitor Information Whalebone Welcome Center. ✉ *2 Rte. 12, , MM 17* ☎ *877/629–4386* ⊕ *www.outerbanks.com/whalebone-junction.html.*

EXPLORING

FAMILY **Jockey's Ridge State Park.** The 420 acres of this park encompass the tallest sand dune system on the East Coast (about 80 to 100 feet). Walk along the 384-foot boardwalk from the visitor center to the edge of the dune. The climb to the top is a challenge; nevertheless, it's a popular spot for hang gliding, kite flying, and sand boarding. You can also explore an estuary, a museum, and a self-guided trail through the park, which also has eight picnic shelters. In summer, join the free Sunset on the Ridge program: watch the sun disappear while you sit on the dunes and learn about their local legends and history. Covered footwear is a wise choice here, as the loose sand gets quite hot (25–30 degrees hotter than air temperature) in the summer months. ✉ *300 W. Carolista Dr., MM 12, off Hwy. 158 Bypass (South Croatan Hwy.)* ☎ *252/441–7132, 252/441–2588 park program reservations* ⊕ *www. jockeysridgestatepark.com* ➔ *Free.*

At Jockey's Ridge State Park you can hike to the top of the tallest natural sand dune in the Eastern United States.

OFF THE
BEATEN
PATH

Lake Phelps. At 16,600 acres, 5 miles across, and about 4 feet deep, Lake Phelps is North Carolina's second-largest natural lake. It's also part of Pettigrew State Park and has long been considered a treasure by boaters and anglers. In 1985 researchers began to prize it for other reasons. Discovered underneath the sand in the beautifully clear water were ancient Native American artifacts, including 30 dugout canoes, one of which dates back some 4,400 years; Native Americans are believed to have settled here some 8,000 years ago. Two canoes are displayed in the Pettigrew Park information center. The park also includes a boat ramp, canoe launch, fishing pier, and camping sites. ⊠ *2252 Lake Shore Rd., Creswell ✛ 56 miles west of Nags Head via U.S. 64; take exit 558 and follow signs for 8 miles to the park office* ☎ *252/797–4475* ⊕ *www. ncparks.gov/pettigrew-state-park* ⊠ *Free; charge for camping.*

OFF THE
BEATEN
PATH

Somerset Place. Drive about an hour inland (or a short detour if you're arriving on U.S. 64 from the west) to see one of North Carolina's best-preserved historic plantations. Somerset Place, now part of Pettigrew State Park and one of North Carolina's 27 official historic sites, once sat on 100,000 acres of land that bordered Lake Phelps. It was one of the state's largest plantations, producing rice, corn, oats, peas, beans, and flax. Its sophisticated sawmills handled thousands of feet of lumber from 1785 to 1865. The 800 slaves who resided here throughout the plantation's 80 years planted and harvested crops, cooked, and washed. Some slaves were also skilled laborers like carpenters, brick masons, cobblers, and weavers. The site, which originally consisted of more than 50 buildings, has nine original 19th-century buildings, and four others have been reconstructed, including slave quarters. Tours of the buildings and grounds last 90 minutes. ⊠ *Pettigrew State Park, 2572 Lake Shore Rd., Creswell* ✛ *52 miles west of Nags Head on U.S. 64; take exit 558, then follow signs to Somerset Place* ☎ *252/797–4560* ⊕ *www.nchistoricsites.org/somerset* ✆ *Free* ⊘ *Closed Sun. and Mon.*

BEACHES

FAMILY **Nags Head Beaches.** Forty-three public Atlantic beach access points plus five sound-side access points make Nags Head the perfect place to hit the shore, no matter what your needs may be. Access points are marked with white signs clearly stating "Public beach access," and 15 of them are suitable for wheelchairs; beach wheelchairs are available at the Bonnett and Hargrove accesses, and the 8th Street access has a stability mat that makes getting a stroller or wheelchair on the beach easy. Many other areas have lifeguards and bathhouses. The town website lists all the accesses and provides a map. No matter where you land, expect clean sand and water. Vehicles are allowed on Nags Head beaches October through April with a town-issue permit. Leashed pets (maximum 10-foot leash) are allowed on Nags Head beaches year-round. **Amenities:** food and drink; lifeguards (late May–early September); parking (fee and no fee); showers; toilets. **Best for:** sunrise; sunset; swimming. ⊠ *S. Croatan Hwy.* ☎ *252/441–5508 town office* ⊕ *www.nagsheadnc.gov* ✆ *Free.*

WHERE TO EAT

$$$$ ✕ **Basnight's Lone Cedar Café.** Hearts were broken when this restaurant,
SEAFOOD owned by powerful North Carolina Senator Marc Basnight and fam-
FAMILY ily, burned in 2007, but it was rebuilt in a contemporary style with simple pine tables, large windows with waterfront views, and a huge glass-walled wine rack. North Carolina produce and seafood star here, including OBX-style clear clam chowder, she-crab soup, pan-blackened bluefish, and whole fried flounder. **Known for:** local seafood and produce; extra-friendly service. Ⓢ *Average main: $28* ⊠ *Nags Head-Manteo Causeway, 7623 S. Virginia Dare Trail* ☎ *252/441–5405* ⊕ *www.lonecedarcafe.com* ⊘ *Closed Mon.–Wed. and Jan.–early Feb. No lunch.*

$$$ ✕ **Blue Moon Beach Grill.** "Once in a blue moon, you have to taste
SEAFOOD life on a sandbar," says the sign over the bar at this small, quirky,
FAMILY and locally popular restaurant set in a small strip center. The gener-
Fodor'sChoice ously portioned fresh seafood and Southern comfort food, lively vibe,
★ friendly bartenders, and an open kitchen make first-timers feel at home and keep regulars returning. **Known for:** moderately priced seafood; Southern comfort food. Ⓢ *Average main: $20* ⊠ *Surfside Plaza, 4104 S. Virginia Dare Trail, MM 13, Shop 16* ☎ *252/261–2583* ⊕ *www.bluemoonbeachgrill.com.*

$ ✕ **John's Drive-in.** When a large milk shake is the only thing that will
FAST FOOD do on a hot summer day, this is the place to head for—locals say they
FAMILY are the best on the Outer Banks, or even on the planet. And when you
Fodor'sChoice just can't take one more night out at a fancy restaurant, John's will
★ come to the rescue with the best handheld food on the Outer Banks: burgers, subs, sandwiches (including grouper), all-beef hot dogs, and sides. **Known for:** milk shakes; sandwiches, hot dogs, and subs. Ⓢ *Average main: $8* ⊠ *3716 N. Virginia Dare Trail* ☎ *252/261–6227* ⊕ *www.johnsdrivein.com* ⊘ *Closed Jan. and Feb.*

Golf courses along the Outer Banks often have beautiful water views.

\$\$\$\$ ✕ **Owens' Restaurant.** Family owned since 1946, this restaurant, housed
SEAFOOD in a replica of an early-19th-century Outer Banks lifesaving station,
FAMILY is more like a museum: classic clapboard construction, pine paneling,
and numerous maritime artifacts. Stick with fresh-off-the-boat local
seafood or the prime beef. **Known for:** local seafood; prime beef; a Nags
Head institution. $ *Average main: $30* ⊠ *7114 S. Virginia Dare Trail
(U.S. 158), MM 16.5* ☎ *252/441–7309* ⊕ *www.owensrestaurant.com*
⊗ *Closed Jan.–early Mar. No lunch.*

\$\$ ✕ **Sam & Omie's.** Named after two fishermen, father and son, this no-
SEAFOOD nonsense shack opened in 1937 and is one of the Outer Banks' oldest
FAMILY restaurants. Fishing photos hang between mounted catches on the
walls, and classic country music twangs in the background. **Known
for:** big breakfasts; local-style steamed and fried seafood. $ *Aver-
age main: $17* ⊠ *7228 S. Virginia Dare Trail (U.S. 158, MM 16.5)*
⚓ *Across from Jennette's Pier* ☎ *252/441–7366* ⊕ *www.samandomies.
net* ⊗ *Closed Dec.–Feb.*

\$\$\$ ✕ **Sugar Creek Seafood Restaurant.** If fiery red sunsets and marinated
SEAFOOD tuna entice you, this is the place to eat. Sip a drink on the pier or
FAMILY in the gazebo to soak in Roanoke Sound's serene views. **Known for:**
large portions of local seafood; market next door with seafood to
go, cooked or uncooked. $ *Average main: $22* ⊠ *Nags Head-Man-
teo Causeway, 7340 S. Virginia Dare Trail* ☎ *252/441–4963* ⊕ *www.
sugarcreekseafood.com.*

WHERE TO STAY

\$\$\$ ⬚ **First Colony Inn.** Stand on the verandas that encircle this old, three-
B&B/INN story, cedar-shingle inn—saved from demolition and moved to the
present site—and admire the ocean views. **Pros:** screened-in porches;

some in-room hot tubs; microwaves and refrigerators in rooms. **Cons:** on a busy highway; you'll have to cross a road to get to the beach. [$] *Rooms from: $235* ✉ *6715 S. Croatan Hwy. (U.S. 158, MM 16)* ☎ *252/441–2343, 800/368–9390* 🌐 *www.firstcolonyinn.com* 🛏 *26 rooms* 🍴 *Breakfast.*

$$$ RESORT FAMILY **Surf Side Hotel.** This midsize beachfront resort near Jennette's Pier is Nags Head's best independent motel. **Pros:** rooms updated in 2016; great views of the beach and ocean; especially friendly and helpful staff. **Cons:** no elevator in the two-story building; some bathrooms are small. [$] *Rooms from: $249* ✉ *6701 S. Virginia Dare Trail* ☎ *252/441–2105, 800/552–7873* 🛏 *76 rooms* 🍴 *Breakfast.*

SPORTS AND THE OUTDOORS

FISHING

FAMILY Fodor'sChoice ★ **Jennette's Pier.** Built in 1939, Jennette's Pier was North Carolina's oldest wooden ocean-fishing pier until 2003 when Hurricane Isabel knocked it down. In 2009, the state of North Carolina came to the rescue, breaking ground for not only a new, 1,000-foot-long concrete pier but also a public beach access point with 262 free parking spaces. Operated by North Carolina Aquariums, this is a great spot for fishing—depending on the time of year you can catch black and red drum, flounder, king mackerel, mahimahi, gray trout, and others—and the website gives a daily fishing report along with details of some notable catches. Nonanglers can walk on the pier, check out educational programs and exhibits offered in the two-story, 16,000-square-foot pier house, or just laze on the wide, clean beach. ✉ *72223 S. Virginia Dare Trail* ✣ *Just north of the U.S. 64/Rte. 12 intersection* 🌐 *www.ncaquariums.com/jennettes-pier* 🎟 *Walk-on $2; fishing $12 (3-day fishing pass $30, 7-day $65, annual $275).*

GOLF

Nags Head Golf Links. Opened in 1986, this Scottish-links-style course borders Roanoke Sound, which is visible from five holes. Sea grass and rolling dunes separate most tees and greens, and brambles growing in the rough make accurate shots a priority. Make sure you bring plenty of spare golf balls. Together with coastal winds and a rugged shoreline, this makes for one of the area's most challenging courses, best suited to long hitters. This is a membership golf club, but the public can play the course. ✉ *5615 S. Seachase Dr., off Rte. 12, MM 15* ☎ *252/441–8073* 🌐 *www.clubcorp.com/Clubs/Nags-Head-Golf-Links* 🎟 *$59–$129 including golf cart, depending on the day and time* 🏌 *18 holes, 6126 yards, par 71; pro shop, driving range, lessons.*

HANG GLIDING

FAMILY **Kitty Hawk Kites.** One of the top hang-gliding outfitters in the country, with 10 locations along the Outer Banks, Kitty Hawk Kites—in business since 1974—gives beginner dune lessons. The only requirement is that you must be able to run approximately 10 yards; kids as young as four and people with most types of physical challenges can be accommodated. Jockey's Ridge is a favorite spot to learn, and instruction packages start at $99. A Hang 1 six-lesson package that starts you on your way to solo hang-gliding is $699. Those with the nerve can try a high-altitude tandem flight that soars up to a mile high. History buffs can try flying a reproduction of the Wright Brothers' 1902 glider. Kitty Hawk Kites also sells wind toys and gives kayaking, kiteboarding, parasailing, surfing, and paddleboarding classes and leads guided walking, Segway, and horseback riding tours. You can pick up sports gear and sportswear, plus souvenirs. ⊠ *Carolista Dr.* ☎ *877/359–8447 reservations, 252/441–2426 Nag's Head Hang-Gliding School* ⊕ *www.kittyhawk.com.*

SCUBA DIVING

Divers come here to explore the many shipwrecks just offshore. One of the favorites, and the first North Carolina Historic Shipwreck Site, is the 175-foot *Huron,* which lies underwater 250 yards off the beach at Nags Head Pier. The iron-hulled ship sank in a November storm in 1877, taking all but a handful of her 124-man crew with her.

Roanoke Island Outfitters & Dive Center. Run by NAUI instructors Matthew and Pam Landrum, Roanoke Island Outfitters & Dive Center has a 36-foot Bertram dive boat docked in Wanchese and a full-service dive shop in Manteo. The dive shop, which runs charters May to October, offers scuba, free diving, and spearfishing classes, beach and night dives, bike rentals, and fishing charters. There are also guided diving trips to more than 20 wreck sites including the *Huron,* a gunship steamer that went down in 1877; the *U-85* U-boat; the *York,* a 253-foot freighter; and the *Benson,* a 465-foot tanker. Half-day dives start at $130 per person, and full-day at $155. ⊠ *312 U.S. 64, Manteo* ☎ *252/473–1356* ⊕ *www.roanokeislandoutfittersanddivecenter.com.*

SURFING

Outer Banks Boarding Company. Rent or buy surfboards, skateboards, skimboards, bodyboards, and stand-up paddleboards. Outer Banks Boarding Company also offers private or group lessons and there's a retail shop. ⊠ *103 E. Morning View Pl. (U.S. 158, MM 11)* ☎ *252/441–1939* ⊕ *www.obbconline.com.*

SHOPPING

Morales Art Gallery. Since 1975 Gallery Row has been a small cluster of art-related businesses that sell everything from beach crafts to original seascapes to diamond earrings. Morales Art Gallery is the fine-arts store that started it all. Most of the gallery owners live on-site. ⊠ *207 E. Gallery Row* ☎ *252/441–6484, 800/635–6035* ⊕ *www.outerbanks. com/morales-art-galleries.html* ☉ *Closed Sun.*

Tanger Outlet Center. Here you'll find about two dozen stores—including Banana Republic, Bass, Coach, Eddie Bauer, J. Crew, and Polo Ralph Lauren—selling designer clothes, shoes, casual attire, books, sunglasses, and more. ⊠ *7100 S. Croatan Hwy.* ☎ *252/441–5634, 800/720–6747* ⊕ *www.tangeroutlet.com/nagshead.*

ROANOKE ISLAND

10 miles southwest of Nags Head.

On a hot July day in 1587, 117 men, women, and children left their boat and set foot on Roanoke Island to form the first permanent English settlement in the New World. Three years later, when a fleet with supplies from England landed, the settlers had disappeared without a trace, leaving a mystery that continues to baffle historians. Much of the 12-mile-long island, which lies between the Outer Banks and the mainland, remains wild. Of the island's two towns, Wanchese is the fishing village and Manteo is tourist oriented, with an aquarium and sights related to the island's history.

GETTING HERE AND AROUND

From the east, drive to the island on U.S. 64; from the Outer Banks, follow U.S. 158 to U.S. 64. Although Manteo's main drag and historic waterfront have sidewalks, a car is useful for visiting the town's various sites. Charter flights are available at Dare County Regional Airport.

ESSENTIALS

Visitor Information Outer Banks Welcome Center on Roanoke Island. ✉ *1 Visitors Center Circle, Manteo* ☎ *877/629–4386, 252/473–2138* ⊕ *www.outerbanks.org.*

EXPLORING

FAMILY **Elizabethan Gardens.** The lush gardens, 3 miles north of downtown Manteo, are a 10-acre re-creation of 16th-century English gardens, established as an elaborate memorial to the first English colonists. Walk through the brick and wrought-iron entrance to see antique statuary, wildflowers, rose gardens, a 400-year-old giant oak tree, and a sunken garden—something will be in bloom almost any time you visit. The gatehouse, designed in the style of a 16th-century orangery, serves as a reception center and gift and plant shop. Many weddings are held in one tranquil garden or another. ■ TIP→ **A smartphone audio tour is available through ONCELL.** ✉ *1411 National Park Dr.* ☎ *252/473–3234* ⊕ *www.elizabethangardens.org* 🎟 *$9* ☉ *Closed Feb.*

FAMILY **Fort Raleigh National Historic Site.** Fort Raleigh is a restoration of the original 1584–90 earthworks that mark the beginning of English-colonial Fodor's Choice history in America. The site has been identified as the original site of ★ the doomed Lost Colonists, and the question that hangs in the air here is, "What happened to the 117 men, women, and children of the 1587 expedition who disappeared without a trace?" ■ TIP→ **Be sure to see the orientation film before taking a guided tour of the fort.** A nature trail through the 513-acre grounds leads to an outlook over Albemarle Sound. Native American and Civil War history is also preserved here. ✉ *1500 Fort Raleigh Rd., Manteo* ☎ *252/473–2111 general information number for all Outer Banks NPS parks* ⊕ *www.nps.gov/fora* 🎟 *Free.*

The Lost Colony. Pulitzer Prize–winner Paul Green's drama was written in 1937 to mark the 350th birthday of Virginia Dare, the first English child born in the New World; in 2013 the show won a Tony Honor for Excellence in the Theatre. Except from 1942 to 1945 (when enemy German U-boats prowled the nearby Atlantic Ocean in during World War II), it has played every summer since in Fort Raleigh National Historic Site's Waterside Theatre, on the same grounds where the doomed English settlers tried to establish their new home. On a huge stage—larger than any on Broadway—and with a cast and crew of more than 130, the story of the first colonists, who settled here in 1587 and mysteriously vanished, is reenacted. Cast alumni include Andy Griffith and Lynn Redgrave. ■TIP→ Try to buy tickets at least a week in advance. Preshow, hour-long backstage tours, dinner packages, and afternoon shows for children are available. ✉ *1409 National Park Dr. ✛ Off U.S. 64, 3 miles north of downtown Manteo* ☎ *252/473–2127 office, 252/473–6000 box office* ⊕ *thelostcolony.org* ✍ *Tickets start at $20; rain insurance is $5* ⊙ *No performances mid-Aug.–mid-May; no performances Sun.*

FAMILY **National Wildlife Refuges Visitor Center.** If you've ever wondered what actually constitutes a national wildlife refuge, this is the place to find out, but don't expect boring science. In a new LEED-certified facility run by the U.S. Fish & Wildlife Service, you'll find lifelike dioramas and fun interactive exhibits, including a virtual "flyover" of 11 national wildlife refuges in a digital Cessna aircraft. Three crackerjack films are shown in a cushy 130-seat auditorium. If you're into native landscaping, you'll appreciate the plantings around the building, consisting entirely of vegetation exclusive to eastern North Carolina. The center has plans for further developments, including trails, gardens, and alternative energy displays. ✉ *100 Conservation Way, Manteo* ☎ *252/473–1131* ⊕ *www. fws.gov/ncgatewayvc* ✍ *Free.*

FAMILY **North Carolina Aquarium at Roanoke Island.** Occupying 68,000 square feet of space overlooking Croatan Sound, 3 miles northeast of Manteo, this aquarium underwent a major $4.5 million renovation in 2014–16, adding seven new (or updated) exhibits on sea turtles, shipwreck marine life, and wild wetlands. *The Graveyard of the Atlantic*—a 285,000-gallon ocean tank containing sharks and the re-created remains of the USS *Monitor,* sunk off Hatteras Island in 1862—remains the centerpiece exhibit. The aquarium hosts a slew of activities and field trips, from feeding fish to learning about medicinal aquatic plants to a workshop on injured sea turtles. It also manages the 1,000-foot-long Jennette's Pier in Nags Head. ✉ *374 Airport Rd., Manteo* ☎ *252/475–2300* ⊕ *www. ncaquariums.com* ✍ *$10.95.*

FAMILY **Roanoke Island Festival Park.** This multifunctional attraction sits on the waterfront in Manteo. Costumed interpreters conduct tours of the 69-foot ship, *Elizabeth II,* a representation of a 16th-century vessel, but you can also help them set the sails, plot a course, and swab the decks. The 25-acre park is home to the interactive Roanoke Adventure Museum, representing 400 years of local history. There's also a re-created 16th-century settlement site, a Native American exhibit, a fossil pit, plays and concerts at indoor and outdoor venues, arts-and-crafts exhibitions, a gift shop, and special programs. ✉ *1 Festival Park, off Budleigh St., Manteo* ☎ *252/475–1500* ⊕ *www.roanokeisland.com* ✍ *$10 good for 2 consecutive days* ⊙ *Closed Jan.–early Mar.*

At Roanoke Island Festival Park, you can help costumed 16th-century "sailors" set the sails and swab the decks of the *Elizabeth II.*

WHERE TO EAT

$$$$ MODERN AMERICAN 🍴 **1587 Restaurant.** This bay-side restaurant in The Tranquil House Inn serves creative cuisine alongside with magical waterfront views. Repeat customers like the ever-changing menu, which highlights local seafood and vegetables. **Known for:** casually elegant dining; fresh local seafood; herbs and vegetables from inn's garden. [$] *Average main: $28* ✉ *Tranquil House Inn, 405 Queen Elizabeth Ave., Manteo* ☎ *252/473–1587* 🌐 *www.1587.com.*

$ DELI FAMILY 🍴 **Poor Richard's Sandwich Shop.** Open since 1984, there is often a long line at the rear of this downtown Manteo institution. Homemade sweet-potato biscuits are breakfast favorites, while cold and grilled classic sandwiches like BLTs, Reubens, tuna melts, and pimento cheese fuel hungry noon crowds. **Known for:** hearty, inexpensive sandwiches. [$] *Average main: $8* ✉ *303 Queen Elizabeth Ave., Manteo* ☎ *252/473–3333* 🌐 *www.poorrichardsmanteo.com.*

WHERE TO STAY

$$$ B&B/INN FAMILY 🏨 **Tranquil House Inn.** This charming 19th-century-style waterfront inn is just steps from shops, restaurants, and Roanoke Island Festival Park. **Pros:** rear porches overlook the water; complimentary evening wine reception; convenient location. **Cons:** on busy commercial waterfront; some rooms need updating. [$] *Rooms from: $230* ✉ *405 Queen Elizabeth Ave., Manteo* ☎ *252/473–1404, 800/458–7069* 🌐 *www.tranquilhouseinn.com* 🕒 *Closed Christmas wk* 🛏 *25 rooms* 🍽 *Breakfast.*

$$$$ B&B/INN 🏨 **White Doe Inn.** Just up the street from Manteo's romantic waterfront, this B&B is listed on the National Register of Historic Places and meets all the criteria for luxury wrapped in serenity. **Pros:** spa and concierge

services; two-person whirlpools in some rooms; four-course breakfast; 24-hour butler's wine pantry. **Cons:** it's a popular wedding venue, so high-season availability can be scarce; rooms not individually climate-controlled. [$] *Rooms from: $275* ✉ *319 Sir Walter Raleigh St., Manteo* ☎ *252/473–9851, 800/473–6091* 🌐 *www.whitedoeinn.com* 🛏 *8 rooms, 1 cottage* 🍴 *Breakfast.*

2

SPORTS AND THE OUTDOORS

SAILING

FAMILY **Pirates Cove Marina.** This 195-slip marina on the west side of Roanoke Sound has a deep-water charter dock as well as a seafood restaurant, a swimming pool, a kiddie pool and playground, a fitness center, and a 13,000-square-foot pavilion for private events. ✉ *2000 Sailfish Dr., Manteo* ☎ *252/473–3906, 800/367–4728* 🌐 *www.fishpiratescove.com.*

CAPE HATTERAS NATIONAL SEASHORE

Fodor's Choice ★ Longtime visitors to the Outer Banks, who see how development has changed these once-unspoiled barrier islands, appreciate that the 70-mile stretch of the Cape Hatteras National Seashore will remain protected. Its pristine beaches, set aside as the first national seashore in 1953, stretch from the southern outskirts of Nags Head to Ocracoke Inlet, encompassing three narrow islands: Bodie, Hatteras, and Ocracoke.

These waters provide some of the East Coast's best fishing and surfing, and they're ideal for other sports such as windsurfing, diving, and boating. Parking is allowed only in designated areas. Fishing piers are in Rodanthe and Avon.

With 300 miles of coastline, there are plenty of beaches that don't have lifeguards on duty. **■TIP→ Only three National Seashore beaches—Coquina Beach, Buxton Beach, and Ocracoke Beach—regularly have lifeguards from late May to early September.**

HATTERAS ISLAND

15 miles south of Nags Head.

The Herbert C. Bonner Bridge, being replaced by a new bridge that's set for completion in 2019, arches for 3 miles over Oregon Inlet and carries traffic to Hatteras Island, a 42-mile-long curved ribbon of sand and starkly beautiful dunes dividing the Atlantic Ocean and Pamlico Sound. At its most distant point (Cape Hatteras), the island is 25 miles from the mainland. About 88% of the island belongs to Cape Hatteras National Seashore and the state of North Carolina; the remainder is privately owned in seven quaint villages strung along the two-lane NC Route 12, the only main road on the island.

Hatteras Island is known as the blue marlin (or billfish) capital of the world. The Continental Shelf, 40 miles offshore, and its current, combined with the nearby Gulf Stream and Deep West Boundary Current, create an unparalleled fish habitat. The total population of the seven villages—from north to south, Rodanthe, Waves, Salvo, Avon, Buxton, Frisco, and Hatteras Village—is around 4,500, but in summer when the hundreds of vacation rental houses fill up, the island's population swells by several-fold. There are not many motels on Hatteras as most visitors stay in vacation houses. Avon is the village with the largest number of vacation rentals. Large waterfront houses with 6 to 10 bedrooms, private swimming pool, an elevator, and even a movie theater can go for $15,000 or more a week in summer, although many more-modest rentals are available.

GETTING HERE AND AROUND

From the north, reach Hatteras Island via U.S. 158. From the east, take U.S. 64 to U.S. 158. South of the Outer Banks on the mainland, U.S. 70 leads to an auto ferry at Cedar Island and U.S. 264 leads to one at Swan Quarter; both take you to Ocracoke village and Route 12. From the north end of Ocracoke Island, another auto ferry gets you to Hatteras village. Small planes can land at the National Park Service's Billy Mitchell Airfield in Frisco. Some charter flights are available from nearby airports.

ESSENTIALS

Visitor Information Hatteras Welcome Center. ⊠ *57190 Kohler Rd., Hatteras Village* ☎ *252/986–2203, 877/629–4386* ⊕ *www.outerbanks.com/hatteras-welcome-center-and-us-weather-bureau-station.html.*

EXPLORING

FAMILY

Fodor's Choice

★

Bodie Island Light Station. The original Bodie (pronounced "body") lighthouse was constructed in 1847 but had to be abandoned in 1859 because of structural issues; the replacement lighthouse was destroyed by Confederate troops in 1861. The current black-and-white banded, 156-foot-tall lighthouse was completed in 1872 and has been restored several times, most recently in 2013. The original light keepers' home, last remodeled in 1992, now serves as a ranger station and information center. From the third Friday in April to Columbus Day, you can climb the 214 steps to the top. (Children must be at least 42 inches tall, and climbers must weigh less than 260 pounds.) ⊠ *Cape Hatteras National Seashore, 8210 Bodie Island Lighthouse Rd., Bodie Island* ☎ *252/475–9000 National Park Service information* ⊕ *www.nps.gov/caha/planyourvisit/bils.htm* ☜ *Grounds and visitor center free; $8 to climb lighthouse* ☉ *Lighthouse tower closed mid-Oct.–late Apr.*

FAMILY

Fodor's Choice

★

Cape Hatteras Lighthouse. Authorized by Congress in 1794 to help prevent shipwrecks, this was the first lighthouse built in the region. The original structure was lost to erosion and Civil War damage; this 1870 replacement, 30 miles south of Rodanthe, is, at 210 feet, the tallest brick lighthouse in the United States. Endangered by the sea, in 1999 the lighthouse, with its distinctive black and white spiral paint and red and tan base, was raised and rolled some 2,900 feet inland to its present location. A visitor center is located near the base of the lighthouse. In summer the Museum of the Sea in the former keeper's quarters is open, and you can climb the lighthouse's 257 narrow steps to the viewing balcony. Children under 42 inches tall aren't allowed to climb. Offshore lie the remains of the USS *Monitor*, a Confederate ironclad ship that sank in 1862. ⊠ *Lighthouse Rd., off Rte. 12, Buxton* ☎ *252/995–4474 National Park Service* ⊕ *www.nps.gov/caha/planyourvisit/climbing-the-cape-hatteras-lighthouse.htm* ☜ *Visitor center and keeper's quarters free, lighthouse climb $8* ☉ *Lighthouse and museum closed mid-Oct.–late Apr.*

FAMILY

Fodor's Choice

★

Chicamacomico Lifesaving Station. Pronounced "chik-a-ma- *com*-i-co," the restored lifesaving station is now a museum that tells the story of the brave people who manned 29 stations that once lined the Outer Banks. These were the precursors to today's Coast Guard, with staff who rescued people and animals from seacraft in distress. Eight buildings on 7 acres include a cookhouse, bathhouse, stables, workshop, and the original 1874 lifesaving station. You'll see original equipment and tools, artifacts, and exhibits. A 1907 cottage moved to the site portrays 19th- and early-20th-century life along the Outer Banks. ✉ *23645 NC Hwy. 12, MM 39.5, Rodanthe* ☎ *252/987–1552 Chicamacomico Historical Association* ⊕ *www.chicamacomico.org* ✉ *$8 (admission good for 1 wk)* ◷ *Closed late Nov.–mid-Apr.*

FAMILY

Frisco Native American Museum & Natural History Center. A collection of Native American artifacts fills this museum. Galleries display native art from across the United States as well as relics from the first inhabitants of Hatteras Island. The museum has been designated as a North Carolina Environmental Education Center. Behind the museum are nature trails, and there's a gift shop. ✉ *53536 Rte. 12, Frisco* ☎ *252/995–4440* ⊕ *www.nativeamericanmuseum.org* ✉ *$5; $15 per household* ◷ *Closed Mon. Winter hrs may vary, call ahead.*

FAMILY

Fodor's Choice

★

Pea Island National Wildlife Refuge. This refuge, at the north end of Hatteras Island, consists of 5,834 acres of marsh on the Atlantic Flyway, plus 25,700 acres of refuge waters. To the delight of birders, more than 365 species have been sighted from its observation platforms and spotting scopes and by visitors who venture into the refuge. Pea Island is home to threatened peregrine falcons, piping plovers, and tundra swans, which winter here, and 25 species of mammals, 24 species of reptiles, and five species of amphibians. A visitor center on Route 12 has an information display and maps of the two trails, including one named for the late broadcaster Charles Kuralt, a Tar Heel native who wrote extensively about the North Carolina coast. On the west side of Route 12 are more than 12 miles of pristine beach. ■TIP→ **Remember to douse yourself in bug spray, especially in spring.** ✉ *15440 Rte. 12, Rodanthe* ☎ *252/473–1131* ⊕ *www.fws.gov/refuge/pea_island* ✉ *Free.*

BEACHES

FAMILY

Coquina Beach. In the Cape Hatteras National Seashore, but just a few miles south of Nags Head off Route 12, at mile marker 26, Coquina is considered by locals to be one of the loveliest beaches in the Outer Banks. The wide-beam ribs of the shipwreck *Laura Barnes* rest in the dunes here. Driven onto the Outer Banks by a nor'easter in 1921, she ran aground north of this location; the entire crew survived. The wreck was moved to Coquina Beach in 1973 and displayed behind ropes, but subsequent hurricanes have scattered the remains and covered them with sand, making it difficult, if not impossible, to discern. **Amenities:** parking (no fee); showers; toilets; lifeguards (late May–early September). **Best for:** swimming; sunrise. ✉ *Hatteras National Seashore, NC Rte. 12* ⊕ *www.nps.gov/caha* ✉ *Free.*

WHERE TO EAT

$ CAFÉ FAMILY

🍴 **Buxton Munch Company.** This casual lunch spot, tucked away in a strip center, has been going strong for nearly 20 years, specializing in wraps, burgers, fish and shrimp tacos, salads, and sandwiches of all kinds. There's nothing fancy here, but prices are reasonable, and there may be a line at peak times. **Known for:** salads, seafood tacos, wraps, burgers, and sandwiches; inexpensive and fairly quick lunch (but it's not fast food). [$] *Average main: $10* ✉ *Osprey Shopping Center, 47359 NC Rte. 12, Buxton* ✥ *Next to ABC store* ☎ *252/995–5502* 🌐 *www.buxtonmunch.com* ⏲ *Closed Sun., Dec.–mid-Mar. No breakfast or dinner.*

$$$$ SEAFOOD Fodor's Choice ★

🍴 **Café Pamlico.** Overlooking Pamlico Sound, Café Pamlico is arguably the best restaurant on Hatteras Island. The understated decor with dark green tones underscores the fact that the focus here is squarely on locally sourced seafood, vegetables from the inn's own garden, and friendly service by local staff. **Known for:** locally sourced seafood; fresh vegetables from the inn's garden; fine-dining atmosphere rare on Outer Banks. [$] *Average main: $30* ✉ *Inn on Pamlico Sound, 49684 NC Rte. 12, Buxton* ☎ *252/995–4500* 🌐 *innonpamlicosound.com.*

$$ AMERICAN FAMILY

🍴 **Oceanas Bistro.** Open year-round for lunch and dinner (seasonally for breakfast), this long-established and popular roadside restaurant is a great spot to get local seafood and a variety of other dishes at moderate prices. Daily specials range from prime rib to tacos and grillers, a cross between a pizza and a quesadilla that's topped with tuna, crab, chicken, or veggies. **Known for:** well-prepared seafood and other dishes; moderate prices; tuna, crab, or chicken grillers. [$] *Average main: $19* ✉ *40774 NC Rte. 12, Avon* ☎ *252/995–4991* 🌐 *www.oceanasbistro.com.*

WHERE TO STAY

$ HOTEL FAMILY

🏨 **Cape Pines Motel.** Though most visitors to Hatteras Island stay in a vacation rental house, this small, 1950s-era motel fills the bill for a night or two. **Pros:** very pet-friendly; large, very clean rooms in main building and new section; swimming pool; modest prices, even in-season. **Cons:** retro style of the main building may be off-putting; not directly on the beach. [$] *Rooms from: $140* ✉ *47497 NC Rte. 12, Buxton* ☎ *252/995–5666* 🌐 *www.capepinesmotel.com* 🛏 *29 rooms* 🍽 *No meals.*

$$$ B&B/INN Fodor's Choice ★

🏨 **The Inn on Pamlico Sound.** You'll feel like an honored houseguest in this casually elegant, full-service boutique hotel, with sweeping waterfront views, intuitive rather than intrusive service, and an indoor-outdoor fine-dining restaurant, Café Pamlico. **Pros:** rooms come in a variety of configurations and price ranges; complimentary fishing gear; 14-seat private theater with film library. **Cons:** sound-side beach isn't as attractive as ocean beaches; popular wedding and event venue may limit availability during high season; no elevators. [$] *Rooms from: $205* ✉ *49684 NC Rte. 12, Buxton* ☎ *866/995–7030* 🌐 *www.innonpamlicosound.com* 🛏 *12 rooms* 🍽 *Breakfast.*

SPORTS AND OUTDOORS

FISHING

Oregon Inlet Fishing Center. This full-service marina, at the north end of Oregon Inlet Bridge on Hatteras Island, offers charter-boat sound and deep-sea fishing excursions and has supplies such as bait, tackle, ice,

OUTER BANKS VACATION RENTALS

Many visitors to the Outer Banks, especially family groups, choose to rent a vacation home rather than staying in a resort, motel, or inn. Rentals on the Outer Banks range from basic condo studio apartments to 10-bedroom, 12-bath beachfront mansions with private pools, movie theaters, gyms, and business centers. In most areas, you have a choice of oceanfront, sound front, water view, or a certain number of blocks back from the beach. Rental prices vary greatly by season, with the highest rates usually being June or July through Labor Day and the lowest from November to April (holiday weeks may be higher). A big beachfront house that might go for $2,000 a week in winter could go for $15,000 on peak weeks in July and August.

OUTER BANKS VACATION RENTALS

Before you check in, here are some rental companies to check out. Some offer rentals all over the Outer Banks, while others focus on, say, just Duck and Corolla, or on Hatteras Island. While most companies have multiple locations, only the address of one, often the main or largest office, is listed, along with the main reservation number and website. **Airbnb** (⊕ *www. airbnb.com*), **Vacation Rentals By Owner** (⊕ *www.vrbo.com*), and other national online rental companies also have many listings on the Outer Banks and, indeed, all along the North Carolina coast.

Midgett Realty. With three offices, Midgett Realty offers rentals in the villages of Rodanthe, Salvo, and Waves on Hatteras Island. ✉ *23198 NC Hwy. 12, Rodanthe* ☎ *866/348–8819* ⊕ *www.midgettrealty.com.*

Ocracoke Island Realty. Ocracoke Island Realty offers vacation rentals on Ocracoke Island. ✉ *1075 Irvin Garrish Hwy., Ocracoke Island* ☎ *866/806–0782* ⊕ *www. ocracokeislandrealty.com.*

Outer Beaches Realty. Outer Beaches Realty offers rentals on Hatteras Island, with offices in Avon, Hatteras Village, and Waves. ✉ *40227 Tigrone Blvd., Avon* ☎ *800/ 627–1850* ⊕ *www.outerbeaches.com.*

Sun Realty. With seven offices, Sun Realty offers vacation rentals over most of the Outer Banks except Ocracoke. ✉ *1500 S. Croatan Hwy., Kill Devil Hills* ☎ *888/853–7770* ⊕ *www.sunrealtync.com.*

2

and fuel for the angler. The National Park Service maintains an adjacent boat launch. ■**TIP➔ A new Oregon Inlet Bridge is under construction.** ✉ *98 Rte. 12* ☎ *252/441–6301, 800/272–5199 toll-free charter boat reservations* ⊕ *www.oregon-inlet.com.*

SHOPPING

FAMILY
Fodor's Choice
★

Buxton Village Books. This independent bookstore in an old cottage on Highway 12 near the middle of town has been a fixture in Buxton for decades. The knowledgeable owner keeps a large selection of regional books as well as used and new books in all genres, plus greeting cards and gifts. The bookshop is open year-round, but only three days a week in winter. ✉ *47918 NC Rte. 12, Buxton* ☎ *252/ 995–4240* ⊕ *www. buxtonvillagebooks.com* ☉ *Closed Sun.–Wed. in winter.*

OCRACOKE ISLAND

Ocracoke Village: 15 miles southwest of Hatteras Village.

Around 950 people live on what is the last inhabited island in the Outer Banks, which can be reached only by water or air. The village, one of the most charming on the entire North Carolina coast, is in the widest part of the island, cradled around a harbor called Silver Lake. Inns, motels, and shops line the main street, while the Ocracoke lighthouse is in a nearby residential area at the end of Lighthouse Road. Man-made canals form the landscape of a smaller residential area called Oyster Creek.

Centuries ago, Ocracoke was the stomping ground of Edward Teach, the pirate better known as Blackbeard, and a major treasure cache from 1718 is still rumored to be hidden somewhere on the island. Fort Ocracoke was a short-lived Confederate stronghold that was abandoned in August 1861 and blown up by Union forces a month later.

Although the island remains a destination for people seeking peace and quiet, silence can be hard to find in summer, when tourists and boaters swamp the place. About 90% of Ocracoke is within Cape Hatteras National Seashore and the island is on the Atlantic Flyway for many migrating land and water birds. The 16 miles of Ocracoke Beach are wild, wide, and pristine, and many argue that it's the best beach in North Carolina.

GETTING HERE AND AROUND

The only way to reach Ocracoke Island is by ferry or private boat. A free auto ferry leaves hourly—and more frequently in peak summer season—from Hatteras Island and arrives 55 minutes later; toll ferries ($15 one way) connect with the mainland at Swan Quarter (2½ hours) and at Cedar Island (2¼ hours). Depending on the season, state ferries land at either end of the island and depart as late as 8 pm to Cedar Island and midnight to Hatteras Island. The ferry to and from Hatteras Island is first-come, first-served, but reservations should be made in advance for Cedar Island and Swan Quarter.

Only one road, Route 12, traverses the island. Quiet streets shoot off to the left and right at the south end. Lots of cyclists come to Ocracoke, and many inns have bikes or golf carts for their guests. Use caution when biking Route 12, especially in summer; traffic can be heavy, and the designated bike path doesn't extend the highway's entire 13-mile length.

ESSENTIALS

Visitor Information National Park Service Visitor Center. ⊠ *NC Rte. 12 (38 Irvin Garrish Hwy.)* ✛ *At Ocracoke village ferry landing* ☎ *252/928–4531* ⊕ *www.nps.gov/caha/planyourvisit/visitor-centers.htm.*

EXPLORING

FAMILY **British Cemetery.** On May 11, 1942, the HMS *Bedfordshire,* an armed British trawler on loan to the United States, was torpedoed by a German U-boat and sank with all 34 hands lost off the coast of Ocracoke Island. The men were buried on Ocracoke in a corner of the community graveyard. The wreck was discovered in 1980 and some artifacts

2

were recovered. It's still frequented by divers. ⊠ *British Cemetery Rd., Ocracoke Village* ☎ *252/926–9171* ⊕ *www.nps.gov/caha/historycul-ture/british-cemetery.htm* ☒ *Free.*

OFF THE BEATEN PATH

Mattamuskeet National Wildlife Refuge. Hyde County's Lake Mattamuskeet is the largest natural lake in North Carolina. Fed only by rainwater and runoff, the lake is 3 feet below sea level. Once drained for farmland, the reclaimed 40,000-acre lake is the centerpiece of a 50,000-acre wildlife refuge that echoes with the calls of some 800 bird and wildlife species including beautiful tundra swans who call the lake their winter home. ⊠ *85 Mattamuskeet Rd., Swan Quarter* ✛ *It's a 2½-hr ferry ride from Ocracoke to Swan Quarter, then a 15-min drive from the Swan Quarter ferry landing* ☎ *252/926–4021 Mattamuskeet National Wildlife Refuge, 800/293–3779 for ferry* ⊕ *www.fws.gov/refuge/mattamuskeet/* ☒ *Free.*

FAMILY
Fodor's Choice
★

Ocracoke Light Station. This lighthouse is a photographer's dream. Built in 1823, it's the second-oldest operating lighthouse in the United States (Sandy Hook, New Jersey, has the oldest). It was first fueled by whale oil, then kerosene, and finally electricity. The lighthouse is built entirely of brick, 5 feet thick at the base and 2 feet thick at the top. The white finish was once achieved with a blend of unslaked lime, glue, rice, salt, and powdered fish. The 77 feet, 5 inches tall structure is no longer open to the public for climbing, but the grounds are accessible year-round. ⊠ *Lighthouse Rd., Ocracoke Village* ☎ *252/475–9000 general park information* ⊕ *www.nps.gov/caha/planyourvisit/ols.htm* ☒ *Free.*

FAMILY

Ocracoke Pony Pen. From the observation platform, 6 miles southwest of the north Hatteras-Ocracoke ferry landing, you can look out at the descendants of the Banker Ponies that roamed wild before the island came under the jurisdiction of Cape Hatteras National Seashore. The Park Service took over management of the ponies in the early 1960s and has helped maintain the population of 25–30 animals; the wild herd once numbered nearly 500. All the animals you see today were born in captivity and are fed and kept on a 180-acre range. Legends abound about the arrival of the island's Banker Ponies. Some believe they made their way to the island after the abandonment of Roanoke's Lost Colony. Others believe they were left by early Spanish explorers or swam to shore following the sinking of the *Black Squall,* a ship carrying circus performers. ⊠ *NC Rte. 12* ☎ *252/475–9000 general park information* ⊕ *www.nps. gov/caha/historyculture/ocracokeponies.htm* ☒ *Free.*

FAMILY

Ocracoke Preservation Society Museum. Run by the local preservation society, the museum is located in a restored American Foursquare house built more than 100 years ago. It was moved to its present location in 1989 and contains photographs and artifacts illustrating the island's lifestyle and history as well as a research library, with photographs and reference materials on island history (viewed by appointment.) On display in the backyard is a round-stern fishing boat from 1934, typical of boats used on the island at that time. The museum is off NC Route 12 on National Park Service land across from the Cedar Island ferry dock in Ocracoke village. ⊠ *49 Water Plant Rd., Ocracoke Village* ☎ *252/928–7375* ⊕ *www.ocracokepreservation.org* ☒ *Free* ☉ *Closed Sun. and early Dec.–late Mar.*

See the descendants of the wild Banker Ponies that used to roam Ocracoke Island at the Ocracoke Pony Pen.

WHERE TO EAT

$$$$
SEAFOOD
FAMILY
Fodor'sChoice
★

✕ **Back Porch Restaurant & Wine Bar.** What looks like a cozy little cottage in the woods actually serves stellar seafood like crab cakes and seared tuna steaks with mango salsa. There are also vegetarian options on the menu as well as meat-based dishes like a pecan-crusted chicken breast in bourbon sauce. **Known for:** fresh local seafood in creative preparations; charming dining space in the woods. Ⓢ *Average main: $27* ⊠ *110 Back Rd., Ocracoke Village* ☎ *252/928–6401* ⊕ *www.backporchocracoke. com* ⊗ *Hrs vary in winter.*

$$$$
SEAFOOD
Fodor'sChoice
★

✕ **The Flying Melon Café.** One of, if not *the*, top restaurant in Ocracoke, the Flying Melon focuses on seafood with Louisiana Creole and Southern twists (the owners lived in New Orleans) creating dishes like seafood gumbo and fried green tomatoes with remoulade sauce. The atmosphere is lively, the service is friendly, and there's a full bar to quench your thirst. **Known for:** fresh seafood provided by local Ocracoke fishermen; some dishes done in a New Orleans Creole style. Ⓢ *Average main: $27* ⊠ *181 Back Rd.* ☎ *252/928–2533* ⊗ *Closed Jan.–early Feb.*

$$
AMERICAN

✕ **Howard's Pub.** This long-established pub is a boisterous and friendly place to eat and drink, with a quick-footed staff who aim to please. Don't miss the fresh-cut pub fries, half-pound burgers, grilled fresh catch, oysters shucked to order, or appetizers like conch fritters or steamed shrimp. **Known for:** large selection of draft and bottled beer; good island bar food like fresh-shucked oysters and conch fritters; burgers and hand-cut pub fries. Ⓢ *Average main: $18* ⊠ *1175 Irvin Garrish Hwy. (NC Rte. 12), Ocracoke Village* ☎ *252/928–4441* ⊕ *www. howardspub.com* ⊗ *Closed mid-Nov.–mid-Mar.*

2

WHERE TO STAY

$$$$ B&B/INN FAMILY Fodor's Choice ★ **Captain's Landing Waterfront Inn.** This small, yellow inn is perched right on Silver Lake in the heart of the village, within walking distance of most restaurants, bars, and the lighthouse. **Pros:** just a few feet from the water; private balconies with views of the harbor and the lighthouse; large suites; very well managed. **Cons:** no elevator; breakfast not included. [$] *Rooms from: $280* ✉ *324 NC Rte. 12 (Irvin Garrish Hwy.), Ocracoke Village* ☎ *252/928–1999* ⇨ *10 rooms* 🍴 *No meals.*

$$ B&B/INN Fodor's Choice ★ **Ocracoke Harbor Inn.** Comfort and convenience are yours in these water-facing rooms, stocked with plenty of amenities like free Wi-Fi, individual climate control, refrigerators, and coffee pots. **Pros:** most upscale inn on island; boat docking free with inn stay; well-managed and meticulously maintained inn; away from busiest part of village but within walking distance. **Cons:** across street from the harbor; some rooms may have noise from adjacent rooms; office not staffed overnight. [$] *Rooms from: $170* ✉ *144 Silver Lake Rd.* ☎ *252/928–5731, 888/456–1998* 🌐 *www.ocracokeharborinn.com* ⏲ *Closed Dec.–mid-Mar.* ⇨ *24 rooms and suites, plus 5 rental cottages* 🍴 *Breakfast.*

SPORTS AND THE OUTDOORS

BEACHES

FAMILY Fodor's Choice ★ **Ocracoke Island Beaches.** The 16 miles of undeveloped shoreline here are often onsidered some of the best beaches in America. These beaches are among the least populated and most beautiful on the Cape Hatteras National Seashore. The shelling is amazing, the solitude unparalleled. Four public-access areas are close to the main beach road, Route 12, and easy to spot; just look for large brown-and-white wooden signs. ■ **TIP→ There are only lifeguards at the day-use beach ½ mile north of Ocracoke Village in late May through early September.** **Amenities:** parking (no fee); toilets; lifeguards. **Best for:** solitude; sunrise; sunset; surfing; swimming; windsurfing. ✉ *Irvin Garrish Hwy. (Rte. 12)* 🌐 *www.nps.gov/caha/planyourvisit/wateractivities.htm* 🎟 *Free.*

SHOPPING

FAMILY **Community Store.** Established in 1918, this combination grocery, general store, and snack bar is located in the middle of the village on the waterfront. It's still locally owned and operated, and you can get just about anything at this little store, from a bag of Doritos or organic foods to marine supplies or toys like potato guns. ✉ *294 Irving Garrish Hwy. (NC Rte. 12), Ocracoke Village* ☎ *252/928–9956.*

CAPE LOOKOUT NATIONAL SEASHORE

3-hr ferry ride southwest of Ocracoke Island via Cedar Island.

Extending for 55 miles from Portsmouth Island to Shackleford Banks, Cape Lookout National Seashore includes 28,400 acres of uninhabited, remote, sandy islands and marsh, which are linked to the mainland by ferries. Loggerhead sea turtles, which are on the federal list of threatened and endangered species, nest here. To the south, wild ponies roam Shackleford Banks. Four-wheel-drive vehicles are allowed on the beach, and primitive camping is allowed. There are primitive cabins (with and without electricity, no linens or utensils) with bunk beds. Ferry service is available from Beaufort to Shackleford Banks, Beaufort, and Harkers Island to the Cape Lookout Lighthouse area, from Davis to Shingle Point, from Atlantic to North Core Banks and Long Point, and from Ocracoke Village to Portsmouth Village.

GETTING HERE AND AROUND
The park's islands are only accessible by boat. Various private ferries run back and forth, and a list of authorized ferry services can be found at the park's website (⊕ *www.nps.gov/calo/planyourvisit/ferry.htm*).

ESSENTIALS
Harkers Island Visitor Center. ⊠ *131 Charles St., Harkers Island* ☎ *252/728–2250* ⊕ *www.nps.gov/calo/planyourvisit/visitorcenters.htm* 🖃 *Park free, ferry ride $15–$35.*

EXPLORING

FAMILY
Fodor's Choice
★

Cape Lookout Lighthouse. When the original 1812 lighthouse proved too short and unstable, the 1859 structure was built to replace it. The double walls allow the tower to rise as tall as required—169 feet—without making the building unstable. This lighthouse on Core Banks island withstood retreating Confederate troops' attempts to blow it up to keep it out of Union hands (they stole the lens instead). With its white-and-black diamond markings, the beacon continues to function as a navigational aid. A small museum inside the Harkers Island Visitor Center over on Harkers Island tells the story of the lighthouse from its first incarnation in 1812. A private ferry, Island Express Ferry Services, runs between Harkers Island and the lighthouse area. It also runs a ferry from the town of Beaufort to the lighthouse area. Anyone 44 inches or taller may climb the tower's 207 steps from mid-May to mid-September. The climb is worth it for an incomparable view of Cape Lookout's wild shores. Tickets must be purchased at the lighthouse on a first-come, first-served basis; reservations are not accepted. ⊠ *Cape Lookout National Seashore Administration Office, 131 Charles St., Harkers Island* ☎ *252/728–7433 Island Express Ferry Services (private ferry), 252/728–2250 Cape Lookout park service information line* ⊕ *www.nps.gov/calo/planyourvisit/lighthouse-climbs.htm* 🖃 *Grounds free; $8 lighthouse; $16 round-trip for pedestrian ferry from Harkers Island, $35 round-trip from Beaufort* ⊘ *Lighthouse closed mid-Sept.–late May; climbing also closed Sun. and Mon. late May–mid-Sept.; Harkers Island and Beaufort ferries closed Oct.–Feb.*

FAMILY
Portsmouth Village. Inhabited from 1753 until the early 1970s, the village listed 685 permanent residents at its peak in 1860, according to the census that year, making it one of the larger settlements on the Outer Banks. It was a "lightering" town, where ships heavy with cargo had to unload to smaller boats that could navigate the shallow Ocracoke Inlet. But the Civil War and the dredging of a deeper inlet at Hatteras were the beginning of the end for Portsmouth. By 1956 there were 17 inhabitants; the last two left in 1971. Today the public can tour the visitor center, the one-room schoolhouse, the post office and general store, and the turn-of-the-20th-century Life Saving Station (a multiroom Coast Guard station). Guided tours are available June 1 to September 1. The walking trails can be difficult because of

standing water, sandy soil, and mosquitoes. Public restrooms are not abundant; bring your own food and water. Rudy Austin's Portsmouth Islands Boat Tours runs a passenger boat from Ocracoke; Morris Marina Ferry Service operates a vehicle and pedestrian ferry from Atlantic, North Carolina, to Long Point Cabin Area with access to Portsmouth Island. ⊠ *Portsmouth Island ✚ Take private ferry from Ocracoke* ☏ *252/728–2250 park information line, 252/928–4361 Rudy Austin's Portsmouth Island Boat Tours (passenger ferry), 252/225–4261 Morris Marina (passenger and vehicle ferries)* ⊕ *www. nps.gov/calo/planyourvisit/visit-portsmouth.htm* 🖾 *Free; passenger ferry $14 round-trip; car ferry $75–$90 round-trip* ☉ *Ranger programs and guided tours don't operate Oct.–May; ferry services don't operate Nov.–Mar.*

SPORTS AND THE OUTDOORS

BEACHES

FAMILY **Cape Lookout Beach.** White sand beaches, blue-green waters, and a tall lighthouse mark this quiet beach at the southern tip of Cape Lookout National Seashore. A boat is the only way to get here. Passenger ferries leave from Harkers Island and Beaufort, while passenger and vehicle ferries leave from Davis and Atlantic. Land on the sound side, then walk across a path to the beach, where you'll be greeted by a long beach strand full of seashells, including large whelk shells. In-season, you can also climb the lighthouse tower or tour a museum in the keeper's quarters. **Amenities:** toilets. **Best for:** solitude; sunrise; sunset; swimming; walking. ⊠ *Cape Lookout National Seashore* ⊕ *www.nps.gov/calo* 🖾 *Beach free; $16 round-trip pedestrian ferry from Harkers Island, $35 from Beaufort; vehicle ferry from Davis is $80 to $150 (pedestrian $16); vehicle ferry from Atlantic $75 to $95 (pedestrian $14)* ☉ *Ferry dates vary but are generally closed Oct. or Nov.–Feb.*

FAMILY **Shackleford Banks.** Wild, wooded, and undeveloped, this 7½-mile-long barrier island, the southernmost part of Cape Lookout National Seashore, is made even more magical by myriad seashells along the shore and about 100 free-roaming horses. Folklore offers two reasons for the Banker Ponies' presence. One tale claims they swam ashore from a long-ago Spanish shipwreck, but some locals say early settlers first put these horses to pasture on the island. The horses may look friendly, but it's best to view them from a distance. The island hosted various settlements in the 1800s, but storms drove residents inland. Today, gravestones here and there are the only remaining evidence of the people who lived here. Island access is by ferry only, from Beaufort and Harkers Island, and although primitive camping is allowed (at no fee), there are no amenities aside from composting toilets. **Amenities:** toilets. **Best for:** solitude; sunrise; sunset; swimming; walking. ⊠ *Shackelford Banks* ☏ *252/728–7433 Island Express Ferry Services (private ferry)* ⊕ *www. nps.gov/calo* 🖾 *Island beaches free; $16 Harkers Island or Beaufort ferry* ☉ *Ferry times vary, closed Oct.–Mar.*

THE CRYSTAL COAST AND NEW BERN

Carteret County, with nearly 80 miles of ocean coastline, is known as the Crystal Coast. It's composed of the south-facing beaches along the barrier island Bogue Banks (Atlantic Beach, Pine Knoll Shores, Indian Beach, Salter Path, and Emerald Isle), three major mainland townships (Morehead City, Beaufort, and Newport), and a series of small, unincorporated "down-east" communities traversed by a portion of U.S. 70, designated a Scenic Byway.

Neighboring Craven County—which contains New Bern, a good chunk of the 157,000-acre Croatan National Forest, and massive Cherry Point Marine Corps air station—is by turns genteel and historic, modern and commercialized, rural and wild. Golfers, boaters, and a growing number of retirees find the area a haven.

BEAUFORT

20 miles west of Harkers Island–Cape Lookout ferry; 150 miles southeast of Raleigh.

There's a feeling of having stepped back in time in this small, historic seaport with a charming boardwalk. Residents take great pride in the city's restored public buildings and homes—and in their homes' histories, which sometimes include tales of pirates and sea captains. ■TIP➔ Don't make the mistake of pronouncing the town's name as "BEW-furt"—that's how South Carolinians pronounce their state's city of Beaufort. North Carolina's Beaufort is pronounced "BOW-furt." Established in 1713, the third-oldest town in North Carolina was named for Henry Somerset, Duke of Beaufort, and it's hard to miss the English influence here, particularly in the historic district's street names. Many are named after British royalty and colonial leaders.

GETTING HERE AND AROUND

Beaufort is near the far eastern end of U.S. 70, which intersects U.S. 17 to the northwest at New Bern. The town has a small airstrip but no commercial flights. For boaters, it's located along the Intracoastal Waterway, and downtown docks are available. The closest airport is in New Bern. The town is a perfect park-and-stroll location, with historic sites, museums, heritage B&Bs, and a retail center all within walking distance of each other.

ESSENTIALS

Visitor Information Beaufort Historic Site Visitor Center and Museum.
✉ *130 Turner St.* ☎ *252/728–5225, 800/575–7483* ⊕ *www.beauforthistoricsite.org.*

EXPLORING

The town retains a strong connection with the sea—everything from motorized dinghies to graceful sailboats to fabulous yachts from around the world anchors here. Boat rides of all types—dolphin watches, dinner cruises, lighthouse excursions, party jaunts, and scenic harbor tours—are available for a fee. Restaurants and shops line the waterfront. Also on the harbor is the private Duke University Marine Laboratory.

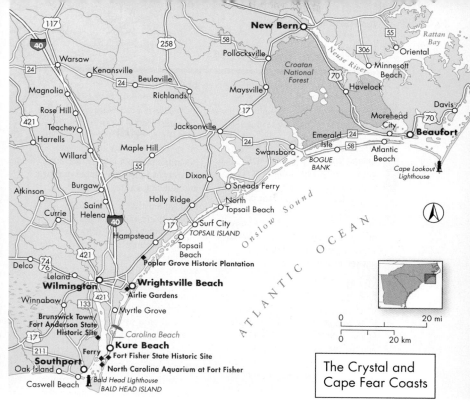

The Crystal and Cape Fear Coasts

FAMILY
Fodor's Choice
★

Beaufort Historic Site. In the center of town, the historic site consists of 10 buildings dating from 1732 to 1859, eight of which have been restored, including the 1796 **Carteret County Courthouse** and the 1859 **Apothecary Shop and Doctor's Office.** Don't miss the **Old Burying Grounds** (1709), where Otway Burns, a privateer in the War of 1812, is buried under his ship's cannon; a nine-year-old girl who died at sea is buried in a rum keg; and an English soldier saluting the king is buried upright in his grave. Tours of the entire 12-block historic site, which is now on the National Register of Historic Places, either on an English-style double-decker bus or by guided walk, depart from the visitor center. For a self-guided tour, download the free walking tour brochure from the website and put on your walking shoes—Beaufort has about 150 historic houses with plaques that list their date of construction and original owner. ⊠ *Turner St.* ☎ *252/728–5225, 800/575–7483* ⊕ *www.beauforthistoric-site.org* ▭ *Guided walking tour $10; bus tour $10; Burying Ground tour $10. Combined tickets: $15 for two tours, $20 for three tours.*

FAMILY
Fodor's Choice
★

North Carolina Maritime Museum. An exhibit about the infamous pirate Blackbeard includes artifacts recovered from the discovery of his flagship, *Queen Anne's Revenge*, near Beaufort Inlet. Other exhibits feature coastal culture and the state's rich marine-science history. You'll see seashells, fossils, duck decoys, and commercial fishing gear. Educational programs

CLOSE UP

North Carolina's Pirates

North Carolina's coast was a magnet for marauding sea dogs during the Golden Age of Piracy, a period in the first quarter of the 18th century.

THE GENTLEMAN PIRATE

Among those who visited North Carolina was Stede Bonnet, the so-called gentleman pirate. For this successful owner of a sugar plantation, piracy seemed the result of a midlife crisis. He should have stayed on the farm: he was cheated by Blackbeard, captured by authorities, and hanged in 1718.

THE FEMALE PIRATE

Anne Bonny was the Irish illegitimate daughter of a lawyer. Married at 16 to a small-time pirate, she fell in love with "Calico Jack" Rackham, and the two ran away together and put together a pirate crew. In 1720 they were attacked and most of the scalawags were too drunk to defend themselves. Rackham was sentenced to be hanged; Bonny claimed she was pregnant and was eventually pardoned. She disappeared from history before the age of 25.

BLACKBEARD

The most notorious buccaneer of them all was Blackbeard, whose two-year reign of terror began in 1716. He cultivated fear by strapping on six pistols and six knives, tying his luxuriant beard into pigtails and, legend has it, tucking lighted matches into it during battle.

A polygamist with at least 12 wives, Blackbeard attacked ships in the Caribbean and settlements along the coasts of Virginia and the Carolinas. At least three of his ships sank in North Carolina's waters; archaeologists are studying artifacts from what is likely the flagship, *Queen Anne's Revenge*, which ran aground on a sandbar near Beaufort Inlet in May 1718.

The following November a seafaring posse caught Blackbeard in one of his favorite playgrounds, Ocracoke Inlet. The pirate was decapitated and his head was hung from one of the conquering ships. Blackbeard's other lost ships and his reputedly fabulous treasure are still being sought today.

---

might include birding treks, sailing lessons, and history tours, and there's a lively schedule of special events. You can also roam the library's extensive maritime collection. The associated **Watercraft Center,** across the street, has lectures and classes on boatbuilding and you can see various projects under construction by professional and amateur boatbuilders. ⊠ *315 Front St.* ☎ *252/728-7317* ⊕ *www.ncmaritimemuseum.org* 🖾 *Free.*

WHERE TO EAT

$$$$
MODERN
AMERICAN

✕ **Beaufort Grocery Co.** Despite the name, Beaufort Grocery Co. is actually a quaint little restaurant in Beaufort's historic district, run by a couple who have formal chef training. Well-known for its lunchtime sandwiches, salads, and gumbo, the dinner menu expands and goes upscale, with the emphasis on duck, pork, and beef, with some local seafood, too. **Known for:** big selection of soups, salads, and sandwiches for lunch; gougeres (Parmesan pastry filled with shrimp or chicken salad); upmarket dinners featuring beef, pork, duck, and seafood. Ⓢ *Average main: $30* ⊠ *17 Queen St.* ☎ *252/728-3899* ⊕ *www.beaufortgrocery.com* ⊙ *Closed Tues.*

$$$ MODERN AMERICAN 🍴 **Blue Moon Bistro.** An instant favorite for many Beaufort visitors, Blue Moon Bistro pairs classic cooking techniques with creative presentations, always emphasizing local seafood, meats, and produce. The restaurant occupies the1827 Dill House, which has been dressed up with oak woodwork, wainscoting, and pressed tin suns and moons. **Known for:** top-notch service; charming setting in a historic old home; innovative takes on local seafood and produce. [$] *Average main: $24* ✉ *119 Queen St.* ☎ *252/728–5800* 🌐 *www.bluemoonbistro.biz* 🕓 *Closed Sun. (except holiday weekends) and Mon. No lunch.*

$$ AMERICAN FAMILY 🍴 **Clawson's 1905 Restaurant & Pub.** A combination of fresh seafood, local beers, and live music make this waterfront restaurant a popular spot, especially for lunch. Housed in a 1900s grocery building, Clawson's is stuffed with memorabilia dedicated to preserving the history and heritage of Beaufort. **Known for:** casual spot for lunch or a hearty dinner; good selection of microbrews; historic memorabilia about Beaufort. [$] *Average main: $18* ✉ *425 Front St.* ☎ *252/728–2133* 🌐 *www.clawsonsrestaurant.com* 🕓 *Closed Sun. Labor Day–Memorial Day.*

$$$$ SEAFOOD 🍴 **The Spouter Inn.** Dining at a shaded table on the Spouter's deck overlooking Beaufort Harbor and Taylor's Creek is one of life's treats; as boats glide by you may see a wild horse or two on Carrot Island just across the way. At dinner prime rib and bourbon barbecue ribs are popular alternatives to local seafood faves such as crab cakes or grilled local fish. **Known for:** casual waterside lunch of sandwiches and light seafood; prime rib and grilled seafood plates for dinner; on-site bakery; new bar area. [$] *Average main: $25* ✉ *218 Front St.* ☎ *252/728–5190* 🌐 *www.thespouterinn.com* 🕓 *Closed Jan.–mid-Feb.*

WHERE TO STAY

$$ B&B/INN 🏨 **Ann Street Inn.** If you like front-porch hospitality, mixing with lively locals and the feeling of being a houseguest in an elegant 1830s home complete with original details such as the wood plank flooring, you'll be in the right place here. **Pros:** intimate environment in quaint 1830s home with many original details; friendly host; delicious hot breakfast. **Cons:** no elevator; some noise from the street; no individual climate control. [$] *Rooms from: $175* ✉ *707 Ann St.* ☎ *252/728–5400* 🌐 *www.annstreetinn.com* 🛏 *3 rooms* 🍽 *Breakfast.*

$$ B&B/INN Fodor's Choice ★ 🏨 **Pecan Tree Inn.** The innkeepers, escapees from Denver winters, are maintaining Pecan Tree Inn's high standards of comfort, cleanliness, and affordability. **Pros:** historic 1860s house with elegantly furnished rooms; maple-butter pecan cookies as afternoon snack; gourmet breakfasts. **Cons:** higher rates April–October and on weekends; two-night minimum most weekends. [$] *Rooms from: $165* ✉ *116 Queen St.* ✥ *Across street from Beaufort Grocery Co.* ☎ *252/728–6733* 🌐 *www.pecantree.com* 🛏 *7 rooms* 🍽 *Breakfast.*

NEW BERN

41 miles northeast of Beaufort.

This city of nearly 30,000 was founded in 1710 by a Swiss nobleman who named it after his home: Bern, Switzerland. Since "bern" means bear in German, the black bear is New Bern's mascot—you'll see them peering from carvings, on the city's seal, on street corners, and in town souvenirs. New Bern had the state's first printing press in 1749, the first newspaper in 1751, and the first publicly funded school in 1764. For nearly 30 years it was the state capital, until it moved to Raleigh in 1792. George Washington even slept in New Bern ... *twice*. In 1898, New Bern cemented its place in pop-culture history when pharmacist Caleb Bradham mixed up a digestive aid that eventually became known as Pepsi-Cola.

Today New Bern has a 20-block historic district that includes more than 150 significant buildings, about a third of which are on the National Register. The diverse architecture covers colonial, Georgian, Federal, Greek Revival, and Victorian styles. Since 1979, more than $200 million has been spent preserving and revitalizing the downtown area, now a pleasant mix of shops, restaurants, and museums. Sailors and sun seekers enjoy the area, too, as the Neuse and Trent rivers provide the perfect environment for such activities as boating, waterskiing, and crabbing. The town has several marinas and seven public or semipublic golf courses that are open year-round.

GETTING HERE AND AROUND

The east–west U.S. 70 and north–south U.S. 17 intersect at New Bern, allowing highway access from all directions. The city also has Coastal Carolina Regional Airport, a medium-size airport with commercial flights on Delta and American. You can walk around downtown, but you'll need a car to maneuver around the city.

ESSENTIALS

Visitor Information New Bern-Craven County Convention and Visitors Bureau. ⊠ *203 S. Front St.* ☎ *252/637–9400* ⊕ *www.visitnewbern.com.*

EXPLORING

FAMILY **Birthplace of Pepsi-Cola.** In honor of the soda's 100th anniversary in 1998, the local bottling company opened the Birthplace in the same corner store where teacher-turned-pharmacist Caleb Bradham brewed his first batch of "Brad's Drink." He later renamed it Pepsi-Cola, began marketing the syrup to other soda fountains, and a conglomerate was born. This old-fashioned shop feels like a museum, with its reproduction of Bradham's fountain and exhibits of memorabilia and gift items. Enjoy a Pepsi float while roaming the new addition next door, full of Pepsi history and souvenirs ranging from T-shirts to thimbles. ⊠ *256 Middle St.* ☎ *252/636–5898* ⊕ *www.pepsistore.com* ⊠ *Free.*

FAMILY
Fodor'sChoice
★
Tryon Palace. This elegant reconstructed 1770 Georgian building was the colonial capitol and originally the home of Royal Governor William Tryon. The palace burned to the ground in 1798, and it wasn't until 1952 that a seven-year, $3.5 million effort to rebuild it took place. Today only the stable and one basement wall are original, and the foundation has been restored to its original footprint. Everything else has been reconstructed from architectural plans, maps, and letters; and the palace is furnished with English and American antiques corresponding to Governor Tryon's inventory. Additionally, 85% of the books in the library are the same titles as those that were there 200 years ago. The stately **John Wright Stanly House** (circa 1783), the **George W. Dixon House** (circa 1830), the **Robert Hay House** (circa 1805), and the **New**

Bern Academy (circa 1809) are also part of the 13-acre Tryon Palace complex. You can also stroll through the 18th-century-style formal gardens, which bloom year-round but are especially popular during spring tulip and fall mum seasons. The complex's 60,000-square-foot **North Carolina History Center** contains two museums providing interactive displays that trace the history of New Bern and the central North Carolina coast. Concerts, lectures, and theater performances also are staged there. ✉ *529 S. Front St.* ☎ *252/639–3500, 800/767–1560* 🌐 *www.tryonpalace.org* 🎟 *Galleries $12; gardens $6; guided tours of galleries and gardens $20.*

WHERE TO EAT

$$ INDIAN FAMILY Fodor's Choice ★ 🍴 **Bay Leaf.** The wonderful smells of freshly prepared curries and tandoori chicken beckon diners to enter this lovely restaurant in the restored Kress Mall. Known for its inexpensive lunch buffet, Bay Leaf is possibly the best restaurant in town, and certainly the best Indian food in the region. **Known for:** inexpensive lunch buffet; appealing atmosphere; exceptionally friendly staff; notable tandoori-style, seafood, and vegetarian dishes. [$] *Average main: $17* ✉ *309 Middle St.* ☎ *252/638–5323* 🌐 *www.bayleafnc.com* 🕒 *Closed Sun.*

$$$ AMERICAN FAMILY 🍴 **Captain Ratty's Seafood & Steakhouse.** Everyone from businesspeople to vacationing families finds something to like at Captain Ratty's. Sandwiches and generous salads are popular lunch items; steaks and seafood, and especially lump crab cakes, are the prime choices for evening meals. **Known for:** sandwiches and salads at lunch; seafood and steaks for dinner. [$] *Average main: $20* ✉ *202 Middle St.* ☎ *252/633–2088* 🌐 *www.captainrattys.com.*

$$$ AMERICAN 🍴 **The Chelsea.** In the former drugstore of the pharmacist who invented Pepsi-Cola, this casual dining spot is a magnet for visitors and local businesspeople wanting a quick sandwich or large salad for lunch. In the evening The Chelsea is more upscale, with entrées in the upstairs dining rooms (there's an elevator) including shrimp and grits and Southern osso buco. **Known for:** sandwiches and lighter fare for lunch; more upscale dishes upstairs in the evening. [$] *Average main: $23* ✉ *335 Middle St.* ☎ *252/637–5469* 🌐 *www.thechelsea.com* 🕒 *Closed Sun.*

$ CAFÉ FAMILY 🍴 **Cow Café.** Nearly everything is "moolicious" at this black-and-white-spotted café—New Bern's only "4-hoof" restaurant—created by the Maola Milk and Ice Cream Company. Today the ice-cream shop and café is privately owned, but cows still rule here, making children squeal with delight. **Known for:** many varieties of ice cream; black-and-white cow toys, gifts, and memorabilia. [$] *Average main: $7* ✉ *319 Middle St.* ☎ *252/672–9269* 🌐 *www.cowcafenewbern.com.*

$$$$ AMERICAN 🍴 **Harvey Mansion Historic Inn and Restaurant.** Dining in this 9,000-square foot home literally puts you inside New Bern history, but you'll feel right at home in the restaurant's intimate dining areas—suitable for both business and casual dinners. The menu downstairs is pub-style, while upstairs features an array of Continental and American dishes such as crab cakes, bacon-wrapped meat loaf, and lamb osso buco. **Known for:** lovely setting in historic home; casual pub menu downstairs; more upscale menu upstairs. [$] *Average main: $29* ✉ *221 S. Front St.* ☎ *252/635–3232* 🌐 *www.theharveymansion.com* 🕒 *No lunch.*

Stroll through 16 acres of 18th-century formal gardens at Tryon Palace.

$$ AMERICAN FAMILY

🍴 **Morgan's Tavern & Grill.** Skylights illuminate exposed redbrick walls and weathered wooden ceiling beams at this downtown, circa 1912 building, originally a garage and filling station. Today, it's probably the town's most popular eatery, with steaks, fried seafood, big burgers, all sorts of salads and sandwiches, and its own craft beers. **Known for:** rustic, appealing, and lively atmosphere; burgers, steaks, and seafood at moderate prices; craft beers. [$] *Average main: $18* ✉ *235 Craven St.* ☎ *252/636–2430* 🌐 *www.morganstavernnewbern.com* 🕒 *Closed Sun.*

WHERE TO STAY

$ B&B/INN Fodor's Choice ★

🏨 **Aerie Bed & Breakfast, Guest House & Conference Center.** The former 1882 Street-Ward residence is now a luxurious bed-and-breakfast that has joined forces with the conference center across the street. **Pros:** affordable rates; gourmet breakfast included; convenient location within walking distance of Tryon Palace and historic district. **Cons:** no elevator; noise from traffic and other guests in some rooms; two suites are in the building across the street. [$] *Rooms from: $142* ✉ *509 and 512 Pollock St.* ☎ *252/636–5553, 800/849–5553* 🌐 *www.aeriebedandbreakfast.com* 🛏 *9 rooms* 🍽 *Breakfast.*

$$ HOTEL FAMILY

🏨 **DoubleTree by Hilton.** At the confluence of the Neuse and Trent rivers within the historic district, this comfortable hotel—with marina facilities—has rooms and suites, some upgraded in 2015, overlooking the Trent River or downtown. **Pros:** free parking; on riverfront away from downtown bustle; recent upgrades and renovations. **Cons:** no complimentary breakfast except for elite Hilton Honors members; rooms are in two separate buildings; needs of meetings and conventions occasionally take precedence over those of individual guests. [$] *Rooms from: $169* ✉ *100 Middle St.* ☎ *252/638–3585, 800/445–8667* 🌐 *www.doubletree3.hilton.com* 🛏 *171 rooms* 🍴 *No meals.*

$ B&B/INN 🏠 **Hanna House.** Innkeepers Camille and Joe Klotz's renovation of the Rudolph Ulrich House (circa 1896) resulted in moderately priced accommodations that attract guests again and again—think sleek, modern plumbing and bath fixtures in antiques-filled rooms. **Pros:** a short walk from downtown shops and a riverfront park; special breakfast requests taken; modest rates. **Cons:** no phones or televisions in rooms; no small children. [$] *Rooms from: $99* ✉ *218 Pollock St.* ☎ *252/635–3209, 866/830–4371* 🌐 *www.hannahousenc.net* 🛏 *5 rooms* 🍴 *Breakfast.*

$ B&B/INN 🏠 **Harmony House Inn.** Crafty wreaths, quilts, and embroidery complement the mix of antiques and reproductions in guest rooms at this 1850 Greek Revival inn that lodged Yankee soldiers during the Civil War. Wine and cheese are served in the evening. **Pros:** on a quiet downtown side street; easy walking distance to shops, restaurants, and the waterfront park; moderate rates. **Cons:** no pets allowed; no elevator. [$] *Rooms from: $119* ✉ *215 Pollock St.* ☎ *252/636–3810, 800/636–3113* 🌐 *www.harmonyhouseinn.com* 🛏 *8 rooms* 🍴 *Breakfast.*

SHOPPING

The success of the downtown revitalization process is obvious in the variety of businesses in these old buildings.

Bear Essentials. This shop specializes in earth-friendly products ranging from cosmetics and lotions to 100% organic cotton baby clothes and women's wear made from bamboo fiber. It also sells inspirational toys and clothes for children, jewelry, candles, and giftware. ✉ *Kress Mall, 309 Middle St.* ☎ *252/637–6663* 🌐 *bearessentialsofnewbern.com* 🕒 *Closed Sun.*

C. Foy Tonsorial Parlor. Located in the historic Kress Mall, C. Foy Tonsorial Parlor and its third-generation owner is bringing back old-fashioned (but upscale) barbering, complete with hot-towel shaves, shoulder massage, and shoe shines. For the ne plus ultra, ask for the New York Mint Julep Cocktail Facial. The Tonsorial Parlor also has hair- and skin-care items for sale. ✉ *Kress Mall, 309 Middle St.* ☎ *252/636–2369* 🌐 *www.cfoyparlor.com* 🕒 *Closed Sun. and Mon.*

Carolina Creations. Fine American crafts and fine art represented by regional and national artists of every genre are the focus at this art gallery and gift shop. You can find blown glass, pottery, jewelry, wood carvings, and all manner of paintings and prints. ✉ *317A Pollock St.* ☎ *252/633–4369* 🌐 *www.carolinacreationsnewbern.com.*

Fine Art @ Baxter's Gallery. This art gallery, located in a former jewelry store with beautiful oak cabinets and black-and-white tile floor, features work by regionally and nationally known artists and craftspeople. Among the work are oil and watercolor paintings, sculpture, functional and decorative pottery, glasswork, and jewelry. ✉ *323 Pollack St.* ☎ *252/671–2724* 🌐 *www.fineartatbaxters.com* 🕒 *Closed Sun.*

WILMINGTON AND THE CAPE FEAR COAST

The greater Cape Fear region stretches from Topsail Island north of Wilmington south to Oak Island. The Cape Fear River basin begins in the Piedmont region and meanders several hundred miles before spilling into the Atlantic Ocean about 20 miles south of downtown Wilmington.

Miles and miles of sand stretch northward to Topsail Island and southward to the South Carolina state line. The beaches offer activities from sunbathing to kayaking, fishing, parasailing, and scuba diving, and towns here have varied accommodations. There are approximately 100 points of public access along the shoreline, marked by orange-and-blue signs.

First settled in 1729, Wilmington is one of North Carolina's two deep-water ports. It also has a 230-block downtown historic district and a picturesque riverfront listed on the National Register of Historic Places. Wilmington seems poised for growth and is beginning to compete with Savannah, Charleston, and Asheville for tourism buzz. South of Wilmington, three distinct island communities are an easy day trip from the city: nearby Wrightsville Beach, quiet Kure (pronounced "*cure*-ee") Beach, and the still rather funky Carolina Beach. Southport, which sits along the west side of Cape Fear River's mouth, has a revitalized waterfront, shaded streets, grand homes, and year-round golf. Such is the personality of the region that it has something for artists, sportspeople, history buffs, naturalists, shoppers, sunbathers, and filmmakers alike. EUE/Screen Gems Studios, with its 50 acres of soundstages and production facilities, is in Wilmington, where more than 400 films and made-for-TV movies have been shot since 1985.

WILMINGTON

89 miles southwest of New Bern; 130 miles south of Raleigh.

The city's long history, including its part in the American Revolution, is revealed in sights downtown and in the surrounding area. The Cotton Exchange is a complex of old mills, warehouses, and cotton export buildings now used as shopping and entertainment centers. *Henrietta III*, a boat resembling the paddle wheelers that once plied the Cape Fear River, has been put into service as a tourist vessel. Wilmington, home to UNC-Wilmington, hosts annual events such as the Azalea Festival, North Carolina Jazz Festival, Christmas candlelight tours, fishing tournaments, and the Cucalorus Film Festival. EUE/Screen Gems Studios has turned out more than 400 film, television, and commercial productions, including *Iron Man 3* for Marvel, *Under the Dome* for CBS, TNT's *Good Behavior*, A +E's *Six*, about a Navy Seal team, and the popular CW network shows *Dawson's Creek* and *One Tree Hill*. Wilmington's sprawling suburban areas are of less interest to visitors, but many of the chain motels and restaurants are located outside the downtown historic sections.

GETTING HERE AND AROUND

Wilmington is at the crossroads of U.S. 17 and the Interstate 40 terminus. Commercial flights land at Wilmington International Airport. The downtown historic district along the riverfront is easily walkable and also offers free trolley service. Downtown parking decks and lots are plentiful and reasonably priced. As you move away from this immediate area, however, a car becomes necessary for visits to places such as the Cameron Art Museum, Airlie Gardens, and the USS *North Carolina* Battleship Memorial. In summer and during rush hours year-round, the major thoroughfares are busy, and seemingly thousands of red lights create stop-and-go traffic, so allow more time than the distance would indicate. Route 132 (College Road), the main north–south road through the city, continues south where Interstate 40 leaves off. U.S. 76/U.S. 17 (Market Street) runs from downtown east to the vicinity of Wrightsville Beach; U.S. 421 goes south to Carolina and Kure beaches.

ESSENTIALS

Visitor Information Cape Fear Coast Convention and Visitors Bureau. ✉ *505 Nutt St., Unit A, Downtown* ☎ *910/341–4030, 877/406–2356* ⊕ *www. wilmingtonandbeaches.com.*

TOURS

Wilmington Ale Trail. Wilmington has joined the North Carolina craft-beer craze and now has about a dozen craft breweries and brewpubs. The Wilmington Ale Trail website and its free magazine help navigate the area's breweries, bottle shops, and taverns. The magazine is available at the Wilmington Tourism & Convention Center, breweries, and most hotels. Several beer festivals are held in Wilmington in October and one in late March. A beer tour, **Port City Brew Bus** (⊕ *www.portcitybrewbus.com*) offers a three-stop brewery tour for $55. ✉ *Wilmington* ☎ *910/679–6023* ⊕ *www.wilmingtonaletrail.com.*

Wilmington Walking Tours. Give yourself chills even on a sultry night. Choose between the Ghost Walk of Old Wilmington, with its stories of privateers, murderers, and unmarked graves ($13); the Haunted Pub Crawl ($17.50), where you wash down tales of madmen and saucy wenches with Dutch courage (must be 21); or Hollywood Location Walk that will take you to real locations and actual sets of movies and television shows that have been or are being filmed in Wilmington ($13). Tours depart from the riverfront at Market and Water Streets and tickets are available online or from the Black Cat Shoppe at 8 Market Street. Tour times and days vary seasonally. ✉ *Market and Water Sts., Downtown* ☎ *910/794–1866 information or buy tickets* ⊕ *www. hollywoodnc.com* 🎟 *$13 ghost walk; $17.50 pub crawl, drinks not included; $13 Hollywood Location Walk.*

EXPLORING
TOP ATTRACTIONS

FAMILY **Airlie Gardens.** Designed first as a European-style garden showcasing plants in all four seasons, Airlie is an example of what conservation, restoration, and preservation can do. Having suffered a serious share of hurricane damage since it was built in the early 1900s and some funding issues, the gardens continue to thrive. Throughout the 67 lush acres in this Southern garden, azaleas, magnolias, and camellias flourish near two freshwater lakes that attract waterfowl. Take note of the greatest specimen in the gardens: a gargantuan 468-year-old Airlie oak. ■TIP➔ **May through October you can flutter among 300 to 400 butterflies in the huge butterfly house.** The last tickets of the day are sold a

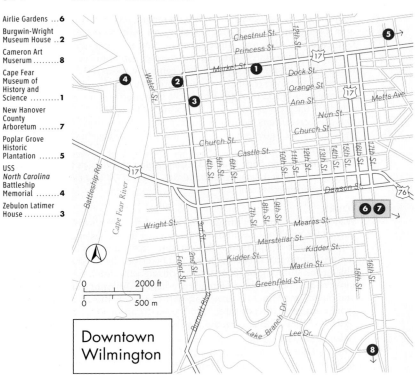

Downtown
Wilmington

half hour before closing. No pets (except service animals) are permitted. ⊠ *300 Airlie Rd., Midtown* ✛ *8 miles east of downtown via U.S. 76* ☎ *910/798–7700* ⊕ *www.airliegardens.org* 🖃 *$9.*

Burgwin-Wright Museum House. The colonial Georgian-style house General Cornwallis used as his headquarters in 1781 was built in 1771 on the foundations of a jail. After a fine, furnished restoration, this colonial gentleman's town house is now a museum that includes seven period gardens, including an orchard, a rose garden, and a kitchen garden, along with an 18th-century debtors prison. ⊠ *224 Market St., Downtown* ☎ *910/762–0570* ⊕ *www.burgwinwrighthouse.com* 🖃 *$12 house tour, gardens free* ۞ *Closed Sun. and Mon.*

Cameron Art Museum. Formerly known as the St. John's Museum of Art, the Cameron, 4 miles south of downtown, is dedicated to the fine arts and crafts of North Carolina. An ambitious changing exhibition schedule of historical and contemporary significance, plus a plethora of public educational programs and a clay studio keep this museum on the cusp of capacity and engagement. The museum's permanent collection, contained in a sleek 40,000-square-foot facility, includes originals by Mary Cassatt and a collection of Seagrove pottery. On the 10-acre grounds are restored Confederate defense mounds built during a battle in the waning days of the Civil War. Jazz@The CAM is a series of concerts (extra cost) on the first Thursday of the month, September through April. ✉ *3201 S. 17th St., South Metro* ☎ *910/395–5999* ⊕ *www.cameronartmuseum.com* 💲 *$10* ☾ *Closed Mon.*

FAMILY **Cape Fear Museum of History and Science.** Trace the natural, cultural, and social history of the lower Cape Fear region from its beginnings to the present in the oldest continuously operating museum in North Carolina (founded 1898). The interactive Cape Fear Stories exhibit provides a chronological history of the region from early Native Americans to the 20th century. A 2017 exhibit, Starring Cape Fear!, explored the more than 400 film projects shot in the Cape Fear area in the past 30 years. Kids can get in touch with the area's environment by feeding Venus flytraps in the Michael Jordan Discovery Gallery (Jordan was born in Wilmington). A fossilized skeleton of a 1.5-million-year-old giant sloth (20 feet long, 6,000 pounds) makes a great photo backdrop. New Hanover County Cape Fear Museum Park with a neat children's playground is adjacent to the museum. ✉ *814 Market St., Downtown* ☎ *910/798–4350* ⊕ *www. capefearmuseum.com* 💲 *Museum $8; park free* ☾ *Museum closed Mon.*

FAMILY **Poplar Grove Historic Plantation.** Take a tour of what was once a major peanut and sweet potato farm in North Carolina, with an 1850 Greek Revival manor house and its outbuildings. Watch a blacksmith at work, see weaving and basket-making demonstrations, and learn about Gullah Geechee heritage. You can also become familiar with farm animals (goats, sheep, horses, geese, and chickens). Tour times vary seasonally. On Wednesday, from 8 to 1, mid-April through late October, local farmers, growers, and artisans sell their produce, plants, and crafts. The site adjoins the 67-acre Abbey Nature Preserve, where birding and hiking are offered. ✉ *10200 U.S. 17, North Metro* ✛ *9 miles northeast of downtown* ☎ *910/686–9518* ⊕ *www.poplargrove.org* 💲 *Guided tours $12* ☾ *Closed Sun.*

FAMILY
Fodor'sChoice
★ **USS *North Carolina* Battleship Memorial.** On the west bank of Cape Fear River, across the river from downtown, take a self-guided tour of a ship that participated in every major naval offensive in the Pacific during World War II. Exploring the floating city, with living quarters, a post office, chapel, laundry, and even an ice-cream shop, takes about two hours. A climb down into the ship's interior is not for the claustrophobic. A 10-minute orientation film is shown throughout the day. The ship, which is open for tours every day of the year, can be reached by car; the river taxi from the downtown waterfront to the ship is no longer operating. Visitors with limited mobility can arrange a "back porch" tour with a minimum four weeks' advance notice. ✉ *1 Battleship Rd., off U.S. 74/76, Downtown* ☎ *910/251–5797* ⊕ *www.battleshipnc.com* 💲 *Boat $14; guided tours $31.*

WORTH NOTING

FAMILY **New Hanover County Arboretum.** Lose yourself along magnolia-lined natural trails among dozens of varieties of shade-loving camellias on this 7-acre site, 6 miles east of downtown. The Japanese teahouse and a gazebo are lovely places to relax, or you could spend a moment of reflection by the water garden. Your little ones will enjoy exploring the children's cottage. The arboretum is part of an NC State University research and educational complex. ✉ *6206 Oleander Dr., off U.S. 76, Midtown* ☎ *910/798–7660* ⊕ *www.nhcgov.com/arboretum/pages/thegardens.aspx* 💲 *Free.*

Kids love touring the USS *North Carolina* battleship, a floating city that saw combat in World War II.

Zebulon Latimer House. Built in 1852 in the Italianate Revival style, this home museum, with 600 Victorian items in its collection, is a reminder of opulent antebellum living. Guided tours are available. The lovely gardens are planted in mid-19th-century style. The Historical Society of the Lower Cape Fear is based here. ✉ *126 S. 3rd St., Downtown* ☎ *910/762–0492* 🌐 *www.lcfhs.org* 🎟 *$12* 🕒 *Closed Sun.*

WHERE TO EAT

$$$ BISTRO Fodor's Choice ★ 🍴 **Caprice Bistro.** Once inside the street-front entrance, you may feel like you're in the 4th *arrondisement* of Paris in a casually elegant bistro. The food here is solid bistro cooking, too, like onion soup, escargots in a garlic-Roquefort sauce, steak frites, a creamy seafood bowl called waterzooi, and many other selections. **Known for:** French bistro food; impeccable service; creative cocktails including an amazing Manhattan. [$] *Average main: $21* ✉ *10 Market St., Downtown* ☎ *910/815–0810* 🌐 *www.capricebistro.com.*

$$$$ SEAFOOD 🍴 **Catch.** Native Wilmingtonian chef Keith Rhodes is a James Beard Award nominee and Southeast finalist who sources local seafood for inspired Asian- and Southern-influenced dishes that have attracted celebrities like Robert Downey Jr. and Gwyneth Paltrow. Copper fish sculptures decorate the dining room's sky blue walls, watching you enjoy lump crab cakes, blackened swordfish, pan-roasted grouper, and other seafood dishes. **Known for:** locally sourced seafood; artistic presentations. [$] *Average main: $29* ✉ *6623 Market St.* ☎ *910/799–3847* 🌐 *www.catchwilmington.com* 🕒 *Closed Sun.*

$$ ASIAN FUSION FAMILY 🍴 **Indochine.** This restaurant has been voted Wilmington's best Asian restaurant every year for more than a decade, and it's easy to see why. Walk through its doors and you'll feel as if you're in another country,

whether you're seated in an authentic Thai hut outdoors or under elaborate Asian artifacts indoors. **Known for:** huge, diverse menu of various Asian dishes; exotic decor; long waits at peak dinner times. [$] *Average main: $18* ✉ *7 Wayne Dr., Midtown* ☎ *910/251–9229* 🌐 *www.indochinewilmington.com* 🕒 *No lunch Sun. and Mon.*

$ MEXICAN FUSION FAMILY 🍴 **K38 Baja Grill.** Named for a popular surfers' point break in Baja, Mexico, where some friends once shared memorable roadside fish tacos, the K38—the mothership of a group of lively local restaurants—menu heavily references Baja culinary traditions. Mexican-American fusion dishes feature seafood, such as tacos with crisp beer-battered fish. **Known for:** Baja-inspired dishes. [$] *Average main: $10* ✉ *5410 Oleander Dr., Midtown* ☎ *910/395–6040* 🌐 *www.liveeatsurf.com.*

$$$$ MODERN AMERICAN Fodor's Choice ★ 🍴 **Manna.** Don't be fooled by the downscale streetscape near Manna, because dining here is a feast for the eyes, a banquet for the palate, and an altar for the soul. Sleek design, creative lighting, and carefully orchestrated music provide a mesmerizing backdrop to Manna's mostly locally sourced ingredients and culinary artistry, and talented mixologists who create cocktails like the Winter Vacation (blackstrap rum, white rum, lime, and bitters). **Known for:** interesting decor; creative, locally sourced dishes; attention to detail. [$] *Average main: $30* ✉ *123 Princess St., Downtown* ☎ *910/763–5252* 🌐 *mannaavenue.com* 🕒 *Closed Mon. No lunch.*

WHERE TO STAY

$$ B&B/INN 🏨 **C. W. Worth House B&B.** This 19th-century Queen Anne–style bed-and-breakfast, with fascinating turrets and period details, is a companionable sister to the family of architectural beauties in Wilmington's 230-block historic district, putting it within easy walking distance of the city's Riverfront shopping, dining, and entertainment areas. **Pros:** complimentary Wi-Fi throughout the house; cozy bedrooms and suites with antique furnishings; innkeepers are welcoming and professional. **Cons:** no elevator; no in-room climate controls. [$] *Rooms from: $160* ✉ *412 S. 3rd St., Downtown* ☎ *910/762–8562* 🌐 *www.worthhouse.com* 🛏 *7 rooms* 🍽 *Breakfast.*

$$ B&B/INN 🏨 **Graystone Inn.** Even the name Graystone evokes an air of elegant sophistication, and the chance to experience a mansion of this caliber with its elegant public rooms and stately bedrooms shouldn't be missed. **Pros:** luxurious lobby and elegant public spaces; most impressive-appearing, mansionlike B&B in the city; spacious, stately rooms. **Cons:** on a busy street with mostly street parking; although recently renovated, some upgrades and improvements still needed, such as better TV; no elevator; nonfunctional fireplaces. [$] *Rooms from: $179* ✉ *100 S. 3rd St., Downtown* ☎ *910/763–2000, 888/763–4773* 🌐 *www.graystoneinn.com* 🛏 *9 rooms* 🍽 *Breakfast.*

$$$ HOTEL 🏨 **Hilton Wilmington Riverside.** The nine-story, fortresslike Hilton Wilmington Riverside may not be your idea of an elegant waterfront hotel, but as the saying goes, this property has location, location, location. **Pros:** convenient to river, downtown restaurants, and shops; short hike up to main part of historic district; Ruth's Chris Steak House in hotel. **Cons:** uninspired architectural design; nothing memorable about rooms. [$] *Rooms from: $229* ✉ *301 N. Water St., Downtown* ☎ *800/416–9753* 🌐 *www.wilmingtonhilton.com* 🛏 *272 rooms* 🍽 *No meals.*

$$
B&B/INN
Fodor's Choice
★

The Verandas. Built in 1853 in the Italianate style, The Verandas suffered a devastating fire in the 1990s, but the new owners redid the mansion to its original glory with elegant and magnificent furnishings and updated safety features like a full sprinkler system. **Pros:** totally renovated and refurbished 8,500-square-foot Italianate mansion; convenient location in historic district; lavishly furnished rooms; gourmet hot breakfasts. **Cons:** high percentage of returning guests can sometimes make availability scarce; no elevator. $ *Rooms from: $189* ⊠ *202 Nun St., Downtown* ☎ *910/251–2212* ⊕ *www.verandas.com* ↪ *8 rooms* ⦿ *Breakfast.*

NIGHTLIFE AND PERFORMING ARTS

The city has its own symphony orchestra, oratorio society, civic ballet, community theater, and concert association. The North Carolina Symphony makes multiple appearances here each year. The old riverfront area—with its restaurants and nightclubs, strolling couples, and horse-drawn carriages—really jumps on weekend nights.

North Carolina Jazz Festival. Since 1979, the North Carolina Jazz Festival has heated up a chilly early February weekend with nightly sets in the Hilton Wilmington Riverside hotel (special overnight rates for festival attendees). World-famous musicians perform in a variety of styles, including swing and Dixieland. ⊠ *Hilton Wilmington Riverside, 301 N. Water St., Downtown* ☎ *910/793–1111* ⊕ *www.ncjazzfestival.com.*

Fodor's Choice
★

Thalian Hall Center for the Performing Arts. A restored opera house in continuous use since 1858, Thalian Hall Center for the Performing Arts hosts dozens of theater, dance, stand-up comedy, cinema society, and musical performances each year. ⊠ *310 Chestnut St., Downtown* ☎ *910/632–2241 office*, *800/523–2820 box office* ⊕ *www.thalianhall.com.*

SPORTS AND THE OUTDOORS

BOATING

Cape Fear Riverboats, Inc. This company runs a variety of cruises on three river boats—*Captain J.N. Maffitt, The John Knox,* and *Jacob's Run*—from docks at Water and Dock Streets. There's a one-hour Wilmington riverfront tour and a four-hour Black River trip. Dinner tours also are offered, as are private charters. ⊠ *101 S. Water St., Downtown* ☎ *800/676–0162* ⊕ *www.cfrboats.com.*

GOLF

Beau Rivage Golf & Resort. Of more than 40 public-access golf courses in the Greater Wilmington area, Beau Rivage is the only one with its own resort, which comprises a collection of 900-square-foot villas overlooking the course. Against a backdrop of Cape Fear (visible from eight holes), the course changes elevation up to 75 feet, challenging players to dance with the wind for accurate placement. A well-equipped practice facility (driving range, chipping and putting area, sand bunkers, rough grass, and putting green) is among a nice group of amenities here. ⊠ *649 Rivage Promenade, South Metro* ☎ *800/628–7080 pro shop* ⊕ *www.beaurivagegolf.com* ⛳ *$54–$65 for 18 holes including cart rental depending on season and time of day* ⅃ *18 holes, 6709 yards, par 72; pro shop, driving range, putting green.*

2

SCUBA DIVING

Aquatic Safaris. Wrecks such as the World War II oil tanker *John D. Gill,* sunk by Germans in 1942 on her second-ever voyage, make for exciting scuba diving off the Cape Fear Coast. In business since 1988, Aquatic Safaris has charter trips to about 30 wrecks and other dive sites on two dive boats. Charters cost $50 to $165 per person, depending on the site and the distance from port in Wrightsville Beach, and take place between May and October when the water is warmer. Lessons and dive certifications are also available. A dive shop is open daily in Wilmington. ⊠ *7220 Wrightsville Ave., Suite A, North Metro* ☎ *910/392–4386* ⊕ *www.aquaticsafaris.com.*

SHOPPING

FAMILY **Cotton Exchange.** Once the headquarters for the largest cotton exporter in the world, this historic warehouse complex now comprises a dense concentration of locally owned boutiques and restaurants—nearly 30 of them—in a rambling maze of courtyards and hallways. Clothing and footwear, arts and crafts, gourmet food supplies, books, and comics are all here. While you're here, check out the Wilmington Walk of Fame honoring local celebrities like David Brinkley, Michael Jordan, Charlie Daniels, Roman Gabriel, and nearly a dozen more. ⊠ *321 N. Front St., Downtown* ☎ *910/343–9896* ⊕ *www.shopcottonexchange.com.*

FAMILY **Old Books on Front Street.** If you're intoxicated by the smell of well-worn books, you'll be addicted as soon as you step inside this store. Among its thousands of treasures are rare paperbacks and recent novels. Tons of gently used cookbooks are shelved next to Sugar, a friendly shop where you can satisfy your sweet tooth over a cuppa jo and a good book. You'll also find the largest collection of African American literature in town, a huge selection of Judaica, as well as theater books and movie and film scripts. The shop hosts events such as a book club and literary walks. ⊠ *249 N. Front St., Downtown* ☎ *910/762–6657* ⊕ *www. oldbooksonfrontst.com.*

WRIGHTSVILLE BEACH

12 miles east of Wilmington.

A short drive from Wilmington, Wrightsville Beach is a good day-trip destination. This is a small (5-mile-long), partly upscale, and quiet island community. Many beach houses have been in the same families for generations, although some striking contemporary homes have been constructed in recent years.

The beaches are serious havens for sunning, swimming, surfing, and surf fishing, and the beach patrol is vigilant about keeping ATVs, glass containers, alcohol, pets, and bonfires off the sands. In summer, when the population skyrockets, parking can be a problem if you don't arrive early; towing is enforced.

GETTING HERE AND AROUND

U.S. 74/76 (Eastwood Drive) is the only road access to this small, friendly town. In town you can walk and bike or boat on the Intracoastal Waterway.

Wrightsville Beach has about 1,500 metered parking spaces, monitored March through October. There are also parking lots and spaces without meters but with pay stations. Parking rules are complex. See the parking section of the town of Wrightsville Beach website for details on costs and permits.

ESSENTIALS

Visitor Information Town of Wrightville Beach. ⊕ *www.townofwrightsvillebeach.com.*

WHERE TO EAT

$$
LATIN AMERICAN
Fodor's Choice
★

✕ **Ceviche's.** Panamanian-inspired food is the focus of this lively rum bar and restaurant about ½ mile from the beach. The eponymous ceviche—traditional Panamanian corvina, lobster, and tuna "cooked" in lime juice—are all wonderful, but *ropa vieja* (flank steak served over coconut rice) and blackened tuna are tasty, too. **Known for:** Panamanian and other Central American dishes; delicious ceviches; big selection of high-quality rum drinks. $ *Average main: $17* ✉ *7210 Wrightsville Ave., Wilmington* ☎ *910/256-3131* ⊕ *www.wbceviche.com.*

$$$
SEAFOOD
FAMILY

✕ **South Beach Grill.** Tight parking on a cramped lot doesn't deter diners from this friendly, slightly retro-looking restaurant, on the site of the first bank in Wrightsville Beach. The fried seafood is good, but the chef shows off with dishes like Lowcountry Frogmore stew or crab-stuffed calamari. **Known for:** Southern and Lowcountry dishes; local seafood just off the boat. $ *Average main: $21* ✉ *100 S. Lumina Ave.* ☎ *910/256-4646* ⊕ *www.southbeachgrillwb.com* ☺ *Closed Mon. No dinner weekends.*

WHERE TO STAY

$$$$
RESORT
FAMILY

⌕ **Blockade Runner Beach Resort.** When you pull up to the parking lot at the seven-story, 1960s-vintage Blockade Runner, your first impression may be "meh," but once inside you'll find one of the area's classier beachfront hotels. **Pros:** prime beachfront location; remodeled, attractive rooms, many with balconies and beach views; free parking; off-season rooms are a good value. **Cons:** unpretentious 1960s-era exterior; hotel can't run A/C and heat at same time, so if you come during a winter hot spell ask for a fan; no microwaves in rooms. $ *Rooms from: $332* ✉ *275 Waynick Blvd.* ☎ *910/256-2251* ⊕ *www.blockade-runner.com* ⇌ *163 rooms and 1 13-bedroom cottage* ⦿ *Breakfast.*

$$$$
RESORT
FAMILY

⌕ **Holiday Inn Resort.** This may be a Holiday Inn, but it's a Holiday Inn with a top beachfront location and a stellar and attentive staff. **Pros:** free airport shuttle; two pools including a heated indoor pool; great views from higher-story rooms on ocean side; kids programs. **Cons:** a few rooms don't have balconies and about 10% have only harbor views; charge for parking; breakfast not included in room rate. $ *Rooms from: $366* ✉ *1706 N. Lumina Ave.* ☎ *910/256-2231, 877/330-5050* ⊕ *www.wrightsville.holidayinnresorts.com* ⇌ *192 rooms* ⦿ *No meals.*

SPORTS AND THE OUTDOORS
BEACHES

FAMILY **Wrightsville Beach.** Clean, wide beaches here provide the setting for all sorts of water sports. Surfers dominate fine morning waves while newbies take lessons on the beach before hitting the respectable swells. Kayakers, parasailers, paddleboarders, bodyboarders, and windsurfers all share the waters here while shoreline runners and walkers hit the sand, which is also perfect for sunbathing, sand-castle building, and people-watching. Anglers can cast lines from the surf or the Johnny Mercer concrete fishing pier. Get to the beach early; parking lots jam up, and most of the 1,500 metered spaces are taken by 9 am in summer. Keep time on the meters; parking enforcement is strict. All pets must be on leashes. **Amenities:** food and drink; lifeguards (Memorial Day to Labor Day); parking (fee); toilets. **Best for:** sunrise; sunset; surfing; swimming; windsurfing. ⊠ *N. Lumina Ave.* ✢ *Take U.S. 76 (Causeway Dr.) to N. Lumina Ave. and turn left or right to find parking* ⊕ *www. townofwrightsvillebeach.com/* ⊠ *Free (fee for most parking Mar.–Oct.).*

KURE BEACH

17 miles southwest of Wrightsville Beach; 21 miles southwest of Wilmington.

A resort community on a strip of sand locals know as Pleasure Island, Kure Beach is home to Fort Fisher State Historic Site, a 712-foot fishing pier, and one of North Carolina's three aquariums. At the southern end of the beach, twisted live oaks still grow behind the dunes. The community has miles of beaches; public access points are marked by orange-and-blue signs.

GETTING HERE AND AROUND

Drive to Kure Beach on U.S. 421 or take the ferry from Route 211 in Southport. Once at the beach, you'll want a car to get up and down the island, although some people walk and bike along the narrow, main highway.

ESSENTIALS

Visitor Information Pleasure Island Visitor Center. ⊠ *1121 N. Lake Park Blvd., Suite B, Carolina Beach* ☏ *910/458–8434* ⊕ *www.pleasureislandnc.org.*

EXPLORING

FAMILY **Fort Fisher State Historic Site.** This is one of the South's largest and most
Fodor's Choice important earthworks fortifications from the Civil War, so tough it
★ was known as the Southern Gibraltar. The fall of the fort in January 1865, closing the last supply lines for the South, helped seal the fate of the Confederacy. You can explore the restored battery with its reconstructed artillery and follow trails with viewpoints and exhibits. Inside, a range of displays ranges from Civil War relics and a fiber-optic battle map to artifacts from sunken blockade runners, weapons, and exhibits about life at the fort for the soldiers and their families. It's also known for its underwater archaeology sites. ⊠ *1610 Fort Fisher Blvd., Kure Beach* ☏ *910/458–5538* ⊕ *www.nchistoricsites.org/fisher* ⊠ *Free* ☉ *Closed early Sept.–late May.*

FAMILY **North Carolina Aquarium at Fort Fisher.** The oceanfront aquarium features a 235,000-gallon saltwater tank that's home to sharks, stingrays, and a Goliath grouper and green moray eel. Twice a day, scuba divers enter the multistory tank and answer questions from the onlookers. There's a touch tank, a tank with glowing jellyfish, an albino alligator, and turtle ponds. Kids love the life-size replica of a megladon shark, complete with fossilized teeth found in North Carolina, and enjoy the daily feeding times and animal encounters. In the Butterfly Bungalow you can wander among hundreds of colorful free-flying butterflies. From April to September, Lorikeet Landing allows kids to interact with the small, tropical birds. ✉ *900 Loggerhead Rd., off U.S. 421, Kure Beach* ☎ *800/832–3474* 🌐 *www.ncaquariums.com* 🎫 *$10.95.*

WHERE TO EAT

$$$ AMERICAN FAMILY 🍴 **Jack Mackerel's Island Grill.** Step through a wood-and-glass hatch door into a dining room where tropical blues and greens accent a bar top fashioned like a wooden boat deck. The Caribbean theme at "Jack Mack's" echoes in the menu, with dishes such as Rasta reef grouper, grilled mahi with sweet chili-lime glaze and, of course, a seafood platter. **Known for:** casual, colorful tropical atmosphere; pretty good seafood; friendly, laid-back staff. [$] *Average main: $23* ✉ *113 K Ave., Kure Beach* ✥ *Near the Kure pier* ☎ *910/458–7668* 🌐 *www.jackmacksgrill.com.*

SPORTS AND THE OUTDOORS

BEACHES

FAMILY **Carolina Beach.** With ice-cream cones and paddleboats, flashing arcade lights and seashell souvenirs, Carolina Beach's old-fashioned boardwalk is steeped in nostalgic charm. Hand-holding, outdoor movies, and bicycles built for two are still favorite pastimes here, but that's not to say you won't find adventure. Stalk giant game fish offshore aboard a choice charter boat. Join surfers riding the waves or skateboarders and in-line devotees winding the local skate park. **Amenities:** food and drink; lifeguards; toilets; parking. **Best for:** sunrise; sunset; surfing; swimming; windsurfing. ✉ *U.S. 421, off U.S. 17, Kure Beach* 🌐 *www.wilmingtonandbeaches.com/Carolina-Beach* 🎫 *Free.*

FAMILY **Kure Beach.** Family memories are made on tall ocean piers where kids reel in their first big catches. You can swim, beachcomb, kiteboard over the big blue sea, or scuba dive down to find some of the Cape Fear Coast's dozens of shipwrecks. Wildlife excursions set off from various nature trails, birding sites, and miles of undeveloped beach. Shorebirds and loggerhead sea turtles inhabit the remote reserve named Zeke's Island. At Fort Fisher, the Confederacy's largest earthen fort, you can track Kure Beach's history. **Amenities:** food and drink; lifeguards (generally Memorial Day to Labor Day); parking (mostly no fee). **Best for:** sunrise; sunset; surfing; swimming; windsurfing. ✉ *U.S. 421, off U.S. 17, Kure Beach* 🌐 *www.wilmingtonandbeaches.com/Kure-Beach* 🎫 *Free.*

SOUTHPORT

10 miles southwest of Kure Beach; 30 miles south of Wilmington.

This small town, quietly positioned at the mouth of Cape Fear River, is listed on the National Register of Historic Places. An increasingly desirable retirement spot, Southport retains its village charm and front-porch hospitality. Stately and distinctive homes, antiques stores, gift shops, and vibrant restaurants line streets that veer to accommodate ancient oak trees. The town, portrayed in Robert Ruark's novel *The Old Man and the Boy,* is ideal for walking; it's also popular with moviemakers—*Crimes of the Heart* (1986) and *Safe Haven* (2013) were filmed here.

GETTING HERE AND AROUND

From U.S. 17, Routes 211 and 133 both land in Southport. A state-operated car ferry arrives every 45 minutes from Kure Beach to the north. Once downtown, you can park your car and walk or bike throughout the waterfront area. Commercial airports are located at nearby Wilmington and Myrtle Beach, South Carolina.

ESSENTIALS

Visitor Information Fort Johnston–Southport Museum & Visitor Center. ⊠ *203 E. Bay St.* ⊹ *Behind N.C. Maritime Museum* ☎ *910/457–7927* ⊕ *www. cityofsouthport.com.*

EXPLORING

Fodor's Choice ★
Southport–Fort Fisher Ferry. If you're approaching the town from Kure Beach and Fort Fisher via U.S. 421, the state-operated year-round car ferry provides a 35-minute Cape Fear River ride between Old Federal Point at the tip of the spit and the mainland. **Bald Head Island Lighthouse** on Bald Head Island is seen en route, as well as the **Oak Island Lighthouse** and the ruins of **Price's Creek Lighthouse**—in fact, this is the only point in the United States where you can see three lighthouses at the same time. It's best to arrive early (30 minutes before ferry departure), as it's first-come, first-served. From April through September the ferry runs 16 times a day each way with departures from 6:15 am to 7 pm from Fort Fisher and from 5:30 am to 6:15 pm from Southport; the rest of the year it makes the trip about 14 times a day. On weekends, the earliest morning ferry is dropped. ⊠ *2422 S. Fort Fisher Bd., Kure Beach* ☎ *800/368–8969 ferry information and reservations, 910/457–6942 direct line to Fort Fisher-Southport ferry* ⊕ *www.ncdot.org/ferry* ⊠ *$5 per car, one way.*

OFF THE BEATEN PATH
Brunswick Town/Fort Anderson State Historic Site. About 10 miles north of Southport, you can explore the ruins and excavations of a colonial town and see the Civil War earthworks of Fort Anderson. The visitor center has a video presentation and a museum of historical items found at the site. Living history events with costumed interpreters range from Civil War reenactments to colonial-era cooking demonstrations. It's a great spot for a picnic too. ⊠ *8884 St. Phillip's Rd. SE, off Rte. 133, Winnabow* ☎ *910/371–6613* ⊕ *www.nchistoricsites.org/brunswic/brunswic.htm* ⊠ *Free.*

WHERE TO EAT AND STAY

$ FAST FOOD 🍴 **Trolly Stop.** An institution in the Cape Fear region (there are also locations in Wrightsville Beach, Wilmington, Chapel Hill), this hot-dog joint is known for various wieners, all with individual names. You have a choice of five kinds of hot dogs, including vegetarian, with 13 choices of toppings. **Known for:** big variety of hot dogs and toppings; casual eating on picnic tables. [$] *Average main: $6* ✉ *111 S. Howe St.* ☎ *910/457–7017* 🌐 *www.trollystophotdogs.com* 💳 *No credit cards.*

$$$$ RESORT FAMILY Fodor's Choice ★ 🏨 **Bald Head Island Resort.** Reached by ferry from Southport, this entire 12,000-acre island bills itself as a resort though it's actually a self-contained, car-free community, complete with a grocery store, restaurants, marina, a 50-room hotel, a 13-room B&B, two "country clubs," and the gorgeous 18-hole George Cobb golf course. **Pros:** friendly small-town feel; secluded and quiet; lots of natural areas and 12 miles of beaches; no cars allowed on island. **Cons:** island is accessible only by ferry; very expensive; activities at the island's recreation clubs are not available to all accommodations. [$] *Rooms from: $300* ✉ *Bald Head Island* ☎ *800/432–7368, 910/457–5003 for ferry reservations* 🌐 *www.baldheadisland.com* ⛳ *18 holes, 6,823 yards, par 72; $85–$125 for 18 holes including cart for guest members with golf privileges; guest club membership fees for those staying on island start at $65 per week; pro shop, lessons, restaurant, bar, putting green, driving range* 🛏 *63 rooms, 200 units* 🍽 *No meals.*

CENTRAL NORTH CAROLINA

The Triangle, the Triad, and Charlotte

WELCOME TO
CENTRAL NORTH CAROLINA

TOP REASONS TO GO

★ **Raleigh museums:** More than a dozen museums and historical sites—several within an easy walk of one another—cover every aspect of North Carolina life, from its prehistoric roots to its arts achievements and sports heroes.

★ **Old Salem:** Costumed guides fill this restored village in the heart of Winston-Salem, founded by the Moravian sect in the mid-18th century.

★ **Golf:** Many of the best golf courses in the Southeast (and some would argue, in the world) surround tiny Pinehurst, a village in the Sandhills.

★ **Wineries:** North Carolina has more than 140 wineries, and many of the finest are in the Piedmont. Sample a few fine vintages in their tasting rooms.

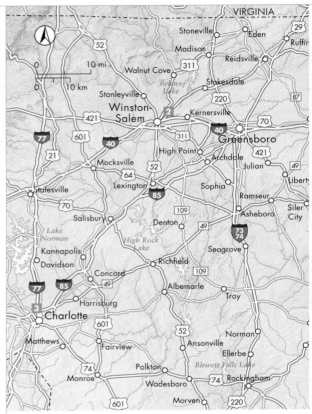

1 **The Triangle: Raleigh, Durham, and Chapel Hill.** The region is home to Duke University, North Carolina State University, and the University of North Carolina at Chapel Hill, so life in the Triangle revolves around basketball and higher education. Leafy campuses offer architectural delights, and the surrounding communities reflect the universities' progressive spirits with a vibrant farm-to-table food scene and a passion for learning and the arts.

2 **The Triad: Greensboro, Winston-Salem, and High Point.** The past and present fuse in fascinating ways in these vastly different cities. History comes to life in the restored Moravian village of

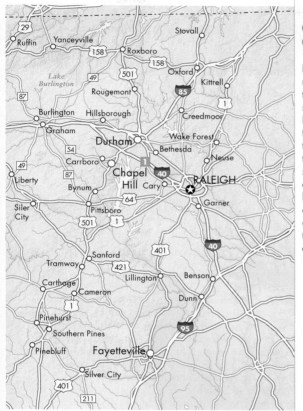

GETTING ORIENTED

North Carolina's dramatic mountains and beaches tend to overshadow the state's central regions. However, visitors who take the time to experience the woodlands and hills that grace the heart of the state will find themselves enchanted by the same sturdy beauty that has nurtured generations of intellectuals and artists, from early-20th-century wit O. Henry to the modern humorist David Sedaris.

Old Salem, and twice a year the furniture-making traditions of the Piedmont thrive at the High Point Market, a home furnishings show. Greensboro, famous for its role in the fight for desegregation half a century ago, continues to be one of the most diverse cities in the state.

3 Charlotte. The Queen City's contemporary facade dazzles, and its skyline gleams with the most impressive modern architecture in the region. Alongside fans cheering the NFL's Carolina Panthers and partiers hitting the city's sleek nightspots, you'll find traditional Southern hospitality and a lot of good eating inspired by regions around the world.

Updated by
Kristen Wile

While visiting the Piedmont, it's easy to forget what state you're in. Though it's in the geographic center of North Carolina, this collection of growing urban areas and college towns is like nothing else in the Tar Heel State. This is a region looking ahead and on the move, and although it does lack a certain amount of tradition and charm, it has something that's perhaps just as special. Here, things are changing all the time, and often for the better. This constant evolution keeps the local culture vital.

The Piedmont's gently rolling hills are home to North Carolina's three major metropolitan areas—the Triangle (Raleigh, Durham, and Chapel Hill), the Triad (Winston-Salem, Greensboro, and High Point), and Charlotte. Though their histories differ, these sprawling population clusters now have much in common. They're full of big-city highlights, like huge sports complexes, sparkling new museums, and upscale restaurants. Hip, progressive elements abound, too, including farmers' markets, indie cinemas, and monthly art walks, which show off the area's growing creative scene. The transition is not only fascinating to watch but also fun to take part in. You should never be at a loss for things to eat, see, or do.

PLANNING

WHEN TO GO
North Carolina's central region shines particularly in spring (April and May) and fall (September and October), when the weather is most temperate and the trees and flowers burst with color.

PLANNING YOUR TIME
Because the areas within the Piedmont are fairly compact, it makes sense to tackle them one at a time. Downtown Raleigh, with its expanding array of restaurants and hotels, makes a good base for exploring

Durham and Chapel Hill on day trips. Take on Charlotte and the Triad separately. In Charlotte, Uptown is centrally located and provides plenty of entertainment, dining, and lodging within walking distance.

GETTING HERE AND AROUND

AIR TRAVEL

The Raleigh-Durham International Airport (RDU), off Interstate 40 between the two cities, is served by most major airlines. RDU Airport Taxi Service provides taxi service from the airport.

3

Charlotte-Douglas International Airport (CLT), served by most major airlines, is west of Charlotte off Interstate 85. From the airport, taxis charge a set fee of $25 to Uptown and surrounding neighborhoods (plus $2 for each additional passenger after the first two) to most destinations in Charlotte. Just west of Greensboro, the Piedmont Triad International Airport (GSO) is off Route 68 north from Interstate 40; it's served by Allegiant Air, American Airlines, Delta, and United. Taxi service to and from GSO is provided by Piedmont Triad Airport Transportation.

Air Contacts Charlotte-Douglas International Airport (*CLT*). ⊠ *5501 Josh Birmingham Pkwy., Airport/Coliseum* ☎ *704/359–4013* ⊕ *www.cltairport.com.* **Piedmont Triad International Airport** (*GSO*). ⊠ *1000 A Ted Johnson Pkwy., Greensboro* ☎ *336/665–5600* ⊕ *www.flyfrompti.com.* **PTI Airport Transportation.** ⊠ *107 Arrow Rd., Greensboro* ☎ *800/588–7787* ⊕ *www.partnc.org/airportshuttle.* **Raleigh-Durham International Airport** (*RDU*). ⊠ *2400 John Brantley Blvd., Morrisville* ☎ *919/840–2123* ⊕ *www.rdu.com.* **RDU Airport Taxi Service.** ⊠ *1600 W. Terminal Blvd., Morrisville* ☎ *919/840–7277* ⊕ *www.rdutaxiinc.com.*

BUS TRAVEL

GoRaleigh is Raleigh's public transport system, Chapel Hill Transit serves Chapel Hill and Carrboro, and GoDurham is Durham's intracity bus system. The fares are $1.25 for Raleigh, and $1 for Durham. Chapel Hill Transit is free.

GoTriangle, which links downtown Raleigh with Cary, Research Triangle Park, Durham, Chapel Hill, and the airport, runs weekdays except major holidays. Rates start at $2.25.

Bus Contacts Chapel Hill Transit. ☎ *919/969–4900* ⊕ *www.chtransit. org.* **GoRaleigh.** ☎ *919/485–7433* ⊕ *www.goraleigh.org.* **GoDurham.** ☎ *919/485–7433* ⊕ *www.godurhamtransit.org.* **GoTriangle.** ☎ *919/485–7433* ⊕ *www.gotriangle.org.*

CAR TRAVEL

Although it's possible to use buses and trains for travel within the Piedmont, they're usually not convenient or quick. Interstates 40, 85, and 77, as well as several state highways, offer easy access to most of the region's destinations. Traffic is an issue in the metropolitan areas during morning and evening rush hours, but this is hardly D.C. or L.A.

Charlotte is a transportation hub; Interstate 77 comes in from Columbia, South Carolina, to the south, and then continues north to Virginia, intersecting Interstate 40 on the way. Interstate 85 arrives from Greenville, South Carolina, to the southwest, and then goes northeast to meet Interstate 40 in Greensboro. From the Triangle, Interstate 85 continues northeast and merges with Interstate 95 in Petersburg, Virginia.

Greensboro and Winston-Salem are on Interstate 40, which runs east–west through North Carolina. From the east, Interstate 40 and Interstate 85 combine coming into the Triad, but in Greensboro, Interstate 85 splits off to go southwest to Charlotte. High Point is off a business bypass of Interstate 85 southwest of Greensboro.

U.S. 1 runs north–south through the Triangle and links to Interstate 85 going northeast. U.S. 64, which makes an east–west traverse across the Triangle, continues eastward all the way to the Outer Banks. Interstate 95 runs northeast–southwest to the east of the Triangle, crossing U.S. 64 and Interstate 40, from Virginia to South Carolina.

TAXI TRAVEL

Taxis and airport vans service all the area towns and airports and are an alternative to renting a car if you don't plan on doing a lot of sightseeing. Reputable companies include Blue Bird Taxi in Greensboro, Central Piedmont Transportation in Winston-Salem, and Crown Cab and Yellow Cab in Charlotte.

Taxi Contacts Blue Bird Taxi. ✉ *1205 W. Bessemer Ave., Suite 208, Greensboro* ☎ *336/272–5112* ⊕ *www.bluebirdtaxigreensboro.blogspot.com.* **Central Piedmont Transportation.** ✉ *6415 Bryan Blvd., Greensboro* ☎ *336/668–9808* ⊕ *www.goservices.com/z/19710/Greensboro-NC/Central-Piedmont-Transportation.* **Crown Cab.** ✉ *1541 St. George St., Charlotte* ☎ *704/334–6666* ⊕ *www.crowncabinc.com.* **Yellow Cab.** ✉ *4257 Golf Acres Dr., Charlotte* ☎ *704/444–4444* ⊕ *www.yellowcabofcharlotte.net.*

TRAIN TRAVEL

From Charlotte there's daily service to Washington, D.C., Atlanta, and points beyond, as well as daily service to the Triangle cities of Raleigh, Durham, and Cary. In Greensboro, Amtrak's *Crescent* stops in before continuing from New York to New Orleans (or vice versa). And the *Carolinian* also stops in Greensboro as it goes from Charlotte to Raleigh and then north to Baltimore, Washington, and New York. The in-state *Piedmont* connects nine cities—including Greensboro—between Raleigh and Charlotte each day.

Train Contacts Amtrak. ☎ *800/872–7245* ⊕ *www.amtrak.com.*

RESTAURANTS

In the Piedmont it's almost as easy to grab a bagel, empanada, or spanakopita as a biscuit. That said, the region is still a center of barbecue: wood-fired, pit-cooked, chopped or sliced pork traditionally served with coleslaw and hush puppies. Southern specialties such as catfish, fried green tomatoes, grits, collard greens, fried chicken, sweet potatoes, and pecan pie are also favorites. *Dining reviews have been shortened. For full information, visit Fodors.com.*

HOTELS

It's not usually a problem to find a place to stay in one of the Piedmont's resorts, bed-and-breakfasts, motels, or hotels. But during the High Point Market, a home-furnishings show held in spring and fall, tens of thousands of people descend on the area, making rooms almost impossible to find. May is graduation time for the region's colleges and universities. If you're planning on visiting the Triangle during these peak times, book accommodations well in advance. ■TIP➔ Because many of the cities in the Piedmont are destinations for business travelers, hotel rates are often much higher during the week than the weekend. You can also expect lots of up-charges in fancier business-oriented hotels for such things as breakfast, parking, and Internet fees. *Hotel reviews have been shortened. For full information, visit Fodors.com.*

3

WHAT IT COSTS				
	$	**$$**	**$$$**	**$$$$**
Restaurants	under $15	$15–$19	$20–$24	over $24
Hotels	under $150	$150–$200	$201–$250	over $250

Restaurant prices are the average cost of a main course at dinner or, if dinner is not served, at lunch. Hotel prices are the lowest cost of a standard double room in high season.

THE TRIANGLE: RALEIGH, DURHAM, AND CHAPEL HILL

The cities of Raleigh (to the east), Durham (to the north), and Chapel Hill (to the west) attract scientists, academics, and businesspeople from all over the world. But the Triangle, as the area's known, is also a nucleus of young, hip energy. Here, things are always in motion, with new "it" bars, galleries, and eateries opening all the time. What never changes, however, is the deep pride in—and rivalry between—the area's three major universities. College basketball is an extremely hot topic, and the NCAA championship tends to trade hands among the three schools.

RALEIGH

85 miles east of Greensboro; 160 miles northeast of Charlotte.

For a state capital, Raleigh is surprisingly approachable. The very walkable downtown, smaller than you might think, is not only home to a multitude of government buildings, but also many friendly pubs and cafés. The shaded parks and the quiet Oakwood Historic District nearby add to the city's comfortable feel. Raleigh has both a sense of history and cutting-edge coolness about it. Home to 11 universities and colleges, this bustling, modern city is a great place to get your fill of urban living (and some great food). Take in a play, visit a museum, and stroll along the wide city streets filled with tall and impressive buildings. When you finally feel the need to connect with nature once more, do as the locals do and grab your running shoes or bike and hit the Capital Area Greenway, Raleigh's well-loved series of trails, more than 68 miles in length and still growing.

GETTING HERE AND AROUND

Like Washington, D.C., Raleigh has a highway that loops around the city. Interstate 440, previously called the "Inner Beltline" and "Outer Beltline," circles the city before meeting Interstate 40 to the south of the city.

If you come by train or bus, you'll step off in Raleigh's Warehouse District, a developing area of cool clubs and restaurants a few blocks west of Downtown. RDU International is a 25-minute cab ride, depending on rush-hour traffic, from Downtown. Buses and taxis serve all parts of the city, including the suburbs. ■ TIP➜ This is the easiest city in the Triangle to get around without a car. Not having your own transportation will make exploration outside the city a pain, however.

TOURS

Historic Raleigh Trolley Tours. Board one of this company's trolleys for a narrated hour-long tour of historic Raleigh. Between March and December, the trolley runs Saturday at 11 am, noon, and 1 and 2 pm. Although the tour starts and ends at Mordecai Historic Park, you can get on board at any stop along the route, including the State Capitol Bicentennial Plaza, the Joel Lane House, and City Market. ☎ 919/996–4364 ⊕ www.raleighnc.gov/parks/content/ParksRec/Articles/Parks/Mordecai.html ≊ $10.

ESSENTIALS

Visitor Information Capital Area Visitor Information. ⊠ 5 E. Edenton St. ☎ 919/807–7950 ⊕ www.nchistoricsites.org/capitol/vc/vc.htm. **Greater Raleigh Convention and Visitors Bureau.** ⊠ 500 Fayetteville St. ☎ 919/834–5900 ⊕ www.visitraleigh.com.

EXPLORING

TOP ATTRACTIONS

City Market. Specialty shops, art galleries, restaurants, and a small farmers' market are found in this cluster of cobblestone streets. ⊠ Martin and Blount Sts., Downtown ☎ 984/232–8661 ⊕ www.historiccitymarket.com ☉ Most stores closed Sun.

Executive Mansion. Since 1891, this 37,500-square-foot brick Queen Anne–style structure, made entirely from materials from the Tar Heel State, with elaborate gingerbread trim and manicured lawns, has been the home of the state's governors. Reservations for tours must be made at least two weeks in advance. ⊠ 200 N. Blount St., Downtown ☎ 919/807–7950 tours ⊕ www.nchistoricsites.org/capitol/exec/exectour.htm ≊ Free.

Joel Lane Museum House. Dating to the 1760s, the oldest dwelling in Raleigh was the home of Joel Lane, known as the "father of Raleigh" because he once owned the property on which the capital city grew. Costumed docents lead tours of the restored house and beautiful period gardens. The last tour starts an hour before closing. ⊠ 728 W. Hargett St., at St. Mary's St., Downtown ☎ 919/833–3431 ⊕ www.joellane.org ≊ $8 ☉ Closed Sun. and Mon. year-round and Tues.–Fri. in mid-Dec.–Feb.

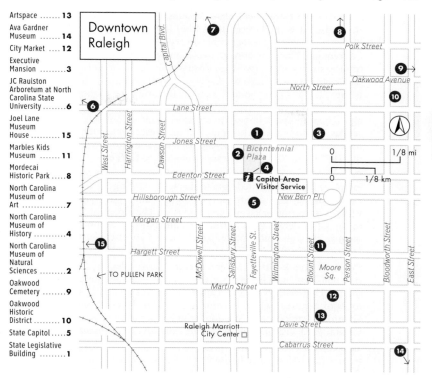

North Carolina Museum of Art. On the west side of Raleigh, the NCMA houses more than 5,000 years of artistic heritage, including one of the nation's largest collections of Jewish ceremonial art. The museum hosts touring exhibitions of works by such artists as Caravaggio and Rodin. There are tours at 11:30 and 1:30 Tuesday to Sunday. A 164-acre park featuring nine monumental works of art, which visitors can view on foot or by bike, adjoins the museum. The light-filled, in-house restaurant, Iris, looks out over gardens. ⊠ *2110 Blue Ridge Rd., North Raleigh* ☎ *919/839–6262* ⊕ *www.ncartmuseum. org* ⊠ *Free* ☉ *Closed Mon.*

North Carolina Museum of History. Founded in 1902, the museum is now in a state-of-the-art facility on Bicentennial Plaza. It houses the N.C. Sports Hall of Fame, which displays memorabilia from hundreds of inductees, from college heroes to pro superstars to Olympic contenders. You can see Richard Petty's race car, Arnold Palmer's Ryder cup golf bag, and Harlem Globetrotter Meadowlark Lemon's uniforms. ■**TIP→** The Capital Area Visitor Services, in the same building, is a great place to plan your downtown itinerary, pick up brochures, or arrange area tours. ⊠ *5 E. Edenton St., Downtown* ☎ *919/807–7900* ⊕ *www. ncmuseumofhistory.org* ⊠ *Free.*

FAMILY **North Carolina Museum of Natural Sciences.** At over 200,000 square feet, this museum is the largest of its kind in the Southeast. Exhibits and dioramas celebrate the incredible diversity of species in the state's various regions. There are enough live animals and insects—including butterflies, snakes, and a two-toed sloth—to qualify as a midsize zoo. Rare whale skeletons are also on display. The pièce de résistance, however, is the "Terror of the South" exhibit, featuring the dinosaur skeleton of "Acro," a giant carnivore that lived in the region 110 million years ago. The impressive bones are the world's most complete acrocanthosaurus dinosaur skeleton. In the Nature Research Center, visitors can have live conversations with scientists. ⊠ *11 W. Jones St., Downtown* 🕾 *919/707–9800* ⊕ *www.naturalsciences.org* 🖾 *Free.*

Oakwood Cemetery. Established in 1869, Oakwood Cemetery is the resting place of 2,800 Confederate soldiers, Civil War generals, governors, and numerous U.S. senators. The carefully cultivated grounds feature willows, towering oaks, and crepe myrtles. The House of Memory next to the Confederate burial ground recalls North Carolinians' involvement in the U.S. military. ⊠ *701 Oakwood Ave., Oakwood Historic District* 🕾 *919/832–6077* ⊕ *www.historicoakwoodcemetery.org.*

Oakwood Historic District. Several architectural styles—including Victorian buildings, which are especially notable—can be found in this tree-shaded 19th-century neighborhood. Brochures for self-guided walking tours of the area, which encompasses 20 blocks bordered by Person, Edenton, Franklin, and Watauga–Linden Streets, are available at the Capital Area Visitor Services on Edenton Street. ⊠ *Downtown.*

State Capitol. This beautifully preserved example of Greek Revival architecture from 1840 once housed all the functions of state government. Today it's part museum, part executive offices. Under its domed rotunda is contained a copy of Antonio Canova's statue of George Washington, depicted as a Roman general. Guided tours are given Saturday starting at 11 and 2. ⊠ *Capitol Sq., 1 E. Edenton St., Downtown* 🕾 *919/733–4994* ⊕ *www.ncstatecapitol.org* 🖾 *Free* ☉ *Closed Sun.*

State Legislative Building. One block north of the State Capitol, this complex hums with lawmakers and lobbyists when the legislature is in session. It's fun to watch from the gallery. Free guided tours are available, but must be scheduled in advance through Capital Area Visitor Information. ⊠ *16 W. Jones St., Downtown* 🕾 *919/733–7928, 919/733–4111* ⊕ *www.ncleg.net* 🖾 *Free.*

WORTH NOTING

Artspace. A nonprofit visual-arts center, Artspace offers open studios, where artists are happy to talk to you about their work. The gift shop showcases the work of the resident artists. ■TIP➜ The place bustles with visitors during the monthly First Friday art walk, when galleries and museums throughout the city host public receptions to show off new work. ⊠ *201 E. Davie St., Downtown* 🕾 *919/821–2787* ⊕ *www.artspacenc.org* 🖾 *Free.*

JC Raulston Arboretum at North Carolina State University. The university's working, research, and teaching garden holds the most diverse collection of hardy temperate-zone plants in the southeastern United States.

There's also a garden featuring plants with white flowers and foliage, and a 300-foot-long perennial border. ✉ *4415 Beryl Rd.* ☎ *919/515–3132* 🌐 *www.ncsu.edu/jcraulstonarboretum.*

FAMILY **Marbles Kids Museum.** This 84,000-square-foot cathedral of play and learning is aimed at children 10 and younger. Everything is hands-on, so your child is free to fill a shopping cart in the marketplace, don a fireman's hat, clamber through the cab of a city bus, scale the crow's nest of a three-story pirate ship, or splash in numerous water stations. Older children can play chess with 2-foot pawns, perform simple science experiments, or learn about the value of cash at the Moneypalooza exhibit. Toddler Hollow, designed with an enchanted forest in mind, is meant for kids under two. The space's wide-open design and its architectural details, including a suspension bridge and a courtyard with a 6-foot marble fountain, give adults something to look at as well. There's also an IMAX theater. ✉ *201 E. Hargett St., Downtown* ☎ *919/834–4040* 🌐 *www.marbleskidsmuseum.org* 🎟 *Museum $5; museum and IMAX $11–$19.*

OUTER RALEIGH

The city is spread out, so you'll need a car to visit museums and parks beyond downtown.

Ava Gardner Museum. Located in the hometown of the legendary movie star, this museum has an extensive collection of memorabilia tracing Gardner's life, from childhood on the farm to her Hollywood glory days. It's about 30 miles southeast of Raleigh in downtown Smithfield. ✉ *325 E. Market St., Smithfield* ☎ *919/934–5830* 🌐 *www.avagardner.org* 🎟 *$10.*

Mordecai Historic Park. You can see the Mordecai family's Greek Revival plantation home and other historically significant structures that have been moved onto the 2-acre property, including the house where President Andrew Johnson was born in 1808. Moses Mordecai, a well-respected lawyer, married two granddaughters of Joel Lane, the "Father of Raleigh." Mordecai's descendants lived in the house until 1964. There are guided tours hourly from 10 to 3 Tuesday to Saturday, and from 1 to 3 on Sunday. ■ **TIP→ The historical figure's name is pronounced MOR-de-key. Using a long "i" will mark you as a newcomer immediately.** ✉ *1 Mimosa St., at Wake Forest Rd., Downtown* ☎ *919/996–4364* 🌐 *www.raleighnc.gov/mordecai* 🎟 *Free; guided tours $5* 🕓 *Visitor center closed Mon.*

WHERE TO EAT

$$$$ STEAKHOUSE Fodor's Choice ★

🍴 **Angus Barn.** Dinner at this huge, rustic barn is a real event, and certainly worth the sizable prices. With its big portions, kitschy surroundings, and 89-page wine and beer list, this steak house is both traditional and fun. **Known for:** classic steaks and baby back ribs; huge wine and beer list; special occasion dining. [$] *Average main: $42* ✉ *9401 Glenwood Ave., North Raleigh* ☎ *919/787–2444* 🌐 *www.angusbarn.com* 🕓 *No lunch.*

$ SOUTHERN

🍴 **Beasley's Chicken + Honey.** Award-winning chef Ashley Christensen's hip fried chicken spot serves the namesake dish as well as modern takes on Southern classics. Sit at the bar and wash down the restaurant's hearty cuisine with a craft cocktail or glass of champagne.

Meet "Acro," the world's most complete acrocanthosaurus dinosaur, at the North Carolina Museum of Natural Sciences.

Known for: elevated Southern classics; fried chicken and honey, duh; hip atmosphere. $ *Average main: $10* ✉ *237 S. Wilmington St., Downtown* ☎ *919/322–0127* ⊕ *www.ac-restaurants.com/beasleys.*

$ ╳ **Big Ed's City Market Restaurant.** This homey breakfast and lunch spot
SOUTHERN was founded by Big Ed Watkins, who claims some of the recipes were handed down from his great-grandfather, a Confederate mess sergeant. Southern cooking doesn't get much more traditional than this place. **Known for:** Southern comfort food; antique political decor; amazing biscuits. $ *Average main: $9* ✉ *220 Wolfe St., City Market, Downtown* ☎ *919/836–9909* ⊕ *www.bigedscitymarket.com* ⊘ *No dinner.*

$$$$ ╳ **Herons.** At this elegant hotel restaurant, the menu shifts with the sea-
SOUTHERN sons and is always filled with new twists on traditional Southern dishes and international fare. Truly farm to fork, the restaurant uses produce from its own sustainable farm, which is less than a mile away. **Known for:** sustainability-driven Southern entrées; always-changing menu with local ingredients; in-house pastry chef. $ *Average main: $35* ✉ *Umstead Hotel & Spa, 100 Woodland Pond Dr., Cary* ☎ *919/447–4200* ⊕ *www. theumstead.com/dining/herons-en.html* ⊘ *No dinner Sun.*

$$$ ╳ **Irregardless Café.** This café's menu—a combination of dishes inspired
ECLECTIC by the seasons for meat eaters as well as vegetarians and vegans— changes daily. Salads are amply portioned, and the breads, soups, and yogurts are made on the premises. **Known for:** meat and vegan options (all local); live music nightly; fantastic brunch menu. $ *Average main: $24* ✉ *901 W. Morgan St., University* ☎ *919/833–8898* ⊕ *www.irre-gardless.com* ⊘ *Closed Mon.*

$$$$ ECLECTIC **Margaux's.** At this North Raleigh fixture, the menu changes daily, with a focus on different world cuisines, including Indian, Asian, and Southern flavors. A stone fireplace warms the room in winter; on the walls frequently changing artworks hang here, there, and everywhere. **Known for:** globally inspired fine dining; nightly three-course prix-fixe menu. *Average main: $30 Brennan Station Shopping Center, 8111 Creedmoor Rd., Suite 111, North Hills 919/846–9846 www.margauxsrestaurant.com Closed Sun. No lunch Sat.–Wed.*

$$$$ AMERICAN **Second Empire.** Wood paneling, muted lighting, and well-spaced tables make for an elegant dining experience in this restored 1879 house. The menu, which changes seasonally, has a regional flavor. **Known for:** high-quality and high-dollar dishes; friendly service; seasonal menu of eclectic American favorites. *Average main: $29 330 Hillsborough St., Downtown 919/829–3663 www.second-empire.com Closed Sun. and Mon. No lunch.*

WHERE TO STAY

$ HOTEL **Hilton North Raleigh/Midtown.** This easy-to-reach hotel is a favorite spot for corporate meetings. **Pros:** close to Interstate 440; free airport shuttle available between 6 am and 10 pm. **Cons:** busy location makes getting in and out of the hotel at rush hour tough; unexciting views from many rooms. *Rooms from: $149 3415 Wake Forest Rd., North Hills 919/872–2323, 800/460–7456 www.hilton.com 333 rooms No meals.*

$$ HOTEL **The Raleigh Marriott City Center.** The 17-story hotel, very close to the city's convention center, is right in the heart of things and has rooms with lots of amenities. **Pros:** great central location with good views; upscale rooms; nice indoor pool. **Cons:** pricier than the chain hotels farther from the city center; parking and Internet usage cost extra; busy during conventions. *Rooms from: $169 500 Fayetteville St., Downtown 919/833–1120 www.marriott.com/hotels/travel/rdumc-raleigh-marriott-city-center 400 rooms No meals.*

$ HOTEL **Raleigh Marriott Crabtree Valley.** Sleek rooms feature modern furnishings in cool grays and whites, with the technology to match, like smart TVs with Netflix capabilities. **Pros:** some of the best shopping in the Triangle is right across the street at Crabtree Valley Mall; there is a free airport shuttle between 7 am and 10 pm; free Wi-Fi in the lobby. **Cons:** traffic from the mall can be terrible; not in walking distance to anywhere charming; high daily rate for Internet. *Rooms from: $123 4500 Marriott Dr., University 919/781–7000, 800/909–8289 www.marriott.com/hotels/travel/rdunc-raleigh-marriott-crabtree-valley 379 rooms No meals.*

$$$$ HOTEL Fodor's Choice ★ **The Umstead Hotel and Spa.** Though close to the airport, this modern and luxurious hotel feels light-years away from the traffic of Interstate 40. **Pros:** luxurious hotel with a restaurant, bar, and spa; lovely natural setting. **Cons:** outside Raleigh and not in walking distance to any sights; allows pets but only at a very high onetime fee. *Rooms from: $309 100 Woodland Pond Rd., Cary 919/447–4000, 866/877–4141 www.theumstead.com 150 rooms No meals.*

NIGHTLIFE AND PERFORMING ARTS

NIGHTLIFE

Goodnight's Comedy Club. This club near the university combines dinner with a night of laughs. Past performers include Jerry Seinfeld, Chris Rock, and Ellen DeGeneres. ✉ *861 W. Morgan St., University* ☎ *919/828–5233* ⊕ *www.goodnightscomedy.com.*

Raleigh Times Bar. Faces of early-20th-century newsboys stare out from a 20-foot photo mural covering one wall at this 1906 newspaper office, artfully restored into a gastropub. The bar features a great selection of Belgian beers and thoughtful wine and cocktail lists. ✉ *14 E. Hargett St., Downtown* ☎ *919/833–0999* ⊕ *www.raleightimesbar.com.*

PERFORMING ARTS

Duke Energy Center for the Performing Arts. The Duke Energy Center for the Performing Arts has several different performance spaces. The 2,277-seat **Memorial Auditorium**, the crown jewel of the complex, is home to the North Carolina Theatre and the nationally acclaimed Carolina Ballet. The 1,700-seat **Meymandi Concert Hall** hosts the North Carolina Symphony. The 600-seat **Fletcher Opera Theater** provides a showcase for the A.J. Fletcher Opera Institute while the 170-seat **Kennedy Theater** stages shows by smaller theater groups. ✉ *2 E. South St., Downtown* ☎ *919/996–8700* ⊕ *www.dukeenergycenterraleigh.com.*

Walnut Creek Amphitheatre. Accommodating up to 20,000 fans, this amphitheater hosts whatever big touring musicians happen to be in town. ✉ *3801 Rock Quarry Rd., Southeast Metro* ☎ *919/831–6400* ⊕ *www.walnutcreekamphitheatre.com.*

SPORTS AND THE OUTDOORS

BASKETBALL

Wolfpack. Raleigh's Atlantic Coast Conference entry, NC State, plays basketball in the PNC Arena, which is also home to the NHL team, the Carolina Hurricanes. ✉ *Raleigh* ☎ *919/865–1510* ⊕ *www.gopack.com.*

GOLF

Hedingham Golf Club. Designed by architect David Postlethwait, this semi-private course has water hazards on eight holes. Watch out for Hole 1, where a large pond affects your play three times. ✉ *4801 Harbour Towne Dr.* ☎ *919/250–3030* ⊕ *www.hedingham.org* ⅃ *18 holes, 6529 yds, par 71. Greens Fee: $20–$30. Facilities: Golf carts, golf academy/lessons.*

Lochmere Golf Club. Designed by Carolina PGA Hall of Famer Gene Hamm, this course meanders through the tree-lined links, challenging players with several different types of water hazards. A tiered green makes Hole 3 a difficult par 3. ✉ *2511 Kildaire Farm Rd., Cary* ☎ *919/851–0611* ⊕ *www.lochmere.com* ⅃ *18 holes, 6627 yds, par 71. Greens Fee: $25–$59. Facilities: Driving range, putting green, golf carts, rental clubs, pro shop, golf academy/lessons, restaurant.*

Neuse Golf Club. About 30 minutes from downtown Raleigh, this semi-private course feels far from the city's hustle and bustle. The 1993 John LaFoy–designed course, which follows the Neuse River, is characterized by rolling fairways and rock outcroppings. ✉ *918 Birkdale Dr., Clayton* ☎ *919/550–0550* ⊕ *www.neusegolf.com* ⅃ *18 holes, 7011 yds, par 72.*

Greens Fee: $35–$69. Facilities: Driving range, golf carts, putting green, rental clubs, pro shop, golf academy/lessons.

HOCKEY

Carolina Hurricanes. The NHL's Carolina Hurricanes play in the PNC Arena, which has a capacity of more than 19,000. ⊠ *PNC Arena, 1400 Edwards Mill Rd., North Raleigh* ☎ *919/467–7825* ⊕ *hurricanes.nhl.com.*

JOGGING

Capital Area Greenway. Nearly 40 years in the making, this series of trails links the city's parks for runners and bikers. It currently consists of 28 trails making up over 100 miles, with new trails opening regularly. ⊠ *Raleigh* ☎ *919/996–3285* ⊕ *www.raleighnc.gov/parks.*

Shelley Lake Park. Runners are drawn to this scenic 53-acre lake and its winding 2-mile paved trail. ⊠ *1400 W. Millbrook Rd.* ☎ *919/996–3285* ⊕ *www.raleighnc.gov/parks.*

SHOPPING

SHOPPING MALLS

Cameron Village Shopping Center. Raleigh's first shopping center is filled with upscale boutiques and restaurants. ⊠ *2034 Cameron St., Cameron Village* ☎ *919/821–1350* ⊕ *www.shopcameronvillage.com.*

Triangle Town Center. H&M, Belk, and Saks Fifth Avenue are just some of the more than 100 stores here. ⊠ *5959 Triangle Town Blvd., North Raleigh* ☎ *919/792–2222* ⊕ *www.triangletowncenter.com.*

FOOD

State Farmers' Market. Open year-round, this 75-acre market is the place to go for locally grown fruits and vegetables, flowers and plants, and North Carolina crafts. There are also a host of restaurants serving down-home cooking. ⊠ *1201 Agriculture St., Southwest Metro* ☎ *919/733–7417* ⊕ *www.ncagr.gov/markets/facilities/markets/raleigh.*

DURHAM

23 miles northwest of Raleigh.

For many, Durham and Duke University are synonymous, and for good reason. Duke's well-manicured lawns, tree-lined streets, and stately buildings run right into town. With more than 37,000 employees, the university is also the city's biggest employer and famous for its renowned medical and research facilities. Having a university of such magnitude in their backyard means that Durhamites and visitors alike can attend all kinds of world-class lectures, exhibits, and sports events. This is not purely a college town, however, but a former tobacco-company town continually growing into a more arts-minded, urbane city. For years, old brick factory buildings have been slowly turned into shopping malls, theater spaces, and trendy restaurants. Although neighboring Chapel Hill often steals its thunder when it comes to attracting visitors, many locals prefer Durham's calmer and more mature vibe. Add Durham's long list of historic sites and museums to its ever-evolving sense of self, and you've got a city that is definitely worth exploring.

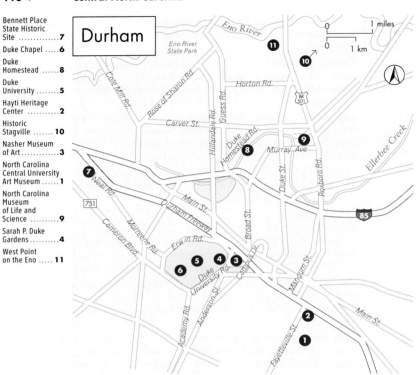

GETTING HERE AND AROUND

Durham's city center has grown rather haphazardly around its universities and commercial districts in the past 100 years. One-way streets and roads that change names can make navigation tricky. Using Durham Freeway, aka Highway 147, as a guide helps. This thoroughfare bisects the city diagonally, connecting Interstates 85 and 40, and most places of interest can be reached via its exits.

ESSENTIALS

Visitor Information Durham Convention and Visitors Bureau. ⊠ *212 W. Main St., Suite 101* ☎ *919/687–0288, 800/446–8604* ⊕ *www.durham-nc.com.*

TOURS

Taste Carolina. For tasting tours of Durham's farm-to-table restaurants, artisanal foods, and craft beer, check out Taste Carolina. They also offer tours in other North Carolina cities, including Raleigh, Chapel Hill, and Winston-Salem. ⊠ *Durham* ☎ *919/237–2254* ⊕ *www.tastecarolina.net* ☛ *From $50.*

EXPLORING

TOP ATTRACTIONS

Fodor's Choice
★

Duke Chapel. A Gothic-style gem built in the early 1930s, this chapel is the centerpiece of Duke University. Modeled after England's Canterbury Cathedral, it has a 210-foot-tall bell tower. Weekly services are held here

Sunday at 11 am. The chapel is a popular wedding spot, so check the website before trying to visit on Saturday. ⊠ *West Campus, Chapel Dr., Duke University* ☎ *919/684–2572* ⊕ *www.chapel.duke.edu.*

Duke Homestead. Washington Duke, patriarch of the now famous Duke family, moved into this house in 1852. It wasn't until he heard how the Union soldiers were enjoying smoking his tobacco that he decided to market his "golden weed." Explore the family's humble beginnings at this State Historic Site, which includes the first ramshackle "factory" as well as the world's largest spittoon collection. Guided tours demonstrate early manufacturing processes; the visitor center exhibits early tobacco advertising. ⊠ *2828 Duke Homestead Rd., Downtown* ☎ *919/477–5498* ⊕ *www.dukehomestead.org* ✉ *Free* ☉ *Closed Sun. and Mon.*

Duke University. A stroll along the tree-lined streets of this campus, founded in 1924, is a lovely way to spend a few hours. Tours of the campus, known for its Georgian and Gothic Revival architecture, are available during the academic year, and can be arranged in advance. ⊠ *Office of Special Events, Smith Warehouse, 114 S. Buchanan Blvd., Duke University* ☎ *919/684–8111* ⊕ *www.duke.edu.*

Fodor'sChoice
★

Historic Stagville. Owned by the Bennehan and Cameron families, Stagville was one of the largest plantations in antebellum North Carolina, at 30,000 acres and with about 900 slaves. The plantation today sits on 71 acres and has many original buildings, including the Bennehan's two-story wood frame home, built in the late 1700s; four two-story slave cabins; the Great Barn, built by slaves; and the family cemetery. Guided tours of the property are given daily at 11, 1, and 3. ⊠ *5828 Old Oxford Hwy.* ☎ *919/620–0120* ⊕ *www.stagville.org* ✉ *Free* ☉ *Closed Sun. and Mon.*

Nasher Museum of Art. A highlight of any Duke visit, this museum displays African, American, European, and Latin American artwork. The collection includes works by Rodin, Picasso, and Matisse. If you like your culture to be more hands-on the museum offers a steady stream of engaging events throughout the year. ⊠ *2001 Campus Dr., Duke University* ☎ *919/684–5135* ⊕ *www.nasher.duke.edu* ✉ *$5.*

FAMILY
Fodor'sChoice
★

North Carolina Museum of Life and Science. Here you can ride in a flying machine, sail a radio-controlled boat on an outdoor pond, view artifacts from space missions, and ride a train through a wildlife sanctuary. The nature center contains such animals as black bears, red wolves, and lemurs. The three-story Magic Wings Butterfly House lets you walk among tropical species in a rain-forest conservatory. In the Insectarium you can see and hear live insects under high magnification and amplification; the Dinosaur Trail gives you a glimpse of what life was like millions of years ago, and comes complete with massive dinosaur replicas. ⊠ *433 W. Murray Ave., off I–85, Downtown* ☎ *919/220–5429* ⊕ *www.lifeandscience.org* ✉ *Museum $16, train ride $4* ☉ *Closed Mon. in mid-Sept.–mid-Mar.*

Sarah P. Duke Gardens. A wisteria-draped gazebo, the Carnivorous Plant Collection, and a Japanese garden with a lily pond teeming with fat goldfish are a few of the highlights of these 55 acres in Duke University's West Campus. More than 5 miles of pathways meander through formal plantings and woodlands. The Terrace Café serves lunch weekdays and brunch Saturday and Sunday. ✉ *426 Anderson St., at Campus Dr., West Campus, Duke University* ☎ *919/684–3698* ⊕ *www.gardens.duke.edu* 💲 *Free.*

WORTH NOTING

Bennett Place State Historic Site. In April 1865 Confederate General Joseph E. Johnston surrendered to U.S. General William T. Sherman in this humble Piedmont farmhouse, 17 days after Lee's surrender to Grant at Appomattox. The two generals then set forth the terms for a "permanent peace" between the South and the North. Live historical events, held throughout the year, demonstrate how Civil War soldiers drilled, lived in camps, got their mail, and received medical care. ✉ *4409 Bennett Memorial Rd., Downtown* ☎ *919/383–4345* ⊕ *www.nchistoricsites.org/bennett* 💲 *Free* ⊘ *Closed Sun. and Mon.*

Hayti Heritage Center. One of Durham's oldest houses of worship houses this center for African American art and culture. In addition to exhibitions of traditional and contemporary art by local, regional, and national artists, the center hosts events like the Bull Durham Blues Festival and the Hayti Heritage Film Festival. ✉ *St. Joseph's AME Church, 804 Old Fayetteville St., Downtown* ☎ *919/683–1709* ⊕ *www.hayti. org* 💲 *Free* ⊘ *Closed Sun.*

North Carolina Central University Art Museum. Located in the first publicly supported liberal-arts college for African Americans, this gallery showcases work by black artists. The permanent collection includes 19th-century masterpieces and 20th-century works created during the Harlem Renaissance. ✉ *580 E. Lawson St., South/NCCU* ☎ *919/530–6211* ⊕ *www.nccu.edu/artmuseum* 💲 *Free* ⊘ *Closed Mon.*

West Point on the Eno. This city park on the banks of the Eno River boasts a restored mill dating from 1778—one of 32 that once dotted the area. Also on-site are a 19th-century Greek Revival farmhouse that was occupied by John Cabe McCown, the onetime owner of the mill, and a museum that showcases early-20th-century photographer Hugh Mangum's pictures of the surrounding area. The three-day Festival for the Eno, held around July 4, includes musicians, artists, and craftspeople from around the region. ✉ *5101 N. Roxboro Rd., U.S. 501N, North Metro* ☎ *919/471–1623* ⊕ *www.enoriver.org* 💲 *Free.*

WHERE TO EAT

$$$ ✕ **Alley Twenty Six.** Enjoy a long and leisurely meal at this seductive spot,
MODERN   which serves gussied-up American classics, such as shrimp and grits or
AMERICAN   a black truffle cheddar burger. Even the most common dishes have an
Fodor'sChoice   unexpected twist here. **Known for:** shared plates of upscale comfort food;
★   late-night menu; craft cocktails with food pairings. 💲 *Average main: $20* ✉ *320 E. Chapel Hill St.* ☎ *984/439–2278* ⊕ *www.alleytwentysix.com.*

$$$ ✕ **The Durham.** James Beard Award–winning chef Andrea Reusing serves
MODERN   local and artisanal ingredients in a dining room meant to feel more like
AMERICAN   a living room than a hotel restaurant. A rooftop bar offers creative cocktails, a full bar menu, and a stunning view. **Known for:** locally sourced, seasonal dishes; unconventional open dining room; great rooftop views. 💲 *Average main: $21* ✉ *The Durham Hotel, 315 E. Chapel Hill St., Downtown* ☎ *919/768–8830* ⊕ *www.thedurham.com/dining.*

$ ✕**Toast.** Tucked into a plain storefront, this low-key Italian sandwich shop
ITALIAN has quite a fan base—you'll likely become a believer, too. Crowd favorites
include panini filled with grilled chicken, roasted peppers, and mozzarella;
and crostini topped with goat cheese, honey, and cracked black pepper.
Known for: Italian-inspired comfort foods; lunch crowds; outdoor dining.
$ *Average main: $8* ✉ *345 W. Main St., Five Points* ☎ *919/683–2183*
⊕ *www.toast-fivepoints.com* ⊗ *Closed Sun. No dinner Mon.*

$$$$ ✕**Watts Grocery.** When slow food enthusiasts say "eat local," this is what
SOUTHERN they mean. The menu of dressed-up regional dishes reflects both the
chef's Southern roots and her French training. **Known for:** chef-driven
Southern dishes; indulgent Sunday brunch; excellent savory meat dishes.
$ *Average main: $25* ✉ *1116 Broad St., Trinity Park* ☎ *919/416–5040*
⊕ *www.wattsgrocery.com* ⊗ *Closed Mon.*

WHERE TO STAY

$$ ⬚**Arrowhead Inn.** This plantation home circa 1775 is a nice treat for
B&B/INN those looking for something a little special. **Pros:** comfortable inn offers
suites and roomy cottages; beautiful country setting; upscale dinners
can be arranged. **Cons:** it's a 15-minute drive to the city center; no
entertainment or dining nearby; old-fashioned decor. $ *Rooms from:*
$159 ✉ *106 Mason Rd., North Metro* ☎ *919/477–8430, 800/528–2207*
⊕ *www.arrowheadinn.com* ↝ *9 rooms* ⧖⧘ *Breakfast.*

$ ⬚**Blooming Garden Inn.** With its yellow exterior, expansive porches,
B&B/INN and lush gardens, this B&B is literally and figuratively a bright spot in
the Holloway Historic District. **Pros:** great location near downtown;
highly regarded service; very comfortable rooms. **Cons:** older bathroom
fixtures; most rooms don't have TVs. $ *Rooms from: $125* ✉ *513 Hol-*
loway St., Downtown ☎ *919/687–0801* ⊕ *www.bloominggardeninn.*
com ↝ *5 rooms* ⧖⧘ *Breakfast.*

$$ ⬚**The Durham.** This boutique hotel with mid-century modern decor
HOTEL emphasizes everything local, from its overall design to the in-room
Fodor's Choice snacks. **Pros:** walking distance to restaurants and sights; friendly staff;
★ great on-site dining and rooftop bar. **Cons:** modern furniture is not for
all; rooftop bar is crowded on nice nights. $ *Rooms from: $199* ✉ *315*
E. Chapel Hill St., Downtown ☎ *919/768–8830* ⊕ *www.thedurham.*
com ↝ *53 rooms* ⧖⧘ *Breakfast.*

$ ⬚**Durham Marriott City Center.** Given this nine-story hotel's excellent
HOTEL downtown location, the rates here are reasonable. **Pros:** located near
plenty of sights; free airport shuttle; warm-toned hallways and room
interiors. **Cons:** not a whole lot of frills; small bathrooms; can get busy
when conventions are in town. $ *Rooms from: $149* ✉ *201 Foster St.,*
Downtown ☎ *919/768–6000* ⊕ *www.marriott.com/hotels/travel/rducv-*
durham-marriott-city-center ↝ *190 rooms* ⧖⧘ *No meals.*

$$ ⬚**21c Museum Hotel.** This innovative hotel is the perfect fusion of art
HOTEL museum and boutique hotel. **Pros:** located in the heart of downtown;
lots of natural light; fun and gorgeous decor throughout. **Cons:** the
check-in desk can be hard to find for newcomers; construction tak-
ing place nearby; modern, minimalist rooms aren't to everyone's taste.
$ *Rooms from: $199* ✉ *111 N. Corcoran St., Downtown* ☎ *919/956–*
6700, 844/301–4629 ⊕ *www.21cmuseumhotels.com/durham* ↝ *125*
rooms ⧖⧘ *No meals.*

3

DID YOU KNOW?

In addition to trying to inspire awe and reverence, the architects of Duke Chapel also added a touch of whimsy. Look for two wooden mice hidden within the intricate woodwork: one is in the choir stalls near the altar; the other is on top of a wooden pillar on the organ. If you still can't find them, take the tour.

3

$$ HOTEL **Washington Duke Inn & Golf Club.** On the campus of Duke University, this luxurious hotel evokes the feeling of an English country inn. **Pros:** well appointed and service-oriented; luxury travelers will feel right at home; allows all pets (for a fee). **Cons:** must be booked well in advance for any stays during graduation or other Duke events; many of the rooms have views of the parking lot. [$] *Rooms from: $179* ✉ *3001 Cameron Blvd., Duke University* ☎ *919/490–0999, 800/443–3853* 🌐 *www.washingtondukeinn.com* 🛏 *313 rooms* 🍴 *No meals.*

NIGHTLIFE AND PERFORMING ARTS

NIGHTLIFE

American Tobacco Campus. This complex, adjacent to the Durham Bulls Athletic Park, houses a theater, bars, and restaurants in a series of beautifully refurbished warehouses left over from the city's cigarette-rolling past. Free summer concerts are staged on a central lawn, in the shadow of a Lucky Strike water tower. ✉ *318 Blackwell St., Downtown* ☎ *919/433–1566* 🌐 *www.americantobaccocampus.com.*

Fullsteam Brewery. Local ingredients are used to make the traditional and experimental beers here, which include year-round options of pilsners, pale ales, and IPAs. Beer-friendly food is served at the tavern. ✉ *726 Rigsbee Ave., Downtown* ☎ *919/682–2337* 🌐 *www.fullsteam.ag.*

James Joyce Irish Pub. Expect frequent live music, trivia nights, and open mics at this Irish bar and popular meeting place. ✉ *912 W. Main St., Downtown* ☎ *919/683–3022* 🌐 *www.jamesjoyceirishpub.com.*

PERFORMING ARTS

American Dance Festival. This internationally known festival, held annually in June and July, brings performances to various locations throughout town. ✉ *715 Broad St., Downtown* ☎ *919/684–6402* 🌐 *www.americandancefestival.org.*

Carolina Theatre. Dating from 1926, this Beaux Arts space hosts classical, jazz, and rock concerts, as well as April's Full Frame Documentary Film Festival and August's North Carolina Gay and Lesbian Film Festival. Check online for a full calendar of indie, retro, and all-around interesting films. ✉ *309 W. Morgan St., Downtown* ☎ *919/560–3030* 🌐 *www.carolinatheatre.org.*

ManBites Dog Theater. ManBites Dog Theater performs original, edgy, socially conscious plays. ✉ *703 Foster St., Downtown* ☎ *919/682–3343* 🌐 *www.manbitesdogtheater.org.*

SPORTS AND THE OUTDOORS

BASEBALL

FAMILY **Durham Bulls.** Immortalized in the hit 1988 movie *Bull Durham* and a tradition since 1902, this AAA affiliate of the Tampa Bay Rays plays in the 10,000-seat Durham Bulls Athletic Park. ✉ *Durham Bulls Athletic Park, 409 Blackwell St., North Metro* ☎ *919/687–6500* 🌐 *www.dbulls.com.*

BASKETBALL

Blue Devils. Durham's Atlantic Coast Conference team plays home games at the 8,800-seat Cameron Indoor Stadium. ✉ *115 Whitford Dr., Duke University* ☎ *919/681–2583* 🌐 *www.goduke.com.*

BASKETBALL RIVALRIES

North Carolinians are famously split when it comes to the sport of basketball. Most locals will tell you that this long tradition of great collegiate basketball is ultimately the product of a larger state commitment to education. North Carolina stands out in the south and indeed the nation as a center for medicine, research, and education. Today "Tobacco Road" runs through a lengthy section of one of the largest medical, pharmaceutical, and tech regions in the nation. For basketball fans "Tobacco Road" is all about the rivalry between the Duke Blue Devils and the Tar Heels of UNC Chapel Hill. While this rivalry is legendary, North Carolina also boasts several other championship schools such as Wake Forest University, North Carolina State University, and Davidson College, who have helped keep the tradition of great basketball strong for half a century.

GOLF

Duke University Golf Club. Twice host of the NCAA men's championship, this course was designed in 1957 by the legendary Robert Trent Jones; his son, Rees Jones, completed a renovation of the links in 1993. The whopping 455-yard par 4 on Hole 18 separates serious players from duffers. ⊠ *3001 Cameron Blvd., at Science Dr.* ☎ *919/681–2288, 800/443–3853* ⊕ *www.golf.duke.edu* ⚑ *18 holes, 7154 yds, par 72. Greens Fee: $55–$100. Facilities: Driving range, golf carts, rental clubs, pro shop, golf academy/lessons, restaurant, bar.*

Hillandale Golf Course. The oldest course in the area, Hillandale was designed by the incomparable Donald Ross, but then redesigned by George Cobb following the course's move in 1960. The course, with a couple of doglegs and a creek running through it, gives even experienced golfers a strategic workout. ⊠ *1600 Hillandale Rd.* ☎ *919/286–4211* ⊕ *www.hillandalegolf.com* ⚑ *18 holes, 6339 yds, par 71. Greens Fee: $18–$25. Facilities: Driving range, golf carts, rental clubs, pro shop, golf academy/lessons, restaurant, bar* ⌂ *Reservations essential.*

HIKING

American Tobacco Trail. This hiking and biking trail runs for more than 22 miles, from downtown Durham into neighboring Chatham and Wake counties. ⊠ *2112 Country Park Dr., Cary* ☎ *919/387–2117* ⊕ *www. triangletrails.org.*

Eno River State Park. This 4,231-acre park includes miles of hiking trails, a picnic area, and backcountry camping sites. Though only 15 minutes from downtown Durham, Eno is a slice of secluded wilderness. ⊠ *6101 Cole Mill Rd., North Metro* ☎ *919/383–1686* ⊕ *www.ncparks.gov.*

SHOPPING

SHOPPING AREAS AND MALLS

Brightleaf Square. In the former Watts and Yuille warehouses, Brightleaf Square is named for the tobacco that once filled these buildings. The two long structures—now filled with stores like James Kennedy Antiques, Schoolkids Records, and Wentworth and Leggett Rare Books and Prints—sandwich an attractive brick courtyard. ⊠ *West Main and Gregson Sts., Duke University* ☎ *919/682–9229* ⊕ *www.historicbrightleaf.com.*

9th Street. Durham's funky 9th Street is lined with shops and restaurants. ✉ *9th St. at Markham Ave., West Metro* ☎ *919/491–9951.*

Streets of Southpoint Mall. At the heart of Durham's shopping scene, this villagelike mall has restaurants, a movie theater, and nearly 150 stores, including Nordstrom and Restoration Hardware. ✉ *6910 Fayetteville Rd., off I–40, Southeast Metro* ☎ *919/572–8808* ⊕ *www.streetsatsouthpoint.com.*

CRAFTS

One World Market. Browse 2,000 square feet of unique, affordable home accessories, children's toys, and other arts and crafts collected from around the world. The market, a nonprofit, sells crafts from fair-trade vendors, which aim to provide artisans in developing countries (and poor areas of the United States) a living wage. ✉ *811 9th St., Duke University* ☎ *919/286–2457* ⊕ *www.shoponeworldmarket.com.*

FOOD

Parker and Otis. Much more than just a grocery store, this shop offers local produce and specialty foods as well as wines, chocolates, teas, coffees, and scads of candy. Breakfast is served until 11, and lunch lasts until 7. Gift baskets can be shipped all over the country. ✉ *112 S. Duke St., Downtown* ☎ *919/683–3200* ⊕ *www.parkerandotis.com.*

CHAPEL HILL

28 miles northwest of Raleigh; 12 miles southwest of Durham.

Chapel Hill is the smallest city in the Triangle, but it probably has the biggest personality. Home to the nation's first state university, the University of North Carolina, this is a college town through and through, one that has never lost its quirky edge, thanks in no small part to its constant influx of young people. With its prestigious yet offbeat reputation, UNC draws all kinds of students, from West Coast hippies to fraternity-loving members of the Southern aristocracy. Part of the fun of the area is the push–pull between this motley crew of students and the wealthy retirees who call Chapel Hill home. Although there are fancy restaurants and hotels, there are also cheap pizza joints and dive bars. Franklin Street, located downtown, caters to both these communities with a mixture of boutiques, restaurants, and galleries. It's just as good a place to buy incense as it is to purchase a designer shirt—and it makes for great people-watching.

GETTING HERE AND AROUND

Chapel Hill is a wonderful place to walk around, and a terrible place to park a car. Find a parking space in one of the lots along Rosemary Street, one block off Franklin, and give yourself a chance to enjoy the Carolina blue skies. Start at the Old Well on Cameron Avenue and wander through campus, or eat, sip, and shop your way down Franklin Street, beginning at the Old Post Office and heading west to Carrboro.

ESSENTIALS

Visitor Information Chapel Hill/Orange County Visitors Bureau. ✉ *501 W. Franklin St.* ☎ *919/245–4320, 888/968–2060* ⊕ *www.visitchapelhill.org.*

EXPLORING

Ackland Art Museum. Come and see one of the Southeast's strongest collections of Asian art, plus an outstanding selection of drawings, prints, and photographs as well as old-master paintings and sculptures. Be sure to say hello to the museum's namesake, William Hayes Ackland, whose modernist tomb is on-site. ✉ *101 S. Columbia St., University* ☎ *919/966–5736* 🌐 *www.ackland.org.*

FAMILY **Morehead Planetarium and Science Center.** The original Apollo astronauts trained here, at what's one of the largest planetariums in the country. You can see planetarium shows, science demonstrations, and exhibits for children and adults. ✉ *250 E. Franklin St., University* ☎ *919/962–1236* 🌐 *www.moreheadplanetarium.org* 🎟 *$7.68* 🕑 *Closed Mon.*

FAMILY Fodor's Choice ★ **North Carolina Botanical Garden.** Part of the University of North Carolina, this tribute to native plants includes wildflowers, shrubs, trees, ferns, and grasses of the Southeast. Other highlights include nature trails that wind through a 300-acre Piedmont forest, a green education center, and an impressive collection of herbs and carnivorous plants. ✉ *100 Old Mason Farm Rd., South Metro* ☎ *919/962–0522* 🌐 *www.ncbg.unc.edu* 🎟 *Free.*

University of North Carolina. Franklin Street runs along the northern edge of the campus, which is filled with oak-shaded courtyards and stately old buildings. Regarded as one of the top public institutions in the United States, UNC Chapel Hill is also one of the country's oldest public universities and was the first to admit students (it opened its doors in 1795). To this day, it remains the very heart of Chapel Hill, which has grown up around it for more than two centuries. ✉ *Visitor Center, 250 E. Franklin St.* ☎ *919/962–1630 Visitor Center* 🌐 *www.unc.edu/visitors.*

Louis Round Wilson Library. Visit the university's library for the largest single collection of North Carolina literature in the nation. ✉ *200 South Rd., University* ☎ *919/962–3765* 🌐 *library.unc.edu/wilson.*

WHERE TO EAT

$ BARBECUE 🍴 **Allen and Son Barbecue.** If you're hankering for the tang of vinegar-based barbecue sauce, then this is the 'cue for you. Located a bit out of town, this family-owned spot has been serving slow-cooked pork plates, sandwiches, and all the traditional fixins' for decades. **Known for:** Eastern Carolina–style barbecue; fresh-cut french fries and legendary hush puppies; old-school style and service. [$] *Average main: $10* ✉ *6203 Millhouse Rd.* ☎ *919/942–7576* 🕑 *Closed Sun. and Mon. No dinner Tues. and Wed.*

$$$ SOUTHERN 🍴 **Crook's Corner.** In business since 1982, this small restaurant has always been an exemplar of Southern chic. The menu, which changes nightly, highlights local produce and regional specialties like hoppin' John and shrimp and grits. **Known for:** Southern classics with local and seasonal ingredients; James Beard Foundation winner; lovely outdoor dining. [$] *Average main: $23* ✉ *610 W. Franklin St., Downtown* ☎ *919/929–7643* 🌐 *www.crookscorner.com* 🕑 *Closed Mon. No lunch Tues.–Sat.*

$$$$ ITALIAN 🍴 **Il Palio.** A real find for food lovers willing to stray from Chapel Hill's lively downtown, this small, independently owned restaurant serves high-class Italian fare with an emphasis on local and seasonal

ingredients (the menu even lists the nearby farms and purveyors used). Although the dishes change frequently, previous offerings have included pappardelle Bolognese and pan-seared scallops served with corn succotash. **Known for:** house-made pasta dishes; intimate dining room; thoughtful, Italian-focused wine list. ⓢ *Average main: $31* ✉ *Siena Hotel, 1505 E. Franklin St.* ☎ *919/929–4000* ⊕ *www.ilpalio.com.*

$

SOUTHERN

✕**Mama Dip's Country Kitchen.** In Chapel Hill, Mildred Cotton Council—better known as Mama Dip—is just about as famous as Michael Jordan. That's because she and her restaurant, which serves authentic home-style Southern meals in a roomy, simple setting, have been on the scene since the late '70s. **Known for:** Southern comfort food, including chicken and dumplings and biscuits; family-run local establishment; friendly service. ⓢ *Average main: $12* ✉ *408 W. Rosemary St., Downtown* ☎ *919/942–5837* ⊕ *www.mamadips.com.*

WHERE TO STAY

$

HOTEL

Aloft Chapel Hill. Embracing a sense of European simplicity, this hip hotel has intentionally sparse rooms that are all furnished with a desk, a small couch, and a plain white bed. **Pros:** good value for an expensive area; unique hotel experience; bus stop across the street for downtown sights. **Cons:** the no-frills approach and youthful vibe might not go over well if your heart's set on luxury; not in walking distance to the university; no on-site restaurant. ⓢ *Rooms from: $136* ✉ *1001 S. Hamilton Rd., Downtown* ☎ *919/932–7772* ⊕ *www.alofthotels.com/chapelhill* ⌑ *134 rooms* ⦿ *No meals.*

$$$$

B&B/INN

Fearrington House Country Inn. The crown jewel of Fearrington Village, this inn sits on a nearly 250-year-old farm that has been remade to resemble a country hamlet. **Pros:** a country inn with up-to-date luxuries; surrounded by plenty of shops and restaurants; fantastic breakfast. **Cons:** visitors may mind the 15-minute drive to the center of Chapel Hill; very expensive; might be too quiet for some. ⓢ *Rooms from: $350* ✉ *2000 Fearrington Village Center, Pittsboro* ☎ *919/542–4000, 800/277–0130* ⊕ *www.fearringtonhouse.com* ⌑ *32 rooms* ⦿ *Breakfast.*

$$$

HOTEL

Fodor'sChoice

★

The Franklin Hotel. Guests come to this boutique hotel, which is just minutes from the UNC campus, to be pampered. **Pros:** great location, with on-site parking; luxurious amenities and friendly staff make stays memorable; cook-to-order breakfast. **Cons:** Franklin Street can get noisy when the campus is buzzing with students; no pool; reservations are scarce during busy times. ⓢ *Rooms from: $239* ✉ *311 W. Franklin St., University* ☎ *919/442–9000* ⊕ *www.franklinhotelnc.com* ⌑ *67 rooms* ⦿ *No meals.*

$$

HOTEL

Siena Hotel. Experience a taste of Italy at this fanciful and friendly hotel, where the lobby and rooms are filled with imported carved-wood furniture, fabrics, and artwork that conjure up the Renaissance. **Pros:** the setting is elegant and close to shopping at Eastgate Mall; friendly staff are extremely helpful; free shuttle service to downtown. **Cons:** not within walking distance to downtown; furnishings in some rooms are a little dated. ⓢ *Rooms from: $179* ✉ *1505 E. Franklin St., North Metro* ☎ *919/929–4000, 800/223–7379* ⊕ *www.sienahotel.com* ⌑ *89 rooms* ⦿ *No meals.*

3

NIGHTLIFE AND PERFORMING ARTS

NIGHTLIFE

The Chapel Hill area is a great place to hear live rock and alternative bands. Many of the best music venues are in adjacent Carrboro, while Chapel Hill's Franklin Street is the spot to create your own pub crawl. As a rule of thumb, the younger crowd heads east of Columbia Street, while the older, postcollege set steers west of it.

Cat's Cradle. This dark and funky venue hosts local and regional bands as well as nationally known indie acts. ⊠ *300 E. Main St., Carrboro* ☎ *919/967–9053* ⊕ *www.catscradle.com.*

The Crunkleton. Setting the standard for craft cocktail bars in North Carolina, the Crunkleton has a knowledgeable staff of mixologists ready to stir and shake drinks. You can also select from a pages-long whiskey list that includes antique spirits. There's beer and wine too. ⊠ *320 W. Franklin St., Downtown* ☎ *919/969–1125* ⊕ *www.thecrunkleton.com.*

Top of the Hill. A restaurant, brewery, and distillery all in one, TOPO has an impressive cocktail list featuring drinks made with homegrown spirits. The top-floor space overlooks Chapel Hill's main street. You can also tour the distillery. ⊠ *505c W. Franklin St., Downtown* ☎ *919/929–8676* ⊕ *www.thetopofthehill.com.*

West End Wine Bar. An affluent crowd seeks out this tony bar, locally owned since 1997, for its comprehensive wine list (more than 50 by the glass), tapas menu, lounge, and outdoor and rooftop patios. Downstairs, the speakeasy-style Cellar has two pool tables and beers on tap. ⊠ *450 W. Franklin St., Downtown* ☎ *919/967–7599* ⊕ *www.westendwinebar.com.*

PERFORMING ARTS

Dean E. Smith Center. Basketball games as well as concerts and other special events are hosted here. ⊠ *300 Skipper Bowles Dr., University* ☎ *919/962–2296, 800/722–4335* ⊕ *www.goheels.com.*

Playmakers Repertory Company. This professional theater company performs a variety of work, from old-time radio dramas to large-scale musicals, using a variety of ingenious sets. ⊠ *Paul Green Theatre, 250 Country Club Rd., University* ☎ *919/962–7529* ⊕ *www.playmakersrep.org.*

SPORTS AND THE OUTDOORS

BASKETBALL

Tar Heels. The University of North Carolina's Tar Heels are Chapel Hill's Atlantic Coast Conference team. They play in the Dean E. Smith Student Activities Center, aka the "Dean Dome." ⊠ *Dean E. Smith Student Activities Center, 300 Skipper Bowles Dr.* ☎ *919/962–2296, 800/722–4335* ⊕ *www.goheels.com.*

GOLF

UNC Finley Golf Club. This public golf course was designed by golf legend Tom Fazio, who gave the links wide fairways and fast greens. ⊠ *500 Finley Golf Course Rd.* ☎ *919/962–2349* ⊕ *www.uncfinley.com* ⅃ *18 holes, 7328 yds, par 72. Greens Fee: $36–$85. Facilities: Driving range, putting green, golf carts, pro shop, golf academy/lessons, restaurant.*

SHOPPING

SHOPPING CENTERS

Eastgate Shopping Center. Minutes from downtown, this lively collection of shops offers everything from antiques to wine. ⊠ *1800 E. Franklin St., at U.S. 15/501 bypass, North Metro* ⊕ *www.shoppingeastgate.com.*

Fearrington Village. Eight miles south of Chapel Hill on U.S. 15/501, this complex has upscale shops selling art, garden items, handmade jewelry, and more. Shoppers can also relax in a spa or one of the center's several restaurants. ⊠ *2000 Fearrington Village Center, Pittsboro* ☎ *919/542–4000* ⊕ *www.fearrington.com.*

BOOKS

McIntyre's Books. You can read by the fire in one of this little shop's cozy rooms. The independent bookstore has a big selection of mysteries, as well as gardening and cookbooks. It also hosts weekly readings. ⊠ *Fearrington Village, 2000 Fearrington Village Center, Pittsboro* ☎ *919/542–3030* ⊕ *www.fearrington.com/mcintyres-books.*

FOOD

A Southern Season. This kitchen supply store stocks everything from classic recipe books to the latest gadgets. Many of the foods, such as barbecue sauces, peanuts, and hams, are regional specialties. Custom gift baskets can be sent anywhere in the world. ⊠ *Eastgate Shopping Center, 201 S. Estes Dr., North Metro* ☎ *919/929–7133* ⊕ *www.southernseason.com.*

THE TRIAD: GREENSBORO, WINSTON-SALEM, AND HIGH POINT

They may be neighbors, but the cities of the Triad are each very distinct. Greensboro, to the east, is a business and cultural hub with a varied, youthful, and surprisingly alternative art scene. Winston-Salem, to the west, is calmer, smaller, and steeped in the past, with two historic villages still preserved for visitors. To the south is High Point, which is off most visitors' radars, unless they're headed to one of its museums or involved in the furniture industry. It's home to the largest furniture trade show in the world.

GREENSBORO

96 miles northeast of Charlotte; 26 miles east of Winston-Salem; 58 miles west of Durham.

With its aging brick buildings and outer ring of small-city sprawl, Greensboro might not seem all that romantic at first. But let it grow on you. There's an energy here, an excitement, a feeling of possibility created by a constant influx of new residents, which include college students, businesspeople, and immigrants from around the world. This mixture of new folks and natives makes this unassuming city diverse in pretty much every aspect of daily life. For a night out, choose between an edgy play, live music, or a second-run movie at the supercheap theater outside town. You can also have your pick of fried chicken, foie gras, or *pho*. Though Greensboro is best known for its textile industry,

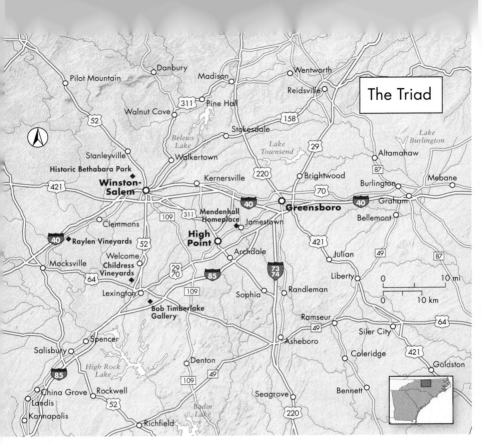

now mostly gone, and its role in the fight for civil rights (the most well-known lunch counter sit-in of the mid-'60s occurred here), this place is creating a brand-new face. To watch this funky work in progress, take an early-evening stroll along South Elm Street, which has housed the city's creative mojo for years. You'll find everything from vintage stores to bubble tea. Things are always evolving in this section of town. With any luck, that represents the future of the city as a whole.

GETTING HERE AND AROUND
Interstates 40 and 85 diverge just to the northeast of Greensboro, which means getting here is easy. Navigating the city is easy, too, especially in the booming and walkable downtown.

ESSENTIALS
Visitor Information Greensboro Area Convention and Visitors Bureau.
✉ 2411 W. Gate City Blvd. ☎ 800/344–2282 ⊕ www.visitgreensboronc.com.

EXPLORING
TOP ATTRACTIONS
Elsewhere. This Greensboro original—a combination art museum, studio, and school—brings complete sensory overload via an astounding explosion of art and artifacts collected over several decades by its former owner, Sylvia Gray, who ran it as a thrift store. Gray sold hardly anything, but that didn't keep her from constantly expanding her vast collection

(or hoard, you could say) of whatnots and thingamajigs. These days, a colorful cast of resident artists creates new work from this musty treasure trove. Expect colorful plumes of fabric hanging from the walls, and toys, books, jewelry, and so much more stuffed into every corner of this large space. You can't buy anything here, but you can touch it all. ■ TIP→ A **great time to visit is during First Friday, when galleries and shops throughout downtown host an open house and art walk. Check out the scene every first Friday of the month, 6–9 pm.** ⊠ *606 S. Elm St., Downtown* ⊕ *www. goelsewhere.org* ⊠ *$1–$5* ⊘ *Closed Sun.–Tues.*

FAMILY **The Greensboro Children's Museum.** The exhibits at this fun museum are designed for children under 12, who can tour an airplane cockpit, explore a fire truck or police car, scale a climbing wall, create crafts out of recycled materials, or learn about buildings in the construction zone. ■ TIP→ **Admission is reduced to $4 Friday 5–8.** ⊠ *220 N. Church St., Downtown* ☎ *336/574–2898* ⊕ *www.gcmuseum.com* ⊠ *$8* ⊘ *Closed Mon.*

The International Civil Rights Center and Museum. With an unflinching eye, this museum documents the beauty and horror of America's civil rights movement of the 1960s. The star attraction is the actual Woolworth lunch counter where countless African Americans staged sit-ins to protest segregation for more than six months in 1960. A guided tour shows viewers how this act of defiance spread to more than 50 cities throughout the South and helped finally bring segregation to an end. Other exhibits uncover the brutality of America's racism throughout the South. ⚠ **Many of the museum's graphic images of historical violence may be too intense for young eyes. Even adults should prepare themselves.** ⊠ *134 S. Elm St., Downtown* ☎ *336/274–9199, 800/748–7116* ⊕ *www.sitinmovement.org* ⊠ *$12* ⊘ *Closed Sun.*

FAMILY **Natural Science Center of Greensboro.** You can roam through a room filled with dinosaurs, learn about gems and minerals, meet a penguin, and see the lemurs and other creatures at this kid-friendly museum. A planetarium, a petting zoo, a reptile and amphibian house, and an aquarium are on the premises. Animal Discovery, a 22-acre science museum and zoological garden, is also here. ⊠ *4301 Lawndale Dr., Northwest Metro* ☎ *336/288– 3769* ⊕ *www.greensboroscience.org* ⊠ *Center $13.50, shows $3–$5.*

Old Greensborough. Elm Street, with its turn-of-the-20th-century architecture, is the heart of this appealing district. Listed on the National Register of Historic Places, it has become one of Greensboro's most vibrant areas, with lively galleries, trendy nightspots, and interesting boutiques and antiques shops. "Friday After Five" brings weekly live music to the district in summer. ■ TIP→ **There's Wi-Fi access throughout the area.** ⊠ *Elm St. between Market and Lee Sts., Downtown* ⊕ *www. downtowngreensboro.net.*

WORTH NOTING

Bicentennial Garden and Bog Garden. Sandwiched between two busy roads, these two gardens flourish almost despite themselves. The garden beds are carefully tended, especially compared to the nearby bog, whose natural setting includes wooden walkways over water and wetlands. ⊠ *Hobbs Rd. and Starmount Farms Dr.* ☎ *336/373–2199* ⊕ *www. greensborobeautiful.org.*

The Blandwood Mansion. The elegant home of former governor John Motley Morehead is considered the prototype of the Italian-villa architecture that swept the country during the mid-19th century. Noted architect Alexander Jackson Davis designed the house, which has a stucco exterior and towers and still contains many of its original furnishings. ✉ *447 W. Washington St., Downtown* ☎ *336/272–5003* 🌐 *www.blandwood.org* 🎟 *$8* 🕒 *Closed Mon.*

Colonial Heritage Center. Situated near Guilford Courthouse National Military Park, this historic park draws you into the life of early settlers with a hands-on approach to history. Among the buildings you'll find here is the restored 19th-century Hoskins House. The center has one of the country's most outstanding collections of original colonial settlement maps. ✉ *2200 New Garden Rd., Northwest Metro* ☎ *336/545–5315* 🌐 *www.visitgreensboronc.com/attractions/colonial-heritage-center* 🎟 *Free* 🕒 *Closed Mon.–Thurs.*

FAMILY **Greensboro Cultural Center.** Home to the offices of more than a dozen art, dance, music, and theater organizations, the cultural center also has several art galleries, a studio theater, an outdoor amphitheater, a sculpture garden, and a restaurant with outdoor seating. ✉ *200 N. Davie St., Downtown* ☎ *336/373–2712* 🌐 *www.greensboro-nc.gov.*

Greensboro Historical Museum. Set in a Romanesque church dating from 1892, the museum has displays about the city's own O. Henry and Dolley Madison. There's also an exploration of the Woolworth sit-in, which launched the civil rights movement's struggle to desegregate eating establishments. Permanent exhibits include collections of Confederate weapons and Jugtown pottery. Behind the museum are the graves of several Revolutionary War soldiers. ✉ *130 Summit Ave., Downtown* ☎ *336/373–2043* 🌐 *www.greensborohistory.org* 🎟 *Free* 🕒 *Closed Mon.*

Guilford Courthouse National Military Park. On March 15, 1781, the Battle of Guilford Courthouse so weakened British troops that they surrendered seven months later at Yorktown. This park was established in 1917 to memorialize that battle, one of the earliest events in the area's recorded history and a pivotal moment in the life of the colonies. There are more than 200 acres here, with wooded hiking trails. ✉ *2332 New Garden Rd., Northwest Metro* ☎ *336/288–1776* 🌐 *www.nps.gov/guco* 🎟 *Free.*

Weatherspoon Art Museum. Set on the campus of North Carolina at Greensboro, the museum is known for its permanent collection, which includes lithographs and bronzes by Henri Matisse, and for its changing exhibitions of 20th-century American art. ✉ *500 Tate St., University* ☎ *336/334–5770* 🌐 *weatherspoon.uncg.edu* 🎟 *Free* 🕒 *Closed Mon.*

WHERE TO EAT

$ INTERNATIONAL 🍴 **Crafted: The Art of Street Food.** The community-style tables here make for a casual dining experience, often with a wait. The no-reservations restaurant serves everything from pho to shrimp skewers along with craft cocktails and local beers. **Known for:** global street food with an Asian focus; community tables; long waits. [$] *Average main: $11* ✉ *600-C Battleground Ave., Downtown* ☎ *336/265–8859* 🌐 *www.eatatcrafted.com* 🕒 *Closed Sun. and Mon.*

$$$$ AMERICAN 🍴 **Liberty Oak Restaurant & Bar.** Situated in a 19th-century building in one of downtown Greensboro's most pleasant areas, this inviting restaurant serves upscale food in nonstuffy surroundings. The constantly shifting menu always includes an array of seafood, steaks, pasta, and vegetarian dishes. **Known for:** stunning seafood and steaks; historic building with patio dining; broad high-end menu. [$] *Average main: $25* ✉ *100–D W. Washington St., Downtown* ☎ *336/273–7057* 🌐 *www.libertyoakrestaurant.com.*

$ BARBECUE 🍴 **Stamey's.** Here the chopped, Eastern-style barbecue is mostly shoulder meat already sauced in the kitchen, though there's also plenty of vinegary Stamey's Secret Sauce at your table. If you're looking for something other than pork, try the Brunswick Stew, a traditional Southeastern thick tomato-based stew. **Known for:** vinegar-based barbecue; traditional Brunswick Stew; homemade peach cobbler. [$] *Average main: $8* ✉ *2206 W. Gate City Blvd.* ☎ *336/299–9888* 🌐 *www.stameys.com* 🕓 *Closed Sun.*

$$$$ AMERICAN Fodor's Choice ★ 🍴 **Table 16.** This magnificent little restaurant is one of the best parts of Greensboro's ever-expanding downtown. The modern menu changes every month to adapt to seasonal produce, and locally grown ingredients are used whenever possible. **Known for:** fine dining menu that changes monthly; knowledgeable staff; five-course tasting menu option with wine pairings. [$] *Average main: $32* ✉ *600 S. Elm St., Downtown* ☎ *336/279–8525* 🌐 *www.table16restaurant.com* 🕓 *Closed Sun.*

WHERE TO STAY

$ HOTEL 🏨 **Biltmore Greensboro Hotel.** In the heart of the central business district, this historic spot has an old-world, slightly faded feel, with 16-foot ceilings, a cage elevator, and a lobby with walnut-panel walls and a fireplace. **Pros:** fans of old hotels will find the setting appealing; great downtown location; one of the best values in town. **Cons:** not very modern; small bathrooms; breakfast is continental only. [$] *Rooms from: $119* ✉ *111 W. Washington St., Downtown* ☎ *336/272–3474, 800/332–0303* 🌐 *www.thebiltmoregreensboro.com* 🛏 *26 rooms* 🍽 *Breakfast.*

$$$$ HOTEL Fodor's Choice ★ 🏨 **O. Henry Hotel.** This boutique hotel, named for the renowned author, who grew up in Greensboro, was constructed in the late 1990s but evokes turn-of-the-20th-century charm; expect lots of wood paneling, leather sofas, mohair club chairs, and an extremely friendly staff. **Pros:** nostalgic setting with modern comforts; in walking distance to the popular Friendly Shopping Center; free airport shuttle (often in a fun London-style taxi). **Cons:** some rooms have views of unattractive commercial properties; not in walking distance from Greensboro's city center; expensive. [$] *Rooms from: $319* ✉ *624 Green Valley Rd., Friendly* ☎ *336/854–2000, 800/965–8259* 🌐 *www.ohenryhotel.com* 🛏 *131 rooms* 🍽 *Breakfast.*

$$$$ HOTEL 🏨 **Proximity Hotel.** With its high ceilings, big windows, and exposed beams, this modern hotel makes you feel like you're in the future—or perhaps just in a loft in a bigger city than Greensboro. **Pros:** blend of luxury and urban cool; free airport shuttle; eco-friendly. **Cons:** the supersleek interior isn't for everyone; outside the city center; on the pricey side. [$] *Rooms from: $319* ✉ *704 Green Valley Rd., Friendly* ☎ *336/379–8200, 800/379–8200* 🌐 *www.proximityhotel.com* 🛏 *147 rooms* 🍽 *No meals.*

NIGHTLIFE AND PERFORMING ARTS
NIGHTLIFE

Blind Tiger. A Greensboro institution, this is one of the best places in the Triad to hear live music. Previous headliners have included Ben Folds Five (their first show, no less) and members of the Neville Brothers. ✉ *1819 Spring Garden St., Coliseum* ☎ *336/272–9888* ⊕ *www. theblindtiger.com.*

Natty Greene's Pub & Brewing Company. Located on lively South Elm Street, this tavern has 12 of its own beers on tap, from a pale ale to a stout. The bar food here's done right, and that includes the potato chips, made in-house. Upstairs is a sports bar with pool tables. In nice weather, you can sit on the patio. ✉ *345 S. Elm St., Downtown* ☎ *336/274–1373* ⊕ *www.nattygreenes.com.*

PERFORMING ARTS

Carolina Theatre. What opened in 1927 as a vaudeville theater has matured and diversified over the years. It now serves as a performing-arts center, showcasing dance, music, films, and plays. The interior, with itsgilded classical-style ornamentation and marble statues, is its own attraction. ✉ *310 S. Greene St., Downtown* ☎ *336/333–2605* ⊕ *www. carolinatheatre.com.*

The Community Theatre of Greensboro. Founded in 1949, this playhouse stages professional shows and a host of children's programs each year in the Old Greensborough historic district. Little-known comedy gems are its specialty. ✉ *520 S. Elm St., Downtown* ☎ *336/333–7470* ⊕ *www.ctgso.org.*

Eastern Music Festival. The Eastern Music Festival, whose guests have included Billy Joel, André Watts, and Wynton Marsalis, brings a month of more than four dozen classical-music concerts to Greensboro's Guilford College and music venues throughout the city. It starts in late June. ✉ *200 N. Davie St., Downtown* ☎ *336/333–7450, 877/833–6753* ⊕ *www.easternmusicfestival.org.*

Greensboro Coliseum Complex. The vast Greensboro Coliseum Complex hosts arts and entertainment events throughout the year, including the Central Carolina Fair as well as roller derby. ✉ *1921 W. Gate City Blvd.* ☎ *336/373–7400* ⊕ *www.greensborocoliseum.com.*

Triad Stage. This downtown professional theater company mixes classic and original plays. ✉ *232 S. Elm St., Downtown* ☎ *336/272–0160, 866/579–8499* ⊕ *www.triadstage.org.*

SPORTS AND THE OUTDOORS
GOLF

Bryan Park & Golf Club. These two public courses, 6 miles north of Greensboro, have 36 holes of great golf. The Players Course, designed by Rees Jones in 1988, features 79 bunkers and eight water hazards. Jones outdid himself on the lovely 1990 Champions Course, in which seven holes hug Lake Townsend. ✉ *6275 Bryan Park Rd., Browns Summit* ☎ *336/375–2200* ⊕ *www.bryanpark.com* 🖐 *Champions Course, Mon.–Thurs. $46, Fri. $49, weekends $54; Players Course, Mon.– Thurs. $44, Fri. $47, weekends $52* 🏌 *Players Course: 18 holes, 7057 yards, par 72; Champions Course: 18 holes, 7255 yards, par 72.*

Grandover Resort & Conference Center. Greensboro's only resort hotel tempts you with 36 holes on the East and West courses, designed by golf architects David Graham and Gary Panks. Golf packages are available; the deluxe package includes dinner for two at the resort's Di Valletta Restaurant. The resort is parallel to Interstate 85, but it's set so deep into 1,500 acres that you'll never think about the traffic. ✉ *1000 Club Rd.* ☎ *336/294–1800, 800/472–6301* ⊕ *www.grandover. com* ⚑ *East Course: 18 holes, 7570 yards, par 72; West Course: 18 holes, 6800 yards, par 72.*

Greensboro National Golf Club. The clubhouse is known for its hot dogs, so you know this course lacks the pretense of others in the area. Called "a golf course for guys who like golf courses," the Don and Mark Charles–designed public links features wide fairways, expansive greens, and layouts that are challenging without resorting to blind spots and other trickery. ✉ *330 Niblick Dr., Summerfield* ☎ *336/342–1113* ⊕ *www.greensboronationalgolfclub.com* ✉ *Weekdays $35–$48, weekends $45–$55* ⚑ *18 holes, 6261 yards, par 72.*

SHOPPING

Replacements, Ltd. Located between Greensboro and Burlington, this is the world's largest seller of discontinued and active china, crystal, flatware, and collectibles. It stocks more than 12 million pieces in 286,000 patterns. Free tours are offered every hour until one hour before closing time. ✉ *I–85/I–40 at Mt. Hope Church Rd., Exit 132, 1089 Knox. Rd., McLeansville* ☎ *800/737–5223* ⊕ *www.replacements.com.*

WINSTON-SALEM

26 miles west of Greensboro; 81 miles north of Charlotte.

Even in the heart of downtown, there's something not entirely modern about Winston-Salem. And that's a good thing. The second-largest city in the Triad blends the past and the present nicely, creating a pleasant and low-key place for both history-minded tourists and nose-to-the-grindstone businesspeople.

Two historical areas—Old Salem and Bethabara—celebrate the hardworking members of the Moravian Church, a Protestant sect that arose in what's now the Czech Republic in the 15th century. For nearly a hundred years, starting in the mid-18th century, the Winston-Salem region was almost entirely populated by Moravian settlers. With its Colonial Williamsburg–like period reconstruction (and tasty, tasty cookies), Old Salem in particular shouldn't be missed, even if you have only an afternoon to spend here.

For a taste of present-day Winston-Salem, check out the Downtown Arts District, centered on the intersection of 6th and Trade Streets. Once known for its bustling tobacco market, this area is now a sea of happening galleries.

With two impressive art museums, a symphony orchestra, a film festival, and the internationally respected North Carolina School of the Arts, there's plenty to do within the city limits.

Watch pottery being made as it was in the 18th and 19th centuries at the Old Salem Museum & Gardens.

GETTING HERE AND AROUND

Easily accessed by Interstate 40, Winston-Salem is laid out in an orderly grid. Parts of the city are great for walking, especially Old Salem and the neighborhoods surrounding it. Parking near most sights is not a problem.

ESSENTIALS

Visitor Information Winston-Salem Convention and Visitors Bureau. ⊠ *200 Brookstown Ave.* ☎ *336/728–4200, 866/728–4200* ⊕ *www.visitwinstonsalem.com.*

EXPLORING

TOP ATTRACTIONS

FAMILY **Historic Bethabara Park.** Set in a wooded 180-acre wildlife preserve, this was the site of the first Moravian settlement in North Carolina. The 1753 community—whose name means "house of passage"—was never intended to be permanent. It fell into decline after Salem's completion. You can tour restored buildings, such as the 1788 Gemeinhaus congregation house, or wander the colonial and medicinal gardens. God's Acre, the first colony cemetery, is a short walk away. Children love the reconstructed fort from the French and Indian War. Brochures for self-guided walking tours are available year-round at the visitor center. ⊠ *2147 Bethabara Rd., University* ☎ *336/924–8191* ⊕ *www. bethabarapark.org* ⊠ *Free, tours $4* ☉ *Closed Mon.*

Museum of Early Southern Decorative Arts. This unique museum on the southern edge of Old Salem showcases the furniture, painting, ceramics, and metalware used in the area through 1820. The bookstore carries hard-to-find books on Southern culture and history. ⊠ *924 S. Main St., Old Salem* ☎ *336/721–7360, 888/653–7253* ⊕ *www.mesda.org* ⊠ *$20, includes admission to Old Salem Museum & Gardens* ☉ *Closed Mon.*

FAMILY
Fodor'sChoice
★

Old Salem Museum & Gardens. Founded in 1766 as a backcountry trading center, Old Salem is one of the nation's most well-documented colonial sites. This living-history museum, a few blocks from downtown Winston-Salem, is filled with dozens of original and reconstructed buildings. Costumed guides explain household activities common in the late-18th and early-19th-century Moravian communities. ■TIP→ Don't miss "America's largest coffeepot," a 12-foot-tall vessel built by Julius Mickey in 1858 to advertise his tinsmith shop. After surviving two separate car collisions, it was moved to its present location at the edge of Old Salem in 1959. ⊠ *900 Old Salem Rd., Old Salem* ☎ *336/721–7300, 888/653–7253* ⊕ *www.oldsalem.org* ✉ *$27, includes admission to Museum of Early Southern Decorative Arts* ☾ *Closed Mon.*

3

QUICK
BITES

Winkler Bakery. No trip to the Old Salem Museum & Gardens is complete without a stop at the Winkler Bakery, where you can buy bread and their pillowy, best-selling sugar cakes, baked in traditional brick ovens. Moravian ginger cookies, paper-thin and dense with spice, are a classic treat. ⊠ *521 S. Main St.* ☎ *336/721–7302* ⊕ *www.oldsalem.org/winkler-bakery.*

RayLen Vineyards. An approximate 20-minute drive from Winston-Salem makes RayLen an easy escape from city life. In its low-key country setting you can tour the vineyard and discover some of the state's most famous wines, including RayLen's Bordeaux-blend showstoppers Eagle's Select and Category 5. ⊠ *3577 Hwy. 158, 20 miles southwest of Winston-Salem, Mocksville* ☎ *336/998–3100* ⊕ *www.raylenvineyards.com.*

WORTH NOTING

OFF THE
BEATEN
PATH

Bob Timberlake Gallery. North Carolina's most successful artist is best known for his landscapes of the rural South, especially his native Lexington. Many of his original paintings, done in a highly detailed "American Realist" style, are exhibited in this gallery about 20 miles from Winston-Salem. You'll also find his personal collections of canoes, furniture, decoys, and quilts. ⊠ *1714 E. Center St. Extension, Exit 94 off I–85, Lexington* ☎ *336/249–4428, 800/244–0095* ⊕ *www.bobtimberlake.com* ✉ *Free* ☾ *Closed Sun.*

OFF THE
BEATEN
PATH

Childress Vineyards. Modeled after an Italian villa, this stately winery provides both an atmosphere and a level of quality that is not what one might expect given that it was created by famous NASCAR driver and team owner Richard Childress. The winery offers more than 30 varieties, including its popular Reserve Chardonnay and Signature Meritage. Within its opulent 35,000-square-foot building, visitors can witness wine making firsthand, or have lunch at the Bistro, which overlooks the vineyards. ⊠ *1000 Childress Vineyards Rd., Lexington* ☎ *336/236–9463* ⊕ *www.childressvineyards.com.*

Reynolda House Museum of American Art. Katharine Smith Reynolds and her husband, Richard Joshua Reynolds, founder of the R. J. Reynolds Tobacco Company, once called this house their home. The 1917 dwelling is filled with paintings, prints, and sculptures by such artists as Thomas Eakins, Frederic Church, and Georgia O'Keeffe. There's also a costume collection, as well as clothing and toys used by the Reynolds children. The museum is next to **Reynolda Village,** a collection of shops, restaurants, and gardens that fill the estate's original outer buildings. ✉ *2250 Reynolda Rd., University* ☎ *336/758–5150, 888/663–1149* 🌐 *www.reynoldahouse.org* 🎟 *$14.*

Southeastern Center for Contemporary Art. Near the Reynolda House Museum of American Art, this museum showcases artwork by nationally and internationally known artists. ✉ *750 Marguerite Dr., University* ☎ *336/725–1904* 🌐 *www.secca.org* 🎟 *Free.*

Tanglewood Park. Once land claimed for Queen Elizabeth by Sir Walter Raleigh, this park is now open to the public for golfing, boating, hiking, fishing, horseback riding, and swimming. There is also a dog park. The Tanglewood Festival of Lights, one of the largest holiday-lights festivals in the Southeast, runs from mid-November to early January. ✉ *4061 Clemmons Rd., Clemmons* ☎ *336/703–6400, 336/703–6420 golf club and stables* 🌐 *www.tanglewoodpark.org* 🎟 *$2 per car.*

TOBACCO BARNS

As you're driving through the Piedmont, you'll notice two-story wooden structures in various states of disrepair. The differences in architecture are subtle but fascinating: a wide tin awning, a small overhang, a roof patched together as abstract art. These are tobacco barns, where tobacco was hung to be cured. Although most have been left to fall apart, some have been transformed into workshops, studios, garages, and small apartments.

WHERE TO EAT

$ GREEK 🍴 **Grecian Corner.** In a white building with blue trim, this eatery has been dishing up gyros and chicken and pork souvlaki since 1970. Patrons, including workers at the nearby hospital and local families, enjoy the friendly service and ample portions of moussaka, spanakopita, and salads, plus more-familiar fare like hamburgers and pizza. **Known for:** classic Greek dishes and wines; family-friendly service; potentially the best gyro in the city. [$] *Average main: $9* ✉ *101 Eden Terr., Downtown* ☎ *336/722–6937* 🌐 *www.greciancorner.com* 💳 *No credit cards* 🕒 *Closed Sun.*

$$$$ AMERICAN 🍴 **Noble's Grille.** New Southern flavors with European accents are the key to the menu here. Typical entrées, grilled or roasted over an oak-and-hickory fire, include filet mignon, seared in a cast-iron pan, and crab cakes. **Known for:** wood-fired meats; fresh and local produce; seasonal menu of American favorites. [$] *Average main: $26* ✉ *380 Knollwood St.* ☎ *336/777–8477* 🌐 *www.noblesgrille.com* 🕒 *Closed Sun. No lunch Sat.*

$$ SOUTHERN 🍴 **Sweet Potatoes.** This restaurant's full name is Sweet Potatoes (Well Shut My Mouth!), and once you have a taste of these Southern classics, you'll know why. Expect friendly service and more food than you could possibly eat. **Known for:** fried chicken, biscuits, and other Southern staples; namesake-worthy sweet potatoes (including in fry and pie form); delicious Sunday brunch. [$] *Average main: $16* ✉ *607 Trade St., Downtown* ☎ *336/727–4844* 🌐 *www.sweetpotatoes.ws* 🕒 *Closed Mon.*

$$ AMERICAN 🍴 **The Tavern in Old Salem.** This landmark has two very distinct personalities. By day, costumed staff serve dishes that hark back to Moravian times, but by night, it morphs into something fancier, with staff wearing black aprons and serving contemporary fare to candlelit tables.

Known for: breads and sweets made from scratch; must-have chicken pies; unique historical vibe. $ *Average main: $19* ✉ *736 S. Main St., Old Salem* 🕿 *336/722–1227* ⊕ *www.thetaverninoldsalem.ws* ☉ *Closed Mon. No dinner Sun.*

WHERE TO STAY

$

B&B/INN

🛏 **Augustus T. Zevely Inn.** The only place to stay in this part of town, this historic house right on Main Street has a way of transporting guests back several centuries; it's also made a name for itself as a romantic getaway. **Pros:** only lodging in Old Salem; guests get a strong sense of history here; modern conveniences like televisions and free Wi-Fi. **Cons:** awfully quiet at night; bathrooms can be small; period furnishings aren't for everyone. $ *Rooms from: $140* ✉ *803 S. Main St., Old Salem* 🕿 *336/748–9299* ⊕ *www.winstonsalembandb.com* ⟿ *12 rooms* ⦿ *Breakfast.*

$

HOTEL

🛏 **Brookstown Inn.** No two rooms are the same in this historic, affordable, and very pleasant lodging, a former textile mill built in 1837. **Pros:** historic setting is unique; walking distance to Old Salem; nice extras. **Cons:** not as posh as newer hotels; some rooms have dim lighting; families might miss having a pool, especially in the sweltering summer. $ *Rooms from: $110* ✉ *200 Brookstown Ave., Old Salem* 🕿 *336/725–1120* ⊕ *www.brookstowninn.com* ⟿ *70 rooms* ⦿ *Breakfast.*

$$

HOTEL

Fodor's Choice

★

🛏 **The Kimpton Cardinal Hotel.** This hotel, located in the building that inspired the Empire State Building, honors the history of Winston-Salem with tartan fabrics that echo the area's textile past and furniture made in the state. **Pros:** architectural touches are stunning; dogs are welcome, and even get their own bed upon request; fun amenities like bowling lanes. **Cons:** rooms fill up quickly during special events at nearby Wake Forest University. $ *Rooms from: $199* ✉ *51 E. 4th St.* 🕿 *336/724–1009, 877/216–3448 reservations* ⊕ *www.thecardinalhotel. com* ⟿ *174 rooms* ⦿ *No meals.*

$

HOTEL

🛏 **Marriott Winston-Salem.** This central and reliable chain hotel is part of Twin City Quarter, a shopping and dining area in downtown Winston-Salem that's adjacent to the Benton Convention Center. **Pros:** it's an easy walk to the arts district and jazz clubs; pool comes in handy on hot days. **Cons:** not overly luxurious; standard experience. $ *Rooms from: $142* ✉ *425 N. Cherry St., Downtown* 🕿 *336/725–3500, 877/888–9762* ⊕ *www.marriott.com* ⟿ *321 rooms* ⦿ *No meals.*

NIGHTLIFE AND PERFORMING ARTS

NIGHTLIFE

Foothills Brewpub. This place has more than a dozen beers on tap, a mix of year-round and seasonal Foothills brews. The pub also serves up classic bar food with a little more thought than your typical drinking hole. Try even more beers at the brewery and tasting room, just outside downtown. ✉ *638 W. Fourth St., Downtown* 🕿 *336/777–3348* ⊕ *www. foothillsbrewing.com.*

The Garage. Check out one of the best places to drink a beer and hear a sampling of mostly regional musicians. There's live music about half the week. ✉ *110 W. 7th St., Downtown* 🕿 *336/777–1127* ⊕ *www. the-garage.ws.*

6th and Vine. For a classy and yet quirky evening out, try this wine bar-café. Outdoor patio seating, North Carolina wines, and frequent dance parties make this a good all-around option. ✉ *209 W. 6th St., Downtown* ☎ *336/725–5577* ⊕ *www.6thandvine.com.*

PERFORMING ARTS

Festival Stage of Winston-Salem. The sister company of the group behind North Carolina Shakespeare Festival stages contemporary and original plays at the Hanesbrands Theatre. ✉ *209 N. Spruce St., University* ☎ *336/747–1414 box office* ⊕ *festivalstage.org.*

National Black Theatre Festival. Every other August, the North Carolina Black Repertory Company hosts this weeklong showcase of African American arts, which attracts tens of thousands of people to venues all over the city. The next festival is scheduled for 2019, though performances occur throughout the year. ✉ *610 Coliseum Dr., University* ☎ *336/723–2266* ⊕ *www.nbtf.org.*

Stevens Center. Many North Carolina School of the Arts musical and dramatic performances are held at this restored 1929 movie palace. ✉ *405 W. 4th St., Downtown* ☎ *336/721–1945* ⊕ *www.uncsa.edu/ performances/stevens-center.*

SPORTS AND THE OUTDOORS

BASKETBALL

Demon Deacons. Winston-Salem's Atlantic Coast Conference entry plays in Lawrence Joel Veterans Memorial Coliseum. ✉ *2825 University Pkwy.* ☎ *336/758–3322, 888/758–3322* ⊕ *wakeforestsports.cstv.com.*

GOLF

Reynolds Park Golf Course. This is the elder statesman of local links: designed by Ellis Maples, the public course opened in 1930. The final hole tests any player's stamina: there's a 425-yard fairway that ends on an elevated green. ✉ *2391 Reynolds Park Rd.* ☎ *336/650–7660, 336/650–7664* ⊕ *www.cityofws.org/departments/recreation-parks/ athletics/golf* 🏌 *$26 weekdays, $31 weekends, includes cart* 🏌 *18 holes, 6534 yards, par 71.*

Tanglewood Park Golf. In addition to Tanglewood Park's Reynolds Course, there's the Championship Course, which was long home to the Vantage Championship. Both courses were designed by Robert Trent Jones in the mid-'50s, and both feature pine-lined fairways (narrower on the Reynolds course) and lakes that come into play several times. Golf cart fees are included in rates for both of these courses. ✉ *U.S. 158 off I–40, 4201 Manor House Cir., Clemmons* ☎ *336/703–6420* ⊕ *www.golf.tanglewoodpark.org* 🏌 *Reynolds Course: Mon.–Thurs. $39, Fri. $41, weekends $49; Championship Course: Mon.–Thurs. $27, Fri. $29, weekends $33; Par 3 Course: weekdays $7.50, weekends $8.50, golf cart $11.* 🏌 *Reynolds Course: 18 holes, 6567 yards, par 72; Championship Course: 18 holes, 7101 yards, par 70; Par 3 Course: 18 holes, 1445 yards, par 54.*

SHOPPING
CRAFTS
Piedmont Craftsmen's Shop & Gallery. Contemporary and traditional works from nearly 400 craftspeople fill this gallery and shop in Winston-Salem's arty hub. The organization has held an annual fair in November since 1963. ⊠ *601 N. Trade St., Downtown* ☎ *336/725–1516* ⊕ *www. piedmontcraftsmen.org* ⊘ *Closed Sun. and Mon.*

HIGH POINT

18 miles southeast of Winston-Salem; 76 miles northeast of Charlotte; 20 miles southwest of Greensboro.

High Point earned its name through simple geography: it was the highest point on the railroad line between Goldsboro and Charlotte. Nowadays the city's "high point" is hosting the semiannual High Point Market, the largest wholesale furniture trade show in the world. Each spring and fall for about a week, so many people flood the town that its population of 108,000 nearly doubles. The rest of the year, the city can be pretty sleepy. Note that High Point does not have that many memorable restaurants; for more varied eats, check out nearby Greensboro or Winston-Salem.

GETTING HERE AND AROUND
High Point is one of the Piedmont's smaller cities, with very little traffic. Navigating it by car is fairly simple, and if you happen to get turned around, friendly folks are ready to offer help with directions.

ESSENTIALS
Visitor Information High Point Convention and Visitors Bureau. ⊠ *1634 N. Main St., Suite 102* ☎ *336/884–5255, 800/720–5255* ⊕ *www.highpoint.org.*

EXPLORING
High Point Museum & Historical Park. You can wander through the 1786 John Haley House and the 1801 Hoggatt House, where rotating exhibits highlight Piedmont history and Quaker heritage with local artifacts. Guests can also schedule guided tours. If you've ever wondered about Quaker cooking or ironwork, you can learn about these aspects of life and more during the museum's monthly living-history events. ⊠ *1859 E. Lexington Ave.* ☎ *336/885–1859* ⊕ *www.highpointmuseum.org* ⚌ *Free* ⊘ *Closed Sun. and Mon.*

Mendenhall Homeplace. A well-preserved example of 19th-century domestic architecture, this park lies a few miles northwest of High Point. As Quakers, the Mendenhalls opposed slavery, and here you can find one of the few surviving false-bottom wagons, used to help slaves escape to freedom on the Underground Railroad. ■**TIP→ Come in July, when kids can learn how to make a corn-husk doll or design a quilt square during the Village Fair.** ⊠ *603 W. Main St., Jamestown* ☎ *336/454–3819* ⊕ *www.mendenhallhomeplace.com* ⚌ *$5* ⊘ *Closed Sun. year-round and Mon.–Thurs. in Jan. and Feb.*

World's Largest Chest of Drawers. In the 1920s, this building shaped like an 18th-century chest of drawers was constructed to call attention to the city's standing as the "furniture capital of the world." The 36-foot-high

CLOSE UP

North Carolina Wineries

For a gentle introduction to the world of wine, look no further than North Carolina. With nearly 140 wineries sprinkled throughout its valleys, mountains, and coastal plain, the state's wine industry is huge yet intimate in its approach.

When touring and tasting around these parts, don't be surprised if you end up sipping your vintage alongside the owner or head grower. Even the wildly successful folks at RayLen and Childress Vineyards, near Winston-Salem, remain approachable and focus on producing quality wine. This is especially true in the Yadkin Valley, the biggest wine-producing region in the state, located on and near the western edge of the Piedmont. Here, nearly 50 wineries have made a name for themselves by bucking North Carolina's centuries-old tradition of producing sweet Muscadine and Scuppernong wines and opting instead for the drier European varieties of the vinifera family. Though they were originally labeled rebels by the state's old-school wine producers, the Yadkin growers are now considered some of the finest in the state. A few of the hot varietals to watch include the white Viognier and the red Cabernet Franc.

building, complete with a 6-foot-long pair of socks dangling from one of its drawers, remains one of the strangest sights in North Carolina to this day. Nearby Furnitureland South has actually built a larger chest of drawers as the facade to one of its showrooms, although it is not freestanding. ✉ *508 N. Hamilton St.*

WHERE TO EAT AND STAY

$$$$ AMERICAN 🍴 **Blue Water Grille.** This intimate spot is one of the best surprises in High Point's sparse culinary scene. The menu, which changes several times a year, is always full of fresh seafood dishes and other Lowcountry favorites, often presented with an Asian flair and a bit of French influence. **Known for:** impressive seafood like ahi tuna; shared plates; classy date-night environment. [$] *Average main: $25* ✉ *126 E. State Ave.* ☎ *336/886–1010* 🌐 *www.bluewatergrillenc.com* 🕓 *Closed Sun. No lunch.*

$ BARBECUE 🍴 **Lexington Barbecue.** The town of Lexington is the base for Carolina's sweet, red-sauce style of barbecue. At Lexington Barbecue, meat is pulled from smoked pork shoulders and served up as a sandwich in a soft bun topped with red slaw. **Known for:** pulled pork smoked over hickory wood; fruit cobblers for dessert; casual barbecue atmosphere. [$] *Average main: $11* ✉ *100 Smokehouse Ln., 20 miles southwest of High Point, Lexington* ☎ *336/249–9814* 🌐 *www.lexbbq.com* 🕓 *Closed Sun.*

$ HOTEL 🏨 **Radisson Hotel High Point.** The central location makes this hotel a favorite with people arriving for weekend shopping trips. **Pros:** close to popular furniture shops and downtown; on-site dining at Bistro 135; reliable service and quality. **Cons:** downtown High Point is usually dead at night; prices are high and availability is low during Market. [$] *Rooms from: $89* ✉ *135 S. Main St.* ☎ *336/889–8888* 🌐 *www.radisson.com/high-point-hotel-nc-27260/usahigh* 🛏 *252 rooms* 🍽 *No meals.*

Don't miss the World's Largest Chest of Drawers in High Point, a city known for its superlative furniture.

PERFORMING ARTS

Theatre Art Galleries. Solo and group shows rotate through several exhibition spaces at this gallery, in the same building as the High Point Theatre. The frequent art openings are always open to the public. ⊠ *220 E. Commerce Ave.* ☎ *336/887–2137* ⊕ *www.tagart.org* ⊙ *Closed during Market.*

SPORTS AND THE OUTDOORS

GOLF

Oak Hollow. Designed by Pete Dye, this public course makes use of its lakeside position by including peninsula greens and an island tee on its par-5 5th hole. ⊠ *3400 N. Centennial St.* ☎ *336/883–3260* ⊕ *www.oak-hollowgc.com* 🍽 *Weekdays $13 for 9 holes, $17 for 18 holes; weekends $22 for 9 holes in last 2 hrs of play, $39 for 18 holes; $15 for golf cart for 18 holes, $9 for golf cart for 9 holes* ⅄ *18 holes, 6564 yards, par 72.*

HIKING

Piedmont Environmental Center. The 376-acre Piedmont Environmental Center has 11 miles of hiking trails and a nearly 10-mile paved greenway adjacent to City Lake Park. ⊠ *1220 Penny Rd.* ☎ *336/883–8531* ⊕ *www.highpointnc.gov/1746/Piedmont-Environmental-Center.*

SHOPPING

Furnitureland South. With more than 1 million square feet of showroom space, this store, the biggest furniture retailer in the world, goes far beyond an average shopping experience; a visit could easily take all day. Customers register with the front desk and are given tips by a Furnitureland consultant on how to maximize their visit to the sprawling store, which includes innumerable galleries from leading manufacturers and a discount center. Meals and refreshments are available at a Starbucks

CLOSE UP

North Carolina Barbecue

Native Americans in what is today North Carolina are the first chapter in one of the longest continuous barbecue traditions anywhere. In fact, Native Americans, African slaves, and German and Scotch-Irish settlers have all had a hand in the evolution of two distinct styles of barbecue.

EAST VS. WEST

Vinegar and pepper sauces in the east highlight the flavor of the meat itself, while western barbecue mixes sweet and smoky flavors in immense variety. Expect more of an eastern influence from Raleigh to the coast. From Charlotte to the mountains the western style dominates. If you find yourself in between these two "barbecue boundaries," treat yourself to a blend of east and west in the form of North Carolina's third barbecue variety: Lexington Style, which adds ketchup to the vinegar-based sauce. However you may slice, chop, or pull it, the barbecue debate has produced great meals and brought friends and family together for generations.

Café and Furnitureland South Café. ✉ *5635 Riverdale Dr., Jamestown* ☎ *336/822–3000* ⊕ *www.furniturelandsouth.com.*

High Point Furniture Sales. Deep discounts are part of the draw to this furniture store. Expect more than 150 well-known brands and some pieces offered at below manufacturer direct prices. The **Discount Furniture Warehouse & Furniture Value & Clearance Center,** at 2035 Brentwood Street, is only one exit from the main store. ✉ *2000 Baker Rd.* ☎ *336/841–5664, 800/334–1875* ⊕ *www.highpointfurnituresales.com.*

CHARLOTTE

Don't expect to hear many Southern accents in this melting pot, the biggest city in the state. Visiting Charlotte is much more of an urban experience than a down-home one, but that's all part of the fun of being in this bustling, forward-focused place. Here, local custom is not to preserve the old, but build new. Although controversial, this tradition is responsible for the ultramodern feel of Uptown Charlotte. With little doubt, it's also why the city is home to so many brand-new sports complexes, museums, and chic lofts. This lack of dwelling in the past brings people from across the country to start new lives—and also to start restaurants, galleries, and high-concept bars.

Things are always in motion here, but history lovers shouldn't despair. Bits and pieces of Charlotte's past still linger. With their antique architecture and shaded streets, neighborhoods like Dilworth and the Fourth Ward offer lovely glimpses of what once was. Other areas, like hip Plaza Midwood, are becoming a fusion of the new and old. There, historic houses have been converted into wine bars and late-night eateries.

Be aware that heavy development has created some typical urban problems throughout town. Yes, the traffic and parking can be terrible, and restaurants are packed on weekends. But don't let that scare you away from the Queen City. When visiting the Piedmont, Charlotte is a must.

GETTING HERE AND AROUND

Charlotte is a driver's town, but its light-rail system makes going without a car possible if you stick to the central areas. Though its route is short and limited, the LYNX blue line is clean and fast. It runs from Uptown, through the convention center, to Interstate 485. Check for routes and schedules at ⊕ *www.charmeck.org/departments/cats/lynx*. You'll be able to walk around Uptown and the historic Fourth Ward.

ESSENTIALS

Visitor Information Visitor Info Center. ⊠ *The Convention Center, 501 S. College St., Uptown* ☎ *800/231–4636* ⊕ *www.charlottesgotalot.com.*

UPTOWN CHARLOTTE

Uptown Charlotte, the city's "downtown," is ideal for walking. The city was laid out in four wards around Independence Square, at Trade and Tryon Streets. The Square, as it is known, is the center of the Uptown area. In recent years, Uptown has become increasingly user-friendly, with restaurants, bars, and museums tightly packed into a small area. If you're in town for only a short while, this is the place to be.

EXPLORING

TOP ATTRACTIONS

Bechtler Museum of Modern Art. With the famed "Firebird" sculpture out front, there's no way you can miss this part of Uptown's art scene. Covered in mirrors and colored class, Niki de Saint Phalle's 17-foot, birdlike creature is just a taste of what Bechtler has to offer inside. The rotating collection might include Warhol's pop art, Giacometti's dark sculptures, and ceramics by Picasso. Founded by the Swiss-born Andreas Bechtler, the museum highlights his family's love affair with art, as well as their deep connections with many of the artists on display. ⊠ *420 S. Tryon St., Uptown* ☎ *704/353–9200* ⊕ *www.bechtler. org* 🖭 *$8* ☉ *Closed Tues.*

FAMILY **Discovery Place Science.** Allow at least two hours for the **aquariums,** the three-story **rain forest,** and the **IMAX Dome Theater.** Lie on a bed of nails, conduct experiments in the interactive labs, or get in touch with your inner innovator as you create shoes from garbage. Check the schedule for special exhibits. ⊠ *301 N. Tryon St., Uptown* ☎ *704/372–6261, 800/935–0553* ⊕ *science.discoveryplace.org* 🖭 *$17; IMAX $10; $22 package for both.*

The Harvey B. Gantt Center for African-American Arts + Culture. Historic Brooklyn, as the once-thriving African American neighborhood here was known, is long gone, but this celebration of black art, history, and culture serves its memory well. Past exhibits have included Tavis Smiley's "American I AM," detailing the imprint of nearly 500 years of black contributions to American culture. The exhibits change frequently, but you can always see John and Vivian Hewitt's collection of African American visual art, including those of Harlem Renaissance–famed and Charlotte-born Romare Bearden. ⊠ *551 S. Tryon St., Uptown* ☎ *704/547–3700* ⊕ *www.ganttcenter.org* 🖭 *$9* ☉ *Closed Mon.*

CLOSE UP

Golfing at Pinehurst

Pinehurst is a New England–style village with quiet, shaded streets and immaculately kept homes ranging from massive Victorians to tiny cottages. It was laid out in the late 1800s in a wagon-wheel pattern by Frederick Law Olmsted, who also designed Asheville's Biltmore Estate and New York City's Central Park. Annie Oakley lived here for a number of years and headed the local gun club. Today Pinehurst is renowned for its golf courses.

Although golfers will be in heaven, their nongolfing friends and family might be at a loss for entertainment around these sleepy parts. Don't expect to find much nightlife here or practically anything open late. Instead, this is a good place to stroll and sleep in. The town operates at a different pace than most of the world, and that's a big part of its charm. ■ TIP→ There are hardly any restaurants in Pinehurst that are not attached to hotels and lodges. When booking your trip, make sure to check out packages that include meals where you're staying.

Pinehurst Resort. Pinehurst is famously known for its golf, and the courses—known by their numbers—can bring a tear to a golfer's eye with their beauty. The courses range from the first, designed in 1898 by legendary Donald Ross, to the most recent, designed in 1995 by Tom Fazio to mark the resort's centennial. No. 2 has hosted more single golf championships than any site in the country, and the U.S. Open will next return there in 2024. The hilly terrain of No. 7 makes it especially tough. ⊠ 80 Carolina Vista Dr., Pinehurst ☎ 855/235–8507 reservations or tee times ⊕ www.pinehurst.com ⛳ $89–$410 ⅃ 9 18-hole courses, 5722–7588 yds, par 68–72.

FAMILY
Fodor'sChoice
★

Levine Museum of the New South. With an 8,000-square-foot exhibit, "Cotton Fields to Skyscrapers: Charlotte and the Carolina Piedmont in the New South," as a jumping-off point, this museum offers a comprehensive interpretation of post–Civil War Southern history. Interactive exhibits and different "environments"—a tenant farmer's house, an African American hospital, a bustling street scene—bring to life the history of the region. ■ TIP→ Admission is free the first Sunday of the month and half price every Sunday. ⊠ 200 E. 7th St., Uptown ☎ 704/333–1887 ⊕ www.museumofthenewsouth.org ⛳ $8.

Mint Museum Uptown. With five stories and 145,000 square feet of space, this is a must-see for art lovers. Expect rotating special exhibits as well as permanent collections of American and contemporary work, plus craft and design. Be sure not to miss the museum's dramatic atrium, which houses a 60-foot-tall glass curtain that offers amazing views of the surrounding cityscape. ■ TIP→ Use your ticket stub for free entrance to Mint Museum Randolph (good for two days). Admission is free at both Mint Museums on Wednesday 5–9 pm. A free shuttle runs between the museums on Wednesday, Friday, and Saturday. ⊠ Levine Center for the Arts, 500 S. Tryon St., Uptown ☎ 704/337–2000 ⊕ www.mintmuseum. org ⛳ $12 ⊘ Closed Mon. and Tues.

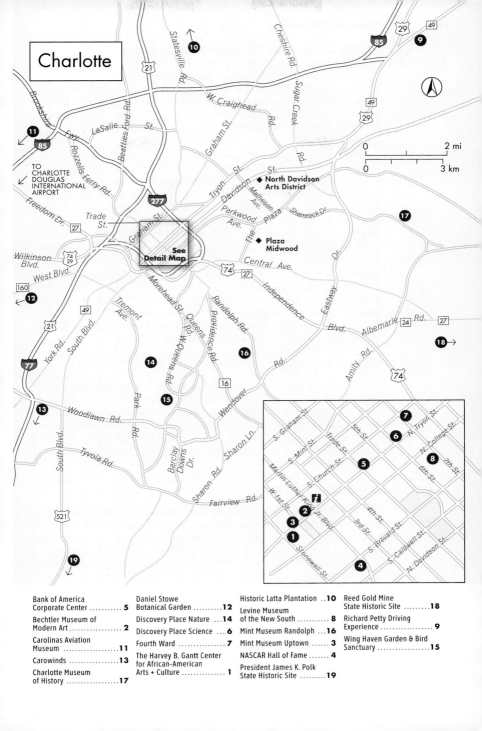

Charlotte

TO CHARLOTTE DOUGLAS INTERNATIONAL AIRPORT

North Davidson Arts District

Plaza Midwood

See Detail Map

0 ——— 2 mi
0 ——— 3 km

FAMILY
Fodor'sChoice
★
NASCAR Hall of Fame. This 150,000-square-foot megamuseum has enough going on to intrigue even non-NASCAR fans. A complete visual overload, the racing palace features exhibits of famous cars, an enormous theater, and countless rotating exhibits. Best of all, the interactive exhibits let visitors travel through the museum as one of their favorite NASCAR heroes. ⊠ *400 E. Martin Luther King Blvd., Uptown* ☎ *704/654–4400, 800/902–6463* ⊕ *www.nascarhall.com* ✉ *$19.95.*

WORTH NOTING

Bank of America Corporate Center. Architecture fans should make time for a trip to see one of the city's most striking buildings. Designed by Cesar Pelli, this structure rises 60 stories to a crownlike top. The main attractions are three monumental lobby frescoes by the world-renowned local painter Ben Long—their themes are making/building, chaos/creativity, and planning/knowledge. Also in the tower are the **North Carolina Blumenthal Performing Arts Center** and the restaurants, shops, and exhibition space of **Founders Hall.** ⊠ *100 N. Tryon St., Uptown.*

Fourth Ward. Charlotte's popular old neighborhood began as a political subsection created for electoral purposes in the mid-1800s. The architecture and sensibility of this quiet, homespun neighborhood provide a glimpse of life in a less hectic time. A brochure with 18 places of historic interest can be picked up at the Visit Charlotte visitor center, at Tryon Street and Martin Luther King Jr. Boulevard. ⊠ *Uptown.*

NORTH DAVIDSON ARTS DISTRICT

Charlotte bills NoDa as "SoHo's little sister." Although this small, historic neighborhood 2 miles north of Uptown is quite a bit sleepier than its New York City sibling, it's still undeniably cool. Creative energy flows through the reclaimed textile mill and little houses, cottages, and commercial spaces. Here you'll find both the kooky and traditional—artists, musicians, dancers, restaurateurs, and even knitters—sharing space.

PLAZA MIDWOOD

Plaza Midwood, one of Charlotte's most diverse areas, is a fascinating place to spend an afternoon or evening. Located northeast of Uptown, on and near Central Avenue and the Plaza, it houses a hipster-approved collection of restaurants, shops, and galleries. After dark, it morphs into a colorful nightlife scene. This is a great spot to simply stroll and people-watch.

GREATER CHARLOTTE

Many of Charlotte's most interesting sights lie outside the city center. From gardens to museums to a racing speedway, there are plenty of reasons to leave Uptown if you have time—and wheels. While you can reach some of these spots by city bus, a car is essential for others.

The NASCAR Hall of Fame displays historic cars and racing memorabilia.

EXPLORING
TOP ATTRACTIONS

Charlotte Museum of History. Built in 1774, this stone building is the oldest dwelling in the county. Hezekiah Alexander and his wife, Mary, reared 10 children in this house and farmed the land. Learn about the lives of early residents in the area through exhibits and displays. ✉ *3500 Shamrock Dr., East Charlotte* ☎ *704/568–1774* ⊕ *www.charlottemuseum.org* 🎟 *$10* ⊗ *Closed Sun. and Mon.*

FAMILY **Discovery Place Nature.** You'll find a butterfly pavilion, bugs galore, live animals, nature trails, a puppet theater, and hands-on exhibits just for children at this museum. ✉ *1658 Sterling Rd., Freedom Park* ☎ *704/372–6261 tickets* ⊕ *nature.discoveryplace.org* 🎟 *$8* ⊗ *Closed Mon.*

OFF THE BEATEN PATH **Historic Latta Plantation.** The last remaining Catawba River plantation open to the public, this living history site interprets 19th-century farm life in North Carolina's backcountry. James Latta, a traveling merchant, built the plantation's Federal-style home in 1800 and soon became a cotton planter. According to family documents, the entire Latta family and more than 30 slaves assisted with production on the 742-acre farm. Today, visitors can tour the home as well as reconstructed slave quarters and a yeoman farmer's home. Historically appropriate farm animals and special weekend programs, such as folk craft demonstrations, round out the experience. ✉ *5225 Sample Rd., Huntersville* ☎ *704/875–2312* ⊕ *www.lattaplantation.org* 🎟 *$8* ⊗ *Closed Mon.*

Mint Museum Randolph. Built in 1836 as the first U.S. Mint, this building has been a home for art since 1936. The holdings in its impressive permanent collections include fashion, ceramics, coins and currency, and art of the ancient Americas. ■TIP→ Your ticket stub gets you free admission to the Mint Museum Uptown (good for two days). ⊠ *2730 Randolph Rd., East Charlotte* ☎ *704/337–2000* ⊕ *www.mintmuseum. org* ⊠ *$12* ⊗ *Closed Mon. and Tues.*

WORTH NOTING

Carolinas Aviation Museum. The star here is the "Miracle on the Hudson" plane—the famed Airbus A320-214 that was safely landed in the Hudson River in January 2009 by the pilot Capt. Chesley B. Sullenberger after both engines failed. A working DC-3, F-14D Super TomCat, and about a dozen other aircraft are also on display. Note that if you're visiting in peak summer there's no air-conditioning here. ⊠ *Charlotte-Douglas International Airport, 4672 First Flight Dr.* ☎ *704/997–3770* ⊕ *www.carolinasaviation.org* ⊠ *$12.*

FAMILY **Carowinds.** Home of Fury 325, the world's tallest and fastest coaster that reaches a height of 325 feet, Carowinds is a place for thrill-seekers. The park, just past the South Carolina border on Interstate 77, also boasts a water park, live concerts and performances, and an interactive 3-D experience. ■TIP→ Check Carowinds's website for current hours and deals. It's usually cheaper to buy tickets online than at the gate. ⊠ *14523 Carowinds Blvd., off I–77 at Carowinds Blvd., South Charlotte* ☎ *704/588–2600* ⊕ *www.carowinds.com* ⊠ *$65.*

Daniel Stowe Botanical Garden. This bright garden is known for its painterly display of colors. There's a perennial garden, wildflower meadow, Canal Garden, an orchid conservatory, and other themed areas. ⊠ *6500 S. New Hope Rd., 20 miles west of downtown Charlotte, Belmont* ☎ *704/825–4490* ⊕ *www.dsbg.org* ⊠ *$12.95.*

President James K. Polk State Historic Site. This state historic site 10 miles south of central Charlotte marks the humble birthplace and childhood home of the 11th U.S. president, nicknamed "Napoléon of the Stump" for his excellent speeches. Guided tours of the log cabins (replicas of the originals) show what life was like for settlers back in 1795. ⊠ *12031 Lancaster Hwy., Pineville* ☎ *704/889–7145* ⊕ *www.nchistoricsites.org/ polk* ⊠ *Free* ⊗ *Closed Sun. and Mon.*

FAMILY **Reed Gold Mine State Historic Site.** This historic site, about 22 miles east of Charlotte, is where America's first documented gold rush began, after Conrad Reed discovered a 17-pound nugget in 1799. Guided underground tours of the gold mine are available, as well as gold panning (from roughly early April to late October), walking trails, and a stamp mill. ⊠ *9621 Reed Mine Rd., north of Rte. 24/27, Midland* ☎ *704/721–4653* ⊕ *www.nchistoricsites.org/reed* ⊠ *Free; gold panning $3* ⊗ *Closed Sun. and Mon.*

Richard Petty Driving Experience. If you want to indulge your inner race-car driver, take lessons through the Richard Petty Driving Experience. You can drive a NASCAR-style stock car at speeds up to 140 mph around the Charlotte Motor Speedway. If you want the thrill of the ride without being in the driver's seat, you can ride with an instructor and go up to 165 mph. Classes are available throughout the year, though only when there's no event at the speedway. Prices start at $449 for eight laps around the track. **■TIP→ You must have a valid driver's license, and you'll need to reserve ahead of time.** ✉ *Charlotte Motor Speedway, 5555 Concord Pkwy. S, Concord* ☎ *704/455–9443, 800/237–3889* 🌐 *www.drivepetty.com.*

Wing Haven Garden & Bird Sanctuary. Set in one of the city's most exclusive neighborhoods, this 4-acre garden is a serene environment for feathered visitors and others. ✉ *248 Ridgewood Ave.* ☎ *704/331–0664* 🌐 *www.winghavengardens.com* 🎟 *$10* 🕒 *Closed Sun.–Tues.*

3

WHERE TO EAT

UPTOWN CHARLOTTE

$$$$ MODERN AMERICAN

🍴 **Halcyon Restaurant, Flavors from the Earth.** This restaurant within the Mint Museum has a stunning view of Tryon Street, Charlotte's main avenue. Expect locally sourced, globally inspired dishes that let the ingredients shine. **Known for:** seasonal menu, all locally sourced; posh atmosphere; central location in Uptown. [$] *Average main: $28* ✉ *500 S. Tryon St., Uptown* ☎ *704/910–0865* 🌐 *www.halcyonflavors.com* 🕒 *Closed Mon. No dinner Sun.*

$ SOUTHERN Fodor's Choice ★

🍴 **Mert's Heart and Soul.** Business executives and arts patrons make their way to Mert's—named for Myrtle, a favorite customer with a sunny disposition. Owners James and Renee Bezzelle serve large portions of Lowcountry and Gullah staples, like fried chicken with greens, mac 'n' cheese, and red beans and rice. **Known for:** classic soul food; pancakes for brunch; famous slow rolls, egg roll wraps filled with black-eyed peas, rice, chicken, and collard greens. [$] *Average main: $12* ✉ *214 N. College St., Uptown* ☎ *704/342–4222* 🌐 *www.mertscharlotte.com.*

$ SOUTHERN

🍴 **Price's Chicken Coop.** If you want to know where the locals eat, just follow the scent of oil to this storefront institution in the historic South End neighborhood, just across Interstate 277 from Uptown. The light, crispy coating that covers the chicken is so juicy you'll begin to understand that there is indeed an art to running a deep fryer. **Known for:** some of the best fried chicken in the state; no dining room—take-out only; cash-only policy. [$] *Average main: $8* ✉ *1614 Camden Rd., South End* ☎ *704/333–9866* 🌐 *www.priceschickencoop.com* 💳 *No credit cards* 🕒 *Closed Sun. and Mon.*

PLAZA MIDWOOD

$ BARBECUE

🍴 **Midwood Smokehouse.** It's notoriously hard to find good barbecue in Charlotte, but this spot with late hours and a full bar bucks the trend. Located in the funky Plaza Midwood neighborhood, it carries a full range of sauces and meats, and keeps its wood-fired smoker burning 24/7. **Known for:** brisket, ribs, and pulled pork; banana pudding for dessert. [$] *Average main: $11* ✉ *1401 Central Ave., Plaza Midwood* ☎ *704/295–4227* 🌐 *www.midwoodsmokehouse.com.*

You can learn about yeoman farmers' lives at the Historic Latta Plantation, a living-history farm and museum.

GREATER CHARLOTTE

$ ECLECTIC 🍴 **The Cowfish.** This fusion spot is all about unexpected combinations: sushi packed with burger and beef components, and burgers stuffed with rice, tempura, rare ahi tuna, and other traditional sushi elements. But even if you're not so adventurous, this fun and always-packed spot will surely have something for you. **Known for:** sushi rolls inspired by burgers; long lines; huge bar menu, including sake. [$] *Average main: $10* ✉ *4310 Sharon Rd., South Park* ☎ *704/365–1922* 🌐 *www.thecowfish.com.*

$$$$ SOUTHERN 🍴 **Dogwood Southern Table & Bar.** Regional cuisine takes up this seasonal menu, located across the street from SouthPark Mall. Guests can share a selection of small plates or order a traditional entrée that highlights the best of North Carolina cuisine. **Known for:** pimento cheese and house-made biscuits; upscale Southern fare; boozy Sunday brunch with craft cocktails. [$] *Average main: $28* ✉ *4905 Ashley Park La., Suite D, South Park* ☎ *704/910–4919* 🌐 *www.dogwoodsoutherntable.com* 🕒 *No lunch Sat.*

$$ AMERICAN 🍴 **300 East.** Operated out of an old home in pleasant Dilworth, this comfortable little spot is the perfect place to hang out and people-watch. The always-changing menu, which has its roots in Southern and Californian styles, includes modern, sophisticated takes on various meat and fish dishes, pizza, salads, and pastas. **Known for:** desserts by one of the best pastry chefs in North Carolina; historic building; creative cocktail list. [$] *Average main: $19* ✉ *300 East Blvd., Dilworth* ☎ *704/332–6507* 🌐 *www.300east.net.*

WHERE TO STAY

UPTOWN CHARLOTTE

$$ HOTEL **The Dunhill Hotel.** You won't find many old buildings in Charlotte, and this 1929 structure in the center of downtown is the city's only historic hotel. **Pros:** great restaurant; one of few historic places in town; central location. **Cons:** rooms can be small; some room appliances are dated. [$] *Rooms from: $169 ✉ 237 N. Tryon St., Uptown ☎ 704/332–4141 🌐 www.dunhillhotel.com 🛏 60 rooms 🍴 Breakfast.*

$$ HOTEL **Hilton Charlotte Center City.** This comfortable hotel is right in the heart of things, just down the block from the Charlotte Convention Center. **Pros:** central location; YMCA on the premises. **Cons:** some rooms have showers only; like most Charlotte hotels, rates vary dramatically depending on the day and time of year. [$] *Rooms from: $179 ✉ 222 E. 3rd St., Uptown ☎ 704/377–1500, 800/445–8667 🌐 www.charlottecentercity.hilton.com 🛏 400 rooms 🍴 No meals.*

$ HOTEL **Omni Charlotte Hotel.** This 16-story hotel is downtown, within walking distance of the convention center as well as many arts and sports venues. **Pros:** location and amenities are great for downtown; adjacent to a mall with tons of restaurant options. **Cons:** busy setting might be too much for some travelers; charges for parking and Internet use add up. [$] *Rooms from: $149 ✉ 132 E. Trade St., Uptown ☎ 704/377–0400 🌐 www.omnicharlotte.com 🛏 374 rooms 🍴 No meals.*

$$ HOTEL **Westin Charlotte.** For an upscale taste of Uptown, it's hard to get much better than this business hotel that's next to the convention center. **Pros:** helpful staff and beautiful surroundings; free Wi-Fi in the lobby and bar; central location. **Cons:** parking and Internet charges can get expensive; gets very busy during conventions. [$] *Rooms from: $159 ✉ 601 S. College St., Uptown ☎ 704/375–2600 🌐 www.westincharlottehotel.com 🛏 722 rooms 🍴 No meals.*

GREATER CHARLOTTE

$$ RESORT **Ballantyne Hotel and Lodge.** On 2,000 acres, this beautiful and stately resort hotel is the best of the best when it comes to luxury in Charlotte. **Pros:** luxury defined; beautiful setting with equally lovely rooms. **Cons:** not convenient for exploring city center; not in walking distance to any interesting sights. [$] *Rooms from: $189 ✉ 10000 Ballantyne Commons Pkwy., South Charlotte ☎ 704/248–4000, 866/248–4824 🌐 www.theballantynehotel.com 🛏 244 rooms 🍴 No meals.*

$$$ B&B/INN **Duke Mansion.** Spending a night at this historic, luxurious inn seems more like borrowing a wealthy friend's estate than spending a night in a hotel. **Pros:** guests get a real sense of history and a neighborhood feel; the surrounding area is a great place to stroll. **Cons:** some bathrooms have older fixtures; not in walking distance to nightlife spots. [$] *Rooms from: $209 ✉ 400 Hermitage Rd., Myers Park ☎ 704/714–4400, 800/808–1009 🌐 www.dukemansion.com 🛏 20 rooms 🍴 Breakfast.*

$ B&B/INN **Morehead Inn.** Built in 1917, this grand Colonial Revival house has rooms filled with period antiques, including several with impressive four-poster beds. **Pros:** cozy and historic; known for its cooked-to-order breakfast. **Cons:** a popular spot for weddings and parties, so it can be

3

noisy; not in walking distance to nightlife. Ⓢ *Rooms from: $129* ✉ *1122 E. Morehead St., Dilworth* ☎ *704/376–3357, 888/667–3432* ⊕ *www. moreheadinn.com* ⤴ *12 rooms* ⍵❘ *Breakfast.*

NIGHTLIFE AND PERFORMING ARTS

NIGHTLIFE
UPTOWN CHARLOTTE
Crave Dessert Bar. Charlotte's only dessert bar serves a wide range of upscale sweets and signature cocktails into the early-morning hours. Crave brings in a young, well-dressed crowd, drawn not only by the place's hip feel, but its wide selection of cupcakes, pies, ice cream, and more. Hookahs are also available, with several different flavors for patrons to toke. ✉ *500 W. 5th St., Suite 120, Uptown* ☎ *704/335–0588* ⊕ *www.cravedessertbar.com.*

Duckworth's Grill & Taphouse. If you love beer, you'll want to plan a stop at this taphouse in the middle of Uptown. Beer taps line the back bar, and if there's a brew you've been meaning to try, chances are this place has it. There are also plenty of televisions, which makes this a prime spot to watch basketball and other local sports. ✉ *330 N. Tryon St., Uptown* ☎ *980/939–1166* ⊕ *www.uptown.duckworths.com.*

NORTH DAVIDSON ARTS DISTRICT
Evening Muse. Hear live music nightly at this popular venue situated in the center of the NoDa Arts District, or wait for "Find Your Muse," its frequent open-mic night. ✉ *3227 N. Davidson St.* ☎ *704/376–3737* ⊕ *www.eveningmuse.com.*

PLAZA MIDWOOD
Thomas Street Tavern. This little bar is one of the best places in Plaza Midwood to grab a beer and play games like corn hole and Ping-Pong on the spacious patio. ✉ *1218 Thomas Ave., Plaza Midwood* ☎ *704/376–1622.*

PERFORMING ARTS
UPTOWN CHARLOTTE
Blumenthal Performing Arts. In addition to the 2,100-seat Belk Theatre, this performing arts center houses several resident companies, including the Charlotte Symphony, Charlotte Ballet, and Opera Carolina. ✉ *130 N. Tryon St., Uptown* ☎ *704/372–1000* ⊕ *www.blumenthalarts.org.*

NORTH DAVIDSON ARTS DISTRICT
Neighborhood Theatre. Once called the Astor Theater this circa-1945 former movie palace is now a venue that has hosted concerts by the likes of the Indigo Girls, Beach House, and Rooney. ✉ *511 E. 36th St., North Davidson* ☎ *704/942–7997* ⊕ *www.neighborhoodtheatre.com.*

PLAZA MIDWOOD
Twenty Two. If you like to look at art with a drink in hand, visit this gallery-bar. The space serves some of the finest craft beer in the area, as well as wine and sake. There's new art monthly. ✉ *1500 Central Ave., Plaza Midwood* ☎ *980/498–7625.*

SPORTS AND THE OUTDOORS

AUTO RACING

Charlotte Motor Speedway. This state-of-the-art facility, with a seating capacity of 89,000, is considered the heart of NASCAR. An estimated 90% of driving teams live within 50 miles. Hosting more than 300 events each year, this is one of the busiest sports venues in the United States. Racing season runs April to November, and tours are offered on non-race days. The Speedway Club, an upscale restaurant, is on the premises. ■TIP➔ When there's a race, the population of Concord can jump from 60,000 to more than 250,000. Make sure you book your hotel well in advance. ⊠ *5555 Concord Pkwy. S, northeast of Charlotte, Concord* ☎ *704/455–3200* ⊕ *www.charlottemotorspeedway.com.*

BOATING

Catawba Queen. On Lake Norman, the *Catawba Queen* paddle wheeler gives dinner cruises and tours. The *Lady of the Lake*, a 90-foot yacht, offers dinner cruises. ⊠ *1459 River Hwy., Mooresville* ☎ *704/663–2628* ⊕ *www.queenslanding.com.*

Lake Norman State Park. Inlets on Lake Norman are ideal for canoeing. You can rent canoes and paddleboats for $5 per hour from the North Carolina Division of Parks and Recreation. ⊠ *759 State Park Rd., Troutman* ☎ *704/528–6350* ⊕ *www.ncparks.gov.*

FOOTBALL

Carolina Panthers. Charlotte's National Football League team plays from August through December, and hopefully into the postseason playoffs, in the 75,000-seat Bank of America Stadium. ⊠ *800 S. Mint St., Uptown* ☎ *704/358–7800* ⊕ *www.panthers.com.*

GOLF

Highland Creek Golf Club. This semiprivate course is lovely to look at and challenging to play. You have to be careful with the water hazards; there are water features on 13 holes. ⊠ *7101 Highland Creek Pkwy.* ☎ *704/875–9000* ⊕ *www.highlandcreekgolfclub.com* ⛳ *$35–$56* ⛳ *18 holes, 7043 yards, par 72.*

Larkhaven Golf Club. The oldest public course in Charlotte, Larkhaven opened in 1958. Mature trees have narrowed the fairways, and there's a 60-foot elevation drop on Hole 9, a par 3. The greens fee includes the use of a cart. ⊠ *4801 Camp Stewart Rd.* ☎ *704/545–4653* ⊕ *www. larkhavengolf.com* ⛳ *Weekdays $30, weekends $39* ⛳ *18 holes, 6717 yards, par 72.*

Paradise Valley Golf Center. This short course is perfect for players without much time: a round takes less than two hours. But don't let that fool you: the course can challenge the best of them. Unique elements include two island tees. There's also a miniature golf course called the Lost Duffer that's set in a 19th-century mining town. ⊠ *110 Barton Creek Dr.* ☎ *704/548–1808* ⊕ *www.charlottepublicgolf.com/paradise_valley_course* ⛳ *18 holes: weekdays $9, weekends $13; mini-golf $5; carts $6* ⛳ *18 holes, 1264 yards, par 54.*

SHOPPING

Charlotte is the largest retail center in the Carolinas. Most stores are in suburban malls; villages and towns in outlying areas have shops selling regional specialties.

ANTIQUES

The nearby towns of Waxhaw, Pineville, and Matthews are the best places to find antiques.

Sleepy Poet Antique Mall. You may get lost among the rows at this antique mall just outside of uptown. Vendors display their wares, ranging from books to furniture. ⊠ *4450 South Blvd., South End* ☎ *704/529–6369* ⊕ *www.sleepypoetstuff.com.*

FOOD

Charlotte Regional Farmers Market. This is the spot for local produce, eggs, plants, and crafts. ⊠ *1801 Yorkmount Rd., Airport/Coliseum* ☎ *704/357–1269* ⊕ *www.ncagr.gov/markets/facilities/markets/charlotte.*

GIFTS

Paper Skyscraper. As the name implies, you'll find books and paper goods here, but you'll also find an assortment of humorous and odd gifts. There is also a selection of Charlotte-themed items to remember the city. ⊠ *330 East Blvd., Dilworth* ☎ *704/333–7130* ⊕ *www. paperskyscraper.com.*

ASHEVILLE AND THE NORTH CAROLINA MOUNTAINS

WELCOME TO ASHEVILLE AND THE NORTH CAROLINA MOUNTAINS

TOP REASONS TO GO

★ **Biltmore Estate:** The 250-room Biltmore House, modeled after the great Renaissance châteaux of the Loire Valley in France, is the largest private home in America.

★ **Blue Ridge Parkway:** This winding two-lane road, which ends at the edge of the Great Smokies and shows off the highest mountains in eastern America, is the most scenic drive in the South and the most-visited National Park site in the country.

★ **Asheville:** Hip, artsy, sometimes funky, with scores of restaurants and active nightlife, Asheville is one of America's coolest places to live, and to visit.

★ **Engaging small towns:** You could easily fall in love with the charm, style, and Southern hospitality of Black Mountain, Blowing Rock, Brevard, and Hendersonville, to name a few.

★ **Mountain arts and crafts:** The mountains are a center of handmade art and crafts, with more than 4,000 working craftspeople.

1 Asheville. Set in a valley surrounded by the highest mountains in eastern America, Asheville is a base for exploring the region, but it is also a destination unto itself. Here you can tour America's largest home and discover why Asheville has a national reputation for its arts, crafts, food, beer, and music scenes.

Coffeehouses, craft breweries, sidewalk cafés, boutiques, antiques shops, clubs, and galleries are everywhere in the city's Art Deco downtown. Just a short drive away are inviting small mountain towns, mile-high vistas that will take your breath away, and enough high-energy outdoor fun to keep your heart rate way up.

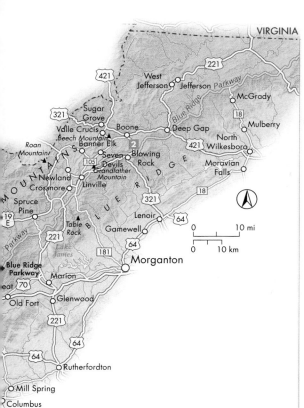

VIRGINIA

West Jefferson · Jefferson Parkway · McGrady

421 · 221

321 · Sugar Grove · Boone · Deep Gap · Mulberry · 18

Valle Crucis · Beech Mountain · North Wilkesboro · 421

Roan Mountain · Banner Elk · Seven Devils · Blowing Rock · Moravian Falls

Newland · Grandfather Mountain · Linville

Crossnore

Spruce Pine · 321 · 18

Table Rock · Lenoir · 64 · U.S. 64

Gamewell

221 · 181 · Lake James · 64 · Morganton

Blue Ridge Parkway · Marion

70 · Old Fort · Glenwood

221 · 64

64 · Rutherfordton

Mill Spring

Columbus

105 · Blue Ridge

0 — 10 mi
0 — 10 km

GETTING ORIENTED

The buzz about the North Carolina Mountains dates back to the early 19th century, when wealthy Lowcountry planters flocked to the highlands to escape the summer heat. Today visitors still come here to enjoy the cool, green mountains and all the activities they provide—hiking, camping, fishing, boating, and just marveling at the scenery. Asheville, the hub of the mountain region, is one of the biggest small cities you'll ever visit, with the artsy élan and dynamic downtown of a much larger burg.

4

2 The High Country. The High Country is the skiing area of the mountains. Boone, Beech Mountain (the highest-elevation incorporated community east of the Mississippi River), Blowing Rock, and Seven Devils together have four ski resorts. Summers here are cooler than elsewhere in the Southeast, and the mountain scenery is notably dramatic.

3 The Southern Mountains. The North Carolina towns here, southwest of Asheville, include Brevard and the chic enclaves of Lake Toxaway, Cashiers, and Highlands. The towns' size, elevation, and attractiveness all vary; if they have anything in common, it's the sky-high real estate prices and a reputation as summer getaways for well-to-do flatlanders.

Updated by
Lan Sluder

The majestic peaks, meadows, shrub-covered balds (big grassy mountaintops where no trees grow), and valleys of the Appalachian, Blue Ridge, and Great Smoky Mountains epitomize the western corner of North Carolina. The Great Smoky Mountains National Park, national forests, hand-made-crafts centers, Asheville's eclectic and sophisticated pleasures, the astonishing Biltmore Estate, and the Blue Ridge Parkway are the area's main draws, providing prime opportunities for shopping, skiing, hiking, bicycling, camping, fishing, canoeing, and just taking in the views.

The city of Asheville is one of the stops on the counterculture trail, as well as being a popular retirement area. Its restaurants regularly make the TV food show circuit, and with craft breweries on nearly every block, it has been named "Beer City USA" for several years in an Internet poll. Thanks to their moneyed seasonal residents and long histories as resorts, even smaller towns like Highlands, Cashiers, Flat Rock, and Hendersonville have restaurants with daring chefs and professional summer theater. In the High Country, where summer temperatures are as much as 15 degrees cooler than in the flatlands, and where snow skiing is a major draw in winter, affluent retirees and hip young entrepreneurs bring panache to even the most rural areas.

Some of the most important arts and culture movements of the 20th century, including Abstract Impressionist painting and the Beat movement, had roots just east of Asheville, at Black Mountain College, where in the 1930s to 1950s the notables included famed artists Josef and Anni Albers, Willem and Elaine de Kooning, Robert Rauschenberg, and Robert Motherwell, choreographer and dancer Merce Cunningham, musician John Cage, futurist Buckminster Fuller, architect Walter Gropius, and the writers Charles Olson and Paul Goodman.

PLANNING

WHEN TO GO

Western North Carolina is a four-season destination. Dates for high season vary from hotel to hotel, but generally it's from Memorial Day through early November. It's most difficult to get a hotel reservation on weekends in October, which is peak leaf-peeping time. June to August draws a lot of families, because kids are out of school. Around ski resorts at the higher elevations, winter, especially the Christmas season and the months of January and February, is prime time; elsewhere, these winter months are slow, and a few hotels close. Spring, late March to late May, is a great time to visit, as the spring wildflowers bloom and the landscape turns green.

PLANNING YOUR TIME

The Asheville area is a convenient base for day visits to Black Mountain and Hendersonville, and even to Brevard, Lake Toxaway, Cashiers, and Highlands in the Southern Mountains. Of course, if you want to see these areas more completely, you're better off spending the night in one or several of these towns. Likewise, it's easy to make day trips to Great Smoky Mountain National Park from Asheville. The Oconaluftee entrance to the Smokies is only an hour and 15 minutes' drive from downtown Asheville. But if you want to spend several days or longer in the Smokies, you'll be better off staying in the park or at one of the small towns at the edge of it, such as Bryson City or Waynesville. *For more information about the park, see Chapter 5: Great Smoky Mountains National Park.* The High Country is too far away to make a comfortable day trip from Asheville, especially considering the winding mountain roads and possible weather conditions (snow in winter and fog almost any time). To explore the High Country in detail, you'll want to make your headquarters in the appealing college town of Boone or one of the other towns nearby, such as Blowing Rock or Banner Elk.

GETTING HERE AND AROUND

AIR TRAVEL

Asheville Regional Airport, one of the most pleasant and modern small airports in the South, is served by Allegiant, Delta, United, and American. Most of the flights are on regional jets. A 2014 study by MIT found that Asheville had the best-connected nonhub airport in the country. There are nonstop flights (some are seasonal) to and from Atlanta, Baltimore, Charlotte, Chicago, Ft. Lauderdale, Ft. Myers, Orlando, Newark, New York's LaGuardia, and St. Petersburg. A new airport garage is adding much-needed parking near the terminals. Charlotte Douglas International Airport (CLT), a major hub for American and with service by Air Canada, Delta, Frontier, Lufthansa, JetBlue, Southwest, and Via, is about a two-hour drive from Asheville or Boone.

Airport Information Asheville Regional Airport *(AVL).* ⊠ *61 Terminal Dr., Fletcher* ☎ *828/209–3660* ⊕ *www.flyavl.com.* **Charlotte Douglas International Airport** *(CLT).* ⊠ *5501 Josh Birmingham Pkwy., Charlotte* ☎ *704/359–4013* ⊕ *www.cltairport.com.*

CAR TRAVEL

The coast-to-coast Interstate 40 runs east–west through Asheville. Interstate 26 runs from Charleston, South Carolina, to Asheville and, partly on a temporary route, continues northwest into Tennessee and the Ohio Valley. Interstate 240 forms a perimeter around the city. U.S. 19/23 is a major north and west route. The Blue Ridge Parkway runs northeast from Great Smoky Mountains National Park to Shenandoah National Park in Virginia, passing Cherokee, Asheville, and the High Country. U.S. 221 runs north to the Virginia border through Blowing Rock and Boone and intersects Interstate 40 at Marion. U.S. 321 intersects Interstate 40 at Hickory and heads to Blowing Rock and Boone.

RESTAURANTS

You can still get traditional mountain food, served family-style, at inns and eateries around the region. Increasingly, though, mountain restaurants serve more elaborate dishes, often with a New Southern style. At many places the emphasis is on the farm-to-table dishes made with locally grown, often organic, ingredients. You can find nearly every U.S. and world cuisine somewhere in Asheville or the rest of the region. *Dining reviews have been shortened. For full information, visit Fodors.com.*

HOTELS

Around the mountains, at least in the larger cities and towns such as Asheville, Hendersonville, and Boone, you can find the usual chain motels and hotels. A building boom is bringing more than a half dozen new hotels to downtown Asheville. For more of a local flavor, look at the many mountain lodges and country inns, some with just a few rooms with simple comforts, others with upmarket amenities like tennis courts, golf courses, and spas. Bed-and-breakfasts bloom in the mountains like wildflowers, and there are scores of them in the region; Asheville alone has more than 50. The mountains also have a few large resorts, including the Omni Grove Park Inn in Asheville. Visiting in the off-season can save you a third or more on hotel rates. Rates are highest during summer weekends and in October, when the leaves change. *Hotel reviews have been shortened. For full information, visit Fodors.com.*

WHAT IT COSTS				
	$	**$$**	**$$$**	**$$$$**
Restaurants	under $15	$15–$19	$20–$24	over $24
Hotels	under $150	$150–$200	$201–$250	over $250

Restaurant prices are the average cost of a main course at dinner or, if dinner is not served, at lunch. Hotel prices are the lowest cost of a standard double room in high season.

VISITOR INFORMATION

Contacts **Brevard/Transylvania County Chamber of Commerce.** ⊠ *175 E. Main St., Brevard* ☎ *800/648–4523, 828/883–3700* ⊕ *www.brevardnc. org.* **Cashiers Area Chamber of Commerce.** ⊠ *202 U.S. 64 W, Cashiers* ☎ *828/743–5191* ⊕ *www.cashiersareachamber.com.* **Haywood Chamber of Commerce.** ⊠ *28 Walnut St., Waynesville* ☎ *828/456–3021.* **High Country Host.** ⊠ *High Country Host Visitor Center, 1700 Blowing Rock Rd., Boone* ☎ *800/438–7500* ⊕ *www.highcountryjourney.com.* **Highlands Chamber of Commerce and Visitor Center.** ⊠ *108 Main St., Highlands* ☎ *828/526–2112* ⊕ *www.highlandschamber.org.*

ASHEVILLE

Asheville is the hippest city in the South. At least that's the claim of its fans, who are legion. Visitors flock to Asheville for its arts and culture, which rivals that of Charleston, South Carolina, or Santa Fe, New Mexico, and to experience its downtown, with myriad restaurants, coffeehouses, microbreweries, museums, galleries, bookstores, antiques shops, and boutiques.

Named "the best place to live" by many books and magazines, Asheville is also a destination for retirees escaping the cold North, or of "halfbacks," those who moved to Florida but who are now coming half the way back North. Old downtown buildings have been converted to upmarket condos for these affluent retirees, and new residential developments seem to be constantly springing up around town.

As a result of this influx, Asheville has a much more cosmopolitan population than most cities of its size (89,000 people in the city; 445,000 in the metro area). Asheville has a diversity you won't find in many cities in the South. There's a thriving gay community, many self-described hippies and hipsters, young-at-heart retirees, and alternative-lifestyle seekers. *Rolling Stone* once called Asheville the "U.S. capital of weird" (sorry, Austin), but with more than 50 microbreweries and brewpubs in the area, and two large national craft breweries, New Belgium and Sierra Nevada, with their East Coast operations here, Asheville prefers the title of Beer City USA. That said, you may be surprised to know that due to state law, bars are illegal in North Carolina. Public establishments that sell mostly alcohol and little food have to operate as private membership clubs. This just means you have to sign up and perhaps pay a nominal onetime membership fee (like a cover charge). You can do this at the door or in advance.

The city really comes alive at night, with restaurants, sidewalk cafés, and coffeehouses; so visit after dark to see the city at its best. Especially on summer and fall weekends, Pack Square, Biltmore Avenue, the "South Slope" area between Biltmore Avenue and Asheland Avenue south of Patton Avenue, Broadway Street, Haywood Street, Wall Street, the Grove Arcade, Pritchard Park (site of a popular drum circle on Friday night), and Battery Park Avenue are busy until late.

GETTING HERE AND AROUND

From the east and west, the main route to Asheville is Interstate 40. The most scenic route to Asheville is via the Blue Ridge Parkway, which meanders between Shenandoah National Park in Virginia and Great Smoky Mountains National Park near Cherokee, North Carolina. Interstate 240 forms a freeway perimeter around Asheville, and Pack Square is the center of the city.

Although a car is virtually a necessity to explore Asheville thoroughly, the city does have a metropolitan bus system with nearly 20 routes radiating from the Asheville Redefines Transit (ART) Center downtown. Asheville also has a hop-on, hop-off sightseeing trolley service and other tour services; tickets are available at the Asheville Visitor Center. The city is highly walkable, and the best way to see downtown is on foot.

ESSENTIALS

Visitor Information Asheville Visitor Center. ⊠ *36 Montford Ave., Downtown* ☎ *828/258–6129, 800/365–8917* ⊕ *www.exploreasheville.com.*

FESTIVALS

Fodor's Choice ★ **Craft Fair of the Southern Highlands.** One of the largest crafts events in the Southeast, the Craft Fair of the Southern Highlands is held for three days twice a year, in mid-July and mid-October. More than 200 of the 900 members of the Southern Highland Craft Guild, who qualify after a stringent jurying process, take over both the concourse and arena of the U.S. Cellular Center in downtown Asheville to display and sell their clay, wood, metal, glass, fiber, leather, jewelry, and other crafts. The fair, which was in its 70th year in 2017, also features live mountain music. ⊠ *U.S. Cellular Center, 87 Haywood St., Downtown* ☎ *828/298–7928 Southern Highland Craft Guild* ⊕ *www.southern-highlandguild.org* ☜ *$8.*

FAMILY
Fodor's Choice ★ **Mountain Dance & Folk Festival.** The oldest folk music festival in the country was established in 1928 by the folk music collector Bascom Lamar Lunsford. It takes place annually "along 'bout sundown" (in fact, 7 to 10 pm) for three nights (Thursday through Saturday) the first weekend of August. You'll see and hear the real thing here—old-timey Appalachian pickers, singers, clog dancers, and more. ■ TIP➜ **Tickets can be purchased at the door but it's best to order in advance online.** ⊠ *Asheville-Buncombe Technical Community College, 340 Victoria Rd., Mission Health Conference Center, Downtown* ☎ *828/398–7901 conference center information* ⊕ *www.folkheritage.org* ☜ *$22 a night, 3-night package $60.*

FAMILY **Shindig on the Green.** Pack a picnic and bring a folding chair or blanket for this free mountain-music concert. Shindig on the Green has been held for more than 50 years most Saturdays from late June through August. The shows, held in Pack Square Park in the heart of Asheville, run from around 7 to 10 pm. ⊠ *Pack Square Park, 121 College St., Roger McGuire Green, Downtown* ☎ *828/258–6101* ⊕ *www.folkheritage.org/shindigonthegreen.htm* ☜ *Free.*

TOURS

Fodor's Choice ★ **Asheville Brewery Tours.** Asheville Brewery Tours' guides are knowledgeable about beer and the booming Asheville craft brewery scene. You hop aboard a van and head out to three or four breweries and brewpubs, with flights of several beers served at each. You'll meet the brewmasters or owners. Some tours visit local hard cider makers. Dog-friendly walking tours of the South Slope brewery section of town are also offered. Tours are available daily year-round, but there are more tours on weekends and from late spring through the fall. ⊠ *101 N. Lexington Ave., Downtown* ☎ *828/233–5006* ⊕ *www.ashevillebrewerytours.com* ⊡ *$49–$59.*

Asheville Food Tours. Asheville Food Tours was the first and arguably still is one of the best of the city's half-dozen walking food tours. You visit six or seven of the better downtown restaurants, usually meeting the chef or owner, and sample the restaurants' food and drink specialties. Around 15 to 20 restaurants and bars participate, with different spots visited on different days. There are two different food tour options and a Saturday brunch tour. The Downtown Food and Brunch tours meet inside the Grove Arcade near the elevators; Food Fan tour meets at WXYZ Bar at Aloft Hotel. Tours last about 3½ hours and tickets must be purchased in advance. ■ TIP→ Tour hours and dates vary by month. ⊠ *Grove Arcade, 1 Page Ave., Downtown* ☎ *828/243–7401* ⊕ *www. ashevillefoodtours.com* ⊡ *$50–$60.*

FAMILY Fodor's Choice ★ **Asheville Urban Trail.** This 1.7-mile walk developed by the City of Asheville has 30 "stations" in five areas of downtown, each with a work of art and plaques marking places of historical or architectural interest. The free self-guided tour begins at Pack Square and takes about two hours to complete. Pick up free maps at the Asheville Visitor Center (36 Montford Avenue), the satellite visitor pavilion (121 College Street) in Pack Square Park, and at various shops in downtown Asheville. You can also download the map and brochure from the City of Asheville website or from the Asheville Visitor Center website. ⊠ *Pack Square Park, 121 College St., Asheville Visitor Center Satellite Pavilion, Downtown* ☎ *828/258–6101 Asheville Visitor Center* ⊕ *www.ashevillenc.gov/Departments/CommunityEconomicDevelopment/PublicArttheUrbanTrail.aspx* ⊡ *Free.*

Fodor's Choice ★ **Eating Asheville.** Eating Asheville made its rep with its classic 2½-hour walking food tour of downtown Asheville, which visits about six restaurants and food shops to sample food and drinks and meet with chefs or owners. Now a High Roller Tour (on weekends only) visits seven higher-end restaurants for food and beverage pairings. The restaurants and sections of town visited vary, but Eating Asheville has relationships with about 30 Asheville eateries. Tours operate year-round, although the number and frequency of tours increase in the summer and fall. Most tours start and finish at the Grove Arcade. ⊠ *Grove Arcade, 1 Page Ave., Downtown* ☎ *828/489–3266* ⊕ *www.eatingasheville.com* ⊡ *Classic tour $54; High Roller $69.*

FAMILY **Gray Line Historic Asheville Trolley Tours.** Gray Line offers hop-on, hop-off tours in and around downtown Asheville in red motorized trolleys. Guided tours leave daily March through December, every 30 minutes from 10 to 3:30, from the Asheville Visitor Center, but you can get on or off and buy tickets at any of nine other stops, including the Omni Grove Park Inn, Biltmore Village, Pack Square, and the River Arts District. In January and February tours operate on a two-hour departure frequency and only on Monday, Friday, and Saturday. The entire tour takes less than two hours, and tickets are good for two consecutive days. ■ **TIP→ A tour without hop-on, hop-off privileges is cheaper.** A 75-minute ghost tour from April to mid-November leaves at 7 pm Monday and Thursday through Saturday from Pack's Tavern at 20 Spruce Street. ✉ *Asheville Visitor Center, 36 Montford Ave., Downtown* ☎ *828/251–8687, 866/592–8687* ⊕ *www.graylineasheville.com* ✉ *$23–$28.*

Fodor's Choice **LaZoom Comedy Tours.** On this very popular and unusual tour, you ride
★ in a big, open-air purple bus while you are entertained by actors who do comedy skits and over-the-top routines about the wacky side of Asheville. If you're over 21, you can bring your own wine or beer (no hard liquor) on the bus. In peak periods such as summer and fall weekends, LaZoom has three or four tours a day, including 90-minute City Comedy Tours, 60-minute Haunted Comedy Tours, 60-minute Kids' Comedy Tours (directed to kids 5–12), and three-hour Band & Beer Tours with live music and visits to three craft breweries. Due to the slightly risqué routines, riders must be at least 13 on the Comedy Tours, 17 on Ghost Tours, and 21 on Band & Beer tours. Many tours sell out, so it's best to reserve in advance by phone, online, or at the LaZoom office; if seats are available you can buy when boarding. City Comedy and Kids' Tours leave from French Broad Co-Op (90 Biltmore Avenue); Haunted Tours leave from behind the Thirsty Monk pub (92 Patton Avenue); Band & Beer Tours leave from Tasty Beverage (162 Coxe Avenue). ✉ *14 Battery Park Ave., Downtown* ☎ *828/225–6932* ⊕ *www.lazoomtours.com* ✉ *$16–$29.*

EXPLORING

DOWNTOWN ASHEVILLE

A city of neighborhoods, Asheville rewards careful exploration, especially on foot. You can break up your sightseeing with stops at the more than 100 restaurants and bars in downtown alone, and at any of hundreds of unique shops (only a couple of downtown Asheville stores are national chains).

Asheville has the largest extant collection of Art Deco buildings in the Southeast outside Miami Beach, most notably the S&W Cafeteria (1929), Asheville City Hall (1928), First Baptist Church (1927), and Asheville High School (1929). It's also known for its architecture in other styles: Battery Park Hotel (1924) is neo-Georgian; the Flatiron Building (1924) is neoclassical; the Basilica of St. Lawrence (1909) is Spanish baroque; and Pack Place, formerly known as Old Pack Library (1925), is in the Italian Renaissance style.

TOP ATTRACTIONS

FAMILY **Asheville Pinball Museum.** One of the more unusual and interesting attractions in town is the Asheville Pinball Museum, a combination museum-arcade of vintage pinball machines and games. You

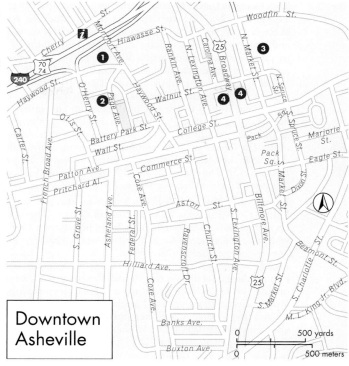

Downtown
Asheville

can come in and look at more than 75 vintage pinball machines and
classic video games, some dating back to the 1930s, at no charge, or
pay $15 for unlimited play on the flashing machines (some old ones
are for display only). There's also a bar serving snacks and craft beers.
Restrooms are labeled Pac Man and Ms. Pac Man. ■**TIP→ There's
often a waitlist to play so allow extra time.** ⊠ *1 Battle Sq., Suite 1A,
Downtown ✛ Just north of Grove Arcade* ☎ *828/776–5671* ⊕ *www.
ashevillepinball.com* ⊡ *Free to visit museum; $15 for unlimited play*
☉ *Closed Tues.*

FAMILY   **Basilica of St. Lawrence.** A collaboration of Biltmore House head architect
Fodor's Choice   Richard Sharp Smith and the Spanish engineer-architect Rafael Gus-
★   tavin, this elaborate Catholic basilica was completed in 1909. It follows
a Spanish Renaissance design, rendered in brick and polychrome tile,
and has a large, self-supporting dome with Catalan-style vaulting. Self-
guided tours are available any time the church is open (free brochures
are available in the vestibule or from the basilica's website). Groups
of five or more can request a guided tour by filling out the form on
the church's website at least a week in advance. ⊠ *97 Haywood St.,
Downtown* ☎ *828/252–6042* ⊕ *www.saintlawrencebasilica.org* ⊡ *Free,
donations requested.*

Fodor's Choice
★

Black Mountain College Museum + Arts Center. The famed Black Mountain College (1933–57), located 16 miles east of Asheville, was important in the development of several groundbreaking 20th-century art, dance, and literary movements. Some of the maverick spirits it attracted in its short lifetime include artists Willem and Elaine de Kooning, Robert Rauschenberg, Josef and Anni Albers, and M. C. Richards; dancer Merce Cunningham; musician John Cage; filmmaker Arthur Penn; futurist Buckminster Fuller; and writers Kenneth Noland, Charles Olson, and Robert Creeley. A small museum and gallery dedicated to the history of the radical college is in downtown Asheville, with space at two locations (56 and 69) on Broadway Street across from each other. The Center puts on exhibits, hosts lectures, and publishes material about the college. Visit the website for current happenings. ✉ *56 Broadway St., Downtown* ☎ *828/350–8484* ⊕ *www.blackmountaincollege.org* 🖅 *Exhibits usually free or $5–$10* ☉ *Closed Tues. and Sun.*

Fodor's Choice
★

Thomas Wolfe Memorial. Asheville's most famous son, novelist Thomas Wolfe (1900–38), grew up in a 29-room Queen Anne–style home that his mother ran as a boardinghouse. In his prime in the 1930s, Wolfe was widely viewed as one of the best writers America had ever produced. The house—memorialized as "Dixieland" in Wolfe's novel *Look Homeward, Angel*—was badly damaged in a 1998 fire; it reopened in 2004 following a painstaking $2.4 million renovation. The house has been restored to its original 1916 condition, including a light canary-yellow paint (though Wolfe called it "dirty yellow") on the exterior. You'll find a visitor center and many displays, and there are hourly guided tours of the house and heirloom gardens. ✉ *52 Market St., Downtown* ☎ *828/253–8304* ⊕ *www.wolfememorial.com* 🖅 *$5* ☉ *Closed Sun. and Mon.*

RIVER ARTS DISTRICT

Asheville's former industrial and warehouse section, just southwest of downtown along the French Broad River, is the up-and-coming art-and-crafts center of the region, with many studios and galleries, plus cafés, breweries, and nightclubs. As industrial companies moved out, artists moved in, seeking cheaper rents for studios and loft apartments. Today the district is home to some 200 working artists—mainly pottery and ceramics artists, painters, fabric artists, and sculptors—and this doesn't include students taking courses. As many as 75 studios in around 20 late-19th- and early-20th-century industrial buildings are open free to the public (hours vary but many are open daily from 9 to 5). You can talk to artists and buy their work, often at lower prices than in galleries. On the second Saturday of each month, studios offer refreshments and demonstrations for visitors. Twice a year, on weekends in early May and early November, the District holds a Studio Stroll, when nearly all the studios and galleries are open to the public. Increasingly, restaurants, bars, and coffeehouses are opening here as well, and a large national craft brewing company, New Belgium, opened its East Coast brewery and distribution center here recently. A large apartment and retail complex is under construction in RAD, and the City of Asheville's new $50 million access and infrastucture project will mean better access to the river, along with new roads, green spaces, and bike and pedestrian paths. For more information on what's going on in the neighborhood, see ⊕ *www.riverartsdistrict.com.*

Biltmore, once the home of George Vanderbilt, is the largest private home in the United States; the estate grounds occupy some 8,000 acres.

Cotton Mill Studios. This 19th-century brick building is a former factory once owned by Moses H. Cone, whose family mansion is on the Blue Ridge Parkway. It's now used by about 15 artists and artisans who specialize in painting, pottery, and textiles. Note the trompe l'oeil mural on the front of the building. Besides seeing working artists and craftspeople in their studios, you can buy some items directly from the artists. The Yuzu Patisserie is also in the building and there's some parking in front. ✉ *122 Riverside Dr., River Arts District* ☎ *828/252–9122* ⊕ *www.thecottonmillstudios.com* ✑ *Free.*

New Belgium Brewery. Fort Collins, Colorado-based national craft brewery New Belgium opened its $175 million Eastern U.S. brewery and distribution headquarters in 2015 at the edge of the River Arts District on the site of the former Asheville Stockyards. Take one of the dozen free brewery tours offered daily (every half hour from 11:30 am to 4:30 pm), or sip beers in the tasting room overlooking the French Broad. It offers a lineup of regular, seasonal, and sour beer brews. ✉ *21 Craven St., River Arts District* ☎ *828/333–6900* ⊕ *www.newbelgium.com* ✑ *Free.*

Fodor'sChoice
★
Odyssey Co-op Gallery. Odyssey Co-op Gallery has a large and high-quality selection of pottery and ceramic works, both functional and decorative, as well as figurative and abstract sculpture, by talented, juried clay artists. The gallery has rotating displays, so new work is on display regularly. As an added plus, you can also visit the numerous studio and student spaces in the Odyssey complex. ✉ *238 Clingman Ave., River Arts District* ☎ *828/285–9700* ⊕ *odysseycoopgallery.com* ☾ *Main gallery closed Mon.*

Fodor's Choice

★

Wedge Studios and Wedge Brewing Company. Once the headquarters of Farmer's Federation, the region's leading agricultural co-op, this large brick building now holds more than 30 independent art and crafts studios, along with the popular Wedge Brewery and other businesses. Each studio sets its own hours, and a few are open only by appointment. The bar at the Wedge, one of the area's most popular craft breweries, has local art on the walls and 8 to 10 beers on tap, including favorites like its Iron Rail IPA (named for the railroad tracks that run near the brewery). Sip your beer inside or grab a bite from one of the food trucks that appear in rotation in the Wedge parking lot and eat at a picnic table outside. (Wedge Brewery has opened a second brewery and pub location in RAD behind Riverview Station and next door to 12 Bones.) ✉ *111–129 Roberts St., River Arts District* ☎ *828/505–2782* ⊕ *www.wedgebrewing.com* ✏ *Free.*

WEST ASHEVILLE

West Asheville, across the French Broad River, has become a hot part of the city, with its main artery, Haywood Road, sporting new restaurants, edgy stores, and popular clubs. Despite the gentrification, some of the area still feels slightly scruffy.

GREATER ASHEVILLE

North Asheville, the historic Montford section (home to more than a dozen B&Bs), and the Grove Park neighborhood all have fine Victorian-era homes, including many remarkable Queen Anne houses from the late 19th century.

TOP ATTRACTIONS

FAMILY

Fodor's Choice

★

North Carolina Arboretum. Part of the original Biltmore Estate, these 434 acres completed Frederick Law Olmsted's dream of creating a world-class arboretum in the western part of North Carolina. The Arboretum is now affiliated with the University of North Carolina and is part of Pisgah National Forest. Highlights include southern Appalachian flora in stunning settings, such as the Blue Ridge Quilt Garden, with bedding plants arranged in patterns reminiscent of Appalachian quilts, and sculptures set among the gardens. The Arboretum has 65 acres of cultivated gardens. A 10-mile network of trails is great for hiking or mountain biking. A bonsai exhibit features miniature versions of many native trees. The 16,000-square-foot Baker Exhibit Center hosts traveling exhibits on art, science, and history. Dogs are welcome on the grounds but must be leashed. ■**TIP→ Admission is free but there is a $12 per car parking fee ($6 the first Tuesday of the month).** ✉ *100 Frederick Law Olmsted Way, Greater Asheville* ⊹ *10 miles southwest of downtown Asheville, at Blue Ridge Pkwy. (MM 393), near I–26 and I–40* ☎ *828/665–2492* ⊕ *www.ncarboretum.org* ✏ *Free; $12 for parking.*

Fodor's Choice

★

Sierra Nevada Brewery. Chico, California-based Sierra Nevada, one of the country's largest national craft breweries, opened its East Coast brewery and distribution center on a 190-acre site on the French Broad River just south of Asheville. The beautifully landscaped complex includes an excellent restaurant, tasting room, gift shop, and hiking and biking trails. You can take a self-guided tour of the facility via the Visitor Corridor, which allows views of the copper-clad brew kettles and a visit to

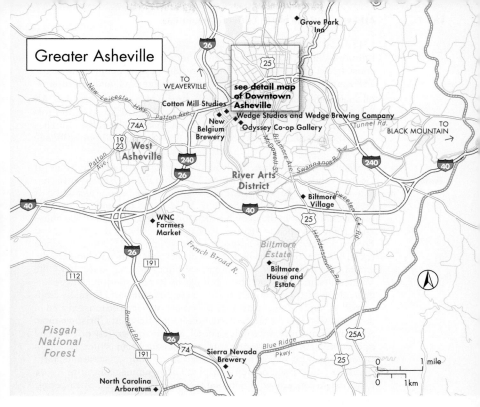

Greater Asheville

Grove Park Inn

TO WEAVERVILLE

Cotton Mill Studios

see detail map of Downtown Asheville

Wedge Studios and Wedge Brewing Company

New Belgium Brewery

Odyssey Co-op Gallery

TO BLACK MOUNTAIN

West Asheville

Patton Ave.

New Leicester Hwy.

Tunnel Rd.

River Arts District

Biltmore Village

WNC Farmers Market

French Broad R.

Biltmore Estate

Biltmore House and Estate

Pisgah National Forest

Sierra Nevada Brewery

Blue Ridge Pkwy.

North Carolina Arboretum

Brevard Rd.

Swannanoa R.

Hendersonville Rd.

Sweeten Ck. Rd.

0   1 mile
0   1 km

the packaging hall and warehouse. Organized tour options include a 30-minute educational tasting; a two-hour moderate hike (with beer) of the forested property the facility sits on; and an intimate three-hour Beer Geek tour, which takes you behind the scenes in the brewing process and includes samples from the tanks in the cellar. ■ **TIP→ The tours of the brewery are often heavily booked so you should reserve as far in advance as possible.** ✉ *Sierra Nevada Brewery, 100 Sierra Nevada Way, near Asheville Regional Airport, Metro South, Greater Asheville* ☎ *828/681–5300, 828/708–6176 tour desk* ⊕ *www.sierranevada.com* ☞ *Tours free–$45.*

WORTH NOTING

FAMILY **WNC Farmers Market.** The highest-volume farmers' market in North Carolina may not have the prettiest exterior, but it's a good place to buy local jams, jellies, honey, stone-ground grits and cornmeal, and, in season, local fruits and vegetables (not all produce is locally grown). A truck section with large sheds below the main retail section (both are open to all) offers produce in bulk. An herb festival is held annually in the spring. On the grounds of the market are a garden supply store and a Southern-style restaurant, Moose Café. ✉ *570 Brevard Rd., Greater Asheville* ✛ *5 miles southwest of downtown Asheville, at Exit 47 of I-40* ☎ *828/253–1691* ⊕ *www.ncagr.gov/markets/facilities/markets/asheville* ☞ *Free.*

BILTMORE VILLAGE

Biltmore Village, across from the entrance to the Biltmore Estate, was constructed at the time that Biltmore House was being built in the 1890s and now holds boutiques, galleries, cigar bars, and restaurants.

FAMILY **All Souls Cathedral.** One of the most beautiful churches in America, All Souls Episcopal Cathedral was designed by Richard Morris Hunt following the traditional Greek Cross plan and inspired by abbey churches in northern England. It opened in 1896. ⊠ *9 Swan St., Biltmore Village* ☏ *828/274–2681* ⊕ *www.allsoulscathedral.org* ✉ *Free.*

FAMILY
Fodor's Choice
★

Biltmore House and Estate. Built in the 1890s as the private home of George Vanderbilt, the astonishing 250-room French Renaissance château is America's largest private house and the number one attraction of its kind in North Carolina. Some of Vanderbilt's descendants still live on the estate (not in the main house, though), but the bulk of the house and grounds is open to visitors. Richard Morris Hunt designed it, and Frederick Law Olmsted landscaped the original 125,000-acre estate (now 8,000 acres). It took 1,000 workers five years to complete the gargantuan project. On view are the antiques and art collected by the Vanderbilts, including notable paintings by Renoir and John Singer Sargent, along with 75 acres of gardens, a conservatory, and formally landscaped grounds. You can also see the on-site winery, the most-visited in America. Candlelight tours of the house are offered at Christmastime. Also on the grounds are a deluxe hotel, a more moderately priced hotel opened in 2016, many restaurants, and an equestrian center. A section called Antler Hill Village houses the new hotel, shops, restaurants, farm buildings, and crafts demonstrations. Each summer, Biltmore Estate hosts music concerts with nationally known entertainers. Most people tour the house on their own, but guided tours are available. Note that there are a lot of stairs to climb, but much of the house is accessible for guests in wheelchairs or with limited mobility. ■TIP→ **At busier times, self-guided visits of the interior of the house require a reservation, so call in advance or book online.** Pricing is complex, varying by month and day of the week, and not inexpensive, but a visit is well worth the cost for its access to the house, gardens, winery, and extensive grounds. The lowest rates are January through March. Save money by buying tickets online rather than at the gate. If you think you'll be back, the best deal is the annual pass, which allows unlimited admission for a year and sometimes costs only a little more than a one-day admission. ⊠ *1 Lodge St., Biltmore Village* ☏ *828/225–1333, 800/411–3812* ⊕ *www. biltmore.com* ✉ *$50–$69 for daytime visits, with access to nearly all parts of the estate; higher rates on holidays* ⊘ *Hrs for admission gate, house, gardens, and winery vary seasonally.*

FAMILY **Biltmore Village.** Across from the main entrance to the Biltmore Estate, Biltmore Village is a highly walkable collection of restored English village–style houses dating from the turn of the 20th century, along with some newer buildings designed to blend with the original architecture. Stroll the brick sidewalks and tree-lined streets and visit antiques stores, clothing and jewelry shops, art galleries, and restaurants. The Grand Bohemian Hotel is in the village, and several B&Bs and motels are nearby. ⊠ *Biltmore Village* ⊕ *www.biltmorevillage.com* ✉ *Free.*

WHERE TO EAT

Because of the large number of visitors to Asheville and the many upscale retirees who've moved here, the city has a dining scene that's much more vibrant and varied than its size would suggest. You'll find everything from Greek to Vietnamese, Nepalese to Southern soul food, and barbecue to sushi. Asheville has more vegetarian restaurants per capita than any other city, and there are local coffeehouses on many corners. Most of the city's many craft breweries also serve food.

DOWNTOWN

$ ECLECTIC

🍴 **Ben's Tune Up.** You can't get any more Asheville than Ben's Tune Up, housed in a converted auto repair shop and offering a slightly bizarre mix of Southern and Japanese dishes along with house-made sake and craft beers. This unique spot is at its best in good weather, when you can enjoy your Japanese-American fusion feast at picnic tables in an open-air beer garden—what remained after the architects took the main roof off the old garage. **Known for:** cool beer and sake garden; Japanese-Southern fusion food; late-night drinks and dancing. [$] *Average main: $12* ✉ *South Slope, 195 Hilliard Ave., Downtown* ☎ *828/424–7580* 🌐 *www.benstuneup.com* 🕒 *Closed Mon.*

$ BARBECUE FAMILY

🍴 **Buxton Hall BBQ.** In a large, open space in what was once a wood-floored skating rink in the now-hip South Slope section, Buxton Hall serves traditional whole-hog, slow-pit-cooked barbecue in the Eastern North Carolina style, infused with chef Elliott Moss's family vinegar mop recipe. The most popular dish here is the pulled-pork plate with a side of brussels sprouts cooked under the hog (available only at dinner). **Known for:** Eastern North Carolina–style whole-hog barbecue; James Beard Award–nominee chef Elliott Moss. [$] *Average main: $13* ✉ *South Slope, 32 Banks Ave., Downtown* ☎ *828/232–7216* 🌐 *www.buxtonhall.com.*

$ INDIAN

🍴 **Chai Pani.** Chai Pani serves "Indian street food" from the chef's hometown of Mumbai in a pleasant small space with photos of India on the walls. Enjoy snacks like *bhel puri* (puffed rice, flour crisps, and chickpea noodles with tamarind chutney) or kale or chicken *pakoras*. **Known for:** street-style snacks like chicken pakoras; many vegetarian-friendly dishes; low prices. [$] *Average main: $11* ✉ *22 Battery Park Ave., Downtown* ☎ *828/254–4003* 🌐 *www.chaipani.net.*

$$$ SOUTHERN Fodor's Choice ★

🍴 **Chestnut.** At this consistently good restaurant on Asheville's thriving "restaurant row," the food is local and seasonal, prices are reasonable, service is agreeable but not fawning, and there's a buzz without being overly loud. Chestnut is in a delightfully refurbished 1920s plumbing supply shop, updated with art from a nearby gallery. **Known for:** dependably good farm-to-table dishes; lively spot; moderate prices for small plates. [$] *Average main: $22* ✉ *48 Biltmore Ave., Downtown* ☎ *828/575–2667* 🌐 *www.chestnutasheville.com.*

$$$ SPANISH Fodor's Choice ★

🍴 **Cúrate.** If you have the blahs, Cúrate, with its extraordinary, authentic tapas and fun atmosphere, is the cure. The nationally known chef-owner, Katie Button, showcases the flavors of Spain in about four dozen small plates (the plates themselves are locally made pottery), with special attention to cured Iberian ham dishes and seafood items such as octopus and calamari. **Known for:** authentic Spanish tapas; fun atmosphere; Iberian hams and Spanish sherries. [$] *Average main: $24* ✉ *11 Biltmore Ave., Downtown* ☎ *828/239–2946* 🌐 *heirloomhg.com/curate* ⏲ *Closed Mon.*

$ CAFÉ
🍴 **Double D's Coffee & Desserts.** Why chase food trucks when you can have coffee and pastries in a red 1963 Lodekka-model double-decker bus from Bristol, England, or out on the adjacent patio. The bus is the main attraction here, but the coffees and pastries aren't bad either. **Known for:** iconic British double-decker bus; specialty coffee; cash-only policy. [$] *Average main: $4* ✉ *41 Biltmore Ave., Downtown* ☎ *828/505–2439* 🌐 *www.doubledscoffee.com* 💳 *No credit cards.*

$ VEGETARIAN
🍴 **Laughing Seed Café.** You'll get more than brown rice and beans at this vegetarian-vegan eatery, a longtime Asheville favorite on charming Wall Street. The extensive menu ranges from fruit drinks to sandwiches and pizzas to dinner specialties influenced by the flavors of India, Cuba, Thailand, Mexico, and Morocco. **Known for:** creative vegetarian-vegan fare; many ingredients from local organic farms. [$] *Average main: $14* ✉ *40 Wall St., Downtown* ☎ *828/252–3445* 🌐 *www.laughingseed.com* ⏲ *Closed Tues.*

$$$$ MODERN MEXICAN
Fodor's Choice ★
🍴 **Limones.** The extraordinary combination of innovative food and drink flavors and this modern Mexican restaurant's upscale setting is the result of the coming together of three special ingredients: a talented chef from Mexico City, North Carolina–sourced ingredients, and a San Francisco bistro atmosphere. Whet your appetite with the ceviche sampler and lobster nachos, washed down with not-to-be-missed blood orange margaritas. **Known for:** Asheville's best margaritas and ceviche; modern Mexican; intelligent, unobtrusive service. [$] *Average main: $27* ✉ *13 Eagle St., Downtown* ☎ *828/252–2327* 🌐 *www.limonesrestaurant.com.*

$ INDIAN FAMILY
🍴 **Mela Indian Restaurant.** Rather than specialize in one type of Indian cuisine, Mela—the best Indian restaurant in the city—offers dishes from across the country. The traditionally prepared Punjab tandoori dishes (chicken, shrimp, and lamb) are especially delicious. **Known for:** classic dishes from all over India; filling, inexpensive luncheon buffet. [$] *Average main: $14* ✉ *70 N. Lexington, Downtown* ☎ *828/225–8880* 🌐 *www.melaasheville.com.*

$ CAFÉ
🍴 **Old Europe.** Old Europe's Hungarian owner creates authentic European pastries, all made fresh daily, and complimented by Mountain City coffee (including the city's best cold-brewed iced coffee), owned by an MIT grad who brings a scientific approach to coffee roasting. Asheville's oldest, but arguably most peripatetic, coffeehouse opens early and stays busy until late. **Known for:** authentic Hungarian and other European pastries; locally roasted and fresh-brewed specialty coffees. [$] *Average main: $5* ✉ *13 Broadway St., Downtown* ☎ *828/255–5999* 🌐 *www.oldeuropepastries.com.*

$$$ CHINESE FUSION
Fodor's Choice ★
🍴 **Red Ginger Dimsum & Tapas.** New in 2016, Red Ginger's chefs extend Chinese dim sum to an all-day menu with tapas-style plates, beautifully presented and served in an upscale setting. Red Ginger does away with rolling carts and lets customers order from an extensive dinner menu of farm-to-table small plates—mostly $5 to $15—such as black truffle shumai, crispy fish, and Shanghai pork dumplings, along with wine from the owner's vineyard and Asian-themed cocktails. **Known for:**

Chinese tapas-style small plates; fresh ingredients from local farms. [$] *Average main: $23* ✉ *82 Patton Ave., Suite 100, Downtown* ✥ *Shares entrance foyer with Asheville Art Gallery* ☎ *828/505–8688* 🌐 *www.redgingerasheville.com.*

$$$$ ECLECTIC Fodor's Choice ★ 🍴 **Rhubarb.** A regular on "top restaurants of the South" lists, Rhubarb brings a dose of creative cuisine and local sourcing to a prime location on Pack Square. Hyper-imaginative chef-owner John Fleer, a five-time James Beard Award Finalist, relishes the unusual, such as rabbit-leek rillettes, octopus salad, and lobster corn dogs. **Known for:** hip, creative menu; James Beard Award Finalist chef-owner John Fleer. [$] *Average main: $27* ✉ *7 S.W. Pack Sq., Downtown* ☎ *828/785–1503* 🌐 *www.rhubarbasheville.com* ⏲ *Closed Tues.*

$ MODERN AMERICAN 🍴 **Wicked Weed.** This wildly popular restaurant and bar is a bit of a step up from a typical brewpub menu, with items like steak tartare, Carolina bison meat loaf, and artisanal cheese plates, which all go well with a Pernicious IPA or another of the 25 available brews. There's a bottle shop, tasting room downstairs, and patio with fire pit. **Known for:** award-winning beers and ales; lively atmosphere; patio with fire pit. [$] *Average main: $13* ✉ *91 Biltmore Ave., Downtown* ☎ *828/575–9599* 🌐 *www.wickedweedbrewing.com.*

$$$ SPANISH Fodor's Choice ★ 🍴 **Zambra.** Zambra's sophisticated tapas, such as grilled octopus in black ink sauce, pistachio-crusted veal sweetbreads with blackberries, and squash gnocchi have made this one of the most interesting restaurants in Asheville. Moorish colors, dim lighting, and a belowground cavelike setting create a romantic atmosphere. **Known for:** Spanish and North African tapas; intimate, romantic atmosphere. [$] *Average main: $23* ✉ *85 Walnut St., Downtown* ☎ *828/232–1060* 🌐 *www.zambratapas.com* ⏲ *No lunch.*

RIVER ARTS DISTRICT

$$$$ SEAFOOD Fodor's Choice ★ 🍴 **The Bull and Beggar.** The Bull and Beggar is decidedly warehouse-hip, with brick walls, old wood floors, and high ceilings. Its slogan is "European-inspired Appalachian cuisine," but its most popular feature is "Burger Monday," when fabulous double-patty burgers with fries go for $10. **Known for:** selection of different oysters on the half shell; "Burger Monday"; hip warehouse atmosphere. [$] *Average main: $32* ✉ *37 Paynes Way, No. 007, River Arts District* ✥ *Near the original Wedge Brewery* ☎ *828/575–9443* 🌐 *www.thebullandbeggar.com* ⏲ *Closed Sun.*

$ BARBECUE Fodor's Choice ★ 🍴 **12 Bones Smokehouse.** Forced out of its original no-frills location by River Arts District gentrification, 12 Bones has a new, larger location (still in the RAD), with twice the seating, new smokers, and a gritty graffiti-covered exterior. The lively crowds still range from hippie potters to downtown suits—former President Barack Obama made 12 Bones his first stop on multiple trips to Asheville—who come for the smoky baby back ribs, pulled pork, beef brisket, and delicious Southern sides like collard greens and corn pudding. **Known for:** smoky baby back ribs to die for; Southern-style sides; staff calling you "Sweetie". [$] *Average main: $10* ✉ *5 Foundy St., River Arts District* ✥ *Next door to new Wedge Brewery location* ☎ *828/253–4499* 🌐 *www.12bones.com* ⏲ *Closed weekends.*

$ ✕ **White Duck Taco Shop.** Popular with penny-pinching artists and crafts-
ECLECTIC   people in the River Arts District, White Duck Taco stays true to its name
with a roast duck taco, but it also has other fusion tacos, including
Thai peanut chicken, lamb gyro, Korean beef *bulgogi*, and Vietnamese
banh mi tofu. Most tacos are under $4, and two make a filling meal.
Known for: roast duck tacos; affordable, filling eats. Ⓢ *Average main:*
$8 ✉ 1 Roberts St., #101, River Arts District ☎ 828/258–1660 ⊕ www.
whiteducktacoshop.com ⊗ Closed Sun.

WEST ASHEVILLE

$$$ ✕ **The Admiral.** Don't be put off by the dowdy cinder-block exterior or the
ECLECTIC   louche neighborhood. Inside this dimly lit, little restaurant that feels like
Fodor'sChoice   a dive bar you'll find some of the most creative cooking in town, with
★   a dinner menu of small and large plates that changes daily. **Known for:**
dive bar atmosphere; super creative chefs; surprising flavors and unusual
combinations. Ⓢ *Average main: $22 ✉ 400 Haywood Rd., Metro West*
☎ 828/252–2541 ⊕ www.theadmiralasheville.com ⊗ No lunch.

$ ✕ **Papas & Beer.** With fajita plates sizzling, cervezas popping, and tables
MEXICAN   packed with hungry families, Asheville's most popular Mexican spot is
FAMILY   a high-energy, noisy experience. You'll find authentic Mexican food, an
expansive menu, delicious margaritas, a free salsa bar, and huge portions
at modest prices. **Known for:** classic Cali-Mex fajitas, enchiladas, and
tacos; huge portions at affordable prices; birthday guests don sombreros
and staff sings "feliz cumpleaños". Ⓢ *Average main: $9 ✉ 1000 Brevard*
Rd., Metro West ☎ 828/665–9070 ⊕ www.papasandbeerasheville.net.

$$ ✕ **Sunny Point Café.** Sunny Point is the quintessential West Asheville eat-
SOUTHERN   ery: food is simple, delicious, and not too expensive; dogs are welcome;
FAMILY   herbs and some veggies come from the restaurant's organic garden next
Fodor'sChoice   door; and there's almost always a line. Breakfast is served all day (with
★   the biggest biscuits in town), and also try the shrimp and grits, juicy
burgers, and meat loaf (regular or vegetarian) with buttermilk mashed
potatoes and sautéed greens. **Known for:** West Asheville style; great
breakfasts served all day; covered outdoor patio dining. Ⓢ *Average*
main: $16 ✉ 626 Haywood Rd., Metro West ☎ 828/252–0055 ⊕ www.
sunnypointcafe.com ⊗ No dinner Sun. or Mon.

GREATER ASHEVILLE

$$ ✕ **Chiesa.** Eponymously named in Italian for its location in a former church
ITALIAN   just a few blocks from downtown Asheville, Chiesa feeds body and soul
FAMILY   with appropriately heavenly fresh-made pastas served under high vaulted
ceilings and in a light and cozy setting. Pasta is most certainly the focus
here, be it house-made fettuccine, angel hair, or orecchiette pasta, served
with flavorful meat or red tomato gravy and paired with Hickory Nut
Gap sweet Italian sausage, shrimp scampi, and chicken marsala. **Known**
for: house-made pastas; friendly, neighborhood feel; tasteful, understated
decor in former church. Ⓢ *Average main: $19 ✉ 152 Montford Ave.,*
Metro North ☎ 828/552–3110 ⊕ www.chiesaavl.com.

$$ ✕ **Ghan Shan Station.** Inspired by the food of Thailand, Vietnam, Laos,
ASIAN FUSION   China, Japan, and Singapore, Ghan Shan Station (Ghan Shan refers to
Fodor'sChoice   a mountain behind the restaurant, Sunset Mountain) has a truly eclectic
★   and inventive selection of fusion dishes. Favorites include coconut squash

soup, red curry shrimp, tofu spread on house-baked naan, and drunken noodles with eggplant and broccoli, served on locally made pottery plates and bowls. **Known for:** creative takes on East Asian cuisines; casual vibe; Sunday Supper series. $ *Average main: $17* ⊠ *143 Charlotte St., Metro North* ☎ *828/774–5280* ⊕ *www.ganshanstation.com* ☾ *Closed Sun.*

$$ VEGETARIAN Fodor'sChoice ★

✕**Plant.** Plant is Asheville's top vegan restaurant, with a sophisticated, frequently changing menu of plant-based dishes from different cultures and cuisines. A typical menu might include Korean tofu chili, lasagna from raw vegetables, and Indian masala *uttapan* of avocado, cabbage, tomato, onion, and coconut chutney, with delicious "ice cream" made with coconut milk for dessert. **Known for:** sophisticated vegan dishes. $ *Average main: $17* ⊠ *165 Merrimon Ave., Metro North* ☎ *828/258–7500* ⊕ *www.plantisfood.com* ☾ *Closed Mon. and Tues. Jan.–early Mar.*

BILTMORE VILLAGE

$$$$ MODERN AMERICAN FAMILY Fodor'sChoice ★

✕**Corner Kitchen.** At one of Asheville's most popular restaurants, the new American menu changes regularly, and many dishes are locally sourced, with entrées such as pecan-crusted mountain trout with ginger sweet potatoes and herb-grilled pork chop with wild rice. The charmingly renovated Victorian cottage in Biltmore Village has wood floors, plaster walls painted in serene colors, a fireplace in one dining room, and alfresco dining on the patio. **Known for:** innovative versions of Southern favorites; charming Biltmore Village location. $ *Average main: $27* ⊠ *3 Boston Way, Biltmore Village* ☎ *828/274–2439* ⊕ *www. thecornerkitchen.com.*

$$$$ MODERN EUROPEAN Fodor'sChoice ★

✕**Dining Room at Inn on Biltmore Estate.** Romantic, impressive, delightful: that just begins to describe the field-to-white-linen-tablecloth dining experience at the Inn on Biltmore Estate. A three-course dinner—perhaps with she-crab soup or foie gras torchon to start, an entrée of lobster and persimmons or beef fillet with roasted root vegetables from the estate farms, and cheesecake napoleon for dessert—is $65. **Known for:** Asheville's most elegant dining; impeccable service; estate-grown or locally sourced ingredients. $ *Average main: $42* ⊠ *Inn on Biltmore Estate, 1 Antler Hill Rd., Biltmore Village* ☎ *828/225–1699* ⊕ *www.biltmore.com.*

$$$$ STEAKHOUSE Fodor'sChoice ★

✕**Ruth's Chris Steak House.** This outpost of the international restaurant group has sizzled its way to the top of the red-meat venues in Asheville. It may be a chain, but prime steaks here are the best in town (by far), the atmosphere is upmarket, service is doting, and the wine list is sophisticated if pricey. **Known for:** serious USDA prime steaks; big steak-house sides; Scotch-and-cigar nights on the patio. $ *Average main: $42* ⊠ *26 All Souls Crescent, Biltmore Village* ☎ *828/398–6200* ⊕ *www.ruths-chris.com/asheville.*

$ VIETNAMESE FAMILY

✕**Wild Ginger Noodle.** What Wild Ginger Noodles lacks in atmosphere, it more than makes up for in delicious pho, noodles, banh mi sandwiches, and other authentic Vietnamese fare at very reasonable prices. Service is very friendly and there's Vietnamese beer. **Known for:** simple, tasty Vietnamese food; Vietnamese beer. $ *Average main: $10* ⊠ *1950 Hendersonville Rd., Suite 12, Metro South* ☎ *828/676–2311* ⊕ *www. wildgingernoodle.com* ☾ *Closed Tues.*

WHERE TO STAY

The Asheville area has a nice mix of B&Bs, motels, and small, owner-operated inns. There are nearly 50 B&Bs in the Asheville area, one of the largest concentrations in the South. Most are in the Montford area near downtown and the Grove Park area. At least a dozen B&Bs in the area promote themselves as gay-owned and actively seek gay and lesbian guests, and others advertise that they are gay-friendly. With the opening of the Aloft, Indigo, Hyatt Place, AC Hotel, Hilton Garden Inn, and Windsor hotels, and the renovation of Haywood Park and some other older properties, the selection of lodging downtown has grown tremendously. Several other major hotels are under construction and due to open in late 2017 or 2018, including Cambria Suites across from the Grove Arcade, the luxury Foundry Inn (a Hilton Curio affiliate) on "The Block," a historically African American business district off Biltmore Avenue, and the conversion of the region's tallest bank building to its tallest hotel, Hotel Arras on West Pack Square.

The boom has spurred a "no more downtown hotels" movement in Asheville, with some proposed properties being rejected by the Asheville City Council. On in-season weekends, downtown hotels and many nearby B&Bs run at more than 90% occupancy, and many of the rooms go for $300 and up. For cheaper options, look at the chain motels in the suburbs. More than 100 chain motel properties are dotted around the metropolitan area, with large clusters on Tunnel Road near the Asheville Mall, on U.S. 25 and Biltmore Avenue near the Biltmore Estate, and southwest near the new Asheville Outlets mall. A few lodges and cabin colonies are found in rural areas around the city. Airbnb is huge here, with some 500 listings.

DOWNTOWN

$$$$ HOTEL 🏨 **AC Hotel.** New in summer 2017, the nine-story AC Hotel, a premium Marriott brand, has a prime central location just north of Pack Square, within walking distance of most downtown restaurants, bars, galleries, and shops. **Pros:** central location in heart of downtown; new in 2017; rooftop terrace and bar. **Cons:** premium Marriott brand not inexpensive. [$] *Rooms from: $299* ✉ *10 Broadway St., Downtown* ☎ *828/258–2522* 🌐 *www.marriott.com/hotels/travel/avlac-ac-hotel-asheville-downtown* 🛏 *132 rooms* 🍴 *No meals.*

$$$$ HOTEL 🏨 **Aloft Asheville Downtown.** With trendy "W xyz" bar and a smashing location just south of Pack Square, this hotel is very, very popular. **Pros:** great central location; easy parking under the hotel; very pet-friendly. **Cons:** perhaps a bit too trendy for some; not designed for most young kids or families; surprisingly pricey. [$] *Rooms from: $366* ✉ *51 Biltmore Ave., Downtown* ☎ *828/232–2838, 877/462–5638* 🌐 *www.starwoodhotels.com/alofthotels* 🛏 *115 rooms* 🍴 *No meals.*

$$$$ HOTEL Fodor's Choice ★ 🏨 **Haywood Park Hotel.** Location is the biggest draw of this all-suites downtown hotel, which is within walking distance of many of Asheville's shops, restaurants, and galleries. **Pros:** great central downtown location; good restaurant on-site and a short stroll from many more. **Cons:** no pool; pricey in-season. [$] *Rooms from: $299* ✉ *1 Battery Park Ave., Downtown* ☎ *828/252–2522* 🌐 *www.haywoodpark.com* 🛏 *33 suites* 🍴 *No meals.*

$$$ HOTEL 🏨 **Hilton Garden Inn.** Hilton brought its mid-tier brand to downtown Asheville in mid-2016 with all its expected conveniences and one unusual feature: a rooftop patio and bar. **Pros:** off-season rates are enticing; new in 2016; on-site parking available at small charge. **Cons:** bit of a walk to main dining, shopping, and entertainment area; chain with limited local atmosphere; free downtown shuttle is a golf cart. [$] *Rooms from: $249* ✉ *309 College St., Downtown* ☎ *828/255–0001* 🌐 *hiltongardeninn3.hilton.com* 🛏 *140 rooms* 🍴 *No meals.*

$$$$ HOTEL 🏨 **Hotel Indigo.** The 12-story Hotel Indigo, part of the IGH Hotels chain, just two blocks from the Grove Arcade and many downtown restaurants and attractions, has furnishings and artwork crafted by local Asheville artists and views of the Blue Ridge Mountains and downtown. **Pros:** short walk to northwest part of downtown; friendly service. **Cons:** no pool; some street noise from nearby expressway; surprisingly pricey in-season. [$] *Rooms from: $405* ✉ *151 Haywood St., Downtown* ☎ *828/239–0239* 🌐 *www.ashevilleindigo.com* 🛏 *100 rooms* 🍴 *No meals.*

4

$$ HOTEL FAMILY 🏨 **Hyatt Place Asheville.** Opened in mid-2016, the eight-story Hyatt Place, in downtown near Montford, is a short walk to the Grove Arcade and restaurants and activities in that area. **Pros:** moderately priced even in-season; walk to both downtown and historic Montford; rooftop bar has great sunset views. **Cons:** fee for on-site parking; expressway-side rooms may have some street noise. [$] *Rooms from: $175* ✉ *199 Haywood St., Downtown* ☎ *828/505–8500* 🌐 *ashevilledowntown.place.hyatt.com* 🛏 *150 rooms* 🍴 *Breakfast.*

$$$$ B&B/INN Fodor's Choice ★ 🏨 **The Windsor Boutique Hotel.** Built in 1907 as a center-of-town hotel, the Windsor had become very run-down indeed until a major renovation led to its reopening with luxurious suites in 2014. **Pros:** large, beautifully decorated suites; perfect location in heart of downtown; decorated with local art. **Cons:** no pool; no on-site parking; often a two- or three-night minimum stay in high season. [$] *Rooms from: $400* ✉ *36 Broadway St., Downtown* ☎ *844/494–6376 toll-free* 🌐 *www.windsorasheville.com* 🛏 *14 rooms* 🍴 *No meals.*

GREATER ASHEVILLE

$$ B&B/INN 🏨 **Albemarle Inn.** This well-established B&B in an upscale North Asheville residential area housed the Hungarian composer Béla Bartók in the early 1940s, when he was creating his "Asheville Concerto"; you can stay in his room on the third floor, although Juliet's Chamber, with its private balcony overlooking lovely gardens, may appeal more to modern Romeos. **Pros:** upscale and historic; lovely residential neighborhood; excellent breakfasts. **Cons:** old-fashioned claw-foot tubs in some rooms may not appeal to all; not within easy walking distance of downtown. [$] *Rooms from: $200* ✉ *86 Edgemont Rd., Grove Park, Metro North* ☎ *828/255–0027* 🌐 *www.albemarleinn.com* 🛏 *12 rooms* 🍴 *Breakfast.*

$$$ B&B/INN Fodor's Choice ★ 🏨 **Chestnut Street Inn.** Even in a city with many excellent B&Bs, Chestnut Street Inn stands out for its location—a short stroll from several good restaurants, within easy walking distance of downtown, yet situated in the quiet, charming Chestnut Hill Historic District away from the city's bustle—and its multilingual innkeepers Emilie and Arturo, who are knowledgeable, engaging, and enthusiastic boosters of their

CLOSE UP

Arts and Crafts Movement

The Arts and Crafts movement was an international movement of the late 19th and early 20th centuries that emphasized local and natural materials, craftsmanship, and a strong horizontal line in architecture and furniture. Inspired by the writings of British art critic John Ruskin, Arts and Crafts, along with the similar American Craftsman style, romanticized the role of the craftsperson and rebelled against the mass production of the Industrial Age. Prominent examples of Craftsman style include the furniture and other decorative arts of Gustav Stickley, first presented in his magazine, *The Craftsman*; the Roycroft community in Ohio, founded by Elbert Hubbard; the Prairie School of architect Frank Lloyd Wright; and the bungalow style of houses popularized in California. At its height between 1880 and 1910, the Arts and Crafts movement flourished in Asheville. The Grove Park Inn's construction was heavily influenced by Arts and Crafts principles, and today the resort hotel has one of the largest collections of Arts and Crafts furniture in the world. Several hundred Asheville bungalows were also built in the Arts and Crafts style. Today, the influence of the Arts and Crafts movement remains strong in the Asheville area, reflected in the large number of working craft studios in the region.

adopted city. **Pros:** award-winning restoration of 1906 house; helpful, welcoming hosts; walking distance to downtown. **Cons:** you'll be tempted to get off your diet with candy and fresh-baked cookies. [$] *Rooms from: $214* ✉ *Chestnut Historical District, 176 E. Chestnut St., Metro North* ☎ *828/285–0705* 🌐 *www.chestnutstreetinn.com* 🛏 *8 rooms* 🍴 *Breakfast.*

$$$ B&B/INN Fodor's Choice ★ 🏨 **1900 Inn on Montford.** Guests are pampered at this Arts and Crafts–style B&B, where most rooms have whirlpool baths, big-screen TVs, and fireplaces. **Pros:** well run; lovely antiques; modern amenities. **Cons:** not for families with small children. [$] *Rooms from: $205* ✉ *296 Montford Ave., Montford, Metro North* ☎ *828/254–9569* 🌐 *www.innonmontford.com* 🛏 *8 rooms, 1 cabin* 🍴 *Breakfast.*

$$$$ RESORT Fodor's Choice ★ 🏨 **Omni Grove Park Inn.** This massive resort, which opened in 1913, has hosted 10 U.S. presidents from Woodrow Wilson to Barack Obama, and it's easy to see why, with its grand views of downtown Asheville and the Blue Ridge Mountains and resort amenities that include a golf course, top-rated spa, and variety of dining options. **Pros:** imposing and historic; wonderful setting; magnificent mountain views; remarkable spa. **Cons:** individual guests sometimes play second fiddle to groups; high rates. [$] *Rooms from: $329* ✉ *290 Macon Ave., Grove Park, Metro North* ☎ *828/252–2711* 🌐 *www.omnihotels.com/hotels/asheville-grove-park* ⛳ *18 holes, 6400 yds, par 70; in-season $85–$140* 🛏 *512 rooms* 🍴 *No meals.*

$$$ B&B/INN Fodor's Choice ★ 🏨 **Reynolds Mansion Bed and Breakfast Inn.** Located in a historic and beautifully restored Colonial Revival mansion built in the 1840s, this inn has 12 fireplaces and 3,000 square feet of porches and it sits on 4 acres on Reynolds Mountain, just north of Asheville. **Pros:** beautiful building; gracious, friendly service; swimming pool (open Memorial Day–Labor

Day). **Cons:** though it's on large grounds, it is in a mixed-use residential and business area. [$] *Rooms from: $215* ⊠ *100 Reynolds Heights, Metro North* ☎ *828/258–1111* ⊕ *www.thereynoldsmansion.com* ↪ *13 rooms* ⃝ *Breakfast.*

BILTMORE VILLAGE

$$$$
HOTEL

⛫ **Grand Bohemian Hotel.** This upscale Marriott hotel is as close as you can get to the main Biltmore gate, and steps from all the shops and restaurants in Biltmore Village. **Pros:** upscale hotel in Biltmore Village; at Biltmore Estate gate; good restaurant. **Cons:** in congested area of Biltmore; very pricey in-season. [$] *Rooms from: $455* ⊠ *11 Boston Way, Biltmore Village* ☎ *828/505–2949, 888/717–8756* ⊕ *www.bohemianhotelasheville.com* ↪ *104 rooms* ⃝ *No meals.*

$$$$
HOTEL
Fodor's Choice
★

⛫ **Inn on Biltmore Estate.** Many people who visit the Biltmore mansion long to stay overnight; if you're one of them, your wish is granted at this posh hilltop property on the estate. **Pros:** superb, romantic restaurant; fine views from some rooms; arguably the most upscale hotel in area; friendly service. **Cons:** very expensive (though there are steep off-season discounts); can be a bit formal. [$] *Rooms from: $409* ⊠ *1 Antler Hill Rd., Metro South* ☎ *828/225–1660* ⊕ *www.biltmore.com/inn* ↪ *201 rooms, 9 suites* ⃝ *No meals.*

$$$$
HOTEL
FAMILY

⛫ **Village Hotel.** Opened in 2016, the Village Hotel is Biltmore Estate's new mid-tier lodging, with rates—while hardly inexpensive—well below those at the Inn on Biltmore Estate. **Pros:** in the middle of the Biltmore Estate at moderate rates; free shuttle around the Estate. **Cons:** more like a motel than a hotel or inn. [$] *Rooms from: $309* ⊠ *Biltmore Estate, 297 Diary Rd., Metro South* ☎ *866/799–9228* ⊕ *www.biltmore.com/stay/hotel* ↪ *209 rooms* ⃝ *No meals.*

NIGHTLIFE AND PERFORMING ARTS

North Carolina does not allow bars. Under state law, public establishments that sell mostly alcohol and little food have to operate as private membership clubs. This just means you have to sign up and perhaps pay a nominal onetime membership fee (like a cover charge). You can do this at the door or in advance.

For the latest information on nightlife, arts, and entertainment in the Asheville area, visit the websites of the *Asheville Citizen-Times* or the *Mountain Xpress.*

NIGHTLIFE

FAMILY

Asheville Pizza and Brewing Company. More than a restaurant, more than a movie theater, Asheville Pizza and Brewing Company, also called Brew 'n' View, is a popular spot to catch a second-run flick on a movie screen while lounging on a sofa, drinking a microbrew, and scarfing a pizza. Kids and dogs are welcome for the food and movie. The same owners have a brewery in downtown Asheville at 77 Coxe Avenue and another pizza joint in South Asheville at 1850 Hendersonville Road. ⊠ *675 Merriman Ave., Metro North* ☎ *828/254–1281* ⊕ *www.ashevillebrewing.com* ▣ *$3 for movies.*

FAMILY   **Bywater.** An unusual combination of outdoor picnic grounds and dive bar, Bywater is on the French Broad River and near the River Arts District. Bring your own food and cook it on one of the charcoal grills beside the bar, or buy from a local food truck. Some folks tube or raft down the French Broad River and stop here for a cold one. ✉ *796 Riverside Dr., Metro North* ☎ *828/232–6967* ⊕ *www.bywaterbar.com* ✉ *Free.*

Grey Eagle. Situated in the River Arts District area, Grey Eagle features popular local and regional bands four or five nights a week, with contra dancing on some other nights. From Monday to Saturday noon to 8 pm, the Grey Eagle doubles as a restaurant, serving tacos, burritos, and nachos. ✉ *185 Clingman Ave., River Arts District* ☎ *828/232–5800* ⊕ *www.thegreyeagle.com.*

Isis Restaurant & Music Hall. What was once a movie house—the marquee and entrance was retained—is now an upscale eatery and a late-night music club. Early in the evening a full dinner, sometimes accompanied by live music, includes buttermilk fried chicken, barbecue tuna, soba noodle salad, and mountain trout with wild-caught shrimp. Then the Isis switches to bar snacks, and the music—bluegrass, blues, reggae, jazz, or rock—ramps up on the main stage downstairs and intimate club upstairs. Isis has 30 local and regional beers on tap, wines, and cocktails. Admission varies but there's often a $10 cover for music events. ✉ *743 Haywood Rd., Metro West* ☎ *828/575–2737* ⊕ *www. isisasheville.com.*

Fodor'sChoice   **Orange Peel Social Aid & Pleasure Club.** Bob Dylan, Hootie and the Blow-
★   fish, Modest Mouse, and the Beastie Boys have played here in a smoke-free setting for audiences of up to 1,100. It's far and away the number one nightspot downtown. There's also a great dance floor, with springy wood slats, as well as a private club (for music, comedy, and drink lovers who are at least 21) on the lower level. ✉ *101 Biltmore Ave.* ☎ *828/225–5851* ⊕ *www.theorangepeel.net* ✉ *Varies.*

Scandals Nightclub. Asheville's best-known gay and lesbian club has a lively dance floor and drag shows most nights that it is open. Club Eleven and Boiler Room are at the same location. ✉ *Grove House, 11 Grove St., Downtown* ☎ *828/505–1612* ⊕ *www.scandalsnightclub. com* ✉ *$5–$10.*

Fodor'sChoice   **Sovereign Remedies.** Offering creative craft cocktails and a classed-up-
★   cool atmosphere (though it's still Asheville casual), Sovereign Remedies is one of Asheville's hottest spots for locally sourced farm-to-table and farm-to-glass delights. The lofty, light-filled space boasts high ceilings, large mirrors, locally built furnishings, and a huge array of spirits in the main bar, but there's also sidewalk seating and a space upstairs, so the bar is even bigger than it first looks. Servers and bartenders are friendly and knowledgeable, and prices are lower than you'd expect for an upscale bar. ✉ *29 N. Market St., Downtown* ☎ *828/919–9518* ⊕ *www.sovereignremedies.com.*

Tressa's Jazz & Blues Club. In a 1913 downtown building, Tressa's features a full bar plus sandwiches and bar snacks in a New Orleans atmosphere. There's live jazz or blues most nights. ✉ *28 Broadway, Downtown* ☎ *828/254–7072* ⊕ *www.tressas.com* ☾ *Closed. Sun.–Mon.*

PERFORMING ARTS

The Asheville area has about 40 theaters and theater companies.

FAMILY **Asheville Community Theatre.** One of the oldest community theater groups in the country, Asheville Community Theatre stages amateur productions year-round in its own theater building. ⊠ *35 E. Walnut St., Downtown* ☎ *828/254–1320* ⊕ *www.ashevilletheatre.org* ☑ *Varies.*

Diana Wortham Theatre. The intimate 500-seat Diana Wortham Theatre is home to more than 200 musical, dance, and theatrical events each year. A $3 million expansion beginning in 2017 will add two more smaller performance spaces and upgrade the main theater. There's parking next to the theater or nearby, under the Aloft Hotel. ⊠ *Pack Place, 2 S. Pack Sq., Downtown* ☎ *828/257–4530* ⊕ *www.dwtheatre.com* ☑ *Varies.*

North Carolina Stage Company. From an alley off Walnut Street, this professional company puts on mostly edgy, contemporary plays. ⊠ *15 Stage La., Downtown* ☎ *828/239–0263* ⊕ *www.ncstage.org.*

Thomas Wolfe Auditorium. The 2,400-seat Thomas Wolfe Auditorium, in the U.S. Cellular Center Asheville (formerly Asheville Civic Center), hosts larger events, including traveling Broadway shows and performances of the Asheville Symphony. ⊠ *87 Haywood St., Downtown* ☎ *828/259–5736 box office* ⊕ *www.uscellularcenterasheville.com* ☑ *Varies.*

SPORTS AND THE OUTDOORS

BASEBALL

FAMILY **Asheville Tourists.** A Class A farm team of the Colorado Rockies, the Asheville Tourists play April to early September at McCormick Field, which opened in 1924, seats 4,000, and is the oldest minor-league park in regular use. It appears briefly in the 1987 movie *Bull Durham*; many well-traveled baseball fans consider McCormick Field one of the most appealing minor-league stadiums in the country. ⊠ *McCormick Pl., 30 Buchanan Pl., Downtown* ☎ *828/258–0428* ⊕ *www.milb.com* ☑ *General admission $8.*

GOLF

FAMILY **Asheville Municipal Golf Course.** This municipal course beside the Swannanoa River, owned by the city of Asheville but since 2012 under private management by Pope Golf, is known for its firm and fast greens. Designed by famed golf architect Donald Ross, it opened in 1927 and is now in the National Register of Historic Places. ⊠ *226 Fairway Dr., East Metro* ☎ *828/298–1867* ⊕ *www.ashevillegc.com* ⚑ *18 holes, 6420 yds, Par 72. Green Fee: $22–$36. Facilities: putting green, pitching area, golf carts, pull carts, rental clubs, pro shop, lessons, snack bar* ⚑ *Reservations essential.*

Fodor's Choice ★ **Omni Grove Park Inn Resort Golf Club.** Formerly the course for the Country Club of Asheville, this beauty first opened in 1899 and was redesigned by Donald Ross in 1926, and last restored in 2001. It has been played by several U.S. presidents, including Barack Obama. Flocks of wild turkeys regularly visit the course. ⊠ *Omni Grove Park Inn, 290 Macon Ave.* ☎ *800/438–5800* ⊕ *www.omnihotels.com/hotels/asheville-grove-park/golf* ⚑ *18 holes, 6400 yds, par 70. Green Fee: $140 weekdays, $160*

*weekends, $85 after 3 pm, mid-Apr.–mid-Nov.; lower rates rest of year.
Facilities: putting green, golf carts, rental clubs, rental shoes, pro shop,
golf lessons, restaurants, bars* ⌂ *Reservations essential.*

HORSEBACK RIDING

FAMILY **Biltmore Estate Trail Rides.** Biltmore offers guided hour-long horseback
rides on the Estate trails ($60) as well as longer private rides, which
must be reserved at least two days in advance ($160 to $230). There's a
weight limit of 200 pounds. ✉ *Biltmore Equestrian Center, Deer Park
Rd., Biltmore Estate, Metro South* ☎ *800/411–3812* ⊕ *www.biltmore.
com/visit/things-to-do/outdoor-activities/horseback-riding* 🎫 *From $60.*

FAMILY **Pisgah View Ranch Trail Rides.** From April through November you can ride
through 2,000 acres of fields and wooded mountainside at this ranch.
If you're not staying at this dude ranch, reserve 24 hours in advance.
Group rides are $40 per person per hour; private rides are $50 an
hour. ✉ *70 Pisgah View Ranch Rd., Candler* ☎ *828/667–9100* ⊕ *www.
pisgahviewranch.net* 🎫 *$40–$50 for tours.*

SKIING

FAMILY **Cataloochee Ranch.** In addition to having skiing and snowboarding, Cataloochee Ranch has cabin rentals and hosts lots of different activities for
the whole family. ✉ *119 Ranch Dr., Maggie Valley* ☎ *828/926–1401,
800/868–1401* ⊕ *www.cataloocheeranch.com.*

FAMILY **Wolf Ridge Ski Resort.** You can "Ski the Wolf" at Wolf Ridge Ski Resort,
which has night skiing and excellent snowmaking capabilities. There
are 17 ski runs, five ski lifts, and two lodges. Weekday all-day and
evening lift tickets are $47, weekends $71. Keep in mind that milder
winters have impacted ski resorts in the South, including Wolf Ridge,
which sometimes closes for a time even in January and February. ✉ *Wolf
Ridge Ski Resort, 578 Valley View Circle, Mars Hill* ☎ *828/689–4111,
800/817–4111* ⊕ *www.skiwolfridgenc.com* 🎫 *Lift tickets $24–$71.*

ZIPLINING

FAMILY **Navitat Canopy Adventures.** Zip through the treetops at Navitat, which
Fodor's Choice has two different zipline complexes in a mountain cove in Madison
★ County, north of Asheville. One has 10 ziplines, ranging from 120 to
1,100 feet in length, with hiking trails, two sky bridges, and two rap-
peling areas. The other has three "racing style" ziplines as long as 3,600
feet. The ziplines have a 70- to 90-pound minimum and 250-pound
maximum weight limit. You need to be able to walk about a mile and be
in generally good health. From the welcome center, it is a seven-minute
ride in a rough-terrain vehicle to the tour entry trail. ■TIP➔ **Make reservations as much as two weeks in advance at peak weekend periods.**
✉ *242 Poverty Branch Rd., 25 miles north of downtown Asheville,
Greater Asheville* ✛ *From Asheville, take I–26/U.S. 19/23 to Jupiter/
Barnardsville exit (Exit 15), then take Barnardsville Hwy. (NC 197)
east 6 miles to Barnardsville. At Barnardsville post office, turn north
on Poverty Branch Road (SR2171) and go 1½ miles to Navitat (on left)*
☎ *828/626–3700, 855/628–4828* ⊕ *www.navitat.com* 🎫 *Tours from
$99* ☉ *Closed Dec.–Mar.*

SHOPPING

SHOPPING CENTERS

FAMILY

Fodor's Choice

★

Downtown Asheville. Shopping is excellent all over downtown Asheville, with around 200 boutiques, including more than 30 art and crafts galleries, and more than a dozen antiques shops. Several streets, notably **Biltmore Avenue, Broadway Street, Lexington Avenue, Haywood Street,** and **Wall Street,** are lined with small, independently owned stores. In fact, there are only two large chain retailers in all of downtown. ✉ *Downtown* ⊕ *www.ashevilledowntown.org.*

FAMILY

Fodor's Choice

★

Grove Arcade. Just before its opening in 1929, the Grove Arcade, which covers an entire city block, was trumpeted as "the most elegant building in America" by its builder, W. E. Grove, the man also responsible for the Grove Park Inn. He envisioned a new kind of retail, office, and residential complex. Grove died before completing the project, and a planned 14-story tower was never built. Still, the building is an architectural wonder, with gargoyles galore. Now it's a public market with about 40 locally owned shops and restaurants, along with apartments and office space. The south end of the Arcade has an outdoor market with about a dozen stalls selling local crafts and farm products. A self-guided architectural tour (download a map from the website) takes about 45 minutes. ✉ *1 Page Ave., Downtown* ☎ *828/252–7799* ⊕ *www.grovearcade.com.*

BOOKS

Fodor's Choice

★

Battery Park Book Exchange and Champagne Bar. At this unusual bookstore, you can relax on an overstuffed chair or sofa while sipping one of 80 wines and champagnes by the glass. The inventory includes some 22,000 secondhand books, with special strength in Civil War, American history, and North Carolina subjects. It's pet-friendly, too, with an "espresso dog bar." ✉ *Grove Arcade, 1 Page Ave., southwest corner, Downtown* ☎ *828/252–0020.*

FAMILY

Fodor's Choice

★

Malaprop's Bookstore and Cafe. This is what an independent bookstore should be, with an intelligent selection of new books, many author appearances and other events, and a comfortable café. Staffers speak many foreign languages, including Hungarian, Russian, Italian, Spanish, French, and German. ✉ *55 Haywood St., Downtown* ☎ *828/254– 6734, 800/441–8829* ⊕ *www.malaprops.com.*

CANDY AND CHOCOLATE

FAMILY

Chocolate Fetish. Chocolate truffles and sea-salt caramels are favorites here, but you can also buy made-on-site items such as chocolate in the shape of cowboy boots and high heels. Most items are sold for takeout, but there's limited in-store seating if you just can't wait to scarf down these delicious sweets with a cup of rich hot chocolate. ✉ *36 Haywood St., Downtown* ☎ *828/258–2353* ⊕ *www.chocolatefetish.com.*

FAMILY

Fodor's Choice

★

French Broad Chocolate Lounge. French Broad Chocolate Lounge—so popular it had to move to this much-larger location on Pack Square in 2014 (though the line is still sometimes out the door)—makes its own delicious chocolate candy, but that's just the start. As its name suggests, it's also a lounge, where you can sit in comfort and enjoy not only truffles

4

and other premium chocolates, but also ice cream, cookies, brownies, various kinds of hot and cold chocolate drinks, and specialty coffees and teas. There's a "grab-and-go" chocolate boutique, if you just want to buy some chocolate. The owners also have a small chocolate factory and tasting room at 21 Buxton Avenue, with free guided tours (reserve in advance) available Saturday at 11 am. ☒ *10 S. Pack Sq., Downtown* ☏ *828/252–4181 lounge and boutique, 828/505–4996 factory* ⊕ *www. frenchbroadchocolates.com.*

FARMERS' MARKETS

The Asheville area has many tailgate markets, usually in parking lots where local growers set up temporary sales stalls on certain days, and farmers' markets, which typically are larger than tailgate markets and often have permanent booths. The website of Appalachian Sustainable Agriculture Market (ASAP) has up-to-date information on all the region's tailgate markets, U-pick farms, and farmers' markets.

ASAP. More than 1,200 small family farms, tailgate markets, farm-to-table restaurants, and similar organizations in the region belong to Asheville-based Appalachian Sustainable Agriculture Project. ASAP lists more than 150 area restaurants and bakeries that buy direct from local farmers. A farm tour is held annually in September. ASAP also publishes a print and online guide to local food sources and tailgate markets. ☒ *306 W. Haywood St., Downtown* ☏ *828/236–1282* ⊕ *www. asapconnections.org.*

FAMILY **Asheville City Market.** Nearly everything at this downtown market is local. Offerings vary, but usually include produce, free-range eggs, homemade breads, and local cheeses from up to 30 local farms. ☒ *161 S. Charlotte St., Downtown* ☏ *828/348–0340* ⊕ *www.asapconnections. org* ☉ *Closed Jan.–Mar.*

FAMILY **North Asheville Tailgate Market.** Asheville's oldest tailgate market has about 40 vendors selling local produce, fruit, meats, breads, and crafts. ☒ *UNC-Asheville, 1 University Heights, Parking Lot C, Metro North* ☏ *828/776–6286* ⊕ *www.northashevilletailgatemarket.org* ☉ *Closed Jan.–mid-Apr.*

GALLERIES

Fodor'sChoice **Blue Spiral 1.** The biggest and arguably the best art gallery in town has
★ changing exhibits of regional sculpture, paintings, fine crafts, and photographs. Blue Spiral owner John Cram also runs the art-film theater next door, the Fine Arts Theater, along with three galleries in Biltmore Village. ☒ *38 Biltmore Ave., Downtown* ☏ *828/251–0202* ⊕ *www. bluespiral1.com.*

FAMILY **CURVE Studios and Garden.** With working studios and exhibits by more than a dozen artists, CURVE Studios displays ceramics, textiles, jewelry, sculpture, and furniture in three buildings. Many items are for sale direct from the artists. CURVE owner Pattiy Torno, who bought the buildings in 1989, was a pioneer in establishing the River Arts District. ☒ *6, 9, and 12 Riverside Dr., River Arts District* ☏ *828/388–3526* ⊕ *www.curvestudiosnc.com.*

FAMILY **Kress Emporium I and II.** In this 1928 landmark building decorated with polychrome terra-cotta tiles, more than 80 artisans show and sell their crafts. In mid-2016, a second location two doors away, Kress Emporium II, opened with about 20 artists. ⊠ *19 and 27 Patton Ave., Downtown* ☎ *828/281–2252 Kress Emporium I, 828/232–7237 Kress Emporium II* ⊕ *www.thekressemporium.com.*

New Morning Gallery. Owned by the arts entrepreneur John Cram, New Morning Gallery has more than 13,000 square feet of exhibit space in a prime location in Biltmore Village. The gallery, which has a national reputation, focuses on more popular and moderately priced ceramics, garden art, jewelry, furniture, and art glass. ⊠ *7 Boston Way, Biltmore Village* ☎ *828/274–2831* ⊕ *www.newmorninggallerync.com.*

Fodor's Choice **Odyssey Co-op Gallery.** Odyssey Co-op Gallery has a large and high-quality
★ selection of pottery and ceramic works, both functional and decorative, as well as figurative and abstract sculpture, by talented, juried clay artists. The gallery has rotating displays, so new work is on display regularly. As an added plus, you can also visit the numerous studio and student spaces in the Odyssey complex. ⊠ *238 Clingman Ave., River Arts District* ☎ *828/285–9700* ⊕ *odysseycoopgallery.com* ⊙ *Main gallery closed Mon.*

FAMILY **Riverview Station.** More than 60 artists, crafters, and entrepreneurs in ceramics, painting, textiles, woodworking, and jewelry work in this complex of studios and galleries in the River Arts District. Several of the artists offer classes and there's lots of free parking. ⊠ *191 Lyman St., River Arts District* ☎ *828/231–7120* ⊕ *www.riverviewstation.com.*

Fodor's Choice **Woolworth Walk.** In a 1938 building that once housed a five-and-dime,
★ Woolworth Walk features the curated work of more than 170 crafts artists, in 20,000 square feet of exhibit space on two levels. There's even a working soda fountain, built to resemble the original Woolworth luncheonette. ⊠ *25 Haywood St., Downtown* ☎ *828/254–9234* ⊕ *www.woolworthwalk.com.*

SIDE TRIPS FROM ASHEVILLE

These small towns, all an easy day trip from Asheville, will charm you with their pleasant change of pace, walkable downtowns, interesting local shops and galleries, and good dining spots.

BLUE RIDGE PARKWAY

Entrance 2 miles east of Asheville.

The Blue Ridge Parkway's 252 miles within North Carolina wind down the High Country through Asheville, ending near the entrance of Great Smoky Mountains National Park. Highlights on and near the parkway include Mt. Mitchell (the highest mountain peak east of the Rockies), Grandfather Mountain, and Mt. Pisgah. Nearly all the towns and cities along the parkway route offer accommodations, dining, and sightseeing. In particular, Boone, Blowing Rock, Burnsville, Asheville, Waynesville, Brevard, and Cherokee are all near popular entrances to the parkway.

VISITOR INFORMATION

FAMILY **Blue Ridge Parkway Visitor Center.** The main Blue Ridge Parkway Visitor Center, part of which has a "living roof" planted in grasses, is located near Asheville and near the Parkway headquarters. Unlike other Parkway visitor centers that are seasonal, this one is open year-round. The main attraction is a 22-foot interactive map of the entire Parkway. Information desk is staffed by rangers, and free maps and brochures are offered, along with books for sale. There's a 24-minute movie on the park. An easy-to-moderate 1.4-mile loop hiking trail begins at the center and connects with the 1,175-mile Mountains-to-the-Sea trail. ⊠ *Blue Ridge Pkwy., 195 Hemphill Knob Rd., MM 384, Metro South* ☎ *828/348–3400 main visitor center line, 828/298–0398 recorded information line with updated weather and closings.*

EXPLORING

TOP ATTRACTIONS

Craggy Gardens. Located at an elevation of 5,500 to 6,000 feet, Craggy Gardens has some of the Parkway's most colorful displays of rhododendrons, usually in June. You can also hike trails and picnic here. Craggy Pinnacle trail offers stunning 360-degree views. ⊠ *Blue Ridge Pkwy., MM 364* ☎ *828/298–0398 Parkway information line* ⊕ *www. nps.gov/blri* ☞ *Free.*

FAMILY
Fodor's Choice
★
Folk Art Center. As the headquarters of the prestigious Southern Highland Craft Guild, the Folk Art Center, located on the Blue Ridge Parkway near Asheville, regularly puts on exceptional quilt, woodworking, pottery, and other crafts shows and demonstrations. This is a top spot to purchase very high quality (and often expensive) crafts, including quilts, baskets, and pottery. ⊠ *Blue Ridge Pkwy., MM 382, East Metro* ☎ *828/298–7928* ⊕ *www.southernhighlandguild.org.*

FAMILY
Fodor's Choice
★
Grandfather Mountain. Soaring to almost 6,000 feet, Grandfather Mountain is just off the Blue Ridge Parkway at milepost 305. The state parks system owns 2,456 acres of Grandfather Mountain, and has conservation easements for 4,000 acres, but another part is privately owned and managed. Admission is charged for the private section, which is famous for its **Mile-High Swinging Bridge,** a 228-foot-long foot bridge that sways over a 1,000-foot drop into the Linville Valley. Winds as high as 121 mph have been recorded at the bridge. The **Natural History Museum** has exhibits on native minerals, flora and fauna, and pioneer life. There are 12 miles of hiking trails and some 100 picnic tables. The annual **Singing on the Mountain** (fourth Sunday in June) is an opportunity to hear old-time gospel music and preaching, and the **Highland Games** (second weekend in July) bring together Scottish clans from all over North America for athletic events and Highland dancing. ⊠ *Blue Ridge Pkwy. and U.S. Hwy. 221, Linville* ☎ *828/733–4337 private attraction, 828/963–9522 state park* ⊕ *www.grandfather.com* ☞ *$20 for Grandfather Mountain private park; state park admission free.*

FAMILY
Fodor's Choice
★
Mt. Mitchell State Park. This park—established in 1915 as North Carolina's first state park—includes the 6,684-foot Mt. Mitchell, the highest mountain peak east of the Rockies. The summit was named after Elisha Mitchell, a professor at UNC–Chapel Hill, who died from a fall while

trying to prove the mountain's true height. At the 1,946-acre park you can climb an observation tower and get food (May–October) at a restaurant there. You can drive to a parking area about 100 feet from the summit and hike the short distance to the summit. Keep an eye on the weather here, as high winds and snow can occur at almost any time, occasionally even in summer. Clouds obscure the views here for at least parts of 8 days out of 10. Keep an eye out for foraging black bears, which have been active in parts of the park. ⚠ **The park may close in winter due to ice and snow so call ahead if you plan to visit that time of year.** ✉ *2388 NC Hwy. 128, off MM 355 Blue Ridge Pkwy., Burnsville* ☎ *828/675–4611 state park, 828/675–1024 restaurant* ⊕ *www.ncparks. gov/Visit/parks/momi/main.php* 🎫 *Free.*

FAMILY
Fodor'sChoice
★

Mt. Pisgah. The 5,721-foot Mt. Pisgah is one of the most easily recognized peaks around Asheville due to the television tower installed there in the 1950s. It has walking trails, a picnic area, an amphitheater where nature programs are given most evenings June through October, and a campground, inn, restaurant, and small grocery a short distance away. The nearby area called **Graveyard Fields** is popular for blueberry picking in midsummer. Fairly easy hiking trails take you to waterfalls. ✉ *Blue Ridge Pkwy., MM 408.6* ☎ *828/271–4779 Parkway headquarters* ⊕ *www.nps. gov/blri* 🎫 *Free* ☾ *In winter may close due to ice and snow.*

WORTH NOTING

FAMILY
Julian Price Park. Green spaces along the Blue Ridge Parkway near Grandfather Mountain include this park, which has hiking, canoeing on a mountain lake, trout fishing, and camping. ✉ *Blue Ridge Pkwy., MM 295–298.1* ☎ *828/298–0398 Parkway information line* ⊕ *www. nps.gov/blri* 🎫 *Free.*

FAMILY
Linville Falls. A ½-mile hike from the visitor center leads to one of North Carolina's most-photographed waterfalls. The easy trail winds through evergreens and rhododendrons to overlooks with views of the series of cascades tumbling into Linville Gorge. There's also a campground and a picnic area. ✉ *Blue Ridge Pkwy., MM 316.3, Spruce Pine* ☎ *828/298– 0398 information line* ⊕ *www.nps.gov/blri* 🎫 *Free.*

FAMILY
Moses H. Cone Park. A turn-of-the-20th-century manor house here is now used for the **Blue Ridge Parkway Craft Center,** which sells fine work by area craftspeople. Here and at the adjoining Julian Price Park near Grandfather Mountain are some 100 picnic sites and the largest campground on the parkway. The park is also known for its cross-country skiing trails. ✉ *Blue Ridge Pkwy., MM 292.7–295* ☎ *828/295–7938 information line* ⊕ *www.nps.gov/blri* 🎫 *Free.*

WHERE TO STAY

$$
B&B/INN
FAMILY
Fodor'sChoice
★

🛏 **Pisgah Inn.** This inn, run by a park-service concessionaire, has motel-like rooms but in a spectacular setting, at 5,000 feet. **Pros:** on a mile-high mountaintop with incredible 30-mile views; rates are reasonable for location; good on-site restaurant. **Cons:** motel-like rooms; very remote setting; often fully booked months in advance. $ *Rooms from: $160* ✉ *Blue Ridge Pkwy., MM 408, Waynesville* ☎ *828/235–8228* ⊕ *www.pisgahinn.com* ☾ *Closed Nov.–Mar.* ⇥ *51 rooms* ❖ *Breakfast.*

BLACK MOUNTAIN

16 miles east of Asheville.

Black Mountain is a small town that has played a disproportionately large role in American cultural history because of the college located near there. For more than 20 years in the middle of the 20th century, from its founding in 1933 to its closing in 1957, Black Mountain College was one of the world's leading centers for experimental art, literature, architecture, and dance, with a list of faculty and students that reads like a *Who's Who* of American arts and letters.

On a different front, Black Mountain is also the home of evangelist Billy Graham. The Graham organization maintains a training center near Black Mountain, and there are several large church-related conference centers in the area, including Ridgecrest, Montreat, and Blue Ridge Assembly. Downtown Black Mountain is small and quaint, with a collection of little shops and several B&Bs.

EXPLORING

Fodor's Choice ★ **Black Mountain College.** Originally housed in rented quarters at nearby Blue Ridge Assembly, southeast of the town of Black Mountain, in 1941 Black Mountain College moved across the valley to its own campus at Lake Eden. Today the site is Camp Rockmont, a privately owned 550-acre summer camp for boys. The school's buildings were originally designed by the Bauhaus architects Walter Gropius and Marcel Breuer, but at the start of World War II the college turned to an American architect, Lawrence Kocher, and several intriguing buildings resulted, including one known as "The Ship," which still stands, with murals by Breuer. Black Mountain College attracted maverick spirits in art, music, and literature, including Willem and Elaine de Kooning, Robert Rauschenberg, Josef and Anni Albers, Buckminster Fuller, M. C. Richards, Merce Cunningham, John Cage, Kenneth Noland, Ben Shahn, Franz Kline, Arthur Penn, Charles Olson, Robert Creeley, and others. ■ **TIP→ During LEAF, a music and poetry festival held in mid-May and mid-October, you can visit and camp at the college. Other times of the year you can rent a cabin on the grounds for overnight stays.** Black Mountain College Museum + Arts Center is in downtown Asheville at 56 Broadway Street. ✉ *375 Lake Eden Rd.* ✣ *5 miles west of Black Mountain* ☎ *828/686–3885 Camp Rockmont, 828/350–8484 Black Mountain College Museum* 🌐 *www.blackmountaincollege.org.*

WHERE TO EAT

$ AMERICAN FAMILY 🍴 **Veranda Café.** With its gingham curtains and checkered tablecloths, this popular downtown café is very cozy, and the food is both unpretentious and tasty. The soups, which change daily, are the best thing on the menu, and the sandwiches are winners, too. **Known for:** homestyle soups and sandwiches. [$] *Average main: $9* ✉ *119 Cherry St.* ☎ *828/669–8864* 🌐 *www.verandacafeandgifts.com* ⏲ *Closed Sun.*

CLOSE UP

Authors of the North Carolina Mountains

They may not be able to go home again, but many famous writers have made their homes in the North Carolina mountains. The one most closely associated with the terrain is Thomas Wolfe (1900–38), author of *Look Homeward, Angel,* who was born and buried in Asheville. His contemporary F. Scott Fitzgerald visited Asheville and environs frequently in the 1930s, staying for long periods at the Grove Park Inn and at other hotels in the area. Fitzgerald's wife, Zelda, an author and artist in her own right, died in a 1948 fire at Highland Hospital, then a psychiatric facility in North Asheville.

William Sydney Porter, who under the pen name O. Henry wrote "The Ransom of Red Chief," "The Gift of the Magi," and many other stories, married into an Asheville-area family and is buried in Asheville at Riverside Cemetery. Carl Sandburg, the Pulitzer Prize–winning poet and biographer of Lincoln, spent the last 22 years of his life on a farm in Flat

Rock. A younger generation of poets, including Jonathan Williams, Robert Creeley, Robert Duncan, and Charles Olson, made names for themselves at Black Mountain College, an avant-garde hotbed for literature during the 1940s and early 1950s.

Novelist Charles Frazier, born in Asheville in 1950, made Cold Mountain, in the Shining Rock Wilderness of the Pisgah National Forest, the setting (and the title) for his best-selling Civil War drama. The mountain can be viewed from the Blue Ridge Parkway at mile marker 412. (The 2003 movie, however, was filmed in Romania.) Enka-Candler native Wayne Caldwell writes eloquently of the people of the Cataloochee section of what is now the Great Smokies in 2007's *Cataloochee* and 2009's *Requiem by Fire.* In several books, Canton native and former North Carolina poet laureate Fred Chappell paints powerful images of his hometown and its odoriferous paper mill.

HENDERSONVILLE

23 miles south of Asheville via I–26.

With about 14,000 residents, Hendersonville has one of the most engaging downtowns of any small city in the South. Historic Main Street, as it's called, extends over 10 winding blocks, lined with about 40 shops, including antiques stores, galleries, and restaurants. Each year from April through October, Main Street has displays of public art. Within walking distance of downtown are several B&Bs.

The Hendersonville area is North Carolina's main apple-growing area, and some 200 apple orchards dot the rolling hills around town. An apple festival, attracting some 200,000 people, is held each year in August. Whereas Asheville is liberal, progressive, and youthful in spirit and reputation, Hendersonville is predominantly a town of retirees and is considered conservative and as "American" as—yes—apple pie.

GETTING HERE AND AROUND

It is about 25 miles from Asheville to Hendersonville, via Interstate 26 East. From I–26, take Four Seasons Boulevard through the typical suburban mix of motels, strip malls, and fast-food restaurants to downtown Hendersonville. Main Street, where there's free parking, runs through the center of town.

WHERE TO EAT AND STAY

$ ✕**West First.** Wood-fired thin-crust pizza made from organic flour is the specialty here, and besides the more usual options, West First also serves unusual pies such as lamb, roasted salmon, and barbecue chicken. The main dining room, a large rectangle, is anchored at one end by the open oven blazing away, and on one side are two large, striking paintings of the owner's grandparents. **Known for:** wood-grilled pizza with unusual ingredients; often a wait; covered patio. Ⓢ *Average main: $12* ⊠ *101b 1st Ave.* W ☎ *828/693–1080* ⊕ *www. flatrockwoodfired.com* ☉ *Closed Sun.*

PIZZA
FAMILY
Fodor's Choice
★

$$$ ⛺ **1898 Waverly Inn.** On a warm afternoon you'll love to "sit a spell" in a rocking chair on the front porch of Hendersonville's oldest inn. **Pros:** historic building; walking distance to downtown; well run. **Cons:** lots of traffic; some rooms are on the small side. Ⓢ *Rooms from: $204* ⊠ *783 N. Main St.* ☎ *828/693–9193* ⊕ *www.waverlyinn.com* ↘ *15 rooms* ⏐◯⏐ *Breakfast.*

B&B/INN

$$ ⛺ **Pinebrook Manor.** The four "bedchambers" in this B&B are named after British Romantic poets—Wordsworth, Lord Byron, Alfred Lord Tennyson, and Elizabeth Barrett Browning—which should give you an idea of what to expect: cozy, charmingly decorated, and, yes, romantic lodging. **Pros:** elegant atmosphere; some rooms have four-poster king bed, whirlpool bath, and fireplace; hospitable hosts serve full breakfasts. **Cons:** not within walking distance of town. Ⓢ *Rooms from: $185* ⊠ *2701 Kanuga Rd.* ☎ *828/698–2707* ⊕ *www.pinebrookmanor. com* ↘ *4 rooms* ⏐◯⏐ *Breakfast.*

B&B/INN

FLAT ROCK

3 miles south of Hendersonville; 26 miles south of Asheville via I–26.

Flat Rock has been a summer resort since the early 19th century. It was a favorite of wealthy planters from Charleston eager to escape the Lowcountry heat. The trip from Charleston to Flat Rock by horse and carriage took as long as two weeks, so you know there must be something here that made the long trek worthwhile. Today, you can tour the home and farm where poet Carl Sandburg spent the last years of his life, take in some summer stock at the official state theater of North Carolina, or play a round of golf.

GETTING HERE AND AROUND

From Asheville, take Interstate 26 East 22 miles to Exit 53. Follow Upward Road about 2½ miles to Flat Rock.

A contestant at the Grandfather Mountain Highland Games throws a 22-pound hammer as part of the Scottish Heavy Athletics competition.

EXPLORING

FAMILY
Fodor's Choice
★

Carl Sandburg Home National Historic Site. "Connemara" is the farm to which the famed poet and Lincoln biographer moved with his wife, Lillian, in 1945; he lived there until his death in 1967. Guided tours of their 1830s house, where Sandburg's papers still are scattered on his desk as if he had just left, and 12,000 of his books are on bookshelves, are given by National Park Service rangers. Kids enjoy a walk around the 264 acres of the farm, which still maintains descendants of the Sandburg family goats. There are miles of trails. ✉ *81 Carl Sandburg Lane, or 1800 Little River Rd.* ☎ *828/693–4178* ⊕ *www.nps.gov/carl* ✉ *House tour $5, grounds free.*

FAMILY
Fodor's Choice
★

Flat Rock Playhouse. This theater, the official State Theater of North Carolina, is known for its high-quality productions, with sophisticated sets and professional actors. The productions are mostly well-known Broadway musicals and other classics. In a converted barnlike building, Flat Rock holds summer and fall college apprentice programs and classes for aspiring actors. The drama season, with about a dozen productions, runs from March to December. Flat Rock Playhouse also puts on plays at a second location in downtown Hendersonville at 125 South Main Street. Seat prices vary but range from $15 to $50. ✉ *2661 Greenville Hwy.* ☎ *828/693–0731* ⊕ *www.flatrockplayhouse.org* ✉ *Prices vary* ☉ *Closed Jan. and Feb.*

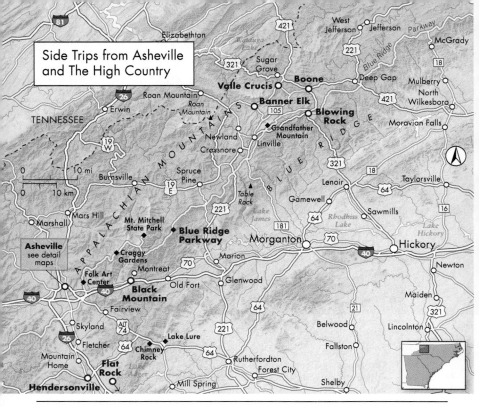

Side Trips from Asheville and The High Country

THE HIGH COUNTRY

Here you'll find the highest, steepest, coldest, snowiest, windiest, and, some say, friendliest parts of the mountains. The High Country, seven counties in the northwest part of the state—Alleghany, Ashe, Avery, Mitchell, Watauga, Wilkes, and Yancey—has not only some of the tallest mountains east of the Rockies, but the highest average elevation in all of eastern America. With temperatures 10 to 15 degrees cooler than in the foothills and flatlands, even folks from Asheville come to the High Country in the summer to cool down.

Unlike the rest of the mountains, winter is the peak season in much of the High Country. Towns like Boone, Blowing Rock, and Banner Elk have boomed in the 40 years since the introduction of snowmaking equipment, and the ski resorts of Beach Mountain, Seven Devils, Sugar Mountain, and Appalachian Ski Mountain attract skiers, snowboarders, and snow-tubers from all over the Southeast. The northern North Carolina portion of Blue Ridge Parkway also winds its way through the High Country. ⚠ Be advised, weather conditions and rock slides may cause temporary closures of sections of the Parkway. Always check the real-time closure map (www.nps.gov/blri/index.htm) before heading to the park.

BLOWING ROCK

86 miles northeast of Asheville; 93 miles west of Winston-Salem.

Blowing Rock, a draw for mountain visitors since the 1880s, has retained the flavor of a quiet New England village, with stone walls and buildings with wood shakes or bark siding. About 1,200 people are permanent residents of this town at a 4,000-foot elevation, but the population swells each summer. On summer afternoons it seems as if most of the town's population is sitting on benches in the town park. To ensure that the town would remain rural, large hotels and motels are prohibited. Blowing Rock is the inspiration for Mitford, the small town in resident writer Jan Karon's novels about country life.

GETTING HERE AND AROUND

To get here from the Blue Ridge Parkway, take U.S. 221/321 at mile marker 292 near Moses H. Cone Park. U.S. 321 makes a loop around the village of Blowing Rock.

EXPLORING

FAMILY **The Blowing Rock.** The Blowing Rock, after which the mountain town is named, is a cliff, which at 4,000 feet looms over the Johns River Gorge about 3,000 feet below. If you throw your hat over the sheer precipice, it may blow back to you, should the wind gods be playful. The story goes that a Cherokee man and a Chickasaw maiden fell in love. Torn between his tribe and his love, he jumped from the cliff, but she prayed to the Great Spirit, and he was blown safely back to her. ⊠ *432 Rock Rd., off U.S. Hwy. 321* ☎ *828/295-7111* ⊕ *www.theblowingrock.com* ⊠ *$7* ⊙ *Inclement weather may cause closures.*

WHERE TO EAT AND STAY

$$$$ ✕ **The Restaurant at Gideon Ridge.** Attached to the Gideon Ridge Inn, this
MODERN intimate 10-table restaurant is your top choice in Blowing Rock. It sticks
AMERICAN with dishes it carries off perfectly, such as strip steak, pork loin chop, or duck breast, but most are sourced from local suppliers, and what's on the menu on a given evening depends on what's available. **Known for:** best dinners in Blowing Rock. $ *Average main: $32* ⊠ *202 Gideon Ridge Rd.* ☎ *828/295-3644* ⊕ *www.gideonridge.com* ⊙ *Closed Sun. and Mon.*

$$$ ⊡ **Gideon Ridge Inn.** At Gideon Ridge Inn, you can take in long-range
B&B/INN views of the mountains from the gardens and stone terraces or relax with a book by the fire in the library or in your own room. **Pros:** beautiful mountaintop views; cozy rooms and suites, all with fireplaces. **Cons:** a few items could stand refurbishing. $ *Rooms from: $230* ⊠ *202 Gideon Ridge Rd.* ☎ *828/295-3644* ⊕ *www.gideonridge.com* ↬ *10 rooms* ⊙| *Breakfast.*

SPORTS AND THE OUTDOORS

RAFTING

FAMILY **High Mountain Expeditions.** This company organizes white-water rafting on the Nolichucky River, Watauga River, and Wilson Creek plus tubing on the New River. A half-day rafting trip on the Watauga River is $65. The company also does caving trips. There are additional locations in Asheville and Banner Elk. ⊠ *1380 Hwy. 105 S, Boone* ☎ *828/266-7238 Boone* ⊕ *www.highmountainexpeditions.com* ⊠ *From $65.*

DID YOU KNOW?

Linville Falls is a great spot to stop and stretch your legs when driving the Blue Ridge Parkway. The falls are a short hike away from the visitor center at mile marker 316.4.

SKIING

FAMILY **Appalachian Ski Mountain.** There's downhill skiing, snowboarding, and ice-skating at this resort, which has a dozen slopes and a half-dozen lifts. There are also cabin rentals and an RV park. ⊠ *940 Ski Mountain Rd.* ☎ *828/295–7828, 800/322–2373* ⊕ *www.appskimtn.com* ✉ *8-hr lift tickets $38 weekdays, $61 weekends.*

BOONE

8 miles north of Blowing Rock.

This college town is home to Appalachian State University and its 17,500 students. Suburban sprawl has arrived, especially along U.S. 321, with its clusters of fast-food restaurants, motels, and a small mall. Closer to ASU, however, you get more of the college-town vibe, with organic-food stores and boutiques. The town was named for frontiersman Daniel Boone, whose family moved to the area when Daniel was 15.

GETTING HERE AND AROUND

Boone, about 100 miles northeast of Asheville, is at the convergence of three major highways—U.S. 321, U.S. 421, and Route 105. From Asheville, take Interstate 40 East to U.S. 64. Follow U.S. 64 to U.S. 321, which leads into Boone.

WHERE TO EAT AND STAY

$$ ✕ **Dan'l Boone Inn.** Near Appalachian State University, in a former hospital surrounded by a picket fence and flowers, Dan'l Boone serves old-fashioned Southern food family style. You can have any or all of the items on the menu, and seconds and thirds if you want them, for the same price—and the portions of fried chicken, country-style steak, ham biscuits, mashed potatoes, and green beans (to name a few) are generous. **Known for:** Southern favorites served family style. $ *Average main: $18* ⊠ *130 Hardin St.* ☎ *828/264–8657* ⊕ *www.danlbooneinn. com* ▬ *No credit cards* ☾ *No breakfast weekdays. No lunch weekdays Jan.–late May* ⚭ *No reservations except for groups of 15-plus; cash or check only.*

SOUTHERN
FAMILY

$$ ✕ **Vidalia.** Named for Georgia's famous sweet onion, this small bistro in the middle of town brings creative regional American cooking to the High Country. The food, much of it from local organic farms, is standout good—for dinner, try the chicken and sweet-potato dumplings, oat-breaded mountain trout, or grilled meat loaf, with, of course, Vidalia onion rings. **Known for:** locally sourced Southern dishes, usually with a creative twist. $ *Average main: $20* ⊠ *831-35 W. King St., across from Watauga Courthouse* ☎ *828/263–9176* ⊕ *www.vidaliaofboonenc. com* ☾ *Closed Mon.*

SOUTHERN
FodorsChoice
★

$$ ⛫ **Lovill House Inn.** Built in 1875 and featuring unusual details such as wormy chestnut woodwork, this two-story restored country farmhouse, the best B&B in the area, occupies 11 wooded acres in a quiet area west of downtown. **Pros:** charming rooms; delicious breakfasts. **Cons:** a bit of a walk into Boone or to App State. $ *Rooms from: $179* ⊠ *404 Old Bristol Rd.* ☎ *828/264–4204, 800/849–9466* ⊕ *www.lovillhouseinn. com* ⚭ *5 rooms, 1 cottage* ⦿⦿ *Breakfast.*

B&B/INN

PERFORMING ARTS

FAMILY **Horn in the West.** A project of the Southern Appalachian Historical Association, *Horn in the West* is an outdoor drama by Kermit Hunter that traces the story of Daniel Boone and other pioneers, as well as the Cherokee, during the American Revolution. The drama has been presented since 1952. Performances are held nightly, Tuesday through Sunday from late June–mid-August. ✉ *Amphitheater, 591 Horn in the West Dr., off U.S. 321* ☎ *828/264–2120* 🌐 *www.horninthewest.com* 🎟 *$24.*

SPORTS AND THE OUTDOORS

CANOEING AND RAFTING

Near Boone and Blowing Rock, the New River, a federally designated Wild and Scenic River (Class I and II rapids) provides excitement for canoeists and rafters, as do the Watauga and Toe rivers and Wilson Creek.

Wahoo's Adventures. This long-established outfitter offers rafting, kayaking, canoeing, stand-up paddleboarding, and tubing on several rivers in Western North Carolina (including the Nolichucky, Watauga, and New rivers), and Class V "extreme rafting" trips on Wilson Creek. Tubing on the New River is the most popular activity. Most activities are available April through October. ✉ *3385 S. U.S. 321* ☎ *828/262–5774, 800/444–7238* 🌐 *www.wahoosadventures.com* 🎟 *From $25.*

GOLF

FAMILY **Sugar Mountain Golf Course.** Designed by Francis Duane, this short par-64 "people's course" sits at a 4,000-foot elevation. Tennis and cottage rentals are also available. ✉ *1054 Sugar Mountain Dr., Sugar Mountain* ☎ *828/898–6464* 🌐 *www.seesugar.com* ⛳ *18 holes, 4560 yds, par 64. Green Fee: $42 weekday/$42 weekend including cart. Facilities: Putting green, pitching area, golf carts, pull carts, rental clubs, pro shop, restaurant* 🕒 *Golf and tennis closed Nov.–Mar.*

VALLE CRUCIS

5 miles west of Boone.

This tiny mountain town has the state's first rural historic district; vintage stores line the downtown streets.

WHERE TO EAT AND STAY

$$ SOUTHERN FAMILY 🍴 **Over Yonder.** Founded by the former chef of Simplicity restaurant at Mast Farm Inn—the two businesses still have a friendly, reciprocal relationship—Over Yonder serves an updated style of Appalachian food, with dishes such as potlikker gumbo and panfried rainbow trout with almonds. Over Yonder is in a charming 1861 farmhouse near the Mast Farm Inn. **Known for:** updated, delicious versions of Appalachian food; 1861 farmhouse. [$] *Average main: $18* ✉ *Valle Crucis, 3608 NC Hwy. 194, Sugar Grove* ☎ *828/963–6301* 🕒 *Closed Tues. and closed Mon. Dec.–Mar.*

$$$ 🛏 **Mast Farm Inn.** You can turn back the clock and still enjoy modern
B&B/INN amenities at this charming and pastoral inn, built in the 1800s and now
FAMILY on the National Register of Historic Places. **Pros:** delightful and historic
Fodor's Choice country inn; personalized service; discounts for teachers. **Cons:** a little
★ off the beaten path; restaurant now only serves breakfast. $ *Rooms
from: $209* ✉ *2543 Broadstone Rd., Banner Elk* 🕾 *828/963–5857*
⊕ *www.themastfarminn.com* ↙ *7 rooms, 8 cottages* ❍❙ *Breakfast.*

SHOPPING

Gallery Alta Vista. If you're looking for a mountain painting, stop by
Gallery Alta Vista, about 10 minutes from Boone. It features the work
of more than 100 artists, many from Western North Carolina. ✉ *2839
Broadstone Rd., Banner Elk* 🕾 *828/963–5247* ⊕ *www.altavistagallery.com.*

Mast General Store. This is the original Mast General Store, first called
The Taylor General Store. Built in 1882–83, the store has plank floors
worn to a soft sheen and an active, old-timey post office. Everything
from ribbons and overalls to yard art and cookware is sold here. You
can take a shopping break by sipping bottled "dope" (mountain talk
for a soda pop) while sitting in a rocking chair on the store's back
porch. For more shopping, an annex is just down the road. Under the
modern ownership of John and Faye Cooper since 1979, Mast General
Store has expanded to nine locations, including ones in Boone,
Asheville, Hendersonville, Winston-Salem, and Waynesville, but as
the first, this one still has the most authentic atmosphere. ✉ *3567 NC
Hwy. 194, Sugar Grove* 🕾 *828/963–6511, 866/367–6278* ⊕ *www.
mastgeneralstore.com.*

BANNER ELK

6 miles southwest of Valle Crucis; 11 miles southwest of Boone.

Surrounded by the lofty peaks of Grandfather, Hanging Rock, Beech,
and Sugar mountains, this ski resort bills itself as the "highest town in
the East." The massively ugly condo tower you'll see on top of Little
Sugar Mountain (not a part of the Sugar Mountain ski resort) is the
only scar on the scenic beauty of the area. At least something good came
of the monstrosity—it so outraged local residents that it prompted the
passing of a ridgeline law preventing future mountaintop development.

SPORTS AND THE OUTDOORS

SKIING

FAMILY **Beech Mountain Resort.** At about 5,500 feet above sea level, Beech Mountain Resort is the highest ski area in the eastern United States. Beech
also offers snowboarding, tubing, and ice-skating. There are a total of
15 ski trails and eight lifts. In warm weather (Memorial Day to Labor
Day), the resort switches to mountain biking and yoga. Beech Mountain
Resort even has a craft brewery. Chalet rentals are available year-round.
✉ *1007 Beech Mountain Pkwy., Beech Mountain* 🕾 *828/387–2011,
800/438–2093* ⊕ *www.beechmountainresort.com* ▤ *Full-day lift/slopes
tickets: $50 weekdays, $77 weekends.*

DID YOU KNOW?

The Blue Ridge Parkway has more than 200 overlooks with breathtaking vistas of the Blue Ridge Mountains, old farmsteads, meadows, and valleys. Be sure to stop and smell the wildflowers as you make your way along America's favorite drive.

Sugar Mountain Resort. One of the larger ski resorts in the High Country, with 17 trails and eight lifts, Sugar Mountain has an equipment shop and lessons, along with snowboarding, tubing, and ice-skating. In warm weather, Sugar also offers rides on the ski lifts, tennis on six clay courts, and an 18-hole, par-64 municipal golf course designed by Frank Duane, open April through October. Vacation rentals are offered year-round. ⊠ *1009 Sugar Mountain Dr., off NC Rte. 184* ☎ *828/898–4521, 800/784–2768, 828/898–6464 golf information and reservations* ⊕ *www.skisugar.com* ✍ *Full-day slope/lift tickets are $43 Mon.–Sat., $72 Sun.; lower rates in Mar.* ⅄ *Par-64, 4,126-yard 18-hole course with pro shop, golf lessons, club rentals; $34 Mar.–late May and mid-Sept.–Oct., $44 late May–mid-Sept.; rates include carts.*

SNOWTUBING

FAMILY **Hawksnest Snow Tubing.** You can no longer ski here but you can try snow tubing on any of 30 tubing lanes at what is claimed to be the largest snow-tubing resort in the East. In either snow or summer heat, Hawksnest also offers ziplining with 20 ziplines that total 4 miles in length. ⊠ *2058 Skyland Dr., Seven Devils* ☎ *828/963–6561, 800/822–4295* ⊕ *www.hawksnesttubing.com* ✍ *$27 per snow-tubing session weekdays, $34 weekends; ziplining $45–$90.*

SHOPPING

FAMILY **Fred's General Mercantile.** For hardware, firewood, a quart of milk, locally grown vegetables, deli sandwiches, pumpkins for Halloween, snowboard and ski rentals, gourmet birdseed, and just about anything else you need, Fred's General Mercantile, half general store and half boutique, is the place to go and has been since 1979, when it was the first store to open at Beech Mountain. ⊠ *501 Beech Mountain Pkwy.* ☎ *828/387–4838* ⊕ *www.fredsgeneral.com.*

THE SOUTHERN MOUNTAINS

The Southern Mountains cover nine North Carolina counties south and west of Asheville. They include Brevard in Transylvania County and also Cashiers, Highlands, and Lake Toxaway, chic summer enclaves where some building lots cost a million dollars.

BREVARD

40 miles southwest of Asheville on Rte. 280.

This small town in the Pisgah National Forest has a friendly, highly walkable downtown. In summer, more than 400 talented music students from around the country attend the music school at the Brevard Music Center, and the Brevard Music Festival features some 80 classical music concerts, some with such noted visiting artists as cellist Yo-Yo Ma, violinists Joshua Bell and Midori, and pianists André Watts and Emanuel Ax.

Brevard residents go nuts over the white squirrels, which dart around the town's parks and the campus of Brevard College. These aren't albinos, but a variation of the eastern gray squirrel. About a quarter of the squirrels in town are white. The white squirrels are thought to have come

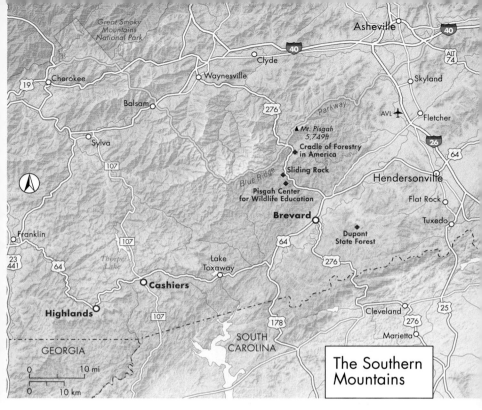

The Southern Mountains

originally from Hawaii by way of Florida; they possibly were released in Brevard by a visitor in the 1950s. Whatever the truth, today Brevard capitalizes on it by holding a White Squirrel Festival in late May.

GETTING HERE AND AROUND

You can reach Brevard via U.S. 64 from Hendersonville, or from the U.S. 276 exit of the Blue Ridge Parkway. North Broad Street and Main Street are the two primary thoroughfares through Brevard. Brevard Music Center is less than a mile west of town—look for directional signs.

EXPLORING

TOP ATTRACTIONS

FAMILY
Fodor'sChoice
★

Cradle of Forestry in America. The home of the first forestry school in the United States is on 6,500 acres in the Pisgah National Forest. Started in 1898 by Carl Schenck, who came here to work for the Biltmore Estate, the school trained some 300 foresters. Here you can visit the school's original log buildings, a restored 1915 steam locomotive, a 1-mile interpretive trail, and a visitor center with many hands-on exhibits of interest to kids and adults. The road from Brevard to the Cradle of Forestry, a scenic byway, continues on to connect with the Blue Ridge Parkway near Mt. Pisgah. ✉ *11250 Pisgah Hwy., off U.S. Hwy. 276 near Brevard, 11 miles from intersection of U.S. 280 and U.S. 276, Pisgah Forest* ☎ *828/877–3130* ⊕ *www. cradleofforestry.com* ✉ *$5, free Tues.* ☉ *Closed early Nov.–mid-Apr.*

FAMILY   **DuPont State Forest.** Between Hendersonville and Brevard you'll find this 11,000-acre North Carolina State Forest with six waterfalls and 80 miles of old dirt roads to explore. It's ideal for biking, hiking, or horseback riding. Fishing and hunting are permitted in-season. ⊠ *U.S. 64 and Little River Rd., Cedar Mountain ✛ From Asheville, take I–26 East to Asheville Airport (Exit 40). Go south on NC 280 for about 16 miles. Turn left on U.S.64 (heading east) for 4 miles. In Penrose, turn right on Crab Creek Rd. for 4 miles to DuPont Rd. Turn right on DuPont Rd. and go 3.1 mile* ☎ *828/877–6527* ⊕ *www. ncforestservice.gov* ⌦ *Free.*

FAMILY   **Pisgah Center for Wildlife Education.** This fish hatchery operated by the state's Department of Wildlife Resources produces more than 400,000 brown, rainbow, and native brook trout each year for release in local streams. You can see the fish up close in 54 large tanks called raceways that channel 3,500 gallons of cold mountain water per minute. There's also a visitor center with information about the life cycle of trout and an educational nature trail. The Davidson River, which runs by the hatchery, is popular for fly-fishing. ⊠ *1401 Fish Hatchery Rd., off U.S. Hwy. 276, Pisgah Forest* ☎ *828/877–4423* ⊕ *www.ncwildlife. org/Learning/EducationCenters/pisgah.aspx* ⌦ *Free* ☉ *Closed Sun. Apr.–Nov.; closed weekends Dec.–Mar.*

FAMILY   **Sliding Rock.** Skid on your tush 60 feet on a natural rock waterslide,
Fodor's Choice   fueled by 11,000 gallons of mountain water a minute, into a clear, cold
★   pool. The pool is 6 to 8 feet deep, so you need to know how to swim. Wear old jeans and tennis shoes and bring a towel. Lifeguards are on duty daily 10–6 from Memorial Day to Labor Day (also usually on weekends September and October); you can slide at other times, but it's at your own risk and changing rooms are closed. On warm summer days the parking area (parking fee $2) is often very crowded. No picnicking is allowed at the Rock, but there are grounds nearby. ⊠ *U.S. 276, Pisgah Forest ✛ About 8 miles north of intersection of Hwys. 280 and 276 in Brevard* ☎ *828/877–3350 National Forest Service, 828/257–4200 National Forest Service office in Asheville* ⊕ *www. fs.usda.gov* ⌦ *Free, $2 parking fee* ☉ *No lifeguard or changing rooms late Oct.–late May.*

WORTH NOTING

FAMILY   **Looking Glass Falls.** Getting to this waterfall is easy, as it's right beside the road in Pisgah National Forest, though parking is limited. Water cascades 60 feet into a clear pool, where you can wade and swim. There's a parking area and a walkway down to the falls. ⚠ **Caution! Rocks around waterfalls are extremely slick.** ⊠ *U.S. Hwy. 276, 6 miles north of Brevard, Pisgah Forest* ☎ *828/877–3265 Pisgah Ranger District, National Forest Service* ⌦ *Free.*

Oskar Blues Brewery. This Colorado-based craft-beer brewer with national distribution, best known for its Dale's Pale Ale, offers brewery tours and tastings at its East Coast headquarters in Brevard (Oskar Blues also has a brewery in Austin, Texas). The Tasty Weasel taproom is open daily with free tours of the brewery, food trucks are on-site for grub, and many evenings there's live music.

The owner, a mountain-biking fan, has purchased a tract of land near the brewery for a planned bike park and a farm. ✉ *342 Mountain Industrial Dr.* ☎ *828/883–2337* ⊕ *www.oskarblues.com/brewery/ brevard* 🖃 *Brewery tours free.*

WHERE TO EAT AND STAY

$$$
SEAFOOD
FAMILY

✕ **The Falls Landing Eatery.** The hands-on owner has made this storefront eatery in downtown Brevard probably the most recommended dining spot in town. The menu skews to seafood (the owner moved here from the U.S. Virgin Islands), with standouts including fish-and-chips, clam chowder, mountain trout, and

MOUNTAIN BIKING

The North Carolina Mountains offer some of the best mountain biking in the East. Among the favorite places for mountain biking are **Tsali**, a peninsula sticking out into Lake Fontana near Bruston City, in the Nantahala National Forest *(see Great Smokies chapter)*; **Dupont State Forest**, just south of Brevard; and the **Bent Creek, Davidson River**, and **Mills River** sections of the Pisgah Ranger District of the National Forest.

blackened mahimahi, but lamb chops and filet mignon are good, too. **Known for:** standout seafood dishes; friendly service. $ *Average main: $23* ✉ *18 E. Main St.* ☎ *828/884–2835* ⊕ *www.thefallslanding.com* ⊘ *Closed Sun.*

$
HOT DOG
FAMILY

✕ **Rocky's Grill & Soda Shop.** This somewhat touristy but fun version of an old-fashioned soda shop—an institution in Brevard since 1943—appeals to kids for its ice-cream creations, like milk shakes, floats, and sundaes. The burgers, hot dogs, and sandwiches are all tasty. **Known for:** ice-cream cones, shakes, and floats; 1940s soda-shop atmosphere. $ *Average main: $8* ✉ *50 S. Broad St.* ☎ *828/877–5375* ⊕ *ddbullwinkels.com/Rockys* ⊘ *No dinner.*

$$
B&B/INN

🛏 **Red House Inn.** One of the oldest houses in Brevard, the Red House Inn was built in 1851 as a trading post and later served as a courthouse, tavern, post office, and school. **Pros:** B&B in historic house; in the center of town; friendly hosts. **Cons:** not for swinging singles; advance reservations important. $ *Rooms from: $160* ✉ *266 W. Probart St.* ☎ *828/884–9349* ⊕ *www.brevardbedandbreakfast.com* ⥲ *4 rooms, 1 cottage, 6 rental houses* ⦿ *Breakfast.*

PERFORMING ARTS

FAMILY
Fodor's Choice
★

Brevard Music Festival. Some 400 talented young music students from nearly every U.S. state and 60 faculty from around the world spend summers at the 180-acre Brevard Music Center. Each year, from mid-June to early August, the Center hosts about 80 public orchestral and chamber music concerts and operas featuring guest performers such as violinist Itzhak Perlman and pianist Garrick Ohlsson. Boston Pops conductor Keith Lockhart is the festival's artistic director. ✉ *349 Andante La.* ☎ *828/862–2100* ⊕ *www.brevardmusic.org* 🖃 *Concert prices vary; some are free.*

For a thrilling ride through Class III and IV rapids, take a guided rafting trip on the Nantahala River.

SPORTS AND THE OUTDOORS

FAMILY **Davidson River Outfitters.** Catch rainbow, brown, or brook trout on the Davidson River, named one of the top 100 trout streams in the United States by Trout Unlimited. Davidson River Outfitters and its 15 guides arrange trips in the Pisgah and Nantahala National Forests and elsewhere, including private trout streams. It also has a fly-fishing school and a fly shop. A full-day guided fly-fishing trip (wading) for two is around $375. ✉ *95 Pisgah Hwy., Pisgah Forest* ☎ *828/877–4181* ⊕ *www.davidsonflyfishing.com* ✐ *Half-day guided trout-fishing trips from $200* ☉ *Closed Sun. Jan.–Feb.*

CASHIERS

63 miles southwest of Asheville via U.S. 74 and NC 107; 14 miles west of Lake Toxaway.

Cashiers (pronounced CASH-ers) is not a quite a town. Until recently, it was just a crossroads, with a store or two, a summer getaway for wealthy South Carolinians escaping the heat. But after the building of many exclusive gated developments, the Cashiers area, at a cool 3,500-foot elevation, now has several new restaurants and stores.

GETTING HERE AND AROUND

From Asheville, take Route 280 to U.S. 64 to get to Cashiers. Everything in Cashiers is within a mile or two of the intersection of Route 107 and U.S. 64.

WHERE TO EAT AND STAY

$$$$
AMERICAN
FAMILY

✕ **Cornucopia.** In the second-oldest building in Cashiers, built in 1892, you can sit on the huge, airy, covered back porch with a metal roof and eat some of the best sandwiches in the area at lunch. Try Cornucopia's most famous sandwich, the Arabian club with turkey and bacon on pita bread, or one of the four burgers. **Known for:** Arabian club sandwich and burgers at lunch; popular with the lunch crowd. $ *Average main: $27* ✉ *16 Cashiers School Rd.* ☎ *828/743–3750* ⊕ *www.cornucopianc. com* ⊙ *Closed Dec.–mid-Mar., closed mid-Mar.–mid-May for dinner.*

$$$$
SOUTHERN
Fodor's Choice
★

✕ **The Orchard.** Located in a century-old farmhouse in an old apple orchard, The Orchard is the best restaurant in Cashiers, putting a Southern twist on traditional American dishes. The decor is comfortable rather than fancy, with a few kitschy Southern touches such as an old Mail Pouch chewing tobacco sign and a Jeep permanently parked out front. **Known for:** catering to upscale visitors and second-home owners; consistently good food; mountain trout. $ *Average main: $28* ✉ *905 Hwy. 107 S* ☎ *828/743–7614* ⊕ *www.theorchardcashiers.com.*

$$$$
RESORT
FAMILY
Fodor's Choice
★

🏨 **High Hampton Inn & Country Club.** With its rustic rooms and cottages, the High Hampton Inn (listed on the National Register of Historic Places) feels unplugged and family-oriented. **Pros:** historic property that's full of tradition. **Cons:** old-fashioned and eccentric; no TVs in rooms; some rooms are small and some need updating. $ *Rooms from: $360* ✉ *1525 NC 107 S* ☎ *828/743–2411, 800/334–2551* ⊕ *www.high-hamptoninn.com* ⊙ *Closed mid-Nov.–late Apr.* ⇱ *116 rooms, 17 cottages, 36 rental homes* ❍ *All meals.*

4

HIGHLANDS

85 miles southwest of Asheville; 11 miles southwest of Cashiers on U.S. 64.

Highlands is a tony town of only 900 people, but the surrounding area swells to 10,000 or more in summer and fall, when those with summer homes here flock back, like wealthy swallows of Capistrano. At 4,118 feet it is usually cool and pleasant when even Asheville gets hot. The five-block downtown is lined with upscale shops, antiques stores, restaurants, and coffeehouses, and there's a sniff of West Palm Beach in the air.

GETTING HERE AND AROUND

From Asheville, you can get to Highlands by two routes. One is via Interstate 40 West, U.S. 23/74 and 441 to Franklin, then Route 28 and U.S. 64 to Highlands. Alternatively, you can drive Route 280 to U.S. 64.

EXPLORING

Cullasaja Gorge. West of Highlands via U.S. 64 toward Franklin, the Cullasaja Gorge (Cul-lah-SAY-jah) is a 7½-mile gorge passing the Cullasaja River, Lake Sequoyah, and several waterfalls, including **Bridal Veil Falls, Dry Falls, Quarry Falls,** and the 200-foot **Cullasaja Falls.** The gorge and falls are in the Nantahala National Forest. ■**TIP**→ **Rocks around waterfalls are slippery, and it is dangerous to try to cross the top of the falls.** ✉ *U.S. 64* ✛ *From Highlands follow U.S. 64W/28N to Franklin* ☎ *828/524–6441 Nantahala Ranger Station, Nantahala National Forest* ⊕ *www.fs.usda.gov/recarea/nfsnc* 🎟 *Free.*

WHERE TO EAT AND STAY

$$$$
ITALIAN
Fodor's Choice
★

✕ **Ristorante Paoletti.** A fixture on Main Street for more than three decades, Ristorante Paoletti serves sophisticated Italian cuisine with first-rate service, although this comes at a price. The menu includes a lengthy section of freshly made pastas, along with many excellent seafood dishes. **Known for:** extensive wine list; upscale Italian food; longtime favorite with many repeat guests. $ *Average main: $38* ✉ *440 Main St.* ☎ *828/526–4906* ⊕ *www.paolettis.com.*

$$$$
ECLECTIC

✕ **Wolfgang's Restaurant & Wine Bistro.** Cheerful and unpretentious, though not inexpensive, Wolfgang's has an eclectic menu ranging from a Wiener schnitzel to venison *au poivre* to Cajun shrimp and grits. Several of the rooms have fireplaces, and in good weather there's outdoor seating. **Known for:** quaint bistro atmosphere; eclectic menu. $ *Average main: $28* ✉ *474 Main St.* ☎ *828/526–3807* ⊕ *www.wolfgangs.net* ☉ *Closed most of Dec.–Feb.*

$$$$
B&B/INN
Fodor's Choice
★

⌶ **Old Edwards Inn and Spa.** Service at this posh inn is first-rate, starting with the complimentary champagne in the lobby and extending to elegantly furnished guest rooms in the main building with period antiques and European linens and more rustic but still luxurious accommodations in the Lodge. **Pros:** deluxe inn with lots of amenities and options; central location in middle of town; top-notch spa. **Cons:** very pricey; often booked months in advance. $ *Rooms from: $450* ✉ *445 Main St.* ☎ *828/526–8008, 866/526–8008 reservations* ⊕ *www.oldedwardsinn. com* ⌷ *43 rooms, 19 suites, 15 cottages, 3 houses* ⌶○⌶ *No meals.*

PERFORMING ARTS

Highlands Playhouse. The well-respected Highlands Playhouse, an Equity theater, puts on four productions each summer. It also doubles as a movie theater, with new and classic films screened year-round. ✉ *362 Oak St.* ☎ *828/526–2695* ⊕ *www.highlandsplayhouse.org.*

SHOPPING

Scudder's Galleries. This high-end antiques dealer and estate liquidator, established in 1925, holds auctions Friday and Saturday nights at 8 pm between mid-June and November. The auctions are entertaining to see, even if you don't plan on buying anything. ✉ *352 Main St.* ☎ *828/526–4111* ⊕ *www.scuddersgallery.com* ☉ *No auctions Dec.– May; shop closed Sun.*

GREAT SMOKY MOUNTAINS NATIONAL PARK

WELCOME TO GREAT SMOKY MOUNTAINS NATIONAL PARK

TOP REASONS TO GO

★ **Witness the wilderness:** This is one of the last remaining big chunks of wilderness in the East. Get away from civilization in more than 800 square miles of tranquility, with old-growth forests, clear streams, meandering trails, wildflowers, and panoramic vistas from mile-high mountains.

★ **Get your endorphins going:** Outdoor junkies can bike, boat, camp, fish, hike, ride horses, white-water raft, watch birds and wildlife, and even cross-country ski.

★ **Experience mountain culture:** Visit restored mountain cabins and tour "ghost towns" in the park, with old frame and log buildings preserved much as they were 100 years ago.

★ **Spot wildlife:** Biologists estimate there are more than 1,500 bears, 6,000 deer, and more than 150 elk now in the park, so your chances of seeing these beautiful wild creatures are quite good.

1 **North Carolina Side.** The North Carolina (or eastern) side of the park boasts the highest mountain in the park—Clingmans Dome—as well as the historic Cataloochee Valley, many scenic overlooks, and great hiking opportunities. It also connects to the famed Blue Ridge Parkway near Cherokee.

2 **Tennessee Side.** The Tennessee (or western) side of the park offers scenic drives to historic parts of the park such as Cades Cove, fun activities like river tubing, excellent hiking, and the only overnight lodge accommodations in the park, Mt. LeConte.

3 Nearby North Carolina Towns. Sometimes called "the quiet side of the park," the North Carolina side of the Smokies is edged with a collection of small, low-key towns. The most appealing of these are Bryson City and Waynesville. Except for these towns, and the city of Asheville about 50 miles east, most of the area around the east side of the park consists of national forest lands and rural areas. On the southwestern boundary of the park is Lake Fontana, the largest lake in Western North Carolina.

GETTING ORIENTED

The Great Smoky Mountains National Park straddles parts of two states, North Carolina and Tennessee. The park headquarters is in Gatlinburg, Tennessee, and many people think of the Smokies as being a Tennessee national park. In fact, slightly more of the park is on the eastern, or North Carolina, side than on the Tennessee side— 276,000 acres to 245,000 acres. The dividing line is at Newfound Gap. Once inside the park, you may not be aware of which state you're in except for practical considerations of geography and the time it takes to get from point to point.

5

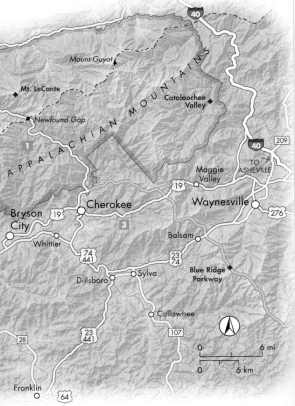

Updated by
Lan Sluder

Great Smoky Mountains National Park is one of the great wild areas of the eastern United States and the most visited national park in the United States. From a roadside lookout or from a clearing in a trail, in every visible direction you can see the mountains march toward a vast horizon of wilderness.

Some of the tallest mountains in the East are here, including 16 peaks over 6,000 feet. The highest in the park, Clingmans Dome, was reputedly the original inspiration for the folk song "On Top of Old Smoky." It rises 6,643 feet above sea level and 4,503 feet above the valley floor. These are also some of the oldest mountains in the world, far older than the Rockies, the Alps, or the Andes. Geologists say the building of what are now the Great Smokies began about a billion years ago.

Today, the park hosts around 11 million visitors each year, more than twice as many as the second-most-visited national park, the Grand Canyon. Even so, with more than 814 square miles of protected land, if you get out of your car you can soon be in a remote cove where your closest neighbors are deer, bobcats, and black bears.

Due to a fortuitous combination of moderate climate and diverse geography, Great Smoky Mountains National Park is one of the most biologically rich spots on Earth. Bears are the most famous animal in the park, but elk are also making the Smokies their home for the first time in 150 years. The Park Service also attempted to reintroduce red wolves to the park, but due to high pup mortality the effort was discontinued in the late 1990s; however, visitors occasionally report seeing what they believe is a wolf. But it is not just large mammals that make it special. The Smokies have been called the "salamander capital of the world," with at least 30 different salamander species. It is also one of the few places on Earth where, for a few evenings in June, you can see synchronous fireflies flashing in perfect unison.

The park offers extraordinary opportunities for other outdoor activities: it has world-class hiking, on more than 850 miles of trails, ranging from easy half-hour nature walks to weeklong backpacking treks. Although backcountry hiking has its wonders, some of the most interesting sights in the park can be seen from the comfort of your car or motorcycle. You can explore old farms and mountain homesteads, or watch cornmeal ground at a working gristmill.

⚠ In November 2016, a fire raged over 11,000 acres of the western (Tennessee) side of the park, particularly in the Chimney Tops area, and swept into developed parts of Gatlinburg and Pigeon Forge, causing the deaths of 14 people and destroying about 2,700 homes and other buildings. While the main tourism areas of Gatlinburg and Pigeon Forge were not damaged, some trails, picnic grounds, and other facilities in the park currently remain closed. While all or nearly all park facilities, except in the Chimney Tops area, are expected to be back to normal operations soon, it's always best to check ahead before you go.

PLANNING

WHEN TO GO

There's not a bad time to visit the Smokies, though summer and the month of October are the most popular times. The biggest month for visitation in the park is July, followed by June, and then October, which is peak fall-color season. Weekends in October are especially crowded, and you should expect traffic delays on U.S. 441 and traffic jams in Cades Cove. Beat the crowds by coming on weekdays and also early in the day, before 10 am. Mid-to-late spring is a wonderful time to visit the park, as wildflowers are in bloom, and it's before the heat, humidity, and crowds of summer. Winter in the park can be beautiful, especially when there's snow on the ground or rime frost on the tree limbs. The air is usually clearer in winter, with less haze, and with leaves off the trees the visibility is excellent. Some park roads, including Clingmans Dome Road, are closed in winter due to ice and snow.

GETTING HERE AND AROUND

Although there are numerous entrances to the North Carolina side of the park, the main entrance is via U.S. 441 near Cherokee and the Oconaluftee Visitor Center.

Another, and much more pleasant (but slower), route to the Smokies is the Blue Ridge Parkway, which has its southern terminus at Cherokee. *For more information on the Blue Ridge Parkway, see Chapter 4: Asheville and the North Carolina Mountains.*

You can enter the park by car at nine different places on the Tennessee side. Most of these entrances take you just a short distance into the park to a developed campground or picnic area. The two major entrances to the park on the western side are from Gatlinburg and Townsend.

AIR TRAVEL

The closest airport on the North Carolina side with national air service is Asheville Regional Airport (AVL), about 60 miles east of the Cherokee entrance. On the Tennessee side, the closest major airport is Knoxville McGhee Tyson Airport (TYS), about 45 miles west of the Sugarlands entrance.

Airport Information **Asheville Regional Airport** (*AVL*). ⊠ *61 Terminal Dr.,
off I-26, Fletcher* ⊕ *www.flyavl.com.* **Knoxville McGhee Tyson Airport** (*TYS*).
⊠ *2025 Alcoa Hwy., Alcoa* ☎ *865/342–3000* ⊕ *www.tys.org.*

CAR TRAVEL

The nearest sizable city to the park in North Carolina is Asheville.
This hip, liberal-minded city is about 50 miles east of Cherokee and
the Oconaluftee Visitor Center. It takes a little more than an hour to
get from Asheville to the Cherokee entrance of the park, via Interstate
40 and U.S. highways 19 and 441. If you aren't pressed for time,
however, we advise traveling via the Blue Ridge Parkway—it takes
longer, but the trip is beautiful.

The closest sizable city to the park in Tennessee is Knoxville, about 40
miles west of the Sugarlands entrance, via U.S. 441.

Coming either from the east or west, Interstate 40 is the main interstate
access route to the Great Smokies; from the north and south, Interstate
75, Interstate 81, and Interstate 26 are primary arteries.

U.S. 441, also called Newfound Gap Road, is the main road through
the park, and the only paved road that goes all the way through. It
travels 31 miles between Cherokee and Gatlinburg, crossing Newfound Gap at nearly a mile high. Once out of the park on the Tennessee side, avoid driving through Gatlinburg (take the bypass option
instead), as even in the off-season, intense traffic means you can spend
an hour crawling through this small town.

RESTAURANTS

The closest thing to fine dining you can find in the park is a hot dog
or burger at the camp store in Cades Cove or a Coke from a vending
machine at a visitor center. If you're up to a 14- or 15-mile round-trip
hike, there is a dining room at LeConte Lodge, which offers a sack lunch
(overnight guests get breakfast and dinner included in the rate and can
spring extra for the lunch). But the best idea for dining in the park is
to create your own gourmet meal with an alfresco picnic at one of the
park's 11 attractive picnic areas.

Outside the park you'll find many more dining options, from fast food
to fine dining, the latter especially in Asheville, which is known for
its farm-to-table, locavore food culture. On the Tennessee side, both
Gatlinburg and Pigeon Forge, which might just rank among the most
touristy towns in the country, have myriad fast-food and family dining
choices. *Dining reviews have been shortened. For full information,
visit Fodors.com.*

HOTELS AND CAMPGROUNDS

The only accommodations actually in the park, besides camping, are
at LeConte Lodge. Outside the park, you have a gargantuan selection
of hotels of every ilk. On the Tennessee side, in Gatlinburg you'll see a
street sign that says "2,000 Hotel Rooms" and points up the hill, and
that's just in one section of town. On the North Carolina side, lodging
is mostly more low-key, but you can choose from old mountain inns,
B&Bs, and motels in the small towns of Bryson City, Waynesville, and
Robbinsville. A seemingly ever-expanding number of hotel towers are

connected to the giant Harrah's casino in Cherokee. With more than 1,200 rooms and at least 600 more under construction, it's the largest hotel in North Carolina, and one of its towers is the tallest building in North Carolina west of Charlotte. About 50 miles away, in and around Asheville, you can choose from among one of the largest collections of B&Bs in the Southeast, along with hip urban hotels and classic mountain resorts.

Camping is abundant and reasonably priced. The park has 939 tent and RV camping spaces at 10 developed campgrounds, two (Cades Cove and Smokemont) open year-round, in addition to more than 100 backcountry campsites, shelters, and horse camps. The cost ranges from $4 per person (backcountry sites and shelters) to $14–$23 per night for front-country sites. All but one of the campgrounds accept RVs and trailers, though most have size limits. Immediately outside the park are many commercial campgrounds and RV parks. Permits are required for all backcountry camping. You can get a backcountry permit online at ⊕ *smokiespermits.nps.gov* or at the backcountry office at Sugarlands Visitor Center. Sites at four campgrounds—Elkmont, Smokemont, Cataloochee, and Cades Cove—can be reserved in advance by calling ☎ *877/444–6777* or visiting ⊕ *www.recreation. gov*; reservations are required only at Cataloochee. Other campgrounds are mostly first-come, first-served, though reservations are available at a few. *Hotel reviews have been shortened. For full information, visit Fodors.com.*

WHAT IT COSTS				
	$	**$$**	**$$$**	**$$$$**
Restaurants	under $15	$15–$19	$20–$24	over $24
Hotels	under $150	$150–$200	$201–$250	over $250

Restaurant prices are the average cost of a main course at dinner or, if dinner is not served, at lunch. Hotel prices are the lowest cost of a standard double room in high season.

VISITOR INFORMATION

There are three main visitor centers in the park: Oconaluftee near Cherokee, Sugarlands near Gatlinburg, and Cades Cove. In addition, there is a visitor contact station at Clingmans Dome, plus four information centers outside the park on the Tennessee side (in Sevierville and Townsend and two in Gatlinburg).

FAMILY **Cades Cove Visitor Center.** This visitor center is located about midway on the highly popular 11-mile Cades Cove Loop on the Tennessee side. What makes this one especially worth visiting is the Cable Mill, which operates spring through fall, and the Becky Cable House, a pioneer home with farm outbuildings. ⊠ *Cades Cove Loop, Great Smoky Mountains National Park* ☎ *865/436–1200 park information line* ⊕ *www.nps.gov/grsm.*

FAMILY **Clingmans Dome Visitor Contact Station.** While not a full-fledged visitor information center, Clingmans Dome has a staffed information kiosk, along with a small park store and bookshop, on the Clingmans Dome trailhead. There are restrooms in the Clingsmans Dome parking lot. ⊠ *Clingmans Dome, Great Smoky Mountains National Park* ☎ *865/436–1200 park information line* ⊕ *www.nps.gov/grsm* ⊗ *Closed Dec.–Mar.*

FAMILY

Fodor's Choice

★

Oconaluftee Visitor Center. The park's only information center on the North Carolina side is 1½ miles from Cherokee and offers interactive displays, a large park and gift shop, ranger-led programs, and assistance from helpful park rangers and volunteers. There are restrooms and vending machines. Adjoining the visitor center, in a large level field next to the Oconaluftee River, is the Mountain Farm Museum. Herds of elk are sometimes seen here. ⊠ *U.S. Hwy. 441, Great Smoky Mountains National Park* ✛ *1½ miles from Cherokee* ☎ *865/436–1200 park information line* ⊕ *www.nps.gov/grsm/planyourvisit/visitorcenters.htm.*

FAMILY **Sugarlands Visitor Center.** The main visitor center on the Tennessee side, Sugarlands features extensive exhibits in a nature museum about park flora and fauna, as well as a 20-minute film about the park. Ranger-led programs are held here from spring to fall. ⊠ *U.S. Hwy. 441, Great Smoky Mountains National Park* ✛ *2 miles south of Gatlinburg* ☎ *865/436–1200 park visitor information line* ⊕ *www.nps.gov/grsm/planyourvisit/visitorcenters.htm.*

FLORA AND FAUNA

A profusion of vegetation defines the Great Smokies; it has one of the richest and most diverse collections of flora in the world. The park is about 95% forested, home to almost 6,000 known species of wildflowers, plants, and trees. Many call the Smokies the "wildflower national park," as it has more flowering plants than any other U.S. national park. In October, hundreds of thousands of visitors jam the roads of the park to view the autumn leaf colors.

You can see wildflowers in bloom virtually year-round: ephemerals such as trillium and columbine in late winter and early spring; bright red cardinal flowers, orange butterfly weed, and black-eyed Susans in summer; and joe-pye weed, asters, and mountain gentian in the fall. However, the best time to see wildflowers in the park is the spring, especially April and early May. The second-best time to see the floral display is early summer. From early to mid-June to mid-July, the hillsides and heath balds blaze with the orange of flame azaleas, the white and pink of mountain laurel, and the purple and white of rhododendron.

Living in Great Smoky Mountains National Park are some 66 species of mammals, more than 200 varieties of birds, 50 native fish species, and more than 80 types of reptiles and amphibians.

The North American black bear is the symbol of the Smokies. Bear populations vary year to year, but biologists think that about 1,500 bears are in the park, a density of about two per square mile. Many visitors to the park see bears, although sightings are never guaranteed.

One Day on the North Carolina Side

If you only have a day to visit the Smokies and are coming from the North Carolina side, start early, pack a picnic lunch, and drive to the **Oconaluftee Visitor Center** to pick up orientation maps and brochures. While you're there, spend an hour or so exploring the **Mountain Farm Museum**. Then drive the half mile to **Mingus Mill** and see corn being ground into meal in an authentic working gristmill. Head on up **Newfound Gap Road** and, via Clingmans Dome Road, to **Clingmans Dome**. The 25-mile drive takes you, in terms of the kinds of plants and trees you'll see at the mountaintop, all the way to Canada. Stretch your legs and walk the ½-mile paved, but fairly steep, trail to the observation tower on Clingmans Dome, the highest point in the Smokies. If you've worked up an appetite, head back down the mountain and stop for a leisurely picnic at **Collins Creek Picnic Area** (MM 25.4). If you want a

moderate afternoon hike, the 4-mile (round-trip) **Kephart Prong Trail** is nearby and wanders for 2 miles along a stream to the remains of a Depression-era Civilian Conservation Corps camp. Alternatively, and especially if it's a hot summer day, save your picnic and hike and instead drive via the **Blue Ridge Parkway** and Heintooga Ridge Road to the **Heintooga Picnic Area** at Balsam Springs. At a mile high, this part of the Smokies is usually cool even in mid-July. If you're up for it, you can hike all or part of the **Flat Creek Trail** (about 5 miles round-trip), which begins near the Heintooga picnic area and is one of the hidden jewels of trails in the park. If you decide not to take a long hike, you may have time to drive the one-way, unpaved **Balsam Mountain Road** to Big Cove Road back to Cherokee. Catch the sunset at an overlook on your drive back. Note that some of these sights are closed in the winter.

The National Park Service has helped reintroduce elk, river otters, and peregrine falcons to the Smokies. Attempts to reintroduce red wolves failed, though visitors occasionally report seeing what they believe is a wolf.

Because of the high elevation of much of the park, you'll see birds here usually seen in more northern areas, including the common raven and the ruffed grouse.

For a few short weeks, usually from late May to mid-June, synchronous fireflies put on an amazing light show. In this illuminated mating dance, the male *Photinus* fireflies blink four to eight times in the air, then wait about six seconds for the females on the ground to return a double-blink response. Inside the park, the Elkmont camping area on the Tennessee side is a popular place to see the fireflies.

Altogether, some 17,000 species of plants, animals, and invertebrates have been documented in the park, and scientists believe that up to 85,000 additional species of life, as yet unidentified, may exist here.

NORTH CAROLINA SIDE

The North Carolina side of the park has a variety of sights and experiences, from high peaks to historical houses. Right at the Oconaluftee Visitor Center at the entrance to the park is the Mountain Farm Museum, one of the best-preserved collections of historic log buildings in the region. Cataloochee Cove is a beautiful valley where you can spot deer, wild turkeys, and elk. Even if you never leave your car, Newfound Gap Road offers plenty of scenic views. If, however, you're ready to lace up your hiking boots, there are hundreds of miles of hiking trails to be explored, including the trail to the top of Clingmans Dome, the highest mountain in the park at 6,643 feet. North Carolina's Mountains to Sea trail starts at Clingmans Dome and ends at Jockey's Ridge on the Outer Banks, and 72 miles of the Appalachian Trail follow the ridgelines of the Smokies, beginning at Lake Fontana on the North Carolina side.

SCENIC DRIVES

FAMILY **Cove Creek Road** (*Old Hwy. 284*). This drive takes you to one of the most beautiful valleys in the Smokies, and to one of its most interesting (and least visited) destinations. The first 7 miles of Cove Creek Road is a mostly paved, winding two-lane road through a scenic rural valley. As you enter the park, the road becomes gravel. Although in the park this is a two-way road, in places it is wide enough only for one vehicle, so you may have to pull over and let an oncoming vehicle pass. At points the curvy road hugs the mountainside, with steep drop-offs, making it unsuitable for large RVs or travel trailers. As you near the Cataloochee Valley, suddenly you're on a nice, paved road again. Follow the paved road, as it is a short cut to the historic old buildings of Cataloochee. (You can also continue on the unpaved Cove Creek Road toward Crosby, Tennessee, and in about 5 miles you can enter Cataloochee from the back side.) Follow the signs for a driving tour of the old houses, barns, churches, a school, and other buildings that are all that remain of the once-thriving Cataloochee community, which at its peak in 1910 had about 1,200 residents. You can stop and walk through most of the buildings. Keep a lookout for elk, wild turkey, deer, and other wildlife here. If you haven't had enough driving for the day, from Cataloochee you can continue on the unpaved Cove Creek Road to Big Creek campground near the North Carolina–Tennessee line, where you can reconnect with Interstate 40 at Exit 451 on the Tennessee side. Cataloochee is better to visit off-season, as you'll face less traffic on Cove Creek Road, and the valley is so peaceful and relaxing. ⊠ *Cove Creek Rd., Great Smoky Mountains National Park* ☎ *865/436–1200 park information line* ⊕ *www.nps.gov/grsm* ✉ *Free.*

FAMILY **Newfound Gap Road** (*U.S. 441*). Newfound Gap Road is the busiest
Fodor's Choice road in the park by far, with more than a million vehicles making the
★ 16-mile climb from 2,000-foot elevation near Cherokee to almost a mile high at Newfound Gap (and then down to Gatlinburg on the Tennessee side). It's the only road that goes all the way through the center of the park, and the only fully paved road through the park. While it's not a

route to escape from the crowds, the scenery is memorable, perhaps more so on the Tennessee than on the North Carolina side. If you don't have time to explore the back roads or to go hiking, Newfound Gap Road will give you a flavor of the richness and variety of the Smokies. Unlike other roads in the park, Newfound Gap Road has mile markers; however, the markers run "backwards" (as far as North Carolinians are concerned), starting at 0 at the park boundary near Gatlinburg to 31.1 at the border of the park at the entrance to the Blue Ridge Parkway near Cherokee. Among the sites on the road are Oconaluftee Visitor Center and Mountain Farm Museum (MM 30.3); Mingus Mill (MM 29.9); Smokemont Campground and Nature Trail (MM 27.2); Web Overlook (MM 17.7), from which there's a good view almost due west of Clingmans Dome; and Newfound Gap (MM 14.7), the start of the 7-mile road to Clingmans Dome. The speed limit on Newfound Gap Road is 45 mph, and less in some places. ⊠ *Newfound Gap Rd. (U.S. Hwy. 441), Great Smoky Mountains National Park* ☎ *865/436–1200 park information line* ⌨ *Free.*

WHAT TO SEE

HISTORIC SIGHTS

There are five historic districts in the Smokies: Cataloochee, Mountain Farm Museum, Cades Cove, Roaring Fork, and Elkmont. Cataloochee and the Mountain Farm Museum are on the North Carolina side, and the other three are on the Tennessee side. All together, the park contains nearly 100 historical buildings that are being preserved, and about 200 old cemeteries. All the historic districts can be reached by car, though exploring them in depth requires a good bit of hiking.

FAMILY

Fodor'sChoice

★

Cataloochee Valley. This is one of the most memorable and eeriest sites in all of the Smokies. At one time Cataloochee was a community of more than 1,200 people, in some 200 buildings. After the land was taken over in 1934 for the national park, the community dispersed. Although many of the original buildings are now gone, more than a dozen houses, cabins, and barns, two churches, and other structures have been kept up. You can visit the Palmer Methodist Chapel, a one-room schoolhouse, Beach Grove School, and the Woody, Caldwell, and Messer homesteads. It's much like Cades Cove on the Tennessee side, but much less visited. On a quiet day you can almost hear the ghosts of the former Cataloochee settlers. Here you will almost always spot elk, reintroduced in 2001, especially in the evening and early morning. You'll also likely see wild turkeys, deer, and perhaps bears. Cataloochee is one of the most remote parts of the Smokies reachable by car, via a narrow, winding, gravel road. The novels of Asheville-area native Wayne Caldwell, *Cataloochee* and *Requiem by Fire,* bring to life the world of Cataloochee before the coming of the park. ⊠ *Cataloochee Valley, Cove Creek Rd., Great Smoky Mountains National Park* ✛ *Take I-40 W to Exit 20 (U.S. Hwy. 276) near Maggie Valley to Cove Creek Rd. and follow signs to Great Smoky Mountains National Park and Cataloochee* ☎ *865/436–1200 park information line* ⊕ *www.nps.gov/grsm* ⌨ *Free* ☽ *Often closed in winter due to snow and ice.*

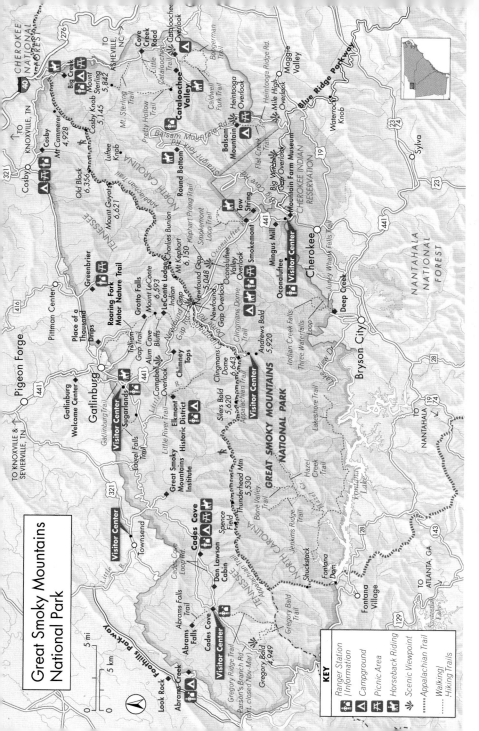

FAMILY **Mingus Mill.** In its time, the late 19th century, this was the state of the art in gristmills, the two large grist stones powered by a store-bought turbine rather than a hand-built wheel. From mid-March to just after Thanksgiving, you can watch the miller make cornmeal, and even buy a pound of it. ⊠ *U.S. Hwy. 441, Great Smoky Mountains National Park ✛ 2 miles north of Cherokee* ☏ *828/497–1904, 865/436–1200 park information line* ⊕ *www.nps.gov/grsm* ✉ *Free* ☾ *Closed late Nov.–mid-Mar.*

FAMILY
Fodor'sChoice
★
Mountain Farm Museum. This is perhaps the best re-creation anywhere of a mountain farmstead. The nine farm buildings, all dating from the late 19th century, were moved in the 1950s to this site, next to the Oconaluftee Visitor Center, from various locations within the park. Besides a furnished two-story chestnut log cabin, there is a barn, apple house, corn crib, smokehouse, beegums, springhouse, chicken coop, and other outbuildings. In season, corn, tomatoes, pole beans, squash, and other mountain crops are grown in the garden, and park staff sometimes put on demonstrations of pioneer activities, such as making apple butter and molasses. Two 1½-mile walking trails (easy) begin near the farm museum. Dogs on leashes are allowed on the trail but not within the farm grounds. Elk are sometimes seen grazing in the pastures adjoining the farm, and occasionally you may see white-tailed deer and wild turkeys. ⊠ *Oconaluftee Visitor Center, U.S. 441, Great Smoky Mountains National Park ✛ 1½ miles from Cherokee* ☏ *828/497–1904, 865/436–1200 park information line* ⊕ *www.nps.gov/grsm/planyourvisit/visitorcenters.htm* ✉ *Free.*

SCENIC STOPS

FAMILY **Andrews Bald.** Getting to Andrews Bald isn't easy. You have to walk the rocky Forney Ridge Trail some 1.8 miles one way, with an elevation gain of almost 600 feet, the equivalent of a 60-story skyscraper. The payoff is several acres of grassy bald at more than 5,800 feet, with stunning views of Lake Fontana and the southeastern Smokies. This is one of only two balds in the Smokies (the other is Gregory Bald on the Tennessee side) that the park service keeps clear. ⊠ *Great Smoky Mountains National Park ✛ 1.8 miles from the Forney Ridge trailhead parking lot, at the end of Clingmans Dome Rd.* ☏ *865/436–1200 park information line* ⊕ *www.nps.gov/grsm* ✉ *Free.*

FAMILY **Big Witch Gap Overlook.** The 2-mile drive on the Blue Ridge Parkway between Big Witch Gap Overlook and Noland Divide Overlook offers fine views into the eastern side of the Smokies, and in May and June the roadsides are heavily abloom with rosebay rhododendron. ⊠ *Blue Ridge Pkwy., MM 461.9, Cherokee* ☏ *828/298–0398 Blue Ridge Parkway information line* ⊕ *www.nps.gov/blri* ✉ *Free.*

FAMILY **Cataloochee Overlook.** Coming from Cove Creek Road onto the paved section of Cataloochee Road, this is your first opportunity to stop and see the broad expanse of Cataloochee Cove. Cataloochee is taken from a Cherokee word meaning "row upon row" or "standing in rows," and indeed you'll see rows of mountain ridges here. The overlook is well marked and has a split-rail fence. ⊠ *Cataloochee Rd., Great Smoky Mountains National Park* ☏ *865/436–1200 park information line* ⊕ *www.nps.gov/grsm* ✉ *Free.*

5

FAMILY **Clingmans Dome.** At an elevation of more than 6,600 feet, this is the
Fodor's Choice third-highest peak east of the Rockies, only a few feet shorter than the
★ tallest, Mt. Mitchell. From the parking lot (where there are restrooms)
at the end of Clingmans Dome Road, walk up a paved, but steep,
½-mile trail to an observation tower offering 360-degree views from the
"top of Old Smoky." There's also a small visitor center and bookshop
(open April to November). Temperatures here are usually 10°F–15°F
lower than at the entrance to the park near Cherokee or Gatlinburg.
Clingmans Dome Road is closed to vehicular traffic in winter, but if
there's snow on the ground you can put on your snowshoes and hike up
to the peak. ⊠ *Clingmans Dome Rd., Great Smoky Mountains National
Park ✢ 7 miles from U.S. 441* ☎ *865/436–1200 park information line*
⊕ *www.nps.gov/grsm* ☒ *Free* ⊗ *Closed Dec.–Mar.*

FAMILY **Heintooga Overlook.** This is one of the best spots to watch the sunset,
with a sweeping view westward of the crest of the Great Smokies.
⊠ *Heintooga Overlook, Heintooga Ridge Rd., Blue Ridge Parkway
MM 458.2, Great Smoky Mountains National Park ✢ 7 miles from
Blue Ridge Parkway* ☎ *865/436–1200 park information line* ⊕ *www.
nps.gov/grsm* ☒ *Free* ⊗ *Closed Nov.–late May.*

FAMILY **Mile High Overlook.** This overlook has a panoramic view of much of
the eastern side of the Smokies. ⊠ *Heintooga Ridge Rd., Great Smoky
Mountains National Park ✢ 1.3 miles from Blue Ridge Pkwy. MM
458.2* ☎ *865/436–1200 park information line* ⊕ *www.nps.gov/blri*
☒ *Free* ⊗ *Often closed in winter due to weather conditions.*

FAMILY **Newfound Gap Overlook.** At 5,048 feet, Newfound Gap is the lowest
drivable pass through the park and provides excellent views of a broad
swath of the Smokies. The ridge at Newfound Gap marks the North
Carolina–Tennessee state line. If you want to say you have been on the
Appalachian Trail, you're just a short and easy walk away from it here.
You will also find the Rockefeller Memorial here (right on the border
of the two states), which commemorates the $5 million donation the
Rockefeller Foundation gave to the park. FDR officially dedicated the
park at this site in 1940. ⊠ *Clingmans Dome Overlook, U.S. Hwy. 441*
☎ *865/436–1200 park information line* ⊕ *www.nps.gov/grsm.*

FAMILY **Oconaluftee Valley Overlook.** From atop the Thomas Divide, just a little
below the crest of the Smokies, you can look down and see the winding Newfound Gap Road. This is also a good spot to view sunrise in
the Smokies. ⊠ *Oconaluftee Valley Overlook, U.S. Hwy. 441, (Newfound Gap Rd.) at MM 15.4, Great Smoky Mountains National Park*
☎ *865/436–1200 park information line* ☒ *Free.*

SPORTS AND THE OUTDOORS

BICYCLING

The North Carolina side of the Smokies offers excellent cycling, and
bicycles are permitted on most roads. However, you have to be selec-
tive about where you bike. ■TIP➔ Vehicular traffic on the main roads,
especially Newfound Gap Road (U.S. 441), can be very heavy. Steep
terrain, and curvy, narrow back roads with narrow shoulders and blind
spots make biking difficult or unsafe in some areas.

Two good places for biking on (mostly) paved roads are Lakeview Drive—the so-called "Road to Nowhere" near Bryson City—and the Cataloochee Valley. Also, Balsam Mountain Road and Cove Creek Road offer pleasant biking with very little auto traffic. Since these roads are unpaved, with mostly gravel surfaces, you should use a mountain bike or an all-terrain hybrid. Helmets are not required by law in the park but are strongly recommended.

FAMILY **Tsali Recreation Area.** Near the Smokies, the Tsali Recreation Area is on a hilly peninsula reaching into Fontana Lake in the Nantahala National Forest, about 15 miles west of Bryson City. With about 42 miles of trails with four excellent loops, it's been named one of the best mountain biking trails by *Outside* magazine. ✉ *NC Hwy. 28 N, Nantahala National Forest, Bryson City* ✛ *From Bryson City, follow U.S. 19/74 to the intersection with NC 28. Follow NC 28 north about 3 miles. Look for a sign for the Tsali Recreation Area; turn right. Follow paved road to the campground and trailhead parking lot; park in the lot with the sign "Bikers park and pay here"* ⊕ *www.fs.usda.gov/nfsnc* 🎫 *$2 per day use fee for bike riders* ☉ *Closed Nov.–Mar.*

BOATING

FAMILY **Fontana Lake and Dam.** More than 29 miles long, and comprising around
Fodor'sChoice 12,000 acres of reservoir, Fontana Lake and Dam border the southern
★ edge of the Great Smokies. Unlike most other lakes in the mountains, Fontana has a shoreline that is almost completely undeveloped, since about 90% of its 240 miles is owned by the federal government. Fishing here is excellent, especially for smallmouth bass, muskie, and walleye. On the downside, the Tennessee Valley Authority (TVA) manages the lake for power generation, and at the peak visitor period in the fall the lake is drawn down, leaving large areas of mudflats. Fontana Dam on the Little Tennessee River, completed in 1944, at 480 feet is the highest concrete dam east of the Rockies. The dam's visitor center gets about 50,000 visitors a year. The Appalachian Trail crosses the top of the dam. ✉ *Fontana Dam Visitor Center, 77 Fontana Dam Rd., Great Smoky Mountains National Park* ✛ *3 miles from Fontana Village off Rte. 28* ☎ *865/632–2101 TVA headquarters, 865/436–1200 park information line, 828/498–2234 Fontana Dam visitor center* ⊕ *www.nps.gov/grsm* 🎫 *Free.*

BOAT RENTALS

Fontana Village Resort Marina. Boat rentals on Fontana Lake, including kayaks, canoes, and pontoon boats, are available at Fontana Village Resort Marina. Pontoon fishing boat rentals are $50 an hour or $275 for a 24-hour overnight rental; canoes and kayaks are $10 an hour or $50 for 24 hours. There's also a $5 launch fee for boats, canoes, and kayaks. Shuttle services across the lake to Hazel and Eagle creeks cost $50 per person round-trip, less for larger groups. Lake boat tours (90 minutes) are $20 per person. ✉ *Fontana Village Resort, 300 Woods Rd., off Hwy. 28 N, Fontana Dam* ☎ *800/849–2258 toll-free in the U.S. and Canada, 828/498–2129* ⊕ *www.fontanavillage.com* ☉ *Closed Nov.–Apr.; call for exact dates.*

FISHING

The North Carolina side of the Smokies has one of the best wild trout fisheries in the East. Deep Creek, Little Cataloochee, and Hazel Creek are streams known to serious anglers all over the country. The North Carolina side has more than 1,000 miles of streams (not all contain trout), and all are open to fishing year-round, except Bear Creek at its junction with Forney Creek, and upstream from there.

Among the best trout streams on this side of the park are Big Creek, Cataloochee Creek, Palmer Creek, Raven Fork, Deep Creek, Hazel Creek, and Noland Creek. Often the best fishing is in higher-elevation streams, in areas that are more difficult to reach. Streams that are easily accessible, such as the Pigeon River, have greater fishing pressure. A free fishing map is available at all visitor centers.

LICENSES

North Carolina Wildlife Resources Commission. You can order a North Carolina inland fishing license, valid throughout the park, by telephone or online, or buy one from fishing shops or guides. The NC license is good throughout the Great Smoky Mountains National Park, even on the Tennessee side (likewise, a Tennessee license is valid throughout the park). A 10-day nonresident fishing license is $18, while an annual license is $36. NC residents pay $7 for a 10-day license and $20 for an annual license. To fish for trout outside the park, you'll also need a trout stamp, which costs an extra $13 for both NC residents and nonresidents. To fish in the Cherokee Reservation (Qualla Boundary), those over 12 need a separate tribal permit, available at shops on the reservation for $10 per day, $17 for two days, $27 for three days, and $47 for five days. A tribal five-day catch-and-release permit is $25. ✉ *1751 Varsity Dr., Raleigh* ☎ *919/707–0391 to buy fishing license* ⊕ *www.ncwildlife.org.*

OUTFITTERS

For backcountry fishing trips, you may want to hire a licensed guide. Full-day trips cost around $225–$300 for one angler, $300–$400 for two. Only guides approved by the National Park Service are permitted to take anglers into the backcountry.

HIKING

Great Smoky Mountains National Park has more than 850 miles of hiking trails, about equally divided between the North Carolina and Tennessee sides. The trails range from short nature walks to long, strenuous hikes that gain several thousand feet in elevation.

Download a copy of the trail guide from the park's website or buy a hiking guide at park stores. You can also call (☎ 865/436–1297) or stop by the park's Backcountry Information office at Sugarlands Visitor Center for information to help plan your backpacking or hiking trip.

EASY

FAMILY **Three Waterfalls Loop.** For the effort of a 2.4-mile hike, this trail will reward you with three pretty waterfalls: Tom Branch, Indian Creek, and Juney Whank. Deep Creek also has a picnic area and campground. Tubing on Deep Creek is fun, too, although it is officially discouraged by the park. Biking also is allowed in this area. ✉ *Deep Creek*

CLOSE UP

Fishing Rules

To fish in the park you must possess a valid fishing license or permit from either Tennessee or North Carolina. Either state license is valid throughout the park, and no trout stamp is required. Persons under 16 don't need a license. Fishing licenses are not available in the park but may be purchased in nearby towns or online. Fishing is permitted year-round within the park; various fishing seasons apply outside it.

Only artificial flies or lures with a single hook can be used—no live bait. Fishing is permitted from a half hour before official sunrise to a half hour after official sunset. The limit for the combined total of brook, rainbow, and brown trout, or smallmouth bass must not exceed five fish each day. You may not have more than five fish in your possession, regardless of whether they are fresh, stored in an ice chest, or otherwise preserved. Twenty rock bass may be kept in addition to the above limit. You can report violations to a park ranger by calling ☎ 865/436–1294.

The minimum size is 7 inches for brook, rainbow, and brown trout, and smallmouth bass. For rock bass there is no minimum size.

If you fish in the stocked streams of the Qualla Boundary, you'll need a tribal fishing license, available at shops in Cherokee and online. Daily trout limit in tribal waters is 10.

Rd., Great Smoky Mountains National Park ✢ Trailhead at end of Deep Creek Rd., near Bryson City entrance to park ☎ 865/436–1200 park information line ⊕ www.nps.gov/grsm ☉ Campground closed Nov.–mid-Apr.

MODERATE

Clingmans Dome Trail. If you've been driving too long and want some exercise along with unbeatable views of the Smokies and an ecological lesson, too, take the ½-mile (1-mile round-trip) trail from the Clingmans Dome parking lot to the observation tower at the top of Clingmans Dome, the highest peak in the Smokies. While paved, the trail is fairly steep, and at well over 6,000 feet elevation you'll probably be gasping for air. Many of the fir trees here are dead, killed by the alien invader, the balsam wooly adelgid, and by acid rain from power plants mostly in the Ohio Valley. There's a small visitor information station on the trail. In the parking lot, often full in-season, there are restrooms. ✉ Clingmans Dome Rd., Great Smoky Mountains National Park ✢ Trail begins at Clingmans Dome parking lot ☎ 865/436–1200 park information line ⊕ www.nps.gov/grsm ☉ Clingmans Dome Rd. is closed Dec.–Mar.

FAMILY **Flat Creek Trail.** This is one of the hidden gems among the park's trails. It's little known, but it's a delightful hike, especially in summer when this higher elevation means respite from stifling temperatures. The path stretches through a pretty woodland, with evergreens, birch, rhododendron, and wildflowers. The elevation gain is about 570 feet. The trail is only 2.6 miles if you use a two-car shuttle, one at the trailhead at mile 5.4 of Heintooga Ridge Road, and the other at the

Heintooga picnic area; if you don't do a two-car shuttle, you'll have to walk 3.6 miles along Heintooga Ridge Road to your car, but even this is pleasant, with spruce and fir trees lining the road and little traffic. Note that Heintooga Ridge Road is closed to vehicle traffic November to late May. ⊠ *Flat Creek Trailhead, Heintooga Ridge Rd., MM 5.4, Great Smoky Mountains National Park* ☎ *865/436–1200 park information line* ⊕ *www.nps.gov/grsm* ☉ *Heintooga Ridge Rd. is closed in winter.*

FAMILY **Kephart Prong Trail.** A 4.2-mile (round-trip) woodland trail, named for one of the early promoters of the park, wanders beside a stream to the remains of a Civilian Conservation Corps camp. Close by, the trail takes a moderate slope to Mt. Kephart, gaining over 900 feet in elevation. ⊠ *U.S. Hwy. 441 (Newfound Gap Rd.), Great Smoky Mountains National Park* ⊹ *Trailhead is 5 miles north of Smokemont Campground on U.S. 441* ☎ *865/436–1200 park information line* ⊕ *www.nps.gov/grsm.*

FAMILY
Fodor's Choice
★
Little Cataloochee. Perhaps no other hike in the Smokies offers a cultural and historic experience like this one. In the early 20th century Cataloochee Cove had the largest population of any place in the Smokies, around 1,200 people. Most of the original structures have been torn down or succumbed to the elements, but a few historic frame buildings remain in the cove and on this remote trail. Some have been restored, such as the Cook log cabin near Davidson Gap, an apple house, and a Baptist church, preserved by park staff. You'll see several of these, along with rock walls and other artifacts, on the Little Cataloochee Trail. The trail is 6 miles (one way) including about a mile at the beginning on Pretty Hollow Gap Trail. It is best hiked with a two-car shuttle, with one vehicle at the Pretty Hollow Gap trailhead in Cataloochee Valley and the other at the Little Cataloochee trailhead at Old Highway 284 (Cove Creek Road). Including the time it takes to explore the historic buildings and cemeteries, you should allow at least six hours for this hike. The Pretty Hollow Gap trailhead is near Beech Grove School in the Cataloochee Valley. ⊠ *Cataloochee Valley, Great Smoky Mountains National Park* ☎ *865/436–1200 park information line* ⊕ *www.nps.gov/grsm.*

FAMILY **Smokemont Loop Trail.** A 6.1-mile (round-trip) loop takes you by streams and, in spring and summer, lots of wildflowers, including trailing arbutus. The trail also passes a field with old chestnut trees killed by the chestnut blight decades ago as well as the old Bradley Cemetery. With access off Newfound Gap Road (U.S. 441) at Smokemont campground near Cherokee, this is an easy trail to get to. ⊠ *Smokemont Campground, U.S. 441, off Newfound Gap Rd., Great Smoky Mountains National Park* ⊹ *Bradley Fork trailhead is at D section of Smokemont campground; follow Bradley Fork Trail to Smokemont Loop Trail* ☎ *865/436–1200 park information line* ⊕ *www.nps.gov/grsm.*

DIFFICULT

FAMILY **Mt. Sterling.** A 5.4-mile (round-trip) hike takes you to an old fire watchtower, which you can climb. The route is steep, with an elevation gain of almost 2,000 feet, so you should consider this a strenuous,

NORTH CAROLINA CAMPGROUNDS

There is no lodging, other than camping, inside the park on the North Carolina side. Two campgrounds on the North Carolina side, Smokemont and Cataloochee, accept reservations. They are required at Cataloochee and advised for Smokemont. Others on the North Carolina side are first-come, first-served. Of the North Carolina campgrounds, only Smokemont is open year-round. Senior and Access National Park cardholders may receive discounts on camping fees.

Balsam Mountain Campground.
If you like a high, cool campground with a beautiful setting in evergreens, Balsam Mountain is it. It's the highest in the park, at more than 5,300 feet. By evening, you may want a campfire—even in summer. The 46 campsites (first-come, first-served) are best for tents, but small trailers or RVs up to 30 feet can fit in some sites. Due to its somewhat remote location off the Blue Ridge Parkway, Balsam Mountain Campground is rarely full even on peak weekends. It's closed mid-October though late May. The camping fee is $14. ⊠ Near end of Heintooga Ridge Rd., Cherokee ☎ 865/436–1200 for park info line ⊕ www.nps.gov/grsm.

Big Creek Campground.
With just 12 campsites, Big Creek is the smallest campground in the park, and the only one that doesn't accept RVs or trailers—it's tents only. This is a walk-in, not hike-in, campground. Five of the 12 first-come, first-served sites (unnumbered) are beside Big Creek, which offers good swimming and fishing.

Carefully observe bear protection rules, as there have been a number of human-bear interactions nearby. It's closed November through early April. The camping fee is $14. ⊠ Cove Creek Rd. (Old Hwy. 284), Newport ☎ 865/436–1200 for park info line ⊕ www.nps.gov/grsm.

Deep Creek Campground.
This campground at the Bryson City entrance to the park is near the most popular tubing spot on the North Carolina side of the Smokies. There's also swimming in several swimming holes. Of the 92 first-come, first-served sites here, Nos. 1–42 are for tents only, and the other sites are for tents and small RVs/trailers up to 26 feet in length. It's closed November through early April. The camping fee is $17. ⊠ 1912 E. Deep Creek Rd., Bryson City ☎ 865/436–1200 for park info line ⊕ www.nps.gov/grsm.

Smokemont Campground.
With 142 sites, Smokemont is the largest campground on the North Carolina side of the park, and it's open year-round. Some of the campsites are a little close together, but the individual sites themselves are spacious. The camping fee ranges from $17 to $20. ⊠ Off U.S. 441 (Newfound Gap Rd.), 6 miles north of Cherokee ☎ 877/444–6777 or ☎ 828/497–9270 ⊕ www.recreation.gov.

5

difficult hike. ✉ *Cataloochee, Old Hwy. 284, Great Smoky Mountains National Park* ✚ *Trailhead on Cove Creek Rd. (Old Hwy. 284), midway between Cataloochee and Big Creek Campground* ☎ *865/436– 1200 park information line.*

HORSEBACK RIDING

Get back to nature and away from the crowds with a horseback ride through the forest. Guided horseback rides are offered by one park concessionaire stable at Smokemont near Cherokee. Rides are at a walking pace, so they are suitable for even inexperienced riders.

Another option is to bring your own horse. Smoky Mountains National Park is one of the best places to ride in the Southeast. There are four horse camps in the Smokies. About 550 miles of the park's hiking trails are open to horses.

OUTFITTERS

FAMILY   **Smokemont Riding Stable.** The emphasis here is on a family-friendly horseback-riding experience, suitable even for novice riders. Choose either the one-hour trail ride ($30) or a 2½-hour waterfall ride (usually departing daily at 9, noon, and 3, $75). There's also a four-hour ride for $120. Riders must be at least five years old and weigh no more than 225 pounds. Smokemont also offers wagon rides ($10). Check with the stable for dates and times. ✉ *135 Smokemont Riding Stable Rd., off U.S. Hwy. 441 near MM 27.2, Cherokee* ☎ *828/497–2373* ⊕ *www. smokemontridingstable.com* ⦿ *Closed mid-Nov.–early Mar.*

TUBING

On a hot summer's day there's nothing like hitting the water. On the North Carolina side, you can swim or go tubing on Deep Creek near Bryson City. The upper section is a little wild and woolly, with white water flowing from cold mountain springs. The put-in is at the convergence of Indian Creek and Deep Creek where the sign reads "No tubing beyond this point." The lower section of Deep Creek is more suitable for kids. Put-in for this section is at the swimming hole just above the first bridge on the Deep Creek Trail. There are several tubing outfitters near the entrance of the park at Deep Creek. Some have changing rooms and showers. Wear a swimsuit and bring towels and dry clothes to change into that you can leave in your car. Most tubing outfitters are open April through October.

OUTFITTERS

You can rent an inner tube for tubing on Deep Creek for around $5 a day at these outfitters, all located near the Deep Creek entrance to the park near Bryson City. Tubes come in a variety of sizes and colors, and some have seats and backrests. Most rental companies are closed from October through March.

Smoky Mountain Campground, Deep Creek Store & Tubes. About 50 yards from the Bryson City entrance to the park, this (highly) commercial operation rents tubes and sells camping supplies. It also has a campground and rental cabins, with free Wi-Fi. ✉ *1840 W. Deep Creek Rd., Bryson City* ☎ *828/488–9665* ⊕ *www.smokymtncampground. com* ⦿ *Closed Nov.–Mar.*

EDUCATIONAL OFFERINGS

Discover the flora, fauna, and mountain culture of the Smokies with scheduled ranger programs and nature walks.

FAMILY **Interpretive Ranger Programs.** The National Park Service organizes all sorts of orientation activities, such as daily guided hikes and talks. The programs vary widely from talks on mountain culture, blacksmithing, and old-time fiddle and banjo music to ranger-led walks through historical areas of the park. Most are free, though ranger-led hayrides in Cades Cove cost $14. Many of the programs are suitable for older children as well as for adults. For schedules, go to the Oconaluftee Visitor Center, Sugarlands, or other park visitor centers and pick up a free copy of the quarterly *Smokies Guide* newspaper, or check online for park events. ☎ *865/436–1200 park information line* ⊕ *www.nps. gov/grsm/planyourvisit/events.htm* ◻ *Most free.*

FAMILY **Junior Ranger Program for Families.** Children ages 5 to 12 can take part in these hands-on educational programs. Kids can pick up a Junior Ranger booklet ($2.50) at Oconaluftee or at other park visitor centers. They're also available at Elkmont and Cades Cove campgrounds and online through the Great Smoky Mountains Association (⊕ *www.shop.smokiesinformation.org*). After they've completed the activities in the booklet, kids can stop by a visitor center to talk to a ranger and receive a Junior Ranger badge. The badges are available year-round but spring through fall the park offers many age-appropriate demonstrations, classes, and programs for Junior Rangers, such as Blacksmithing, Stream Splashin', Critters and Crawlies, Cherokee Pottery for Kids, and—our favorite—Whose Poop's on My Boots? ⊠ *Oconaluftee Visitor Center* ☎ *865/436–1200 park information line* ⊕ *www.nps.gov/grsm/forkids/index.htm* ◻ *$2.50.*

WHERE TO EAT

There are no restaurants within the park (other than at the remote Le Conte Lodge and a snack bar within the camp store at Cades Cove on the Tennessee side). Picnic areas, however, provide amenities such as restrooms—some with pit toilets and some with flush toilets, but not all have running water in the bathrooms (bring hand sanitizer) or potable drinking water. Most picnic areas in the park have raised grills for cooking. Picnic grounds in the park are free, except for group pavilions at several grounds, which can be reserved in advance and charge from $20 to $75 per group. To avoid future problems with bears, clean your grill and picnic area thoroughly before leaving.

PICNIC AREAS

FAMILY **Big Creek Picnic Area.** This is the smallest picnic area in the park, with only 10 picnic tables. It's accessible via Exit 451 of Interstate 40, or the unpaved Cove Creek Road from Cataloochee. There's a small campground here and restrooms but no pavilion. Several good hiking trails can be reached from the picnic area. Big Creek has some Class IV rapids nearby. ⊠ *Big Creek Picnic Area, Waynesville* ✛ *Off I–40 at Exit 451 (Waterville). Follow the road past the Walters Power Generating Station to a four-way intersection. Continue straight through*

5

and follow signs ☎ *865/436–1200 park information number* ⊕ *www. nps.gov/grsm* ☽ *Closed Nov.–mid-Apr.*

FAMILY **Collins Creek Picnic Area.** The largest developed picnic area in the park, Collins Creek has 182 picnic tables. Collins Creek, which runs near the picnic area, is a small stream with above-average trout fishing (license required). The site has restrooms with flush toilets, potable water, and a 70-seat pavilion for groups that can be reserved in advance for $20. ⊠ *U.S. Hwy. 441 (Newfound Gap Rd.), at MM 25.4, Great Smoky Mountains National Park* ⊹ *About 8 miles from Cherokee* ☎ *865/436–1200 park information number* ⊕ *www.nps. gov/grsm* ☽ *Closed Nov.–Mar.*

FAMILY **Deep Creek Picnic Area.** Deep Creek offers more than picnicking. You
Fodor's Choice can go tubing (rent a tube for the day for around $5 at nearby com-
★ mercial tubing centers), hike about 2 miles to three pretty waterfalls, or go trout fishing. You can even go mountain biking here, as this is one of the few park trails where bikes are allowed. The picnic area, open year-round (but no running water in winter), has 58 picnic tables, plus a pavilion that seats up to 70 (reserve in advance, fee $20). There's also a campground here. ⊠ *1912 E. Deep Creek Rd., Bryson City* ⊹ *From downtown Bryson City, follow signs for 3 miles to Deep Creek* ☎ *865/436–1200 park information line.*

FAMILY **Heintooga Picnic Area.** This is our favorite developed picnic area in the
Fodor's Choice park. Located at more than a mile high and set in a stand of spruce
★ and fir, the picnic area has 41 tables. Nearby is Mile High Overlook, which offers one of the most scenic views of the Smokies and is a great place to enjoy the sunset. For birders, this is a good spot to see golden-crowned kinglets, red-breasted nuthatches, and other species that prefer higher elevations. You're almost certain to see the common raven here. Nearby are a campground and trailheads for several good hiking trails, including Flat Creek. You can return to Cherokee via an unpaved back road, Balsam Mountain Road, which is one way, to Big Cove Road. The disadvantage is that due to the high elevation (and the risk of snow and ice) the picnic area is only open from late May to mid-October. ⊠ *Heintooga Ridge Rd., Great Smoky Mountains National Park* ⊹ *Near end of Heintooga Ridge Rd. From Cherokee, take the Blue Ridge Pkwy. 11 miles to the turnoff for Heintooga Ridge Rd. Follow Heintooga Ridge Rd. about 9 miles to picnic area* ☎ *865/436–1200* ⊕ *www.nps.gov/grsm* ☽ *Closed mid-Oct.–mid-May.*

TENNESSEE SIDE

The Tennessee side of the park, like the nearby tourism-oriented communities of Pigeon Forge and Gatlinburg, gets a lot of visitors. Some 2 million people a year tour Cades Cove, and on a busy fall weekend the traffic on the Cades Cove Loop may remind you of midtown Manhattan, without the taxis and Ubers. The Tennessee side also has the largest and busiest campgrounds and picnic areas. *A November 2016 fire burned down 11,000 acres of the park, killed 14 people, and destroyed about 2,700 homes and businesses in the Gatlinburg area. There are currently several closures that may continue for an unknown period of time, including the Chimneys picnic grounds and Chimney Top Trail. Driving U.S. 441 on the Tennessee side, you will see blackened and fallen trees by the side of the road, though the fire left some areas untouched. The worst fire damage was in remote areas away from main roads.*

SCENIC DRIVES

FAMILY

Fodor's Choice

★

Cades Cove Loop Road. This 11-mile loop through Cades Cove is the most popular route in the park and arguably the most scenic part of the entire Smokies. The one-way, one-lane paved road starts 7.3 miles from the Townsend entrance. Stop at the orientation shelter at the start of the loop and pick up a Cades Cove Tour booklet ($1.50). The drive begins with views over wide pastures to the mountains at the crest of the Smokies. Few other places in the Appalachians offer such views across wide valley bottoms with hayfields and wildflower meadows, framed by split-rail fences and surrounded by tall mountains. Along the way, you'll pass three 19th-century churches and many restored houses, log cabins, and barns—all are open for exploration. A highlight of the loop road, about midway, is the Cable Mill area, with a visitor center, working water-powered gristmill, and a restored farmstead. The Cades Cove Loop Road is also an excellent place to see wildlife, including black bears (especially in late summer and fall), white-tailed deer, and wild turkeys. The road, open year-round, is closed from sunset to sunrise. On Wednesday and Saturday mornings until 10 am the loop is open only to bicyclists and walkers. On almost any day, even in winter but especially on weekends during peak visitor months, you can expect traffic delays, as passing points on the one-way road are few and far between, and if just one vehicle stops, scores of vehicles behind it also have to stop and wait. Allow at least two to three hours just to drive the loop, longer if you want to stop and explore the historic buildings. If you get frustrated with delays, there are two points at which you can cut across the loop on improved gravel roads, exiting sooner. A campground and picnic area open year-round are near the beginning point of the Loop Road, and a horse camp is nearby. ⊠ *Cades Cove Loop Rd., Great Smoky Mountains National Park* ⊕ *www.nps.gov/grsm.*

FAMILY

Foothills Parkway. A long-planned 71-mile scenic parkway, Foothills parallels the northern and western edges of the Great Smoky Mountains National Park. Construction began in 1960, but due to funding problems to date only three sections of the parkway have been completed and opened to the public, a 17.5-mile western section from U.S. 321 near Townsend to U.S. 129 at Chilhowee Lake, a 6-mile portion from Cosby (at TN 32) to Interstate 40, plus the Gatlinburg Bypass between Pigeon Forge and the park, which also is considered part of the Parkway. The 17.5-mile western section is particularly scenic, with stunning views of the western edge of the park. The entire unfinished section between Walland and Wears Valley is currently closed to all public use until 2018 due to construction. ■TIP➔ **Known as the "Tail of the Dragon" for its 318 curves in 11 miles, U.S. 129 is popular with motorcycle and sports-car enthusiasts. It connects with the end of the Foothills Parkway at Chilhowee.** ⊠ *Foothills Pkwy., Gatlinburg* ⊕ *www.nps.gov/grsm.*

Continued on page 231

GREAT SMOKY MOUNTAINS THROUGH THE SEASONS
SPRING, SUMMER, AND FALL
by Lan Sluder

The changing seasons bring new experiences to the Great Smoky Mountains National Park. In spring you can tiptoe through the wildflowers; in fall a curtain of fiery red and gold leaves sets the trees ablaze; in summer shady paths and cool mountain streams beckon. Throughout the seasons, miles of hiking trails and wilderness await exploration beyond the car window.

Above: Newfound Gap, Great Smoky Mountains

Spring arrives at the lower elevations in March and April. With it, the wild-flowers—buttercups, columbine, arbutus, and hundreds more—bloom, carpeting meadows and popping up near forest streams. Wildflower walks are a popular activity and the Spring Wildflower Pilgrimage in late April is a must for budding botanists.

The warm, hazy days of *summer* begin in June as do many of the park's best activities. You can hike to a cool,

high peak in the clouds, walk part of the Appalachian Trail, splash or tube in a stream, or fish for native brook trout.

In *autumn,* the flaming golds of sugar maples, the rich reds of sumac and sourwoods, and the mellow yellows of birch and poplar make for memorable leaf peeping. Because elevations in the park range from 1,000 to over 6,000 feet, autumn color lasts for up to two months. Fall foliage generally peaks in mid- to late-October.

TOP SPRING WILDFLOWERS

❶ Trillium

The large flowered trillium, with blooms three to four inches across, is the most common of ten trillium varieties in the park. To identify this impressive flower, look for sets of three: three large pointed green leaves, three sepals, and three white petals. Trilliums bloom on woody slopes and along roadsides and trails at elevations up to 3,500 feet from April to May. **See it:** Middle Prong Trail (TN), Oconaluftee River Trail (NC).

❷ Lady Slippers

These delicate orchids come in pink, yellow, and white. The slender stalk rises from a pair of green leaves, and then bends a graceful neck to suspend the paper-thin flower, which resembles a woman's slipper. They favor wooded areas in dappled sunlight, often under oaks. **See it:** Cove Hardwood Nature Trail (TN).

❸ Fire pink

These brilliant red flowers have five notched petals and bloom in dry rocky areas in April and May. Look for the ruby-throated hummingbirds that pollinate the flowers. **See it:** Chestnut Top Trail (TN).

❹ Rhododendron

The park is famous for its displays of rhododendron. The rosebay's big clumps of white flowers appear in June around streams at the lower and middle elevations and as late as July at higher elevations. The Catawba, with stunning purple flowers, blooms at higher elevations in June. **See it:** rosebay, trails below 5,000 feet; Catawba, Newfound Gap Road (NC and TN).

❺ Flame azalea

Blooms can be found in white, peach, yellow, and red, but the most striking color is the namesake flame orange. They bloom in April and May at low to mid-elevation, and June to early July on the mountaintops. **See it:** Gregory Bald (TN), Andrews Bald (NC), Balsam Mountain Road (NC).

TOP TREES FOR FALL COLOR

❶ Tulip poplar
With its tall, straight trunk and light yellow leaves in the fall, the tulip poplar is hard to miss. Poplars are among the first to turn and often grow in stands of hundreds of trees, at elevations under 4,500 feet. **See it:** Cove Hardwood Nature Trail (TN), Fontana Lake (NC), Ramsey Cascades Trail (TN).

❷ Sugar maple
Sugar maples are the kings of the fall forest with brilliant orange-to-yellow leaves that appear like fire against the blue autumn sky. Each leaf has five multi-pointed lobes. Maples turn early in the season and are found at elevations up to 4,500 feet. **See it:** Sugarlands Valley (TN), Cataloochee (NC), Newfound Gap Road (NC and TN).

❸ Sumac
Sumac are small shrubs, but inch for inch they pack more fall color than almost any other tree in the mountains. You'll recognize them for their bright scarlet leaves and oblong clusters of red fruit. Staghorn sumac grows along roadsides at up to 5,500 feet. **See it:** Newfound Gap Road (NC and TN).

❹ Sourwood
In the fall, the sourwood leaves are among the first to turn, glowing deep red and orange. At this time the sourwood also bears sprays of small green fruit. The leaves have a slight sour taste. **See it:** low to middle elevations off Parson Branch Road (TN).

❺ Sweetgum
The spiny ball-shaped fruits of the American sweetgum can be annoying to step on, but the trees' showy fall colors make up for it. Orange-yellow and red leaves mix with dark purple and smoky brown. Sweetgums turn around the middle of the season. These medium-size hardwoods, grow at the lower elevations, especially near creeks and streams. **See it:** Cades Cove (TN), Lower Little Pigeon River (TN).

⬤ =Common ⬤ =Somewhat Common ⬤ =Rare

5

IN FOCUS GREAT SMOKY MOUNTAINS THROUGH THE SEASONS

CHOOSE YOUR DAY HIKE

Whether you just want to stretch your legs or you have a yen to climb a mountain, the Smokies has a hike for you. Here are a few of our favorite hikes to waterfalls, scenic overlooks, and historic sites.

Tom Branch waterfall, Deep Creek

BEST HIKES TO WATERFALLS

ABRAMS FALLS, TN

Moderate, 5 miles round-trip, 3 hours

From the trailhead off Cades Cove Loop Road, follow Abrams Creek to Abrams Falls, where you can take a dip in a lovely natural pool below the falls framed by laurel and rhododendron.

LAUREL FALLS, TN

Easy, 2.6 miles round-trip, 1.5 hours

Off Little River Road, this popular trail to 75-foot, multi-level Laurel Falls is paved and offers a mostly gentle walk in the woods. It's suitable for kids and strollers, though the trail is narrow in places with steep drop-offs.

THREE WATER- FALLS LOOP, NC

Easy, 2.4 miles round-trip, 1.5 hours

About 3 miles by car from Bryson City, Deep Creek offers something for the entire family, with river tubing, mountain biking, fishing, and several loop trails including this easy loop, which takes you by three small falls.

TRILLIUM GAP TRAIL TO GROTTO FALLS, TN

Moderate, 2.6 miles round-trip, 2 hours

From the trailhead off Roaring Fork Motor Trail, Trillium Gap Trail gains over 400 feet in elevation, crossing several small streams and passing old-growth hemlocks before reaching 30-foot Grotto Falls, the only falls in the park that you can walk behind.

BEST HIKES TO OVERLOOKS

CLINGMANS DOME TRAIL, NC

Moderate, 1 mile round-trip, 1 hour

Paved but steep, this trail leads you to the 6,643-foot Clingmans Dome, crosses the Appalachian Trail, and ends at a 54-foot tall observation tower with stunning views of the Smokies.

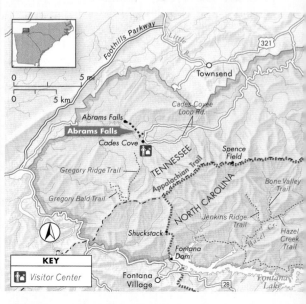

BEST HIKES TO HISTORIC SITES

KEPHART PRONG, NC

Moderate, 4 miles
round-trip, 3 hours

Named for Horace Kephart, who was an advocate for the establishment of the park, the trail crosses the Oconaluftee River six times over footbridges, passing remains of a 1930s Civilian Conservation Corps camp that was later used to house conscientious objectors during World War II.

Hikers in Great Smoky Mountains National Park

LITTLE CATALOOCHEE TRAIL, NC

Moderate, 5.9 miles
one way, 6 hours

The Little Cataloochee Trail is one of the Smokies' most historically rich hikes, passing several old cabins and houses, cemeteries, a church, school, and other relics of early 20th-century life in the Cataloochee Valley before the coming of the national park. We recommend using a two-car shuttle for this hike.

Clingmans Dome

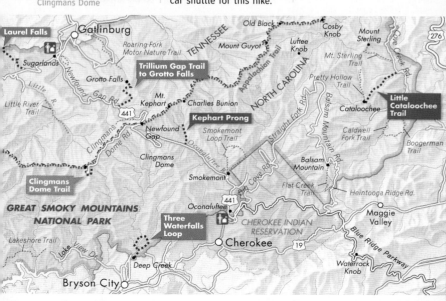

FUN SUMMER ACTIVITIES

Rafting on the Nantahala River

Summer is prime time for outdoor fun in the park and nearby.

BIKING

Main roads have a lot of traffic and lack bike lanes. For safer biking, choose back roads such as Balsam Mountain Road (NC) and Cove Creek Road (NC). A hybrid or mountain bike is best on these unpaved roads. For mountain biking, try the Tsali Recreation Area.

Best places to bike: Cades Cove Loop (TN), an 11-mile paved road, is closed to motor vehicles Wednesday and Saturday mornings until 10. Cataloochee Valley (NC) is another good place to bike.

BOATING

Rent a powerboat or pontoon boat and enjoy a lazy day on the water.

Best place for boating: Fontana Lake, bordering the southern edge of the park in North Carolina, has power and pontoon boats for rent.

FISHING

There's top-notch trout fishing in the 2,100 miles of trout streams in the park. You can catch rainbow, brown, and the native brook trout. Only artificial lures and flies can be used, not live bait.

Best places to fish: In North Carolina, Deep Creek, Little Cataloochee, and Hazel Creek are good trout streams. Little River, Abrams Creek, and Little Pigeon River are good choices on the Tennessee side.

RAFTING

Ride the white water! You can take a guided rafting trip, or rent your own raft on several rivers in and near the Smokies.

Best places to raft: The Nantahala just outside the park on the North Carolina side is the most popular river for rafting. On the Tennessee side, the Big Pigeon River offers rafting in mild white water.

TUBING

Few things are more pleasant than floating down a refreshing stream on a hot day. You can rent a large inner tube for less than $10 a day.

Best places to tube: Deep Creek (NC) and Little River (TN).

CLOSE UP

One Day on the Tennessee Side

If you have one day and are entering the park from the Tennessee side, start early, pack a picnic lunch, and drive to the **Sugarlands Visitor Center** to orient yourself to the park. Beat the crowds to the **Cades Cove Loop Road** and drive the 11-mile loop, stopping to explore the preserved farmsteads and churches. Spend some time in the **Cable Mill** area, visiting the gristmill, **Gregg-Cable House,** and other outbuildings. Depending on your timing, you can picnic at one of the stops in Cades Cove or Metcalf Bottoms. Take **Newfound Gap Road** up to

Newfound Gap. **Clingmans Dome Road** is just over the state line, but if you've come this far you'll want to drive up. Stretch your legs and walk to the observation tower on **Clingmans Dome.** Return down Clingmans Dome and Newfound Gap roads and then proceed on to **Roaring Fork Motor Nature Trail.** Stop to explore the preserved cabins and other sites along the trail. At Auto Tour site no. 5, park in the parking lot at the Trillium Gap trailhead and—if you have the time and are up to a moderate 2.6-mile (round-trip) hike—walk to **Grotto Falls.**

5

FAMILY

Fodor's Choice

★

Newfound Gap Road. In a little more than 14 miles, Newfound Gap Road (U.S. 441) climbs more than 3,500 feet from Gatlinburg to the gap through the crest of the Smokies at 5,046 feet. It takes you through Southern cove hardwood, pine-oak, and Northern hardwood forests to the spruce-fir forest at Newfound Gap. Unlike other roads in the park, Newfound Gap Road has mile markers, starting at the park entrance near Gatlinburg. Sugarlands Visitor Center is at mile marker 1.7. You'll probably see a lot of cars parked at Alum Cave trailhead (MM 10.4), which follows Alum Cave Creek to Arch Rock, a natural tunnel caused by weathering, and then to Alum Cave Bluffs, a site of a potash alum and epsomite mine briefly operated by Epsom Salts Company before the Civil War. The trail eventually leads to LeConte Lodge on Mt. LeConte. At Newfound Gap (MM 14.7), you can straddle the Tennessee–North Carolina state line and also hike some of the Appalachian Trail. The two-lane, paved Newfound Gap Road has a 45 mph speed limit, with lower limits in some areas. It is frequently closed in winter due to ice and snow or rockslides. ⚠ **Part of this area was affected in the November 2016 fire. The Chimney Tops trail and picnic area are currently closed and may potentially remain closed well into 2018.** ⊠ *U.S. Hwy. 441, Great Smoky Mountains National Park* ⊕ *www.nps.gov/grsm.*

FAMILY

Fodor's Choice

★

Roaring Fork Motor Nature Trail. Roaring Fork offers a dramatic counterpoint to Cades Cove Loop Road. Where Cades Cove Loop meanders through a wide open valley, Roaring Fork closes in, with the forest sometimes literally just inches from your car's fender. The one-way, paved road is so narrow in places that RVs, trailers, and buses are not permitted. The 6-mile Roaring Fork Motor Nature Trail starts just beyond the Noah "Bud" Ogle farmstead and the Rainbow Falls trailhead. Stop and pick up a Roaring Fork Auto Tour booklet ($1) at the information shelter.

Numbered markers along the route are keyed to 16 stops highlighted in the booklet. Along the road are many opportunities to stop your car and get closer to nature. Among the sites are several old cabins and the Alfred Reagan place, which is painted in the original blue, yellow, and cream, "all three colors that Sears and Roebuck had," according to a story attributed to Mr. Reagan. At one point the roadside is littered with fallen and now decaying chestnut trees that were killed by the chestnut blight in the early part of the 20th century. There are several good hiking trails starting along the road, including Trillium Gap Trail that leads to Mt. LeConte. The road follows Roaring Fork Creek a good part of the way, and the finale is a small waterfall called "The Place of a Thousand Drips," right beside the road. ⊠ *Gatlinburg* ✛ *To get to Roaring Fork from Gatlinburg from the Parkway (U.S. 441), turn onto Historic Nature Trail at stoplight number 8 in Gatlinburg and follow it to the Cherokee Orchard entrance of the park* ☎ *865/436–1200 park information line* ⊕ *www.nps.gov/grsm* ☉ *Closed Dec.–Mar. (dates vary).*

WHAT TO SEE

HISTORIC SIGHTS

FAMILY

Fodor's Choice

★

Cades Cove. A 6,800-acre valley surrounded by high mountains, Cades Cove has more historic buildings than any other area in the park. Driving, hiking, or biking the 11-mile Cades Cove Loop Road, you can see three old churches (Methodist, Primitive Baptist, and Missionary Baptist), a working gristmill (Cable Mill), a number of log cabins and houses in a variety of styles, and many outbuildings, including cantilevered barns, which used balanced beams to support large overhangs. The Cherokee name for this valley is Tsiyahi, place of otters, but today you're more likely to see bears, deer, and wild turkeys. For hundreds of years Cherokee Indians hunted in Cades Cove, but there is no evidence of major settlements. Under the terms of the Calhoun Treaty of 1819, the Cherokee forfeited their rights to Cades Cove, and the first white settlers came in the early 1820s. By the middle of the 19th century, well over 100 families lived in the cove, growing corn, wheat, oats, cane, and vegetables. For a while, when government-licensed distilleries were allowed in Tennessee, corn whiskey was the major product of the valley, and even after Tennessee went dry in 1876, illegal moonshine was still produced. After the establishment of the park in the 1930s, many of the nearly 200 buildings were torn down to allow the land to revert to its natural state. More recently, however, the bottomlands in the cove have been maintained as open fields, and the remaining farmsteads and other structures have been restored to depict life in Cades Cove as it was from around 1825 to 1900. The NPS mows areas near the road for wildlife viewing. Keep in mind: the Loop Road gets 2 million visitors per year; at peak times traffic in and out of here can be extremely slow. ⊠ *Cades Cove Loop Rd., Great Smoky Mountains National Park* ☎ *865/436–1200 park information line* ⊕ *www.nps.gov/grsm.*

FAMILY

Fodor's Choice

★

Elkmont Historic District. What began as a logging town in the early years of the 20th century evolved into a summer colony for wealthy families from Knoxville, Chattanooga, and elsewhere in Tennessee.

Cades Cove has a number of historical houses, log cabins, and barns.

In 1910, Little River Lumber Company deeded a tract of 50 acres of land to some prominent Knoxvillians who belonged to a fishing and hunting club called the Appalachian Club. Later, exclusive hunting and fishing rights on a 40,000-acre tract above Elkmont were sold to the club and many cottages were built as summer getaways. Other prominent east Tennessee families bought land here and built the Wonderland Hotel. Eventually, the park was established, taking the Elkmont land. Parts of the Elkmont community were placed on the National Registry of Historic Places in 1994. Today, Elkmont is primarily a campground, although many of the original 74 cottages remain along Jakes Creek and Little River. ⚠ Some cottages are falling down so be careful when visiting them. Most of the cottages are at the far end of the campground—follow the Elkmont Nature Trail, or you can drive a separate paved road off Little River Road to the collections of old buildings. The Wonderland Hotel, in disrepair, began to collapse in 2005–06, and the Park Service demolished most of what was left. The remains of the hotel are just northwest of the campground. In recent years, the Park Service has been stabilizing and restoring several homes along Jakes Creek. The Appalachian Clubhouse has been restored to its 1930s appearance, complete with rocking chairs on the porch. Some 19 structures in "Daisy Town" are being restored, but more than 50 other cottages have been, or are slated to be, torn down, despite objections from some conservation groups. ✉ *Little River Rd., Great Smoky Mountains National Park* ✢ *4½ miles west of Gatlinburg entrance to park* ☎ *865/436–1200 park information line* ⊕ *www.nps.gov/grsm.*

FAMILY **Roaring Fork.** You can visit several preserved mountain cabins and other buildings in the Roaring Fork area near Gatlinburg. Roaring Fork was settled by Europeans in the 1830s and '40s. At its height around the turn of the 20th century, there were about two dozen families in the area. Most lived a simple, hardscrabble existence, trying to scrape out a living from the rough mountain land. The Noah "Bud" Ogle self-guided nature trail, on Orchard Road just before entering the one-way Roaring Fork Motor Nature Trail, offers a walking tour of an authentic mountain farmstead and surrounding hardwood forest. Highlights include a log cabin, barn, streamside tub mill, and a wooden flume system to bring water to the farm. Among the historic structures on the Motor Nature Trail, all open for you to explore, are the Jim Bales cabin, the Ephraim Bales cabin, and the Alfred Reagan house, one of the more "upscale" residences at Roaring Fork. ⊠ *Orchard Rd. and Roaring Fork Motor Nature Trail, Roaring Fork* ☎ *865/436–1200 park information line* ⊕ *www. nps.gov/grsm* ☉ *Closed late Nov.–late Mar.*

SCENIC STOPS

FAMILY **Campbell Overlook.** Named for Carlos Campbell, a conservationist who was instrumental in helping to establish the park, Campbell Overlook provides a good view up a valley to Bull Head peak and, farther up, to Balsam Point. An exhibit at the overlook explains the different types of forests within the park. ⊠ *Newfound Gap Rd. (U.S. 441), MM 3.9, Great Smoky Mountains National Park* ⊕ *www.nps.gov/grsm.*

FAMILY **Chimney Tops Overlook.** From any of the three overlooks grouped together on Newfound Gap Road, you'll have a good view of the Chimney Tops—twin peaks that cap 2,000-foot-high cliffs. You also see hundreds of dead Fraser fir and spruce trees, along with some dead hemlocks, victims of woolly adelgids and air pollution. ⊠ *Newfound Gap Rd. (U.S. 441), MM 7.1, Gatlinburg* ⊕ *www.nps.gov/grsm.*

FAMILY **Dan Lawson Cabin.** From many points along the 11-mile, one-way Cades Cove Loop Road, you'll enjoy iconic views of the broad Cades Cove valley. The Park Service keeps hayfields and pastures cleared, so you can see how the valley may have looked in the late 19th century when it was farmed by more than 100 families. Typical is the view across the valley from the front porch of the Dan Lawson cabin, the original portion of which was built in 1856. ⊠ *Cades Cove Loop Rd., Townsend* ⊕ *www.nps.gov/grsm.*

FAMILY **Gregory Bald/Gregory Ridge Trail.** From almost 5,000 feet on Gregory Bald, you have a breathtaking view of Cades Cove and Rich Mountain to the north, and the Nantahala and Yellow Creek mountains to the south. You can also see Fontana Lake to the southeast. Many hybrid rhododendrons grow on and around the bald. Gregory Bald is one of only two balds in the Smokies that are being kept cleared of tree growth by the Park Service. This is a view that just a few thousand people a year will see, as it's reachable only by a strenuous hike via Gregory Ridge trail of more than 11 miles round-trip. The trailhead is at the end of Forge Creek Road in Cades Cove. ⊠ *Hike the Gregory Ridge Trail (5.5 miles one way) from Cades Cove, Gatlinburg* ⊕ *www.nps.gov/grsm.*

Deer are a common sight throughout the Great Smoky Mountains, especially in the early morning and at dusk.

FAMILY **Look Rock.** The overlooks looking east on the western section of the Foothills Parkway around Look Rock have remarkable views. This is also a great spot to enjoy the sunrise over the Smokies. Stargazers gather at the five overlooks south of the Look Rock exit where light pollution is especially low. ✉ *Look Rock Overlook, Foothills Pkwy.* ☎ *865/436–1200 park info* ⊕ *www.nps.gov/grsm.*

SPORTS AND THE OUTDOORS

BICYCLING

Tennessee requires that children age 16 and under wear a helmet, and it's strongly recommended that all riders do so, regardless of age.

Cades Cove. Arguably the best place to bike, the 11-mile loop road is mostly level, and being on a bike allows you to get around traffic back-ups. However, traffic can be heavy, especially on weekends in summer and fall, and the road is narrow. ■TIP→ **The best time to bike the Cove is from early May to late September on Wednesday and Saturday mornings until 10 am when it is closed to motor vehicles.** Bicycles and helmets can be rented ($20 per day) in summer and fall at an annex behind Cades Cove Campground Store (✉ *Cades Cove Campground* ☎ *865/448–9034*).

Foothills Parkway West. The 17.5-mile road has light vehicular traffic and is a scenic and fairly safe place for bicycling. Safe biking also is available on the lightly used access roads to **Greenbrier** picnic area and **Cosby** campground.

FISHING

There are more than 200 miles of wild trout streams on the Tennessee side of the park. Trout streams are open to fishing year-round. Among the best trout streams on the Tennessee side are Little River, Abrams Creek, and Little Pigeon River.

Tennessee Wildlife Resources Agency. A Tennessee fishing license, required of anyone 13 and over, is valid throughout the Great Smokies park and also for fishing in other areas of Tennessee. A one-day, nonresident adult fishing license good for all types of fish including trout is $16; a three-day license is $40.50; 10-day is $61.50; and an annual nonresident license is $99. Licenses for Tennessee residents vary, but cost less. A special trout-fishing nonresident license for the Gatlinburg area (outside the park) costs $13.50 for one day and doesn't require a state license. ■TIP➔ North Carolina fishing licenses are cheaper, and since either an NC or TN license is good anywhere in the park, you'll save by buying a NC license, even if you just want to fish on the Tennessee side. ✉ *3030 Wildlife Way, Morristown* ☎ *800/332–0900 info for East Tennessee, 615/781–6585 buy fishing license by phone* ⊕ *www.tn.gov/twra.*

OUTFITTERS

For backcountry trips, you may want to hire a guide. Full-day fishing trips cost about $250–$300 for one angler, $250–$350 for two. Only guides approved by the National Park Service are permitted to take anglers into the backcountry.

Little River Outfitters. This large fly-fishing shop and school has been in business since 1984. It specializes in teaching beginners to fly-fish. Although it does not offer guide services, it can hook you up with guides for fishing in the Smokies or elsewhere. ✉ *106 Town Square Dr., Townsend* ☎ *865/448–9459* ⊕ *www.littleriveroutfitters.com.*

Smoky Mountain Angler. This well-equipped fly-fishing shop offers equipment rentals, fishing licenses, and half-day and full-day fly- and spin-fishing trips with one of its half dozen guides. Full-day guided trout fishing trips (wading) in the park are around $250 for one person and an extra $50 for each additional person (tips not included). ✉ *466 Brookside Village Way, Gatlinburg* ☎ *865/436–8746* ⊕ *www.smokymountainangler.com.*

HIKING

EASY

FAMILY **Elkmont Nature Trail.** This 1-mile loop is good for families, especially if you're camping at Elkmont. It passes by many of the remaining buildings in the Elkmont Historic District. Pick up a self-guided brochure (50¢) at the start of the trail. ✉ *Near Elkmont campground* ☎ *865/436–1200 park info* ⊕ *www.nps.gov/grsm.*

FAMILY **Gatlinburg Trail.** This is one of only two trails in the park (the other one is Oconaluftee River Trail on the North Carolina side) where dogs and bicycles are permitted. Dogs must be on leashes. The trail, which starts at Sugarlands Visitor Center, follows the Little Pigeon River. The first 0.3 mile of the 1.9-mile trail (one way) is through the park headquarters and on a service road. ✉ *Trailhead at Sugarlands Visitor Center, Sugarlands Visitor Center, off U.S. Hwy. 441, Gatlinburg* ☎ *865/436–1200 park info line* ⊕ *www.nps.gov/grsm.*

FAMILY **Laurel Falls.** This paved trail is fairly easy. It takes you past a series of cascades to a 60-foot waterfall and a stand of old-growth forest. The trail is extremely popular in summer and on weekends almost anytime (trolleys from Gatlinburg stop here), so don't expect solitude. The 1.3-mile paved trail to the falls is wheelchair accessible. Wooden posts mark every one-tenth of a mile, and the total round-trip hike is 2.6 miles. ⊠ *Trailhead is on the west side of Little River Rd. between Sugarlands Visitor Center and Elkmont campground, about 3.9 miles west of Sugarlands, Gatlinburg* ⊕ *www.nps.gov/grsm.*

FAMILY **Little River Trail at Elkmont.** This 5.1-mile loop (if Cucumber Gap and Jakes Creek trails are included) offers a little of everything—historical buildings, fly-fishing, a waterfall, and wildflowers. The first part of the trail wanders past remnants of old logging operations and cottages that were once the summer homes of wealthy Tennesseans. Huskey Branch Falls appears at about 2 miles. The Little River Trail passes the junction with three other trails, offering the possibility for even longer hikes—Cucumber Gap at 2.3 miles, Huskey Gap at 2.7 miles, and Goshen Prong Trail at 3.7 miles. The trail is normally open even in winter. At any point you can try your hand at fly-fishing for trout in the Little River, one of the best trout streams in the park (license required). Parking at the trailhead has been improved and expanded. This is the habitat of the synchronous fireflies, which put on their light show on June evenings. ⊠ *Gatlinburg* ✛ *Trailhead is near Elkmont campground. Turn left just before entrance to campground and go 0.6 mile to a fork in the road. The trail is a continuation of the left fork* ⊕ *www. nps.gov/grsm.*

FAMILY **Sugarlands Valley Trail.** The easiest trail in the park, it's only 0.25 mile one way, virtually level, and paved, so it's suitable for young children, strollers, and wheelchairs. A brochure available at the start (50¢) explains the numbered exhibits and features of the trail. ⊠ *U.S. Hwy. 441 (Newfound Gap Rd.), Gatlinburg* ✛ *Trailhead is 0.3 mile south of Sugarlands Visitor Center* ⊕ *www.nps.gov/grsm.*

FAMILY **Trillium Gap Trail to Grotto Falls.** Grotto Falls is the only waterfall in the park that you can walk behind. The Trillium Gap Trail, off the Roaring Fork Motor Nature Trail, which leads to Grotto Falls, is primarily through a hemlock forest (many of the hemlocks have been killed by the hemlock woolly adelgid). Only 1.3 miles long, with an easy slope, this trail is suitable for novice hikers and is one of the most popular in the park. The total round-trip distance to Grotto Falls is 2.6 miles.

THE APPALACHIAN TRAIL

Each spring about 1,500 hikers set out to conquer the Appalachian Trail (AT), the 2,190-mile granddaddy of all hikes. Most hike north from Springer Mountain, Georgia, toward Mt. Katahdin, Maine. By the time they get to the Great Smokies, 160 miles from the trailhead in Georgia, about half the hikers will already have dropped out. Typically, only about 400 hikers per year complete the entire AT. At Newfound Gap Overlook, you can get on it for a short hike on the North Carolina–Tennessee line.

5

Trillium Gap Trail continues on to LeConte Lodge, a total one-way distance of about 8 miles. It is a horse trail, and llamas resupplying the lodge also use it. The Roaring Fork Motor Trail is closed in winter. ✉ *Off Roaring Fork Motor Tr., Gatlinburg* ✢ *Take Roaring Fork Motor Nature Trail to stop no. 5 on the auto tour, then look for trailhead for Trillium Gap Trail* ⊕ *www.nps.gov/grsm.*

MODERATE

FAMILY **Abrams Falls.** This 5-mile round-trip trail is one of the most popular in the Smokies, in part due to the trailhead location near stop no. 10 on the loop road in Cades Cove, which gets more than 2 million visitors a year. Beginning at the wooden bridge over Abrams Creek, the trail first goes along a pleasant course through rhododendron. It becomes somewhat steep at a couple of points, especially near Arbutus Ridge. The path then leads above Abrams Falls and down to Wilson Creek. Though only about 20 feet high, the falls are beautiful, with a good volume of water and a broad pool below. ✉ *Cades Cove Loop Rd., Townsend* ✢ *Parking lot is on an unpaved side road between signposts 10 and 11* ⊕ *www.nps.gov/grsm.*

FAMILY **Appalachian Trail at Newfound Gap.** For those who want to say they hiked part of the AT (⊕ *www.nps.gov/appa*), which runs some 72 miles through the Great Smokies, this section is a great place to start; it's easy to get to and not too steep. Park in the Newfound Gap Overlook parking lot and cross the road to the trail. From Newfound Gap to Indian Gap the trail goes 1.7 miles through spruce-fir high-elevation forest, and in late spring and summer there are quite a few wildflowers. The total round-trip distance is 3.4 miles. ✉ *Appalachian Trail, U.S. Hwy. 441 (Newfound Gap Rd.), Great Smoky Mountains National Park* ✢ *Park at Newfound Gap Overlook parking lot* ⊕ *www.nps.gov/grsm.*

HORSEBACK RIDING

Several hundred miles of backcountry trails on the Tennessee side are open to horseback riders. Horses are restricted to trails specifically designated for use; check the park trail map ($1) for horse trails and rules and regulations about riding in the backcountry. You can also download a map from ⊕ *www.nps.gov/grsm/planyourvisit/horseriding.htm.*

OUTFITTERS

FAMILY **Cades Cove Riding Stables.** This park concessionaire offers carriage rides ($12), hayrides ($12), and ranger-guided hayrides ($14), along with horseback riding ($30 an hour). It's first-come, first-served with no reservations except for large groups. Call the stables to find out times and dates of ranger-led hayrides. Horseback riders must be at least six years old and weigh no more than 250 pounds. ✉ *Cades Cove Campground, 10018 Campground Dr., Townsend* ☎ *865/448–9009* ⊕ *www. cadescovestables.com* ⊗ *Closed early Dec.-mid-Mar.*

TUBING

Tubing requires little skill beyond the ability to let yourself float down a river and can be done at almost any age. Little River is the most popular tubing river on the west side of the Smokies. It flows east to west from its headwaters in the park through the town of Townsend. The Little River is mostly flat water (Class I), with a few mild Class II rapids.

Although you can tube on the Little River within the park, several outfitters in Townsend rent tubes and life jackets and provide shuttle buses or vans that drop you at an entry point from which you can float a mile or two downriver to the outfitter's store. Expect to pay from $8 to $13 per person, which includes a full day's tube and life-jacket rental plus unlimited use of the shuttle. Kayak rentals are also offered by some outfitters. Typically the cost is $15 for the kayak rental and the first shuttle trip, and $5 each for additional shuttle trip. Outfitters are generally open May through September or October.

OUTFITTERS

FAMILY **Smoky Mountain River Rat.** This outfitter, the best of the bunch in the Townsend area, offers tubing on the Little River during warm-weather months. Tube rental, life jacket, and all-day shuttle is $15. A season pass is available for about $30. ✉ *205 Wears Valley Rd., Townsend* ☎ *865/448–8888* 🌐 *www.smokymtnriverrat.com* 🕓 *Closed Oct.–Apr.*

EDUCATIONAL OFFERINGS

FAMILY **Great Smoky Mountains Institute at Tremont.** Located within the park at Tremont, this residential environmental education center offers a variety of programs year-round for student groups, teachers, and families. The adult and teacher programs include photography, crafts, naturalist certification, and backpacking nature trips. Summer camp programs are offered for children 9–17, starting at around $589. Family camp weekends and weeks are also offered. Many programs book up early. Go to the Tremont website to download a programs brochure. Accommodations at Tremont are in Caylor Lodge, a heated and air-conditioned dormitory that sleeps up to 125 people, and also in tents on platforms. Meals are served family-style in a large dining hall. Some 5,000 students and adults attend programs at the Institute each year. ✉ *9275 Tremont Rd., Townsend* ☎ *865/448–6709* 🌐 *www.gsmit.org.*

FAMILY **Smoky Mountain Field School.** The University of Tennessee's Smoky Mountain Field School offers noncredit workshops, hikes, and outdoor adventures for adults and families. About 700 participants each year choose from among some 30 experts teaching around 50 sessions. Classes are held at various locations, usually within the park itself. Fees vary, ranging from around $79 to $195. ✉ *UT Smoky Mountain Field School, 600 Henley St., 313 Conference Center Bldg., Knoxville* ☎ *865/974–0150* 🌐 *smfs.utk.edu.*

WHERE TO EAT

$ FAST FOOD FAMILY 🍴 **Cades Cove Camp Store Snack Bar.** The only eating establishment in the park, other than the restaurant at LeConte Lodge, is a little snack bar inside the Cades Cove camp store. Here, you can buy hot dogs, burgers, sandwiches, soup, and other snacks. **Known for:** convenience-store atmosphere; campground food basics; ice-cream shop next door. [$] *Average main: $6* ✉ *Cades Cove Campground, Cades Cove Loop Rd., Great Smoky Mountains National Park* ☎ *865/448–9034 campground store* 🌐 *www.nps.gov/grsm* 🕓 *Closed Dec.–Feb.*

PICNIC AREAS

Cades Cove Picnic Area. This picnic area, near the beginning of the Cades Cove loop, has 81 picnic tables. Its big advantage is that it's near beautiful Cades Cove valley; the disadvantage is that as many as 2 million people come through this area each year. Also, at only 1,800 feet high, it can be hot and humid in summer. Potable water and flush toilets are available. Bears are fairly common, so closely observe food storage precautions. Spence Field, Anthony Creek, and Thunderhead trailheads are at the picnic area. There is a campground store here that sells hot dogs, burgers, ice cream, basic grocery supplies, and firewood; it also rents bikes. ⊠ *Great Smoky Mountains National Park* ✛ *9 miles east of Townsend, near the entrance to Cades Cove Loop and near the Cades Cove campground* ⊕ *www.nps.gov/grsm.*

FAMILY **Metcalf Bottoms Picnic Area.** This large, 122-table picnic area is midway between Sugarlands Visitor Center and Cades Cove. Only part of the picnic area is open in winter. The Little River is nearby, where you can fish or take a cooling dip. There are restrooms with flush toilets, potable water, and a 70-seat pavilion (open March through October) that can be reserved in advance. Two easy hiking trails, Metcalf Bottoms and Little Brier, begin at the picnic area. ⊠ *Great Smoky Mountains National Park* ✛ *Off Little River Rd., about 11 miles west of Gatlinburg* ⊕ *www.nps.gov/grsm.*

WHERE TO STAY

$$$$
RESORT
FAMILY
Fodor'sChoice
★
Blackberry Farm. Sprawled over more than 4,200 acres with fantastic views of the Smoky Mountains, this rustic estate, complete with red barn, hides a luxurious country retreat with refined service. **Pros:** wonderful setting and hospitality; plenty of activities including children's programs; huge wine cellar. **Cons:** remote and rural; dedicated urbanites may have difficulty adjusting to the quiet and stillness; very expensive. $ *Rooms from: $745* ⊠ *1471 West Millers Cove Rd., Walland* ☎ *865/984–8166, 800/648–2348 toll-free reservations* ⊕ *www. blackberryfarm.com* ↩ *68 rooms* ⫙ *Some meals.*

$$$$
B&B/INN
FAMILY
Fodor'sChoice
★
LeConte Lodge. Set at 6,360 feet near the summit of Mt. LeConte, this hike-in lodge is remote, rustic, and remarkable; it is not, however, luxurious. **Pros:** unique setting high on Mt. LeConte; a true escape from civilization; a special experience available only to a few. **Cons:** books up far in advance; hike-in access only, difficult for physically challenged or those not in good condition; simplest of accommodations with few modern conveniences. $ *Rooms from: $290* ⊠ *Mt. LeConte Lodge, Great Smoky Mountains National Park* ☎ *865/429–5704 reservations* ⊕ *www.lecontelodge.com* ☾ *Closed late Nov.– late Mar.* ↩ *7 cabins, 2 group sleeping cabins, all with shared bath* ⫙ *Some meals.*

LeConte Lodge has no electricity, no running water, and the only way to get there is to hike up a mountain; it rewards guests with peace, quiet, and fantastic views.

FESTIVALS AND EVENTS

FAMILY
Fodor's Choice
★

Spring Wildflower Pilgrimage. Each year in mid-to-late April, the Great Smoky Mountains National Park and the Great Smoky Mountains Association host the Spring Wildflower Pilgrimage. It attracts wildflower enthusiasts from all over the country for five days of wildflower and natural-history walks, seminars, classes, photography tours, and other events. Instructors include National Park Service staff, along with outside experts. Most activities are at various locations in the park, both on the North Carolina and Tennessee sides, but registration is in Gatlinburg at the W. L. Mills Conference Center adjoining the Gatlinburg Convention Center. Begun in 1951, the pilgrimage has grown to more than 140 different walks, classes, and events. Advance registration online begins in February of the year of the conference, and some events quickly sell out. Check the website for current details and dates. ⊠ *W. L. Mills Conference Center, 303 Reagan Dr., beside Gatlinburg Convention Center, Gatlinburg* ☎ *865/436–7318 Great Smoky Mountains Association, 888/898–9102 GSMA toll-free* ⊕ *www.springwildflowerpilgrimage.org* ⊠ *Registration $50 for 1 day, $75 for 2 or more days; some events free.*

TENNESSEE CAMPGROUNDS

Campgrounds at Cades Cove, Cosby, and Elkmont on the Tennessee side accept reservations, which can be made up to six months in advance. The America the Beautiful pass does not provide discounts for camping; however, the Senior and Access passes do provide discounts on camping fees.

Abrams Creek Campground. This first-come, first-served small campground (16 sites) is on the extreme western edge of the park, way off the beaten path. It can be hot and humid here in summer. Several trails, including Gold Mine, Cane Creek, Rabbit Creek, and Little Bottoms begin at or near the campground. It's closed mid-October through late May. The camping fee is $14. ⊠ *Off Happy Valley Rd. On western section of Foothills Pkwy., turn southeast on Happy Valley Rd. and follow approx. 2 miles to sign at access road to Abrams Creek Campground* ☎ *865/436–1200 for park info line* ⊕ *www.nps.gov/grsm.*

Cades Cove Campground. This is one of the largest campgrounds in the Smokies, with 159 sites, the one with the most on-site services, and one of only two in the park open year-round (the other is Smokemont on the North Carolina side). It has a small general store with a snack bar, bike rentals, horse stables, hayrides, an amphitheater, picnic area, and an RV dump station. This is a popular campground and often fills up in summer and fall. Reservations must be made at least one day ahead of arrival and can be made up to six months in advance. The camping fee is $17–$20. ⊠ *10042 Campground Dr., at entrance to Cades Cove Loop Rd.* ☎ *877/444–6777 or 865/448–2472 for information* ⊕ *www.recreation.gov.*

Cosby Campground. This large campground is set among poplars, hemlocks, and rhododendrons, near Cosby and Rock creeks. Most of the campsites are for tents only, and RVs/trailers are limited to just 25 feet. Of the 157 total sites, 26 can be reserved in advance by telephone or online. Bears are in the area, and several campsites may be closed temporarily due to aggressive bear activity. Nearby are many opportunities for hiking, with trailheads for Snake Den Ridge and Gabes Mountain trails. This campground is rarely very busy and nearly always has sites available even when others are full. It's closed November through early April. The camping fee is $14. ⊠ *127 Cosby Park Rd., off TN 32* ☎ *877/444–6777 or 423/487–2683 to check site availability* ⊕ *www.recreation.gov.*

Elkmont Campground. Easy hiking trails and the ability to wade, tube (bring your own inner tubes), fish, and swim in Little River, which runs through the campground, make Elkmont ideal for kids. Even though it is the largest campground in the Smokies, with 200 tent/RV sites plus 20 walk-in sites, it is often fully booked. Rates are $17–$23; reserve in advance by phone or online (reservations must be made at least one week ahead and can be made up to six months in advance). It's closed late November through mid-March. ⊠ *434 Elkmont Rd.* ☎ *877/444–6777 or 865/430–5560 for information* ⊕ *www. recreation.gov.*

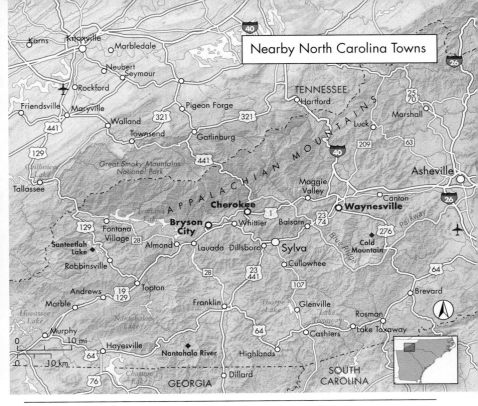

NEARBY NORTH CAROLINA TOWNS

Whether you're looking for a hot meal and a comfy bed after days of camping out or just want some "unnatural" diversion, these small towns have everything from a big casino to quaint potteries to keep you entertained.

CHEROKEE

178 miles east of Charlotte; 51 miles west of Asheville; 2 miles from entrance to Great Smoky Mountains National Park.

The 56,700-acre Cherokee reservation is known as the Qualla Boundary, and the town of Cherokee is its capital. Truth be told, there are two Cherokees: There's the Cherokee with the often-tacky pop culture, with junky gift shops full of cheap plastic "Indian crafts." These are designed to appeal to the lowest common denominator of the tourist masses. But there's another Cherokee that's a window into the rich heritage of the tribe's Eastern Band. Although now relatively small in number—Eastern Band tribal enrollment is 14,000—these Cherokee and their ancestors have been responsible for keeping alive the Cherokee culture. They are the descendants of those who hid in the Great Smoky Mountains to avoid the Trail of Tears, the forced removal of the Cherokee Nation to

Oklahoma in the 19th century. They are survivors, extremely attached to the hiking, swimming, trout fishing, and natural beauty of their ancestral homeland. You'll note that due to tribal efforts, all official signs in the Qualla Boundary, and many private commercial ones, are in the Cherokee language as well as in English. The reservation is dry, with no alcohol sales, except at the huge Harrah's casino complex. This means that there are few upscale restaurants in the area (because they depend on wine and cocktail sales for much of their profits), just fast-food and mom-and-pop places.

GETTING HERE AND AROUND

The Blue Ridge Parkway's southern terminus is at Cherokee, and the parkway is by far the most beautiful route to Cherokee and to Great Smoky Mountains National Park. A faster option is U.S. 23 and U.S. 74/U.S. 441, connecting Cherokee with Interstate 40 from Asheville or from Franklin in the south. The least pleasant route is U.S. 19 from Interstate 40, a mostly two-lane road pocked with touristy roadside shops.

ESSENTIALS

FAMILY **Cherokee Welcome Center.** This visitor center partners with and provides tourism information for a number of worthy local organizations including Qualla Arts & Crafts, Museum of the Cherokee Indian, Cherokee Fishing, Cherokee Chamber of Commerce, and the Cherokee Historical Association. ✉ *Cherokee Welcome Center, 498 Tsali Blvd., aka U.S. Hwy. 441 Business* ☎ *800/438–1601 toll-free in U.S. and Canada* 🌐 *www.visitcherokeenc.com.*

EXPLORING

FAMILY Fodor's Choice ★ **Museum of the Cherokee Indian.** The Museum of the Cherokee Indian, with displays and artifacts that cover 12,000 years, is one of the best Native American museums in the United States. Computer-generated images, lasers, specialty lighting, and sound effects help re-create events in the history of the Cherokee: for example, you'll see children stop to play a butter-bean game while adults shiver along the snowy Trail of Tears. The museum has an art gallery, a gift shop, and an outdoor living exhibit of Cherokee life in the 15th century. ✉ *589 Tsali Blvd., aka U.S. Hwy. 441* ☎ *828/497–3481* 🌐 *www.cherokeemuseum.org* 🎟 *$11.*

FAMILY **Oconaluftee Indian Village.** At the historically accurate, re-created Oconaluftee Indian Village, guides in native costume lead you through a 1760-era Cherokee village, while others demonstrate traditional skills such as weaving, pottery, canoe construction, and hunting techniques. ✉ *564 Tsali Blvd.* ☎ *828/497–2315* 🌐 *www.visitcherokeenc.com/play/attractions/oconaluftee-indian-village* 🎟 *$18.40* ⏲ *Closed mid-Apr.–mid-Nov.*

WHERE TO EAT AND STAY

$ AMERICAN FAMILY 🍴 **Peter's Pancakes & Waffles.** Pancake houses are big in Cherokee, and Peter's is at the top of the stack. Many locals are regulars here, and you'll see why when you try the blueberry pancakes with country ham. **Known for:** traditional pancakes with country ham; lots of locals; views of the Oconaluftee River. [$] *Average main: $8* ✉ *1384 Tsali Blvd., aka U.S. Hwy. 441* ☎ *828/497–5116* ⏲ *No dinner.*

$$$$ HOTEL Fodor'sChoice ★ **Harrah's Cherokee Casino Hotel.** The high-rise towers of the largest hotel in North Carolina, with nearly 1,200 rooms and suites currently and another 800 under construction, loom over the mom-and-pop motels nearby. **Pros:** fitness center, indoor pool, and resort golf course nearby; only place within the reservation to buy alcohol; 10 diverse restaurants options. **Cons:** hotel often heavily booked; some public areas reek of tobacco smoke; huge casino environment not for everyone. [$] *Rooms from: $450* ✉ *U.S. Hwy. 19 at U.S. Hwy. 441 Business, 777 Casino Dr.* ☎ *800/223–7277 reservations, 828/497–7777* 🌐 *www.harrahscherokee.com* 🛏 *1,118 rooms* 🍴 *No meals.*

NIGHTLIFE AND PERFORMING ARTS

NIGHTLIFE

Harrah's Casino. Owned by the Eastern Band of the Cherokee, Harrah's Casino has live blackjack, roulette, craps, and poker games along with some 5,000 electronic gaming machines in a huge casino the size of more than three football fields. Alcohol is available in the casino and its restaurants and bars (the rest of the Cherokee Indian Reservation is dry). Smoking is allowed in most of the casino, but restaurants and some public areas are smoke-free. Big-name stars such as Chris Rock, Willie Nelson, and Reba McEntire provide entertainment at the casino's 3,000-seat theater. Whatever one thinks of gambling, the highly successful casino has made a big impact on the 13,000 members of the Eastern Band of the Cherokee; recently, each member of the tribe received $11,700 from casino profits. In 2016, the tribe opened a second, $140 million casino and 300-room hotel complex about an hour west of Cherokee in Murphy, North Carolina. ✉ *777 Casino Dr., U.S. 19 at U.S. 441 Business* ☎ *828/497–7777, 800/427–7247 Reservations* 🌐 *www.harrahscherokee.com.*

PERFORMING ARTS

FAMILY ***Unto These Hills.*** This colorful, well-staged history of the Cherokee begins at the time of Spanish explorer Hernando de Soto's visit in 1540 and continues to the infamous Trail of Tears. The show runs from early June to mid-August. First presented in 1950, the drama has been updated with a new script and new costumes. More than 6 million people have seen the play over the years. Contemporary plays are presented in the Mountainside Theater as well. ✉ *Mountainside Theater on Drama Rd., off U.S. 441 N, 564 Tsali Blvd.* ☎ *828/497–2111, 866/554–4557 toll-free ticket reservations* 🌐 *www.cherokeesmokies.com/unto_these_hills.html* 🎟 *$20–$23.*

SPORTS AND THE OUTDOORS

FISHING

FAMILY **Cherokee Indian Reservation.** There are 30 miles of regularly stocked trout streams on the Cherokee Indian Reservation. The public can fish on most of the Raven Fork, Oconaluftee River, and Soco watersheds. To fish in these tribal waters you need a tribal catch-and-keep fishing permit, available at many reservation businesses or online. (Kids under 12 don't need a permit.) The $10 permit is valid for one day. Permits for longer periods are available: $17 for a two-day, $27 for a three-day, and $47 for a five-day. Creel limit is 10 per day per permit holder. A season's permit is available for $250. A three-day catch-and-release permit for Raven Creek is $25. Catch-and-keep waters are closed for two weeks before the last Saturday in March, but otherwise fishing is permitted year-round, from dawn to one hour before dusk. Only artificial lures are permitted. A North Carolina fishing license and trout stamp are not required for reservation fishing. ⌧ *Fisheries & Wildlife Management, 498 Tsali Blvd., at Cherokee Welcome Center* ☎ *828/497–6700* ⊕ *www.fishcherokee.com.*

GOLF

Sequoyah National Golf Club. Associated with Harrah's Cherokee Hotel and Casino and owned by the Eastern Band of the Cherokee Nation, Sequoyah National is open to the public as well as to those staying at Harrah's. The challenging 18-hole, par-72, 6,600-yard course, in a valley surrounded by mountains, was designed by Robert Trent Jones II. It has groomed bent grass greens with bluegrass fairways. Tee times may be booked by phone or online. Pricing varies significantly by day, time, and season. ⌧ *79 Cahons Rd., Whittier* ☎ *828/538–4246 to book tee times, 828/497–3000 pro shop* ⊕ *www.sequoyahnational.com* ⚑. *18 holes, 6600 yds, par 72. Greens Fee: varies depending on day and date, starting at $45. Facilities: Driving range, putting green, pitching area, golf carts, pull carts, rental clubs, pro shop, golf academy/lessons, restaurant, bar* ⚓ *Reservations essential.*

HIKING

FAMILY **Oconaluftee Islands Park & Trail.** In the downtown area of Cherokee you can cross the Oconaluftee River on a footbridge to the well-kept Oconaluftee Islands Park & Trail. The park has nice picnic facilities and walking trails. In warm weather, you can wade, tube, and swim in the river. On Thursday, Friday, and Saturday evenings in summer there's a bonfire and often a Cherokee storyteller. ⌧ *Tsali Blvd., off U.S.Hwy. 441, across from Cherokee Elementary School* ☎ *800/438–1601 Cherokee Welcome Center* ⊕ *www.visitcherokeenc.com.*

SHOPPING

FAMILY **Qualla Arts and Crafts Mutual.** The Qualla Arts and Crafts Mutual, across Fodor'sChoice the street from the Museum of the Cherokee Indian, is a cooperative ★ that displays and sells items created by 300 Cherokee craftspeople. The store has a large selection of extraordinary high-quality baskets, masks, and wood carvings, some of which can cost hundreds of dollars. Many items are of museum or near-museum quality, and there's a central gallery with truly wonderful Cherokee arts and crafts on display (items in the gallery are not for sale). ⌧ *Tsali Manor Dr., across from Museum of the Cherokee off U.S. Hwy. 441* ☎ *828/497–3103* ⊕ *www. quallaartsandcrafts.com.*

BRYSON CITY

65 miles east of Asheville; 11 miles southwest of Cherokee.

Bryson City is a little mountain town on the Nantahala River, one of the lesser-known gateways to the Great Smokies. The town's most striking feature is the former city hall with a four-sided clock. Since becoming the depot and headquarters of the Great Smoky Mountains Railroad, the downtown shopping area has been rejuvenated, mostly with gift shops, restaurants, and ice-cream stands.

GETTING HERE AND AROUND

Bryson City is a 15-minute drive from Cherokee on U.S. 19. Near Bryson City are two entrances to the Great Smokies.

EXPLORING

FAMILY **Great Smoky Mountains Railroad.** The popular train rides of the Great Smoky Mountains Railroad include excursions from the railroad's Bryson City depot and a number of special trips. Diesel-electric and, occasionally, steam locomotives travel 44 miles along the Nantahala Gorge to Nantahala Outdoor Center. The 32-mile Tuckasegee River to Dillsboro and back trips are both offered year-round, but with very limited schedules January to March. Open-sided cars or standard coaches are ideal for picture-taking as the mountain scenery glides by. There also are refurbished first-class, climate-controlled cars, with deluxe seating and meals. Combination rail excursions and Nantahala River rafting trips are offered in summer and early fall. The railroad also does special event excursions at various times during the year, including wine and beer tastings and an adult-only Moonshine trip. For kids, the railroad offers special excursions, including a Wizard of Oz train in summer and Polar Express trip at Christmas. Excursion schedules change frequently so check the railroad's website for the latest information. There are many discount deals available—for seniors, local residents, military, and others. ✉ *225–226 Everett St.* ☎ *800/872–4681 toll-free reservations line* 🌐 *www.gsmr.com* 🎟 *Nantahala and Tuckasegee excursions: $51–$106; prices vary for special event trips.*

FAMILY Fodor's Choice ★ **Nantahala River.** The most popular river in western North Carolina for rafting and kayaking is the Nantahala River, which races through the scenic Nantahala Gorge, a 1,600-foot-deep gorge that begins about 13 miles west of Bryson City on U.S. 19. Class III and Class IV rapids (Class V are the most dangerous) make for a thrilling ride. A number of outfitters run river trips or rent equipment. At several points along the river you can park your car and watch rafters run the rapids—on a summer day you'll see hundreds of rafts and kayaks going by. ✉ *U.S. 19, beginning 13 miles west of Bryson City* ☎ *828/524–6441 Nantahala Ranger District, National Forest Service* 🌐 *www.fs.usda.gov.*

WHERE TO EAT AND STAY

$$$ MODERN AMERICAN FAMILY Fodor's Choice ★ 🍴 **Cork & Bean Bistro.** This bistro and bar brings big city cool to Bryson City, with burgers, crepes, soups, and sandwiches for lunch, and hearty dinner entrées like bison meat loaf, mountain trout with quinoa, and venison osso buco. It's in a rustic, woody space in a 1908 building that formerly housed Bryson City Bank. **Known for:** rustic dining room in historic space; hearty meals with organic, local twists; craft beers. [$] *Average main: $22* ✉ *16 Everett St.* ☎ *828/488–1934* 🌐 *www.brysoncitycorkandbean.com* 🕒 *Closed Mon.*

$ FAST FOOD FAMILY 🍴 **The Filling Station Deli and Sub Shop.** This little sandwich shop is downtown Bryson City's most popular place to grab a Cuban, foot-long kosher hot dog, French dip (roast beef hoagie), corned beef on rye, or other sandwich—or a bowl of chili. While you're waiting, you can look at the old service-station memorabilia. **Known for:** filling, fresh sandwiches to go; ice cream sandwich cookies for dessert. [$] *Average main: $7* ✉ *145 Everett St.* ☎ *828/488–1919* 🌐 *www.thefillingstationdeli.com* 🕒 *Closed Sun.*

$

AMERICAN

FAMILY

✕ **River's End at Nantahala Outdoor Center.** The casual riverside setting and high-energy atmosphere at NOC's eatery draws lots of hungry people returning from an invigorating round of rafting or hiking. Every seat has a view of the Nantahala River, and the menu is mostly salads, soups, pizzas, and sandwiches. **Known for:** different types of chili; views of the Nantahala River. $ *Average main: $12* ⊠ *Nantahala Outdoor Center, 13077 Hwy. 19 W* ☎ *828/488–7172* ⊕ *www.noc.com.*

$$$$

B&B/INN

FAMILY

Fodor's Choice

★

🛏 **Everett Hotel.** Upstairs from the Cork and Bean Bistro, the bistro owners have turned the second and third floors of this 1909 brick building into a charming boutique hotel. **Pros:** rustically elegant rooms in historic building; good location in rejuvenated part of town; rooftop terrace with nice view and a fire pit. **Cons:** no elevator; no pool; priced a little higher than chain motels in area. $ *Rooms from: $269* ⊠ *Courthouse Square, 16 Everett St.* ☎ *828/488–1976* ⊕ *www.theeveretthotel.com* ⇗ *9 rooms* ⊙ *Breakfast.*

$$

B&B/INN

FAMILY

🛏 **Hemlock Inn.** This folksy, friendly mountain inn on 55 acres on a hilltop near Bryson City is the kind of place where you can rock, doze, catch up on reading, and play Scrabble. **Pros:** unpretentious, family-oriented inn; delicious Southern-style food; very welcoming atmosphere. **Cons:** no Wi-Fi, televisions, or in-room phones; no alcohol served; very basic rooms. $ *Rooms from: $189* ⊠ *Galbraith Creek Rd.* ☎ *828/488–2885* ⊕ *www.hemlockinn.com* ⊙ *Closed Jan.–mid-Apr.* ⇗ *19 rooms, 4 cottages* ⊙ *Some meals.*

SPORTS AND THE OUTDOORS

RIVER RAFTING AND KAYAKING

FAMILY

Fodor's Choice

★

Nantahala Outdoor Center (NOC). This center claims to be America's largest outdoor recreation company, with more than 1 million visitors a year arriving to raft on the Nantahala and six other rivers: the Chattooga, Cheoah, French Broad, Nolichucky, Ocoee, and Pigeon. Rates vary depending on the length of the trip and the river; trips on the Nantahala are around $30 to $70. Other rafting trips cost up to $150. NOC also rents kayaks, ducks, mountain bikes, and other equipment. The bustling 500-acre NOC complex is a tourist attraction itself, especially for young people, with three restaurants, an inn, five restaurants and zip-line adventures, several stores, a fly-fishing shop, and a stop for the Great Smoky Mountains Railroad. The company has expanded to offer paddling, wilderness medicine, and rafting and swift-water rescue training. NOC also has outlets in Asheville and Gatlinburg. ⊠ *13077 Hwy. 19 W* ☎ *800/905–7238* ⊕ *www.noc.com.*

WAYNESVILLE

17 miles east of Cherokee on U.S. 19.

This is where the Blue Ridge Parkway meets the Great Smokies. Waynesville is the seat of Haywood County. About 40% of the county is occupied by Great Smoky Mountains National Park, Pisgah National Forest, and the Harmon Den Wildlife Refuge. The town of Waynesville is a rival of Blowing Rock and Highlands as a summer and vacation-home retreat for the well-to-do, though the atmosphere here is a bit more countrified.

Folkmoot USA, a two-week international festival that began in Waynesville in 1984 and is held annually in July, brings music and dancing groups from around the world to various venues in Waynesville and elsewhere in western North Carolina.

GETTING HERE AND AROUND

Waynesville is about 30 miles southwest of Asheville. From Asheville, take Interstate 40 West. At Exit 27, take U.S. 74 West to U.S. 23/74 West. At Exit 102, take U.S. 276 to Waynesville. If coming from Cherokee, about 19 miles west of Waynesville, you can take U.S. 74 East to U.S. 23 to Waynesville; the longer but much more scenic route is via the Blue Ridge Parkway. South Main Street is the main commercial street in Waynesville, lined for several blocks with small shops, craft breweries, and art galleries.

EXPLORING

FAMILY **Cold Mountain.** The vivid best-selling novel by Charles Frazier, *Cold Mountain,* and its movie adaptation have made a destination out of the real Cold Mountain. About 15 miles from Waynesville in the Shining Rock Wilderness Area of Pisgah National Forest, the 6,030-foot rise had long stood in relative anonymity. But with the success of Frazier's book, people want to see the region that Inman and Ada, the book's Civil War–era protagonists, called home. For a view of the splendid mass, stop at any of a number of overlooks off the Blue Ridge Parkway. Try the Cold Mountain Overlook, just past mile marker 411.9; the Wagon Road Gap parking area, at mile marker 412.2; or the Waterrock Knob Interpretative Station, at mile marker 451.2. You can climb the mountain, but be prepared; the hike to the summit is strenuous. No campfires are allowed in Shining Rock, so you'll need a stove if you wish to cook. ⊠ *Blue Ridge Pkwy., MM 411.9, Cold Mountain Overlook* ☎ *828/298–0398 parkway information line* ⊕ *www.nps.gov/blri.*

Museum of North Carolina Handicrafts. Exhibits of 19th-century heritage crafts are on display at the Museum of North Carolina Handicrafts, located in the Shelton House (circa 1875). ⊠ *49 Shelton St., at corner of U.S. Hwy 276 S* ☎ *828/452–1551* ⊕ *www.sheltonhouse.org* ▨ *$5* ⊙ *Closed Nov.–Apr.*

WHERE TO EAT AND STAY

$$$$ ✕ **Chef's Table.** Here at Waynesville's ultimate special-occasion restaurant,
MODERN the chef-owner uses ingredients from his own farm or other local farms
AMERICAN to prepare dishes in an open kitchen. Menu items like lamb shank, osso
FAMILY buco, and roasted duck breast are created with wine pairings in mind. **Known for:** hands-on chef-owner who uses local ingredients; wine-country cuisine with wine pairings. $ *Average main: $27* ⊠ *30 Church St.* ☎ *828/452–6210* ⊕ *www.thechefstableofwaynesville.com* ⊙ *Closed Sun.*

$$$$ ✕ **Frogs Leap Public House.** Frogs Leap partners with more than a dozen
SOUTHERN natural and organic producers to find the ingredients needed to create
FAMILY its rigorous "farm-to-fork" modern Southern menu, which changes frequently depending on what's in season. Several signature dishes, such as Sunburst trout and Hickory Nut Farm grass-fed meat loaf, do stay on the menu, and those are always dependable. **Known for:** charming rustic atmosphere; always changing organic, farm-to-table menu. $ *Average main: $26* ⊠ *44 Church St.* ☎ *828/456–1930* ⊕ *www.frogsleappublichouse.com* ⊙ *Closed Sun.*

5

$$
SOUTHERN

✕**The Sweet Onion.** This casual restaurant in downtown Waynesville serves delicious Southern comfort food like roast beef, country fried steak, bacon-wrapped meat loaf, blackberry barbecue short ribs, and shrimp and grits. Entrées come with two sides, like mashed potatoes, collards, or fried okra. **Known for:** Southern comfort food; cheerful, friendly staff. $ *Average main: $18* ⊠ *39 Miller St.* ☎ *828/456–5559* ⊕ *www.sweetonionrestaurant.com* ��� *Closed Sun.*

$$
B&B/INN
Fodor'sChoice
★

Andon-Reid Bed & Breakfast Inn. Inside this large, 6,000-square-foot 1902 restored Victorian house near downtown Waynesville all is light and comfort; the two suites and three large rooms, plus the carriage house, are nicely decorated in a crafty, early American style, with wood floors. **Pros:** hospitable owners; cozy rooms and suites with fireplaces; delicious breakfasts. **Cons:** a bit of a walk to the main downtown area; no pool; no elevator. $ *Rooms from: $155* ⊠ *92 Daisy Ave.* ☎ *828/452–3089* ⊕ *www.andonreidinn.com* ⟿ *7 rooms* ⟊ *Breakfast.*

$$$$
B&B/INN
Fodor'sChoice
★

The Swag Country Inn. The Swag sits at 5,000 feet, high atop the Cataloochee Divide, with its 250 wooded acres bordering the Great Smoky Mountains National Park, and with guest rooms and cabins assembled from authentic log structures and transported here. **Pros:** small luxury inn with personality; fabulous location on a nearly mile-high mountaintop; delicious meals included. **Cons:** remote; very expensive; no TV, no bar, no a/c (but rarely needed at this elevation). $ *Rooms from: $520* ⊠ *2300 Swag Rd.* ☎ *828/926–0430, 800/789–7672 toll-free reservations in U.S. and Canada* ⊕ *www.theswag.com* ��� *Closed late Nov.–mid-Apr.* ⟿ *14 rooms* ⟊ *All meals.*

$$
B&B/INN

The Yellow House on Plott Creek Road. Just outside town, this lovely two-story Victorian, painted a sunflower yellow, sits on 5 acres on a low knoll, with colorful surrounding gardens and hammocks under shady trees. **Pros:** well-run bed-and-breakfast; lovely grounds; romantic. **Cons:** very couples-oriented; not within walking distance of restaurants and shops in town; no TV in rooms. $ *Rooms from: $165* ⊠ *89 Oak View Dr., at Plott Creek Rd., 1 mile west of Waynesville* ☎ *828/452–0991, 800/563–1236 toll-free reservations* ⊕ *www.theyellowhouse.com* ⟿ *10 rooms* ⟊ *Breakfast.*

NIGHTLIFE

Frog Level Brewing Company. Little Waynesville now has four craft brewers and they're all good, but the original one in the historic Frog Level section is still the best. Frog Level Brewing has a large, comfortable tasting room with lots of exposed brick and natural wood. In good weather you can sit outside by the creek. There's live music some nights. ⊠ *56 Commerce St.* ☎ *828/454–5664* ⊕ *www.froglevelbrewing.com* ��� *Closed Sun.*

SHOPPING

FAMILY
Downtown Waynesville. The main shopping area in downtown Waynesville stretches several long blocks along Main Street, with a number of small boutiques, bookstores, antiques shops, restaurants, and a bakery. Side streets in this charming small town also offer shopping and dining. A few blocks away, Frog Level is an up-and-coming dining and entertainment section in a former industrial area. ⊠ *Main St.* ☎ *828/456–3517 Downtown Waynesville Association* ⊕ *www.downtownwaynesville.com.*

MYRTLE BEACH, SC, AND THE GRAND STRAND

WELCOME TO MYRTLE BEACH, SC, AND THE GRAND STRAND

TOP REASONS TO GO

★ **Sixty miles of beach:** From North Myrtle Beach south to Pawleys Island, Grand Strand sand is silky-smooth—perfect for sunbathing and biking.

★ **Golf, golf, and more golf:** More than 100 golf courses for all skill levels meander through pine forests, dunes, and marshes.

★ **Southern culture:** Explore Southern culture and history on a plantation tour; taste it in the form of barbecue and other local foods; bring it home with a hammock woven right in Pawleys Island.

★ **Brookgreen Gardens:** More than 500 works from American artists are set among 250-year-old oaks, palms, and flowers in America's oldest sculpture garden.

★ **Water world:** Thanks to the area's rivers, waterways, inlets, and Atlantic coastline, you'll find yourself surrounded by water while you're here. Explore it anyway you like: drop a hook, dip a toe or an oar, or dive right in and make your own waves.

1 The Myrtle Beach Area. Myrtle Beach has a colorful case of multiple personalities in its makeup, from exclusive resorts to gritty nostalgia and everything in between. And that's what makes it unique. Try local muscadine wine, fill up at restaurants by renowned chefs, touch heaven in the SkyWheel Ferris wheel, play Skee-Ball at an oceanfront arcade, take in shops and variety shows, and, of course, enjoy the miles of sandy beaches. North Myrtle Beach, including the small, waterfront fishing towns of Little River and Cherry Grove, has a diverse assortment of entertainment options, from casino riverboats to scuba-diving artificial reefs and shipwrecks to fishing off the Cherry Grove Pier. At the Shagger's Hall of Fame, learn about South Carolina's state dance, the shag, born on Ocean Drive.

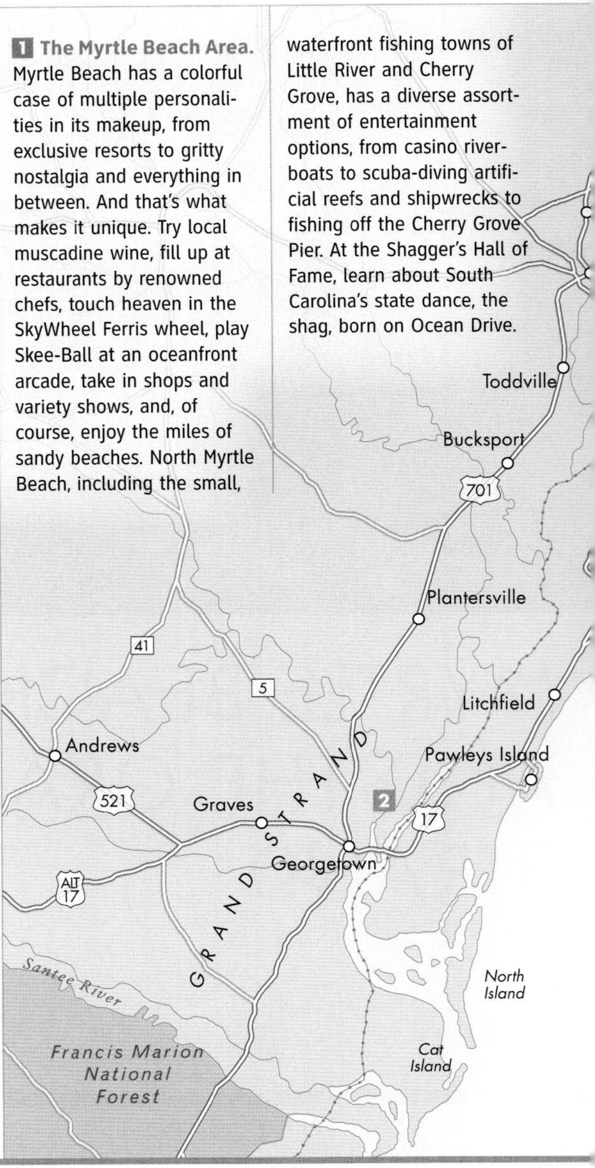

Toddville

Bucksport

701

Plantersville

41

5

Litchfield

Andrews

Pawleys Island

521

Graves

2

17

AlT 17

Georgetown

GRAND STRAND

Santee River

North Island

Francis Marion National Forest

Cat Island

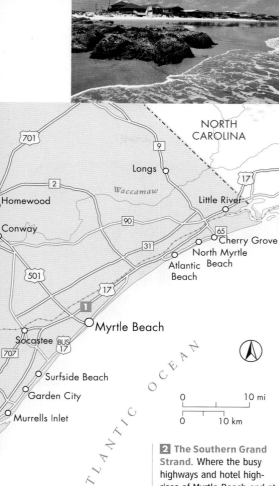

NORTH CAROLINA

Longs

Waccamaw

Homewood

Conway

Little River

Cherry Grove

North Myrtle Beach

Atlantic Beach

Myrtle Beach

Socastee

Surfside Beach

Garden City

Murrells Inlet

ATLANTIC OCEAN

0   10 mi

0   10 km

GETTING ORIENTED

Although most resort communities have beaches and water activities, the Grand Strand—the 60-mile stretch of beaches from Little River to Georgetown—is known for much more. Lush botanical gardens, elegant waterfronts, quirky art galleries, theatrical shows, high-end and kitschy shopping, and tasty seafood are just some of the Strand's assets. Although other coastal communities, such as Charleston or Hilton Head Island, may cater to a wealthier lifestyle, the Grand Strand can accommodate both the budget-conscious as well as the high-end traveler.

6

2 The Southern Grand Strand. Where the busy highways and hotel high-rises of Myrtle Beach end at the border of Horry and Georgetown counties, the South Strand begins. The coastal communities of Georgetown County— seafood-centric Murrells Inlet, arrogantly shabby Pawleys Island, and historic Georgetown—boast a slow-paced, rustic elegance. Poke around small shops surrounded by live oaks or sample the fresh catch of the day, with no pretense in sight.

MYRTLE BEACH AND THE GRAND STRAND BEACHES

The broad, flat beaches along the Grand Strand are a patchwork of colorful coastal scenes—from the high-energy section of Myrtle Beach backed by a wall of hotel high-rises to the laid-back leisure of Pawleys Island, accessible only by two causeway bridges that cross the salt marsh.

The family-oriented Grand Strand is world-renowned as one of the Eastern Seaboard's megavacation centers. The main attraction, of course: 60 miles of white sand, stretching from the North Carolina border south to Georgetown, with Myrtle Beach as the hub. From North Myrtle Beach all the way down to Pawleys Island, the Grand Strand's silky sand invites you to take your shoes off and relax. Low-tide, packed sand makes way for early-bird joggers, bikers, and dog walkers next to the crashing waves. If you're lucky, you'll see dolphins, which often come in close in the early morning or just before sunset.

(above) Low tide is the perfect time for kids to splash in the waves. (lower right) Family beach days are easy with so many amenities nearby. (upper right) You can rent sailboats along the beach.

GOLF

The Myrtle Beach area is the place to go for golf while at the beach. The award-winning Barefoot Resort offers four courses and vistas along the Intracoastal Waterway on the north end. The renowned, private Dunes Club course features breathtaking ocean views, and the Jack Nicklaus–designed Pawleys Plantation on the south end will have you putting amongst the pluff mud at low tide in the marshes.

MYRTLE BEACH

It's no secret **Myrtle Beach** is a big hit with families. The international praise it has received as a family destination put it on the summer vacation map, so if you're seeking a quiet spot on the sand, this isn't the place for you. What you will find here is a buzz of activity, from music spilling out of beachfront tiki bars, to an overflow of excitement from the stretch of boardwalk shops and cafés between the piers at 14th and 2nd Avenues North. There is still plenty of natural beauty to be found, including shelling along the beach in the morning. For sunseekers who prefer more peace, Myrtle Beach's residential section between 38th and 48th Avenues North, which is short on beach access parking (and thus, people), is the best bet. **Myrtle Beach State Park,** just south of Springmaid Pier, is another peaceful spot with picnic areas, wooded nature trails, a children's activity center, playgrounds, and a fishing pier.

NORTH MYRTLE BEACH

North Myrtle Beach is less crowded, but it's certainly no less appealing. You'll find a hodgepodge of smaller hotels, high-rises, and beach cottages along the coastline. Sunbathers, shellers, and walkers love the wide beaches. North Myrtle's population increases in spring and fall when two national shag-dance gatherings take over the streets. The old shag dance clubs, as well as oodles of

cute restaurants, still thrive along North Myrtle's Main Street. You may even see a few shaggers shuffling the dance steps on the sand, like they first did more than 50 years ago.

SURFSIDE BEACH AND GARDEN CITY BEACH

Surfside Beach is a small, southern suburb of Myrtle Beach, touted as a family beach that has a tight community of locals, parks, and a pier flanked by a block of seafood restaurants for visitors. **Garden City Beach** is south of Surfside off the Atlantic Avenue causeway, which ends at the Garden City Pier, boasting a fun arcade, fishing, and a one-of-a-kind bar that hosts live bands on summer nights. Garden City not only features beaches ocean-side, but a popular secluded beach inlet-side, called the Point, accessible by boat.

LITCHFIELD BEACH AND PAWLEYS ISLAND

When you go to the South Strand's **Litchfield Beach** and **Pawleys Island**, it's time to relax, slow down your stride, and breathe in the fragrance of the saltwater marshes. Pawleys Island was once a summertime retreat for wealthy rice plantation owners who lived inland and remains perfect for quiet relaxation. Kissing the northern cusp of Litchfield is **Huntington Beach State Park,** a coastal haven for hikers, bird-watchers, or history buffs.

6

Updated
by Stratton
Lawrence

The coastal beauty of the Myrtle Beach area is priceless, but its affordability for families has also ranked this resort area as one of the most accessible beach destinations in the world. And, as Myrtle Beach's reputation as a family-friendly destination has grown, so have the size, sophistication, and number of activities available.

The main attraction is the broad, beckoning beach known as the Grand Strand—60 miles of white sand, stretching nearly from the North Carolina border in Little River and North Myrtle Beach south to Surfside Beach, Garden City Beach, Murrells Inlet, Pawleys Island, and Georgetown, with Myrtle Beach centered at the hub. People come to "the Strand" for all of the traditional beach-going pleasures: swimming, sunbathing, sailing, surfing, shell hunting, fishing, jogging, and strolling. Away from the water, golfers have more than 100 courses to choose from, designed by the likes of Arnold Palmer, Robert Trent Jones, and Jack Nicklaus.

Golfing and beaching are far from "it" in Myrtle Beach, however. When it comes to diversions, you could hardly be better served, with acclaimed seafood restaurants, giant shopping complexes, trendy markets, factory outlets, Vegas-style live performance and concert venues, nightlife hot spots, amusement and water parks, arcades, a dozen shipwrecks for divers to explore, beachfront campgrounds, antique-car and wax museums, an award-winning aquarium, the world's largest outdoor sculpture garden, and a museum dedicated entirely to rice.

PLANNING

WHEN TO GO

The Grand Strand was developed as a summer resort, and with its gorgeous beaches, flowering tropical plants, palmetto trees, and warm weather, it continues to shine during the height of the summer season. That said, the fall and spring shoulder seasons may be even better. Warm temperatures allow for beach activities, but the humidity drops, the crowds thin, and the heat of summer passes.

Winter—November through February—isn't usually considered a time to visit the beach, but the region can be quite pleasant. There are certainly cold days, but for the most part golfers, tennis players, and other outdoors enthusiasts can enjoy their pursuits during these months—at rock-bottom prices.

■ **TIP➔ In the third and fourth weeks of May, much of the Grand Strand is inhabited by bikers in town for the Harley-Davidson Spring Rally and the Atlantic Beach Bike Fest. Traffic and noise problems are common, and hotel space is scarce.**

PLANNING YOUR TIME

Many visitors do Myrtle Beach in a long weekend; beach or golf by day, and nightlife, dining, and shows by night. But with the area's bounty of beaches, amusements parks, mini-golf courses, and waterslides, you could easily fill a week, especially if you've got kids in tow. Enjoy the great outdoors by water or land (boardwalk, mini-golf, and Market Common festivals year-round) or pass rainy days in indoor playgrounds with aquariums, museums, and arcades galore. If history is your passion, spend at least a day exploring Georgetown on foot, by boat, or with a guided tour. With all this to explore, we recommended you rent a car, as these treasures are spread out.

GETTING HERE AND AROUND
AIR TRAVEL
The Myrtle Beach International Airport (MYR) is served by Allegiant, American, Delta, Elite, Porter, Spirit, United, and WestJet, flying nonstop to more than 30 cities. The terminal's 12 gates over two concourses include an array of shops and restaurants.

Air Contacts Myrtle Beach International Airport (MYR). ✉ 1100 Jetport Rd., Myrtle Beach ☎ 843/448–1580 ⊕ www.flymyrtlebeach.com.

CAR TRAVEL
Midway between New York and Miami, the Grand Strand isn't connected directly to any interstate highways but is within an hour's drive of Interstate 95, Interstate 20, Interstate 26, and Interstate 40 via Route 22 (Veterans Highway), U.S. 501, and the newer Route 31 (Carolina Bays Parkway). U.S. 17 Bypass and U.S. 17 Business are the major north–south coastal routes through the Strand.

■ **TIP➔ In summer, to bypass incoming southbound traffic jams on U.S. 501, take Interstate 95 to Interstate 40 to U.S. 17 (at Wilmington) to Route 31, which connects to Myrtle Beach via Route 544 or the tail end of U.S. 501.**

MOPED TRAVEL
Rent a moped for a fun way to travel with the slower traffic along Ocean Boulevard (state law maximum speed for mopeds is 30 mph), anywhere along the Grand Strand. Helmets are strongly advised within Myrtle Beach city limits and are required for riders under 21.

Contacts East Coast Golf Carts and Scooters. ✉ 410 Sea Mountain Hwy., North Myrtle Beach ☎ 843/424–2644 ⊕ www.eastcoastgolfcarts.com. **Mopeds, Bikes & Surf.** ✉ 106 N. Kings Hwy., Myrtle Beach ☎ 843/626–6900.

TAXI TRAVEL

Taxi services are available at several locations along the Grand Strand. Uber and Lyft are both available in Myrtle Beach and are permitted at the airport for pickups and drop-offs—Uber is more popular and generally faster to get a car. Diamond Taxi Transportation serves the North Myrtle Beach area, Creekside Cab serves the South Strand, and Absolute Taxi serves the central Myrtle Beach area.

Taxi Contacts Absolute Taxi. ☎ *843/333–3333* ⊕ *www.absolutetaxi.com.* **Creekside Cab.** ☎ *843/357–8444.* **Diamond Cab.** ☎ *843/448–8888* ⊕ *www. myrtlebeachdiamondcab.com.*

RESTAURANTS

With the sand at your feet, seafood will most likely be on your mind. The nearly 2,000 restaurants on the Grand Strand boast all types of seafood, whether you're seeking a buffet or a more intimate dining spot. The summer months see an influx of visitors, so waits at popular restaurants can reach up to an hour or more. ■ TIP→ To avoid long waits, take advantage of early-bird dinner specials, make a reservation, or opt for takeout. Many spots oblige with free delivery to hotels. *Dining reviews have been shortened. For full information, visit Fodors.com.*

HOTELS

High-rise hotels line the Grand Strand, but kitschy beach motels, beachside camping, luxury resorts, and weekly beach house or cottage rentals are popular choices, too. Most accommodations have pools, and many high-rises up the ante with lazy rivers or water-play areas. Advance reservations are recommended for the majority of beach properties. Ask about special packages that include golf, shows, and shopping. *Hotel reviews have been shortened. For full information, visit Fodors.com.*

WHAT IT COSTS			
	$	**$$**	**$$$**	**$$$$**
Restaurants	Under $15	$15–$19	$20–$24	over $24
Hotels	Under $150	$150–$200	$201–$250	over $250

Restaurant prices are the average cost of a main course at dinner or, if dinner is not served, at lunch. Hotel prices are the lowest cost of a standard double room in high season.

DISCOUNTS AND DEALS

Visitor centers and grocery stores throughout the Grand Strand have free coupon books with discounts for mini-golf, 18-hole golf courses, personal watercraft rentals, and parasailing, to name a few. Kiosks on the boardwalk and in area malls also have special offers.

TOURS

Palmetto Tour & Travel, Sunway Charters & Tours, and Gray Line offer tour packages and guide services.

Tour Contacts Gray Line Tours Myrtle Beach. ☏ *843/448–9483* ⊕ *www. graylinemyrtlebeach.com.* **Palmetto Tour & Travel.** ☏ *843/236–5722* ⊕ *www. palmettotourandtravel.com.* **Sunway Charters & Tours.** ☏ *843/293–2100* ⊕ *www.sunwaychartersandtours.com.*

THE MYRTLE BEACH AREA

Myrtle Beach was a late bloomer. Until 1901 it didn't have an official name; that year the first hotel went up, and oceanfront lots were selling for $25. Today, more than 15 million people a year visit the region, and no wonder: lodging, restaurants, shopping, and entertainment choices are varied and plentiful. The many award-winning golf courses in the area add to the appeal. What's more, Myrtle Beach has taken a big step toward extending its reputation beyond a frenzied collection of all-you-can-eat buffets, T-shirt shops, and gritty bars with the unveiling of an oceanfront boardwalk that meanders between the 14th Avenue North and 2nd Avenue North piers. There is a renewed interest in the oceanfront shops, ice-cream parlors, restaurants, and arcades, and the beautiful new boardwalk is recapturing a pedestrian- and family-friendly Myrtle Beach that was alive with the Pavilion amusement park (demolished in 2006) in its 1960s heyday. The Myrtle Beach Boardwalk is constantly expanding with amusements and attractions, including the SkyWheel, the largest Ferris wheel on the East Coast by day (and a sky-high spectacle at night).

Neon lights still light up noisy blocks of Ocean Boulevard ("the Strip"), Kings Highway, and Restaurant Row (sometimes called the Galleria area), but the Strip and boardwalk are generally safe and clean. Nearby attractions such as Family Kingdom amusement park, Broadway at the Beach, Broadway Grand Prix, and Myrtle Waves Water Park add a dose of fun to your afternoon.

If a quiet vacation is more your speed, opt for dining in sophisticated restaurants following days lolling on relatively uncrowded beaches adjacent to the residential areas of Myrtle Beach at either end of the Strip.

■TIP➔ **Be sure to take note of whether an establishment is on U.S. 17 Business or U.S. 17 Bypass—confusing the two could lead to hours of frustration. U.S. 17 Business is also referred to as Kings Highway.**

MYRTLE BEACH

94 miles northeast of Charleston; 138 miles east of Columbia.

Myrtle Beach, with its high-rises and hyper-development, is the nerve center of the Grand Strand and one of the major seaside destinations on the East Coast. Visitors are drawn here for the swirl of classic vacation activity, from beaches to golf to nightlife to live music and theater shows.

To capture the flavor of the place, take a stroll along the sidewalks or boardwalk of Ocean Boulevard. Here you'll find an eclectic assortment of restaurants and gift and novelty shops. When you've had your fill, turn east and make your way back onto the beach amid the sunbathers, parasailers, kite fliers, and kids building sand castles.

GETTING HERE AND AROUND

Most routes to Myrtle Beach run via Interstates 95 and 40, and connect to either U.S. 501, Route 31, Route 22, or U.S. 17. The main thorough-fares through the Grand Strand are U.S. 17 Bypass and U.S. 17 Business (aka Kings Highway); both run parallel to the beach. Most of the city's main streets are numbered and are designated north or south.

ESSENTIALS

Visitor Information Myrtle Beach Area Convention and Visitors Bureau Welcome Centers. ⊠ *1200 N. Oak St.* ☎ *843/626–7444, 800/356–3016* ⊕ *www.visitmyrtlebeach.com* ✉ *Myrtle Beach International Airport* ☎ *843/626–7444, 800/356–3016* ⊕ *www.visitmyrtlebeach.com.*

EXPLORING

TOP ATTRACTIONS

FAMILY

Fodor's Choice

★

Broadway Grand Prix Family Race Park. This go-cart race park features seven different tracks, including one indoor slick track. The 26-acre facility also has racing memorabilia, a "Sky Coaster" thrill ride, an arcade, and miniature golf. ⊠ *1820 21st Ave. N, at U.S. 17 Bypass, Central Myrtle Beach* ☎ *843/839–4080* ⊕ *www.broadwaygrandprix. com* ✉ *Single-ride tickets from $2; unlimited day passes sold by height: $24.95 under 47", $29.95 48"–59"; $34.95 60" and up* ☉ *Closed Nov.–Mar.*

FAMILY

Family Kingdom. Dominated by a gigantic white wooden roller coaster called the Swamp Fox, **Family Kingdom amusement park** is quite an experience, and it's right on the ocean. There are thrill and children's rides, a log flume, go-cart track, old-fashioned carousel, and the Sling-shot Drop Zone, which rockets riders straight down a 110-foot tower. It's a bit like going to a state fair that runs all summer long. Bring your bathing suit and cross the street for more fun at **Splashes Oceanfront Water Park.** Operating hours can vary, so it's worthwhile to call before visiting, especially on Saturday when the parks are sometimes rented by groups. Money-saving bundled tickets and multiday passes are readily available; check the website for more information. ⊠ *300 S. Ocean Blvd., The Strip* ☎ *843/626–3447 amusement park, 843/916–0400 water park* ⊕ *www.familykingdomfun.com* ✉ *free; single-ride tickets $1.15 each; 1-day unlimited access to most rides $27.95 amusement park, $21.95 water park; amusement and water park combo pass $37.90* ☉ *Closed Oct.–Mar.*

Fodor's Choice

★

Franklin G. Burroughs-Simeon B. Chapin Art Museum. A hidden gem in a 1920s beach cottage on the southern cusp of Ocean Boulevard, this museum has a permanent collection that will open your eyes to the art community that thrives on the Grand Strand. Impressive national touring exhibits stop here year-round. ⊠ *3100 S. Ocean Blvd., South Myrtle Beach* ☎ *843/238–2510* ⊕ *www.myrtlebeachartmuseum.org* ✉ *Donations accepted* ☉ *Closed Mon.*

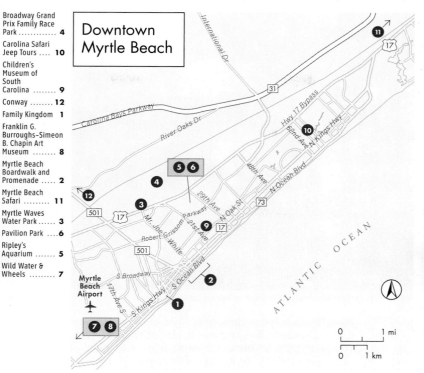

Downtown Myrtle Beach

FAMILY **Myrtle Beach Boardwalk and Promenade.** It's a mile-long oceanfront destination in itself, day or night, drawing in visitors of all ages. The boardwalk stretches from the 14th Avenue Pier, where seafood restaurant–café Pier 14 roosts, to the newly renovated 2nd Avenue Pier and its Pier House restaurant and open-air rooftop lounge. Take a sky-high seat on the SkyWheel, the largest Ferris wheel on the East Coast at 175 feet tall with enclosed gondolas for a smooth ride (don't miss the light show at night), then stop in for a bite to eat at Jimmy Buffett's LandShark restaurant located right at the entrance. You can also take the kids to play in the old-time arcade, zip across the Myrtle Beach Zipline Adventures aerial course, break for a soft-serve ice-cream cone, shop for a souvenir at the world-famous Gay Dolphin, shuck oysters at Dirty Don's, pull up a stool at the Bowery (the legendary bar that gave country band Alabama its start), or just stroll or sit, taking in the beach scene. A schedule of free live concerts, performances, fireworks, and children's carnivals abounds in summer at the boardwalk's Plyler Park. And don't miss the holiday, family-friendly block parties year-round. ⚠ **Bikes, pets, and skateboards are prohibited on the boards May–September.** ✉ *14th Ave. N to 2nd Ave. N and Ocean Blvd.* ⊕ *www.myrtlebeachdowntown.com* ✆ *Free.*

Myrtle Beach's mile-long boardwalk is lined with restaurants to grab a bite.

Myrtle Beach Safari. A three-hour Wild Encounters tour at The Institute of Greatly Endangered and Rare Species (T.I.G.E.R.S.) transports you away from Myrtle Beach on an African walking safari. A team of animal handlers, led by nationally renowned trainer Dr. Bhagavan "Doc" Antle, allows you to hold baby tigers, pose with a 900-pound liger, hug orangutans, feed an elephant, and more. You leave with a life-changing experience, captured on a personalized DVD, plus a disc with hundreds of professional photos taken of you as you pose with animals throughout the day. The tour is intended to be both entertaining and educational; entrance fees fund conservation of the animals at this sanctuary and conservation projects in Africa. Driving to the sanctuary is not permitted; tour reservations can be made from the T.I.G.E.R.S. Preservation Station at Barefoot Landing, where they will brief you on directions to the sanctuary (and you can see a live tiger through glass for free). Children must be at least six years old for the tour. ⊠ *Barefoot Landing: Preservation Station, 4898 S. Hwy. 17* ☎ *843/361–4552* ⊕ *www.myrtlebeachsafari.com* ✉ *$299* ⊘ *Closed Nov.–Feb.*

FAMILY **Myrtle Waves Water Park.** At South Carolina's largest water park you can shoot through twisty chutes, swim in the Ocean in Motion Wave Pool, race your friends down Snake Mountain, or ride a boogie board on the Racin' River. Even the toddlers will enjoy splashing in Bubble Bay and Saturation Station playground. There's beach volleyball, too, for when you've had enough water. Shaded areas with lounge chairs offer respite from the sun, and private cabanas, complete with waitstaff, are available to rent for the day. Lifeguards on duty are aplenty, and lockers are available to keep money and valuables safe. Wear a well-secured swimsuit on the big slides, or you may reach the end of the slide before your suit does. ✉ *3000 Mr. Joe White Ave., Central Myrtle Beach* ☎ *843/913–9250* ⊕ *www.myrtlewaves.com* ⛱ *Full day $27.99; all tickets include next day free* ☉ *Closed Oct.–Apr.*

FAMILY **Pavilion Park.** The historic oceanfront Pavilion (razed in 2006) lives on through its amusement rides that are now split between three sections at Broadway at the Beach. East Park features original Pavilion rides like the famous Herschell-Spillman Carousel, dating back to 1912. West Park is home to kiddie rides and the Myrtle Turtle coaster, while Central Park includes an array of modern thrill rides. In between, hit the snack stands vending funnel cakes and snow cones. ✉ *Broadway at the Beach, 1171 Celebrity Circle, Central Myrtle Beach* ☎ *843/839–0303* ⊕ *www. pavilion-park.com* ⛱ *$2 ride tickets; $25 unlimited ride pass* ☉ *Closed Jan. Limited hours and attractions Nov.–Mar.*

FAMILY
Fodor'sChoice
★
Ripley's Aquarium. Glide underwater (no need for a wet suit) through a winding tunnel exhibit that's longer than a football field, where sharks of all kinds and exotic marine creatures, including poisonous lionfish, moray eels, and an octopus, swim over and around you (or below you, if you spring for the glass-bottom boat tour). Children can examine horseshoe crabs and stingrays in touch tanks, and mermaid shows are offered regularly. Special exhibits are often included in the price of aquarium admission. Admission discounts are available when combined with price of Ripley's Ocean Boulevard attractions. ✉ *Broadway at the Beach, 1110 Celebrity Circle, Central Myrtle Beach* ☎ *843/916–0888* ⊕ *www.ripleyaquariums.com/myrtlebeach* ⛱ *$26.99.*

FAMILY **Wild Water & Wheels.** This water park has 24 water-oriented rides and activities, along with go-carts and mini-golf. If your children are old enough to navigate the park on their own, spend a few minutes at the adults-only lounge pool, where you can sit immersed in Jacuzzi-like bubbles, or rest in your own private cabana. ■**TIP→ Admission is lower after 2 pm and even lower on Friday evenings after 5.** ✉ *910 U.S. 17 S, Surfside Beach* ☎ *843/238–3787* ⊕ *www.wild-water.com* ⛱ *Full day $27.98; afternoon only $19.98* ☉ *Closed Oct.–Apr.*

WORTH NOTING

FAMILY **Carolina Safari Jeep Tours.** Visit everything from a plantation house to an alligator-laden salt marsh to an 18th-century church on these tours. Along the way, learn fun facts and scary ghost stories, told from a script that keeps even history-phobes entertained. The 3½-hour tour, which includes some walking, provides a complete overview of the region and beautiful views of the Grand Strand's varied ecosystem. Call to make a reservation; you'll be picked up at your hotel in a jeep that seats about a dozen people. ✉ *Myrtle Beach* ☎ *843/497–5330* ⊕ *www. carolinasafari.com* ⛱ *$40.*

FAMILY **Children's Museum of South Carolina.** Bring the kids here to beat the heat or take cover on a rainy day. Create giant bubbles, pet turtles, and play dentist or doctor. It's educational, it's hands-on, and it's entertaining for parents, too. ✉ *2204 N. Oak St., Central Myrtle Beach* ☎ *843/946–9469* ⊕ *www.cmsckids.org* ⛱ *$8.*

6

OFF THE
BEATEN
PATH
Conway. For a break from the beach, or as a pleasant way to spend a cool or cloudy day, take a day trip to the historic town of Conway. Conway is a 15-mile trip inland on Route 501 North to Route 501 Business across the bridge that arches over the Waccamaw River and onto the town's Main Street. A huge source for lumber in the 1870s, the town is now an eclectic hub for art studios and the arts (take a glassblowing class at Conway Glass!), antiques stores, and a growing number of foodie hot spots, including the celebrated Rivertown Bistro. Conway's Riverwalk, along the Waccamaw River, offers a peaceful respite for walkers, joggers, and bikers. If you're charmed and want to stay the night, the elegant Cypress Inn is a luxurious respite worlds away from the busy attractions of the Grand Strand. ⊠ *Conway.*

WHERE TO EAT

$$
ITALIAN

✕ **Angelo's Steak & Pasta.** Cut, trimmed, and seasoned to order, steaks sizzle on their way to the tables and then melt in your mouth at this Italian-style steak house. Pasta is served up on the daily Italian buffet, featuring standard favorites such as spaghetti, meatballs, lasagna, and tortellini alfredo. **Known for:** tableside magic shows; longevity—Angelo's has been a fixture for four decades. $ *Average main: $20* ⊠ *2311 S. Kings Hwy., South Myrtle Beach* ☎ *843/626–2800* ⊕ *www. angelosteakandpasta.com* ◷ *No lunch weekdays.*

$$$$
ECLECTIC

✕ **Collectors Café and Gallery.** A successful restaurant, art gallery, and coffeehouse rolled into one, this unpretentiously artsy spot has bright, funky paintings and tile work covering its walls and tabletops. The seasonal menu is among the most inventive in the area. **Known for:** hot spot for locals on weekend evenings; being a far cry from standard Myrtle Beach fish-house fare. $ *Average main: $30* ⊠ *7740 N. Kings Hwy., North End* ☎ *843/449–9370* ⊕ *www.collectorscafeandgallery. com* ◷ *Closed Sun. No lunch Sat.*

$
AMERICAN

✕ **Dagwood's Deli.** Comic-strip characters Dagwood and Blondie could split one of the masterful meat-packed sandwiches at Dagwood's Deli, where locals line up on their lunch break. There are the usual suspects—ham, turkey, and homemade chicken salad—but you won't regret trying one of the more distinctive creations like the Hogpound, pork tenderloin doused in melted Swiss and provolone. **Known for:** delivery to most of the Myrtle Beach area; catering for family and business groups. $ *Average main: $8* ⊠ *400 Mr. Joe White Ave., Central Myrtle Beach* ☎ *843/448–0100* ⊕ *www.dagwoodsdeli.com* ◷ *Closed Sun. No dinner.*

$$
ASIAN

✕ **Indo Thai Sushi & Hibachi.** Owner Laura Smith is legendary in Myrtle Beach for her sushi artistry. In addition to sushi masterpieces she creates a slew of authentic Thai noodle dishes and signature seafood creations like Coco Shrimp and jumbo soft-shell crabs. **Known for:** elaborate sushi rolls; Indonesian-style seafood specialties. $ *Average main: $19* ⊠ *980 82nd Pkwy., North End* ☎ *843/692–7000* ⊕ *www. indothairestaurant.com.*

$
MODERN
MEXICAN

✕ **Nacho Hippo.** If you're a hungry hippo, then slide a stool over to a maximo plate of nachos here at this duo of hip corner cantinas in The Market Common and in North Myrtle Beach. It's bold, fresh, and fun—from the funky wall and ceiling decor to the creative Mexican dishes. **Known for:** budget-priced margaritas; massive, creative nachos piled high in seafood, vegan, and kamikaze versions. [$] *Average main: $10* ✉ *The Market Common, 1160 Farrow Parkway, South Myrtle Beach* ☎ *843/839–9770* 🌐 *www.nachohippo.com.*

$$$ SEAFOOD Fodor's Choice ★ 🍴 **Sea Captain's House.** The windowed porch overlooking the ocean houses the best seats at this nautical-themed restaurant in a 1930s beach cottage. Menu highlights include sautéed crab cakes and jambalaya; it's the rare Myrtle Beach seafood restaurant that offers vegetarian and gluten-free menus. **Known for:** historic oceanfront locale—an island of history amid high-rises; hearty breakfasts that are a step above the Strip's pancake-house fare. [$] *Average main: $22* ✉ *3002 N. Ocean Blvd., The Strip* ☎ *843/448–8082* 🌐 *www.seacaptains.com.*

$ JAPANESE FUSION 🍴 **Sobaya Japanese Bistro.** Tucked into a cozy corner of St. James Square, this bistro packs a lot of punch into its tiny frame. Expect attentive service and authentic Japanese-Korean fusion flavors in entrées like seasoned beef bibimbap or seared ahi salad with yuzu dressing. **Known for:** hibachi bento boxes at lunch; authentic Asian cuisine. [$] *Average main: $10* ✉ *3590 St. James Ave., Unit A, Central Myrtle Beach* ☎ *843/839–4899* 🌐 *www.sobayabistro.com* 🕒 *Closed Sun. and Mon.*

$$$ ITALIAN 🍴 **Villa Romana.** It's all about family at Villa Romana, where owners Rinaldo and Franca come in early to make the gnocchi and stick around to greet customers. It's hard to resist filling up on the *stracciatella* (Italian egg-drop) soup, bruschetta, salad, and rolls (perhaps the best on the Strand) that accompany every meal, but try. **Known for:** homemade sauces, pastas, and gnocchi; live Italian accordion music during service. [$] *Average main: $20* ✉ *707 S. Kings Hwy., Central Myrtle Beach* ☎ *843/448–4990* 🌐 *www.villaromanamyrtlebeach.com* 🕒 *No lunch.*

$ BURGER 🍴 **Wahlburgers.** The Myrtle Beach outpost of the burger joint owned by Mark Wahlberg and his family is airy, bright, and spacious. Order a specialty burger or sandwich at the counter with names like the Beast and the O.F.D (Originally from Dorchestah), or perch at the bar for a cold beer and a relaxed respite from the busy goings-on at Broadway at the Beach. **Known for:** decadent frappes and floats; a thick turkey burger called the Thanksgiving Day Sandwich. [$] *Average main: $10* ✉ *Broadway at the Beach, 1320 Celebrity Circle, Unit 195, Central Myrtle Beach* ☎ *843/213–1254* 🌐 *www.wahlburgersrestaurant.com.*

WHERE TO STAY

$$$$ RESORT 🏨 **Anderson Ocean Club and Spa.** Small touches of heavenly Moroccan luxury greet you upon arrival, from the fountain in the front plaza to the stately double-door entrance flanked by large lanterns. **Pros:** upscale furnishings will wow you; central location convenient to Broadway at the Beach dining and entertainment options; one of the most well-appointed resort complexes in the area. **Cons:** proximity of Magnolia's restaurant is only a plus if you love basic country cookin'; lots of resorts in this area can make for a crowded beach; no true lobby or indoor communal space. [$] *Rooms from: $300* ✉ *2600 N. Ocean Blvd., The Strip* ☎ *843/213–5340* 🌐 *www.oceanaresorts.com/anderson* 🛏 *289 units* 🍽 *No meals.*

GRAND STRAND VACATION RENTALS

If a hotel just won't suit the size of your crew, the Grand Strand can accommodate with beach-house or cottage rentals aplenty.

Here are a few agencies to check out before you check in:

Beachcomber Vacations. ⊠ *Myrtle Beach* ☎ *800/334–3798* ⊕ *www. beachcombervacations.com.*

Dunes Realty. ⊠ *Myrtle Beach* ☎ *888/889–0312, 843/651–2116* ⊕ *www.dunes.com.*

Elliott Realty. ⊠ *North Myrtle Beach* ☎ *888/669–7853* ⊕ *www. elliottrealty.com.*

Garden City Realty. ⊠ *Garden City Beach* ☎ *877/767–7737* ⊕ *www. gardencityrealty.com.*

Grand Strand Vacations. ⊠ *North Myrtle Beach* ☎ *800/722–6278* ⊕ *www.grandstrandvacations.com.*

Seaside Rentals. ⊠ *Surfside Beach* ☎ *866/252–9930* ⊕ *www.seasiderentalsonline.com.*

Surfside Realty Company. ⊠ *Surfside Beach* ☎ *800/833–8231* ⊕ *www.surfsiderealty.com.*

$$$$
RESORT
FAMILY

Breakers Resort Hotel. This sprawling seven-tower oceanfront hotel, which is in the middle of the Myrtle Beach Strip, has airy and spacious rooms complete with contemporary furnishings. **Pros:** excellent views from the tower rooms; kids activities are included; multiple on-site dining options. **Cons:** pool areas can be crowded in high season; presence of families and children can detract from a romantic getaway; it's located in a high-traffic area of the beach. Ⓢ *Rooms from: $260* ⊠ *2006 N. Ocean Blvd., The Strip* ☎ *855/861–9550, 855/861–9550* ⊕ *www. breakers.com* ⌁ *672 units* ⦿ *No meals.*

$$
RESORT
FAMILY

The Caravelle Resort. She may be over the hill (built in 1960 and fully renovated in 2007), but she's as youthful and tropically trendy as ever, with a bright yellow exterior, superchic condos, and the Wild Water pool area running the length of one side of the hotel, which receives rave giggles and shrieks of delight from kids; the complex has more then 10 pools. **Pros:** on-site Santa Maria Restaurant is a Myrtle Beach institution; sunny glass-roofed seventh-floor indoor pool; one of only a few Myrtle Beach hotels with access to the private Dunes Club Golf Course. **Cons:** lobby and concierge are across the street making check-in confusing, especially during heavy summertime traffic; it's a walk from some of the buildings to the main pool area. Ⓢ *Rooms from: $192* ⊠ *6900 N. Ocean Blvd., North End* ☎ *800/297–3413* ⊕ *www. thecaravelle.com* ⌁ *540 condos* ⦿ *No meals.*

$$$$
RESORT
FAMILY

Caribbean Resort and Villas. Four different properties make up the Caribbean, each offering access to the other's amenities. **Pros:** Cayman Tower's floor-to-ceiling windows afford expansive views of the beach and ocean from most rooms; great family-geared water facilities. **Cons:** not for couples looking for a quiet romantic stay; pools and water-activity areas are designed for families. Ⓢ *Rooms from: $292* ⊠ *3000 N. Ocean Blvd., The Strip* ☎ *855/421–6947* ⊕ *www.caribbeanresort. com* ⌁ *465 rooms* ⦿ *No meals.*

$$ ⬚ **Grande Shores Ocean Resort.** Grande Shores is a combination of rent-
RESORT able condos with full kitchens and standard hotel rooms outfitted with
FAMILY refrigerators, coffeemakers, and, in a few cases, kitchenettes. **Pros:**
water features for all age groups; spacious rooms with full kitchens
are great for families; rooftop pool. **Cons:** only a select group of rooms
actually face the ocean; less flashy and fancy than newer competitors.
Ⓢ *Rooms from: $170* ✉ *201 77th Ave. N, The Strip* ☎ *855/707–4712*
⊕ *www.grandeshores.com* ⤳ *136 rooms* ⁜❘*No meals.*

$$$$ ⬚ **Hampton Inn and Suites Oceanfront.** This property combines the reli-
RESORT ability of an established hotel chain with the joys of a beach resort. **Pros:**
crisp white bed linens lend rooms a tropical, beachy feel; on-site day
spa. **Cons:** it's a drive or over a mile walk to the boardwalk and attrac-
tions along the Strip. Ⓢ *Rooms from: $289* ✉ *1803 S. Ocean Blvd.,
South Myrtle Beach* ☎ *888/407–0422* ⊕ *www.hamptoninnoceanfront.
com* ⤳ *227 rooms* ⁜❘*Breakfast.*

$$$ ⬚ **Island Vista Resort.** Nestled along the residential north end of the
RESORT Strand, this resort has room to breathe, instead of being smack up
FAMILY against the clutter of hotels clogging the coastline farther south. **Pros:**
free on-site kids activities; room furnishings are tastefully tropical, not
tacky; less crowded beach area than its peers. **Cons:** you'll need a car
to reach the boardwalk; there's less to do in walking distance than at
other resorts. Ⓢ *Rooms from: $233* ✉ *6000 N. Ocean Blvd., North End*
☎ *855/732–6250* ⊕ *www.islandvista.com* ⤳ *149 rooms* ⁜❘*No meals.*

$$$$ ⬚ **Kingston Plantation.** This 145-acre ocean-side complex includes three
RESORT hotels, as well as restaurants, shops, and one- to three-bedroom condo-
FAMILY miniums and villas. **Pros:** lushly landscaped property; award-winning
beachfront restaurant, Café Amalfi, on-site; expansive on-site water
park with whirlpools, lazy river, and waterslides. **Cons:** some condos
may include a sleeper sofa in the bed count; it's a drive to popular attractions along the Strip. Ⓢ *Rooms from: $289* ✉ *10000 Beach Club Dr.,
North End* ☎ *800/876–0010* ⊕ *www.kingstonplantation.com* ⤳ *1458
units* ⁜❘*No meals.*

$$$ ⬚ **Marina Inn at Grande Dunes.** From the rich wood and sumptuous car-
RESORT pet in the lobby to the manicured lawns and amenities, this inn along
FAMILY the Intracoastal Waterway is a little slice of paradise. **Pros:** exemplary
service; views of the Waterway and Grand Dunes golf greens; daily
schedule of activities for families and children. **Cons:** Highway 17 runs
adjacent to the complex; it's a drive to get to the beach. Ⓢ *Rooms from:
$229* ✉ *8121 Amalfi Pl., North End* ☎ *843/913–1333* ⊕ *www.mari-
nainnatgrandedunes.com* ⤳ *210 rooms* ⁜❘*No meals.*

$$$$ ⬚ **Myrtle Beach Marriott Resort & Spa at Grande Dunes.** Entering this plan-
RESORT tation-chic high-rise resort, with its airy wicker furniture, giant palms,
and mahogany details, will take you away from the hubbub of Myrtle
Beach and straight to a tropical locale. **Pros:** striped hammocks swing
near the dunes with views of the ocean; several pools and water features
are available. **Cons:** it's a bit of a drive south to the hub of Myrtle Beach
shopping; the pool area can be crowded in-season. Ⓢ *Rooms from:
$329* ✉ *8400 Costa Verde Dr.* ☎ *843/449–8880* ⊕ *www.myrtlebeach-
marriott.com* ⤳ *400 rooms* ⁜❘*No meals.*

6

$$$$ RESORT 🏨 **Ocean 22.** Hilton's most recent construction on the Strip is a sleek, ultramodern array of suites with full kitchens and spacious, well-appointed living areas with ocean views. **Pros:** close proximity to the boardwalk and attractions along the Strip; free entry to Wild Water & Wheels Water Park; top-notch fitness center. **Cons:** pool complex doesn't feature the kid-oriented aspects of other resorts; close proximity of other resorts can make for a crowded beach. [$] *Rooms from: $399* ✉ *2200 North Ocean Blvd., The Strip* ☎ *843/848–0022* 🌐 *www.hilton.com* 🛏 *220 suites* 🍴 *No meals.*

NIGHTLIFE AND PERFORMING ARTS

CLUBS AND LOUNGES

Fodor's Choice ★ **The Boathouse Waterway Bar & Grill.** If you're up for a rowdy evening of entertainment (and a worthy basket of grub for dinner), grab a spot in the backyard April–September for the annual free Sunday Summer Concert Series featuring national touring acts; Fridays check out free local acts. It's quite a sight, as fleets of boats anchor for a waterway view of the stage and the landlocked crowd packs the bank. ✉ *201 Fantasy Harbour Blvd., Fantasy Harbor* ☎ *843/903–2628* 🌐 *www.boathousemb.com.*

FAMILY **Broadway at the Beach.** South Carolina's only Hard Rock Cafe, Jimmy Buffett's Margaritaville restaurant, daiquiri bar Fat Tuesday, dueling piano bar Crocodile Rocks, and karaoke haven Broadway Louie's are just a few of the hot spots at Broadway at the Beach, which also has shopping and recreational activities like an amusement park, WonderWorks interactive museum, speedboat rides on the lakes and a towering zipline over Lake Broadway. ✉ *U.S. 17 Bypass, between 21st and 29th Aves. N, Central Myrtle Beach* ☎ *843/444–3200* 🌐 *www.broadwayatthebeach.com.*

2001 Entertainment Complex. This 21-and-older complex showcases a little bit of everything under one roof, from live music on stage to a mainstream dance club. ✉ *920 Lake Arrowhead Rd., North End* ☎ *843/449–9434* 🌐 *www.2001nightclub.com.*

FILM

Big D Theater. A former IMAX theater, the Big D features large-format digital movies on a giant three-story-high screen, plus luxury leather seating. ✉ *Broadway at the Beach, U.S. 17 Bypass, between 21st and 29th Aves. N, Central Myrtle Beach* ☎ *843/445–1600* 🌐 *www.carmike.com.*

MUSIC AND LIVE SHOWS

FAMILY **Carolina Opry.** A Myrtle Beach show staple since 1986, The Carolina Opry is a family-oriented variety show featuring country, light rock, show tunes, and gospel. There's also a "Time Warp" show that pays tribute to the '60s, '70s, and '80s; a laser light show; and a Christmas Special. ✉ *8901 N. Kings Hwy., North End* ☎ *800/843–6779* 🌐 *www.thecarolinaopry.com.*

Comedy Cabana. Touring comedians—some of whom have made cable TV appearances—make their way to Comedy Cabana, a little comedy club that's inspired belly laughs for over 20 years on the north side of town. There's an on-site restaurant serving pizza and burgers. ✉ *9588 N. Kings Hwy., North End* ☎ *843/449–4242* 🌐 *www.comedycabana.com.*

Legends in Concert. This venue features high-energy shows by impersonators of Elvis, Garth Brooks, Michael Jackson, and the Blues Brothers, plus more current pop stars like Britney Spears and Lady Gaga. ✉ *Broadway at the Beach, 2925 Hollywood Dr., Central Myrtle Beach* ☎ *800/960–7469* ⊕ *www.legendsinconcert.com/myrtle-beach.*

FAMILY **Pirates Voyage.** This Dolly Parton–owned production features a 15-foot-deep water lagoon staged with Crimson and Sapphire pirate ships. Ye families will enjoy a four-course feast while watching swashbuckling fights, pyrotechnics, acrobats, high dives, and mermaids in flight. ✉ *8907 N. Kings Hwy., North End* ☎ *843/497–9700* ⊕ *www.pirates-voyage.com* ✍ *$49.99.*

SPORTS AND THE OUTDOORS

BASEBALL

FAMILY **Myrtle Beach Pelicans Baseball.** Catch a minor-league baseball game April–September with this proud Chicago Cubs–affiliated team at TicketReturn.com Field. Look for specials and promos, like the "all-you-can-eat" seats and Thirsty Thursdays. Distractions include a super-size playground and inflatable rides for kids, and contests and entertainment between innings. A sandy beach section, picnic area, and luxury suites can be reserved for groups. ✉ *1251 21st Ave. N, Central Myrtle Beach* ☎ *843/918–6002* ⊕ *www.myrtlebeachpelicans.com.*

BEACHES

Regardless of whether you're staying on the beach, you shouldn't have too much trouble getting to a spot of sand. There are nearly 150 public beach access points in the city, all marked with signs. Most are located off Ocean Boulevard and have parking and "shower towers" for cleaning up; few have restroom facilities. Parking can be scarce, but during summer the city allows metered parallel parking on Ocean Boulevard.

Because much of Myrtle Beach's coastline is dominated by high-rise hotels, there are plenty of places to get lunch or a cool drink without having to get back in your car. Many of these hotels also rent beach chairs, umbrellas, and boogie boards. Some have nets set up for beach volleyball. ■TIP➜ **For a quieter beach experience, look for beach access away from the high-rise hotels. The Strand's residential section between 30th and 48th Avenues North are good bets.**

Dogs, kayaks, and surfboards are limited on many beaches from May through September. Be sure to read the ordinances posted at each access point for details. ■TIP➜ **Summer heat can be brutal, and the sand can scorch: don't step out of the hotel barefoot.**

FAMILY **Garden City Beach.** In Horry County's southernmost coastal town of the same name, this diverse landscape of beachfront along the Atlantic is backed by a causeway that crosses creeks and tributaries feeding into marinas and the southern village of Murrells Inlet. The coastline is a curious collection of a few high-rise hotels, older condo buildings, and cute, stilted beach houses. Beachfront disappears at high tide farther south—so much so that it slaps up against the pilings and sea wall. The Garden City Pier is a must for fishing (free), strolling, playing arcade games, or dancing to live music at the partially covered bar perched at

6

the very end. Other beach activities include kayaking, Jet Skiing, kite-boarding, parasailing, banana-boat rides, and boogie boarding. **Best for:** sunrise; surfing; swimming; walking. **Amenities:** food and drink; lifeguards (sometimes); parking; showers; toilets; water sports. ✉ *At-lantic Ave. and S. Waccamaw Dr., Garden City Beach.*

FAMILY **Myrtle Beach.** The beachfront of the city of Myrtle Beach stretches from the Springmaid Pier at the south end up to 82nd Avenue North. That's a lot of real estate to choose from for your chair or blanket. Expect the entire length of this popular family beach to be busy from May to October with people fishing, boogie boarding, parasailing, surfing (only allowed after 5 pm), and sunbathing. In the off-season (November–February) you can take horseback rides on the beach. Restaurants and shops line the boardwalk section of 2nd to 14th Avenues. A beachfront trail of workout stations lines the north end. Note that an ordinance bans tents over 7½ feet in diameter from Memorial Day to Labor Day. **Best for:** partiers; sunrise; swimming; walking. **Amenities:** lifeguard (May–September; no lifeguards in residential section of 38th–48th Avenues north); parking (free at north-end beach access areas; metered on street along Ocean Boulevard; pay-by-day or -hour at Pavilion Parking Garage at 8th Avenue North); showers; toilets; water sports. ✉ *32nd Ave. S to 82nd Ave. N, Central Myrtle Beach.*

FAMILY **Myrtle Beach State Park.** This state-protected parcel of land has a mile-long beach, 350 campsites, picnic pavilions, hiking trails in the woods beyond the dunes, a fishing pier complete with an ice-cream shop, playgrounds, and a quaint boardwalk. There are year-round family or children's activities offered through the park, like crabbing and nature programs. Note that there are no lifeguards. **Best for:** sunrise; swimming; walking. **Amenities:** food and drink; parking (free with $5 admission to park); showers; toilets. ✉ *4401 S. Kings Hwy., South Myrtle Beach* ⊕ *www.southcarolinaparks.com/myrtlebeach* 🖾 *$5.*

FAMILY **Surfside Beach.** Dubbed "the Family Beach," this small strand just south of Myrtle Beach offers up about 2 miles of white sand. Here, the hotel high-rises, bright lights, and big city of Myrtle Beach disappear, replaced by beach houses, cottages, and peaceful views. The centerpiece Surfside Pier is the site of most of the town's festivals, burger and fried fish joints, and a kickin' karaoke bar. **Best for:** solitude; sunrise; surfing; swimming; walking. **Amenities:** food and drink; lifeguards (May–September); parking (lots with meters at 12 out of 36 beach access areas); showers; toilets. ✉ *17th Ave. N to Melody La., Surfside Beach.*

FISHING

Fishing along the Grand Strand is best during the warm waters of late spring through December. Anglers can fish from 10 piers and jetties for amberjack, sea trout, and king mackerel. Surf casters may snare bluefish, whiting, flounder, pompano, and channel bass. In the South Strand, the tidal creeks weaving through the salt marsh yield flounder, blues, croakers, spots, shrimp, clams, oysters, and blue crabs.

■**TIP**➜ **Swimmers, steer clear of the piers. Fishermen's bait is known to lure unwelcome sharks to the water as well.**

Grand Strand Fishing Rodeo. For more than 50 years, from April through October, the Grand Strand Fishing Rodeo has held a fish-of-the-month contest on participating area piers, with prizes for the largest catch of a designated species. There's no registration fee; entrants must take their catch to designated weigh stations for consideration. ⊠ *Myrtle Beach* ⊕ *www.Facebook.com/GrandStrandFishingRodeo.*

GOLF

Known as the Golf Capital of the World, the Grand Strand is home to more than 100 courses. Many are championship layouts and most are public.

Arrowhead Country Club. Known for its top-notch condition, regardless of the season, Arrowhead is the only Raymond Floyd–designed course in the region. Many of the scenic 27 holes, uniquely grouped into 9-hole themes, run along the Intracoastal Waterway. All greens are MiniVerde Bermudagrass, a grass species developed to tolerate high temperatures. Chomping at the bit? Arrowhead offers showers, towels, and amenities so you can sneak in one last round before heading to the airport, which is five minutes away. ⊠ *1201 Burcale Rd., West Myrtle Beach* ☎ *800/236–3243, 843/236–3243* ⊕ *www.arrowheadcc. com* ⊠ *$79* ⚑ *27 holes. 6180 yds. Par 72.* ⚒ *Reservations essential* ⚐ *Facilities include a driving range, golf academy/lessons for juniors, and a restaurant.*

Indigo Creek Golf Club. Beauty and bargains await at Indigo Creek, a course cut through forests of huge oaks and pines that once surrounded an indigo plantation. The Willard Byrd design boasts tall oaks, meandering creeks, and stellar maintenance of the Tift Dwarf Bermuda greens and tees. ⊠ *9480 Indigo Club Dr., Murrells Inlet* ☎ *800/718–1830, 843/650–1809* ⊕ *www.indigocreekgolfclub.com* ⊠ *$75* ⚑ *18 holes. 6747 yds. Par 72.* ⚒ *Reservations essential* ⚐ *Facilities include a driving range, pitching area, golf academy/lessons, and a restaurant.*

Pine Lakes. Built in 1927 and listed on the National Register of Historic Places, Pine Lakes is reputed as the Grand Strand's "Granddaddy" of courses. The patriarch, however, is carefully maintained and was redesigned in 2009, unveiling newer holes near the new north-end entrance off Grissom Parkway. A conversation here led to the creation of *Sports Illustrated* magazine, a piece of trivia proudly displayed on the walls of the clubhouse. ⊠ *5603 Granddaddy Dr., Central Myrtle Beach* ☎ *877/283–2122* ⊕ *www.pinelakes.com* ⊠ *$95* ⚑ *18 holes. 6675 yds. Par 70.* ⚒ *Reservations essential* ⚐ *Facilities include a pitching area, golf academy/lessons, and a restaurant.*

Resort Club at Grande Dunes. This course has some of the widest and purportedly fairest fairways in Myrtle Beach, a veritable kingdom of golf, with majestic, nationally award-winning views of the tranquil waterway. ⊠ *8700 Golf Village La., North End* ☎ *877/283–2122* ⊕ *www. grandedunesgolf.com* ⊠ *$128* ⚑ *18 holes. 7618 yds. Par 72.* ⚒ *Reservations essential* ⚐ *Facilities include a pitching area, golf academy/ lessons, and a restaurant.*

6

The Tournament Players Club Myrtle Beach. Designed by the legendary Tom Fazio, this former home to the Senior PGA Tour Championship has also been solid training grounds for PGA Tour star and Myrtle Beach local Dustin Johnson, who founded the Dustin Johnson Golf School here. The scenery is both beautiful and challenging, with plenty of towering pines, wetlands, and water hazards. ⊠ *1199 TPC Blvd., Murrells Inlet* ☎ *877/283–2122* ⊕ *www.tpcmyrtlebeach. com* ✉ *$128* ⅃ *18 holes. 6950 yds. Par 72.* ⚲ *Reservations essential* ☞ *Facilities include a driving range, pitching area, golf academy/ lessons, and a restaurant.*

The Witch. Dan Maples–designed, this course is off the beaten Myrtle Beach path amid the pines along Route 544. True to its name, it can be quite bewitching throughout its 500-acre rolling layout over higher elevations and the lower wetlands connected by a mile of bridges. ⊠ *1900 Hwy. 544, Conway* ☎ *843/347–2706* ⊕ *www.witchgolf.com* ✉ *$79* ⅃ *18 holes. 6796 yds. Par 71.* ⚲ *Reservations essential* ☞ *Facilities include a driving range, rental clubs, and golf academy/lessons.*

HELICOPTER RIDES

For a bird's-eye view of the beach, take to the sky in a helicopter to scoot along the coastline or explore more customized tours inland. The tours are great for aerial photo ops.

Helicopter Adventures. ⊠ *1860 21st Ave. North, Central Myrtle Beach* ☎ *800/359–4386* ⊕ *www.helicopteradventures.com* ✉ *Flights start at $20.*

Oceanfront Helicopters. ⊠ *3000 S. Kings Hwy., South Myrtle Beach* ☎ *843/946–0022* ⊕ *www.huffmanhelicopters.com* ✉ *Flights start at $20.*

MINI-GOLF

Nearly 50 mini-golf courses, also known as "putt-putt" around here, are in full swing along the Grand Strand. It's practically a subculture of Myrtle Beach that will have you climbing through caverns, scaling volcanic mountains, crossing rapids, and dodging fire-breathing dragons to master the 18-hole mini-greens. Beat the crowds by putt-putting in the morning or before the after-dinner rush.

FAMILY **Cancun Lagoon Mayan Adventure Golf.** Putt over 27 holes inside or out of Cancun's massive 50-foot Mayan pyramid. It's open weekends only during winter. ⊠ *2101 S. Kings Hwy., South Myrtle Beach* ☎ *843/444– 1098* ⊕ *www.paradiseadventuregolf.com* ✉ *$9.50 (age 10 and up); all-day pass $15.*

FAMILY **Dragon's Lair Fantasy Golf.** Mini-golf goes medieval, as you maneuver through castle lookouts and caverns while dodging the 30-foot fire-breathing dragon that intermittently pops up from his lair. ⊠ *Broadway at the Beach, 1197 Celebrity Circle, Central Myrtle Beach* ☎ *843/913–9301* ⊕ *www.dragonslairfantasygolf.com* ✉ *$9 before 6 pm, $10 after 6.*

Hawaiian Rumble. Host of the U.S. ProMiniGolf Association's Masters Championship, this course takes mini-golf to a whole new level, especially with its centerpiece: a 40-foot-tall, fire-erupting volcano mountain that "rumbles" the ground every 20 minutes. ✉ *3210 U.S. 17 S, North Myrtle Beach* ☎ *843/272–7812* ⊕ *www.hawaiianrumbleminigolf.com* ☜ *$9 (age 5 and up).*

FAMILY **Mt. Atlanticus Minotaur.** Indoor and outdoor greens race around a giant mountain, past waterfalls, and into lagoons of this tiki-themed 36-hole course. ✉ *707 N. Kings Hwy., off 7th Ave. N, near U.S. 501, Central Myrtle Beach* ☎ *843/444–1008* ⊕ *www.mountatlanticus.com* ☜ *$10.*

SCUBA DIVING
You don't have to go far off the coast of the Grand Strand to explore the underwater world. Man-made reefs boast an array of fish including sea fans, sponges, reef fish, anemones, urchins, and crabs. A number of shipwrecks are also worth exploring under the waves. Paddle wheelers, freighters, and cargo ships lie in ruins off the coast, and are popular scuba spots. ■ TIP➔ **Always wanted to dive but never learned how? Most dive shops can have you PADI certified in a weekend.**

Nu Horizons Dive & Travel. Certification classes and equipment rentals, as well as an indoor dive tank, are available at this diving headquarters in the Sports Corner shopping center. ✉ *515 U.S. 501, Suite A, Central Myrtle Beach* ☎ *800/505–2080, 843/839–1932* ⊕ *www.southcarolinadive.com.*

TENNIS
There are more than 200 courts on the Grand Strand. Facilities include hotel and resort courts, as well as free municipal courts in Myrtle Beach, North Myrtle Beach, and Surfside Beach. ■ TIP➔ **Many tennis clubs offer weekly round-robin tournaments that are open to players of all levels.**

Grande Dunes Tennis Club. A full fitness facility with 10 Har-Tru courts (eight lit), the club also offers lessons, clinics, camps, and match opportunities. ✉ *U.S. 17 Bypass at Grande Dunes Blvd., North End* ☎ *843/449–4486* ⊕ *www.grandedunestennis.com.*

Prestwick Tennis Club. This club offers court time, instruction, and tournament opportunities on adult and junior levels; 11 clay and two hard courts are lighted for nighttime play. ✉ *1375 McMaster Dr., South Myrtle Beach* ☎ *843/831–0117* ⊕ *www.prestwicktennisclub.com.*

WATER SPORTS
Don't forget to bring your own towels and sunscreen when you head out.

Fodor's Choice **Downwind Sails.** Hobie Cats, personal watercraft, Jet Skis, and ocean
★ kayaks are available for rent at Downwind Sails, a trusted company here at the beach since 1981; they also have banana-boat rides (where you're towed in a long, yellow inflatable raft) and parasailing. ✉ *2985 S. Ocean Blvd., South Myrtle Beach* ☎ *843/448–7245* ⊕ *www.downwindsailsmyrtlebeach.com.*

Island Adventure Watersports. For water fun along the Waterway, this rental spot at the Socastee Swing Bridge offers the standard watersport vessels, plus wakeboards, paddle boards, and Jet Ski tours. ✉ *5843 Dick Pond Rd., Socastee* ☎ *843/650–7003* ⊕ *www.islandadventurewatersports.com.*

6

Ocean Watersports. This outfit specializes in parasailing and also rents all kinds of water-sports equipment, from Jet Skis to jet boats. ⊠ *405 S. Ocean Blvd., on the beach at 3rd Ave. S, The Strip* ☎ *843/445–7777* ⊕ *www.parasailmyrtlebeach.com.*

Village Surf Shoppe. Learn how to ride the waves with a rental board or surfing lesson from the crew at Village Surf Shoppe, led by Kelly Richards and his son Cam. Richards shapes his own Perfection Surfboards at the shop, while his national surf champion sons and staff (including four USA Team members) take aspiring surfers out for camps and some hands-on action near the Garden City Pier, a tradition since 1969. ⊠ *500 Atlantic Ave., Garden City Beach* ☎ *843/651–6396* ⊕ *www.villagesurfshoppe.com.*

SHOPPING

FAMILY **Broadway at the Beach.** There are more than 100 mostly name-brand shops selling everything from high-end apparel and candy to Harley-Davidson and comic-book-themed gifts. ⊠ *U.S. 17 Bypass, , between 21st and 29th Aves. N, Central Myrtle Beach* ☎ *800/386–4662, 843/444–3200* ⊕ *www.broadwayatthebeach.com.*

Coastal Grand Mall. With more than 1 million square feet of retail space, this is the area's most significant indoor mall with department stores—and it's the second largest in the state. The blocks surrounding the mall contain a cool restaurant district, a movie theater, and tons of specialty shops. ⊠ *2000 Coastal Grand Circle, Central Myrtle Beach* ☎ *843/839–9100* ⊕ *www.coastalgrand.com.*

FAMILY **The Market Common.** Combining high-end shopping with upscale living and dining spaces, the 114-acre Market Common features stores like Banana Republic, Anthropologie, Barnes & Noble, and Tommy Bahama. A movie theater, playgrounds, bountiful year-round outdoor festivals, and a park with a man-made lake and bike path make it a day-trip destination. ⊠ *4017 Deville St., off Farrow Pkwy., between U.S. 17 Business and U.S. 17 Bypass, South Myrtle Beach* ☎ *843/839–3500* ⊕ *www.marketcommonmb.com.*

Fodor's Choice ★

Tanger Factory Outlet Center. This large outlet center has two locations in Myrtle Beach. Nike, Polo, Brooks Brothers, and J.Crew are some of the stores found at the location on U.S. 501. The North End location has 75 factory outlet stores, including Gap, Banana Republic, and Old Navy. ⊠ *4635 Factory Stores Blvd., off U.S. 501* ☎ *843/236–5100* ⊕ *www.tangeroutlet.com.*

NORTH MYRTLE BEACH

5 miles north of Myrtle Beach via U.S. 17.

North Myrtle Beach, best known as the site where the shag, South Carolina's state dance, originated, is made up of the beach towns Cherry Grove, Crescent Beach, Windy Hill, and Ocean Drive. Entering North Myrtle Beach from the south on U.S. 17, you'll see Barefoot Landing, a huge shopping and entertainment complex that sits on the Intracoastal Waterway. As you make your way east toward the ocean, then north on Ocean Boulevard South, high-rises give way to small motels, then to single beach houses, many of which are available for rent. This end of the Strand marks the tip of a large peninsula, and there are lots of little islands, creeks, and marshes between the ocean and the intracoastal to explore by kayak or canoe. **■ TIP→ Mosquitoes can be a problem on the marsh, especially in the early evening. Be sure to pack repellent.**

GETTING HERE AND AROUND

North Myrtle Beach is an easy jaunt up U.S. 17 or Route 31 from Myrtle Beach (Route 22 or Main Street exits) or just south of Little River. Once inside the city limits, the numbered cross streets connect to Ocean Drive, the beachfront road.

EXPLORING

FAMILY **Alligator Adventure.** Interactive reptile shows, including an alligator-feeding demonstration, are the main attractions at this wildlife park. Boardwalks lead through marshes and swamps on the 15-acre property, where you'll see wildlife of the wetlands, including a pair of rare white albino alligators, the largest known crocodile in captivity, giant Galápagos tortoises, river otters, and all manner of reptiles, including boas, pythons, and anacondas. Unusual plants and exotic birds, as well as lemurs and bats, also thrive here. ✉ *U.S. 17 at Barefoot Landing* ☎ *843/361–0789* 🌐 *www.alligatoradventure.com* 🎫 *$19.99.*

6

WHERE TO EAT

$$$$ ECLECTIC 🍴 **Greg Norman's Australian Grille.** Overlooking the Intracoastal Waterway, this large restaurant in Barefoot Landing has leather booths, Australian aboriginal art on the walls, an extensive wine list, an outdoor patio with a fire pit, and a classy bar, the Shark Pub. The menu features grilled meats and seafood, and many of the selections have an Asian flair. **Known for:** holiday and seasonal wine dinners; hearty surf-and-turf entrées. [$] *Average main: $32* ✉ *4930 U.S. 17 S* ☎ *843/361–0000* 🌐 *www.gregnormansaustraliangrille.com.*

$$$$ ECLECTIC Fodor's Choice ★ 🍴 **Parson's Table.** It's a heavenly experience at this Little River staple housed in an old country church that dates back to 1885. Renowned chef-owner Ed Murray Jr. brings the finest steaks and local seafood and produce to the table. **Known for:** success as a local, independent, fine-dining restaurant amidst Myrtle Beach's sea of chain spots; thoughtful wine and craft-cocktail lists. [$] *Average main: $25* ✉ *4305 McCorsley Ave., Little River* ☎ *843/249–3702* 🌐 *www.parsonstable.com* 🕒 *No lunch.*

$$$ SEAFOOD 🍴 **Rockefellers Raw Bar.** Yes it's a raw bar—and a good one, with a bounty of fresh seafood—but don't sell the cooked items short at this small, casual locals' joint. The seasoned boiled shrimp are the real deal, and the iron pot of steamed mussels, clams, scallops, and other goodies is a terrific version of a Lowcountry staple. **Known for:** comfy boat captain chairs lining the wraparound bar; authentic, local hospitality (and attitude). [$] *Average main: $20* ✉ *3613 U.S. 17 S* ☎ *843/361–9677* 🌐 *www.rockefellersrawbar.com.*

$$$$ CONTEMPORARY 🍴 **SeaBlue.** Don't let the strip-mall location put you off; this restaurant's seafood and locally sourced entrées stand out. Blue mood lighting, a glowing aquarium, and abstract art combine to give this restaurant more of a Miami Beach than Myrtle Beach feel. **Known for:** contemporary,

inspired cuisine from quality ingredients; chic, trendy vibe; hopping on weekends. [$] *Average main: $30* ✉ *503 Hwy. 17 N* ☎ *843/249–8800* 🌐 *www.seabluewinebar.com* 🕓 *No lunch. Closed Sun.*

WHERE TO STAY

$$ RESORT FAMILY 🏨 **Best Western Ocean Sands Resort.** One of the few family-owned resort properties left in North Myrtle Beach, the Ocean Sands has a beachfront tiki bar and updated one- and two-bedroom suites with full kitchens. **Pros:** friendly, available staff; continental breakfast included. **Cons:** annex building is down the street away from the central hotel; not as flashy as newer competitors. [$] *Rooms from: $160* ✉ *1525 S. Ocean Blvd.* ☎ *843/272–6101, 800/588–3570* 🌐 *www.oceansands.com* 🛏 *95 suites* 🍴 *Breakfast.*

$$$ RESORT FAMILY 🏨 **Myrtle Beach Barefoot Resort.** This luxury golf resort includes more than 160 one- to four-bedroom condominium units and Barefoot Yacht Club Villas. **Pros:** pretty views of the Intracoastal Waterway surround the resort; Barefoot Landing shopping and entertainment center is just across the inlet. **Cons:** going to the Strip or boardwalk requires driving across a busy highway; condos are spread throughout golf course complex; you can't simply walk out onto the beach like at similarly priced oceanfront resorts. [$] *Rooms from: $225* ✉ *Barefoot Resort Bridge Rd.* ☎ *800/548–9904* 🌐 *www.myrtlebeachbarefootresort.com* 🛏 *322 condos* 🍴 *No meals.*

$$$ RESORT FAMILY Fodor's Choice ★ 🏨 **North Beach Plantation.** The Plantation's towering design rises above White Point Swash and turns heads everywhere along the coast. **Pros:** sky-high surroundings make you feel like royalty; Cinzia Spa and fitness center are incomparable on the Grand Strand; the water park and pool complex is the area's largest. **Cons:** spa and fitness center are not in the towers; location is somewhat isolated from other attractions. [$] *Rooms from: $250* ✉ *719 N. Beach Blvd.* ☎ *855/904–4858* 🌐 *www.northbeachrentals.com* 🛏 *300 condos* 🍴 *No meals.*

NIGHTLIFE AND PERFORMING ARTS

CLUBS AND LOUNGES

Spanish Galleon Nightclub. This club hosts DJs and a regular rotation of live rock and beach music bands. ✉ *Ocean Drive Beach & Golf Resort, 100 N. Ocean Blvd.* ☎ *800/438–9590* 🌐 *www.spanishgalleon-nightclub.com.*

MUSIC AND LIVE SHOWS

Live music acts from all genres are a big draw on the Grand Strand. Music lovers have many family-oriented shows to choose from.

Alabama Theatre. The 2,250-seat Alabama Theatre has a regular variety show of singing and dancing with a wonderful patriotic closing; the theater also hosts guest music and comedy artists during the year and a holiday-themed show. ✉ *Barefoot Landing, 4750 U.S. 17 S* ☎ *843/272–1111* 🌐 *www.alabama-theatre.com.*

House of Blues. The House of Blues showcases big names and up-and-coming talent and national names in blues, rock, jazz, country, and R&B in its 2,000-seat concert hall and on stages in its Southern-style restaurant and patio. The Sunday gospel brunch is a great deal. ✉ *Barefoot Landing, 4640 U.S. 17 S* ☎ *843/272–3000 for tickets* 🌐 *www.houseofblues.com.*

Pirate's Cove Bar & Grill. The dance floor and rooftop bar at Pirate's Cove are packed every weekend for rock and R&B bands. ⊠ *205 Main St.* ☎ *843/249–8942* ⊕ *www.piratescovelounge.com.*

SHAG DANCE

Contrary to views on the other side of the pond, "shag" isn't a dirty word in North Myrtle Beach; it's a dance that has defined the area since the first pitter-patter-shuffle of footwork on Ocean Drive in the 1940s. A slower-paced sister of the swing, the shag is still celebrated nightly in a number of clubs, biannually with the Society of Stranders citywide festivals in April and September, and annually with the National Shag Dance Championships held in North Myrtle Beach in March.

Duck's Night Club. You can dance the shag and take lessons from the pros at Duck's Beach Club. The club often hosts shag events throughout the year for dedicated and novice dancers. There's also an on-site café. ⊠ *229 Main St.* ☎ *843/663–3858* ⊕ *www.ducksatoceandrive.com.*

Fodor's Choice ★ **Fat Harold's Beach Club.** Step back to a bygone era when you enter the jukebox front door of this hip-movin' shag spot that's constantly hosting shag contests. ⊠ *212 Main St.* ☎ *843/249–5779* ⊕ *www.fatharolds.com.*

OD Arcade & Lounge. This place might be small but it's big on the shag moves, cold drinks, and fish baskets. It also hosts rock bands and karaoke nights. ⊠ *100 S. Ocean Blvd.* ☎ *843/249–6460* ⊕ *www.odarcade.net.*

SPORTS AND THE OUTDOORS

BEACHES

FAMILY **Cherry Grove Oceanfront Park.** In the quiet community of Cherry Grove, this small oceanfront park with pretty, budding landscaping has amenities for families, like a shaded gazebo, bench swings, and a ramp to the sand for strollers. **Best for:** solitude; sunrise; swimming; walking. **Amenities:** lifeguards; showers; toilets. ⊠ *2108 N. Ocean Blvd., near 21st Ave. N* ⊕ *www.parks.nmb.us/parks-and-grounds/cherry-grove-oceanfront-park.*

FAMILY **North Myrtle Beach.** Choose from more than 240 access points to this beach, which is populated with fewer sunbathers than Myrtle Beach—especially farther south and north of Main Street's stretch of beachfront. Ocean Park, at 101 South Ocean Boulevard, offers a nice setting, with a beachfront picnic shelter and a giant, 40-foot-tall inflatable triple waterslide, dubbed the Trippo, open in summer. **Best for:** sunrise; surfing; swimming; walking; windsurfing. **Amenities:** food and drink; lifeguards; parking (metered); showers; toilets; water sports. ⊠ *Ocean Blvd., from 63rd Ave. N to 47th Ave. S.*

FISHING

FAMILY **Cherry Grove Fishing Pier.** This pier has a two-story observation deck and reaches 985 feet into the ocean, making it the place to catch pompano, bluefish, and mackerel. You can rent tackle and buy bait at the pier. Early morning and late afternoon are the best time to catch fish. ⊠ *3500 N. Ocean Blvd.* ☎ *843/249–1625* ⊕ *www.cherrygrovepier.com* 🖃 *$2 for walkers; $7 per rod to fish.*

Little River Fishing Fleet. This outfitter offers half- and full-day excursions, as well as night fishing and dolphin cruises. ⊠ *1903 Hwy. 17 S* ☎ *843/361–3323* ⊕ *www.littleriverfleet.com.*

GOLF

Fodor'sChoice

★

Barefoot Resort & Golf. The four 18-hole championship courses at Barefoot were designed by Tom Fazio, Davis Love III, Pete Dye, and Greg Norman with all skill levels in mind. Notable details include a replica of plantation ruins on the Love course and only 60 acres of mowable grass among the natural vegetation on the Norman course. The Dye course is the chosen site of the annual Monday After the Masters celebrity tournament, hosted by Hootie and the Blowfish. ⊠ *4980 Barefoot Resort Bridge* ☎ *866/638–4818,* ⊕ *www.barefootgolf.com* ⌨ *$155* ⚑ *72 holes. Dye 7343 yds; par 71. Fazio 6834 yds; par 71. Love 7000 yds; par 72. Norman 7200 yds; par 72.* ⚓ *Reservations essential* ☞ *Facilities include a driving range, pitching area, golf academy/lessons, and restaurants.*

Tidewater Golf Club. Designed by Ken Tomlinson, the magnificent Tidewater peninsula is one of only two courses in the area with an ocean view; the marshes and waterway border other well-crafted parts of the course. The challenging fairways and high bluffs are reminiscent of Pebble Beach. ⊠ *1400 Tidewater Dr.* ☎ *843/466–8754* ⊕ *www.tidewatergolf.com* ⌨ *$170* ⚑ *18 holes. 7044 yds. Par 72.* ⚓ *Reservations essential* ☞ *Facilities include a driving range, pitching area, golf academy/lessons, and a bar.*

WATER SPORTS

Coastal Scuba. Learn to scuba dive, take a dive trip, or just rent equipment at Coastal Scuba, which is PADI certified. ⊠ *1903 U.S. 17 S* ☎ *843/361–3323* ⊕ *www.coastalscuba.com.*

Myrtle Beach Water Sports. You can rent your own pontoon boats or Jet Skis, try parasailing, or book a dolphin cruise aboard the *Sea Screamer,* touted, at 72 feet, as the world's largest speedboat. ⊠ *Harbourgate Marina, 2100 Sea Mountain Hwy., on the docks* ☎ *843/280–7777* ⊕ *www.myrtlebeachwatersports.com.*

SHOPPING
MALLS

FAMILY **Barefoot Landing.** This complex features more than 100 specialty shops, bars, and restaurants, along with numerous entertainment activities, including children's amusement rides. In summer, check out the fireworks displays every Monday night. ⊠ *4898 U.S. 17 S* ☎ *843/272–8349* ⊕ *www.bflanding.com.*

Myrtle Beach Mall. This indoor mall sits in the Briarcliffe section just north of Tanger Outlets and just south of Barefoot Landing, offering department store and boutique standards, as well as a monstrous Bass Pro Shop, a movie theater, and an improv comedy club. ⊠ *10177 N. Kings Hwy.* ☎ *843/272–4040* ⊕ *www.mymallmyrtlebeach.com.*

MUSIC

Judy's House of Oldies. Beach-music lovers have been finding their long-lost favorites at the family-owned Judy's House of Oldies for years. Find classics on cassette and CD at this small but packed-to-the-gills music emporium. ⊠ *300 Main St.* ☎ *843/249–8649* ⊕ *www.judyshouseofoldies.com.*

THE SOUTHERN GRAND STRAND

Unlike the more developed area to the north, the southern end of the Grand Strand—Murrells Inlet, Litchfield, Pawleys Island, and Georgetown—has a barefoot, laid-back vibe that suits its small restaurants, shops, galleries, outdoors outfitters, and natural beauty. Locals pride themselves on their "shabby-chic" mentality.

MURRELLS INLET

15 miles south of Myrtle Beach via U.S. 17.

Murrells Inlet, a fishing village with some popular seafood restaurants, is a perfect place to rent a fishing boat or join an excursion. A notable garden and state park provide other diversions from the beach. Though there are a few chain hotels, they aren't anywhere near the water. The village makes a fine day trip, unless you've rented a waterfront cottage.

GETTING HERE AND AROUND

Driving south on U.S. 17 takes you through Murrells Inlet. If you stay on U.S. 17 Bypass, though, you'll miss some of the town's character. Try taking U.S. 17 Business to get a taste of the real Murrells Inlet. Most cross streets connect to the bypass if you get turned around.

6

EXPLORING

Fodor's Choice ★ **Brookgreen Gardens.** One of the Grand Strand's most magnificent hidden treasures, the 9,100-acre Brookgreen Gardens is the oldest and largest sculpture garden in the United States, with more than 550 examples of figurative American sculpture by such artists as Frederic Remington and Daniel Chester French. Each sculpture is carefully set within garden rooms and outdoor galleries graced by sprawling live oak trees, colorful flowers, and peaceful ponds. The gardens are lush and full in spring and summer, and in winter splashes of color from winter-blooming shrubs are set off against the stark surroundings.

The property was purchased as a winter home for industrialist Archer Huntington and his wife, Anna Hyatt Huntington, in 1929, but they quickly decided to open it to the public as a sculpture garden and wildlife sanctuary. You'll find a Lowcountry Zoo, an aviary, a cypress swamp, nature trails, an education center, and a butterfly house. Several tours, including a boat tour of tidal creeks and a jeep excursion into the preserve, leave from Brookgreen. Summer concerts under the stars and the garden's breathtaking Night of a Thousand Candles during Christmas season are Brookgreen traditions. The gardens are just beyond *The Fighting Stallions*, the Anna Hyatt Huntington sculpture alongside U.S. 17. ⊠ *1931 Brookgreen Garden Dr.* ✛ *3 miles south of Murrells Inlet on Hwy. 17* ☎ *843/235–6000* ⊕ *www.brookgreen.org* ✉ *$16.*

FAMILY
Fodor's Choice ★ **Huntington Beach State Park.** This 2,500-acre former estate of Archer and Anna Huntington lies east of U.S. 17, across from Brookgreen Gardens. The park's focal point is **Atalaya** (circa 1933), their Moorish-style 30-room home. There are nature trails, ample areas for biking (including a new bicycle path from Huntington Beach to Litchfield

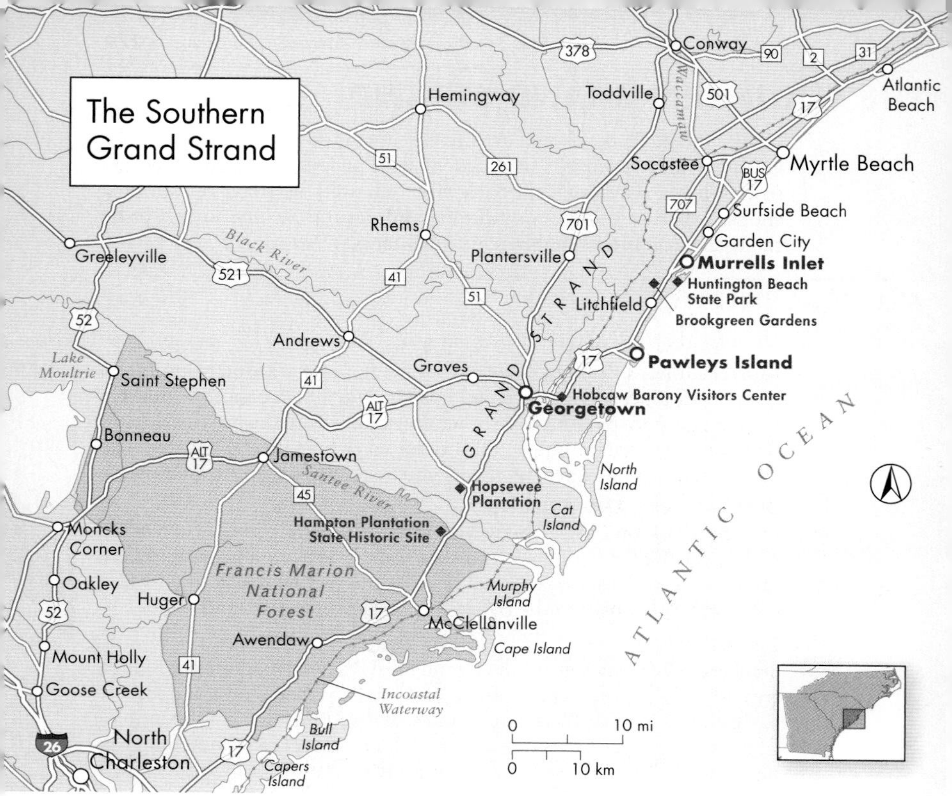

Beach), fishing, an education center with aquariums and a loggerhead sea turtle–nesting habitat, picnic areas, bird-watching expeditions, a playground, concessions, and a campground. ✉ *Murrells Inlet* ✥ *East of U.S. 17, 3 miles south of Murrells Inlet* ☎ *843/237–4440* 🌐 *www.huntingtonbeachstatepark.net* 🎟 *$5.*

WHERE TO EAT

$$$$ ITALIAN Fodor's Choice ★ 🍴 **Costa.** Although it's billed as Italian, the focus at this popular bistro is fresh, local seafood, from savory local clams to juicy shrimp and diver scallops, tossed with pastas and worked into creative appetizers. The interior features open ceilings and a classy nautical theme in cool blues. **Known for:** thoughtful wine list; impeccable clams and mussels. [$] *Average main: $25* ✉ *4606 Hwy. 17 Business* ☎ *843/299–1970* 🌐 *www.costamyrtlebeach.com.*

$$$$ SEAFOOD Fodor's Choice ★ 🍴 **Lee's Inlet Kitchen.** They're closed at lunchtime and on Sunday; they don't take reservations or have a view, but nobody fries up a mess of seafood like Lee's, which is something they've been doing since 1948. Even the biggest eaters will get their fill when they order the Shore Dinner: fried or broiled flounder, shrimp, oysters, scallops, deviled crab, and lobster, along with a shrimp cocktail, clam chowder, hush puppies, fries, and coleslaw. **Known for:** huge platters of fried seafood; Lowcountry authenticity. [$] *Average main: $25* ✉ *4460 U.S.*

17 Business ☎ *843/651–2881* ⊕ *www.leesinletkitchen.com* ⊙ *No lunch. Closed Sun.*

$$$ ✕ **Nance's Creek Front Restaurant.** You can smell the brine and Old Bay SEAFOOD seasoning the minute you leave your car and head toward the front door of Nance's. Oysters, the small local ones that taste of saltwater, are the specialty, available fried or steamed in an iron pot and served with butter. **Known for:** steamed local oysters; 10-layer chocolate cake for dessert. $ *Average main: $20* ✉ *4883 U.S. 17 Business* ☎ *843/651–2696* ⊙ *No lunch.*

$$ ✕ **Prosser's BBQ.** This ain't your four-star fine-dining eatery, and it's prac-BARBECUE tically a requirement to lick your fingers clean. Lip-smacking pulled pork is served along with Lowcountry goodies like collard greens, mashed potatoes, fried chicken, macaroni and cheese, banana pudding, and peach cobbler. **Known for:** all-you-can-eat Southern barbecue buffet; bang-for-your-buck value. $ *Average main: $15* ✉ *3750 U.S. 17 Business* ☎ *843/357–6146* ⊕ *www.prossersbbq.com.*

$$ ✕ **Salt Water Creek.** Set under a giant live oak tree along the bypass AMERICAN and beyond a lovely brick patio, this café serving elevated Lowcountry cuisine is anything but typical. Cool, coastal inspirations are cleverly combined with comforting Southern hospitality. **Known for:** weekend brunch; laid-back atmosphere. $ *Average main: $18* ✉ *4660 U.S. 17 Bypass* ☎ *843/357–2433* ⊕ *www.saltwatercreekcafe.com.*

$$$ ✕ **Wahoo's Fish House.** Whether you choose to sit inside the contem-SEAFOOD porary confines of this casual, fine-dining waterfront restaurant or outside at the tropical-tiki Raw Bar, you can't go wrong with atmosphere or cuisine. The menu features seafood and sushi, as well as Lowcountry-inspired dishes. **Known for:** an amalgam of sushi and fried seafood platters; live music in the evenings. $ *Average main: $22* ✉ *3993 U.S. 17 Business* ☎ *843/651–5800* ⊕ *www.wahoosfishhouse. com* ⊙ *No lunch.*

NIGHTLIFE

Hot Fish Club. This happening waterfront joint serves seafood and sushi and features live music on its gazebo stage every Friday and Saturday night. ✉ *4911 U.S. 17 Business* ☎ *843/357–9175* ⊕ *www.hotfishclub. com* ⊙ *Closed Mon.*

FAMILY **Murrells Inlet Marshwalk.** You can have a drink, watch boats come back from a day of fishing, hear a blend of live music, and enjoy the evening breeze with a stroll along the Murrells Inlet Marshwalk, a picturesque boardwalk that connects eight waterfront bars and restaurants, from Drunken Jack's on the north end to Wicked Tuna at the Crazy Sister Marina on the south end. On the Fourth of July, the Marshwalk serves as your front-row seat to the wildly popular Boat Parade. Also included along the way are colorful waterfront stops with fanciful names like Dead Dog Saloon, Creek Ratz, Bubba's Love Shak, and Wahoo's. ✉ *Murrells Inlet* ⊕ *www.marshwalk.com.*

The drive from the Grand Strand to peaceful Pawleys Island makes for an excellent road trip.

PAWLEYS ISLAND

10 miles south of Murrells Inlet via U.S. 17.

Fodor'sChoice ★ About 4 miles long and a half-mile wide, Pawleys, sometimes referred to as "arrogantly shabby," began as a resort before the Civil War, when wealthy planters and their families summered here. It's mostly made up of weathered old summer cottages nestled in groves of oleander and oak trees. You can watch the famous Pawleys Island hammocks being made and bicycle around admiring the beach houses, many dating to the early 1800s. Golf and tennis are nearby. ■ **TIP→ Parking is limited on Pawleys and facilities are nil, so arrive early and bring what you need.**

GETTING HERE AND AROUND

Pawleys Island is south of Murrells Inlet on U.S. 17. Take North Causeway Drive off the main highway to experience the natural beauty of the island. A 2-mile-long historic district is home to rustic beach cottages, historic buildings, and even a church.

WHERE TO EAT

$$$$ ECLECTIC 🍴 **Frank's.** This local favorite serves dishes that give traditional cooking methods and ingredients a new twist. The former 1930s grocery store has transformed into fine dining, with wood floors, framed French posters, and cozy fireside seating. **Known for:** local seafood dishes like grouper and shrimp with Dijon cream sauce and grits; informal vibe with sophisticated food. [$] *Average main: $28* ✉ *10434 Ocean Hwy.* ☎ *843/237–3030* 🌐 *www.franksandoutback.com* ⏲ *Closed Sun. No lunch.*

$ MEXICAN 🍴 **Habaneros.** The fish tacos here are to die for, but the full menu of Mexican favorites at this colorful cantina proves that Pawleys Island is not just about seafood. Take a seat inside or on the festive deck, which is the place to be on Cinco de Mayo, and order a burrito with secret sauce and a margarita. **Known for:** the sunny outdoor bar and deck; margaritas priced right. [$] *Average main: $10* ✉ *11151 Ocean Hwy.* ☎ *843/235–9595* 🌐 *www.habanerosrestaurant.com.*

$ BARBECUE-SEAFOOD 🍴 **Hog Heaven BBQ and Raw Bar.** Part barbecue joint, part raw bar (after 5), Hog Heaven has a wonderful smoky aroma that perfumes U.S. 17 for miles. Pulled-pork barbecue has the tang of vinegar and the taste of long hours in the pit. **Known for:** a generous all-you-can-eat buffet; the curious wedding of pork barbecue and fried seafood. [$] *Average main: $10* ✉ *7147 Ocean Hwy.* ☎ *843/237–7444* 🌐 *www.hogheaveninc.com.*

$ ITALIAN 🍴 **Landolfi's.** This fourth-generation-owned Italian pastry shop, deli, and restaurant has excellent coffee, hearty hoagies, pizzas, homemade sorbet, and delicious and authentic pastries, including cannoli and *pasticciotti* (a rich cookielike pastry filled with jam). Both counter and table service is available. **Known for:** wood-fired pizza and panini; laid-back atmosphere. [$] *Average main: $10* ✉ *9305 Ocean Hwy.* ☎ *843/237–7900* ⏲ *Closed Sun. and Mon.*

6

WHERE TO STAY

$$ HOTEL 🏨 **Hampton Inn Pawleys Island.** Ongoing upgrades keep this hotel in tip-top condition. **Pros:** cute turtles populate the pond outside and beg for treats; continental breakfast included. **Cons:** the beach isn't within walking distance; as a chain hotel, it lacks the charm of other area options. [$] *Rooms from: $199* ✉ *150 Willbrook Blvd.* ☎ *843/235–2000* 🌐 *www.hamptoninn.com* 🛏 *66 rooms* 🍽 *Breakfast.*

$$ RESORT Fodor's Choice ★ 🏨 **Litchfield Beach & Golf Resort.** This beautifully landscaped 4,500-acre resort features a nearly 2-mile stretch of oceanfront accommodations that range from condos to the 160-room Litchfield Inn. Other options, such as high-rise condos, duplexes, and even Charleston-style beach houses, overlook fairways, lakes, or the marsh. **Pros:** geared to all kinds of travelers; beautiful natural surroundings; modern amenities. **Cons:** some properties are at least a 15-minute walk to the beach; minimum stays during high season. [$] *Rooms from: $200* ✉ *14276 Ocean Hwy.* ☎ *843/237–3000, 888/734–8228* 🌐 *www.litchfieldbeach.com* 🛏 *560 units* 🍽 *No meals.*

$$$$ B&B/INN Fodor's Choice ★ 🏨 **Sea View Inn.** A "barefoot paradise," Sea View is a no-frills beachside boardinghouse (there are no TVs or in-room phones) with long porches. **Pros:** quaint, quiet oceanfront experience is completely unlike the megaresorts on the Grand Strand; all meals are included. **Cons:** not wheelchair-accessible; some showers are outside the room. [$] *Rooms from: $275* ✉ *414 Myrtle Ave.* ☎ *843/237–4253* 🌐 *www.seaviewinn.com* 💳 *No credit cards* ⏲ *Closed Dec.–Mar.* 🛏 *15 rooms, 1 cottage* 🍽 *All meals.*

PERFORMING ARTS

Pawleys Island Festival of Music & Art. Pawleys Island comes alive each September and early October during the Pawleys Island Festival of Music & Art, which brings national and local artists together for a month of concerts, exhibitions, and readings. Past performers have included David Sanborn and Delbert McClinton. ⊠ *Pawleys Island* ☎ *843/626–8911* ⊕ *www.pawleysmusic.com.*

SPORTS AND THE OUTDOORS

BEACHES

FAMILY
Fodor'sChoice
★

Litchfield Beach/Pawleys Island. Over 3 miles of tranquil and natural beach runs along the shoreline of Pawleys Island. The surrounding architecture consists only of beach cottages and low-lying resorts, so it's a peaceful retreat. Lack of crowds allows for bicycling on packed sand, shelling, or napping on a hammock. Note that there aren't any lifeguards. **Best for:** solitude; sunrise; sunset; surfing; swimming; walking; windsurfing. **Amenities:** parking (limited; on side streets). ⊠ *Pawleys Island* ⊕ *www. townofpawleysisland.com.*

GOLF

Caledonia Golf & Fish Club. Designed by Mike Strantz, this course on a former Southern rice plantation is a stunning Lowcountry beauty, from its entrance avenue of live oaks, continuing around pretty streams, and ending with an 18th hole that borders an old rice field. ⊠ *369 Caledonia Dr.* ☎ *843/237–3675* ⊕ *www.caledoniagolfandfishclub. com* 🏌 *$159* ⅄ *18 holes. 6526 yds. Par 70.* 🏌 *Reservations essential* ☞ *Facilities include a driving range, pitching area, golf academy/lessons, and a restaurant.*

Pawleys Plantation Golf & Country Club. This Jack Nicklaus–designed course demands respect from golfers for its several tricky holes surrounded by saltwater marshes. Off the course, many reserve the posh clubhouse and patio for four-course wedding receptions, with the 18th hole as a backdrop. ⊠ *70 Tanglewood Dr.* ☎ *877/283–2122* ⊕ *www. pawleysplantation.com* 🏌 *$89* ⅄ *18 holes. 7026 yds. Par 72.* 🏌 *Reservations essential* ☞ *Facilities include a driving range, pitching area, golf academy/lessons, and a restaurant.*

Tradition Golf Club. Rated as one of the best-maintained courses on the Grand Strand, this Ron Garl–designed beauty is also affordable. ⊠ *1027 Willbrook Blvd.* ☎ *877/283–2122* ⊕ *www.traditionclubmyrtlebeach. com* 🏌 *$74* ⅄ *18 holes. 6313 yds. Par 72.* 🏌 *Reservations essential* ☞ *Facilities include a driving range, pitching area, golf academy/lessons, and a restaurant.*

Willbrook Plantation. Dan Maples designed this course with nature in mind, on two former rice plantations that now wind past historical markers, a slave cemetery, and a tobacco shack. Polls have ranked Willbrook high on the list with women, in particular, for its Southern hospitality and leafy surrounds. ⊠ *379 Country Club Dr.* ☎ *877/283– 2122* ⊕ *www.willbrookgolf.com* 🏌 *$89* ⅄ *18 holes. 6704 yds. Par 72.* 🏌 *Reservations essential* ☞ *Facilities include a driving range, pitching area, golf academy/lessons, and a restaurant.*

TENNIS

Litchfield Country Club. You can get court time, rental equipment, and instruction at Litchfield Country Club. There are 17 clay courts, four of which are lighted. ⊠ *619 Country Club Rd.* ☎ *843/237–3983* ⊕ *www. litchfieldgolf.com/racquet-club* ⊿ *$15 walk-in guest.*

SHOPPING

Hammock Shops Village. The Hammock Shops Village is an outdoor complex of two dozen boutiques, gift shops, and restaurants built with old beams, timber, and ballast brick under a canopy of live oaks. Outside the Original Hammock Shop, in the Hammock Weavers' Pavilion, craftspeople demonstrate the 19th-century art of weaving the famous cotton-rope Pawleys Island hammocks. Also look for jewelry, toys, antiques, and designer fashions. ⊠ *10880 Ocean Hwy.* ☎ *843/235–6355* ⊕ *www.thehammockshops.com.*

Litchfield Books. This independent bookstore is the place to pick up a beach read or regional-interest book. It's also the home base for authors who want to return home after making it on the bestsellers' list during the store's Moveable Feast series. ⊠ *Fresh Market Commons, 14421 Ocean Hwy.* ☎ *843/237–8138* ⊕ *litchfieldbooks.com* ⊘ *Closed Sun.*

GEORGETOWN

13 miles south of Pawleys Island via U.S. 17.

Founded on Winyah Bay in 1729, Georgetown was once the center of America's colonial rice empire. A rich plantation culture developed on a scale comparable to Charleston's, and the historic district is among the prettiest in the state (though reconstruction on eight buildings along Front Street is still underway after a fire in September 2013). Today, oceangoing vessels still come to Georgetown's busy port, and the **Harborwalk,** the restored waterfront, hums with activity. ■**TIP➜ Many of the restaurants along the river side of Front Street have back decks overlooking the water that come alive in the early evening for happy hour.**

GETTING HERE AND AROUND

Georgetown is accessible from U.S. 17, as well as Route 701. The heart of the town is near the waterfront—an easy trip off the highway down any side street is worth it. Take Cannon Street to Front Street to see the harbor.

ESSENTIALS

Visitor Information Georgetown County Chamber of Commerce. ⊠ *531 Front St.* ☎ *843/546–8436, 800/777–7705* ⊕ *www.visitgeorge.com.*

EXPLORING

TOP ATTRACTIONS

Fodor's Choice ★ **Hampton Plantation State Historic Site.** This 18th-century plantation house was the home of Archibald Rutledge, poet laureate of South Carolina for 39 years until his death in 1973. The Lowcountry mansion's exterior has been restored; cutaway sections in the finely crafted interior show the changes made through the centuries. The grounds are

6

landscaped, and there are picnic areas. ⊠ *1950 Rutledge Rd., McClellanville* ☎ *843/546–9361* ⊕ *www.southcarolinaparks.com/hampton* ⌨ *Mansion $7.50, grounds free.*

Hobcaw Barony Visitors Center. Discover this historic landmark that was once the vast estate of the late Wall Street financier Bernard M. Baruch. Franklin D. Roosevelt and Winston Churchill came here to confer with him. A small interpretive center has exhibits on coastal ecology and history, with special emphasis on the Baruch family. There are aquariums, touch tanks, video presentations, and guided two-hour tours of the 16,000-acre wildlife refuge. ⊠ *22 Hobcaw Rd., off U.S. 17, 2 miles north of Georgetown* ☎ *843/546–4623* ⊕ *www.hobcawbarony. org* ⌨ *Visitor center free; tours $20* ⊘ *Closed Sun.*

Kaminski House Museum. Overlooking the Sampit River from a bluff is this sprawling historic home (circa 1769) that's notable for its collections of regional antiques and furnishings, its Chippendale and Duncan Phyfe furniture, Royal Doulton vases, and silver. Events at the Kaminski House include summer outdoor concerts on the lawn. ⊠ *1003 Front St.* ☎ *843/546–7706* ⊕ *www.kaminskimuseum.org* ⊘ *Closed Sun.*

FAMILY   **Rice Museum.** A graceful market and meeting building in the heart of Georgetown, topped by an 1842 clock and tower, has been converted into a unique museum, with maps, tools, and dioramas that outline the history of rice in Georgetown. At the museum's Prevost Gallery next door is the Brown's Ferry river freighter, the oldest American-built water-going vessel in existence. The museum gift shop has local pine needle baskets, African dolls, and art (including baskets made from whole cloves), as well as South Carolina rice and honey. ⊠ *633 Front St.* ☎ *843/546–7423* ⊕ *www.ricemuseum. org* ⌨ *$7* ⊘ *Closed Sun.*

WORTH NOTING

Hopsewee Plantation. This amazing plantation, a National Historic Landmark, overlooks the North Santee River and is surrounded by moss-draped live oaks, magnolias, and tree-size camellias. The circa-1740 mansion has a fine Georgian staircase and hand-carved lighted-candle moldings. The River Oak Cottage Tea Room on-site serves a full menu of Southern treats. ⊠ *494 Hopsewee Rd., off U.S. 17, 12 miles south of Georgetown* ☎ *843/546–7891* ⊕ *www.hopsewee.com* ⌨ *$20* ⊘ *Closed Sun. and Mon.*

Prince George Winyah Episcopal Church. Named after King George II, this church still serves the parish established in 1721. It was built in 1737 with bricks brought from England. ⊠ *300 Broad St.* ☎ *843/546–4358* ⊕ *www.pgwinyah.org* ⌨ *Donations accepted* ⊘ *Closed Oct.–Feb. except for services.*

WHERE TO EAT

$$$ ✕ **River Room.** The dining room at the River Room has Sampit River
SEAFOOD   views from most tables, which is especially romantic at night, when
Fodor's Choice   the oil lamps and brass fixtures cast a warm glow on the dark wood
★   and brick interior of the early-20th-century building. Menu highlights include char-grilled fish (especially the Carolina grouper), Cajun fried oysters, seafood pastas, and steaks. **Known for:** fresh

fish entrées; lively waterfront atmosphere. $ *Average main: $22* ✉ *801 Front St.* ☎ *843/527–4110* ⊕ *www.riverroomgeorgetown. com* ☾ *Closed Sun.*

$ ✕ **Thomas Café.** Though it might look the part, this isn't a greasy spoon:
SOUTHERN the luncheonette dishes up great fried chicken, homemade biscuits, and pie, plus grits, eggs, country ham, and other breakfast favorites. Join the regulars at the counter, or sit in one of the booths or café tables in the 1920s storefront building. **Known for:** classic Southern lunch fare; famous fried chicken. $ *Average main: $10* ✉ *703 Front St.* ☎ *843/546– 7776* ☾ *Closed Sun. No dinner.*

WHERE TO STAY

$$ ⛉ **Hampton Inn Georgetown Marina.** Watch boats cruise up and down the
HOTEL river at this riverside resort with spectacular views of the Intracoastal Waterway. **Pros:** there is a marina outside the hotel if you'd like to arrive by boat; walkable to Georgetown's old village. **Cons:** as a chain hotel, it lacks the unique aspects of some other hotels; the pool is a small, typical hotel pool. $ *Rooms from: $159* ✉ *420 Marina Dr.* ☎ *843/545–5099* ⊕ *www.hamptoninn.com* ⤳ *98 rooms* ⦿❘ *Breakfast.*

$$ ⛉ **The Keith House Inn.** Expect Southern hospitality at this historic
B&B/INN home with easy access to Front Street's restaurants and waterway. **Pros:** Front Street location means you can park the car if Georgetown is your primary destination; provides an authentic taste of life in the village. **Cons:** the beaches farther north are a drive, and downtown Georgetown itself may not appeal for more than a day; can fill up easily, so book in advance. $ *Rooms from: $159* ✉ *1012 Front St.* ☎ *843/485–4324* ⊕ *www.thekeithhouseinn.com* ⤳ *4 rooms* ⦿❘ *Breakfast.*

SPORTS AND THE OUTDOORS

BOATING

FAMILY **Cap'n Rod's Lowcountry Plantation Tours.** Cruise up the river with Captain Rod, past abandoned rice plantations, and hear stories about the belles who lived there; another tour visits a lighthouse and an unspoiled barrier island beach. ✉ *701 Front St.* ☎ *843/477–0287* ⊕ *www.lowcountrytours.com* ✉ *$35.*

FAMILY **Rover Boat Tours.** Book a three-hour tour with Rover Boat Tours, sailing the high seas since 1995, to an untouched barrier island past the Winyah Bay Lighthouse for an exclusive afternoon of shelling. Pack snacks for the nearly hour-long trip to and from the island. ✉ *735 Front St., on the harbor* ☎ *843/546–8822* ⊕ *roverboattours.com* ✉ *$38.*

Wallace Sailing Charters. Feel the spray on your face as you explore Winyah Bay aboard a 40-foot yacht with Captain Dave of Wallace Sailing Charters. Each trip is limited to six passengers, so it feels like you're touring on a private yacht. ✉ *525 Front St.* ☎ *843/902–6999* ⊕ *www.wallacesailingcharters.com* ✉ *$300 for 6 guests* ↻ *All cruises are by appointment only.*

FAMILY **Wooden Boat Show.** Each October for more than 20 years, Front Street in Georgetown has been transformed into an iconic event: the Wooden Boat Show. Craftsmen showcase their works in the wooden boat exhibits, plus there is an intense boatbuilding competition (finished off by a rowing race on the river), kids' model-building contest, live music, and arts and crafts. All proceeds from the show are donated to the Harbor Historical Association's maritime museum. ⊠ *Georgetown* ☎ *843/520–0111* ⊕ *www.woodenboatshow.com.*

CANOEING AND KAYAKING

Fodor'sChoice
★

Black River Outdoors Center. This outfitter offers naturalist-guided canoe and kayak tours of the tidelands and swamps of Georgetown County. Guides are well versed not just in the wildlife but also in local lore. Tours take kayakers past settings such as Drunken Jack's (the island that supposedly holds Blackbeard's booty), and Chicora Wood plantation, where dikes and trunk gates mark canals dug by slaves to facilitate rice growing in the area. It's said that digging the canals required as much manual labor as Egypt's pyramids. Wildlife tends to be more active during the early morning or late afternoon; there's a good chance you'll hear owls hooting on the evening tours, especially in fall. It also rents and delivers kayaks throughout the southern Grand Strand. ⊠ *Georgetown* ☎ *843/546–4840* ⊕ *www.blackriveroutdoors.com.*

CHARLESTON, SC

WELCOME TO CHARLESTON, SC

TOP REASONS TO GO

★ **Dining out:** Charleston has become one of the country's biggest culinary destinations, with talented chefs who offer innovative twists on the city's traditional Lowcountry cuisine.

★ **Seeing art:** The city abounds with galleries, so you'll never run out of places to see remarkable art.

★ **Spoleto Festival USA:** If you're lucky enough to visit in late May and early June, you'll find a city under a cultural siege: Spoleto's flood of indoor and outdoor performances (opera, music, dance, and theater) is impossible to miss.

★ **The Battery:** The views from the terminus of Charleston's peninsula—the elegant waterfront mansions that line White Point Garden and across the harbor to Fort Sumter—are the loveliest in the city.

★ **Historic homes:** Step back in time in Charleston's preserved 19th-century houses like the Nathaniel Russell House, or visit plantations like Boone Hall outside the city.

1 **North of Broad.**
You'll find the lion's share of Charleston's restaurants, hotels, and shops along King and Market Streets, two intersecting thorough-fares that bisect the peninsula.

2 **South of Broad.**
The southern part of the downtown peninsula's Historic District is a living museum of historical homes and harbors a few B&Bs.

3 **Mount Pleasant and Vicinity.** Across the Arthur Ravenel Jr. Bridge, spanning the Cooper River, sits Mount Pleasant, an affluent suburb that's home to Boone Hall Plantation and historic Shem Creek.

4 **West Ashley and James Island.** The subur-ban areas across the Ashley River from downtown beckon visitors to Folly Beach and to three major historic plantations on Ashley River Road.

GETTING ORIENTED

The heart of the city is on a peninsula, sometimes just called "downtown" by the 700,000 residents who populate the tri-county metro area. Walking Charleston's peninsula is the best way to get to know the city.

7

Concord St.

Pritchard St.

Market St.

Vendue Range

Unity Alley

East Bay St.

Exchange St.

Elliot St.

Battery

Cooper River

0   1/8 mile

0   200 meters

Updated
by Stratton
Lawrence

Wandering through the city's French Quarter and South of Broad neighborhoods, one might mistake Charleston for a movie set. Dozens of church steeples punctuate the low skyline, and horse-drawn carriages pass centuries-old mansions and town houses, their stately salons offering a crystal-laden and parquet-floored version of Southern comfort. Outside, magnolia-filled gardens overflow with carefully tended heirloom plants. At first glance, the city resembles an 18th-century etching come to life—but look closer and you'll see that block after block of old structures have been restored. Happily, after three centuries of wars, epidemics, fires, and hurricanes, Charleston has prevailed and is now one of the South's best-preserved cities.

Although home to Fort Sumter, where the bloodiest war in the nation's history began, Charleston is also famed for its elegant houses. These handsome mansions are showcases for the "Charleston style," a distinctive look that is reminiscent of the West Indies, and for good reason. Before coming to the Carolinas in the late 17th century, many early British colonists first settled on Barbados and other Caribbean islands. In that warm and humid climate they built homes with high ceilings and rooms opening onto broad "piazzas" (porches) at each level to catch welcome sea breezes. As a result, to quote the words of the Duc de La Rochefoucauld, who visited in 1796, "One does not boast in Charleston of having the most beautiful house, but the coolest."

Preserved through the hard times that followed the Civil War and an array of natural disasters, many of Charleston's earliest public and private buildings still stand. Thanks to a rigorous preservation movement and strict Board of Architectural Review guidelines, the city's new structures blend in with the old. In many cases, recycling is the name of the game—antique handmade bricks literally lay the foundation for new homes. But although locals do dwell—on certain literal levels—in the past, the city is very much a town of today.

Take, for instance, the internationally heralded Spoleto Festival USA. For 17 days every spring, arts patrons from around the world come to enjoy international concerts, dance performances, operas, and plays at various venues citywide. Day in and day out, diners can feast at upscale restaurants, shoppers can look for museum-quality paintings and antiques, and lovers of the outdoors can explore Charleston's outlying beaches, parks, and marshes. But as cosmopolitan as the city has become, it's still the South, and just beyond the city limits are farm stands cooking up boiled peanuts, the state's official snack.

PLANNING

WHEN TO GO

There really is no bad time to visit Charleston. Spring and fall are high season, when the temperatures are most comfortable and hotel rates and occupancy are at their highest. Art shows, craft fairs, and music festivals (including the famous Spoleto USA festival) occur throughout the year. In fall, golfers are out in full force, and though it may be too cool to swim, beachcombing is a popular activity out on the sea islands. During the high season it's important to make your reservations as far in advance as possible for both hotels and restaurants.

PLANNING YOUR TIME

The best way to get acquainted with Charleston is to take a carriage ride or walking tour, especially one that takes you through the South of Broad neighborhood. You can get acquainted with Charleston's Historic District at your leisure, especially if you can devote at least three days to the city, which will allow time to explore some of the plantations west of the Ashley River. With another day, you can explore Mount Pleasant, and if you have even more time, head out to the coastal islands, where golf and beach activities are the order of the day.

GETTING HERE AND AROUND

AIR TRAVEL

Charleston International Airport is about 12 miles north of downtown. Charleston Executive Airport on John's Island is used by private (noncommercial) aircraft, as is Mount Pleasant Regional Airport.

Several cab companies, including Uber and Yellow Cab, serve the airport. An average trip to or from downtown is $25.

Airport Information Charleston International Airport. ⊠ *5500 International Blvd., North Charleston* ☎ *843/767-7000* ⊕ *www.iflychs.com.*

BOAT AND FERRY TRAVEL

Boaters—many traveling the Intracoastal Waterway—dock in Charleston Harbor at Ashley Marina and City Marina. The Charleston Water Taxi is a delightful way to travel between Charleston and Mount Pleasant. It also offers dolphin cruises and harbor boat rides, and some people take the $10 round-trip journey just for fun. The water taxi departs from the Charleston Harbor Marina in Mount Pleasant daily every hour from 9 am to 7 pm, and every hour between 9:30 am and 7:30 pm from the Charleston Maritime Center in downtown Charleston. Do not confuse its address at 10 Wharfside Street as being near the area of Adger's Wharf, which is on the lower peninsula.

Boat and Ferry Contacts Charleston Water Taxi. ✉ *Charleston Maritime Center, 10 Wharfside St., Ansonborough* ☎ *843/330–2989* ⊕ *www.charlestonwatertaxi.com.*

CAR TRAVEL

You'll need a car in Charleston if you plan on visiting destinations off the downtown peninsula, or if you plan to take trips to Edisto Island, Beaufort, or Hilton Head.

Interstate 26 traverses the state from northwest to southeast and terminates at Charleston. U.S. 17, the coastal road, also passes through Charleston. Interstate 526, also called the Mark Clark Expressway, runs primarily east–west, connecting the West Ashley area, North Charleston, Daniel Island, and Mount Pleasant.

PUBLIC TRANSPORTATION

The Charleston Area Regional Transportation Authority (CARTA), the city's public bus system, takes passengers around the city and to the suburbs. Bus Route 11, which goes to the airport, is convenient for travelers. CARTA operates DASH, which runs buses that look like vintage trolleys along three downtown routes. All trips are free on DASH. CARTA buses go to James Island, West Ashley, and Mount Pleasant.

Public Transportation Contacts Charleston Area Regional Transportation Authority (CARTA). ✉ *Downtown Historic District* ☎ *843/724–7420* ⊕ *www.ridecarta.com.*

TAXI TRAVEL

Circling the Historic District, pedicabs are a fun way to get around in the evening, especially if you are barhopping. Three can squeeze into one pedicab, which averages $5 per person for a 10-minute ride.

Fares within the city average $5 to $10 per trip with the regular cab companies.

Taxi Contacts Bike Taxi. ☎ *843/532–8663* ⊕ *www.biketaxi.net.* **Charleston Green Taxi.** ☎ *843/819–0846* ⊕ *www.charlestongreentaxi.com.* **Yellow Cab of Charleston.** ☎ *843/577–6565* ⊕ *www.yellowcabofcharleston.com.* **Uber.** ⊕ *www.uber.com*

DISCOUNTS AND DEALS

A $52.95 Charleston Heritage Passport, sold at the Charleston, North Charleston, and Mount Pleasant visitor centers, gets you into the Charleston Museum, the Gibbes Museum of Art, Drayton Hall, Middleton Place, and five historic houses for two consecutive days. Three- and seven-day passes are also available.

TOURS

BOAT TOURS

FAMILY **Charleston Harbor Tours.** This company offers excursions that give the colonial history of the harbor and its forts. ⊠ *Charleston Maritime Center, 10 Wharfside St., Ansonborough* ☎ *843/722–1112* ⊕ *www. charlestonharbortours.com* ⌨ *From $25.*

FAMILY **Sandlapper Tours.** These tours focus on regional history, coastal wildlife, and nocturnal ghostly lore. ⊠ *Charleston Maritime Center, 10 Wharf- side St., Ansonborough* ☎ *843/849–8687* ⊕ *www.sandlappertours.com* ⌨ *From $27.*

FAMILY **Schooner Pride.** On the 84-foot-tall schooner *Pride,* you can enjoy an eco-friendly sail and the natural sounds of Charleston harbor on a two-hour harbor cruise, a dolphin cruise, a sunset cruise, or romantic full-moon sails. ⊠ *Aquarium Wharf, 360 Concord St., Ansonbor- ough* ☎ *800/344–4483, 843/722–1112* ⊕ *www.schoonerpride.com* ⌨ *From $35.*

FAMILY **SpiritLine Cruises.** Another way to experience the harbor is with SpiritLine Cruises. These come with a live narrator, as well as an option for a dinner cruise that includes a three-course dinner and dancing to music by a local DJ. ⊠ *Aquarium Wharf, 360 Concord St., Ansonborough* ☎ *843/722–2628* ⊕ *www.spiritlinecruises.com* ⌨ *From $24.*

CARRIAGE TOURS

Carriage tours are a great way to see Charleston. The going rate is around $25 per person. Carolina Polo and Carriage Company, Old South Carriage Company, and Palmetto Carriage Works run horse-drawn carriage tours of the Historic District. Each follows one of four routes (determined by a city-operated bingo lottery at the start of each tour) and lasts about one hour. Most carriages queue up at North Market and Anson Streets. In addition to public tours, each carriage company offers private tours and wedding rentals.

Carriage Tour Contacts Carolina Polo and Carriage Company. ⊠ Double-Tree by Hilton Historic District, 181 Church St., Market ☎ 843/577–6767 ⊕ www. cpcc.com. **Old South Carriage Company.** ⊠ 14 Anson St., Market ☎ 843/723–9712 ⊕ www.oldsouthcarriagetours.com. **Palmetto Carriage Works.** ⊠ 8 Guignard St., Market ☎ 843/853–6125 ⊕ www.palmettocarriage.com.

ECOTOURS

FAMILY **Barrier Island Eco Tours.** Located at the Isle of Palms Marina, Barrier Island Eco Tours runs three-hour pontoon-boat tours to the uninhab- ited Capers Island. ⊠ *Isle of Palms Marina, 50 41st Ave., Isle of Palms* ☎ *843/886–5000* ⊕ *www.nature-tours.com* ⌨ *From $36.*

FAMILY
Fodor's Choice
★ **Coastal Expeditions.** This company has half-day and full-day naturalist-led kayak, SUP, and motorboat tours on local rivers, plus a ferry to Bulls Island in the Cape Romain National Wildlife Refuge. ⊠ *514-B Mill St., Mount Pleasant* ☎ *843/884–7684* ⊕ *www.coastalexpeditions. com* ⌨ *From $40.*

The Joseph Manigault House is one of the finest examples of Federal-style architecture in Charleston.

WALKING TOURS

Walking tours on various topics—horticulture, slavery, or women's history—are available from several city-certified tour companies, mostly located around the Market area. Bulldog Tours and Tour Charleston each offer popular ghost walks that explore the city's supernatural side and visit historic graveyards after dark.

Both Charleston Sole and Charleston 101 specialize in general history tours, while Bulldog Tours also offers culinary tours that stop into restaurants throughout the Historic District.

Walking Tour Contacts Bulldog Tours. ⊠ *18 Anson St., Market* ☎ *843/722–8687* ⊕ *www.bulldogtours.com.* **Charleston 101 Tours.** ⊠ *Powder Magazine, 79 Cumberland St., Market* ✢ *1 block from the City Market* ☎ *843/556–4753* ⊕ *www.charleston101tours.com.* **Charleston Sole.** ⊠ *The Old Exchange Building, 122 East Bay St., Broad Street* ☎ *843/364–8272* ⊕ *www.charleston-sole.com.* **Tour Charleston.** ⊠ *2A Cumberland St., Market* ☎ *843/723–1670* ⊕ *www.tourcharleston.com.*

VISITOR INFORMATION

The Charleston Area Convention & Visitors Bureau runs the Charleston Visitor Center, which has information about the city and its surrounding neighborhoods, plantations, beaches, and islands. The Preservation Society of Charleston has information on house tours.

Visitor Information Charleston Visitor Center. ⊠ *375 Meeting St., Upper King* ☎ *800/774–0006* ⊕ *www.charlestoncvb.com.* **Preservation Society of Charleston.** ⊠ *147 King St., Lower King* ☎ *843/722–4630* ⊕ *www.preservation-society.org.*

EXPLORING CHARLESTON

Everyone starts a tour of Charleston in downtown's famous Historic District. Roughly bounded by Lockwood Boulevard on the Ashley River to the west, Calhoun Street to the north, East Bay Street on the Cooper River to the east, and the Battery to the south, this fairly compact area of 800 acres contains nearly 2,000 historic homes and buildings. The peninsula is divided up into several neighborhoods, starting from the south and moving north, including the Battery, South of Broad, Lower King Street, and Upper King Street ending near "the Crosstown," where U.S. 17 connects downtown to Mount Pleasant and West Ashley.

Beyond downtown, the Ashley River hugs the west side of the peninsula; the region on the far shore is called West Ashley. The Cooper River runs along the east side of the peninsula, with Mount Pleasant on the opposite side and Charleston Harbor in between. Lastly, there are outlying sea islands: James Island, John's Island, Wadmalaw Island, Kiawah Island, Seabrook Island, Isle of Palms, and Sullivan's Island. Each has its own appealing attractions. Everything that entails crossing the bridges is best explored by car or bus.

NORTH OF BROAD

During the early 1800s, large tracts of land were available North of Broad—as it was outside the bounds of the original walled city—making it ideal for suburban plantations. A century later the peninsula had been built out, and today the resulting area is a vibrant mix of residential neighborhoods and commercial clusters, with verdant parks scattered throughout. The district comprises three primary neighborhoods: Upper King, the Market area, and the College of Charleston. Though there are a number of majestic homes and pre-Revolutionary buildings in this area (including the Powder Magazine, the oldest public building in the state), the main draw is the rich variety of stores, museums, restaurants, and historic churches.

As you explore, note that the farther north you travel (up King Street in particular), the newer and more commercial development becomes. Although pretty much anywhere on the peninsula is considered prime real estate these days, the farther south you go, the more expensive the homes become.

TOP ATTRACTIONS

Fodor'sChoice **Aiken-Rhett House Museum.** One of Charleston's most stately mansions, ★ built in 1820 and virtually unaltered since 1858, has been preserved rather than restored, meaning visitors can see its original wallpaper, paint, and some furnishings. Two of the former owners, Governor Aiken and his wife, Harriet—lovers of all things foreign and beautiful—bought many of the chandeliers, sculptures, and paintings in Europe. The carriage house remains out back, along with a building that contained the kitchen, laundry, and slave quarters, making this the most intact property to showcase urban life in antebellum Charleston. Take the audio tour, as it vividly describes both the ornate family rooms and the slave quarters, giving historical and family details throughout. ⌧ *48 Elizabeth St., Upper King* ☎ *843/723–1159* ⊕ *www.historiccharleston. org* ⬚ *$12; $18 with admission to Nathaniel Russell House.*

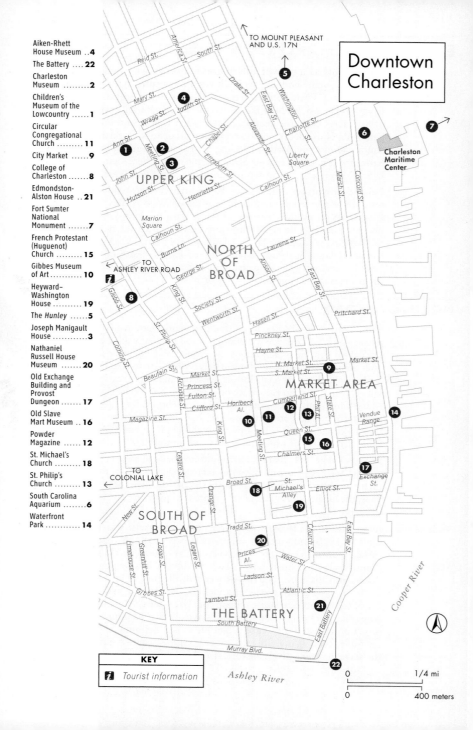

Aiken-Rhett
House Museum ..4

The Battery 22

Charleston
Museum 2

Children's
Museum of the
Lowcountry 1

Circular
Congregational
Church 11

City Market 9

College of
Charleston 8

Edmondston-
Alston House ..21

French Protestant
(Huguenot)
Church 15

Fort Sumter
National
Monument 7

Gibbes Museum
of Art 10

Heyward–
Washington
House 19

The *Hunley* 5

Joseph Manigault
House 3

Nathaniel
Russell House
Museum 20

Old Exchange
Building and
Provost
Dungeon 17

Old Slave
Mart Museum ..16

Powder
Magazine 12

St. Michael's
Church 18

St. Philip's
Church 13

South Carolina
Aquarium 6

Waterfront
Park 14

KEY

i Tourist information

FAMILY **Charleston Museum.** Although housed in a modern-day brick complex, this institution was founded in 1773 and is the country's oldest museum. To the delight of fans of *Antiques Roadshow,* the collection is especially strong in South Carolina decorative arts, from silver to snuffboxes. There's also a large gallery devoted to natural history (don't miss the giant polar bear). Children love the permanent Civil War exhibition and the interactive "Kidstory" area, where they can try on reproduction clothing in a miniature historic house. The Historic Textiles Gallery features rotating displays that showcase everything from uniforms and flags to couture gowns to antique quilts and needlework. Combination tickets that include the Joseph Manigault House and the Heyward-Washington House are a bargain at $25. ⊠ *360 Meeting St., Upper King* ☎ *843/722–2996* ⊕ *www.charlestonmuseum.org* ⊒ *$12; $18 combination ticket with Heyward-Washington House or Joseph Manigault House; $25 combination ticket all three sites.*

FAMILY **Children's Museum of the Lowcountry.** Hands-on interactive exhibits at this top-notch museum will keep kids—from babies on up to age 10—occupied for hours. They can climb aboard a Lowcountry pirate ship, drive an antique fire truck, race golf balls down a roller coaster, and create masterpieces in the art center. ⊠ *25 Ann St., Upper King* ☎ *843/853–8962* ⊕ *www.explorecml.org* ⊒ *$10* ⊘ *Closed Mon.*

Circular Congregational Church. The first church building erected on this site in the 1680s gave bustling Meeting Street its name. The present-day Romanesque structure, dating from 1890, is configured on a Greek-cross plan and has a breathtaking vaulted ceiling. While the sanctuary is not open to visitors except during Sunday morning service, you are welcome to explore the graveyard, which is the oldest English burial ground in the city, with records dating back to 1695. ⊠ *150 Meeting St., Market* ☎ *843/577–6400* ⊕ *www.circularchurch.org* ⊘ *Graveyard closed Sat.*

FAMILY **City Market.** Most of the buildings that make up this popular attraction were constructed between 1804 and the 1830s to serve as the city's meat, fish, and produce market. These days you'll find the open-air portion packed with stalls selling handmade jewelry, crafts, clothing, jams and jellies, and regional souvenirs. A major renovation transformed the market's indoor section, creating a beautiful backdrop for 20 stores and eateries. Local craftspeople are on hand, weaving sweetgrass baskets—a skill passed down through generations from their African ancestors. From March through December, a night market on Friday and Saturday hosts local artists and food vendors. This shopping mecca's perimeters (North and South Market Streets) are lined with restaurants and shops. ⊠ *N. and S. Market Sts. between Meeting and E. Bay Sts., Market* ⊕ *www.thecharlestoncitymarket.com.*

College of Charleston. With a majestic Greek revival portico, Randolph Hall—an 1828 building designed by Philadelphia architect William Strickland—presides over the college's central Cistern Yard. Draping oaks envelop the lush green quad, where graduation ceremonies and concerts, notably during Spoleto Festival USA, take place.

7

Women in Charleston keep alive the art of sweetgrass basket weaving brought over by enslaved people from Africa.

Scenes from films like *Cold Mountain* and *The Notebook* have been filmed on the historic campus of this liberal arts college, founded in 1770. ⊠ *Cistern Yard, 66 George St., College of Charleston Campus* ☎ *843/805–5507* ⊕ *www.cofc.edu.*

FAMILY
Fodor's Choice
★

Fort Sumter National Monument. Set on a man-made island in Charleston's harbor, this is the hallowed spot where the Civil War began. On April 12, 1861, the first shot of the war was fired at the fort from Fort Johnson across the way. After a 34-hour battle, Union forces surrendered and Confederate troops occupied Fort Sumter, which became a symbol of Southern resistance. The Confederacy managed to hold it, despite almost continual bombardment from August 1863 to February of 1865. When it was finally evacuated, the fort was a heap of rubble. Today, the National Park Service oversees it, and rangers give interpretive talks.

To reach the fort, take a private boat or one of the ferries that depart from Patriots Point in Mount Pleasant and downtown's Fort Sumter Visitor Education Center, which includes exhibits on the antebellum period and the Civil War. There are seven trips daily to the Fort between mid-March and mid-August, fewer the rest of the year. ☎ *843/883–3123* ⊕ *www.nps.gov/fosu* ⊠ *Fort free; ferry $21.*

French Protestant (Huguenot) Church. The circa-1845 Gothic-style church is home to the nation's only practicing Huguenot congregation. English-language services are held Sunday at 10:30, with a tour given to any visitors afterward at 11:15. ⊠ *136 Church St., Market* ☎ *843/722–4385* ⊕ *www.huguenot-church.org.*

Fodor'sChoice ★ **Gibbes Museum of Art.** Housed in a beautiful Beaux Arts building, this museum boasts a collection of 10,000 works, principally American with a local connection. Different objects from the museum's permanent collection are on view in "The Charleston Story," offering a nice overview of the region's history. ⊠ *135 Meeting St., Market* ☎ *843/722–2706* ⊕ *www.gibbesmuseum.org* ✍ *$12* ☉ *Closed Mon.*

Joseph Manigault House. An extraordinary example of Federal architecture, this 1803 residence and National Historic Landmark reflects the urban lifestyle of a well-to-do rice-planting family and the Africans they enslaved. Engaging guided tours reveal a stunning spiral staircase, rooms that have been preserved in period style, and American, English, and French furniture from the early 19th century. Outside, stroll through the artfully maintained period garden with a classical Gate Temple and interpretive signs that note where historic buildings once stood. ⊠ *350 Meeting St., Upper King* ☎ *843/723–2926* ⊕ *www. charlestonmuseum.org* ✍ *$12; $18 combination ticket with Heyward-Washington House or Charleston Museum; $25 combination ticket all three sites.*

Fodor'sChoice ★ **Old Slave Mart Museum.** This is thought to be the state's only existing building that was used for slave auctioning, a practice that ended here in 1863. It was once part of a complex called Ryan's Mart, which also contained a slave jail, kitchen, and morgue. It is now a museum that shares the history of Charleston's role in the slave trade, a horrific part of the city's history, but one that is important to understand. Charleston was a commercial center for the South's plantation economy, and slaves were the primary source of labor both within the city as well as on the surrounding plantations. Galleries are outfitted with interactive exhibits, including push buttons that allow you to hear voices relating stories from the age of slavery. The museum sits on one of the few remaining cobblestone streets in town. ⊠ *6 Chalmers St., Market* ☎ *843/958–6467* ⊕ *www.charleston-sc.gov* ✍ *$8* ☉ *Closed Sun.*

FAMILY Fodor'sChoice ★ **South Carolina Aquarium.** Get up close and personal with more than 5,000 creatures at this waterfront attraction, where exhibits invite you to journey through distinctive habitats. Step into the Mountain Forest and find water splashing over a rocky gorge as river otters play. Enter the open-air Saltmarsh Aviary to feed stingrays and view herons, diamondback terrapins, and puffer fish. And gaze in awe at the two-story, 385,000-gallon Great Ocean Tank, home to sharks, jellyfish, and a loggerhead sea turtle. Kids love the Touch Tank, and tours of the Sea Turtle Hospital are well worth the extra $15. ⊠ *100 Aquarium Wharf, Ansonborough* ☎ *800/722–6455, 843/577–3474* ⊕ *www.scaquarium.org* ✍ *$24.95.*

St. Philip's Church. Founded around 1680, St. Philip's didn't move to its current site until the 1720s, becoming one of the three churches that gave Church Street its name. The first building in this location (where George Washington worshipped in 1791) burned down in 1835 and was replaced with the Corinthian-style structure seen today. A shell that exploded in the churchyard while services were being held during the Civil War didn't deter the minister from finishing his sermon (the

Take the ferry to Fort Sumter National Monument to see where the first shots of the Civil War were fired.

congregation gathered elsewhere for the remainder of the war). Amble through the churchyards, where notable South Carolinians such as John C. Calhoun are buried. If you want to tour the church, call ahead, as open hours depend upon volunteer availability. ✉ *142 Church St., Market* ☎ *843/722–7734* ⊕ *www.stphilipschurchsc.org.*

FAMILY **Waterfront Park.** Enjoy the fishing pier's "front-porch" swings, stroll along the waterside path, or relax in the gardens overlooking Charleston Harbor. The expansive lawn is perfect for picnics and family playtime. Two fountains can be found here: the oft-photographed Pineapple Fountain and the Vendue Fountain, which children love to run through on hot days. ✉ *Vendue Range at Concord St., Market* ⛱ *Free.*

WORTH NOTING

The Hunley. In 1864, the Confederacy's H. L. *Hunley* sank the Union warship USS *Housatonic*, becoming the world's first successful submarine. But moments after the attack, it disappeared mysteriously into the depths of the sea. Lost for more than a century, it was found in 1995 off the coast of Sullivan's Island, and raised in 2000. The *Hunley* is now being preserved and excavated in a 90,000-gallon tank, which you can see during an informative guided tour. An exhibit area includes artifacts excavated from the sub and interactive displays. There's also a full-size replica of the *Hunley* outside the Charleston Museum. ✉ *1250 Supply St., Old Charleston Naval Base, North Charleston* ☎ *877/448–6539 for tours* ⊕ *www.hunley.org* ⛱ *$16* ⊗ *Closed weekdays.*

Powder Magazine. Completed in 1713, the oldest public building in South Carolina is one of few that remain from the time of the Lords Proprietors. The city's volatile—and precious—gunpowder was kept here during the Revolutionary War, and the building's thick walls were designed to contain an explosion if its stores were detonated. Today, it's a small museum with a permanent exhibit on colonial and Revolutionary warfare. ⊠ *79 Cumberland St., Market* ☎ *843/722–9350* ⊕ *www. powdermag.org* ⧉ *$5.*

SOUTH OF BROAD

The heavily residential area south of Broad Street brims with beautiful private homes, many of which have plaques bearing brief descriptions of the property's history. Mind your manners, but feel free to peek through iron gates and fences at the verdant displays in elaborate gardens. Although an open gate once signified that guests were welcome to venture inside, that time has mostly passed—residents tell stories of how they came home to find tourists sitting in their front-porch rockers. But you never know when an invitation to have a look-see might come from a friendly owner-gardener. Several of the city's lavish house museums call this famously affluent neighborhood home.

TOP ATTRACTIONS

FAMILY

Fodor'sChoice

★

The Battery. During the Civil War, the Confederate army mounted cannons in the Battery, at the southernmost point of Charleston's peninsula, to fortify the city against Union attack. Cannons and piles of cannonballs still line the oak-shaded park known as White Point Garden—kids can't resist climbing them. Where pirates once hung from the gallows, strollers now take in the serene setting from Charleston benches (small wood-slat benches with cast-iron sides). Stroll the waterside promenades along East Battery and Murray Boulevard and you can enjoy views of Charleston Harbor, the Ravenel Bridge, and Fort Sumter on one side, with some of the city's most photographed mansions on the other. You'll find locals dangling their fishing lines, waiting for a catch. ⊠ *East Battery St., at Murray Blvd., South of Broad* ⧉ *Free.*

Heyward-Washington House. This Georgian-style double house was the town home of Thomas Heyward, patriot leader and signer of the Declaration of Independence. The city rented the residence for George Washington's use during the president's weeklong stay in Charleston in 1791. Inside, visitors find historic Charleston-made furniture, notably the withdrawing room's Holmes Bookcase, considered to be one of the most exceptional examples of American colonial furniture. Also significant is the 1740s kitchen building, as it's the only one of its kind open to the public in Charleston. Don't miss the formal gardens, which contain plants commonly used in the area in the late 18th century. ⊠ *87 Church St., South of Broad* ☎ *843/722–0354* ⊕ *www.charlestonmuseum.org* ⧉ *$12.*

Fodor'sChoice

★

Nathaniel Russell House Museum. One of the nation's finest examples of Federal-style architecture, the Nathaniel Russell House was built in 1808 and is restored to a 19th-century aesthetic. Its grand beauty is proof of the immense wealth Russell accumulated as one of the city's leading merchants. In addition to the famous "free-flying" staircase that spirals up three stories with no visible support, the ornate interior is distinguished by Charleston-made furniture as well as paintings and works on paper by well-known American and European artists,

7

DID YOU KNOW?

The original steeple bells of St. Philip's (Episcopal) Church were given to the Confederate army to be melted into cannon. Four of the 11 bells were replaced in 1976 and now chime from 8 in the morning to 8 at night.

including Henry Benbridge, Samuel F. B. Morse, and George Romney. The extensive formal garden is worth a leisurely stroll. ⌧ *51 Meeting St., South of Broad* ☎ *843/724–8481* ⊕ *www.historiccharleston.org* ⌧ *$12; $18 with admission to Aiken-Rhett House Museum.*

St. Michael's Church. Topped by a 186-foot steeple, St. Michael's is the city's oldest surviving church building. The first cornerstone was set in place in 1752 and, through the years, other elements were added: the steeple clock and bells (1764); the organ (1768); the font (1771); and the altar (1892). A claim to fame: George Washington worshipped in pew number 43 in 1791. Listen for the bell ringers on Sunday mornings before worship services. ⌧ *78 Meeting St., corner of Meeting and Broad Sts., South of Broad* ☎ *843/723–0603* ⊕ *www.stmichaelschurch.net.*

WORTH NOTING

Edmondston-Alston House. In 1825, Charles Edmondston built this house in the Federal style on Charleston's High Battery. About 13 years later, second owner Charles Alston began transforming it into the Greek Revival structure seen today. The home is furnished with family antiques, portraits, silver, and fine china. ⌧ *21 E. Battery, South of Broad* ☎ *843/722–7171* ⊕ *www.edmondstonalston.com* ⌧ *$12.*

FAMILY **Old Exchange Building & Provost Dungeon.** Built as a customshouse in 1771, this building once served as the commercial and social center of Charleston. It was the site of many historic events, including the state's ratification of the Constitution in 1788 and two grand celebrations hosted for George Washington. However, the place was also used by the British to house prisoners during the Revolutionary War, an ordeal detailed in one of the exhibits. Costumed interpreters bring history to life on guided tours, and kids are fascinated by the period mannequins on display in the dungeon. ⌧ *122 E. Bay St., South of Broad* ☎ *843/727–2165* ⊕ *www.oldexchange.org* ⌧ *$10.*

MOUNT PLEASANT AND VICINITY

East of Charleston, across the Arthur Ravenel Jr. Bridge—one of the longest cable-stay bridges in North America—is the town of Mount Pleasant, named not for a mountain but for a plantation founded there in the early 18th century. In its Old Village neighborhood are antebellum homes and a sleepy, old-time town center with a drugstore where patrons still amble up to the soda fountain and lunch counter for egg-salad sandwiches and floats. Along Shem Creek, where the local fishing fleet brings in the daily catch, several seafood restaurants serve the area's freshest (and most deftly fried) seafood. Other attractions in the area include military and maritime museums, plantations, and, farther north, the Cape Romain National Wildlife Refuge.

TOP ATTRACTIONS

FAMILY

Fodor's Choice

★

Boone Hall Plantation & Gardens. A drive through a ½-mile-long live-oak alley draped in Spanish moss introduces you to this still-functioning plantation, the oldest of its kind. Tours take you through the 1936 mansion, the butterfly pavilion, and the heirloom rose garden. Eight slave cabins on the property have been transformed into the Black

Boone Hall is one of the country's oldest working plantations and continues to grow crops like strawberries, tomatoes, and pumpkins.

History in America exhibit, displaying life-size figures, recorded narratives, audiovisual presentations, photos, and historical relics. Seasonal Gullah cultural performances are perennial crowd favorites. Stroll along the winding river, or pluck in-season fruits (like strawberries, peaches, and pumpkins) from the fields. Across the highway is Boone Hall's Farm Market, with fresh local produce, a café, and a gift shop. The miniseries *North and South* was filmed here, as was the movie adaptation of Nicholas Spark's *The Notebook*. ■TIP→ **Plan your visit to coincide with annual events like the Lowcountry Oyster Festival in January or the Scottish Games and Highland Gathering in September.** ✉ *1235 Long Point Rd., off U.S. 17 N, Mount Pleasant* ☎ *843/884–4371* ⊕ *www. boonehallplantation.com* ✉ *$24.*

FAMILY **Fort Moultrie.** A part of the Fort Sumter National Monument, this is the site where Colonel William Moultrie's South Carolinians repelled a British assault in one of the first patriot victories of the Revolutionary War. Completed in 1809, the fort is the third fortress on this site on Sullivan's Island, 10 miles southeast of Charleston. Set across the street, the companion museum is an unsung hero. Although much is made of Fort Sumter, this smaller historical site is creatively designed, with figurines in various uniforms that make military history come alive. A 20-minute educational film that spans several major wars tells the colorful history of the fort. There's also an exhibit focusing on the slave trade and Sullivan's Island's role in it. ■TIP→ **Plan to spend the day bicycling through Sullivan's Island, where you'll find a cluster of century-old beach houses.** ✉ *1214 Middle St., Sullivan's Island* ☎ *843/883–3123* ⊕ *www.nps.gov/fosu* ✉ *$3.*

FAMILY
Fodor'sChoice
★

Mount Pleasant Memorial Waterfront Park. Sprawling beneath the Ravenel Bridge, this beautifully landscaped green space invites lounging on the grass with views of Charleston Harbor. You can also take a path up to the bridge for a stroll. Find helpful info in the visitor center, chat with Gullah locals selling traditional baskets in the Sweetgrass Cultural Arts Pavilion, and spend a quiet moment listening to the waterfall fountain in the Mount Pleasant War Memorial. Kids love the playground modeled after the Ravenel Bridge, and parents appreciate that it's fenced, with benches galore. A 1,250-foot-long pier stretches into the water—grab a milk shake from the Snack Bar and Tackle Shop and a seat on one of the double-sided swings to watch folks fishing for their supper. ✉ *71 Harry Hallman Blvd., Mount Pleasant* ☎ *843/762–9946* ⊕ *www.ccprc.com.*

FAMILY

Patriots Point Naval and Maritime Museum. Climb aboard the USS *Yorktown* aircraft carrier—which contains the Congressional Medal of Honor Museum—as well as the destroyer USS *Laffey.* A life-size replica of a Vietnam support base camp showcases naval air and watercraft used in that military action. ✉ *40 Patriots Point Rd., Mount Pleasant* ☎ *843/884–2727* ⊕ *www.patriotspoint.org* ✎ *$22.*

WORTH NOTING

Cape Romain National Wildlife Refuge. Maritime forests, barrier islands, salt marshes, beaches, and coastal waterways make up this 66,287-acre refuge established in 1932 as a migratory bird haven. The **Sewee Visitor & Environmental Education Center** has information and exhibits on the property and its trails, as well as an outdoor enclosure housing endangered red wolves (feedings are Thursday at 3 pm and Saturday at 11:30 am). The refuge is aiding the recovery of the threatened loggerhead sea turtle, and a video details the work. ■**TIP→ From the mainland refuge, you can take a $40 ferry ride to Bulls Island to explore its boneyard beach and freshwater ponds teeming with alligators.** ✉ *Sewee Center, 5821 U.S. 17 N, Awendaw* ☎ *843/928–3368* ⊕ *www.fws.gov/caperomain* ✎ *Free* ⊙ *Closed Sun.–Tues.*

Charles Pinckney National Historic Site. This site includes the last 28 acres of the plantation owned by Charles Pinckney, a drafter and signer of the U.S. Constitution. You can tour an 1820s coastal cottage, constructed after Pinckney's death, that features interpretive exhibits about the man, the Constitution, and slave life. A nature trail leads to the archaeological foundations of three slave houses. ✉ *1254 Long Point Rd., off U.S. 17 N, Mount Pleasant* ☎ *843/881–5516* ⊕ *www.nps.gov/chpi* ✎ *Free.*

FAMILY

Old Village. The historic center of Mount Pleasant, this neighborhood is distinguished by white picket fences, storybook cottages, antebellum homes with wide porches, tiny churches, and lavish waterfront homes. It's a lovely area for a stroll or bike ride, and Pitt Street offers a couple of locally loved eateries and boutiques. Head south along Pitt Street to the Otis M. Pickett Bridge & Park, popular for picnicking, fishing, and sunset views. ✉ *Pitt St. and Venning St., Mount Pleasant.*

7

The pastel houses of Rainbow Row on East Bay Street are a popular photo op.

WEST OF THE ASHLEY RIVER

Ashley River Road (Route 61) begins a few miles northwest of downtown Charleston, over the Ashley River Bridge. Sights are spread out along the way, and those who love history, old homes, and gardens may need several days to explore places like Drayton Hall, Middleton Place, and Magnolia Plantation and Gardens. Spring is a peak time for the flowers, although many of them are in bloom throughout the year.

TOP ATTRACTIONS

FAMILY

Fodor's Choice

★

Magnolia Plantation & Gardens. Pick and choose from a variety of exhibits at Magnolia Plantation, established in the 1670s by Thomas Drayton after he moved from Barbados. The extensive garden—the oldest public one in the country—was begun in the late 17th century and has evolved into a Romantic-style green space overflowing with plants, including a vast array of azaleas and camellias, along with some themed areas (a biblical garden, for example) and a topiary maze. Take a train or boat to tour the grounds, or traverse more than 500 acres of trails by foot or bike (bring your own). The 60-acre Audubon Swamp Garden invites a good, long stroll on its network of boardwalks and bridges. There's also a petting zoo, a nature center, and a reptile house. Five pre- and post-Emancipation cabins have been restored and serve as the focal point of an interpreter-led tour called From Slavery to Freedom. And be sure to visit the 19th-century plantation house, which originally stood near Summerville. The home was taken apart, floated down the Ashley River, and reassembled here. ⊠ *3550 Ashley River Rd., West Ashley* ☎ *843/571–1266* ⊕ *www.magnoliaplantation.com* ✉ *Grounds $15; house tour $8; tram $8; boat $8; From Slavery to Freedom exhibit $8; Audubon Swamp $8.*

FAMILY **Middleton Place.** Established around 1742, Middleton Place was at the
Fodor's Choice center of the Middleton family's empire of rice plantations, which
★ consisted of 63,000 acres and 3,500 slaves on properties throughout
the South Carolina Lowcountry. With its massive three-story brick
manor home and prized gardens, Middleton Place was a grand statement of wealth.

The original manor home was destroyed in the Civil War, but one of
its flanking buildings, which served as the gentlemen's guest quarters,
was salvaged and transformed into the family's postbellum residence.
It now serves as a house museum, displaying impressive English silver,
furniture, original paintings, and historic documents, including an early
silk copy of the Declaration of Independence. In the stable yards, historic interpreters use authentic tools to demonstrate spinning, weaving,
blacksmithing, and other skills from the plantation era. Heritage-breed
farm animals, such as water buffalo and cashmere goats, are housed
here, along with peacocks.

To get the complete picture of life on a rice plantation, be sure to allow
time for the African American Focus tour. The tour begins at Eliza's
House, a restored 1870s sharecropper's home. Inside the house, a small
exhibit provides details on the lives of the Middleton slaves.

Restored in the 1920s, the breathtakingly beautiful gardens are considered the oldest landscaped gardens in the country, begun in 1741 by
Henry Middleton, second president of the First Continental Congress.
From camellias to roses, blooms of all seasons form floral *allées* (alleys)
along terraced lawns and around a pair of ornamental lakes that are
shaped like butterfly wings.

If all this leaves you feeling peckish, head over to the cozy Middleton Place Restaurant for excellent Lowcountry specialties for lunch
and dinner. You can also stay overnight at the contemporary Inn at
Middleton Place, where floor-to-ceiling windows splendidly frame the
Ashley River. ⊠ *4300 Ashley River Rd., West Ashley* ☎ *800/782–3608,*
843/556–6020 ⊕ *www.middletonplace.org* ✉ *General admission $28,*
house tour $15, carriage tours $18; $49 combination ticket includes
Edmonston-Alston House.

WORTH EXPLORING

Drayton Hall. Considered the nation's finest example of Palladian-
inspired architecture, Drayton Hall is the only plantation house on the
Ashley River to have survived the Civil War intact. A National Trust
Historic Site built between 1738 and 1742, it's an invaluable lesson in
history as well as in architecture. The home has been left unfurnished
to highlight the original plaster moldings, opulent hand-carved woodwork, and other ornamental details. Regular tours, with guides known
for their in-depth knowledge, depart on the half hour and paint a vivid
picture of the people who once inhabited this fabled house. Visitors
can also see the African American cemetery and even take part in the
45-minute "Connections" program that uses maps and historic documents to trace the story of Africans from their journey to America,
through slavery, and into the 20th century. ⊠ *3380 Ashley River Rd.,*
West Ashley ☎ *843/769–2600* ⊕ *www.draytonhall.org* ✉ *$22.*

WHERE TO EAT

It's hard to beat Charleston when it comes to eating out. The city is blessed with a bevy of Southern-inflected selections, from barbecue parlors to fish shacks to casual places serving Lowcountry fare like shrimp and grits. And if you'd like to sample something new, there are plenty of places serving updated versions of classic dishes. Before you leave, you'll definitely see why Charleston is considered one of the great food cities in the world.

As for attire, Charleston invites a crisp yet casual atmosphere. Don't forget, Charleston was recognized as the Most Mannerly City in the union by Marjabelle Young Stewart, which means that residents are slow to judge (or, at the least, that they do so very quietly). On the whole, the city encourages comfort and unhurried, easy pacing. The result is an idyllic setting in which to enjoy oysters on the half shell and other homegrown delicacies from the land and sea that jointly grant the city its impressive culinary standing.*Dining reviews have been shortened. For full information, visit Fodors.com. Use the coordinate (⊕ 1:B2) at the end of each listing to locate a site on the corresponding map.*

PRICES

Fine dining in Charleston can be expensive. One option to keep costs down might be to try several of the small plates that many establishments offer. To save money, drive over the bridges or go to the islands, including James and Johns islands.

WHAT IT COSTS				
	$	$$	$$$	$$$$
Restaurants	under $15	$15–$19	$20–$24	over $24

Restaurant prices are for a main course at dinner, or if dinner is not served, at lunch.

NORTH OF BROAD

$$ THAI

🍴 **Basil.** There's a reason that this corner restaurant in the heart of downtown has been lauded again and again for its Asian fare. Dinner hours generate extended wait times—no reservations allowed—as patrons angle for an outdoor or window table to sample the eclectic dishes. **Known for:** sidewalk dining in the heart of Upper King Street; tons of vegetarian options; long waits for a table. [$] *Average main: $16* ✉ *460 King St., Upper King* ☎ *843/724–3490* 🌐 *www.eatatbasil.com* ⊕ *A1.*

$ MODERN AMERICAN Fodor's Choice ★

🍴 **Butcher & Bee.** Healthy and light but always satisfying, this local favorite has grown into new digs and expanded its lunch and dinner menus. The seasonal menu features creative salads, craft sandwiches, rice bowls, and a scrumptious breakfast menu that leaves patrons wanting to stick around for lunch. **Known for:** locally sourced, seasonal ingredients used in eclectic ways; drool-worthy sandwiches; big patio for outside dining. [$] *Average main: $12* ✉ *1085 Morrison Dr., North Morrison* ☎ *843/619–0202* 🌐 *www.butcherandbee.com* ⊕ *B1.*

$$$$ SOUTHERN Fodor's Choice ★ 🍴 **Charleston Grill.** Quite simply, this restaurant provides what many regard as the city's highest gastronomic experience. Chef Michelle Weaver creates the groundbreaking New South cuisine, while sommelier Rick Rubel stocks 1,300 wines in his cellar, with many served by the glass. **Known for:** impeccable service; a wine selection that rivals the world's best; nightly tasting menu that spans genres. [$] *Average main: $30* ✉ *Charleston Place Hotel, 224 King St., Market* ☎ *843/577–4522* 🌐 *www.charlestongrill.com* ⏲ *No lunch* ⊕ *C4.*

$$$ FRENCH Fodor's Choice ★ 🍴 **Chez Nous.** The menu may be illegible, the space miniscule, and the tucked-away location like finding Waldo, but the food is almost always sublime. Each night only two appetizers, two entrées (like snapper with a vin jaune sauce or gnocchi with chanterelles), and two desserts are offered. **Known for:** romantic hideaway dining; unique French, Spanish, and Italian fare; constantly changing menu. [$] *Average main: $24* ✉ *6 Payne Ct., off Coming St., Upper King* ☎ *843/579–3060* 🌐 *cheznouschs.com* ⏲ *Closed Mon.* ⊕ *A1.*

$$$$ MODERN AMERICAN 🍴 **Circa 1886.** Located on-site at the Wentworth Mansion, this former residential home is full of hand-carved marble fireplaces and stained-glass windows. The award-winning eatery emphasizes seasonal offerings, while also showing off the chef's Texas roots. **Known for:** romantic outdoor dining in the courtyard on warm evenings; views of the city from the cupola atop the mansion; jerk-brined antelope procured from a Texas hill country farm. [$] *Average main: $32* ✉ *149 Wentworth St., Lower King* ☎ *843/853–7828* 🌐 *www.circa1886.com* ⏲ *Closed Sun.* ⊕ *A4.*

$ BAKERY FAMILY 🍴 **Cupcake DownSouth.** This cute shop features more than 50 flavors of cupcakes. A daily flavor chart reveals the collection of pocket-sized pleasures on offer. **Known for:** sweet treats to please all ages; catering for parties and weddings; flavors like peanut butter banana fluff, praline, and death by chocolate. [$] *Average main: $4* ✉ *433 King St., Upper King* ☎ *843/853–8181* 🌐 *www.freshcupcakes.com* ⊕ *B2.*

$$$$ ECLECTIC 🍴 **Cypress Lowcountry Grille.** In a renovated 1834 brick building with striking contemporary decor, this eatery has leather booths, a ceiling with light sculptures that change color, and a "wine wall" packed with 4,500 bottles. The cuisine is high-end Southern American, with fresh local ingredients accented with exotic flavors, notably from the Pacific Rim. **Known for:** acclaimed charcuterie program; gourmet burgers at the upstairs bar; fantastic wine list. [$] *Average main: $35* ✉ *167 E. Bay St., Market* ☎ *843/727–0111* 🌐 *www.cypresscharleston.com* ⏲ *No lunch* ⊕ *H6.*

$$$$ SOUTHERN 🍴 **Edmund's Oast.** It's not just what's in the pint glasses at this upscale brewpub that has locals raving. The kitchen dishes up heritage chicken and Carolina Gold rice porridge, roasted grouper with cowpea and fennel salad, and braised lamb meatballs. **Known for:** the best of the best for beer nerds; foodie-oriented Sunday brunch; sunshine-filled patio. [$] *Average main: $25* ✉ *1081 Morrison Dr., North Central* ☎ *843/727–1145* 🌐 *www.edmundsoast.com* ⏲ *No lunch* ⊕ *C1.*

$$$$ SOUTHERN Fodor's Choice ★ 🍴 **FIG.** Spend an evening here for fresh-off-the-farm ingredients cooked with unfussy, flavorful finesse. The menu changes frequently, but the family-style vegetables might be as simple as young beets in sherry vinegar served in a plain white bowl. **Known for:** local, seasonal fare that consistently sets the standard for Charleston dining; nationally

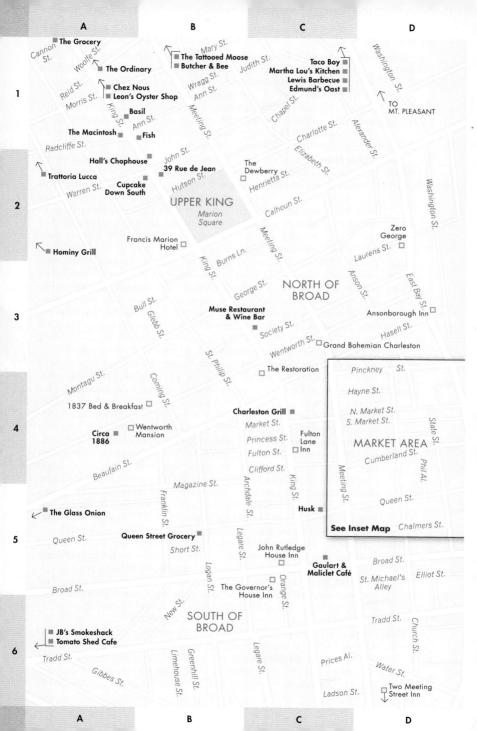

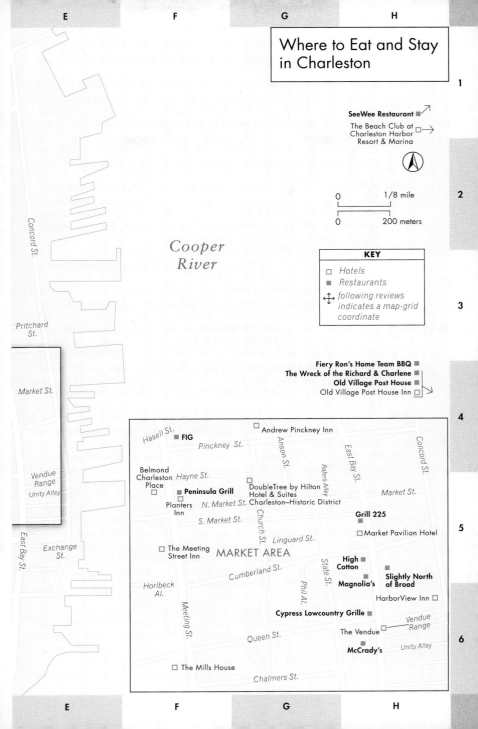

Where to Eat and Stay in Charleston

SeeWee Restaurant ■ ↗

The Beach Club at □ →
Charleston Harbor
Resort & Marina

0 ———— 1/8 mile
0 ———— 200 meters

Cooper River

KEY

□ Hotels
■ Restaurants
⟷ following reviews
indicates a map-grid
coordinate

Fiery Ron's Home Team BBQ ■
The Wreck of the Richard & Charlene ■
Old Village Post House ■
Old Village Post House Inn □ ↘

Concord St.

Pritchard St.

Market St.

Vendue Range
Unity Alley

East Bay St.

Exchange St.

Hasell St. ■ FIG
Pinckney St.

□ Andrew Pinckney Inn

Anson St.

Rajers Alley

East Bay St.

Concord St.

Belmond
Charleston Hayne St.
Place
□
■ Peninsula Grill
Planters N. Market St.
Inn
S. Market St.

□
DoubleTree by Hilton
Hotel & Suites
Charleston–Historic District

Market St.

Church St.

Grill 225

□ Market Pavilion Hotel

□ The Meeting
Street Inn   MARKET AREA

Linguard St.

Cumberland St.

Horlbeck
Al.

Meeting St.

State St.

Phil Al.

High ■
Cotton

Magnolia's ■

Cypress Lowcountry Grille ■

The Vendue □

■
McCrady's

■
Slightly North
of Broad

HarborView Inn □

Vendue
Range

Unity Alley

Queen St.

□ The Mills House

Chalmers St.

recognized wine program; lively bar scene. $ *Average main: $30* ✉ *232 Meeting St., Market* 🕾 *843/805–5900* ⊕ *www.eatatfig.com* ◷ *No lunch* ✛ *F4.*

$$$$
ECLECTIC

✕ **Fish.** Savvy foodies were the first to embrace the inventive French-Asian cuisine at this Upper King stalwart. The steamed local clams or mussels are a great start, while the daily whole fish special is as fine a plate of seafood as you'll find anywhere in town, although it's difficult to bypass the slow-cooked short ribs. **Known for:** creative craft cocktails with flair; lively after-work happy hour scene at the bar; seafood dishes with unique flavors. $ *Average main: $26* ✉ *440–442 King St., Upper King* 🕾 *843/722–3474* ⊕ *www.fishrestaurantcharleston.com* ◷ *No lunch* ✛ *B1.*

$$$$
STEAKHOUSE

✕ **Grill 225.** This atmospheric establishment has been stockpiling accolades over the years, and it's never been better. The cuisine—combined with a staggering array of excellent wines and professional, caring service—make Grill 225 a popular special-occasion spot. **Known for:** glitz and glamour in the heart of Market Street; one of the best steaks in town; the signature Nitrotini cocktail. $ *Average main: $40* ✉ *Market Pavilion Hotel, 225 E. Bay St., Market* 🕾 *843/723–0500* ⊕ *www.marketpavilion.com/grill225.cfm* ✛ *H5.*

$$$$
MODERN
AMERICAN
Fodor's Choice
★

✕ **The Grocery.** Executive chef and owner Kevin Johnson's restaurant sits in impressive quarters near the corner of Cannon and King Streets. The menu suggests a humble, considerate approach, as the dishes represent local flavors: the wood-roasted carrots come with feta, raisins, and pistachio crumble, while the wood-roasted black bass is delivered with salsa verde. **Known for:** down-to-earth dishes designed for sharing; a monstrous wood-fired oven used to excellent effect; decadent cassoulet of chorizo, pork belly, and duck confit. $ *Average main: $25* ✉ *4 Cannon St., Market* 🕾 *843/302–8825* ⊕ *www.thegrocerycharleston.com* ◷ *No lunch* ✛ *A1.*

$$$$
STEAKHOUSE
Fodor's Choice
★

✕ **Hall's Chophouse.** Thanks to its impressive 28-day aged USDA steaks, Hall's Chophouse has quickly established itself as one of the top steak houses in town. Recommended are the 28-ounce Tomahawk rib eye, the New York strip, and the slow-roasted prime rib. **Known for:** hopping upscale bar scene; first-class service from the Hall family; amazing variety of steaks. $ *Average main: $45* ✉ *434 King St., Upper King* 🕾 *843/727–0090* ⊕ *www.hallschophouse.com* ◷ *No lunch* ✛ *B2.*

$$$$
SOUTHERN

✕ **High Cotton.** This Charleston classic remains unchanged by time: lazily spinning paddle fans, lush palm trees, and exposed brick walls. The kitchen serves up regional classics like Lowcountry boil and bacon-wrapped stuffed rabbit loin. **Known for:** live jazz and bluegrass music at the bar; one of the city's finest weekend brunches; high-rising peanut butter pie for dessert. $ *Average main: $30* ✉ *199 E. Bay St., Market* 🕾 *843/724–3815* ⊕ *www.highcottoncharleston.com* ◷ *No lunch weekdays* ✛ *H5.*

$$
SOUTHERN

✕ **Hominy Grill.** The wooden barber poles from the last century still frame the door of this homespun café and Lowcountry landmark. Chef Robert Stehling is a Carolina boy who lived in New York; that dichotomy shows in his "uptown" comfort food. **Known for:** the standard bearer for shrimp and grits in a town that hangs its name on the dish; the Charleston Nasty, a heart-stopping chicken biscuit with gravy;

low-key Southern charm and hospitality. Ⓢ *Average main: $18* ✉ *207 Rutledge Ave., Cannonborough* ☎ *843/937–0930* ⊕ *www.hominygrill. com* ◷ *No dinner Sun.* ✛ *A2.*

$$$$
SOUTHERN
Fodor'sChoice
★

✕ **Husk.** With an abundance of accolades, Husk serves an ambitious menu steeped in the South, and the South alone—celebrated chef Sean Brock forbids the inclusion of items from other regions or provinces. A large chalkboard lists the ever-changing artisanal dishes available, as the menu sometimes varies twice daily. **Known for:** the Husk burger, modeled after In-N-Out's famous offering; the throwback stand-alone bar with its great bourbon menu; smoky bacon cornbread for a side. Ⓢ *Average main: $29* ✉ *76 Queen St., Market* ☎ *843/577–2500* ⊕ *www. huskrestaurant.com* ✛ *C5.*

$$
SOUTHERN

✕ **Leon's Oyster Shop.** Casual, quirky, and a tad Wes Anderson-y, this oyster shop sports a kitschy ambience and blues-heavy soundtrack. Fried chicken sammies come towering, dressed in fresh slaw and nestled on perfectly prepared rolls. **Known for:** lively stand-up bar scene; extensive champagne list; old-school soft-serve ice cream. Ⓢ *Average main: $15* ✉ *698 King St., Upper King* ☎ *843/531–6500* ⊕ *www.leonsoystershop.com* ✛ *A1.*

$
BARBECUE
Fodor'sChoice
★

✕ **Lewis Barbecue.** Austin pitmaster John Lewis transformed Charleston's smoked meat scene when he opened this Texas-style joint that serves prime rib, pulled pork, and "hot guts" by the pound. Opt for the monster "El Sancho Loco" sandwich if you just can't decide. **Known for:** Tex-Mex Tuesdays and smoked prime rib Wednesdays; inducing food comas; margaritas and other refreshing cocktails. Ⓢ *Average main: $12* ✉ *464 N. Nassau St., North Morrison* ☎ *843/805–9500* ⊕ *www. lewisbarbecue.com* ◷ *Closed Mon.* ✛ *C1.*

$$$$
MODERN
AMERICAN
Fodor'sChoice
★

✕ **The Macintosh.** Here's another name to tuck into your sweetgrass basket filled with great Charleston chefs: Jeremiah Bacon. Bacon shows off his fondness for the little-regarded deckle—a highly marbled, delicious piece of rib eye—as well as local cobia, clams, and grouper. **Known for:** creative, seasonal starters worthy of over-ordering; bone marrow bread pudding for dessert; sophistication without pretense. Ⓢ *Average main: $30* ✉ *478 King St., Upper King* ☎ *843/788–4299* ⊕ *www.themacintoshcharleston.com* ◷ *No lunch* ✛ *A1.*

$$$$
SOUTHERN

✕ **Magnolias.** The theme at this extremely popular tourist destination is evident in the vivid paintings of creamy white blossoms that adorn the walls. A visit from Oprah Winfrey revived the reputation of "Mags," a pioneer here of innovative Lowcountry cuisine. **Known for:** collard green and tasso ham egg rolls that spawned a Southern-fusion revolution; classic, dependable renditions of upscale Southern fare; affordable Sunday brunch. Ⓢ *Average main: $26* ✉ *185 E. Bay St., Market* ☎ *843/577–7771* ⊕ *www.magnoliascharleston.com* ✛ *H5.*

$
SOUTHERN

✕ **Martha Lou's Kitchen.** Martha Lou Gadsden has made her pink cinderblock building into a palace of soul food. And although the building is quirky, with a huge mural of the owner visible from a mile down the road, the food quickly convinces skeptics what all the fuss is about. **Known for:** authentic Southern soul food; the low-key experience of the humble dining room; collard greens, giblet rice, and chitterlings. Ⓢ *Average main: $12* ✉ *1068 Morrison Dr., Charleston* ☎ *843/577–9583* ⊕ *www.marthalouskitchen.com* ▬ *No credit cards* ✛ *C1.*

7

$$$$
AMERICAN
Fodor's Choice
★

✕ **McCrady's.** Sean Brock has reinvented his original Charleston kitchen, converting the first McCrady's into McCrady's Tavern, which now serves the most elevated pub fare in town. McCrady's proper moved next door and became a 22-seat, ticket prix-fixe menu that plays out over 16 ever-changing courses. **Known for:** communal dinner style at a wraparound bar; the adventure of trying everything on a menu that changes nightly; ticketed reservation system. $ *Average main: $125* ✉ *115 East Bay St., Market* ☎ *843/577–0025* ⊕ *www.mccradysrestaurant.com* ☾ *Closed Mon. and Tues. No lunch* ✛ *H6.*

$$$$
MEDITERRANEAN

✕ **Muse Restaurant & Wine Bar.** Set in a pale yellow building on Society Street, Muse lays bare Mediterranean stylings in sophisticated, relaxed quarters. The bar functions as a drawing room, permitting easy introductions and closer inspection of the restaurant's impressive, 100-plus-bottle wine list. **Known for:** dining alfresco; late-night weekend menu; delicious fried sea bass. $ *Average main: $26* ✉ *82 Society St., Lower King* ☎ *843/577–1102* ⊕ *www.charlestonmuse. com* ☾ *No lunch* ✛ *C3.*

$$$$
SEAFOOD

✕ **The Ordinary.** Award-winning chef Mike Lata delivers every possible type of underwater delight here, from Capers Inlet clams to jumbo blue crab Louie. The two-story dining room of this former bank building fills up fast, but you can always belly up to the stunning bar while you wait and enjoy a variety of clever cocktails. **Known for:** heady wine pairings; daily plat du jour; excellent oyster bar. $ *Average main: $28* ✉ *544 King St., Market* ☎ *843/414–7060* ⊕ *www.eattheordinary.com* ☾ *Closed Mon. No lunch* ✛ *A1.*

$$$$
SOUTHERN

✕ **Peninsula Grill.** Chef Graham Dailey incorporates Lowcountry produce and seafood into traditional Peninsula dishes, at once eyeing the past and the future. The dining room fixtures (walls covered in olive-green velvet and 18th-century-style portraits and wrought-iron chandeliers on the ceiling) serve as an excellent backdrop for "sinfully grilled" Angus steaks, as well as jumbo sea scallops and Berkshire pork chops. **Known for:** the sought-after coconut cake dessert; special-occasion splurging; knowledgeable and friendly sommelier. $ *Average main: $35* ✉ *Planters Inn, 112 N. Market St., Market* ☎ *843/723–0700* ⊕ *www.peninsulagrill.com* ☾ *No lunch* ✛ *F5.*

$
AMERICAN

✕ **Queen Street Grocery.** For crepes and cold-pressed coffee, locals turn to this venerable Charleston institution. Built in 1922, the corner building has served many purposes throughout the years: butcher shop, candy shop, and late-night convenience store, and now stays true to its roots as a neighborhood grocery store with much of the produce and other goods sourced from local growers. **Known for:** mouthwatering croissant sandwiches; grab-and-go picnic items (including wine); long history as a dependable, old-school corner store. $ *Average main: $9* ✉ *133 Queen St., Market* ☎ *843/723–4121* ✛ *B5.*

$$$$
SOUTHERN

✕ **Slightly North of Broad.** This former warehouse with atmospheric brick-and-stucco walls has a chef's table that looks directly into the open kitchen. Many of the specialties, including wild game and other less common meats, are served as small plates that are perfect for sharing. **Known for:** bustling lunchtime service popular with local notables; forefather of farm-to-table movement in Charleston;

divine braised lamb shank. $ *Average main: $30* ✉ *192 E. Bay St., Market* ☎ *843/723–3424* ⊕ *www.snobcharleston.com* ☾ *No lunch weekends* ✛ *H5.*

$ ✕ **Taco Boy.** Accommodating locals and out-of-towners alike, Taco Boy
MEXICAN delivers tasty Mexican American treats to a bustling patio crowd. The
FAMILY ambience is half the allure of this eclectic outpost featuring rehabbed
or reclaimed materials—right down to the bar counter, carved from
a fallen North Carolina walnut tree, and the funky Mexican folk art
adorning every inch of wall space. **Known for:** funky, eclectic decor;
creative, gourmet tacos; some mean margaritas and micheladas. $ *Average main: $12* ✉ *217 Huger St., North of Broad* ☎ *843/789–3333* ⊕ *www.tacoboy.net* ✛ *C1.*

$ ✕ **The Tattooed Moose.** If it looks like a cross between a veterans' hall and
AMERICAN a dive bar, that's because the Tattooed Moose is going for a decidedly
unpretentious vibe. With 90-plus beers on the menu and a large moose
head behind the counter, the place cuts a distinctive figure. **Known for:**
showstopper duck club sandwich; live bluegrass and roots music; chill
and eclectic vibe. $ *Average main: $10* ✉ *1137 Morrison Dr., Market* ☎ *843/277–2990* ⊕ *www.tattooedmoose.com* ✛ *B1.*

$$$ ✕ **39 Rue de Jean.** With a backdrop of classic French-bistro style—gleam-
FRENCH ing wood, cozy booths, and white-papered tables—Charleston's trendy
set wines and dines until the wee hours here on such favorites as steamed
mussels in a half-dozen preparations. Order them with *pomme frites*, as
the French do. **Known for:** lively social scene, especially before shows at
the Charleston Music Hall next door; top-notch sushi, an unexpected
addition at a French joint; nightly specials, including amazing burgers
and bouillabaisse. $ *Average main: $24* ✉ *39 John St., Upper King* ☎ *843/722–8881* ⊕ *www.39ruedejean.com* ✛ *B2.*

$$$$ ✕ **Trattoria Lucca.** Chef Ken Vedrinski's first wonder, Trattoria Lucca, is a
ITALIAN welcoming invitation to the world of Italian food in Charleston. Come
Fodor'sChoice in for the warm cauliflower *sformatino* (with farm-fresh eggs, pancetta,
★ and Parmesan cheese), stay for the pasta dishes made with locally milled
organic semolina. **Known for:** Monday night family supper; handmade,
authentic Italian fare. $ *Average main: $26* ✉ *41 Bogard St., North of
Broad* ☎ *843/973–3323* ⊕ *www.luccacharleston.com* ☾ *Closed Sun.
No lunch* ✛ *A2.*

SOUTH OF BROAD

$ ✕ **Gaulart and Maliclet Café.** This local favorite, also known as Fast and
FRENCH French, has been a fixture in the neighborhood for over 30 years, thanks
to the consistent food, the esprit de corps of the staff, and the family-
style tables for sharing breakfast, lunch, or dinner. Thursday brings a
crowd for fondue, but opt to get your cheese fix with the wonderful
Bucheron cheese salad. **Known for:** gourmet bites in an area of town
short of restaurants; charming ambience; nightly specials, including
fondue night. $ *Average main: $14* ✉ *98 Broad St., South of Broad* ☎ *843/577–9797* ⊕ *www.fastandfrenchcharleston.com* ☾ *Closed Sun.
No dinner Mon.* ✛ *C5.*

7

MOUNT PLEASANT AND VICINITY

$$$$ SOUTHERN 🍴 **Old Village Post House.** Many residents of this tree-lined village consider this their neighborhood tavern. Expect contemporary takes on Southern favorites like lump crab cakes, shrimp and grits, and fresh vegetables like a butter beans mélange. **Known for:** charming atmosphere of a 19th-century inn; celebrated Southern cuisine; popular weekend brunch. [$] *Average main: $26* ✉ *101 Pitt St., Mount Pleasant* ☎ *843/388–8935* 🌐 *www.oldvillageposthouseinn.com/restaurant* ✥ *H4.*

$$ SOUTHERN FAMILY 🍴 **SeeWee Restaurant.** This former general store is about 25 minutes from downtown Charleston, but it's worth the trip for the Southern-style flashback. The veteran waitresses will call you "hon" and recommend their favorites, a lot of which are Southern-fried: pickles, green tomatoes, chicken, oysters, and fresh local shrimp. **Known for:** real Lowcountry cookin'; charm that's not at all contrived; outdoor seating and live music Saturday nights. [$] *Average main: $18* ✉ *4808 Hwy. 17 N, Awendaw* ☎ *843/928–3609* ⏲ *No dinner Sun.* ✥ *H1.*

$$$ SEAFOOD FAMILY Fodor's Choice ★ 🍴 **The Wreck of the Richard & Charlene.** At first glance, the odd name appears to refer to this waterfront restaurant's exterior, topped off with a shabby screened-in porch (in actuality, the *Richard and Charlene* was a trawler that slammed into the building during a hurricane in 1989). Located in the old village of Mount Pleasant, the kitchen serves up Southern tradition on a plate: boiled peanuts, fried shrimp, and stone-crab claws. **Known for:** generous platters of fried seafood; old-school ambience right on the shrimp docks. [$] *Average main: $22* ✉ *106 Haddrell St., Mount Pleasant* ☎ *843/884–0052* 🌐 *www.wreckrc.com* 💳 *No credit cards* ⏲ *No lunch* ✥ *H4.*

GREATER CHARLESTON

$ SOUTHERN FAMILY 🍴 **Fiery Ron's Home Team BBQ.** This bar and restaurant has swiftly earned the endorsement of even the old-school barbecue set (the restaurant's newfangled pork tacos notwithstanding). And Home Team has done so with time-honored adherence to the oft-preferred technique of low-and-slow grilling, producing St. Louis–style ribs, and traditional smoked pork and chicken. **Known for:** pulled pork and rich mac 'n' cheese; live blues and rock music at all three locations; unique tableside sauces. [$] *Average main: $10* ✉ *1205 Ashley River Rd., West Ashley* ☎ *843/225–7427* 🌐 *www.hometeambbq.com* ✥ *H4.*

$$ SOUTHERN 🍴 **The Glass Onion.** Established by a trio of Louisiana expats, the Glass Onion fashions a taut bond between Charleston and New Orleans, dishing up *beaucoup* Southern eats. Take a peek at the menu: deviled eggs, meat loaf, fried catfish po'boys, and overstuffed pimiento-cheese sandwiches, along with sweets like bread pudding with whiskey sauce. **Known for:** addictive deviled eggs; consistent, seasonal Southern fare; delectable Saturday brunch that often sells out. [$] *Average main: $18* ✉ *1219 Savannah Hwy., Johns Island* ☎ *843/225–1717* 🌐 *www.ilovetheglassonion.com* ⏲ *Closed Sun.* ✥ *A5.*

$ SOUTHERN FAMILY 🍴 **JB's Smokeshack.** If you're hankering for a country barbecue joint, JB's will do ya. Most patrons choose the reasonably priced buffet, which consists of barbecue pork, apple-wood-smoked chicken, a selection of

Broad Street divides Charleston's historic district into North and South of Broad.

Southern veggies—usually including okra gumbo, butter beans, and coleslaw—and desserts like banana pudding. **Known for:** all-you-can-eat buffet; banana pudding like grandma made it; award-winning Angus beef brisket. [$] *Average main: $9* ✉ *3406 Maybank Hwy., Johns Island* ☎ *843/577–0426* ⏲ *Closed Sun.* ✣ *A6.*

$$ SOUTHERN Fodor's Choice ★ 🍴 **Tomato Shed Cafe.** This Johns Island roadside joint presents a banquet of locally raised delicacies. Owners and farmers Pete and Babs Ambrose maintain a 135-acre farm on Wadmalaw Island, sourcing grounds for the restaurant. **Known for:** tomato pie when it's in season; take-and-bake meals, perfect for visitors staying in rentals on Kiawah. [$] *Average main: $16* ✉ *842 Main Rd., Johns Island* ☎ *843/599–9999* 🌐 *www.stonofarmmarket.com* ⏲ *Closed Sun.* ✣ *A6.*

WHERE TO STAY

Charleston is a city known for its lovingly restored mansions that have been converted into atmospheric bed-and-breakfasts, as well as deluxe inns, all found in the residential blocks of the Historic District. Upscale, world-class hotels share space downtown with boutique hotels that provide a one-of-a-kind experience. Chain hotels pepper the busy, car-trafficked areas (like Meeting Street). In addition, there are chain properties in the nearby areas of West Ashley, Mount Pleasant, and North Charleston. Mount Pleasant is considered the most upscale suburb; North Charleston is the least, but if you need to be close to the airport, are participating in events at its Coliseum and Convention Center, or aim to shop the outlet malls there, it is a practical, less expensive alternative. *Hotel reviews have been shortened. For more information, visit*

Fodors.com. Use the coordinate (⊕ 1:B2) at the end of each listing to locate a site on the corresponding map.

PRICES

Charleston's downtown lodgings have three seasons: high season (March to May and September to November), mid-season (June to August), and low season (late November to February). Prices drop significantly during the short low season, except during holidays and special events like the Southeastern Wildlife Exposition each February. High season is summer at the island resorts; rates drop for weekly stays and during the off-season. Although prices have gone up at the B&Bs, don't forget that a full breakfast for two is generally included, as well as an evening wine reception, which can take the place of happy hour and save on your bar bill.

WHAT IT COSTS

	$	$$	$$$	$$$$
Hotels	under $150	$150–$200	$201–$250	over $250

Prices in the reviews are the lowest cost of a standard double room in high season.

VACATION HOME RENTALS

Dunes Properties. For a wide selection of house and condo rentals on Folly Beach and Isle of Palms (including Wild Dunes Resort), call the Isle of Palms branch of locally owned Dunes Properties. ✉ *1400 Palm Blvd., Isle of Palms* ☎ *843/886–5600* 🌐 *www.dunesproperties.com.*

Wyndham Vacation Rentals. For condo and house rentals on Kiawah Island, Seabrook Island, and Isle of Palms (including Wild Dunes Resort), contact Wyndham Vacation Rentals. ✉ *354 Freshfields Dr., Johns Island* ☎ *843/768–5000* 🌐 *www.wyndhamvacationrentals.com.*

NORTH OF BROAD

$$ B&B/INN

🏨 **Andrew Pinckney Inn.** Nestled in the heart of Charleston, this West Indies–inspired inn offers a range of accommodations, from charming rooms perfect for couples to two-level suites big enough for the whole family. **Pros:** the town houses are ideal for longer stays; afternoon gourmet tea and coffee service with fresh-baked cookies. **Cons:** elevator access for standard rooms only; bustling neighborhood and nearby horse stables can be noisy. [$] *Rooms from: $199* ✉ *40 Pinckney St., Market* ☎ *843/937–8800, 800/505–8983* 🌐 *www.andrewpinckneyinn.com* 🛏 *41 rooms* 🍴 *Breakfast* ⊕ *G4.*

$$$ B&B/INN Fodor'sChoice ★

🏨 **Ansonborough Inn.** At this boutique hotel you can relax in your comfortable suite or indulge in evening wine and cheese on the rooftop terrace while enjoying views of the city and Cooper River. **Pros:** lots of period details; 24-hour upscale supermarket across the street; easy walking distance to the Market. **Cons:** not that close to King Street shops; some rooms open to a central atrium directly over the lobby. [$] *Rooms from: $219* ✉ *21 Hasell St., Market* ☎ *800/723–1655* 🌐 *www.ansonboroughinn.com* 🛏 *45 suites* 🍴 *Breakfast* ⊕ *D3.*

$$$$ HOTEL 🏨 **Belmond Charleston Place.** Even casual passersby enjoy gazing up at the immense handblown Murano glass chandelier in this hotel's open lobby, clicking across the Italian marble floors, and browsing the gallery of upscale shops that completes the ground-floor offerings of this hotel. **Pros:** full of antiques from Sotheby's; on the best shopping street in the Historic District; pet-friendly (with an additional fee). **Cons:** rooms aren't as big as one might expect for the price; hosts lots of conference groups in shoulder seasons; lacks the charm of more historic properties. [$] *Rooms from: $279* ✉ *205 Meeting St., Market* ☎ *843/722–4900, 888/635–2350* 🌐 *www.belmond.com/charleston-place* 🔑 *483 rooms* 🍴 *Some meals* ✥ *F5.*

$$$$ HOTEL 🏨 **The Dewberry.** Built in the renovated Federal Building overlooking Marion Square, the Dewberry exudes style and sophistication from the travertine marble to the mahogany and walnut that adorn the lobby and in-house bar and restaurant. **Pros:** one of the city's best cocktail bars on-site; perfectly central location; world-class spa. **Cons:** sheer indulgence doesn't come free; the planned rooftop bar was shut down by the city. [$] *Rooms from: $499* ✉ *334 Meeting St., Middle King* ☎ *888/550–1450* 🌐 *www.thedewberrycharleston.com* 🔑 *155 rooms* 🍴 *No meals* ✥ *B2.*

$$$ HOTEL FAMILY 🏨 **DoubleTree by Hilton Hotel & Suites Charleston–Historic District.** With a beautifully restored entrance portico from 1874, this former bank building offers spacious suites with nice touches like antique reproductions and canopy beds. **Pros:** an easy walk to King Street shopping and a charming stroll to the South of Broad residential area; family-friendly vibe; complimentary warm chocolate chip cookies. **Cons:** no free breakfast, although there is an on-site café; lacks the historic atmosphere of an independent inn; no self-parking available. [$] *Rooms from: $209* ✉ *181 Church St., Market* ☎ *843/577–2644* 🌐 *www.doubletree.com* 🔑 *202 rooms and suites* 🍴 *No meals* ✥ *G5.*

$$ B&B/INN Fodor's Choice ★ 🏨 **1837 Bed & Breakfast.** A hospitable staff helps give you a sense of what it would be like to live in one of Charleston's grand old homes. **Pros:** a very good concierge will help you plan your days; reasonable rates; relaxing porch to rest up after exploring. **Cons:** limited on-site parking; period furniture and decor won't carry as much appeal to younger generations; surrounding college district can be noisy on weekend nights. [$] *Rooms from: $165* ✉ *126 Wentworth St., Market* ☎ *843/723–7166, 877/723–1837* 🌐 *www.1837bb.com* 🔑 *9 rooms* 🍴 *Breakfast* ✥ *B4.*

$$$ HOTEL 🏨 **Francis Marion Hotel.** Wrought-iron railings, crown moldings, and decorative plasterwork speak of the elegance of 1924, when the Francis Marion was the largest hotel in the Carolinas. **Pros:** in the midst of the peninsula's best shopping; on-site day spa; some of the best city views. **Cons:** rooms are small, as is closet space; on a busy intersection. [$] *Rooms from: $219* ✉ *387 King St., Upper King* ☎ *843/722–0600* 🌐 *www.francismarioncharleston.com* 🔑 *235 rooms* 🍴 *No meals* ✥ *B2.*

$$$ B&B/INN 🏨 **Fulton Lane Inn.** This inn is both lovely and quirky: its Victorian-dressed rooms (some with four-poster beds, handsome fireplaces, and jetted tubs) are laid out in a bit of a floor-creaking maze, but it adds to the inn's individuality. **Pros:** location is tops; charming choice of rooms;

evening wine, cheese, and sherry. **Cons:** price fluctuates dramatically between weekdays and weekends; street noise does seep in. S *Rooms from: $219* ⊠ *202 King St., Lower King* ☎ *843/720–2600, 800/720– 2688* ⊕ *www.fultonlaneinn.com* ⇆ *45 rooms* ⦿ *Breakfast* ✛ *C4.*

$$$$
HOTEL
⛨ **Grand Bohemian Charleston.** One of the entrances to this luxurious Marriott-affiliated hotel steers guests directly into an art gallery, an indication of the modern, creative flair that awaits inside. **Pros:** in-house wine-blending program offered for guests; one of the best rooftop bars in town; central location for walking the Historic District. **Cons:** priced higher than some competitors; the unique emphasis on art won't appeal to everyone. S *Rooms from: $425* ⊠ *55 Wentworth St., Market* ☎ *843/722–5711* ⊕ *www.grandbohemiancharleston.com* ⇆ *50 rooms* ⦿ *No meals* ✛ *C3.*

$$$$
HOTEL
⛨ **HarbourView Inn.** If you ask for a room with a view or even a private balcony here, you can gaze out on Charleston Harbor and onto the kid-friendly fountain at the center of Waterfront Park. **Pros:** continental breakfast can be delivered to your room or the rooftop; location is tops; service is notable. **Cons:** rooms are off long, modern halls, giving the place more of a chain hotel feel; not as new and exciting as similarly priced options. S *Rooms from: $279* ⊠ *2 Vendue Range, Market* ☎ *843/853–8439* ⊕ *www.harbourviewcharleston.com* ⇆ *52 rooms* ⦿ *Breakfast* ✛ *H6.*

$$$$
HOTEL
⛨ **Market Pavilion Hotel.** The hustle and bustle of one of the city's busiest corners vanishes as soon as the uniformed bellman opens the lobby door of the Market Pavilion Hotel to reveal wood-paneled walls, antique furnishings, and chandeliers hung from high ceilings; it resembles a European grand hotel from the 19th century, and you feel like you're visiting royalty. **Pros:** opulent furnishings; architecturally impressive, especially the tray ceilings; conveniently located for everything. **Cons:** the gym is small; some may find the interior over the top. S *Rooms from: $279* ⊠ *225 E. Bay St., Market* ☎ *843/723–0500* ⊕ *www.marketpavilion.com* ⇆ *70 rooms* ⦿ *Breakfast* ✛ *H5.*

$$
B&B/INN
⛨ **The Meeting Street Inn.** Guest rooms in this 1874 stucco house with porches on the second, third, and fourth floors overlook a lovely courtyard with fountains and a heated spa tub. **Pros:** some of the more expensive rooms have desks and other extras; bathrooms sport nice marble fixtures; fun wine-and-cheese nights. **Cons:** decor could use some updating; some rooms overlook an adjacent parking lot; parking is pricey. S *Rooms from: $189* ⊠ *173 Meeting St., Market* ☎ *843/723–1882, 800/842–8022* ⊕ *www.meetingstreetinn.com* ⇆ *56 rooms* ⦿ *Breakfast* ✛ *F5.*

$$$
HOTEL
⛨ **The Mills House.** A favorite local landmark that serves as a departure point for several historic tours, the Wyndham-managed Mills House is the modern iteration of the original 1853 hotel by the same name, where General Robert E. Lee once slept. **Pros:** convenient to Historic District; a popular Sunday brunch spot; a concierge desk so well regarded that locals call for neighborly assistance and advice. **Cons:** rooms are rather small, which is typical of hotels of this time period; it's on a busy street; parking is valet-only and expensive. S *Rooms from: $209* ⊠ *115 Meeting St., Market* ☎ *843/577–2400* ⊕ *www.millshouse.com* ⇆ *215 rooms* ⦿ *No meals* ✛ *F6.*

$$$$
B&B/INN ⬚ **Planters Inn.** Part of the Relais & Châteaux group, this boutique property with well-appointed and beautifully maintained rooms is a stately sanctuary amid the bustle of Charleston's Market. **Pros:** double-pane and interior shuttered windows render the rooms soundproof; front desk staff knows your name upon arrival; exceptional full breakfast (included only as part of a package). **Cons:** no pool; no fitness center; parking is pricey and by valet only. $ *Rooms from: $339* ✉ *112 N. Market St., Market* ☎ *843/722–2345* ⊕ *www.plantersinn.com* ⇱ *64 rooms* ❄ *No meals* ✢ *F5.*

$$$$
B&B/INN ⬚ **The Restoration.** Charleston architect Neil Stevenson designed this boutique hotel to be swank and suave to the hilt, even featuring a rooftop terrace with sleek sofas and prime views. **Pros:** complimentary passes to nearby workout facilities; room service comes via neighboring restaurants; free bike rentals. **Cons:** no gym on the premises, but there are some within easy walking distance; prices are steep. $ *Rooms from: $299* ✉ *75 Wentworth St., Market* ☎ *877/221–7202* ⊕ *www.therestorationhotel.com* ⇱ *16 suites* ❄ *Breakfast* ✢ *C3.*

$$$$
B&B/INN ⬚ **The Vendue.** Thanks to its gorgeous art-filled space, the Vendue feels as much like a contemporary art museum as it does a boutique hotel. **Pros:** free bike rentals; soundproofing masks street noise; great restaurant and coffee shop. **Cons:** no complimentary breakfast; some halls and spaces are small as in centuries past. $ *Rooms from: $275* ✉ *19 Vendue Range, Market* ☎ *843/577–7970, 800/845–7900* ⊕ *www.thevendue.com* ⇱ *84 rooms* ❄ *No meals* ✢ *H6.*

$$$$
B&B/INN ⬚ **Wentworth Mansion.** The grandest inn in town features Second Empire antiques and reproductions, elaborate woodwork, and original stained-glass windows, as well as the sweeping views from the rooftop cupola. **Pros:** fantastic on-site restaurant and spa; opulent guest rooms; free parking. **Cons:** style can strike some people as forbidding; outside the tourist areas. $ *Rooms from: $400* ✉ *149 Wentworth St., College of Charleston Campus* ☎ *888/466–1886* ⊕ *www.wentworthmansion.com* ⇱ *21 rooms* ❄ *Breakfast* ✢ *A4.*

$$$$
HOTEL
Fodor's Choice
★ ⬚ **Zero George.** Five restored 19th-century residences have been joined together to create this hideaway in the heart of Charleston's leafy Ansonborough neighborhood that's surrounded by well-heeled homes, and just a short walk from East Bay restaurants, City Market, and Liberty Square. **Pros:** convenient and quiet location; local charm; free Wi-Fi and breakfast. **Cons:** it's a bit of a walk to the Market and to King Street; style and luxury don't come cheap. $ *Rooms from: $299* ✉ *0 George St., Ansonborough* ☎ *843/817–7900* ⊕ *www.zerogeorge.com* ⇱ *18 rooms* ❄ *Breakfast* ✢ *D2.*

SOUTH OF BROAD

$$$$
B&B/INN ⬚ **The Governor's House Inn.** The stately architecture of this quintessential Charleston lodging radiates the grandeur, romance, and civility of the city's bountiful colonial era. **Pros:** pets are allowed in some rooms; chairs and beach towels provided for day trips; free off-street parking in an elegant courtyard. **Cons:** kids not allowed in the main-building rooms; the period decor isn't as trendy as newer options. $ *Rooms from: $265* ✉ *117 Broad St., South of Broad* ☎ *843/720–2070, 800/720–9812* ⊕ *www.governorshouse.com* ⇱ *11 rooms* ❄ *Breakfast* ✢ *C5.*

7

$$$$ B&B/INN 🏨 **John Rutledge House Inn.** In 1791, George Washington visited this elegant mansion, then the residence of one of South Carolina's most influential politicians, John Rutledge; you can follow in his footsteps by booking one of the spacious accommodations within this National Historic Landmark. **Pros:** decor makes you feel like a true Charlestonian; quiet back courtyard; friendly staff. **Cons:** you can hear some street and kitchen noise in the first-floor rooms; the two carriage houses are not as grand as the main house. [$] *Rooms from: $289* ✉ *116 Broad St., South of Broad* ☎ *800/476–9741* 🌐 *www.johnrutledgehouseinn.com* 🛏 *19 rooms* 🍴 *Breakfast* ✣ *C5.*

$$$ B&B/INN 🏨 **Two Meeting Street Inn.** As pretty as a wedding cake, this 1892 Queen Anne–style mansion wears overhanging bays, colonnades, balustrades, and a turret; two original Tiffany stained-glass windows (worth as much as the house itself), carved-oak paneling, and a crystal chandelier dress up the public spaces. **Pros:** free on-street parking; community refrigerator on each floor; ringside seat for a Battery view and horse-drawn carriages clipping by. **Cons:** no credit cards accepted; not equipped for handicapped guests; the decor is on the grandmotherly side. [$] *Rooms from: $225* ✉ *2 Meeting St., South of Broad* ☎ *843/723–7322* 🌐 *www.twomeetingstreet.com* 💳 *No credit cards* 🛏 *9 rooms* 🍴 *Breakfast* ✣ *D6.*

MOUNT PLEASANT

$$$ RESORT FAMILY 🏨 **The Beach Club at Charleston Harbor Resort & Marina.** Mount Pleasant's finest hotel sits on Charleston Harbor, so you can gaze at the city's skyline with your feet on this resort's sandy beach or from the waterfront pool. **Pros:** the most accessible hotel to downtown that's not in downtown (approximately 6 miles away); large pool and extensive grounds are perfect for enjoying a sunset glass of wine; on-site gym. **Cons:** a bit removed from the action; not pet-friendly; no complimentary breakfast. [$] *Rooms from: $223* ✉ *20 Patriots Point Rd., Mount Pleasant* ☎ *843/856–0028* 🌐 *www.charlestonharborresort.com* 🛏 *125 rooms* 🍴 *No meals* ✣ *H1.*

$$ B&B/INN 🏨 **Old Village Post House Inn.** This white wooden building anchoring Mount Pleasant's Historic District is three-in-one—an excellent restaurant, a neighborly tavern, and a cozy inn set at the top of a high staircase. **Pros:** prices are as affordable as some chain motels on the highway; in the most picturesque and walkable neighborhood in Mount Pleasant; close to Sullivan's Island and Isle of Palms. **Cons:** shares some public spaces with the downstairs restaurant; some minor old building woes, including creaky wood floors; not a traditional hotel, so service can be quirky. [$] *Rooms from: $184* ✉ *101 Pitt St., Mount Pleasant* ☎ *843/388–8935* 🌐 *www.oldvillageposthouseinn.com* 🛏 *6 rooms* 🍴 *Breakfast* ✣ *H4.*

ELSEWHERE IN CHARLESTON

$$$$ RESORT 🏨 **Kiawah Island Golf Resort.** Choose from one- to four-bedroom villas, three- to eight-bedroom private homes, or the Sanctuary at Kiawah Island, an amazing 255-room luxury waterfront hotel and spa that is one of the most prestigious resorts in the country and yet is still kid-friendly. **Pros:** smaller villas are more affordable; restaurant is an ideal venue for an anniversary or a proposal; the golf courses and tennis programs are ranked among the country's best. **Cons:** not all rooms have ocean views; pricey and a long drive from town. [$] *Rooms from: $285* ✉ *1 Sanctuary Beach Dr., Kiawah Island* ☎ *843/768–2121, 800/576–1570* 🌐 *www.kiawahresort.com* 🛏 *745 rooms* 🍴 *No meals.*

$$$ RESORT FAMILY 🏨 **Wild Dunes Resort.** Guests at this 1,600-acre island beachfront resort can choose from a long list of recreational options, including Tom Fazio–designed golf courses and a nationally ranked tennis program. **Pros:** golf courses are first-class; free shuttle runs from 7 am to 11 pm to wherever you need to go within the complex; it's rarely crowded on the beach. **Cons:** in summer, kids dominate the pool areas and the boardwalk; it's at least a 30-minute drive to downtown Charleston, and summer beach traffic can make day trips a headache. [$] *Rooms from: $246* ✉ *5757 Palm Blvd., Isle of Palms* ☎ *866/359–5593, 843/886–6000* 🌐 *www.destinationhotels.com/wild-dunes* 🛏 *493 rooms* 🍴 *No meals.*

7

NIGHTLIFE AND PERFORMING ARTS

For a midsize city, Charleston has a surprisingly varied and sophisticated arts scene, though the city really shines during its major annual arts festival, Spoleto Festival USA. The nightlife scene is similarly comprehensive, with nocturnal venues for all ages and tastes.

NIGHTLIFE

You can find it all here, across the board, for Charleston loves a good party. The more mature crowd goes to the sophisticated spots, and there are many: piano bars, wine bars, lounges featuring jazz groups or a guitarist-vocalist, and cigar lounges. Rooftop bars are a particular Charleston tradition, and the city has several good ones. Many restaurants offer live entertainment on at least one weekend night, and these tend to cater to an older crowd. The Upper King area especially has grown in recent years, overtaking the Market area in terms of popularity and variety. ■ **TIP→ A city ordinance mandates that bars must close by 2 am and that patrons must be out of the establishment and doors locked by that hour. Last call is usually 1:30.**

NORTH OF BROAD

BARS AND PUBS

Bin 152. Husband-and-wife Patrick and Fanny Panella ply their guests with selections from more than 130 bottles of wine and 40 varieties of cheeses and charcuterie, freshly baked breads, contemporary art, and antique furniture. All of it is imminently available, too, from the Sauvignon Blanc and Shiraz to the tables and chairs. Cast in low lighting, the wine bar serves as a comfortable backdrop for a pre- or postdinner drink, or an entire evening. ⊠ *152 King St., Lower King* ☎ *843/577–7359* ⊕ *www.bin152.com.*

Gin Joint. The cocktails here—frothy fizzes, slings, smashes, and juleps— are retro, some dating back to before Prohibition. The bartenders don bow ties and suspenders, but the atmosphere is utterly contemporary, with slick gray walls and subtle lighting. The kitchen serves up small plates like cheeses, pork buns, and buttermilk-fried chicken hearts. ⊠ *182 East Bay St., Market* ☎ *843/577–6111* ⊕ *www.theginjoint.com.*

The Griffon. Dollar bills cover just about every square inch of the Griffon, helping the bar achieve nearly legendary status around the city. It's wood interior is dark, dusty, and well-worn, yet somehow still seems charming. A rotating selection of draft beers comes from local breweries like Westbrook, Coast, and Holy City. It's a popular lunchtime and happy hour watering hole, and hosts live music on weekend nights. ⊠ *18 Vendue Range, Market* ☎ *843/723–1700* ⊕ *www.griffoncharleston.com.*

Fodor'sChoice
★
Pavilion Bar. Atop the Market Pavilion Hotel, the swanky outdoor Pavilion Bar offers panoramic views of the city and harbor, set around the hotel's posh swimming pool. Enjoy appetizers like lobster and duck with one of the specialty mojitos or martinis. The dress code dictates no flip-flops, baseball caps, visors, or tank tops. ⊠ *Market Pavilion Hotel, 225 E. Bay St., Market* ☎ *843/723–0500* ⊕ *www.marketpavilion.com.*

The Rooftop Bar at Vendue. Have a cocktail and appetizer as you watch the colorful sunset behind the church steeples. There are actually two bars at this venue atop the recently renovated Vendue Inn; the lower Deck Bar has tables and chairs shaded by umbrellas, but the view of the water is partially obscured by condo towers. Keep going to the higher-level bar, which offers a 360-degree panorama and an open-air atmosphere. You'll find live music by local and regional bands on weekends. Get here early, as it closes at midnight. ⊠ *Vendue Inn, 19 Vendue Range, Market* ☎ *843/577–7970* ⊕ *www.thevendue.com.*

The Royal American. This place isn't really a dive bar—it just looks like one, thanks to dim lighting and an expansive deck that backs up to the train tracks. The bar serves an array of canned beers and a tasty trio of punches with rum, bourbon, or vodka poured over crushed ice. Hungry? Feast on blue-collar eats like fried bologna sandwiches, loaded baked potatoes, and house-made beef jerky. There's also live music throughout the week on an intimate indoor stage. ⊠ *970 Morrison Dr., North Morrison* ☎ *843/817–6925* ⊕ *www.theroyalamerican.com.*

LIVE MUSIC

Fodor'sChoice
★
Charleston Grill. The elegant Charleston Grill hosts live jazz seven nights a week, drawing from the city's most renowned musicians. Performers range from the internationally acclaimed Brazilian guitarist Duda Lucena to the Bob Williams Duo, a father and son who play classical guitar and violin. The place draws an urbane thirtysomething crowd. Down the hall, the neighboring Thoroughbred Club offers nightly live music and an impressive selection of bourbons. ⊠ *Charleston Place Hotel, 224 King St., Market* ☎ *843/577–4522* ⊕ *www.charlestongrill.com.*

UPPER KING
BARS AND PUBS

Fodor'sChoice **The Belmont.** This place doesn't seek attention—heck, it won't even list
★ its phone number. But with a soaring tin ceiling, exposed-brick walls,
and a penchant for projecting black-and-white films onto the wall,
the charisma comes naturally. An inventive cocktail menu served up
by sharply dressed mixologists helps, too. Try their take on the spicy-
sweet Brown Derby, a bourbon drink made with jalapeño-infused
honey, or the Bells of Jalisco, featuring *reposado* tequila, more jalapeño honey, and lime juice. There's also a light menu of panini, char-
cuterie, and homemade pop tarts. ⊠ *511 King St., Upper King* ⊕ *www.
thebelmontcharleston.com.*

Closed for Business. This "draught emporium" offers more than 40 taps
pouring pints and liters of local and seasonal brews. With pale wood
paneling, leather club chairs, and lightbulbs flickering in a fireplace, the
place has plenty of charm. CFB also features a tasty menu of upscale
pub fare, including Chicago-style hot dogs and a fried pork cutlet sandwich called the Pork Slap. ⊠ *453 King St., Upper King* ☎ *843/853–8466*
⊕ *www.closed4business.com.*

The Cocktail Club. This establishment characterizes the craft cocktail
movement with its "farm-to-shaker" seasonal selection of creative concoctions. The bar showcases exposed-brick walls and wooden beams
inside its lounge areas, though warm evenings are best spent outside on
the rooftop patio. Inside, some of Charleston's best (and best-looking)
bartenders muddle and shake clever mixtures like Safety Word, made
from habañero-spiked tequila, muddled kiwi, and lime juice, and the
Double Standard, a serrano-pepper-infused gin and cucumber vodka
blend. ⊠ *479 King St., #200, Upper King* ☎ *843/724–9411* ⊕ *www.
thecocktailclubcharleston.com.*

DANCE CLUBS

Trio Club. Funky sounds from the '70s and '80s mix with the latest club
anthems at this perennially popular dance club. Listen to the cover
bands at the downstairs bar, mingle on the outdoor patio, or head
upstairs for the DJ-led dance party. It's only open Friday and Saturday
nights. ⊠ *139 Calhoun St., Upper King* ⊕ *www.triocharleston.com.*

GAY AND LESBIAN

Dudley's on Ann. A local landmark, the city's oldest gay bar hosts lively
karaoke parties, DJs and dancing on weekends, and rollicking drag
shows. ⊠ *42 Ann St., Upper King* ☎ *843/577–6779* ⊕ *www.dudleyso-
nann.com.*

LIVE MUSIC

Music Farm. Once a train depot, this massive space is filled to the max
when popular bands like Galactic, the North Mississippi Allstars, and
Passion Pit play. Tickets typically range from $15 to $25. The bar is
only open on nights when a concert is scheduled. ⊠ *32 Ann St., Upper
King* ☎ *843/577–6989* ⊕ *www.musicfarm.com.*

PERFORMING ARTS

FESTIVALS

Spoleto USA is only the beginning—there are dozens of festivals held throughout the city each year. Some focus on food and wine, whereas others are concerned with gardens and architecture.

Charleston Wine + Food. Since 2005, this annual fete has served as the city's marquee event for foodies. Spread over four days, it brings together the nation's leading chefs (including local James Beard award winners), food writers, and, of course, regular diners who love to eat and drink. Held the first full weekend of March, it emphasize the Low-country's culinary heritage. Marion Square serves as the hub with its Culinary Village, but savvy attendees grab up tickets quickly for the numerous dinners and special events held around the city. ⊠ *Charleston* ☎ *843/727–9998* ⊕ *www.charlestonwineandfood.com.*

MOJA Arts Festival. Held each year in late September and early October, this festival celebrates the region's African heritage and Caribbean influences on local culture. It includes theater, dance, and music performances, art shows, films, lectures, and tours of the Historic District. ⊠ *Charleston* ☎ *843/724–7305* ⊕ *www.mojafestival.com.*

FAMILY **Piccolo Spoleto Festival.** The spirited companion festival of Spoleto Festival USA showcases the best in local and regional talent from every artistic discipline. There are as many as 700 events—from jazz performances to puppet shows, military band concerts, and expansive art shows in Marion Square—from mid-May through early June. Many of the performances are free or inexpensive, and hundreds of these cultural experiences are kid-friendly. ⊠ *Charleston* ☎ *843/724–7305* ⊕ *www.piccolospoleto.com.*

FAMILY **Southeastern Wildlife Exposition.** One of Charleston's biggest annual events, this celebration of the region's flora and fauna takes place in mid-February, offering fine art by renowned wildlife artists, bird of prey demonstrations, dog competitions, an oyster roast, and a gala. Spread across three days, the expo generally attracts more than 500 artists and 40,000 participants to various venues around the city. ⊠ *Charleston* ☎ *843/723–1748* ⊕ *www.sewe.com.*

Fodor's Choice **Spoleto Festival USA.** For 17 glorious days in late May and early June,
★ Charleston gets a dose of culture from the Spoleto Festival USA. This internationally acclaimed performing-arts festival features a mix of distinguished artists and emerging talent from around the world. Performances take place in magical settings, such as the College of Charleston's Cistern beneath a canopy of ancient oaks or inside a centuries-old cathedral.

A mix of formal concerts and casual performances is what Pulitzer Prize–winning composer Gian Carlo Menotti had in mind when, in 1977, he initiated the festival as a complement to his opera-heavy Italian festival. He chose Charleston because of its European look and because its residents love the arts—not to mention any cause for celebration. He wanted the festival to be a "fertile ground for the young" as well as a "dignified home for the masters."

The finale is a must-do, particularly for the younger crowd. Staged outdoors at Middleton Place, the plantation house and lush landscaped gardens provide a dramatic backdrop. The inexpensive seating is unreserved and unlimited. The lawn is covered with blankets and chairs, and many families bring lavish spreads to munch and sip on. Recent performances have included bluegrass legend Del McCoury and local favorites Shovels & Rope, followed by spectacular fireworks exploding over the Ashley River.

Some 45 events—with most tickets averaging between $25 and $50—include everything from improv to Shakespeare, from rap to chamber music, from ballet to salsa. Because events sell out quickly, buy tickets several weeks in advance (book hotel rooms and make restaurant reservations early, too). Tickets to midweek performances are a bit easier to secure. ⊠ *Charleston* ☎ *843/579–3100* ⊕ *www.spoletousa.org.*

VENUES

Fodor'sChoice
★
Charleston Music Hall. Regularly hosting big-name bluegrass, blues, and country acts, the beautiful 928-seat Charleston Music Hall shines. Home to the Charleston Jazz Orchestra, it's in the heart of Upper King and within easy walking distance of numerous popular bars and restaurants for pre- and postshow refreshments. ⊠ *37 John St., Upper King* ☎ *843/853–2252* ⊕ *www.charlestonmusichall.com.*

Dock Street Theatre. Incorporating the remains of the old Planter's Hotel (circa 1809), this theater is hung with green velvet curtains and has wonderful woodwork, giving it a New Orleans French Quarter feel. Charleston Stage Company performs full seasons of family-friendly fare, and the Spoleto Festival USA uses the stage for productions in May and June. ⊠ *135 Church St., Broad Street* ☎ *843/720–3968* ⊕ *www. charlestonstage.com/dock-street-theatre.html.*

North Charleston Performing Art Center. Touring Broadway productions and big-name bands frequent the 2,300-seat North Charleston Performing Art Center. In recent years, performers such as David Byrne, Tony Bennett, and Willie Nelson have taken the stage. ■TIP➜ It's worth paying extra for seats in the front half of the venue. ⊠ *5001 Coliseum Dr., North Charleston* ☎ *843/529–5000* ⊕ *www.northcharlestoncoliseumpac.com.*

SPORTS AND THE OUTDOORS

Charleston is a wonderful place to get outdoors. The region's beaches are taupe sand, and the Carolina sun warms them some nine months out of the year. You'll find an amazing number of low-cost options, from biking to canoeing and kayaking and nature walks. Area golf courses are reasonably priced compared to, say, Hilton Head, the public courses being the least expensive.

BASEBALL

FAMILY **Charleston RiverDogs.** The local minor-league baseball team plays at "the Joe," on the banks of the Ashley River near the Citadel. Kids love the mascot, Charlie T. Riverdog. After games, fireworks often illuminate the summer sky in honor of this all-American pastime. The season runs from April through September. Tickets cost a reasonable $7 to $12. ⊠ *Joseph P. Riley Jr. Stadium, 360 Fishburne St., Hampton Park Terrace* ☎ *843/577–3647* ⊕ *www.riverdogs.com.*

BEACHES

There are glorious beaches just outside the Charleston city limits. You and your kids can build sand castles, gather seashells after high tide, or bring a kite and let it loose on a long lead. The Charleston area's mild climate means you can swim from March through October.

Folly Beach. Anchored by Folly Beach Pier, this is the Lowcountry's most iconic summer playground. Head out early to avoid traffic if you're visiting over a weekend. Street parking is free, but to avoid a ticket, all four wheels have to be off the pavement. If you're a surfer, keep driving until you reach Folly's Washout. Stock up on snacks and sandwiches at Bert's Market on E. Ashley Avenue or grab a taco with the locals at Chico Feo across the street. **Amenities:** food and drink; lifeguards; parking (fee). **Best for:** swimming; surfing. ⊠ *Folly Beach* ⊕ *www.cityoffollybeach.com.*

FAMILY **Isle of Palms County Park.** Play beach volleyball or soak up the sun in a lounge chair on this wide stretch of sand. This beach is as good as the island's idyllic name. The sands are golden and the waves are gentle, so it's great for families with small children. People seeking to avoid the crowds and those seeking peace and quiet can venture a few blocks north down the beach. The county park is the only lifeguard-protected area on the Isle of Palms. **Amenities:** food and drink; lifeguards; parking (fee). **Best for:** sunrise; swimming; walking ⊠ *Ocean Blvd., 1st to 14th Ave., Isle of Palms* ☎ *843/762–9957* ⊕ *www.ccprc. com* ⊞ *$10 per car weekdays, $15 on weekends.*

FAMILY
Fodor's Choice
★

Kiawah Beachwalker Park. This public park about 28 miles southwest of Charleston has a wide beach at low tide, often ranked among the country's best. Stunningly beautiful Kiawah is one of the Southeast's largest barrier islands, with 10 miles of wide, immaculate ocean beaches. You can walk safely for miles, shelling and beachcombing to your heart's content. The beach is complemented by the Kiawah River, with lagoons filled with birds and wildlife, and golden marshes that make the sunsets even more glorious. **Amenities:** food and drink; lifeguards; parking (fee); showers; toilets. **Best for:** solitude; sunset; swimming; walking. ⊠ *1 Beachwalker Dr., Kiawah Island* ☎ *843/762–9964* ⊕ *www.ccprc. com* ⊞ *$10 per car weekdays, $15 on weekends.*

FAMILY **Sullivan's Island Beach.** This is one of the most pristine beaches in the Charleston area. The beachfront is owned by the town—some 190 acres of maritime forest overseen by the Lowcountry Open Land Trust. The downside is that there are no amenities like public toilets and showers. There are, however, a number of good small restaurants on nearby Middle Street, the island's main drag. There are approximately 30 public-access paths (four are wheelchair accessible) that lead to the beach. "Sully's" is a delightful island with plenty to see, including Fort Moultrie National Monument. **Amenities:** none. **Best for:** sunrise; sunset; walking; windsurfing. ⊠ *Atlantic Ave., Sullivan's Island* ⊕ *www. sullivansisland-sc.com.*

BIKING

Cycling at your own pace is one of the best ways to see Charleston. Those staying at the nearby island resorts, particularly families with children, almost always rent bikes, especially if they are there for a week.

Affordabike. The name says it all: bike rentals at this shop start at $25 for 24 hours (or $55 a week), and that includes a helmet, lock, and basket. Conveniently located in the Upper King area, it's open on Sunday—the best day for riding around downtown Charleston or across the Ravenel Bridge. ⊠ *563 King St., Upper King* ☎ *843/789–3281* ⊕ *www. affordabike.com.*

Bicycle Shoppe. Open seven days a week, this shop rents simple beach cruisers for $7 per hour, $28 per day, or $50 per week, and that includes a helmet, basket, and lock. For those wanting to tackle the Ravenel Bridge, the store offers hybrids for $10 per hour or $40 per day. There's a second branch at 1539 Johnnie Dodds Boulevard in Mount Pleasant, and they offer free delivery to local beaches. ⊠ *281 Meeting St., Market* ☎ *843/722–8168* ⊕ *www.thebicycleshoppe.com.*

FAMILY **Island Bike & Surf Shop.** Rent beach bikes for a very moderate weekly rate (starting at $35 per week), or check out hybrids, mountain bikes, bicycles built for two, and a wide range of equipment for everyone in the family. The shop will even deliver to Kiawah and Seabrook islands. ⊠ *3665 Bohicket Rd., Johns Island* ☎ *843/768–1158* ⊕ *www.island-bikeandsurf.com.*

BOATING

Kayak through isolated marshes, rivers, and estuaries to outlying islands, or explore Cape Romain National Wildlife Refuge.

AquaSafaris. If you want a sailboat or yacht charter, a cruise to a private beach barbecue, or just a day of offshore fishing, contact AquaSafaris. Captain John Borden takes veteran and would-be sailors out daily on *Serena*, a 50-foot sloop, leaving from Shem Creek and Isle of Palms. A sunset cruise on the *Palmetto Breeze* catamaran offers panoramic views of Charleston Harbor set to a soundtrack of Jimmy Buffett tunes. Enjoy beer and cocktails as you cruise in one of the smoothest sails in the Lowcountry. ⊠ *A-Dock, 24 Patriots Point Rd., Mount Pleasant* ☎ *843/886–8133* ⊕ *www.aqua-safaris.com.*

FAMILY **Charleston Kayak Company.** Guided kayak tours with Charleston Kayak Company depart from the grounds of the Inn at Middleton Place. You'll glide down the Ashley River and through brackish creeks in a designated State Scenic River Corridor. Naturalists tell you about the wetlands and the river's cultural history. It's not uncommon to spot an alligator, but thankfully they take no interest in kayakers. Tours last two hours (reservations essential) and cost $49 per person. There are private tours available, as well as trips through an adjacent swamp and to the marshes behind Folly Beach. For self-guided trips, both single and tandem kayak rentals are available starting at $30, including all safety gear. ⊠ *Middleton Place Plantation, 4290 Ashley River Rd., West Ashley* ☎ *843/628–2879* ⊕ *www.charlestonkayakcompany.com.*

FAMILY
Fodor's Choice
★

Coastal Expeditions. Outings for individuals, families, and large groups are arranged by Coastal Expeditions. A kayak or SUP tour with a naturalist guide starts at $52 per adult, and kayak rentals start at $45 for a half day. The company provides exclusive access to Cape Romain National Wilderness Area on Bulls Island via the Bulls Island Ferry. The ferry departs from Garris Landing in Awendaw and runs Tuesday and Thursday to Saturday from April through November. It costs $40 round-trip. Bulls Island has rare natural beauty, a "boneyard beach," shells galore, and nearly 300 species of migrating and native birds. Coastal Expeditions has additional outlets at Crosby's Seafood on Folly Beach and at Isle of Palms Marina. ✉ *Shem Creek Maritime Center, 514B Mill St., Mount Pleasant* ☎ *843/884–7684* ⊕ *www.coastalexpeditions.com.*

Ondeck Charleston. Learn how to command your own 26-foot sailboat on Charleston's beautiful harbor with the guidance of an instructor at Ondeck Charleston. This academy can teach you and your family how to sail comfortably on any size sailboat, and can take you from coastal navigation to ocean proficiency. Instructors are fun and experienced, and are U.S. Sailing–certified professionals. Skippered charters are also available and start at $285. ✉ *24 Patriots Point Rd., Mount Pleasant* ☎ *843/971–0700* ⊕ *www.ondecksailing.us.*

GOLF

With fewer golfers than in Hilton Head, the courses in the Charleston area have more prime tee times available. Even if you're not a guest, you can arrange play at private island resorts, such as Kiawah Island, Seabrook Island, and Wild Dunes. Don't be surprised to find a white-tailed deer grazing on a green or an alligator floating in a water hole. For top courses like Kiawah's Ocean Course, expect to pay in the $200 to $300 range during peak season in spring and early fall. Municipal golf courses are a bargain, often costing less than $25 for 18 holes.

Charleston Municipal Golf Course. This walker-friendly public course isn't as gorgeous as the resort courses—a highway bisects it—but it does have a lot of shade trees, and the price is right. About 6 miles from downtown and 20 miles from the resort islands of Kiawah and Seabrook, the course has a simple snack bar serving breakfast and lunch, as well as beer and wine. ✉ *2110 Maybank Hwy., James Island* ☎ *843/795–6517* ⊕ *www. charleston-sc.gov/golf* 🏌 *$17–$24* ⚑ *18 holes, 6450 yds, par 72.*

Charleston National Golf Club. The best nonresort golf course in Charleston tends to be quiet on weekdays, which translates into lower prices. The setting is captivating, carved along the Intracoastal Waterway and traversing wetlands, lagoons, and pine and oak forests. Finishing holes are set along golden marshland. Diminutive wooden bridges and a handsome clubhouse that looks like an antebellum mirage add to the natural beauty of this well-maintained course. ✉ *1360 National Dr., Mount Pleasant* ☎ *843/203–9994* ⊕ *www.charlestonnationalgolf.com* 🏌 *$66–95* ⚑ *18 holes, 6412 yds, par 72.*

Dunes West Golf & River Club. Designed by Arthur Hill, this championship course has great marsh and river views and lots of modulation on the Bermuda-covered greens shaded by centuries-old oaks. The generous

Check out the shrimp boats and spot bottlenose dolphins from a kayak tour on Shem Creek.

fairways have greens that may be considered small by today's standards, making approach shots very important. Located about 15 miles from downtown Charleston, it's in a gated residential community with an attractive antebellum-style clubhouse. ⊠ *3535 Wando Plantation Way, Mount Pleasant* ☎ *843/856–9000* ⊕ *www.duneswestgolfclub.com* ⌦ *$52–$92* ⚐ *18 holes, 6871 yds, par 72.*

Patriots Point Links. A partly covered driving range and spectacular harbor views make this golf course feel special. It's just across the spectacular Ravenel Bridge, and if you drive here you can take advantage of the free public parking. You could also take the water taxi from downtown and arrange for a staffer to pick you up. Four pros offer one-on-one instruction, as well as lessons and clinics. There's a junior camp during the summer. ⊠ *1 Patriots Point Rd., Mount Pleasant* ☎ *843/881–0042* ⊕ *www. patriotspointlinks.com* ⌦ *$50–$89* ⚐ *18 holes, 6900 yds, par 72.*

TENNIS

Charleston is the home of the world-class Volvo Car Open (formerly the Family Circle Cup), a professional women's tournament. Held over nine days every April at the Family Circle Tennis Center, it attracts some 90,000 fans from around the globe and boasts a roster of former and current champions, including Chris Evert, Martina Navratilova, Jennifer Capriati, and Venus and Serena Williams.

FAMILY
Fodor'sChoice
★

Family Circle Tennis Center. This world-class facility is, without question, one of the top places to play tennis in the Southeast. Open to the public, the 17 courts (13 clay, 4 hard) are lighted for night play. Rates are $10 for the hard courts, $15 for clay. Four miniature courts for kids ages four to eight make this a destination for the whole family. With one of the best-qualified teaching staffs in the country, the MW Tennis Academy offers private lessons and clinics for players of all ages. The Volvo Car Open, a signature event for women's tennis, is hosted here each April. Not coincidentally, this is also the city's top venue for concerts under the stars. ⊠ *161 Seven Farms Dr., Daniel Island* ☎ *843/849–5300* ⊕ *www.familycircletenniscenter.com.*

SHOPPING

One-of-a-kind, locally owned boutiques, where the hottest trends in fashion hang on the racks, make up an important part of the contemporary Charleston shopping experience. Charleston has more than 25 fine-art galleries, making it one of the top art towns in America. Local Lowcountry art, which includes both traditional landscapes of the region as well as more contemporary takes, is among the most prevalent styles here.

SHOPPING DISTRICTS

City Market. This cluster of shops, covered stands, and restaurants fills Market Street between Meeting and East Bay Streets. Sweetgrass basket weavers work here amidst trinket and souvenir booths, T-shirt shops, and upscale clothing boutiques. In the covered market, vendors have stalls selling everything from jewelry to purses to paintings of Rainbow Row. The middle section of the market is enclosed and air-conditioned. ⊠ *E. Bay and Market Sts., Market* ⊕ *www.thecharlestoncitymarket.com.*

King Street. The city's main shopping strip is divided into informal districts: Lower King (from Broad Street to Market Street) is the Antiques District, lined with high-end dealers; Middle King (from Market Street to Calhoun Street) is the Fashion District, a mix of national chains like Anthropologie and Pottery Barn and locally owned boutiques; and Upper King (from Calhoun Street to Spring Street) has been dubbed the Design District, known for both its restaurant scene and furniture and interior-design stores. Check out Second Sundays on King, when the street closes to cars from Calhoun Street to Queen Street. Make sure to visit the Saturday farmers' market in Marion Square throughout the spring and summer months. ⊠ *Charleston.*

NORTH OF BROAD

ANTIQUES

George C. Birlant & Co. You'll find mostly 18th- and 19th-century English antiques here, but keep your eye out for a Charleston Battery bench (which you can spot at White Point Garden), for which they are famous. Founded in 1922, Birlant's is fourth-generation family-owned. ⊠ *191 King St., Lower King* ☎ *843/722–3842* ⊕ *www.birlant.com* ☉ *Closed Sun.*

Jacques' Antiques. As the name suggests, most of the antiques here are imported from France, and the rest are either European or English from the 17th to the 20th centuries. Decorative arts include ceramics, porcelains, and crystal. From the candlesticks to the armoires, all are in exquisite taste. ✉ *160 King St., Lower King* ☎ *843/577–0104* ⊕ *www. jacantiques.com* ⊘ *Closed Sun.*

ART GALLERIES

Anglin Smith Fine Art. This gallery exhibits contemporary paintings by Betty Anglin Smith and her talented triplets, Jennifer, Shannon, and Tripp. Her son, Tripp, is a nature photographer specializing in black-and-white images. The bronze wildlife sculptures are by nationally recognized Darrell Davis; the acclaimed oil paintings by Kim English are attention-getters. ✉ *9 Queen St., Market* ☎ *843/853–0708* ⊕ *www.anglinsmith.com.*

Corrigan Gallery. Owner Lese Corrigan displays her own paintings and the works of some 16 other painters and photographers. Most pieces fit the genre of contemporary Southern art. ✉ *62 Queen St., Market* ☎ *843/722–9868* ⊕ *www.corrigangallery.com* ⊘ *Closed Sun.*

Gallery Chuma. This gallery showcases Gullah art, ranging from inexpensive prints to original works by artists like Jonathan Green. The vibrantly colored paintings of this highly successful South Carolina artist have helped popularize Gullah culture. ✉ *188 Meeting St., Market* ☎ *843/722–1702* ⊕ *www.gallerychuma.com.*

Horton Hayes Fine Art. This gallery carries sought-after Lowcountry paintings depicting coastal life by Mark Kelvin Horton, who also paints architectural and figurative works. Shannon Rundquist is among the 13 Lowcountry artists shown; she has a fun, whimsical way of painting local life and is known for her blue-crab art. ✉ *30 State St., Market* ☎ *843/958–0014* ⊕ *www.hortonhayes.com.*

Fodor's Choice ★ **Robert Lange Studios.** The most *avant* of the contemporary galleries, this striking, minimalist space is a working studio for Robert Lange and other exceptionally talented young artists. Most of the work has a hyperrealistic style with surreal overtones. This is also home base for the work of lauded, whimsical painter Nathan Durfee and local-scene veteran Karen Ann Myers. ✉ *2 Queen St., Market* ☎ *843/805–8052* ⊕ *www.robertlangestudios.com.*

BOOKS

Fodor's Choice ★ **Blue Bicycle Books.** Look for out-of-print and rare books, including hardcover classics, at this locally adored bookstore with a large selection of everything from military history to cookbooks. They host frequent signings by local authors like Dorothea Benton Frank and the Lee Brothers. ✉ *420 King St., Upper King* ☎ *843/722–2666* ⊕ *www. bluebicyclebooks.com.*

CLOTHING

Ben Silver. Charleston's own Ben Silver, premier purveyor of blazer buttons, has more than 800 designs, including college and British regimental motifs. The shop also sells British neckties, embroidered polo shirts, and blazers. This Charleston institution was founded in the 1960s. ✉ *149 King St., Lower King* ☎ *843/577–4556* ⊕ *www.bensilver.com* ⊘ *Closed Sun.*

Berlin's. Family-owned since 1883, this Charleston institution has a reputation as a destination for special-occasion clothing. The store, which for generations sold preppy styles, has now added European designers. There is a complimentary parking lot across the street. ⊠ *114–116 King St., Lower King* ☎ *843/722–1665* ⊕ *www.berlinsclothing.com* ⊘ *Closed Sun.*

Christian Michi. This shop carries tony women's clothing and accessories. Designers from Italy, such as Piazza Sempione, are represented, as is Hoss Intropia from Spain. Known for its evening wear, the shop has pricey but gorgeous gowns and a fine selection of cocktail dresses. High-end fragrances add to the luxurious air. ⊠ *220 King St., Lower King* ☎ *843/723–0575.*

Copper Penny. This longtime local clothier sells trendy dresses and women's apparel from designers like Trina Turk, Millie, Tibi, and Diane Von Furstenberg. There's also an accompanying shoe store next door, and two satellite locations in Mount Pleasant. ⊠ *311 King St., Middle King* ☎ *843/723–2999* ⊕ *www.shopcopperpenny.com.*

Ellington. Chic and classy, this shop is known for its washable, packable clothing made of feel-good fabrics like silk, linen, and cashmere. Its fashions have classic lines, but always feel up-to-date. ⊠ *24 State St., Market* ☎ *843/722–7999* ⊘ *Closed Sun.*

Finicky Filly. This boutique carries exceptional women's apparel and accessories by such designers as Lela Rose, Schumacher, All Dressed Up, and Etro. It appeals to women from college age to seniors. ⊠ *303 King St., Middle King* ☎ *843/534–0203* ⊕ *www.thefinickyfilly.com.*

Hampden Clothing. One of the city's trendiest boutiques attracts the young and well-heeled, who come here for an edgier style. Hot designers like Yigal Azrouël, Vena Cava, Alexander Wang, and Jenni Kayne help make it a premier destination for the latest in fashion. ⊠ *314 King St., Middle King* ☎ *843/724–6373* ⊕ *www.hampdenclothing.com.*

Ibu. Artisans from 34 countries contribute the elaborate and intricate textiles used to make the mostly women's clothing for sale here. The brightly colored shop is nestled in an upstairs nook on Lower King. Purchases support the communities where the clothing and supplies originate. ⊠ *183B King St., Lower King* ☎ *843/327–8304* ⊕ *www.ibumovement.com* ⊘ *Closed Sun.*

FAMILY **Kids on King.** This shop's world-traveling owners offer the finest in children's apparel, accessories, and toys from just about everywhere. You'll be transported to other lands with the handcrafted designs. ⊠ *310 King St., Middle King* ☎ *843/720–8647* ⊕ *www.kidsonking.com.*

The Trunk Show. This upscale consignment shop sells designer dresses, handbags, and shoes. The back room has been converted into a men's department, with mostly new clothes but some vintage items as well. The shop is also known for its estate jewelry and custom-made jewelry from semiprecious stones. There's an excellent selection of gowns and evening wear. ⊠ *281 Meeting St., Market* ☎ *843/722–0442* ⊘ *Closed Sun.*

Worthwhile. Designer women's clothing, shoes, and jewelry make it fun to shop at this boutique in a historic home. You can also find artsy and hip baby gear. ✉ *268 King St., Middle King* ☎ *843/723–4418* ⊕ *www.shopworthwhile.com.*

FOOD AND WINE

Caviar & Bananas. This upscale specialty market and café features out-of-the-ordinary items like duck confit, pâté, and truffles. Note the locally produced items such as Callie's Pimiento Cheese and Jack Rudy Cocktail Co. Small Batch Tonic Water. ✉ *51 George St., Middle King* ☎ *843/577–7757* ⊕ *www.caviarandbananas.com.*

FAMILY **Market Street Sweets.** Stop here for melt-in-your-mouth pralines, bear claws, fudge, and the famous glazed pecans—cinnamon and sugar is the favorite. ✉ *100 N. Market St., Market* ☎ *843/722–1397* ⊕ *www.riverstreetsweets.com.*

O'Hara & Flynn. One of Charleston's best-known wine shops also has a wine bar, open Monday through Saturday. If you buy a bottle of wine at retail price, you can drink it at the tables or right at the wine bar for a $10 corkage fee. Meats (including imported sausage and salami), cheeses, and fresh olive oil are sold here, and you can order some as small appetizer plates. There's live jazz and acoustic music on Thursday and Friday evenings. ✉ *225 Meeting St., Market* ☎ *843/534–1916* ⊕ *www.oharaandflynn.com* ⊘ *Closed Sun.*

Ted's Butcherblock. In addition to gourmet meals to go, this elevated café offers wines, cheeses, cold meats, and olive oils. Attend one of the frequent wine tastings, or stop by to see what's cooking on the patio grill. ✉ *334 E. Bay St., Ansonborough* ☎ *843/577–0094* ⊕ *www.tedsbutcherblock.com* ⊘ *Closed Sun. and Mon.*

SOUTH OF BROAD

ART GALLERIES

Ann Long Fine Art. Serious art collectors head to Ann Long Fine Art for neoclassical and modern works. This world-class gallery features outstanding, albeit pricey, works by gifted American and European artists. Many are painted with Old Master techniques. In addition, the gallery manages the estate of Otto Neumann. ✉ *54 Broad St., South of Broad* ☎ *843/577–0447* ⊕ *www.annlongfineart.com.*

Charleston Renaissance Gallery. This gallery carries museum-quality art—in fact, more than half of the beautifully framed works are sold to museums. Visit, nonetheless—these are paintings of rare beauty. ✉ *103 Church St., South of Broad* ☎ *843/723–0025* ⊕ *www.fineartsouth.com* ⊘ *Closed weekends.*

Ellis-Nicholson Gallery. Showcasing painters and sculptors from those just starting their careers to veterans with international reputations, this gallery has a top-of-the-line selection of works. They also have an impressive selection of handcrafted jewelry. ✉ *1½ Broad St., South of Broad* ☎ *843/722–5353* ⊕ *www.ellis-nicholsongallery.com.*

Fodor's Choice **Martin Gallery.** In a former bank building, this grand space is the city's
★ most impressive gallery. It sells works by nationally and internationally
acclaimed artists, sculptors, and photographers, and is especially well-
known for its bronzes and large wooden sculptures, as well as glass
pieces and custom-designed jewelry. ⊠ *18 Broad St., South of Broad*
☎ *843/723–7378* ⊕ *www.martingallerycharleston.com.*

GREATER CHARLESTON

CANNONBOROUGH

CLOTHING

Indigo & Cotton. This men's store is the go-to boutique for the latest in
gentlemen's tailoring featuring brands such as Gitman Vintage, Filson
Red Label bags, and Raleigh Denim. The Cannonborough shop is also
brimming with bow ties, handkerchiefs, and other accessories. ⊠ *79
Cannon St., Cannonborough* ☎ *843/718–2980* ⊕ *www.indigoandcot-
ton.com* ☾ *Closed Sun.*

GIFTS

Mac & Murphy. This hole-in-the-wall is for anyone who favors old-fashioned methods of communication, with the trendiest in notepads, pens,
wrapping paper, and stationery, including Cheree Berry, Crane & Co.,
and Dude and Chick. ⊠ *74½ Cannon St., Cannonborough* ☎ *843/576–
4394* ⊕ *www.macandmurphy.com* ☾ *Closed Sun.*

NORTH CHARLESTON

MALLS AND SHOPPING CENTERS

Tanger Outlet. If you are a dedicated outlet shopper, head to Tanger
Outlet in North Charleston. This spiffy, contemporary mall houses 80
name-brand outlets like Loft, J.Crew, Timberland, and Saks OFF 5TH.
⊠ *Centre Pointe Dr., off I–26, North Charleston* ☎ *843/529–3095*
⊕ *www.tangeroutlet.com.*

HILTON HEAD, SC, AND THE LOWCOUNTRY

WELCOME TO HILTON HEAD, SC, AND THE LOWCOUNTRY

TOP REASONS TO GO

★ **Beachcombing:** Hilton Head Island has 12 miles of beaches. You can swim, soak up the sun, or walk along the sand.

★ **Challenging golf:** Hilton Head's nickname is "Golf Island," and its many challenging courses have an international reputation.

★ **Serving up tennis:** Home to hundreds of tennis courts, Hilton Head is one of the nation's top tennis destinations.

★ **Staying put:** This semitropical island has been a resort destination for decades, and it has all the desired amenities for visitors—a vast array of lodgings, an endless supply of restaurants, and excellent shopping.

★ **Beaufort:** This small antebellum town offers large doses of heritage and culture; nearly everything you might want to see is within its downtown historic district.

1 Hilton Head Island. One of the Southeast coast's most popular tourist destinations, Hilton Head is known for its golf courses and tennis courts. It's a magnet for time-share owners and retirees. Bluffton is Hilton Head's neighbor to the west. The old-town area is laden with history and charm.

2 Beaufort. This charming town just inland from Hilton Head is a destination in its own right, with a lively dining scene and cute bed-and-breakfasts.

3 Daufuskie Island. A scenic ferry ride from Hilton Head, Daufuskie is now much more developed than it was during the days when Pat Conroy wrote *The Water Is Wide*, but it's still a beautiful island to explore, even on a day trip. You can stay for a few days at a variety of fine rental properties, tool down shady dirt roads in a golf cart, and delight in the glorious, nearly deserted beaches.

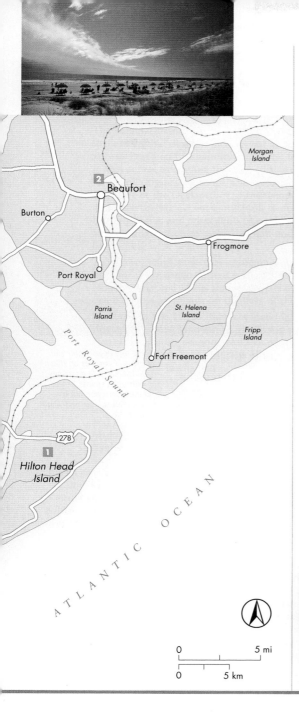

GETTING ORIENTED

Just north of South Carolina's border with Georgia, Hilton Head is best explored by car, as its points of interest spread over a flat coastal plain that is a mix of wooded areas, marshes, and sea islands, the latter of which are sometimes accessible only by boat or ferry. The 42-square-mile island is shaped like a foot, hence the reason locals often describe places as being at the "toe." Hilton Head's neighbor, Bluffton, is a quirky, artsy town rich with history. In the last several years it has grown from 1 square mile to about 50 square miles. South of Hilton Head is the city of Savannah, which is about a 45-minute drive from the island. North of Hilton Head is Beaufort, a cultural treasure and a graceful antebellum town. Beaufort is also about 45 minutes from Hilton Head.

8

BEST BEACHES IN HILTON HEAD AND THE LOWCOUNTRY

Hilton Head's beaches are good for the soul. The 12 glorious miles of white-sand beaches are perfect for sunbathing, bike riding, or simply taking a peaceful walk. The Atlantic Ocean waters are generally smooth thanks to the island's geographic location.

There are several beaches on Hilton Head Island that range from the bucolic and peaceful to ones perfect for families. All beaches are open to the public, but many access points are open only to resort or hotel guests. There are several public access points that take beachgoers over small walkways or boardwalks surrounded by sand dunes and sea oats. Beachgoers might see a variety of critters, including crabs, sand dollars, starfish, pelicans, great blue herons, and many other species. The beaches are wide, particularly at low tide, and the sand at the mid-tide point is packed hard, making it great for bike riding. The waters are generally tame, although under certain weather conditions you'll see surfers riding the waves.

(above and upper right) With 12 miles of beaches on Hilton Head Island, there are plenty of wide-open spaces. (lower right) Conservation efforts assure critters large and small a home.

SEA TURTLES

Between May and August, loggerhead sea turtles build their nests and lay their eggs on the beaches of Hilton Head. The hatchlings emerge from their nests at night and are guided by the light on the horizon to the ocean. Any artificial light will disorient them, causing them to go toward the dunes instead of into the water. Due to this, all light sources along the beaches must be off by 10 pm.

HILTON HEAD'S BEST BEACHES

ALDER LANE BEACH PARK

Alder Lane Beach Park is a nice spot for a swim or a romantic walk. This beach, which has lifeguards on patrol during the summer months, is less crowded than some of the more popular areas, like Coligny Beach. There are restrooms, outdoor showers, and vending machines. The beach, like almost all public beaches on Hilton Head, is wheelchair accessible. Alder Lane Beach Park is on the south end (near the toe) of Hilton Head Island, next to the Marriott Vacation Club Grande Ocean off South Forest Beach Drive.

BURKES BEACH

If you're looking to get away from the crowds, **Burkes Beach** is a great choice. It's located midisland, adjacent to the Chaplin Community Park at the end of Burkes Beach Road off William Hilton Parkway (U.S. 278). There are no lifeguards, so it's quieter than many of the other Hilton Head beaches. It's a great place for a quiet walk along the shore. If you get up early it's also a perfect spot to catch an amazing sunrise.

COLIGNY BEACH PARK

This south-end beach, located off Coligny Circle, is by far the most popular beach on Hilton Head Island. The entrance to the beach has choreographed fountains for children to play

under, showers and changing rooms, large restroom facilities, swinging benches, and a boardwalk to the beach. Throughout the summer months there is children's entertainment starting at 6:30 pm weekdays at Coligny Plaza, which is within walking distance to the beach. There are chairs and umbrellas for rent, volleyball nets, and even Wi-Fi. For the grown-ups, the outdoor Tiki Hut bar at the Beach House, a Holiday Inn Resort, is a local favorite spot to drink a cool beverage while enjoying the ocean view. Parking is free at **Coligny Beach Park.**

DRIESSEN BEACH AND FOLLY FIELD BEACH

These beaches are near the heel of Hilton Head Island and are great spots for families. In fact, on many summer days you'll see bicyclists enjoying the day, beachgoers flying colorful kites, and children building sand castles. **Driessen Beach** is accessible at Bradley Beach Road off William Hilton Parkway. Follow along a wooden boardwalk, which weaves over a small tidal marsh, to get to the beach. It's a hike, but the beach is worth the walk. There are barbecue grills, a playground, outdoor showers, restrooms, and a picnic pavilion. **Folly Field Beach** is next to Driessen Beach off Folly Field Road, and also boasts outdoor showers, restrooms, and lifeguards during the summer months.

8

LOWCOUNTRY CUISINE

To understand Lowcountry cuisine, you have to dig in to the "what" and the "where" of its historic culinary conglomeration.

(above) Shrimp po'boys are menu staples in the Lowcountry. (lower right) Once you taste shrimp and grits you may crave it morning, noon, and night. (upper right) Hoppin' John is often topped with salsa.

Although you can find Lowcountry cuisine along most of coastal South Carolina all the way down to Savannah, the food's foundation feeds off the pulse of Lowcountry, the Holy City of Charleston, where, centuries ago, European aristocrats would share kitchens with their African slaves. The result was a colonial European fusion with Caribbean and West African, otherwise known as Gullah, influences.

Seafood—shrimp, crabs, fish, and oysters—from the marshlands, combined with rice pulled from the countless coastal rice plantations' paddies, are the core ingredients of this specific cuisine. Add to that a twist of exotic African spices and citrus zest, as well as locally grown okra, corn, and benne seeds and you have Lowcountry staples like shrimp and grits, she-crab soup, hoppin' John, and perlau.

First-time visitors to the area will quickly realize that Lowcountry cuisine is pure Southern comfort.

A SWEET SIDE

While, it's true, you can't eat this Lowcountry must with a fork, sweet tea is an undoubtedly essential sidekick to South Carolina cuisine. Sugar is added to the brew before it cools, which makes this supersaturated beverage all the more sweet. Lowcountry visitors beware: when ordering at a restaurant, iced tea will most likely arrive as sweet tea.

Here are some Lowcountry staples:

SHRIMP AND GRITS

If you're not convinced that South Carolina is serious about grits, consider this: in 1976, it declared grits the official state food. In the South, grits are most commonly paired with its coastal-waters counterpart, making shrimp and grits a standard dish for breakfast, lunch, and dinner. Today, foodies will delight in discovering the dish to be dressed up with everything from sausage, bacon, and Cajun seasoning to cheese, gravy, and tomato-based sauces.

SHE-CRAB SOUP

Rich and creamy, with lumps of crabmeat and a splash of dry sherry, she-crab soup is to the Lowcountry as chowder is to New England. The "she" of this signature dish actually comes from the main ingredient, a female crab's orange crab roe. It is delicious as an appetizer, and quite filling as an entrée.

STEAMED OYSTERS

Oyster beds are plentiful in the creeks and inlet waters along the Lowcountry coast. Also plentiful are those who can't get enough of shucking the fresh meat out of clasped shells and dipping it into warm, drawn butter or cocktail sauce. Oysters are usually served by the half dozen, with a side of Saltine crackers.

HOPPIN' JOHN

This rice-and-bean concoction is not only a favorite Lowcountry dish, but a lucky one at that. Families throughout the Lowcountry prepare hoppin' John on New Year's Day for lunch or dinner in hopes that it will provide them with a year's worth of good luck. It's all in the classic Lowcountry ingredients: black-eyed peas symbolize pennies (a side of collard greens adds to the wealth in the new year). Rice, chopped onions, bacon (or ham), and peppers are added to the peas. Add garnishes like a spoonful of salsa or a dollop of sour cream for an interesting Southwest spin.

PERLAU

South Carolina takes great pride in its perlau, more lovingly known at the table as "chicken bog." This rice-based dish is cooked with chunks of tender chicken and sausage slices, simmered in the chef's choice of Southern seasonings. For more than 30 years, in fact, the tiny town of Loris has been hosting its annual Loris Bog-off Festival, where hundreds of chefs compete to be awarded with the best bowl of bog.

8

Updated by
Sally Mahan

Hilton Head Island is a unique and incredibly beautiful resort town that anchors the southern tip of South Carolina's coastline. What makes this semitropical island so unique? At the top of the list is the fact that visitors won't see large, splashy billboards or neon signs. What they will see is an island where the environment takes center stage, a place where development is strictly regulated.

There are 12 miles of sparkling white-sand beaches, amazing world-class restaurants, top-rated golf courses—Harbour Town Golf Links annually hosts the Heritage Golf Tournament, a PGA Tour event—and a thriving tennis community. Wildlife abounds, including loggerhead sea turtles, alligators, snowy egrets, wood storks, great blue heron, and, in the waters, dolphins, manatees, and various species of fish. There are lots of activities offered on the island, including parasailing, charter fishing, kayaking, and many other water sports.

The island is home to several private gated communities, including Sea Pines, Hilton Head Plantation, Shipyard, Wexford, Long Cove, Port Royal, Indigo Run, Palmetto Hall, and Palmetto Dunes. Within these you'll find upscale housing (some of it doubling as vacation rentals), golf courses, shopping, and restaurants. Sea Pines is one of the most famous of these communities, as it is known for the iconic candy-cane-striped Hilton Head Lighthouse. There are also many areas on the island that are not behind security gates.

PLANNER

WHEN TO GO
The high season follows typical beach-town cycles, with June through August and holidays year-round being the busiest and most costly. Mid-April, during the annual RBC Heritage Golf Tournament, is when rates tend to be highest. Thanks to the Lowcountry's mostly moderate

year-round temperatures, tourists are ever-present. Spring is the best time to visit, when the weather is ideal for tennis and golf. Autumn is almost as active for the same reason.

To get a good deal, it's imperative that you plan ahead. The choicest locations can be booked six months to a year in advance, but booking agencies can help you make room reservations and get good deals during the winter season, when the crowds fall off. Villa-rental companies often offer snowbird rates for monthly stays during the winter season. Parking is always free at the major hotels, but valet parking can cost from $20 to $32; the smaller properties have free parking, too, but no valet service.

PLANNING YOUR TIME

No matter where you stay, spend your first day relaxing on the beach or hitting the links. After that, you'll have time to visit some of the area's attractions, including the Coastal Discovery Museum or the Sea Pines Resort. You can also visit the Tanger outlet malls on U.S. 278 in Bluffton. Old-town Bluffton is a quaint area with many locally owned shops and art galleries. If you have a few more days, visit Beaufort on a day trip or even spend the night there. This historic antebellum town is rich with history. Savannah is also a short drive away.

GETTING HERE AND AROUND

AIR TRAVEL

Most travelers use the Savannah/Hilton Head International Airport, less than an hour from Hilton Head, which is served by Air Canada, Allegiant, American Eagle, Delta, JetBlue, United, and Suncountry. Hilton Head Island Airport is served by American Airlines.

Air Contacts Hilton Head Island Airport. ✉ *120 Beach City Rd., North End* ☎ *843/255–2950* ⊕ *www.hiltonheadairport.com.* **Savannah/Hilton Head International Airport.** ✉ *400 Airways Ave., Northwest* ☎ *912/964–0514* ⊕ *www.savannahairport.com.*

BOAT AND FERRY TRAVEL

Hilton Head is accessible via boat, with docking available at Harbour Town Yacht Basin, Skull Creek Marina, and Shelter Cove Harbor.

Boat Docking Information Harbour Town Yacht Basin. ✉ *Sea Pines, 149 Lighthouse Rd., South End* ☎ *843/363–8335* ⊕ *www.seapines.com.* **Shelter Cove Marina.** ✉ *Shelter Cove, 1 Shelter Cove La., Mid-Island* ☎ *800/466–7894* ⊕ *www.palmettodunes.com/shelter-cove/marina-hilton-head.* **Skull Creek Marina.** ✉ *1 Waterway La., North End* ☎ *843/681–8436* ⊕ *www.theskullcreek-marina.com.*

BUS TRAVEL

The Lowcountry Regional Transportation Authority, known as the Palmetto Breeze, has buses that leave Bluffton in the morning for Hilton Head, Beaufort, and some of the islands. The fare is $2.50, and exact change is required.

Bus Contacts Lowcountry Regional Transportation Authority. ☎ *843/757–5782* ⊕ *www.palmettobreezetransit.com.*

CAR TRAVEL

Driving is the best way to get onto Hilton Head Island. Off Interstate 95, take Exit 8 onto U.S. 278 East, which leads you through Bluffton (where it's known as Fording Island Road) and then to Hilton Head. Once on Hilton Head, U.S. 278 forks: on the right is William Hilton Parkway, and on the left is the Cross Island Parkway (a toll road that costs $1.25 each way). If you take the Cross Island (as the locals call it) to the south side where Sea Pines and many other resorts are located, the trip will take about 10 to 15 minutes. If you take William Hilton Parkway the trip will take about 30 minutes. Be aware that at check-in and checkout times on Friday, Saturday, and Sunday, traffic on U.S. 278 can slow to a crawl. ■TIP➔ Be careful of putting the pedal to the metal, particularly on the Cross Island Parkway. It's patrolled regularly.

Once on Hilton Head Island, signs are small and blend in with the trees and landscaping, and nighttime lighting is kept to a minimum. The lack of streetlights makes it difficult to find your way at night, so be sure to get good directions.

TAXI TRAVEL

There are several taxi services available on Hilton Head, including Hilton Head Taxi and Limousine and Diamond Transportation, which has SUVs and passenger vans available for pickup at Savannah/Hilton Head International Airport and Hilton Head Airport. Prices range from $20 to $120, depending on where you're headed.

Taxi Contacts Diamond Transportation. ☎ 843/247–2156 ⊕ hiltonheadrides. com. **Hilton Head Taxi and Limousine.** ☎ 843/785–8294 ⊕ yellowcabhhi.net.

TRAIN TRAVEL

Amtrak gets you as close as Savannah or Yemassee.

Train Contacts Savannah Amtrak Station. ✉ 2611 Seaboard Coastline Dr., Savannah ☎ 800/872–7245 ⊕ www.amtrak.com.

RESTAURANTS

The number of fine-dining restaurants on Hilton Head is extraordinary, given the size of the island. Because of the proximity to the ocean and the small farms on the mainland, most locally owned restaurants are still heavily influenced by the catch of the day and seasonal harvests. Most upscale restaurants open at 11 and don't close until 9 or 10, but some take a break between 2 and 4. Many advertise early-bird menus, and sometimes getting a table before 6 can be a challenge. During the height of the summer season, reservations are a good idea, though in the off-season you may need them only on weekends. There are several locally owned breakfast joints and plenty of great delis where you can pick up lunch or the fixings for a picnic. Smoking is prohibited in restaurants and bars in Bluffton, Beaufort, and on Hilton Head. Beaufort's restaurant scene has certainly evolved, with more trendy restaurants serving contemporary cuisine moving into the downtown area. *Dining reviews have been shortened. For full information, visit Fodors.com.*

HOTELS

Hilton Head is known as one of the best vacation spots on the East Coast, and its hotels are a testimony to its reputation. The island is awash in regular hotels and resorts, not to mention beachfront or golf-course-view villas, cottages, and luxury private homes. You can expect the most modern conveniences and world-class service at the priciest places. Clean, updated rooms and friendly staff are everywhere, even at lower-cost hotels—this is the South, after all. Staying in cooler months, for extended periods of time, or commuting from nearby Bluffton can save money. *Hotel reviews have been shortened. For full information, visit Fodors.com.*

WHAT IT COSTS				
	$	**$$**	**$$$**	**$$$$**
Restaurants	under $15	$15–$19	$20–$24	over $24
Hotels	under $150	$150–$200	$201–$250	over $250

Restaurant prices are for a main course at dinner, excluding sales tax. Hotel prices are for two people in a standard double room in high season, excluding service charges and tax.

TOURS

Tour Contacts Adventure Cruises. ⊠ *Shelter Cove Marina, 9 Harbourside La., Mid-Island* ☎ *843/785–4558* ⊕ *www.cruisehiltonhead.com.* **Gullah Heritage Trail Tours.** ⊠ *Coastal Discovery Museum, 70 Honey Horn Dr., North End* ☎ *843/681–7066* ⊕ *www.gullaheritage.com.* **Harbour Town Yacht Basin.** ⊠ *Sea Pines, 149 Lighthouse Rd., South End* ☎ *843/363–2628* ⊕ *harbourtownyachtbasin.com.* **Low Country Nature Tours.** ⊠ *Shelter Cove Marina, 1 Shelter Cove La., Mid-Island* ☎ *843/683–0187* ⊕ *www.lowcountrynaturetours.com.* **Pau Hana & Flying Circus Sailing Charters.** ⊠ *Palmetto Bay Marina, 86 Helmsman Way, South End* ☎ *843/686–2582* ⊕ *www.hiltonheadislandsailing.com.*

VISITOR INFORMATION

As you're driving into town, you can pick up brochures and maps at the Hilton Head Island–Bluffton Chamber of Commerce and Visitor and Convention Bureau.

Visitor Information Hilton Head Island-Bluffton Chamber of Commerce and Visitor and Convention Bureau. ⊠ *1 Chamber of Commerce Dr., Mid-Island* ☎ *843/785–3673* ⊕ *www.hiltonheadisland.org.*

8

HILTON HEAD ISLAND

Hilton Head Island is known far and wide as a vacation destination that prides itself on its top-notch golf courses and tennis programs, world-class resorts, and beautiful beaches. But the island is also part of the storied American South, steeped in a rich, colorful history. It has seen Native Americans and explorers, battles from the Revolutionary War to the Civil War, plantations and slaves, and development and environmentally focused growth.

More than 10,000 years ago, the island was inhabited by Paleo-Indians. From 8000 to 2000 BC, Woodland Indians lived on the island. A shell ring made from their discarded oyster shells and animal bones from that period can be found in the Sea Pines Nature Preserve.

The recorded history of the island goes back to the early 1500s, when Spanish explorers sailing coastal waters came upon the island and found Native American settlements. Over the next 200 years, the island was claimed at various times by the Spanish, the French, and the British. In 1663, Captain William Hilton claimed the island for the British crown (and named it for himself), and the island became home to indigo, rice, and cotton plantations.

During the Revolutionary War and the War of 1812, the British harassed islanders and burned plantations, but the island recovered from both wars. During the Civil War, Union troops took Hilton Head in 1861 and freed the more than 1,000 slaves on the island. Mitchelville, one of the first settlements for freed blacks, was created. There was no bridge to the island, so its freed slaves, called "Gullah," subsisted on agriculture and the seafood-laden waters.

Over the years, much of the plantation land was sold at auction. Then, in 1949, General Joseph Fraser purchased 17,000 acres, much of which would eventually become various communities, including Hilton Head Plantation, Palmetto Dunes, and Spanish Wells. The general bought another 1,200 acres, which his son, Charles, used to develop Sea Pines. The first bridge to the island was built in 1956, and modern-day Hilton Head was born.

What makes Hilton Head so special now? Charles Fraser and his business associates focused on development while preserving the environment. And that is what tourists will see today: an island that values its history and its natural beauty.

GETTING HERE AND AROUND

Hilton Head Island is 19 miles east of Interstate 95. Take Exit 8 off Interstate 95 and then U.S. 278 east, directly to the bridges. If you're heading to the southern end of the island, your best bet to save time and avoid traffic is the Cross Island Parkway toll road. The cost is $1.25 each way.

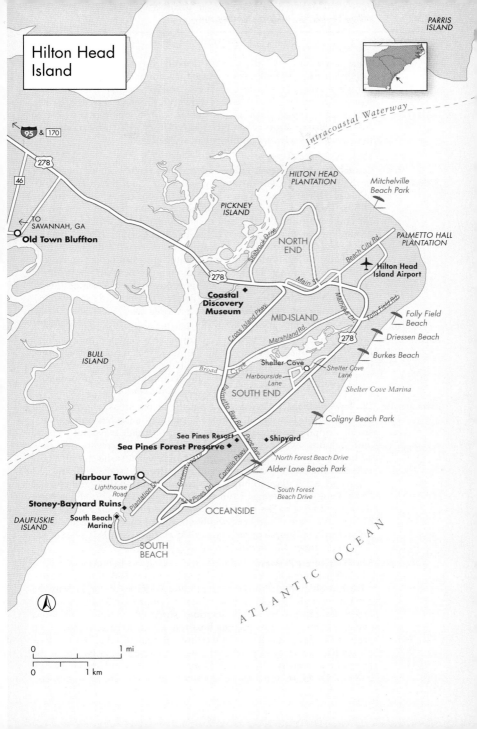

EXPLORING

Your impression of Hilton Head depends on which of the island's developments you make your temporary home. The oldest and best known of Hilton Head's developments, Sea Pines occupies 4,500 thickly wooded acres. It's not wilderness, however; among the trees are three golf courses, tennis clubs, riding stables, and shopping plazas. A free trolley shuttles visitors around the resort. Other well-known communities are Palmetto Dunes and Port Royal Plantation.

TOP ATTRACTIONS

FAMILY

Fodor's Choice

★

Coastal Discovery Museum. This wonderful museum tells about the history of the Lowcountry. For instance, you'll learn about the early development of Hilton Head as an island resort from the Civil War to the 1930s. There is also a butterfly enclosure, various hands-on programs for children, guided walks, and much more. Take a walk around the grounds to see marshes, open fields, live oaks dripping with Spanish moss, as well as South Carolina's largest southern red cedar tree, which dates back to 1595. Admission is free, but lectures and tours on various subjects cost between $5 and $10. Although the museum is just off the Cross Island Parkway, the peaceful grounds make it feel miles away. ⊠ *70 Honey Horn Dr., off Hwy. 278, North End* ☎ *843/689–6767* ⊕ *www.coastaldiscovery.org* ✆ *Free* ☉ *Closed Sun.*

FAMILY

Fodor's Choice

★

Harbour Town. The closest thing the Sea Pines development has to a downtown is Harbour Town, a charming area centered on a circular marina that's filled with interesting shops and restaurants. Rising above it all is the landmark candy-cane-stripe Hilton Head Lighthouse, which you can climb to enjoy a view of Calibogue Sound. ⊠ *Lighthouse Rd., South End* ☎ *866/561–8802* ⊕ *www.seapines.com.*

Fodor's Choice

★

Old Town Bluffton. Tucked away from the resort areas, charming Old Town Bluffton has several historic homes and churches on oak-lined streets dripping with Spanish moss. The Promenade was built recently and includes several new bars and restaurants. There are also new additions to Old Town, including a microbrewery. At the end of Wharf Street in this artsy community is the Bluffton Oyster Company (63 Wharf Street), a place to buy fresh raw local shrimp, fish, and oysters. Grab some picnic fixings from the Downtown Deli (27 Mellichamp Drive) and head to the boat dock at the end of Pritchard Street for a meal with a view. Another incredibly beautiful spot for a picnic is the grounds of the Church of the Cross. ⊠ *May River Rd. and Calhoun St., Bluffton* ⊕ *www.oldtownbluffton.com.*

FAMILY

Sea Pines Forest Preserve. Walking and biking trails take you past a stocked fishing pond, a waterfowl pond, and a 3,400-year-old Native American shell ring at this 605-acre public wilderness tract. Pick up the extensive activity guide at the Sea Pines Welcome Center to take advantage of goings-on—moonlight hayrides, storytelling around campfires, and alligator- and bird-watching boat tours. The preserve is part of the grounds at Sea Pines Resort. Overlooking a small lake, the outdoor chapel has five wooden pews and a wooden lectern engraved with the Prayer of St. Francis. ⊠ *Sea Pines Resort, 32 Greenwood Dr., South End* ☎ *843/363–4530, 866/561–8802* ⊕ *www.seapines.com* ✆ *$6 per car.*

DID YOU KNOW?

Bluffton, 12 miles west of
Hilton Head Island, is a quaint
town with historic homes,
an active artists' colony, and
several good restaurants.

WORTH NOTING

Stoney-Baynard Ruins. Check out the Stoney-Baynard Ruins, the remnants of a plantation home and slave quarters built in the 1700s by Captain John "Saucy Jack" Stoney. A cotton planter named William Edings Baynard bought the place in 1840. On the National Register of Historic Sites, only parts of the walls are still standing. The ruins are not easy to find, so ask for directions at the Sea Pines Welcome Center at the Greenwood Drive gate. ✉ *Plantation Dr., near Baynard Cove Rd., South End* 🎟 *Free.*

WHERE TO EAT

$$$ SEAFOOD

🍴 **Black Marlin Bayside Grill.** If you want to dine with a view of the "blue," then head to this seafood eatery in Palmetto Bay Marina. The place draws a steady stream of customers most days, but Saturday and Sunday brunch are the highlights for eggs Benedict and live entertainment. **Known for:** a hopping happy hour; an outdoor Hurricane Bar with a Key West vibe. [$] *Average main: $23* ✉ *Palmetto Bay Marina, 86 Helmsman Way, South End* ☎ *843/785–4950* 🌐 *www.blackmarlinhhi.com.*

$$$ SEAFOOD FAMILY

🍴 **Captain Woody's.** If you're looking for a fun, casual, kid-friendly seafood restaurant, Captain Woody's is the place to go. Start with the creamy crab bisque, oysters on the half shell, or the sampler platter, which includes crab legs, shrimp, and oysters. **Known for:** grouper sandwiches, including the buffalo grouper, grouper melt, and grouper Reuben; a lively atmosphere. [$] *Average main: $22* ✉ *6 Target Rd., South End* ☎ *843/785–2400* 🌐 *www.captainwoodys.com.*

$$$$ ITALIAN

🍴 **Frankie Bones.** This restaurant, which is dedicated to Frank Sinatra, appeals to an older crowd that likes the traditional Italian dishes on the early dining menu. But during happy hour, the bar and the surrounding cocktail tables are populated with younger patrons who order flatbread pizzas and small plates. **Known for:** cool twists on traditional dishes; drinks for dessert (the tiramisu martini is to die for). [$] *Average main: $26* ✉ *1301 Main St., North End* ☎ *843/682–4455* 🌐 *www.frankiebonesbhi.com.*

$ AMERICAN

🍴 **Harold's Country Club & Grill.** Not the "country club" you might expect, Harold's Country Club & Grill is a remodeled gas station in the little town of Yemassee, just east of Interstate 95, south of Charleston. There's a buffet every Thursday, wings and things like seafood baskets and hamburgers on Friday, and steak or chicken with a variety of sides on Saturday. **Known for:** cheerful ladies slapping meat on your plate cafeteria-style; great music; kitschy dining rooms. [$] *Average main: $13* ✉ *97 U.S. 17A, Yemassee* ☎ *843/589–4360* 🌐 *www.haroldscountryclub.com* 🕒 *Closed Sun.–Wed.*

$$$ JAPANESE Fodor's Choice ★

🍴 **Hinoki.** A peaceful oasis awaits you at Hinoki, which has some of the best sushi on Hilton Head. Try the Hilton Head roll, which is whitefish tempura and avocado, the Hinoki roll with asparagus and spicy fish roe topped with tuna and avocado, or one of the more than 50 sushi and sashimi choices. **Known for:** superfresh sushi; extensive sake menu. [$] *Average main: $23* ✉ *Orleans Plaza, 37 New Orleans Rd., South End* ☎ *843/785–9800* 🌐 *hinokihhi.com* 🕒 *Closed Sun.*

$$
MEXICAN

✕ **Mi Tierra.** There's nothing fancy here, just great Mexican food and decor that has a Southwestern feel, with tile floors, colorful sombreros, and paintings of chili peppers hanging on the walls. Start with a margarita and the chips and salsa, and don't forget to order the guacamole and bean dip as well. **Known for:** delicious comfort food; authentic Mexican dishes; extensive menu and daily specials. Ⓢ *Average main: $15* ✉ *130 Arrow Rd., South End* ☎ *843/342–3409* ⊕ *www.mitierrabluffton.com* ⊘ *No lunch weekends.*

$$$$
ITALIAN
Fodor'sChoice
★

✕ **Michael Anthony's.** Owned by a talented, charismatic Philadelphia family, this restaurant has a convivial spirit, and its innovative pairings and plate presentations are au courant. You can expect fresh, top-quality ingredients, simple yet elegant sauces, and waiters who know and care about the food and wine they serve. **Known for:** cooking demonstrations/classes; on-site market with fresh pasta; wine tastings. Ⓢ *Average main: $30* ✉ *Orleans Plaza, 37 New Orleans Rd., Suite L, South End* ☎ *843/785–6272* ⊕ *www.michael-anthonys.com* ⊘ *Closed Sun. No lunch.*

$$$$
EUROPEAN

✕ **Old Fort Pub.** Overlooking the sweeping marshlands of Skull Creek, this romantic restaurant has almost panoramic views. It offers one of the island's best overall dining experiences: the building is old enough to have some personality, and the professional staffers diligently do their duty. **Known for:** amazing, decadent entrées beautifully presented; a lovely Sunday brunch; gorgeous views; romantic atmosphere. Ⓢ *Average main: $33* ✉ *Hilton Head Plantation, 65 Skull Creek Dr., North End* ☎ *843/681–2386* ⊕ *www.oldfortpub.com* ⊘ *No lunch.*

$$
BARBECUE
FAMILY

✕ **One Hot Mama's.** This heavenly barbecue joint is a Hilton Head institution because of its upbeat atmosphere, graffiti-strewn walls, and melt-in-the-mouth pulled pork and fall-off-the-bone ribs. But the place also offers some unusual choices: the wings, which have won multiple awards at Hilton Head's Rib Burnoff and Wing Fest, come with tasty sauces ranging from strawberry-jalapeño to Maui Wowii. **Known for:** lots of fun in the "Barmuda Triangle" (other bars are just steps away). Ⓢ *Average main: $19* ✉ *7A Greenwood Dr., South End* ☎ *843/682–6262* ⊕ *onehotmamas.com.*

$$$$
AMERICAN
Fodor'sChoice
★

✕ **Red Fish.** This seafood eatery's "naked" catch of the day—seafood grilled with olive oil, lime, and garlic—is a heart-healthy specialty that many diners say is the best thing on the menu. The restaurant's wine cellar is filled with some 1,000 bottles, and there's also a retail wine shop so you can take a bottle home. **Known for:** fabulous food; fabulous service; gluten-free selections. Ⓢ *Average main: $30* ✉ *8 Archer Rd., South End* ☎ *843/686–3388* ⊕ *www.redfishofhiltonhead.com* ⊘ *No lunch Sun.*

$$$$
SOUTHWESTERN

✕ **Santa Fe Cafe.** Walk through the doors and you're greeted by the sights, sounds, and aromas of New Mexico: Native American rugs, Mexican ballads, steer skulls and horns, and the pungent smells of chilies and mesquite on the grill. The restaurant is perhaps best experienced on a rainy, chilly night when the adobe fireplaces are cranked up. **Known for:** rooftop cantina with fireplace, music; tasty margaritas. Ⓢ *Average main: $28* ✉ *807 William Hilton Pkwy., Mid-Island* ☎ *843/785–3838* ⊕ *santafehhi.com* ⊘ *No lunch weekends.*

8

$ AMERICAN Fodor's Choice ★ 🍴 **Signe's Heaven Bound Bakery & Café.** Every morning, locals roll in for the deep-dish French toast, crispy polenta, and whole wheat waffles. Since 1972, European-born Signe has been feeding islanders her delicious soups and quiches, curried chicken salad, and loaded hot and cold sandwiches. **Known for:** to-die-for baked goods; the "beach bag" (a lunch packed with goodies to take to the beach); cozy, friendly atmosphere. [$] *Average main: $8* ✉ *93 Arrow Rd., South End* ☎ *843/785–9118* 🌐 *www.signesbakery.com* 🕒 *Closed Sun. Dec.–Feb. No dinner.*

$$ AMERICAN FAMILY Fodor's Choice ★ 🍴 **Skull Creek Boathouse.** Soak up the salty atmosphere in this pair of dining areas where almost every table has a view of the water. Outside is a third dining area and a bar called the Buoy Bar at Marker 13 where Adirondack chairs invite you to sit back, relax, and catch the sunset. **Known for:** great views; fun atmosphere; seafood from the "Dive Bar"; tasty sandwiches and po'boys with a Southern twist. [$] *Average main: $17* ✉ *397 Squire Pope Rd., North End* ☎ *843/681–3663* 🌐 *www.skullcreekboathouse.com.*

$$$ AMERICAN 🍴 **Truffles Cafe.** When a restaurant keeps its customers happy for decades, there's a reason: you won't find any of the namesake truffles on the menu, but instead there's grilled salmon with a mango-barbecue glaze and barbecued baby back ribs. There's a second Hilton Head location on Pope Avenue, and a Bluffton branch that has a lovely outdoor seating area. **Known for:** wide-ranging menu; very popular with locals. [$] *Average main: $20* ✉ *Sea Pines Center, 71 Lighthouse Rd., South End* ☎ *843/671–6136* 🌐 *www.trufflescafe.com* 🕒 *Closed Sun. No lunch.*

$$$$ STEAKHOUSE 🍴 **WiseGuys.** The red-and-black decor is modern and sophisticated at this restaurant—it's a little art deco, a little contemporary. The food is a spin on the classics, starting with seared tuna sliders and an incredible beef tenderloin carpaccio topped with baby arugula and horseradish cream. **Known for:** cool urban atmosphere; mouthwatering steaks. [$] *Average main: $32* ✉ *1513 Main St., North End* ☎ *843/842–8866* 🌐 *wiseguyshhi.com* 🕒 *No lunch.*

BLUFFTON

$$$$ EUROPEAN Fodor's Choice ★ 🍴 **Claude & Uli's Bistro.** It's hard to go wrong with a chef who has cooked at Maxim's in Paris, the Connaught Hotel in London, and Ernie's in San Francisco. Chef Claude Melchiorri, who grew up in Normandy, France, and his wife, Uli, offer divine food at this atmospheric restaurant tucked away in a strip mall right before the bridges to Hilton Head. **Known for:** intimate ambience; French-bistro feel. [$] *Average main: $28* ✉ *Moss Creek Village, 1533 Fording Island Rd., Bluffton* ☎ *843/837–3336* 🌐 *claudebistro.com* 🕒 *No lunch Sun.–Tues. No lunch in summer.*

WHERE TO STAY

$$$ RESORT FAMILY Fodor's Choice ★ 🏨 **Beach House Hilton Head Island.** On one of the island's most popular stretches of sand, the Beach House Hilton Head Island is within walking distance of lots of shops and restaurants. **Pros:** the location cannot be beat; renovations have made this a very desirable destination; professional staff. **Cons:** in summer the number of kids raises the noise

volume; small front desk can get backed up. $ *Rooms from: $249* ⊠ *1 S. Forest Beach Dr., South End* ☎ *843/785–5126* ⊕ *www.beachhouse-hhi.com* ⮑ *202 rooms* ⦾ *No meals.*

$$$$
RESORT
FAMILY

⛱ **Disney's Hilton Head Island Resort.** The typical cheery colors and whimsical designs at Disney's Hilton Head Island Resort create a look that's part Southern beach resort, part Adirondack hideaway. **Pros:** family-friendly vibe; young and friendly staffers; plenty of space to spread out. **Cons:** it's a time-share property; expensive rates. $ *Rooms from: $414* ⊠ *22 Harbourside La., Mid-Island* ☎ *843/341–4100* ⊕ *hiltonhead.dis-ney.go.com* ⮑ *123 units* ⦾ *No meals.*

$$$
HOTEL
FAMILY

⛱ **Hampton Inn on Hilton Head Island.** Although it's not on the beach, this attractive hotel is a good choice for budget travelers. **Pros:** good customer service; moderate prices; more amenities than you might expect. **Cons:** not on a beach; parking lot views. $ *Rooms from: $219* ⊠ *1 Dillon Rd., Mid-Island* ☎ *843/681–7900* ⊕ *www.hamptoninn.com* ⮑ *103 rooms, 12 studios* ⦾ *Breakfast.*

$$$$
HOTEL
FAMILY
Fodor's Choice
★

⛱ **Hilton Head Marriott Resort & Spa.** Private balconies with views of the palm-shaded grounds are the best reason to stay at this resort facing the Atlantic Ocean. **Pros:** steps from the beach; lots of amenities; one of the best-run operations on the island. **Cons:** rooms could be larger; in summer kids are everywhere. $ *Rooms from: $359* ⊠ *1 Hotel Circle, Palmetto Dunes, Mid-Island* ☎ *843/686–8400* ⊕ *www.marriott.com/hotels/travel/hhhgr-hilton-head-marriott-resort-and-spa* ⮑ *513 rooms* ⦾ *No meals.*

$$$$
HOTEL
Fodor's Choice
★

⛱ **The Inn at Harbour Town.** The most buzzworthy of Hilton Head's properties, this European-style boutique hotel has a proper staff clad in kilts that pampers you with British service and a dose of Southern charm. **Pros:** a service-oriented property; central location; three golf courses: Heron Point; Atlantic Dunes, and Harbour Town Golf Links; complimentary parking. **Cons:** no water views; two-day minimum on most weekends. $ *Rooms from: $309* ⊠ *Sea Pines, 7 Lighthouse La., South End* ☎ *843/785–3333* ⊕ *www.seapines.com* ⮑ *60 rooms* ⦾ *No meals.*

$$$$
RESORT
FAMILY

⛱ **Omni Hilton Head Oceanfront Resort.** At this beachfront hotel with a Caribbean sensibility, the spacious accommodations range from studios to two-bedroom suites. **Pros:** competes more with condos than hotels because of the size of its accommodations; lots of outdoor dining options. **Cons:** wedding parties can be noisy; cell phone service is spotty. $ *Rooms from: $349* ⊠ *23 Ocean La., Palmetto Dunes, Mid-Island* ☎ *843/842–8000* ⊕ *www.omnihiltonhead.com* ⮑ *323 rooms* ⦾ *No meals.*

$$
HOTEL

⛱ **Park Lane Hotel & Suites.** The island's only all-suites property has a friendly feel, which is probably why many guests settle in for weeks. **Pros:** one of the island's most reasonably priced lodgings; parking and Wi-Fi are free; playground for the kids. **Cons:** doesn't have an upscale feel; more kids means more noise, especially around the pool area. $ *Rooms from: $176* ⊠ *12 Park La., South End* ☎ *843/686–5700* ⊕ *www.hiltonheadparklanehotel.com* ⮑ *156 suites* ⦾ *No meals.*

8

$$$$ RESORT FAMILY 🏨 **Sonesta Resort Hilton Head Island.** Set in a luxuriant garden that always seems to be in full bloom, the Sonesta Resort is the centerpiece of Shipyard Plantation, which means you'll have access to all its various amenities, including golf and tennis. **Pros:** close to all the restaurants and nightlife in Coligny Plaza; spacious rooms; free parking. **Cons:** Wi-Fi and cell phone service can be a problem; service is sometimes impersonal. [$] *Rooms from: $299* ✉ *Shipyard Plantation, 130 Shipyard Dr., South End* ☎ *843/842–2400, 800/334–1881* 🌐 *www.sonesta.com/hiltonheadisland* 🛏 *340 rooms* 🍴 *No meals.*

$$$$ RESORT FAMILY Fodor's Choice ★ 🏨 **Westin Hilton Head Island Resort & Spa.** A circular drive winds around a sculpture of long-legged marsh birds as you approach this beachfront resort, whose lush landscape lies on the island's quietest stretch of sand. **Pros:** great for destination weddings; the beach here is absolutely gorgeous; pampering spa; guests have access to the Port Royal Golf & Racquet Club. **Cons:** lots of groups in the off-season. [$] *Rooms from: $314* ✉ *2 Grass Lawn Ave., Port Royal Plantation, North End* ☎ *800/933–3102, 843/681–4000* 🌐 *www.westinhiltonheadisland.com* 🛏 *416 rooms* 🍴 *No meals.*

BLUFFTON

$ HOTEL 🏨 **Candlewood Suites.** At this suites-only hotel, the guest rooms are comfortable and tastefully decorated in muted browns and beiges. **Pros:** location makes it convenient to Hilton Head, Beaufort, and Savannah; every room has a full kitchen; free guest laundry. **Cons:** cell phone service is hit-or-miss; set back from road, it can be difficult to find. [$] *Rooms from: $129* ✉ *5 Young Clyde Court, Bluffton* ☎ *843/705–9600* 🌐 *www.candlewoodsuites.com/blufftonsc* 🛏 *124 suites* 🍴 *No meals.*

$$$$ B&B/INN Fodor's Choice ★ 🏨 **Montage Palmetto Bluff.** About 15 minutes from Hilton Head, the Lowcountry's most luxurious resort sits on 20,000 acres that have been transformed into a perfect replica of a small island town, complete with its own clapboard church. **Pros:** 18-hole May River Golf Club on-site; tennis/bocce/croquet complex has an impressive retail shop; the river adds both ambience and boat excursions. **Cons:** the mock Southern town is not the real thing; not that close to the amenities of Hilton Head. [$] *Rooms from: $580* ✉ *1 Village Park Sq., Bluffton* ☎ *843/706–6500, 866/706–6565* 🌐 *www.montagehotels.com/palmettobluff* 🛏 *50 cottages, 75 inn rooms* 🍴 *No meals.*

PRIVATE VILLA RENTALS

Hilton Head has some 6,000 villas, condos, and private homes for rent, almost double the number of the island's hotel rooms. Villas and condos seem to work particularly well for families with children, especially if they want to avoid the extra costs of staying in a resort. Often these vacation homes cost less per diem than hotels of the same quality. Guests on a budget can further economize by cooking some of their own meals.

Villas and condos are primarily rented by the week, Saturday to Saturday. It pays to make sure you understand exactly what you're getting before making a deposit or signing a contract. For example, a property owner in the Hilton Head Beach & Tennis Club advertised that his villa sleeps six. That villa had one small bedroom, a foldout couch, and a hall closet with two very narrow bunk beds. That's a far cry from the three-bedroom villa you might have expected. ■ TIP➔ **Before calling a vacation rental company, make a list of the amenities you want.** Ask for pictures of each room and ask when the photos were taken. If you're looking for a beachfront property, ask exactly how far it is to the beach. Make sure to ask for a list of all fees, including those for parking, cleaning, pets, security deposits, and utility costs. Finally, get a written contract and a copy of the refund policy.

RENTAL AGENTS

Hilton Head Vacation Rentals. Representing more than 250 vacation rentals ranging in size from one to seven bedrooms, Hilton Head Vacation Rentals has villas, condos, and homes with oceanfront views. It offers various packages that include golf and other activities. Rentals are generally for three to seven days. ⊠ *578 William Hilton Pkwy., Hilton Head Island* ☎ *843/785–8687* ⊕ *www.hiltonheadvacation.com* ⟲ *0.*

Resort Rentals of Hilton Head Island. This company represents some 275 homes and villas, including many located inside the gated communities of Sea Pines, Palmetto Dunes, and Shipyard Plantation. Others are in North and South Forest Beach and the Folly Field area. Stays are generally Saturday to Saturday during the peak summer season; three- or four-night stays may be possible off-season. Most of the properties are privately owned, so decor and amenities can vary. ⊠ *32 Palmetto Bay Rd., Suite 1B, Mid-Island* ☎ *800/845–7017* ⊕ *www.hhivacations.com* ⟲ *0.*

Sea Pines Resort. The vast majority of the overnight guests at Sea Pines Resort rent one of the 500 suites, villas, and beach houses. One- and two-bedroom villas have a minimum stay of four nights. For stays of four or more nights, you must arrive on Saturday, Sunday, Monday, or Tuesday. Three- and four-bedrooms villas have a minimum stay of seven nights, and you've got to check in on Saturday. All houses have Internet access, and most have Wi-Fi. Housekeeping is usually an additional charge. ⊠ *32 Greenwood Dr., South End* ☎ *843/785–3333, 866/561–8802* ⊕ *www.seapines.com/vacation-rentals.*

NIGHTLIFE AND PERFORMING ARTS

NIGHTLIFE

Bars, like everything else on Hilton Head, are often in gated communities or shopping centers. Some are hangouts frequented by locals, and others get a good mix of both locals and visitors. There are a fair number of clubs, many of them restaurants that crank up the music after diners depart.

Big Bamboo. Decked out like a World War II–era officers' club, this South Pacific–themed bar and restaurant features live music most nights of the week. ⊠ *Coligny Plaza, 1 N. Forest Beach Dr., South End* ☎ *843/686–3443* ⊕ *www.bigbamboocafe.com.*

Comedy Magic Cabaret. Several nights a week this lounge brings top-flight comedic talent to Hilton Head. Start off with dinner and drinks downstairs at Pelican's Point Seafood & Steakhouse, then head upstairs for the comedy. Tickets are $22 to $26 per person. ■ TIP➔ **Book ahead, because the shows sell out fairly quickly.** ⊠ *South Island Square, 843 William Hilton Pkwy., South End* ☎ *843/681–7757* ⊕ *www.comedymagiccabaret.com.*

Fodor'sChoice **The Jazz Corner.** The elegant supper-club atmosphere at this popular spot
★ makes it a wonderful setting in which to enjoy an evening of jazz, swing,
or blues. There's a special martini menu, an extensive wine list, and a
late-night menu. ■ TIP→ The club fills up quickly, so make reservations.
⊠ *The Village at Wexford, 1000 William Hilton Pkwy., Suite C-1, South
End* 🕾 *843/842–8620* ⊕ *www.thejazzcorner.com.*

Reilley's Plaza. Dubbed the "Barmuda Triangle" by locals, the bars at this
plaza include One Hot Mama's, Reilley's, the Lodge Martini, and Jump
& Phil's Bar & Grill. It's the closest thing Hilton Head Island has to a
raging club scene. ⊠ *Hilton Head Plaza, Greenwood Dr., right before
gate to Sea Pines, South End.*

FAMILY **The Salty Dog Cafe.** If there's one thing you shouldn't miss on Hilton Head
Fodor'sChoice Island, it's the iconic Salty Dog Cafe. It's the ideal place to escape, sit
★ back, and enjoy the warm nights and ocean breezes in a tropical setting
at the outdoor bar. There's live music (think Jimmy Buffett) seven nights
a week during high season. Bring the family along for kid-friendly entertainment, including music, magic, and face painting at 7 pm throughout
the summer. ⊠ *South Beach Marina, 224 S. Sea Pines Dr., South End*
🕾 *843/671–5199* ⊕ *www.saltydog.com.*

Santa Fe Cafe. A sophisticated spot for cocktails in the early evening, the
Santa Fe Cafe is also a great place to lounge in front of the fireplace or
sip top-shelf margaritas at the rooftop cantina. ⊠ *807 William Hilton
Pkwy., Mid-Island* 🕾 *843/785–3838* ⊕ *www.santafehhi.com.*

PERFORMING ARTS

Fodor'sChoice **Arts Center of Coastal Carolina.** Locals love the exhibits at the Walter
★ Greer Gallery and the theater productions at the Arts Center of Coastal
Carolina. Programs for children are also popular. ⊠ *14 Shelter Cove
La., Mid-Island* 🕾 *843/686–3945* ⊕ *www.artshhi.com.*

FAMILY **Hilton Head Island Gullah Celebration.** This showcase of Gullah life through
arts, music, and theater is held at a variety of sites throughout the Lowcountry in February. 🕾 *843/255–7304* ⊕ *www.gullahcelebration.com.*

Fodor'sChoice **Hilton Head Symphony Orchestra.** A selection of summer concerts—includ-
★ ing the popular Symphony Under The Stars—are among the year-round
performances by the symphony. Most events are at the First Presbyterian Church. ⊠ *First Presbyterian Church, 540 William Hilton Pkwy.,
Mid-Island* 🕾 *843/842–2055* ⊕ *www.hhso.org.*

FAMILY **Main Street Youth Theatre.** A variety of performances showcasing young
local talent are presented by Main Street Youth Theatre. ⊠ *25 New
Orleans Rd., Mid-Island* 🕾 *843/689–6246* ⊕ *www.msyt.org.*

SPORTS AND THE OUTDOORS

Hilton Head Island is a mecca for the sports enthusiast and for those
who just want a relaxing walk or bike ride on the beach. There are 12
miles of beaches, 24 public golf courses, more than 50 miles of public
bike paths, and more than 300 tennis courts. There's also tons of water
sports, including kayaking and canoeing, parasailing, fishing, sailing,
and much more.

BEACHES

A delightful stroll on the beach can end with an unpleasant surprise if you don't put your towels, shoes, and other earthly possessions way up on the sand. Tides here can fluctuate as much as 7 feet. Check the tide chart at your hotel.

FAMILY **Alder Lane Beach Park.** A great place for solitude even during the busy summer season, this beach has hard-packed sand at low tide, making it great for walking. It's accessible from the Marriott Grand Ocean Resort. **Amenities:** lifeguards; showers; toilets. **Best for:** solitude; walking; swimming. ⊠ *Alder La., off South Forest Beach Rd., South End.*

Burkes Beach. This beach is usually not crowded, mostly because it is a bit hard to find and there are no lifeguards on duty. **Amenities:** none. **Best for:** solitude; sunrise; swimming; windsurfing. ⊠ *60 Burkes Beach Rd., at William Hilton Pkwy., Mid-Island.*

FAMILY
Fodor's Choice
★
Coligny Beach. The island's most popular beach is a lot of fun, but during high season it can get very crowded. Accessible from the Beach House Hilton Head Island and several other hotels, it has choreographed fountains that delight little children, bench swings, and beach umbrellas and chaise longues for rent. If you have to go online, there's also Wi-Fi access. **Amenities:** lifeguards; food and drink; parking (no fee); showers; toilets. **Best for:** windsurfing; swimming. ⊠ *1 Coligny Circle, at Pope Ave. and South Forest Beach Dr., South End.*

FAMILY **Driessen Beach.** A good destination for families, Driessen Beach is peppered with people flying kites, making it colorful and fun. There's a long boardwalk to the beach. **Amenities:** parking; lifeguards; toilets; showers. **Best for:** walking; sunrise; swimming. ⊠ *43 Bradley Beach Rd., at William Hilton Pkwy., Mid-Island.*

Folly Field Beach Park. Next to Driessen Beach, Folly Field is a treat for families. It can get crowded in high season, but even so it's a wonderful spot for a day of sunbathing and swimming. The first beach cottages on Hilton Head Island were built here in the 1950s. **Amenities:** lifeguards; parking; toilets; showers. **Best for:** swimming; sunrise; walking. ⊠ *55 Starfish Dr., off Folly Field Rd., North End.*

Mitchelville Beach Park. Not ideal for swimming because of the many sharp shells on the sand and in the water, Mitchelville Beach Park is a terrific spot for a walk or beachcombing. It is not on the Atlantic Ocean, but rather on Port Royal Sound. **Amenities:** parking; toilets. **Best for:** solitude; walking. ⊠ *124 Mitchelville Rd., Hilton Head Plantation, North End.*

BIKING

More than 50 miles of public paths crisscross Hilton Head Island, and pedaling is popular along the firmly packed beach. The island keeps adding more to the boardwalk network as visitors are using it and because it's such a safe alternative for kids. Bikes with wide tires are a must if you want to ride on the beach. They can save you a spill should you hit loose sand on the trails. Keep in mind when crossing streets that, in South Carolina, vehicles have the right-of-way. ■ TIP→ **For a map of trails, visit www.hiltonheadislandsc.gov.**

Biking is popular on the hard-packed sand at low tide.

Bicycles from beach cruisers to mountain bikes to tandem bikes can be rented either at bike stores or at most hotels and resorts. Many can be delivered to your hotel, along with helmets, baskets, locks, child carriers, and whatever else you might need.

FAMILY **Hilton Head Bicycle Company.** You can rent bicycles, helmets, and adult tricycles from the Hilton Head Bicycle Company. ⊠ *112 Arrow Rd., South End* ☎ *843/686–6888, 800/995–4319* ⊕ *www.hiltonheadbicycle.com.*

FAMILY **Pedals Bicycles.** Rent beach bikes for adults and children, kiddy karts, jogging strollers, and mountain bikes at Pedals. ⊠ *71A Pope Ave., South End* ☎ *843/842–5522, 888/699–1039* ⊕ *www.pedalsbicycles.com.*

FAMILY **South Beach Bike Rentals.** Rent bikes, helmets, tandems, and adult tricycles at this spot in Sea Pines. ⊠ *230 South Sea Pines Dr., Sea Pines, South End* ☎ *843/671–2453* ⊕ *www.south-beach-cycles.com.*

CANOEING AND KAYAKING
This is one of the most delightful ways to commune with nature on this commercial but physically beautiful island. Paddle through the creeks and estuaries and try to keep up with the dolphins.

FAMILY **Outside Hilton Head.** Boats, canoes, kayaks, and paddleboards are available for rent. The company also offers nature tours and dolphin-watching excursions. ⊠ *Shelter Cove Marina, 1 Shelter Cove La., Mid-Island* ☎ *843/686–6996, 800/686–6996* ⊕ *www.outsidehiltonhead.com.*

Fodor's Choice
★

FISHING
Although anglers can fish in these waters year-round, in April things start to crank up and in May most boats are heavily booked. May is the season for cobia, especially in Port Royal Sound. In the Gulf Stream you

can hook king mackerel, tuna, wahoo, and mahimahi. ■TIP➔ A fishing license is necessary if you are fishing from a beach, dock, or pier. They are $11 for 14 days. Licenses aren't necessary on charter fishing boats because they already have their licenses.

FAMILY **Bay Runner Fishing Charters.** With more than four decades of experience fishing these waters, Captain Miles Altman takes anglers out for trips lasting three to eight hours. Evening shark trips are offered May to August. ✉ *Shelter Cove Marina, 1 Shelter Cove La., Mid-Island* ☎ *843/290–6955* ⊕ *www.bayrunnerfishinghiltonhead.com.*

FAMILY **Bulldog Fishing Charters.** Captain Christian offers his guests 4-, 6-, 8-, and 10-hour fishing tours on his 32-foot boat. ✉ *1 Hudson Rd., departs from docks at Hudson's Seafood House on the Docks, Mid-Island* ☎ *843/422–0887* ⊕ *bulldogfishingcharters.com.*

FAMILY
Fodor's Choice
★
Capt. Hook Party Boat. Deep-sea fishing tours are available on this large party boat, which sells concessions as well. The friendly crew teaches children how to bait hooks and reel in fish. ✉ *Shelter Cove Marina, 1 Shelter Cove La., Mid-Island* ☎ *843/785–1700* ⊕ *www.captainhookhiltonhead.com.*

FAMILY **Fishin' Coach.** Captain Dan Utley offers a variety of fishing tours on his 22-foot boat to catch redfish and other species year-round. ✉ *2 William Hilton Pkwy., North End* ☎ *843/368–2126* ⊕ *www.fishincoach.com.*

FAMILY **Gullah Gal Sport Fishing.** Fishing trips are available on a pair of 34-foot boats, the *Gullah Gal* and *True Grits.* ✉ *Shelter Cove Marina, 1 Shelter Cove La., Mid-Island* ☎ *843/842–7002* ⊕ *www.hiltonheadislandcharterfishing.com.*

FAMILY **Integrity.** The 38-foot charter boat *Integrity* offers offshore and near-shore fishing. ✉ *Harbour Town Yacht Basin, Mariners Way, Sea Pines, South End* ☎ *843/671–2704, 843/422–1221* ⊕ *www.integritycharterfishing.com.*

FAMILY **Palmetto Bay Charters.** This company offers a wide variety of charters on various size boats. ✉ *Palmetto Bay Marina, 86 Helmsman Way, South End* ☎ *843/785–7131.*

FAMILY **Palmetto Lagoon Charters.** Captain Trent Malphrus takes groups for half- or full-day excursions to the region's placid saltwater lagoons. Redfish, bluefish, flounder, and black drum are some of the most common trophy fish. ✉ *Shelter Cove Marina, 1 Shelter Cove La., Mid-Island* ☎ *866/301–4634* ⊕ *www.palmettolagooncharters.com.*

FAMILY **The Stray Cat.** The Stray Cat will help you decide whether you want to fish "in-shore" or go offshore into the deep blue. ✉ *2 Hudson Rd., North End* ☎ *843/683–5427* ⊕ *www.straycatcharter.com.*

GOLF

Hilton Head is nicknamed "Golf Island" for good reason: the island itself has 24 championship courses (public, semiprivate, and private), and the outlying area has 16 more. Each offers its own packages, some of which are great deals. Almost all charge the highest greens fees in the morning and lower fees as the day goes on. Lower rates can also be found in the hot summer months. It's essential to book tee times in advance, especially in the busy spring and fall months;

8

resort guests and club members get first choices. Most courses can be described as casual-classy, so you will have to adhere to certain rules of the greens. ■TIP➔ The dress code on island golf courses does not permit blue jeans, gym shorts, or jogging shorts. Men's shirts must have collars.

Fodor'sChoice
★

The Heritage PGA Tour Golf Tournament. The most internationally famed golf event in Hilton Head is the annual RBC Heritage PGA Tour Golf Tournament, held mid-April. There are a wide range of ticket packages available. Tickets are also available at the gate. ⊠ *Sea Pines Resort, 2 Lighthouse La., South End* ⊕ *www.rbcheritage.com.*

GOLF SCHOOLS

Golf Learning Center at Sea Pines Resort. The well-regarded golf academy offers hourly private lessons by PGA-trained professionals and one- to three-day clinics to help you perfect your game. ⊠ *Sea Pines, 100 N. Sea Pines Dr., South End* ☎ *843/785–4540* ⊕ *www.golfacademy.net.*

Palmetto Dunes Golf Academy. There's something for golfers of all ages at this academy: instructional videos, daily clinics, and multiday schools. Lessons are offered for ages three and up, and there are special programs for women. Free demonstrations are held with Doug Weaver, former PGA Tour pro and director of instruction for the academy. Take advantage of the free swing evaluation and club-fitting. ⊠ *Palmetto Dunes Oceanfront Resort, 7 Trent Jones La., Mid-Island* ☎ *843/785– 1138* ⊕ *www.palmettodunes.com.*

GOLF COURSES

Arthur Hills and Robert Cupp at Palmetto Hall. There are two prestigious courses at Palmetto Hall Plantation: Arthur Hills and Robert Cupp. Arthur Hills is a player favorite, with its trademark undulating fairways punctuated with lagoons and lined with moss-draped oaks and towering pines. Robert Cupp is a very challenging course, but is great for the higher handicappers as well. ⊠ *Palmetto Hall, 108 Fort Howell Dr., North End* ☎ *843/689–9205* ⊕ *www.palmettodunes.com* ▣ *$109* ⚲. *Arthur Hills: 18 holes, 6257 yds, par 72. Robert Cupp: 18 holes, 6025 yds, par 72.* ⚱ *Reservations essential.*

Country Club of Hilton Head. Although it's part of a country club, the course is open for public play. A well-kept secret, it's rarely too crowded. This 18-hole Rees Jones–designed course is a more casual environment than many of the other golf courses on Hilton Head. ⊠ *Hilton Head Plantation, 70 Skull Creek Dr., North End* ☎ *843/681–4653, 866/835–0093* ⊕ *www.clubcorp.com/Clubs/Country-Club-of-Hilton-Head* ▣ *$105* ⚲. *18 holes, 6543 yds, par 72.*

Golden Bear Golf Club at Indigo Run. Located in the upscale Indigo Run community, Golden Bear Golf Club was designed by golf legend Jack Nicklaus. The course's natural woodlands setting offers easygoing rounds. It requires more thought than muscle, yet you will have to earn every par you make. Though fairways are generous, you may end up with a lagoon looming smack ahead of the green on the approach shot. And there are the fine points—the color GPS monitor on every cart and women-friendly tees. After an honest, traditional test of golf, most golfers finish up at the plush clubhouse with some food and drink

The Golden Bear Golf Club at upscale Indigo Run was designed by Jack Nicklaus.

at Just Jack's Grille. ✉ *Indigo Run, 100 Indigo Run Dr., North End* ☎ *843/689–2200* ⊕ *www.goldenbear-indigorun.com* ▭ *$109* 🏌 *18 holes, 6643 yds, par 72.*

Fodor's Choice ★ **Harbour Town Golf Links.** Considered by many golfers to be one of those must-play-before-you-die courses, Harbour Town Golf Links is extremely well known because it has hosted the RBC Heritage Golf Tournament every spring for the last four decades. Designed by Pete Dye, the layout is reminiscent of Scottish courses of old. The Golf Academy at the Sea Pines Resort is ranked among the top 10 in the country. ✉ *Sea Pines Resort, 11 Lighthouse La., South End* ☎ *843/842–8484, 800/732–7463* ⊕ *www.seapines.com/golf* ▭ *$350* 🏌 *18 holes, 7099 yds, par 71* ⚐ *Reservations essential.*

Robert Trent Jones at Palmetto Dunes. One of the island's most popular layouts, this course's beauty and character are accentuated by the 10th hole, a par 5 that offers a panoramic view of the ocean (one of only two on the entire island). It's among the most beautiful courses in the Southeast, with glittering lagoons punctuating 11 of the 18 holes. ✉ *Palmetto Dunes, 7 Robert Trent Jones La., North End* ☎ *843/785–1138* ⊕ *www.palmettodunes.com* ▭ *$95* 🏌 *18 holes, 6570 yds, par 72* ⚐ *Reservations essential.*

BLUFFTON GOLF COURSES

There are several beautiful golf courses in Bluffton, which is just on the other side of the bridges to Hilton Head Island. These courses are very popular with locals and can often be cheaper to play than the courses on Hilton Head Island.

Crescent Pointe. An Arnold Palmer Signature Course, Crescent Pointe is fairly tough, with somewhat narrow fairways and rolling terrain. There are numerous sand traps, ponds, and lagoons, making for some demanding yet fun holes. Some of the par 3s are particularly challenging. The scenery is magnificent, with large live oaks, pine-tree stands, and rolling fairways. Additionally, several holes have spectacular marsh views. ⊠ *Crescent Pointe, 1 Crescent Pointe, Bluffton* ☎ *843/706–2600* ⊕ *www.crescentpointegolf.com* ⊠ *$52–$63* 🏌 *18 holes, 6447 yds, par 71.*

Eagle's Pointe. This Davis Love III–designed course—located in the Eagle's Pointe community in Bluffton—is one of the area's most playable. Eagle's Pointe attracts many women golfers because of its women-friendly tees, spacious fairways, and large greens. There are quite a few bunkers and lagoons throughout the course, which winds through a natural woodlands setting that attracts an abundance of wildlife. ⊠ *Eagle's Pointe, 1 Eagle's Pointe Dr., Bluffton* ☎ *843/757–5900* ⊕ *www.eaglespointegolf.com* ⊠ *$35–$55* 🏌 *18 holes, 6399 yds, par 72.*

Island West Golf Club. Fuzzy Zoeller and golf course designer Clyde Johnston designed this stunningly beautiful course set amid the natural surroundings at Island West. There are majestic live oaks, plenty of wildlife, and expansive marsh views on several holes. Golfers of all skill levels can find success on this succession of undulating fairways. There are several holes where the fairways are rather generous, while others can be demanding. This is a fun and challenging course for golfers of all handicaps. ⊠ *Island West, 40 Island West Dr., Bluffton* ☎ *843/689–6660* ⊕ *www.islandwestgolf.net* ⊠ *$35–$45* 🏌 *18 holes, 6208 yds, par 72.*

Fodor's Choice ★ **The May River Golf Club.** An 18-hole Jack Nicklaus course, this has several holes along the banks of the scenic May River and will challenge all skill levels. The greens are Champion Bermuda grass and the fairways are covered by Paspalum, the latest eco-friendly turf. Caddy service is always required. No carts are allowed earlier than 9 am to encourage walking. ⊠ *Palmetto Bluff, 476 Mount Pelia Rd., Bluffton* ☎ *843/706–6500* ⊕ *www.palmettobluff.com* ⊠ *$315* 🏌 *18 holes, 7171 yds, par 72* ⌕ *Reservations essential.*

Old South Golf Links. There are many scenic holes overlooking marshes and the intracoastal waterway at this Clyde Johnson–designed course. It's a public course, but that hasn't stopped it from winning awards. It's reasonably priced, and reservations are recommended. ⊠ *50 Buckingham Plantation Dr., Bluffton* ☎ *843/785–5353* ⊕ *www.oldsouthgolf.com* ⊠ *$60–$75* 🏌 *18 holes, 6772 yds, par 72.*

PARASAILING

For those looking for a bird's-eye view of Hilton Head, it doesn't get better than parasailing. Newcomers will get a lesson in safety before taking off. Parasailers are then strapped into a harness, and as the boat takes off, the parasailer is lifted about 500 feet into the sky.

FAMILY **H2O Sports.** You can soar above Hilton Head and can check out the views up to 25 miles in all directions with this popular company located in Sea Pines. ✉ *149 Lighthouse Rd., Sea Pines, South End* ☎ *843/671–4386, 877/290–4386* ⊕ *www.h2osports.com.*

FAMILY

Fodor'sChoice

★

Parasail Hilton Head. You can glide 500 feet in the air over Palmetto Bay Marina and Broad Creek on a trip with this company. ✉ *Broad Creek Marina, 18 Simmons Rd., Mid-Island* ☎ *843/842–2566* ⊕ *www. parasailhiltonhead.com.*

TENNIS

There are more than 300 courts on Hilton Head. Tennis comes in at a close second as the island's premier sport after golf. It is recognized as one of the nation's best tennis destinations. Hilton Head has a large international organization of coaches. ■**TIP➜ Spring and fall are the peak seasons for cooler play, with numerous tennis packages available at the resorts and through the schools.**

FAMILY

Fodor'sChoice

★

Palmetto Dunes Tennis & Pickleball Center. Ranked among the best in the world, this facility at the Palmetto Dunes Oceanfront Resort has 26 clay tennis courts (six of which are lighted for night play) and eight pickleball courts. There are lessons geared to players of every skill level given by enthusiastic staffers. Daily round-robin tournaments add to the festive atmosphere. ✉ *Palmetto Dunes Oceanfront Resort, 6 Trent Jones La., Mid-Island* ☎ *843/785–1152* ⊕ *www.palmettodunes.com.*

FAMILY **Port Royal Racquet Club.** The occasional magnolia tree dots the grounds of the Port Royal Racquet Club, which has 10 clay and four hard courts. The professional staff, stadium seating, and frequent tournaments are why it is ranked among the best in the world. ✉ *Port Royal Plantation, 15 Wimbledon Court, Mid-Island* ☎ *843/686–8803* ⊕ *www.portroyalgolfclub.com.*

FAMILY **Sea Pines Racquet Club.** The highly rated club has 21 clay courts, as well as instructional programs and a pro shop. There are special deals for guests of Sea Pines. ✉ *5 Lighthouse La., Sea Pines Resort, South End* ☎ *843/363–4495* ⊕ *www.seapines.com/tennis.*

Fodor'sChoice

★

Van der Meer Tennis Center. Recognized for its tennis instruction for players of all ages and skill levels, this highly rated club in Shipyard Plantation has 17 hard courts, four of which are covered and lighted for night play. The Van der Meer Tennis Center also offers courts at the Shipyard Racquet Club, which has 20 courts. ✉ *19 DeAllyon Ave., Shipyard Plantation, South End* ☎ *800/845–6138* ⊕ *www.vandermeertennis.com.*

ZIPLINE TOURS

FAMILY

Fodor'sChoice

★

ZipLine Hilton Head. Take a thrilling tour of Hilton Head on a zipline over ponds and marshes and past towering oaks and pines. This company offers eight ziplines, two suspended sky bridges, and a dual-cable racing zipline. Guests are harnessed and helmeted, and must be at least 10 years old and weigh between 80 and 250 pounds. ✉ *33 Broad Creek Marina Way, Mid-Island* ☎ *843/682–6000* ⊕ *ziplinehiltonhead.com.*

8

SHOPPING

Hilton Head is a great destination for those who love shopping, starting with the Tanger outlet malls. Although they're officially in Bluffton, visitors drive by the outlets on U.S. 278 to get to Hilton Head Island. Tanger Outlet I has been completely renovated and reopened with many high-end stores, including Saks OFF 5th, DKNY, Michael Kors, and more.

ART GALLERIES

Fodor's Choice ★ **Ben Ham Images.** The extraordinary photography of Ben Ham focuses on Lowcountry landscapes. ⊠ *90 Capital Dr., Suite 104, Mid-Island* ☎ *843/842–4163* ⊕ *www.benhamimages.com.*

Red Piano Gallery. Original art by contemporary artists can be found at this upscale gallery. ⊠ *220 Cordillo Pkwy., Mid-Island* ☎ *843/842–4433* ⊕ *redpianoartgallery.com.*

Walter Greer Gallery. Part of the Arts Center of Coastal Carolina, this modern gallery showcases local artists. ⊠ *Arts Center of Coastal Carolina, 14 Shelter Cove La., Mid-Island* ☎ *843/681–5060* ⊕ *www.artshhi.com/greer-gallery.*

GIFTS

Fodor's Choice ★ **Markel's.** The very helpful and friendly staff at Markel's is known for wrapping gifts with giant bows. You'll find unique Lowcountry gifts, including hand-painted wineglasses and beer mugs, lawn ornaments, baby gifts, greeting cards, and more. ⊠ *1008 Fording Island Rd., Bluffton* ☎ *843/815–9500* ⊕ *www.markelsgifts.com.*

Pretty Papers. Fine stationery and gifts are available at Pretty Papers. ⊠ *The Village at Wexford, 1000 William Hilton Pkwy., Suite E7, Mid-Island* ☎ *843/341–5116* ۻ *Closed Sun.*

Fodor's Choice ★ **Salty Dog T-Shirt Factory.** You can't leave Hilton Head without a Salty Dog T-shirt, so hit this factory store for the best deals. The iconic T-shirts are hard to resist, and there are lots of choices for kids and adults in various colors and styles. ⊠ *69 Arrow Rd., South End* ☎ *843/842–6331* ⊕ *www.saltydog.com.*

FAMILY **The Storybook Shoppe.** Charming, whimsical, and sweet describe this children's bookstore. It has a darling area for little ones to read as well as educational toys for infants to teens. ⊠ *41A Calhoun St., Bluffton* ☎ *843/757–2600* ⊕ *www.thestorybookshoppe.com* ۻ *Closed Sun.*

FAMILY **Top of the Lighthouse Shop.** The Hilton Head Lighthouse is the island's iconic symbol, and this shop celebrates the red-and-white-striped landmark. ⊠ *149 Lighthouse Rd., Sea Pines, South End* ☎ *866/305–9814* ⊕ *www.harbourtownlighthouse.com/shop.*

JEWELRY

Bird's Nest. Local handmade jewelry, accessories, and island-themed charms are available at this popular spot. ⊠ *Coligny Plaza, 1 N. Forest Beach Dr., #21, South End* ☎ *843/785–3737* ⊕ *www.thebirdsnesthiltonhead.com.*

Forsythe Jewelers. This is the island's leading jewelry store, offering pieces by famous designers. ⊠ *71 Lighthouse Rd., Sea Pines, South End* ☎ *843/671–7070* ⊕ *www.forsythejewelers.biz* ۻ *Closed Sun.*

Goldsmith Shop. Classic jewelry, much of it with island themes, is on sale at the Goldsmith Shop. ⊠ *3 Lagoon Rd., South End* ☎ *843/785–2538* ⊕ *www.thegoldsmithshop.com.*

MALLS AND SHOPPING CENTERS

Coligny Plaza. Things are always humming at this shopping center, which is within walking distance of the most popular beach on Hilton Head. Coligny Plaza has more than 60 shops and restaurants, including unique clothing boutiques, souvenir shops, and the expansive Piggly Wiggly grocery store. There are also bike rentals and free family entertainment throughout summer. ⊠ *Coligny Circle, 1 N. Forest Beach Dr., South End* ☎ *843/842–6050.*

FAMILY **Harbour Town.** Distinguished by a candy-striped lighthouse, Harbour Town wraps around a marina and has plenty of shops selling colorful T-shirts, casual resort wear, and beach-themed souvenirs. ⊠ *Sea Pines, 32 Greenwood Dr., South End* ☎ *866/561–8802* ⊕ *www.seapines.com/recreation/harbour-town.*

FAMILY **Old Town Bluffton.** A charming area, Old Town features local artist galleries, antiques, and restaurants. ⊠ *Downtown Bluffton, May River Rd. and Calhoun St., Bluffton* ☎ *843/706–4500* ⊕ *www.oldtownbluffton.com.*

Shops at Sea Pines Center. Clothing for men and women, the best local crafts, and fine antiques are the draw at this outdoor shopping center. You can even get a massage at the on-site day spa. ⊠ *71 Lighthouse Rd., South End* ☎ *843/363–6800* ⊕ *www.theshopsatseapinescenter.com.*

South Beach Marina. Looking like a New England fishing village, South Beach Marina is the place for beach-friendly fashions. ⊠ *232 South Sea Pines Dr., South End.*

Fodor's Choice **Tanger Outlets.** There are two halves to this popular shopping center: ★ Tanger Outlet I has more than 40 upscale stores, as well as popular eateries like Olive Garden, Panera Bread, and Longhorn Steakhouse. Tanger Outlet II has Abercrombie & Fitch, Banana Republic, the Gap, and Nike, along with 60 others stores. There are also several children's stores, including Gymboree, Carter's, and Baby Gap. ⊠ *1414 Fording Island Rd., Bluffton* ☎ *843/837–5410, 866/665–8679* ⊕ *www.tangeroutlet.com/hiltonhead.*

The Village at Wexford. Upscale shops, including Lilly Pulitzer and Le Cookery, as well as several fine-dining restaurants can be found in this shopping area. There are also some unique gift shops and luxe clothing stores. ⊠ *1000 William Hilton Pkwy., Hilton Head Island* ⊕ *www.villageatwexford.com.*

SPAS

Spa visits have become a recognized activity on the island, and for some people they are as popular as golf and tennis. In fact, spas have become one of the top leisure-time destinations, particularly for "golf widows." And this popularity extends to the men as well; previously spa-shy guys have come around, enticed by couples massage, deep-tissue sports massage, and even the pleasures of the manicure and pedicure.

8

There are East Indian–influenced therapies, hot-stone massage, Hungarian organic facials—the treatments span the globe. Do your research, go online, and call or stop by the various spas and ask the locals their favorites. The therapists island-wide are noteworthy for their training, certifications, and expertise.

Faces. This place has been pampering loyal clients for more than three decades, thanks to body therapists, stylists, and cosmetologists who really know their stuff. Choose from the line of fine cosmetics, enjoy a manicure and pedicure, or have a professional do your evening makeup for that special occasion. ⊠ *The Village at Wexford, 1000 William Hilton Pkwy., South End* ☎ *843/785–3075* ⊕ *www.facesdayspa.com.*

Fodor'sChoice **Heavenly Spa by Westin.** This is the quintessential spa experience on
★   Hilton Head. Known internationally for its innovative treatments, the Heavenly Spa incorporates local traditions. Prior to a treatment, clients are told to put their worries in a basket woven from local sweetgrass; de-stressing is a major component of the therapies here. The relaxation room with its teas and healthy snacks and the adjacent retail area with products like sweetgrass scents are heavenly, too. In-room spa services are available, as are romance packages. ⊠ *Westin Resort Hilton Head Island, 2 Grasslawn Ave., Port Royal Plantation, North End* ☎ *843/681–1019* ⊕ *www.westinhiltonheadisland.com.*

Spa Montage Palmetto Bluff. Dubbed the "celebrity spa" by locals, this two-story facility is the ultimate pamper palace. The names of the treatments, which often have a Southern accent, are almost as creative as the treatments themselves. There are Amazing Grace and The Deep South body therapies, and sensual soaks and couples massage. The spa also offers a variety of other services, including pedicures and manicures, facials and other skin treatments, and a hair salon. ⊠ *Palmetto Bluff, 1 Village Park Sq., Bluffton* ☎ *843/706–6270* ⊕ *spamontage.com.*

Spa Soleil. A wide variety of massages and other treatments are offered at Spa Soleil. The tantalizing teas and snacks make your time here a soothing, therapeutic experience. This is an amazing island treasure. ⊠ *Hilton Head Marriott Resort & Spa, 1 Hotel Circle, Palmetto Dunes, Mid-Island* ☎ *843/686–8420* ⊕ *www.marriott.com/hotels/travel/ hhhgr-hilton-head-marriott-resort-and-spa.*

BEAUFORT

38 miles north of Hilton Head via U.S. 278 and Rte. 170; 70 miles southwest of Charleston via U.S. 17 and U.S. 21.

Charming homes and churches grace this old town on Port Royal Island. Come here on a day trip from Hilton Head, Savannah, or Charleston, or to spend a quiet weekend at a B&B while you shop and stroll through the historic district. Beaufort continues to gain recognition as an art town and supports a large number of galleries for its diminutive size. Visitors are drawn equally to the town's artsy scene and to the area's water-sports possibilities. The annual Beaufort Water Festival, which takes place over 10 days in July, is the premier event. For a calendar of Beaufort's annual events, check out ⊕ *www.beaufortsc.org.*

More and more transplants have decided to spend the rest of their lives here, drawn to Beaufort's small-town charms, and the area is burgeoning. A truly Southern town, its picturesque backdrops have lured filmmakers here to shoot *The Big Chill, The Prince of Tides,* and *The Great Santini,* the last two being Hollywood adaptations of best-selling books by the late author Pat Conroy. Conroy waxed poetic about the Lowcountry and called the Beaufort area home.

To support Beaufort's growing status as a tourist destination, it has doubled the number of hotels in recent years. Military events like the frequent graduations (traditionally Wednesday and Thursday) at the marine base on Parris Island tie up rooms.

GETTING HERE AND AROUND

Beaufort is 25 miles east of Interstate 95, on U.S. 21. The only way to get here is by private car or Greyhound bus.

ESSENTIALS

Well-maintained public restrooms are available at the Beaufort Visitors Center. You can't miss this former arsenal; a crenellated, fortlike structure, it is now beautifully restored and painted ocher.

The Beaufort County Black Chamber of Commerce (⊕ *www.bcbcc. org*) puts out an African American visitor's guide, which takes in the surrounding Lowcountry. The Beaufort Visitors Center gives out copies.

Visitor Information Beaufort Visitors Center. ⊠ *713 Craven St., Beaufort* ☎ *843/525–8500* ⊕ *www.beaufortsc.org.* **Beaufort Regional Chamber of Commerce.** ⊠ *1106 Carteret St., Beaufort* ☎ *843/525–8500* ⊕ *www.beaufort-chamber.org.*

EXPLORING

TOP ATTRACTIONS

FAMILY
Fodor'sChoice
★
Henry C. Chambers Waterfront Park. Off Bay Street, this park is a great place to survey the scene. Trendy restaurants and bars overlook these 7 beautifully landscaped acres along the Beaufort River. At night everyone strolls along the river walk. ⊠ *1006 Bay St., Beaufort* ☎ *843/525–7000* ⊕ *www.cityofbeaufort.org.*

Fodor'sChoice
★
Parish Church of St. Helena. The 1724 church was turned into a hospital during the Civil War, and gravestones were brought inside to serve as operating tables. While on church grounds stroll the peaceful cemetery and read the fascinating inscriptions. ⊠ *505 Church St., Beaufort* ☎ *843/522–1712* ⊕ *www.sthelenas1712.org.*

St. Helena Island. About 9 miles southeast of Beaufort, St. Helena Island is a stronghold of the Gullah culture. Several African American–owned businesses in its tight-knit community of Frogmore make this quite the tourist magnet. ⊠ *Rte. 21, St. Helena Island* ⊕ *www.beaufortsc.org/ area/st.-helena-island.*

FAMILY
York W. Bailey Museum. The museum at the Penn Center has displays on the heritage of Sea Island African Americans; it also has pleasant grounds shaded by live oaks. Dating from 1862, Penn Center was the

The World of Gullah

In the Lowcountry, Gullah refers to several things: a language, a people, and a culture. Gullah (the word itself is believed to be derived from *Angola*), an English-based dialect rooted in African languages, is the unique language, more than 300 years old, of the African Americans of the Sea Islands of South Carolina and Georgia. Most locally born African Americans of the area can understand, if not speak, Gullah.

GULLAH HISTORY

Descended from thousands of slaves who were imported by planters in the Carolinas during the 18th century, the Gullah people have maintained not only their dialect but also their heritage. Much of Gullah culture traces back to the African rice-coast culture and survives today in the art forms and skills, including sweetgrass basket making, of Sea Islanders. During the colonial period, when rice was king, Africans from the West African rice kingdoms drew high premiums as slaves. Those with basket-making skills were extremely valuable because baskets were needed for agricultural and household use. Made by hand, sweetgrass baskets are intricate coils of marsh grass with a sweet, haylike aroma.

GULLAH FOOD

Nowhere is Gullah culture more evident than in the foods of the region. Rice appears at nearly every meal—Africans taught planters how to grow rice and how to cook and serve it as well. Lowcountry dishes use okra, peanuts, *benne* (a word of African origin for sesame seeds), field peas, and hot peppers. Gullah food reflects the bounty of the islands: shrimp, crabs, oysters, fish, and such vegetables as greens, tomatoes, and corn. Many dishes are prepared in one pot, a method similar to the stewpot cooking of West Africa.

GULLAH TODAY

On St. Helena Island, near Beaufort, Penn Center is the unofficial Gullah headquarters, preserving the culture and developing opportunities for Gullahs. In 1852 the first school for freed slaves was established at Penn Center. You can delve into the culture further at the York W. Bailey Museum.

On St. Helena, many Gullahs still go shrimping with hand-tied nets, harvest oysters, and grow their own vegetables. Nearby on Daufuskie Island, as well as on Edisto, Wadmalaw, and John's islands near Charleston, you can find Gullah communities. A famous Gullah proverb says, "*If oonuh ent kno weh oonuh dah gwine, oonuh should kno weh oonuh come f'um.*" Translation: "If you don't know where you're going, you should know where you've come from."

first school for the newly emancipated slaves. These islands are where Gullah, a musical language that combines English and African languages, developed. This museum and the surrounding community of St. Helena Island are a major stop for anyone interested in the Gullah history and culture of the Lowcountry. ⊠ *16 Penn Center Circle W, St. Helena Island* ☎ *843/838–2432* ⊕ *www.penncenter.com* ✉ *$5.*

WORTH NOTING

Barefoot Farm. Check out this farm stand for perfect watermelons, rhubarb, and strawberry jam. ✉ *939 Sea Island Pkwy., St. Helena Island* ☎ *843/838–7421.*

John Mark Verdier House Museum. Built in the Federal style, this 1804 house has been restored and furnished as it would have been prior to a visit by Marquis de Lafayette in 1825. It was the headquarters for Union forces during the Civil War. ✉ *801 Bay St., Downtown Historic District* ☎ *843/379–6335* 🌐 *historicbeaufort.org* 🎟 *$10* 🕒 *Closed Sun.*

WHERE TO EAT

$$$$ ECLECTIC Fodor's Choice ★ 🍴 **Breakwater Restaurant & Bar.** This downtown restaurant offers small tasting plates such as tuna tartare and fried shrimp, but if you prefer not to share there are main dishes like lamb meat loaf and filet mignon with a truffle demi-glace. The presentation is as contemporary as the decor. **Known for:** contemporary approach to Lowcountry cuisine; elegant atmosphere. [$] *Average main: $30* ✉ *203 Carteret St., Downtown Historic District* ☎ *843/379–0052* 🌐 *www.breakwatersc.com* 🕒 *Closed Sun. No lunch.*

$$ AMERICAN 🍴 **Johnson Creek Tavern.** There are times when you just want a cold one accompanied by some raw oysters. Head to Johnson Creek Tavern and sit outside to take advantage of the marsh views. **Known for:** decorated dollar bills stapled to the wall; fresh seafood; $1 happy hour beers. [$] *Average main: $19* ✉ *2141 Sea Island Pkwy., Harbor Island* ☎ *843/838–4166* 🌐 *www.johnsoncreektavern.com.*

$$$ AMERICAN 🍴 **Plums.** This hip restaurant began its life in 1986 in a homey frame house with plum-color awnings shading the front porch. An oyster bar that looks out to Bay Street, Plums still uses old family recipes for its soups, crab-cake sandwiches, and curried chicken salad. **Known for:** raw bar; inventive burgers, sandwiches for lunch; sophisticated dinner menu. [$] *Average main: $22* ✉ *904 Bay St., Downtown Historic District* ☎ *843/525–1946* 🌐 *www.plumsrestaurant.com.*

$$$$ AMERICAN Fodor's Choice ★ 🍴 **Saltus River Grill.** The hippest eatery in Beaufort, Saltus River Grill wins over diners with its sailing motifs, breezy patio, and modern Southern menu. The bar opens at 4 pm, as does the raw bar with its tempting array of oysters and sushi specials. **Known for:** signature she-crab soup; steaks, seafood, and sushi; breathtaking views. [$] *Average main: $32* ✉ *802 Bay St., Downtown Historic District* ☎ *843/379–3474* 🌐 *www.saltusrivergrill.com* 🕒 *No lunch.*

WHERE TO STAY

Even though accommodations in Beaufort have increased in number, prime lodgings can fill up fast, so do call ahead.

$$$ B&B/INN 🏨 **Beaufort Inn.** This 1890s Victorian inn charms you with its handsome gables and wraparound verandas. **Pros:** in the heart of the historic district; beautifully landscaped space. **Cons:** atmosphere in the main building may feel too dated for those seeking a more contemporary

hotel; no water views. $ *Rooms from: $209* ✉ *809 Port Republic St., Downtown Historic District* ☎ *843/379–4667* ⊕ *www.beaufortinn.com* ⊲ *32 rooms, 4 apartments* ⦿ *Breakfast.*

$$$ 🛏 **Beaulieu House.** From the French for "beautiful place," Beaulieu

B&B/INN House is the only waterfront bed-and-breakfast in Beaufort on Cat Island—it's a quiet, relaxing inn with airy rooms decorated in Caribbean colors. **Pros:** great views; scrumptious gourmet hot breakfast; short drive to Beaufort historic district. **Cons:** thin walls; hot water can be a problem; a bit off the beaten path. $ *Rooms from: $205* ✉ *3 Sheffield Ct., Beaufort* ☎ *843/770–0303* ⊕ *beaulieuhouse.com* ⊲ *5 rooms* ⦿ *Breakfast.*

$$ 🛏 **Best Western Sea Island Inn.** This well-maintained motel in the heart of

HOTEL the Historic District puts you within walking distance of many shops and restaurants. **Pros:** only swimming pool in downtown Beaufort; directly across from marina and an easy walk to art galleries and restaurants; breakfast included. **Cons:** air-conditioning is loud in some rooms; breakfast room can be noisy. $ *Rooms from: $179* ✉ *1015 Bay St., Beaufort* ☎ *843/522–2090* ⊕ *www.sea-island-inn.com* ⊲ *43 rooms* ⦿ *Breakfast.*

$$ 🛏 **City Loft Hotel.** This 1960s-era motel was cleverly transformed by its

HOTEL hip, young owners to reflect their high-tech, minimalist style. **Pros:** stylish decor; use of the adjacent gym; very accommodating staff. **Cons:** the sliding Asian screen that separates the bathroom doesn't offer full privacy; no lobby or public spaces. $ *Rooms from: $189* ✉ *301 Carteret St., Downtown Historic District* ☎ *843/379–5638* ⊕ *www.citylofthotel. com* ⊲ *22 rooms* ⦿ *No meals.*

$$$ 🛏 **Cuthbert House Inn.** Named after the original Scottish owners, who

B&B/INN made their money in cotton and indigo, this 1790 home is filled with 18th- and 19th-century heirlooms and retains the original Federal fireplaces and crown and rope molding. **Pros:** owners are accommodating; complimentary wine and hors d'oeuvres service; great walk-about location. **Cons:** some furnishings are a bit busy; some artificial flower arrangements; stairs creak. $ *Rooms from: $225* ✉ *1203 Bay St., Downtown Historic District* ☎ *843/521–1315* ⊕ *www.cuthberthouse-inn.com* ⊲ *7 rooms, 3 suites* ⦿ *Breakfast.*

$$ 🛏 **Two Suns Inn.** With its unobstructed bay views and wraparound

B&B/INN veranda complete with porch swing, this historic home—built in 1917 by an immigrant Lithuanian merchant—offers a distinctive Beaufort experience. **Pros:** most appealing is the Charleston room, with its own screened-porch and water views; it's truly peaceful. **Cons:** decor is unsophisticated; although on Bay Street it's a bike ride or short drive downtown; third-floor skylight room is cheapest but least desirable. $ *Rooms from: $169* ✉ *1705 Bay St., Downtown Historic District* ☎ *843/522–1122, 800/532–4244* ⊕ *www.twosunsinn.com* ⊲ *6 rooms* ⦿ *Breakfast.*

FRIPP ISLAND

There are more than 200 private villas for rent on Fripp Island (but no hotels). Fripp Island Golf & Beach Resort (⊕ *www.frippislandresort. com*) offers a range of rental options, including homes, villas, and golf cottages, many with oceanfront or golf views.

$$$$ RESORT FAMILY 🏨 **Fripp Island Resort.** On the island made famous in *Prince of Tides*, with 3½ miles of broad, white beach and unspoiled scenery, this resort has long been known as one of the more affordable and casual on the island. **Pros:** fun for all ages; the beach bar has great frozen drinks and live music; two golf courses: Ocean Creek and Ocean Point. **Cons:** far from Beaufort; some dated decor; could use another restaurant with contemporary cuisine. [$] *Rooms from: $374* ✉ *1 Tarpon Blvd., Fripp Island* ✣ *19 miles south of Beaufort* ☎ *855/602–5893* 🌐 *www.frippislandresort.com* 🛏 *210 units* 🍴 *No meals.*

NIGHTLIFE

Emily's. This fun hangout is populated with locals who graze on tapas while eyeing one of the four wide-screen TVs. The piano sits idle until a random patron sits down and impresses the crowd. The bar is full of local characters. There is a separate dining room. ✉ *906 Port Republic St., Downtown Historic District* ☎ *843/522–1866* 🌐 *www.emilysrestaurantandtapasbar.com.*

Luther's. A late-night waterfront hangout, Luther's is casual and fun, with a young crowd watching the big-screen TVs or dancing to rock music live bands on Thursday, Friday, and Saturday nights. Luther's also has a terrific late-night menu. The decor features exposed brick, pine paneling, and old-fashioned posters on the walls. ✉ *910 Bay St., Downtown Historic District* ☎ *843/521–1888.*

SPORTS AND THE OUTDOORS

BEACHES

FAMILY Fodor's Choice ★ **Hunting Island State Park.** This secluded park 18 miles southeast of Beaufort has 4 miles of public beaches—some dramatically eroding. The light sand beach decorated with driftwood and the subtropical vegetation is breathtaking. The state park was founded in 1938 to preserve and promote the area's natural wonders, and it harbors 5,000 acres of rare maritime forests. You can kayak in the tranquil lagoon; stroll the 1,300-foot-long fishing pier (among the longest on the East Coast); and go fishing or crabbing. For sweeping views, climb the 167 steps of the 1859 **Hunting Island Lighthouse**. Bikers and hikers can enjoy 8 miles of trails. The nature center has exhibits, an aquarium, and lots of turtles; there is a resident alligator in the pond. **Amenities:** none. **Best for:** solitude; sunrise; swimming; walking. ✉ *2555 Sea Island Pkwy., St. Helena Island* ☎ *866/345–7275* 🌐 *www.southcarolinaparks.com* 🎟 *$5.*

BIKING

Beaufort looks different from two wheels. In town, traffic is moderate, and you can cruise along the waterfront and through the historic district. However, if you ride on the sidewalks or after dark without a headlight and a rear red reflector, you run the risk of a city fine of nearly $150. If you stopped for happy hour and come out as the light is fading, walk your bike back "home." Some inns lend or rent out bikes to guests, but alas, they may not be in great shape and usually were not the best even when new. ■ **TIP→ The Spanish Moss Trail is the perfect place to ride bikes.**

FAMILY   **Lowcountry Bicycles.** If you want a decent set of wheels, contact Low-country Bicycles. Bikes are $8 an hour or $25 a day. ⊠ *102 Sea Island Pkwy., Beaufort* ☎ *843/524–9585* ⊕ *www.lowcountrybicycles.com.*

FAMILY   **Spanish Moss Trail.** The trail, which opened in 2016, is the Lowcountry's answer to the Rails to Trail movement. This nearly 10-mile trail (14 miles when complete) currently connects Beaufort, Port Royal, and Burton. It's open to walkers, runners, bikers, fishers, skaters, and scooters and offers great water and marsh views as well as opportunities to view coastal wildlife and historic landmarks. ■ TIP➜ **The website offers a downloadable trail guide.** ⊠ *Beaufort* ⊕ *spanishmosstrail.com.*

BOATING

Beaufort is where the Ashepoo, Combahee, and Edisto rivers form the A.C.E. Basin, a vast wilderness of marshes and tidal estuaries loaded with history. For sea kayaking, tourists meet at the designated launching areas for fully guided, two-hour tours.

FAMILY   **Barefoot Bubba's.** Less than 1 mile from Hunting Island, Barefoot Bubba's rents bikes and kayaks and will deliver them to the park or anywhere in the area. ⊠ *2135 Sea Island Pkwy., St. Helena Island* ☎ *843/838–9222* ⊕ *barefootbubbasurfshop.com.*

FAMILY   **Beaufort Kayak Tours.** Owner-operators Kim and David Gundler of Beaufort Kayak Tours are degreed naturalists and certified historical guides.
Fodor's Choice   The large cockpits in the kayaks make for easy accessibility and the
★   tours go with the tides, not against them, so paddling isn't strenuous. The tours meet at various public landings throughout Beaufort County. ☎ *843/525–0810* ⊕ *www.beaufortkayaktours.com* ✉ *$50.*

GOLF

Most golf courses are about a 10- to 20-minute scenic drive from Beaufort.

Dataw Island. This upscale island community is home to Tom Fazio's Cotton Dike golf course, with spectacular marsh views, and Arthur Hill's Morgan River golf course, with ponds, marshes, and wide-open fairways. The lovely 14th hole of the latter overlooks the river. To play you must be accompanied by a member or belong to another private club. ⊠ *100 Dataw Club Rd., Dataw Island* ✛ *6 miles east of Beaufort* ☎ *843/838–8250* ⊕ *www.dataw.org* ✉ *$69–$120* ⅞*. Cotton Dike: 18 holes, 6787 yds, par 72. Morgan River: 18 holes, 6657 yds, par 72.*

Fripp Island Golf & Beach Resort. This resort has a pair of championship courses. Ocean Creek Golf Course, designed by Davis Love, has sweeping views of saltwater marshes. Designed by George Cobb, Ocean Point Golf Links runs alongside the ocean the entire way. This is a wildlife refuge, so you'll see plenty of animals, particularly the graceful marsh deer. In fact, the wildlife and ocean views may make it difficult for you to keep your eyes on the ball. To play, nonguests must belong to a private golf club. ⊠ *2119 Sea Island Pkwy., Fripp Island* ☎ *843/838–3535, 843/838–1576* ⊕ *www.frippislandresort.com* ✉ *$75–$99* ⅞*. Ocean Creek: 18 holes, 6613 yds, par 71. Ocean Point: 18 holes, 6556 yds, par 72.*

Sanctuary Golf Club at Cat Island. This is a semiprivate club, so members get priority. Its scenic course is considered tight with plenty of water hazards. ✉ *Cat Island, 8 Waveland Ave., Beaufort* ☎ *843/524–0300* ⊕ *catisland-sanctuarygolf.com* ⌦ *$40–$80* ⛳ *18 holes, 6673 yds, par 72.*

SHOPPING

ART GALLERIES

Longo Gallery. The colorful designs of Suzanne and Eric Longo decorate the Longo Gallery. Suzanne creates ceramic sculpture—couples dancing and mothers with children are among her favorite motifs. Eric's whimsical paintings often feature fish. ✉ *103 Charles St., Downtown Historic District* ☎ *843/522–8933.*

Fodor'sChoice ★ **Red Piano Too Gallery.** More than 150 Lowcountry artists are represented at the Red Piano Too Gallery, considered one of the area's best (if not the best) art spaces. It carries folk art, books, fine art, and much more. Much of the art at the gallery represents the Gullah culture. ✉ *870 Sea Island Pkwy., St. Helena Island* ☎ *843/838–2241* ⊕ *redpianotoo.com.*

Rhett Gallery. The Rhett Gallery sells Lowcountry art by four generations of the Rhett family, including remarkable wood carvings. There are also antique maps, books, Civil War memorabilia, and Audubon prints. ✉ *901 Bay St., Downtown Historic District* ☎ *843/524–3339* ⊕ *rhettgallery.com.*

DAUFUSKIE ISLAND

8

13 miles (approximately 45 minutes) from Hilton Head via ferry.

From Hilton Head you can take a 45-minute ferry ride to nearby Daufuskie Island, the setting for Pat Conroy's novel *The Water Is Wide,* which was made into the movie *Conrack.* The boat ride may very well be one of the highlights of your vacation. The Lowcountry beauty unfolds before you, as pristine and unspoiled as you can imagine. The island is in the Atlantic, nestled between Hilton Head and Savannah. Many visitors come just for the day to have lunch or dinner; kids might enjoy biking or horseback riding. On weekends, the tiki hut at Freeport Marina whirrs out frozen concoctions as a vocalist sings or a band plays reggae and rock and roll. The island also has acres of unspoiled beauty. On a bike, in a golf cart, or on horseback, you can easily explore the island. You will find remnants of churches, homes, and schools—some reminders of antebellum times. Guided tours include such sights as an 18th-century cemetery, former slave quarters, a "praise house," an 1886 African Baptist church, the schoolhouse where Pat Conroy taught, and the Haig Point Lighthouse. There are a number of small, artsy shops like the Iron Fish Gallery.

GETTING HERE AND AROUND

The only way to get to Daufuskie is by boat, as it is a bridgeless island. The public ferry departs from Broad Creek Marina on Hilton Head Island several times a day. On arrival to Daufuskie you can rent a golf cart (not a car) or bicycle or take a tour. Golf carts are the best way to get around on the island. Enjoy Daufuskie (⊕ *www.enjoydaufuskie. com*) offers golf cart rentals to tourists when they come to visit. If you are coming to Daufuskie Island for a multiday stay with luggage and/or groceries, and perhaps a dog, be absolutely certain that you allow a full hour to park and check in for the ferry, particularly on a busy summer weekend. Whether you are staying on island or just day-tripping, the ferry costs $25 round-trip. Usually the first two pieces of luggage are free, and then it is $10 apiece.

Freeport Marina, where the public ferry disembarks on Daufuskie Island, includes the Freeport General Store, a restaurant, overnight cabins, and more. A two-hour bus tour of the island by local historians will become a true travel memory. The ferry returns to Hilton Head Island on Tuesday night in time to watch the fireworks at Shelter Cove at sundown.

Live Oac, based on Hilton Head, is an owner-operated company that offers Lowcountry water adventures such as nature tours, fishing excursions, and dolphin cruises. On its first-class hurricane-deck boats you are sheltered from sun and rain; tours, usually private charters, are limited to six people. Captains are interpretive naturalist educators and U.S. Coast Guard–licensed.

Take a narrated horse-drawn carriage tour of historic Beaufort with Southurn Rose Buggy Tours and learn about the city's fascinating history and its antebellum and Victorian architecture.

Tour Contacts Live Oac. ⊠ *43 Jenkins Rd., North End* ☎ *888/254–8362* ⊕ *www.liveoac.com.* **Southurn Rose Buggy Tours.** ⊠ *1002 Bay St., Downtown Historic District* ☎ *843/524–2900* ⊕ *www.southurnrose.com.*

WHERE TO EAT AND STAY

$$
\begin{array}{l}
\end{array}
$$

$$ **SEAFOOD** **FAMILY** ✕ **Old Daufuskie Crab Company Restaurant.** This outpost, with its rough-hewn tables facing the water, serves up surprisingly good fare. The specialties are deviled crab and chicken salad on buttery grilled rolls; many diners also enjoy the Lowcountry buffet with its pulled pork and sides like butter beans and potato salad. **Known for:** incredible sunsets; colorful bar; reggae and rock music. ⓢ *Average main: $17* ⊠ *Freeport Marina, 1 Cooper River Landing Rd., Daufuskie Island* ☎ *843/342–8687* ⊕ *www.enjoydaufuskie.com/daufuskie-crab-company.*

$$$$ **RENTAL** 🏠 **Sandy Lane Villas.** A luxurious, oceanfront low-rise condominium complex, the twin Sandy Lane Villas buildings look out to the simple boardwalk that leads directly to a nearly deserted beach. **Pros:** spacious and private; unobstructed ocean views. **Cons:** not a homey beach cottage; 20 minutes from Freeport Marina. ⓢ *Rooms from: $475* ⊠ *Sandy Lane Villas, 2302 Sandy La., Daufuskie Island* ☎ *843/785–8021* ⊕ *www.daufuskieislandrentals.com* ⤳ *32 villas* ⦿*No meals.*

9

THE MIDLANDS AND
THE UPSTATE, SC

WELCOME TO THE MIDLANDS AND THE UPSTATE, SC

TOP REASONS TO GO

★ **Small-town charm:** Small towns—most of them with shady town squares, small shops, and a café—dot this region. Abbeville and Aiken are a couple of the nicest.

★ **Rafting the Chattooga:** The fact that the movie *Deliverance* was filmed here doesn't scare away rafting enthusiasts from some of the best white water in the country.

★ **Antiquing in Camden:** Camden's Antiques & Arts District, which comprises most of the downtown area, is a trove of well-priced furniture, ironwork, and high-quality paintings.

★ **Congaree Swamp National Park:** Wander through 20 miles of trails or follow the 2½-mile boardwalk that meanders over lazy creeks and under massive hardwoods.

★ **Waterfalls:** There are more than 25 waterfalls in the Upstate; some, like 75-foot Twin Falls, are an easy walk from the road. Others, such as Raven Cliff Falls, are a 2-mile hike away.

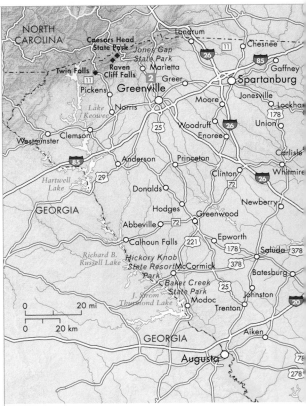

1 Columbia and the Midlands. Columbia is swarming with activity, from the University of South Carolina campus to the halls of the State House. Day or night, there is always something to do. It's worth it, though, to slow down the pace and take a drive out of town. With thick forests, quaint towns, and scores of local home-cooking restaurants, the Midlands will take you back to a simpler time.

2 The Upstate. The Upstate is a treasure trove of natural and historic sites. Hiking trails and waterfalls abound for visitors of all fitness levels. Even the most robust will enjoy the river and trails in Falls Park,

GETTING ORIENTED

South Carolina's gleaming coasts and rolling mountains are linked by its lush Midlands. Swells of sandy hills mark where the state's coastline once sat, and as you drive farther inland you'll be greeted by the beauty of the Smoky Mountain foothills. What lies between is a mixture of Southern living—in cities and rural farms—that is truly remarkable.

9

right in the heart of downtown Greenville. History buffs will love following the South Carolina National Heritage Corridor through the area. The drive stretches through lush landscapes, making stops at historic sites and homes along the way.

Updated
by Stratton
Lawrence

Lying between the coastal Lowcountry and the mountains, South Carolina's varied Midlands region holds swamps and rivers, fertile farmland—perfect for horse-raising—and hardwood and pine forests. Lakes have wonderful fishing, and the many state parks are popular for hiking, swimming, and camping. Small towns with bed-and-breakfasts in former mansions are common, and the many public and private gardens provide bursts of color throughout the year.

At the center of the region is the state capital, Columbia, an engaging contemporary city enveloping cherished historic elements. Just outside town, Congaree National Park has the largest intact tract of old-growth floodplain forest in North America. Aiken, the center of South Carolina's Thoroughbred country, is where the champions Sea Hero and Pleasant Colony were trained. Towns such as Abbeville and Camden preserve and interpret the past, with old house museums, history re-creations, and museum exhibits.

The Upstate of South Carolina is a land of waterfalls and wide vistas, cool pine forests, and fast rapids. Camping, hiking, white-water rafting, and kayaking are less than an hour from downtown Greenville and a paddle's throw from the small hamlets that are scattered about. Greenville itself, artsy and refined, is a modern Southern city with a thriving downtown full of trendy restaurants, boutiques, and galleries.

PLANNING

WHEN TO GO

Central South Carolina comes alive in spring, beginning in early March, when the azaleas, dogwoods, wisteria, and jasmine turn normal landscapes into fairylands of pink, white, and purple shaded by a canopy of pines. The heat of late May through September can be oppressive, particularly in the Midlands. Festivals celebrating everything from peaches to okra are held in summer. Fall will bring the state fair in Columbia,

SEC and ACC football to the University of South Carolina and Clemson University, rich yellows and reds of the changing trees in the mountains, and a number of art and music festivals.

FESTIVALS

Summer kicks off the festival season in the Midlands, and there's plenty to celebrate. Check out ⊕ *www.scbarbeque.com* for information on South Carolina barbecue festivals.

Lexington County Peach Festival. Every Fourth of July, indulge in fresh peach ice cream, or just bite into a sun-warmed peach while enjoying the peach parade and the evening fireworks. ⊠ *Gilbert* ☎ *803/892–5207* ⊕ *www.lexingtoncountypeachfestival.com* ⊠ *Free.*

Okra Strut. September's Okra Strut in Irmo is slimy fun, including live music and carnival rides. ⊠ *Irmo* ☎ *803/781–7050* ⊕ *www. theokrastrut.com* ⊠ *Free.*

South Carolina Peanut Party. The peanut is king at this annual fest held in Pelion each August, featuring rides, a parade, and a pageant. ⊠ *951 Pine St., Pelion* ⊕ *discoversouthcarolina.com/products/2116* ⊠ *Free.*

PLANNING YOUR TIME

The Midlands and Upstate have a good mix of larger cities and small towns. Columbia and Greenville are destinations on their own, with plenty of sights, stores, and high-end restaurants. The surrounding towns offer great day trips and shopping excursions, especially if you're looking to go antiquing. In Aiken you can spend the day with the horses at events like the Triple Crown each spring and Sunday polo matches every fall.

Miles of forested land and winding rivers offer plenty of reasons to stay outdoors. With options covering everything from hiking and mountain biking to motorcycle paths and bridle trails, it's easy to find an excuse to head into the woods. The Palmetto Trail stretches across the entire state and can be walked in segments. The South Carolina National Heritage Corridor allows visitors to take a driving tour of some of South Carolina's major historic sites from the foothills of the Smokies to the coast of Charleston. The Ninety Six National Historic Site offers a mile-long loop through the woods, past Revolutionary War battlegrounds.

GETTING HERE AND AROUND

AIR TRAVEL

Columbia Metropolitan Airport (CAE), 10 miles west of downtown Columbia, is served by American Airlines, Delta, and United. Greenville–Spartanburg International Airport (GSP), off Interstate 85 and between the two cities, is served by Allegiant, American Airlines, Delta, Southwest, and United.

Air Contacts Columbia Metropolitan Airport (*CAE*). ⊠ *3250 Airport Blvd., West Columbia* ☎ *803/822–5000* ⊕ *www.columbiaairport.com.* **Greenville Spartanburg International Airport** (*GSP*). ⊠ *2000 GSP Dr., Greer* ☎ *864/877– 7426* ⊕ *www.gspairport.com.*

CAR TRAVEL

Interstate 77 leads into Columbia from the north, Interstate 26 runs through northwest–southeast, and Interstate 20 east–west. Interstate 85 provides access to Greenville, Spartanburg, Pendleton, and Anderson. Interstate 26 runs from Charleston through Columbia to the Upstate, connecting with Interstate 385 into Greenville. Car rental by all the national chains is available at the airports in Columbia and Greenville.

TAXI TRAVEL

Companies providing service in Columbia include Blue Ribbon and Checker Yellow Cab. American VIP Limo provides citywide service as well as service to other cities statewide. It's about $20 to $25 from the airport to downtown Columbia. Greenville services include Budget Cab Company and Yellow Cab of Greenville. Fares from the Greenville airport to downtown Greenville will run around $25.

Taxi Contacts American VIP Limo. ☎ 803/238–6669 ⊕ www.theviplimo. com. **Budget Cab Company.** ☎ 864/233–4200. **Checker Yellow Cab.** ☎ 803/799–3311 ⊕ www.checkeryellowcab.com. **The Original Blue Ribbon Taxi Company.** ☎ 803/754–8163 ⊕ www.originalblueribbontaxi.com. **Yellow Cab Greenville.** ☎ 864/233–6666.

TRAIN TRAVEL

Across the state, Amtrak makes stops at Camden, Charleston, Clemson, Columbia, Denmark, Dillon, Florence, Greenville, Kingstree, Spartanburg, and Yemassee.

Train Contacts Amtrak. ☎ 800/872–7245 ⊕ www.amtrak.com.

RESTAURANTS

Most of the smaller towns have at least one dining choice that may surprise you with its take on sophisticated fare. Larger cities such as Columbia and Greenville have both upscale foodie haunts and ultracasual grits-and-greens joints. Plan ahead: many places close on Sunday. *Dining reviews have been shortened. For full information, visit Fodors.com.*

HOTELS

For an authentic taste of South Carolina's heartland, your best bet is to stay at an inn or B&B. Count on a handful of rooms, hearty breakfasts, and perhaps a garden for wandering and a restored town square nearby. What you gain in charm, however, you may have to give up in convenience. Our local writers vet every hotel to recommend the best lodging in each price category. Unless otherwise specified, you can expect private bath, phone, and TV in your room. For expanded reviews, facilities, and current deals, visit Fodors.com. *Hotel reviews have been shortened. For full information, visit Fodors.com.*

WHAT IT COSTS				
	$	$$	$$$	$$$$
Restaurants	under $15	$15–$19	$20–$24	over $24
Hotels	under $150	$150–$200	$201–$250	over $250

Restaurant prices are the average cost of a main course at dinner or, if dinner is not served, at lunch. Hotel prices are the lowest cost of a standard double room in high season.

COLUMBIA AND THE MIDLANDS

The state capital may be the only large city in the wide swath of land that makes up the Midlands, but the profusion of small and medium-size towns makes this area a patchwork quilt of history and activity. The local museums and historic homes that line the shady streets often house surprisingly deep collections on Civil or Revolutionary War battles or the lifestyle on early-1800s plantations. Well-informed and friendly docents are happy to share stories, or even tips on who's got the best peach pie in town.

COLUMBIA

112 miles northwest of Charleston via I–26; 101 miles southeast of Greenville via I–385 and I–26.

Old as Columbia may be, trendy and collegiate neighborhoods have given the city an edge. The symphony, two professional ballet companies, several theaters that stage live, often locally written, productions, and a number of engaging museums keep the arts thriving. The city is a sprawling blend of modern office blocks, suburban neighborhoods, and the occasional antebellum home. Here, too, is the expansive main campus of the University of South Carolina. Out of town, 550-acre Lake Murray is full of pontoon boats and Jet Skis, and Congaree National Park's swamps, creeks, and hiking trails are waiting to be explored.

In 1786, South Carolina's capital was moved from Charleston to Columbia, along the banks of the Congaree River. One of the nation's first planned cities, Columbia has streets that are among the widest in America, because it was then thought that stagnant air in narrow streets fostered the spread of malaria. The city soon grew into a center of political, commercial, and cultural activity, but in early 1865, General William Tecumseh Sherman invaded South Carolina and incinerated two-thirds of Columbia. Only a few homes, public buildings, and historic sights survived. The First Baptist Church, where secession was declared, still stands because a janitor directed Sherman's troops to a Presbyterian church instead.

9

GETTING HERE AND AROUND

Columbia lies in the heart of the state. It's two hours from the coast and just a little more than that from the mountains. Major interstates, along with airport, train, and bus terminals, make the city very accessible. Most of the action happens in the downtown neighborhoods of the Vista and Five Points. Devine Street, in the Shandon neighborhood, also offers plenty of boutique shopping and fine dining, and the university's football stadium, fairground, zoo, and gardens are all a short drive away. Historic Columbia runs guided house, garden, and walking tours of Columbia and rents storied properties and gardens for events.

ESSENTIALS

Tour Contacts Historic Columbia Foundation. ☎ 803/252–7742 ⊕ www.historiccolumbia.org.

Visitor Information Columbia Metropolitan Convention Center and Visitors Bureau. ✉ 1101 Lincoln St. ☎ 803/545–0001 ⊕ www.columbiaconventioncenter.com.

EXPLORING

TOP ATTRACTIONS

Columbia Museum of Art. This attractive, expansive gallery contains art from the Kress Foundation collection of Renaissance and baroque treasures, sculpture, and decorative arts. There are prominent paintings by European and American masters, including a Monet and a Botticelli, as well as temporary exhibitions that have featured world-famous works by artists like Salvador Dalí. ✉ 1515 Main St., Main Street Area ☎ 803/799–2810 ⊕ www.columbiamuseum.org ⧆ $12; free every second Sun. ⊘ Closed Mon.

FAMILY
Fodor's Choice
★

EdVenture Children's Museum. With more than 90,000 square feet for climbing, exploring, painting, playing, building—oh, and learning, too—this museum is a full day of hands-on fun. Eddie, a 40-foot-tall statue of a boy that can be climbed on (and in) by children and adults, is the centerpiece. Each of nine galleries has a theme, such as Planet Putt and Play, Wags & Whiskers, or Maker Works. Kids can shop in their own grocery store, act as firefighters in a full-size fire truck, and pretend to be newscasters. ✉ 211 Gervais St., Vista ☎ 803/779–3100 ⊕ www.edventure.org ⧆ $11.50.

FAMILY
Fodor's Choice
★

Riverbanks Zoo & Garden. This top-notch zoo contains more than 2,000 animals and birds in natural habitats, including a sea lion exhibit added in 2016. Walk through landscaped gardens to see elephants, Siberian tigers, koalas, and penguins. The South American primate collection has won international acclaim, and the park is noted for its success in breeding endangered species. The Aquarium Reptile Complex has regional, desert, tropical, and marine specimens. Ride the carousel, and take a tram over the Saluda River to the 70-acre botanical gardens. A forested section with walking trails has spectacular views of the river and passes Civil War ruins. Stop by the Saluda Factory Interpretive Center for more information about the site's history and its connection to the Civil War. ✉ 500 Wildlife Parkway at I–126 and U.S. 76, West Columbia ☎ 803/779–8717 ⊕ www.riverbanks.org ⧆ $15.95.

A tour of the South Carolina State House reveals the location of six cannon hits made by General Sherman's army during the Civil War.

FAMILY **South Carolina State Museum.** Exhibits in this refurbished textile mill explore the state's natural history, archaeology, and historical development. An iron gate made for the museum by Phillip Simmons, the "dean of Charleston blacksmiths," is on display, as is an exhibit on South Carolina's astronauts and artifacts associated with the state's cotton industry and slavery. Recent exhibits are geared toward the younger set, including a 4-D theater and nature-oriented rotating films shown in the new planetarium. ■ TIP→ When skies are clear, the observatory stays open until 10 pm on Tuesdays. ⊠ *301 Gervais St., Vista* ☎ *803/898–4921* ⊕ *www.scmuseum.org* 🖾 *$8.95.*

State House. Six bronze stars on the western wall mark where direct hits were made by General Sherman's cannons. The Capitol building, started in 1851 and completed in 1907, is made of native blue granite in the Italian-Renaissance style. The interior is richly appointed with brass, marble, mahogany, and artwork. Guided tours are available throughout the day. ⊠ *1100 Gervais St., Main Street Area* ☎ *803/734–2430* ⊕ *www. southcarolinaparks.com* 🖾 *Free.*

WORTH NOTING

Hampton-Preston Mansion & Gardens. Dating from 1818, this grand home is filled with lavish furnishings collected by three generations of two influential families. Buy tickets at the Robert Mills House. ⊠ *1615 Blanding St., Main Street Area* ☎ *803/252–7742* ⊕ *www.historiccolumbia. org* 🖾 *$8* ⊙ *Closed Mon.*

Lake Murray. This 41-mile-long lake has swimming, boating, picnicking, and superb fishing. There are many marinas and campgrounds in the area. A 1.7-mile pedestrian walkway stretches across the Dreher Shoals

Dam offering panoramic views. The lake is off Interstate 26, 15 miles west of Columbia. In summer a massive flock of purple martins fills the sky at sunset, when the birds return to their roost on Bomb Island. ✉ *2184 N. Lake Dr.* ☎ *803/781–5940* 🌐 *www.lakemurraycountry.com.*

Mann-Simons Site. This cottage and outdoor museum was the home of Celia Mann, one of only 200 free African Americans in Columbia in the mid-1800s. Buy tickets at the Robert Mills House. ✉ *1403 Richland St., Main Street Area* ☎ *803/252–7742* 🌐 *www.historiccolumbia.org* 🎟 *$8* 🕒 *Closed Mon.*

FAMILY **Riverfront Park and Historic Columbia Canal.** Where the Broad and Saluda rivers form the Congaree River is the site of the city's original waterworks and hydroelectric plant. Interpretive markers describe the area's plant and animal life and tell the history of the buildings. A 2½-mile paved trail weaves between the river and the canal and is filled with runners and walkers. ✉ *312 Laurel St., Vista* ☎ *803/733–8613* 🎟 *Free.*

Robert Mills House and Gardens. The classic, columned 1823 house was named for its architect, who later designed the Washington Monument. It has opulent Regency furniture, marble mantels, and spacious grounds. This is the home of the Historic Columbia Foundation, where you can get maps of walking and driving tours of historic districts and buy tickets to the Hampton-Preston Mansion and Gardens and the Mann-Simons Cottage. ✉ *1616 Blanding St., Main Street Area* ☎ *803/252–7742* 🌐 *www.historiccolumbia.org* 🎟 *$8* 🕒 *Closed Mon.*

FAMILY **Tunnelvision Mural.** This glowing optical illusion painted on the wall of the Federal Land Bank Building in 1976 by local artist Blue Sky gives the appearance of a tunnel leading to the mountains. ✉ *Taylor and Marion Sts., Main Street Area.*

University of South Carolina. A highlight of this sprawling university is its original campus, founded in 1801. Stroll the historic buildings and gardens of the Horseshoe, or dive into the special collections at the S.C. Library, the first stand-alone college library in the nation. The McKissick Museum on campus features exhibits on geology, gemstones, and local folklife. ✉ *Sumter St., USC Campus* ☎ *803/777–7251 McKissick Museum* 🌐 *www.sc.edu/visitorcenter.*

Woodrow Wilson Family Home. This boyhood home of President Woodrow Wilson, which reopened in 2014 after an eight-year renovation, displays the gaslights, arched doorways, and ornate furnishings of the Victorian period. Museum exhibits explore the life of Woodrow Wilson and the south in the 1870s. **■ TIP → Buy tickets at the Robert Mills House.** ✉ *1705 Hampton St., Main Street Area* ☎ *803/252–7742* 🌐 *www.historiccolumbia.org* 🎟 *$8* 🕒 *Closed Mon.*

WHERE TO EAT

$ CAFÉ 🍴 **The Gourmet Shop.** Mirrors and art adorn the walls at this French-inspired bakery and café serving coffee, sandwiches, soups, and cheese plates. Next door, the retail shop sells wine, kitchen gadgets, French table linens, and fancy food items. **Known for:** fresh baguettes and cookies; chicken salad sandwiches. [$] *Average main: $10* ✉ *724 Saluda Ave., Five Points* ☎ *803/799–3705* 🌐 *www.thegourmetshop.net* 🕒 *No dinner.*

$$$$ ✕ **Hampton Street Vineyard.** Inside one of the first buildings constructed
AMERICAN in the city after Sherman's infamous march, Hampton Street Vineyard
is a cozy bistro where exposed brick walls, arched windows, and original wide-plank floors set the tone. Dinners are creative but never over
the top, with upscale American fare such as seared breast of duck and
sautéed crab cakes. **Known for:** massive wine selection; locally inspired,
seasonally changing menu. $ *Average main: $28* ✉ *1201 Hampton
St., Downtown* ☎ *803/252–0850* ⊕ *www.hamptonstreetvineyard.com*
⊗ *Closed Sun. No lunch Sat.*

$ ✕ **Little Pigs Barbecue.** Grab a plate, get in the buffet line, and load up
SOUTHERN on pulled pork barbecue, fried chicken, ribs, and fried fish, along with
fixings such as collards, coleslaw, and macaroni and cheese. Since Little
Pigs uses mustard-, tomato-, and vinegar-base barbecue sauces, you can
sample all three and pick your favorite. **Known for:** all-you-can-eat buf-
fet; real country cooking, priced right. $ *Average main: $10* ✉ *4927
Alpine Rd., Northeast* ☎ *803/788–8238* ⊕ *www.littlepigs.biz* ⊗ *Closed
Mon. and Tues. No dinner Sun. and Wed.*

$ ✕ **Mediterranean Tea Room.** The name is a bit of a misnomer, since this
MIDDLE EASTERN friendly little restaurant serves Middle Eastern and Greek food. The
marinated chicken breast keeps people coming back, but the *kofta*
(spiced meatball), hummus, and vegetarian dishes offer patrons a break
from the rich Southern cooking elsewhere. **Known for:** gyros and falafel;
cheery atmosphere. $ *Average main: $10* ✉ *2601 Devine St., Shandon*
☎ *803/799–3118* ⊗ *Closed Sun. No lunch Sat.*

$$$$ ✕ **Motor Supply Co. Bistro.** The daily changing menu at this stalwart of
ECLECTIC the Columbia dining scene highlights the best of what local farmers
Fodor's Choice and purveyors have to offer, worked into eclectic dishes that span from
★ European to Asian influences. The artsy interior and thoughtful service
make it a standout in the city's dining scene. **Known for:** curated beer
and wine selection; farm-to-table menu that changes daily. $ *Average
main: $26* ✉ *920 Gervais St., Vista* ☎ *803/256–6687* ⊕ *www.motorsup-
plycobistro.com* ⊗ *Closed Mon.*

$$$ ✕ **Mr. Friendly's New Southern Cafe.** Who knew that barbecue sauce
SOUTHERN could be the base for such tasty salad dressing or that pimento cheese
could elevate a fillet to near perfection? Appetizers of fried pickles and
country ham and spinach dip only add to the creative thinking that
makes Mr. Friendly's such a local treasure; the ever-changing wine-
by-the-glass menu is another. **Known for:** seafood specials; impressive
wine and beer list. $ *Average main: $22* ✉ *2001 A Greene St., Five
Points* ☎ *803/254–7828* ⊕ *www.mrfriendlys.com* ⊗ *No lunch Sat.
Closed Sun.*

$$ ✕ **The War Mouth.** Named after a freshwater sunfish and set in a former
SOUTHERN auto repair garage, this casual-cool joint serves up whole hog from its
wood-fired outdoor barbecue pit as well as hearty Southern specialties like chicken bog, quail legs, and catfish stew. Stick around for
nightcap craft cocktails at the popular bar. **Known for:** wood-fired
meats; lively happy hour; craft cocktails. $ *Average main: $18* ✉ *1209
Franklin St., Main Street Area* ☎ *803/569–6144* ⊕ *www.thewarmouth.
com* ⊗ *Closed Mon.*

9

WHERE TO STAY

$$ HOTEL **Aloft Columbia Downtown.** A short walk from the convention center and hot spot restaurants and nightlife, and housing a lively bar of its own, downtown's newest hotel is also its most modern, outfitted with contemporary art and light fixtures, and flooded with natural light in its loftlike public spaces. **Pros:** contemporary decor and gym; lively bar; close to convention center and area nightlife. **Cons:** no pool; no dining room or room service. [$] *Rooms from: $180* ✉ *823 Lady St., Downtown* ☎ *803/445–1900* 🌐 *www.starwoodhotels.com* 🛏 *107 rooms* 🍴 *No meals.*

$ HOTEL **Comfort Suites at Harbison.** A short drive down the access road from a mall, shopping center, and cinema complex, the Comfort Suites is off Interstate 26 just west of downtown Columbia. **Pros:** great for avoiding heavy downtown traffic; exercise room and indoor pool. **Cons:** too far away to go anywhere on foot; could do with some upgrades. [$] *Rooms from: $146* ✉ *750 Saturn Pkwy., Exit 103, Harbison* ☎ *803/407–4444* 🌐 *www.choicehotels.com* 🛏 *82 rooms* 🍴 *Breakfast.*

$$ HOTEL **Embassy Suites by Hilton Columbia Greystone.** In the spacious seven-story atrium lobby—with skylights, fountains, pool, and live plants—you can enjoy your breakfast and evening cocktails. **Pros:** across from the zoo and botanical gardens. **Cons:** not close to restaurants or nightlife. [$] *Rooms from: $199* ✉ *200 Stoneridge Dr., Greystone* ☎ *803/252–8700* 🌐 *www.columbiagreystone.embassysuites.com* 🛏 *218 rooms* 🍴 *Breakfast.*

$$ B&B/INN **Hampton Inn Downtown Historic District.** This classy outpost is within walking distance of restaurants and nightlife in the Vista neighborhood. **Pros:** outdoor saltwater pool. **Cons:** rooms along Gervais Street can be noisy. [$] *Rooms from: $179* ✉ *822 Gervais St., Vista* ☎ *803/231–2000* 🌐 *www.hamptoninncolumbia.com* 🛏 *122 rooms* 🍴 *Breakfast.*

NIGHTLIFE AND PERFORMING ARTS

NIGHTLIFE

Art Bar. In the hopping Vista neighborhood, this funky spot has neon-painted walls, colorful string lights, and a lively crowd, making it the perfect setting for karaoke and dancing to live bands. ✉ *1211 Park St., Vista* ☎ *803/929–0198* 🌐 *www.artbarsc.com.*

Blue Tapas Bar and Cocktail Lounge. An ice bar, multiple water features, and a decent tapas menu create a big-city feel at this popular local nightspot. ✉ *721A Lady St., Vista* ☎ *803/251–4447.*

Fodor's Choice ★ **Hunter-Gatherer Brewery & Alehouse.** In 2017, this venerable local beer hall celebrated its 20th anniversary of serving an excellent selection of beers and a menu of elevated pub fare. It also hosts occasional live bands. ✉ *900 Main St., USC Campus* ☎ *803/748–0540* 🌐 *huntergathererbrewery.com.*

The Whig. Directly across from the State House, the subterranean Whig draws an eclectic mix of patrons who are drawn to its dive bar vibe by the great drink specials, classic pub fare, and the wildly popular Taco Tuesday. ✉ *1200 Main St., basement, Main Street Area* ☎ *803/931–8852* 🌐 *www.thewhig.org.*

PERFORMING ARTS

Colonial Life Arena. The largest arena in the state hosts major concerts and entertainment events, as well as University of South Carolina basketball games. ⊠ *801 Lincoln St., Vista* ☎ *803/576–9200* ⊕ *www. coloniallifearena.com.*

Koger Center for the Arts. This performing arts center presents national and international theater, ballet, and musical groups, as well as individual performers. ⊠ *1051 Greene St., at Assembly St., USC Campus* ☎ *803/777–7500* ⊕ *kogercenterforthearts.com.*

Town Theatre. Founded in 1919, the Town Theatre is on the National Register of Historic Places and stages eight plays a year. ⊠ *1012 Sumter St., USC Campus* ☎ *803/799–2510* ⊕ *www.towntheatre.com.*

Trustus. This local professional theater group presents new and original plays throughout the year. ⊠ *520 Lady St., Vista* ☎ *803/254–9732* ⊕ *www.trustus.org.*

Workshop Theatre. This publicly funded local theater hosts a number of plays and productions each year. ⊠ *635 Elmwood Ave., Downtown* ☎ *803/799–4876* ⊕ *www.workshoptheatre.com.*

SPORTS AND THE OUTDOORS

CANOEING AND KAYAKING

The Saluda River near Columbia has challenging, seasonal Class III and IV rapids. Saluda access is out of town in Gardendale and Saluda Shoals Park, as well as at the Riverbanks Zoo. The Broad and the Saluda rivers meet in the center of town to become the calmer Congaree River. There's public access for the Congaree behind EdVenture on Senate Street at the Senate Street Landing.

FAMILY **Adventure Carolina.** Guided Saluda, Broad, and Congaree river trips and swamp canoeing excursions (Saluda and Broad have rapids, Congaree is calm) can be arranged from this company, as can ski and snowboard rentals and trips in the winter. ⊠ *1107 State St., Cayce* ⌖ *1 mile southwest of Columbia* ☎ *803/796–4505.*

River Runner Outdoor Center. This local outfitter rents and sells canoes, kayaks, and gear, and can point you in the right direction for river or swamp expeditions. ⊠ *905 Gervais St., Vista* ☎ *803/771–0353* ⊕ *www.riverrunner.us.*

PARKS

FAMILY
Fodor's Choice
★
Congaree National Park. The alluvial floodplain, bordered by high bluffs, in this nearly 27,000-acre park (the only national park in South Carolina) contains many old-growth bottomland hardwoods, the oldest and largest trees east of the Mississippi River. The water and trees are beautifully eerie. Self-guided canoe trails and 22 miles of hiking trails line the park, which is full of wildlife, including otters, deer, and woodpeckers, as well as the occasional wild boar. There's also a 2.5-mile boardwalk through the swamp. ⊠ *100 National Park Rd., 20 miles southeast of Columbia, Hopkins* ☎ *803/776–4396* ⊕ *www. nps.gov/cong* ⊠ *Free.*

FAMILY **Saluda Shoals Park.** Canoe and kayak rentals are available for exploring the Saluda River at this 400-acre park. There are also picnic shelters, an observation deck, trails, and a water park. ⊠ *5605 Bush River Rd., 12 miles northwest of downtown Columbia* ☎ *803/731–5208* ⊕ *www. icrc.net* 🖪 *$5 per car.*

FAMILY **Sesquicentennial State Park.** The 1,419-acre Sesquicentennial State Park is not far from downtown but feels as if it's deep in the country. A 30-acre lake sits at the heart of the park, allowing for fishing and nonmotorized boating. Enjoy picnicking areas, playgrounds, and miles of nature, hiking, and mountain-biking trails. ⊠ *9564 Two Notch Rd., Northeast* ☎ *803/788–2706* ⊕ *www.southcarolinaparks.com* 🖪 *$5.*

SHOPPING

Many of Columbia's antiques outlets, boutique shops, and restaurants are in the Vista neighborhood around Huger and Gervais Streets, between the State House and the river. A number of intriguing shops and cafés are in Five Points, around Blossom and Harden Streets, as well as along Devine Street in the Shandon neighborhood to the east. There are also antiques shops across the river on Meeting and State Streets in West Columbia.

Old Mill Antique Mall. You'll find a wide array of furniture, glassware, jewelry, and books at this sprawling complex with over 75 dealers. ⊠ *310 State St., West Columbia* ☎ *803/796–4229* ⊕ *oldmillantiquemall.com.*

FAMILY
Fodor'sChoice
★
Soda City Market. Every Saturday morning from 9 am to 1 pm, Soda City Market comes to life along Main Street, with artists and artisans joining the farm stands, often to the sounds of local musicians. In all there are about 100 vendors. ⊠ *1500 Block Main St., Main Street Area* ⊕ *www.sodacitysc.com.*

State Farmers' Market. One of the 10 largest in the country, the State Farmers' Market, open daily, features fresh vegetables, along with flowers, plants, seafood, and more. ⊠ *3483 Charleston Hwy., West Columbia* ☎ *803/737–4664* ⊕ *www.scstatefarmersmarket.com.*

CAMDEN

35 miles northeast of Columbia via I–20.

A town with horse history and grand colonial homes, charming Camden has never paved some of its roads for the sake of the hooves that regularly trot over them. Both the Carolina Cup and the Colonial Cup are run here.

Camden is South Carolina's oldest inland town, dating from 1732. British General Lord Cornwallis established a garrison here during the Revolutionary War and burned most of the town before evacuating it. A center of textile trade from the late 19th century through the 1940s, Camden blossomed when it became a refuge for Northerners escaping the cold winters. Because General Sherman spared the town during the Civil War, most of its antebellum homes still stand.

DID YOU KNOW?

Rangers provide free, guided canoe trips on weekends along Cedar Creek in Congaree National Park. The trips are an excellent way to experience the floodplain forest, which contains some of the tallest trees in eastern North America. You might also spot river otters, turtles, snakes, and wild pigs.

GETTING HERE AND AROUND

A roughly 40-minute drive northeast of Columbia will take you to Camden, which makes a great day trip. A distinct downtown holds many stores carrying antiques, collectibles, and one-of-a-kind art. Outside the downtown area you will find historical homes, museums, and horse-race courses. Camden Carriage Company can take you on a tour on a horse-drawn carriage through Camden's loveliest neighborhood and down unpaved roads.

ESSENTIALS

Tour Information Camden Carriage Company. ☎ *803/425–5737* 🌐 *www.camdencarriage.com.*

EXPLORING

Bonds Conway House. This home was built by the first African American in Camden to buy his freedom. The circa-1812 home has the fine details of a skilled craftsman, including wonderful woodwork and heart-pine floors. It now serves as the home of the Kershaw County Historical Society. ✉ *811 Fair St.* ☎ *803/425–1123* 🌐 *www.kershawcountyhistoricalsociety.org* 🎟 *Free.*

FAMILY **Historic Camden Revolutionary War Site.** This 107-acre outdoor museum complex emphasizes the period surrounding the British occupation of 1780. Several structures dot the site, including the 1789 **Craven House**, the **Blacksmith Shed**, and the **Kershaw House**, a reconstruction of the circa-1770 home of Camden's founder, Joseph Kershaw, which also served as Cornwallis's headquarters; it's furnished with period pieces. A nature trail, fortifications, powder magazine, picnic area, and crafts shop are also here. Guided tours are available. ✉ *U.S. 521, 222 Broad St.* ✥ *1½ miles north of I–20* ☎ *803/432–9841* 🌐 *discoversouthcarolina.com/products/1657* 🎟 *$5* 🕒 *Closed Mon.*

Kershaw County Chamber of Commerce. When you stop in for brochures and information, take note of the Chamber's building: it was designed by Robert Mills, the architect of the Washington Monument. Upstairs, the old courthouse is open for viewing. ✉ *607 S. Broad St.* ☎ *803/432–2525* 🌐 *www.kershawcountychamber.org.*

National Steeplechase Museum. This museum at the historic Springdale Race Course contains the largest collection of racing memorabilia in the United States. The Equisizer, a training machine used by jockeys for practice, lets you experience the race from the jockey's perspective; don't stay on too long, unless you want to feel the race all day. ✉ *200 Knights Hill Rd.* ☎ *803/432–6513* 🌐 *www.steeplechasemuseum.org* 🎟 *Free.*

WHERE TO EAT AND STAY

$$$$ STEAKHOUSE 🍴 **Mill Pond Steak House.** It's all about steak here, and what steaks they are: aged for at least 35 days before they're cut, the fillets, rib eyes, and strips are juicy, tender, and packed with flavor. You can dine alfresco overlooking the sprawling pond or enjoy the vintage saloon-style bar. **Known for:** views across the namesake pond; high-end Southern cuisine; locally sourced produce. [$] *Average main: $33* ✉ *84 Boykin Mill Rd., 10 miles south of Camden, Rembert* ☎ *803/425–8825* 🌐 *www.themillpondsteakhouse.com* 🕒 *Closed Sun. and Mon. No lunch.*

$$$$
SEAFOOD
✕ **Sam Kendall's.** The exposed brick wall and high-back booths offer the perfect upscale backdrop for steak or seafood. The menu also features an extensive list of more than 100 wines. **Known for:** fine dining in historic digs; signature cocktails; extensive wine list. $ *Average main: $28* ✉ *1043 Broad St.* ☎ *803/424–2005* ⊕ *www.samkendalls. com* ⊙ *Closed Sun.*

$$
B&B/INN
▦ **Bloomsbury Inn.** Noted Civil War diarist Mary Boykin Chestnut wrote much of her famous account in this house, which was built in 1849 by her husband's family. **Pros:** impressive breakfast; richly decorated rooms; electric car charging stations on-site. **Cons:** no elevator. $ *Rooms from: $175* ✉ *1707 Lyttleton St.* ☎ *803/432–5858* ⊕ *www. bloomsburyinn.com* ⇨ *4 rooms* ▯◎▯ *Breakfast.*

SHOPPING

Camden is known for its antiques shopping, with the heart of the antiques and arts district along Broad Street, as well as on neighboring Rutledge, DeKalb, and Market Streets.

Camden Antiques Market. Well-priced furniture and decorative art dating back to the 18th century is on offer here. ✉ *830 S. Broad St.* ☎ *803/432–0818* ⊕ *www.camdenantiquesmarket.com.*

Mulberry Market Bake Shop. Sample almond Danish pastries, lemon bars, and macaroons at this delightful confectionery. European-style (high-fat) butter is the key to the divine cheese sticks. ✉ *536 E. DeKalb St.* ☎ *803/424–8401* ⊙ *Closed Sun.*

Rutledge Street Gallery. The paintings, textiles, and sculpture of two dozen local and regional artists are on display at this light-filled studio. ✉ *508 Rutledge St.* ☎ *803/425–0071* ⊕ *www.rutledgestreetgallery.com* ⊙ *Closed Sun. and Mon.*

AIKEN

9

89 miles southwest of Camden via I–20; 56 miles southwest of Columbia via I–20 and U.S. 1.

This is Thoroughbred country. Aiken first earned its fame in the 1890s, when wealthy Northerners wintering here built stately mansions and entertained one another with horse shows, hunts, and lavish parties. Many up-to-60-room houses stand as a testament to this era of opulence. The town is still a center for all kinds of outdoor activity, including the equestrian events of the Triple Crown, as well as tennis and golf.

GETTING HERE AND AROUND

An hour's drive southwest of Columbia will take you to the rolling green horse country of Aiken. Though not a concise town square, Laurens Street and the surrounding streets offer plenty of shopping, dining, and entertainment. If you're headed to the polo matches or races, the horse district is only a five-minute drive outside the downtown area.

ESSENTIALS

Visitor Information Aiken Visitors Center and Train Museum. ✉ *406 Park Ave. SE* ☎ *803/293–7846* ⊕ *www.visitaikensc.com.* **Aiken Chamber of Commerce.** ✉ *121 Richland Ave. E* ☎ *803/641–1111* ⊕ *www.aikenchamber.net.*

EXPLORING

FAMILY   **Aiken County Historical Museum.** One wing of this 1860 estate is devoted to early regional culture, including Native American artifacts, firearms, an authentically furnished 1808 log cabin, a schoolhouse, and a miniature circus display. ⊠ *433 Newberry St. SW* ☎ *803/642–2015* ⊕ *www. aikenmuseum.us* ✍ *Donations suggested.*

Aiken Thoroughbred Racing Hall of Fame and Museum. The area's horse farms have produced many national champions, which are commemorated here. Exhibits include horse-related decorations, paintings, and sculptures, plus racing silks and trophies. The Hall of Fame is on the grounds of the 14-acre **Hopelands Gardens,** where you can wind along paths past quiet terraces and reflecting pools. There's also a Touch and Scent Trail with Braille plaques. ⊠ *135 Dupree Pl., off Whiskey Rd.* ☎ *803/642–7631* ⊕ *www.aikenracinghalloffame.com* ✍ *Free* ☉ *Closed Mon.*

FAMILY   **Hitchcock Woods.** At 2,100 acres and three times the size of New York's Central Park, this is one of the largest urban forests in the country and is listed on the National Register of Historic Places. Make use of the maps available at the entrances, because it's easy to get lost. Note that there are seven entrances to the woods; the ones with best parking are at 2180 Dibble Road SW and 430 South Boundary Road. ⊠ *2180 Dibble Rd. SW* ☎ *803/642–0528* ⊕ *www.hitchcockwoods.org.*

Old Edgefield Pottery. Stephen Ferrell has an extensive collection of Edgefield pottery on display at this shop operated by the Edgefield County Historical Society. Ferrell, like his father, is an accomplished potter in his own right. ■TIP→ **Ask to see original pieces crafted by the famed and prolific African American potter known only as Dave. While a slave, he created some of the first "face jugs."** ⊠ *230 Simpkins St., 15 miles northwest of Aiken, Edgefield* ☎ *803/634–1634.*

FAMILY   **Redcliffe Plantation State Historic Site.** Home to James Hammond, who is credited with being first to declare that "Cotton is King," this wood-frame house remained in the family until 1975. The 13,000-square-foot mansion (which now sits on 369 acres) remains just as it was, down to the 19th-century books on the carved shelves. Former slave quarters contain photograph and textile exhibits. Once you've toured the house, be sure to explore the grounds on the 1-mile trail. ■TIP→ **Take note: the house has no central heat or air-conditioning.** ⊠ *181 Redcliffe Rd., 15 miles southwest of Aiken, Beech Island* ☎ *803/827–1473* ⊕ *www.southcarolinaparks.com* ✍ *Park entrance free, house tours $7.50.*

WHERE TO EAT

$$$ ✕ **Linda's Bistro.** Chef Linda Rooney elevates traditional European favor-
EUROPEAN   ites, turning out excellent mushroom-Gruyère tarts, risotto with roasted mushrooms and Asiago cheese, and steak frites. Main courses come with a salad, a vegetable, and potatoes. **Known for:** seasonal wild game dinners; rotating selection of entrées priced below $20. $ *Average main: $22* ⊠ *135 York St. SE* ☎ *803/648–4853* ⊕ *www.lindasbistro-aiken. com* ☉ *Closed Sun. and Mon. No lunch.*

$$$$
ECLECTIC
Fodor'sChoice
★

✕ **Malia's.** Locals love this busy contemporary restaurant, with dim lighting and dark decor that conveys a cool class. The menu changes monthly and may include American, Caribbean, French, and Italian entrées. **Known for:** white tablecloth dining; small-town farm-to-table cuisine. $ *Average main: $28* ✉ *120 Laurens St. SW* ☎ *803/643–3086* ⊕ *www.maliasrestaurant.com* ⊘ *Closed Sun. and Mon. No dinner Tues.*

$
AMERICAN

✕ **New Moon Café.** Here you can pair Aiken's best coffee (the coffee beans are roasted right next door) with freshly baked muffins and sweet rolls, panini sandwiches and salads, and homemade soups. The crab bisque is particularly good. **Known for:** healthy food made with heart; smoothies and milk shakes. $ *Average main: $9* ✉ *116 Laurens St. NW* ☎ *803/643–7088* ⊕ *www.newmooncafes.com* ⊘ *No dinner.*

WHERE TO STAY

$
B&B/INN
Fodor'sChoice
★

🛏 **Carriage House Inn.** Located in Aiken's historic downtown, this charming inn is within walking distance of local boutiques and restaurants. **Pros:** central location; special "pet suites" available; pleasant grounds. **Cons:** no elevator, but ADA compliant rooms are available. $ *Rooms from: $125* ✉ *139 Laurens St. NW* ☎ *803/644–5888* ⊕ *www.aikencarriagehouse.com* ⮌ *37 rooms* ♨ *Breakfast.*

$$
B&B/INN
Fodor'sChoice
★

🛏 **The Willcox.** Winston Churchill, Franklin D. Roosevelt, and the Astors have slept at this 19th-century inn, where luxurious facilities—including a spa, restaurant, and outdoor pool—and authentic Southern hospitality come together to make an outstanding getaway. **Pros:** breakfast is a huge step above normal fare; pets are allowed; on-site spa. **Cons:** a bit of a walk to downtown shops and restaurants. $ *Rooms from: $189* ✉ *100 Colleton Ave. SW* ☎ *803/648–1898* ⊕ *www.thewillcox.com* ⮌ *22 rooms* ♨ *Breakfast.*

SPORTS AND THE OUTDOORS

Aiken Polo Club. Polo matches are played at Whitney Field on Sundays at 3 pm, September through November and April through June. ✉ *420 Mead Ave.* ☎ *803/643–3611* ⊕ *www.aikenpolo.org.*

Triple Crown. Three weekends in late March and early April are set aside for the local Triple Crown, which includes Thoroughbred trials of promising yearlings, a steeplechase, and harness races by young horses making their debut. ✉ *538 Two Notch Rd. SE* ☎ *803/648–9641* ⊕ *www.aikensteeplechase.com.*

ABBEVILLE

25 miles west of Ninety Six via Rte. 34 and Rte. 72; 102 miles west of Columbia.

Abbeville is one of inland South Carolina's most satisfying lesser-known towns. An appealing historic district includes the old business areas, early churches, and residential areas. What was called the "Southern cause" by supporters of the Confederacy was born and died here: it's where the first organized secession meeting was held and where, on May 2, 1865, Confederate president Jefferson Davis officially disbanded the defeated armies of the South in the last meeting of his war council.

GETTING HERE AND AROUND

Abbeville is a little more than an hour west of Columbia. Most of the sites, including the opera house, are around its quaint town square, with shopping and restaurants all within walking distance. A short drive—or a long walk—past the square is the historic Burt-Stark Mansion.

ESSENTIALS

Visitor Information Greater Abbeville Chamber of Commerce. ✉ *107 Court Sq.* ☎ *864/366–4600* 🌐 *www.abbevillechambersc.com.*

EXPLORING

Abbeville Opera House. Built in 1908 along the old town square, this auditorium has been renovated to reflect the grandeur of the days when lavish road shows and stellar entertainers took center stage. Current productions range from contemporary light comedies to local renderings of Broadway musicals. Self-guided tours available. ✉ *100 Court Sq.* ☎ *864/366–2157* 🌐 *www.theabbevilleoperahouse.com.*

Burt-Stark Mansion. It was here that Jefferson Davis disbanded the Confederate armies, effectively ending the Civil War. Built in 1820, the house was a private residence until 1971, when Mary Stark Davis died. She willed the house to the Abbeville County Historic Preservation Commission, with a provision that nothing be added or removed from the house. It's filled with lovely antiques, carved-wood surfaces, and old family photos. Her clothing is still in the dresser drawers. ✉ *400 N. Main St.* ☎ *864/366–0166* 🌐 *www.burtstark.com* 🎟 *$10* 🕒 *Closed Sun.–Thurs.*

Trinity Episcopal Church. Built in 1860, this is the town's oldest standing church. Complete with a 125-foot spire, the Gothic Revival structure has an original chancery window imported from England, and a rare working 1860 John Baker tracker organ. ✉ *200 Church St.* ☎ *864/366–5186* 🎟 *Free.*

WHERE TO EAT AND STAY

$$ AMERICAN 🍴 **Village Grill.** The menu goes from hamburgers to fillets, but many locals frequent the Village Grill because of the herb rotisserie chicken. Burgers are ground on the spot and salads consist of locally grown organic vegetables. **Known for:** integrity in ingredient sourcing; chicken and ribs. [$] *Average main: $15* ✉ *110 Trinity St.* ☎ *864/366–2500* 🌐 *www.abbevillevillagegrill.com* 🕒 *Closed Sun. and Mon.*

$ AMERICAN 🍴 **Yoder's Dutch Kitchen.** Try some authentic Pennsylvania Dutch home cooking in this unassuming South Carolina redbrick building. There's a weekend lunch buffet and evening smorgasbord with fried chicken, stuffed cabbage, Dutch meat loaf, breaded veal Parmesan, and plenty of vegetables. **Known for:** unique country cooking; all-you-can-eat buffet. [$] *Average main: $10* ✉ *809 E. Greenwood St., east of downtown* ☎ *864/366–5556* 🕒 *Closed Sun.–Wed. No dinner Thurs.*

$ B&B/INN 🏨 **Belmont Inn.** Because of the theater-dining-and-lodging packages, the Belmont Inn is a popular overnight stop for opera-house-goers. **Pros:** ideal location near opera house and town square; veranda has great views of town; period furnishings and building. **Cons:** the inn hosts weddings, so rooms book fast. [$] *Rooms from: $129* ✉ *104 E. Pickens St.* ☎ *864/459–9625* 🌐 *www.belmontinn.net* 🛏 *26 rooms* 🍽 *No meals.*

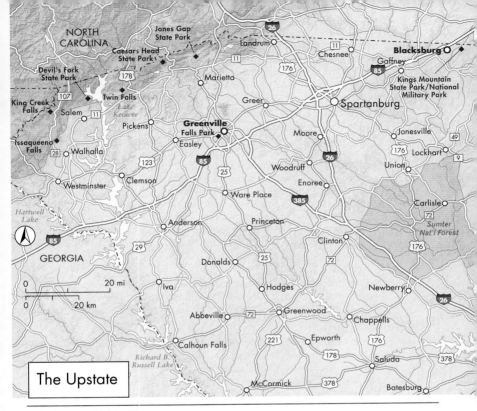

The Upstate

THE UPSTATE

The Upstate, also known as the Upcountry, in the northwest corner of the state, has long been a favorite for family vacations because of its temperate climate and natural beauty. The abundant lakes and waterfalls and several state parks (including Caesars Head, Keowee-Toxaway, Oconee, Table Rock, and the Chattooga National Wild and Scenic River) provide all manner of recreational activities. Beautiful anytime, the 130-mile Cherokee Foothills Scenic Highway (Route 11), which goes through the Blue Ridge Mountains, is especially delightful in spring (when the peach trees are in bloom) and in autumn.

GREENVILLE

100 miles northwest of Columbia via I–26 and I–385.

Once known for its textile and other manufacturing plants, Greenville has reinvented itself as a trendy and sophisticated city able to support a surprising number of restaurants, galleries, and boutiques along a tree-lined Main Street that passes a stunning natural waterfall. Anchored by two performance centers, the city's business district is alive well into most evenings with couples and families enjoying the energy of this revitalized Southern city. Downtown development has been so successful that many young professionals are moving here and creating interesting living spaces from old warehouses and retail establishments. Festivals are held many weekends along tree-lined Main Street.

GETTING HERE AND AROUND

Greenville is a little more than two hours northwest of Columbia. The Greenville area lies in the foothills of the Appalachian Mountains, so there is plenty of hiking and numerous waterfalls just outside town. The revitalized Main Street area, a long tree-lined stretch of shops, restaurants, and hotels, is a great base camp for your stay. To the south, the road runs through Falls Park and passes Fluor Field, home of the Greenville Drive baseball team. The northern end is home to Heritage Green, a block of museums, theaters, and a library. Be prepared when driving around the outskirts of Greenville—Interstate 185, a connector loop of Interstate 85 and Interstate 385, is a toll road, so have your dollars ready.

ESSENTIALS

Visitor Information Discover Upcountry Carolina Association. ☎ 800/849–4766 ⊕ www.upcountrysc.com. **VisitGreenvilleSC Visitor Center.** ✉ 206 S. Main St. ☎ 864/233–0461, 800/717–0023 ⊕ www.visitgreenvillesc.com.

EXPLORING

FAMILY **Caesars Head State Park.** Part of the Mountain Bridge Wilderness Area and best known for the Raven Cliff Falls here, Caesar's Head State Park is about 30 miles north of Greenville. The trail leading to the 420-foot-tall falls can be reached a mile north of the park's main entrance; along the way there are spectacular views of river gorges and pine-covered mountains. Cross Matthews Creek on a suspension bridge; the view of the falls is worth the terror of knowing you're held in the air by nothing but wire. ✉ 8155 Geer Hwy., U.S. 276, Cleveland ☎ 864/836–6115 ⊕ www.southcarolinaparks.com/caesarshead ☑ Overlook is free, $2 for use of hiking trails.

FAMILY **Children's Museum of the Upstate.** This 80,000-square-foot facility is packed with hands-on exhibits that cover everything from science and music to construction and race cars. There are also special areas for kids five and under. ✉ 300 College St., Heritage Green ☎ 864/233–7755 ⊕ www.tcmupstate.org ☑ $10 ☼ Closed Mon. during winter.

FAMILY **Devils Fork State Park.** This park on Lake Jocassee has luxurious villas and camping facilities, hiking, boating, and fishing. Lower Whitewater Falls plunges more than 200 feet over huge boulders to splash into the lake waters. The falls can be viewed from an overlook or from a boat on the lake. ✉ 161 Holcombe Cr., off Rte. 11, north of Salem, 45 miles northwest of Greenville, Salem ☎ 864/944–2639 ⊕ www.southcarolinaparks.com ☑ $2.

FAMILY **Falls Park.** In this outdoor oasis, sloping green hills, giant boulders, and winding walkways offer great views of the Reedy River, but it's along the Liberty Bridge that you'll find the best views of the waterfalls. Guided tours of the gardens are available (reserve ahead of time). The Peace Center amphitheater hosts moonlight movies,

The unique Twin Falls, 24 miles outside of Greenville, is also one of the easiest local waterfalls to get to.

Shakespeare plays, and open-air concerts during the year. ⊠ *601 S. Main St.* ☏ *864/467–4355* ⊕ *www.fallspark.com* ☑ *Free.*

Fodor's Choice
★

Greenville County Museum of Art. This Southern-focused gallery is home to American paintings dating from the colonial era, along with more-modern works by Andy Warhol, Georgia O'Keeffe, and Jasper Johns. It hosts the world's largest public collection of Andrew Wyeth watercolors, and admission is free. ⊠ *420 College St., Heritage Green* ☏ *864/271–7570* ⊕ *www.gcma.org* ☑ *Free* ⊘ *Closed Mon. and Tues.*

9

FAMILY
Fodor's Choice
★

Jones Gap State Park. Famous for its trout fishing and the Rim of the Gap trail, which has views of Rainbow Falls, Jones Gap State Park is 6 miles east of U.S. 276 and is part of the Mountain Bridge Wilderness Area. Be sure to pick up a trail map and register before venturing into the wilderness; some of the trails are long and strenuous. ⊠ *303 Jones Gap Rd., 6 miles east off U.S. 276, Marietta* ☏ *864/836–3647* ⊕ *www.southcarolinaparks.com/jonesgap* ☑ *$5.*

Shoeless Joe Jackson Museum and Baseball Library. This collection is housed in the former home of baseball great Joe Jackson, who along with seven other White Sox players, was accused of throwing the 1919 World Series. Though he was found not guilty, Jackson was banned from playing baseball. The museum has records, artifacts, photographs, and a film, along with a library of baseball books donated from fans around the country. At the end of each summer, staffers challenge their peers at Georgia's Ty Cobb Museum to a vintage baseball game. ⊠ *356 Field St., across from Fluor Field, Historic West End* ☏ *864/346–4867* ⊕ *www.shoelessjoejackson.org* ☑ *Free.*

THE PALMETTO TRAIL

Beginning in Oconee State Park in the Upstate and ending along the coast just north of Charleston, the Palmetto Trail is the perfect way to travel the state on foot or by mountain bike. Marked for travel in both directions by way of standard trail blazes and occasional signs, the route spans 425 miles of South Carolina's mountains, piedmont, and coastal plain. That mileage is broken into more than 20 passages that vary in length from a short 7-mile section to a multiday hike that's roughly 50 miles. The trail winds through state parks and national forests and past Revolutionary War battlefields—all with glorious views. Visit ⊕ www. palmettoconservation.org to plan your hike.

OFF THE BEATEN PATH

Twin Falls. It's a scenic drive and then an easy hike to these picturesque double falls, where the left and larger of the falls pitches from a height of 75 feet and white water swooshes over wide gray boulders on the right. Don't give in to the temptation to climb the rocks leading to the top of the falls; not only is the view not much better but the stones are very slippery. The trail is on public property, a ¼-mile hike one way. ⊠ Water Falls Road, Pickens ✛ Take Cleo Chapman Rd. to Eastatoe Community Rd. to Water Falls Rd. (gravel).

Upcountry History Museum. Exhibits focus on the history of the 15 counties of the South Carolina Upstate. There are two floors of interactive displays and a small theater where special programs are regularly presented. ⊠ 540 Buncombe St., Heritage Green ☎ 864/467–3100 ⊕ www. upcountryhistory.org ➔ $6 ♥ Closed Mon.

WHERE TO EAT

$$$$
AMERICAN

✕ **Augusta Grill.** The daily changing menu at this fine dining stalwart includes seafood like tempura soft shell crabs, hearty steaks, and braised duck. Order ahead to be sure the kitchen hasn't run out of its signature blackberry cobbler. **Known for:** small plate options designed for sharing; varied, seasonal menu; blackberry cobbler. $ Average main: $26 ⊠ 1818 Augusta St. ☎ 864/242–0316 ⊕ www.augustagrill.com ♥ Closed Sun. and Mon. No lunch.

$$$$
SOUTHERN
Fodor's Choice
★

✕ **Soby's New South Cuisine.** The palette of plums and golds is a stunning contrast to the original brick and wood that was uncovered during the renovation of this 19th-century cotton exchange building. Although the menu changes seasonally, perennial favorites—a layered appetizer of fried green tomatoes and jalapeño pimento cheese, shrimp, and locally ground grits, and the wonderful white-chocolate banana-cream pie—are always available. **Known for:** popular Sunday brunch; one of the city's best wine lists. $ Average main: $25 ⊠ 207 S. Main St., Downtown ☎ 864/232–7007 ⊕ www.sobys.com ♥ No lunch.

$
DINER

✕ **Stax Omega Diner.** Sit at the booths or the half-circle counter with stools and peruse this contemporary diner's menu, which features a little of everything, from bacon and eggs, burgers, and souvlaki, to Greek-style chicken, shrimp, and grits. When you're done with your meal, check out the sweets menu from the Stax bakery next door. **Known for:** Greek and Italian desserts; popular local catering service; classic diner fare. [$] *Average main: $12* ✉ *72 Orchard Park Dr.* ☎ *864/297–6639* 🌐 *www.staxs.net.*

$ DELI 🍴 **Two Chefs Cafe & Market.** Mix and match from the selection of homemade sandwiches and healthy entrée options like roasted-potato salad and dried-cranberry-and-grilled-chicken salad. Tempting desserts include apple-brandy cake, flourless chocolate cake, and fruit tarts. **Known for:** salad-sandwich combos; daily entrée specials; grab-and-go market. [$] *Average main: $8* ✉ *644 N. Main St., Suite 107* ☎ *864/370–9336* 🌐 *www.twochefscafeandmarket.com* 🕒 *Closed Sun.*

WHERE TO STAY

$$$ HOTEL 🏨 **Aloft Greenville Downtown.** One of the city's newest lodging options, this colorful, modern hotel offers rooms adorned with art and nouveau furnishings, including spacious suites. **Pros:** central location downtown; outdoor swimming pool is open late; pet-friendly. **Cons:** not directly on Main Street. [$] *Rooms from: $220* ✉ *5 N. Laurens St., Downtown* ☎ *864/297–6100* 🌐 *www.aloftgreenvilledowntown.com* 🛏 *144 rooms* 🍽 *No meals.*

$$$ HOTEL 🏨 **Hyatt Regency Greenville.** Conveniently located in the middle of the revitalized downtown of shops and restaurants, this lauded chain's rooms come with one king or queen bed or two doubles. **Pros:** easy access to Main Street and Falls Park; popular on-site restaurant, Roost. **Cons:** the breakfast buffet served at the restaurant is not included. [$] *Rooms from: $249* ✉ *220 N. Main St., Downtown* ☎ *864/235–1234* 🌐 *www.greenville.hyatt.com* 🛏 *327 rooms* 🍽 *No meals.*

$$$$ HOTEL 🏨 **The Westin Poinsett.** This 11-story downtown hotel combines old-fashioned appeal (it was built in 1925) with modern upgrades courtesy of Westin. **Pros:** central location on Main Street; on-site coffee shop; fitness studio and spa. **Cons:** daily parking fee. [$] *Rooms from: $265* ✉ *120 S. Main St.* ☎ *864/421–9700* 🌐 *www.westinpoinsettgreenville.com* 🛏 *223 rooms* 🍽 *No meals.*

PERFORMING ARTS

Bon Secours Wellness Arena. This 15,000-seat arena hosts major concerts and sporting events. ✉ *650 N. Academy St.* ☎ *864/241–3800* 🌐 *www.bonsecoursarena.com.*

The Peace Center. Situated along the Reedy River, The Peace Center's theater, concert hall, and amphitheater present star performers, touring Broadway shows, dance companies, chamber music, and local groups. ✉ *300 S. Main St.* ☎ *864/467–3000* 🌐 *www.peacecenter.org.*

SPORTS AND THE OUTDOORS

Upstate golf courses are less crowded and are usually a bit less hot than those on the coast. The area's rolling hills provide an added challenge. Further afield, on the border of Georgia and South Carolina, the Chattooga River offers one of the country's best white-water experiences.

Links O'Tryon. This 18-hole course with stunning views of the Blue Ridge Mountains and fieldstone bridges and walls was designed by Tom Jackson. ✉ *11250 New Cut Rd., Campobello* ☎ *864/468–5099* 🌐 *www.linksotryon.com* 🎫 *$32 weekdays, $42 weekends* ⛳ *18 holes, 6877 yds, par 72.*

The Rock at Jocassee. Also called Bear Valley, this mountain course features plenty of water hazards; its signature hole has a waterfall view. ⊠ *171 Sliding Rock Rd., Pickens* ☎ *864/878–2030* ⊕ *www.bearvalleygolf.com* 🖃 *$22 weekdays, $38 weekends* ⅃. *18 holes, 6710 yards, par 72.*

SHOPPING

The shopping area along Greenville's Main Street and adjoining West End may be just a half-mile long, but it's chockablock with interesting shops and growing by the year.

Augusta Twenty. This friendly shop is filled with racks of designer clothing and has frequent sales. ⊠ *20 Augusta St., at S. Main St., Downtown* ☎ *864/233–2600* ⊕ *www.augustatwenty.com* ⊗ *Closed Sun.*

FAMILY **O.P. Taylor's.** Even adults love this supercool toy emporium. ⊠ *117 N. Main St.* ☎ *864/467–1984* ⊕ *www.optaylors.com.*

Perdeaux Fruit Farm. Stop here if you're driving the Cherokee Foothills Scenic Highway between June and November. Perdeaux Fruit Farm sells an always-changing selection of locally grown fruits, such as peaches, blackberries, pears, apples, and raspberries. Owner Dick Perdue also makes the jams, jellies, applesauce, and ciders that fill the shelves, along with local honey. ⊠ *2400 SC Hwy. 11, Travelers Rest* ☎ *864/979–8378* ⊗ *Closed in winter and on Mon. and Tues. in summer.*

BLACKSBURG

70 miles northeast of Greenville via I–85.

Once a booming center during the "iron rush" of the late 1800s, Blacksburg is a quiet little town with a lot of history. Home to both Kings Mountain State Park and Kings Mountain National Military Park, the town celebrates the historic Battle of Kings Mountain each October with battlefield tours, enactments, and living history interpreters.

EXPLORING

Kings Mountain National Military Park. A Revolutionary War battle considered an important turning point was fought here on October 7, 1780. Colonial Tories were soundly defeated by ragtag patriot forces from the southern Appalachians. Visitor center exhibits, dioramas, and an orientation film describe the action. A paved self-guided trail leads through the battlefield. ⊠ *Off Exit 2, I–85* ☎ *864/936–7921* ⊕ *www. nps.gov/kimo* 🖃 *Free.*

FAMILY **Kings Mountain State Park.** This 6,000-acre park, adjacent to the National Military Park, has camping, fishing, boating, and nature and hiking trails. ⊠ *Off Exit 2, I–85* ☎ *803/222–3209* ⊕ *www.southcarolinaparks. com/kingsmountain* 🖃 *$2.*

SAVANNAH, GA

WELCOME TO SAVANNAH, GA

TOP REASONS TO GO

★ **Winsome architecture:** Savannah has no shortage of architectural or historical marvels. The many building styles make strolling the tree-lined neighborhoods a delight.

★ **Midnight in the Garden of Good and Evil:** John Berendt's famous 1994 book about a local murder and the city's eccentric characters still draws travelers to the places described in the novel.

★ **Famous Southern restaurants:** Savannah's elegant restaurants, notably Elizabeth on 37th and the Olde Pink House, have exquisite Southern cuisine.

★ **Historic inns and bed-and-breakfasts:** One of Savannah's unique pleasures is the opportunity to stay in a historic home fronting a prominent square.

★ **Savannah by night:** Ubiquitous "to-go" cups make barhopping a popular pastime. Ghost tours are another fun nocturnal activity.

1 The Historic District. A link to the past is a big part of Savannah's allure. The 2½-square-mile landmark Historic District is the nation's largest. It is where the city's historic squares and most of its accommodations, restaurants, and shops are located.

2 Tybee Island. Formerly known as Savannah Beach, Tybee Island has been a destination since the 1920s, when a train connected downtown to the beach pavilion where jazz bands played. These days the island is a mix of kitschy shops and interesting

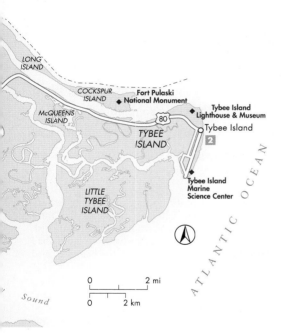

GETTING ORIENTED

Although it's commonly referred to as "downtown," the Historic District lies on the northern edge of Savannah, just across the river from Hutchinson Island and South Carolina. The borders of the district are River Street to the north, Gaston Street to the south, and East Broad Street and Martin Luther King Jr. Boulevard to the east and west.

Tybee Island is 18 miles east of Savannah via Victory Drive (U.S. 80).

10

restaurants. Whether you're looking to work on your tan, spend a day on a fishing charter, or maneuver a Jet Ski, this is a must-see during the summer months.

Updated by
Summer Teal
Simpson Hitch

Savannah is such a warm, welcoming city that you may find it especially easy to get acquainted with the "Hostess City," as it is known to those smitten by its hospitality and charm. As America's first planned city, Savannah is perhaps most recognized for its 22 squares, the diverse group of parks that dot the Historic District. The city also remains connected with its namesake river; it is home to a busy commercial port, and towering cargo ships are a common sight along River Street.

Savannah, Georgia's oldest city, began its modern history on February 12, 1733, when James Oglethorpe and 120 colonists arrived at Yamacraw Bluff on the Savannah River to what would be the last British colony in the New World. For a century and a half the city flourished as a bustling port, and was the departure point for cotton being shipped around the world.

Although Savannah was spared during the Civil War, the city fell on hard times soon afterward. Cobwebs replaced cotton in the dilapidated riverfront warehouses. Historic buildings languished; many were razed or allowed to decay. The tide finally turned in the 1950s, when residents began a concerted effort—which continues to this day—to restore and preserve the city's unique architectural heritage.

The past plays an important role in Savannah. Standing in a tranquil square surrounded by historic homes, it's easy to feel as if you have stumbled through a portal into the past. Don't be fooled though, as the city offers much more than antebellum nostalgia for moonlight and magnolias. Savannah is home to several colleges and universities, including the prestigious Savannah College of Art and Design (SCAD), and in the last decade in particular has seen a surge of creative energy. A new crop of cultural events lends a youthful vibe to the Hostess City.

PLANNING

PLANNING YOUR TIME

Savannah is not large, but it is atmospheric, and you want to allow sufficient time to soak in the ambience. You'll need a minimum of two or three days to fully appreciate the Historic District and its many sights, not to mention the food, which is an integral part of the Savannah experience. You'll need another day or two to see the sights in the surrounding area, including a jaunt out to Tybee Island for a fishing trip, kayaking tour, or relaxing on the beach. Some travelers head north to Hilton Head or Charleston to round out their Lowcountry experience.

GETTING HERE AND AROUND

You can fly into Savannah and catch a cab downtown, which is largely walkable. But you'll probably need a car if you want to explore beyond the Historic District.

AIR TRAVEL

Savannah and Hilton Head share an airport. Savannah/Hilton Head International Airport (SAV) is 11 miles west of downtown. The airport is only 20 minutes by car from the Historic District and around 40 minutes from Hilton Head Island. There are plenty of taxis waiting outside the baggage claim area, and some of the larger hotels offer shuttles. ■ TIP➔ If the flights into Savannah/Hilton Head International Airport aren't convenient, consider Jacksonville International Airport. The drive time to Savannah is just shy of 2½ hours.

Airport Information Savannah/Hilton Head International Airport. ✉ *400 Airways Ave., Northwest* ☎ *912/964–0514* ⊕ *www.savannahairport.com.*

CAR TRAVEL

Interstate 95 slices north–south along the Eastern Seaboard, intersecting 10 miles west of town with east–west Interstate 16, which dead-ends in downtown Savannah. U.S. 17, the Coastal Highway, also runs north–south through town. U.S. 80 is another east–west route through Savannah.

Downtown parking can be a challenge; there are often more options in nearby residential neighborhoods. Tourists may purchase one- and two-day parking passes for $8 and $14 from the Savannah Visitors Center, the Parking Services Department, and some hotels and inns (several properties give you this pass for free if you're staying with them). Rates vary at local parking garages, but in a City of Savannah–owned lot you should expect to pay at least $1 to $2 per hour during business hours on weekdays, a $2 flat rate in the evenings, and a flat rate of $5 to $10 on the weekends.

10

PUBLIC TRANSPORTATION

Chatham Area Transit (CAT) operates buses in Savannah and Chatham County Monday through Saturday from 6 am to just shy of midnight, and Sunday from 7 am to 9 pm. (Some lines stop running earlier or may not run on Sunday.) A free shuttle runs a loop throughout the Historic District. The Riverfront Trolley—a refurbished 1930s streetcar—runs the length of River Street Thursday to Sunday.

Public Transit Contacts Chatham Area Transit (CAT). ☎ *912/233–5767* ⊕ *www.catchacat.org.*

TAXI TRAVEL

AAA Adam Cab is a locally owned and operated, dependable 24-hour taxi service. Calling ahead for reservations could yield a flat rate. Yellow Cab Company is another reliable ride. Both companies charge $1.92 per mile. Mobile on-demand cab services like Uber and Lyft are also popular in the area.

Savannah Pedicab offer rides in people-powered vehicles that cost $45 per hour. They operate from 10 am to midnight (until 2 am on weekends).

Contacts AAA Adam Cab. ☎ *912/927–7466.* **Savannah Pedicab.** ☎ *912/232–7900* ⊕ *www.savannahpedicab.com.* **Yellow Cab.** ☎ *912/236–1133, 912/224–3298* ⊕ *www.yellowcabofsavannah.com.*

TOURS

CARRIAGE TOURS

Carriage Tours of Savannah. Operating out of City Market, Carriage Tours of Savannah travels the Historic District at a 19th-century clip-clop pace, with coachmen spinning tales and telling ghost stories along the way. ☎ *912/236–6756* ⊕ *www.carriagetoursofsavannah.com* ✉ *From $22 per person.*

TROLLEY TOURS

Old Savannah Tours. This is the city's award-winning company with years of experience and the widest variety of tours. Popular options include the historic hop-on, hop-off trolley tour, the 90-minute Historic Overview, and the ghost tour that includes dinner at Pirates' House. ☎ *800/517–9007* ⊕ *www.oldsavannahtours.com* ✉ *From $20.*

Old Town Trolley Tours. With Old Town Trolley Tours, you'll find 90-minute tours traversing the Historic District. Trolleys stop at 16 designated stops every 30 minutes daily from 9 to 5 (August to March) or 9 to 6 (April to July). You can hop on and off as you please. ☎ *855/245–8992 toll-free* ⊕ *www.trolleytours.com/savannah* ✉ *From $33.*

WALKING TOURS

Creepy Crawl Haunted Pub Tour. This tour is a great option for anyone who loves a good ghost story and a visit to local watering holes. Believers say there are so many ghosts in Savannah they're actually divided into subcategories. These charismatic guides specialize in tavern ghosts, and they'll regale you with tales of secret sub-basements, possessed gum-ball machines, and animated water faucets. Tours traditionally depart from the Six Pence Pub at 8 pm and last for 2½ hours. ☎ *912/238–3843* ⊕ *www.savannahtours.com/creepy-crawl-pub-tour* ✉ *From $25.*

Ghost Talk Ghost Walk Tour. This tour should send chills down your spine during an easygoing 1-mile jaunt through the old colonial city. Tours, lasting 1½ hours, leave from the middle of Reynolds Square, at the John Wesley Memorial at 7:30 pm and 9:30 pm, weather permitting. Reservations are required. ☎ *912/233–3896* ⊕ *www.ghosttalkghostwalk.com* ✉ From $10.

VISITOR INFORMATION

Visitor Information Contacts Savannah Visitor Information Center. ✉ *301 Martin Luther King Jr. Blvd., Historic District* ☎ *912/944–0455* ⊕ *www.visitsavannah.com.* **Tybee Island Visitor Information Center.** ✉ *802 1st St., Tybee Island* ☎ *877/344–3361* ⊕ *www.visittybee.com.*

EXPLORING

With an eclectic array of shops, restaurants, museums, and monuments spread across the Historic District, the best way to explore downtown Savannah is on foot. Whether you plan a route ahead of time or just wander aimlessly, a leisurely stroll will always result in unique discoveries. If your feet start to ache, flag down a pedicab driver—these people-powered vehicles are a great way to get around, and the drivers usually tell a good story or two.

THE HISTORIC DISTRICT

Georgia's sage founder, General James Oglethorpe, laid out the city on a grid as logical as a geometry solution. The Historic District is neatly hemmed in by the Savannah River, Gaston Street, East Broad Street, and Martin Luther King Jr. Boulevard. Streets are arrow-straight, and public squares are tucked into the grid at precise intervals. Bull Street, anchored on the north by City Hall and the south by Forsyth Park, charges down the center of the grid and maneuvers around the five public squares that stand in its way. The squares all have some historical significance; many have elaborate fountains, monuments to war heroes, and shaded resting areas with park benches. Beautiful homes and mansions speak lovingly of another era.

TOP ATTRACTIONS

Andrew Low House. Built on the site of the city jail, this residence was constructed in 1848 for Andrew Low, a native of Scotland and one of Savannah's merchant princes. Designed by architect John S. Norris, the residence later belonged to Low's son, William, who inherited his father's wealth and married his longtime sweetheart, Juliette Gordon. The couple moved to England and several years after her husband's death, Juliette returned to this house and founded the Girl Scouts here on March 12, 1912. The house has 19th-century antiques, stunning silver, and some of the finest ornamental ironwork in Savannah, but it is the story and history of the family—even a bedroom named after the family friend and visitor General Robert E. Lee—that is fascinating and well told by the tour guides. ✉ *329 Abercorn St., Historic District* ☎ *912/233–6854* ⊕ *www.andrewlowhouse.com* ✉ *$10; $21 includes admission to Davenport House and Ships of the Sea Museum* ♡ *Closed early Jan.*

Chippewa Square. Anchoring this square is Daniel Chester French's imposing bronze statue of General James Edward Oglethorpe, founder of both the City of Savannah and the State of Georgia. The bus-stop scenes of *Forrest Gump* were filmed on the northern end of the square. Savannah Theatre, on the corner of Bull and McDonough Streets, claims to be the oldest continuously operated theater site in North America and offers a variety of family-friendly shows. ✉ *Bull St., between Hull and Perry Sts., Historic District.*

City Market. Although the 1870s City Market was razed years ago, its atmosphere and character are still evident. Adjacent to Ellis Square, the area is a lively destination because of its galleries, boutiques, street performers, and open-air cafés. New to the block is Byrd Cookie Co.,

10

DID YOU KNOW?

Midnight in the Garden of Good and Evil by John Berendt brought so much fame to Savannah, it is known simply as "the book" here. Fans make the pilgrimage to the Mercer House on Monterey Square, where Jim Williams once had his antique business.

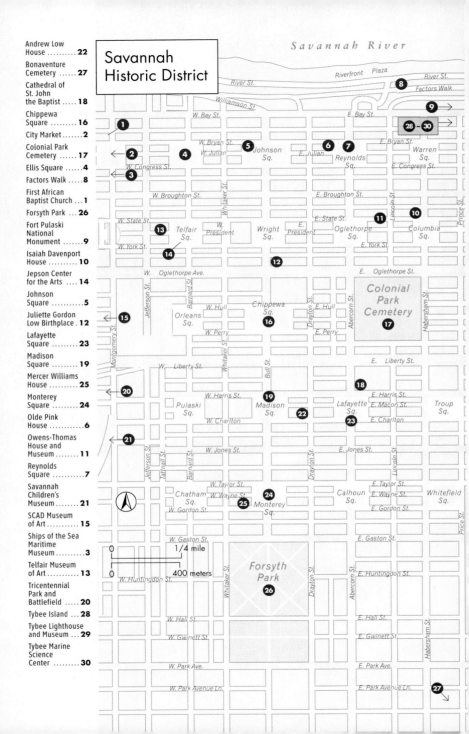

Savannah Historic District

a popular local bakery with great edible souvenirs, and Savannah Pie Society, offering specialty British meat pies. City Market is also a good spot to purchase trolley tickets or take a ride in a horse-drawn carriage. ⊠ *W. St. Julian St., between Barnard and Montgomery Sts., Historic District* ☎ *912/232–4903* ⊕ *www.savannahcitymarket.com.*

Colonial Park Cemetery. Stroll the shaded pathways and read some of the old tombstone inscriptions in this park, the final resting place for Savannahians who died between 1750 and 1853. Many of those interred here succumbed during the yellow fever epidemic in 1820. Notice the dramatic entrance gate on the corner of Abercorn and Oglethorpe Streets. Local legend tells that when Sherman's troops set up camp here, they moved some headstones around and altered inscriptions for their own amusement, which partially explains the headstones mounted against the far wall. This spooky spot is a regular stop for ghost tours. ⊠ *Oglethorpe and Abercorn Sts., Historic District.*

FAMILY
Fodor'sChoice
★

Ellis Square. Converted from a public square to a parking garage in the 1970s, Ellis Square has been restored in recent years and is once again one of Savannah's most popular spots. Near the western end stands a statue of legendary songwriter Johnny Mercer, a Savannah native. Nearby is a visitor center with a touch-screen city guide, maps and brochures, and public restrooms. To the east is a life-size chess board; the pieces can be requested at the visitor center. A treat for youngsters (and the young at heart) is the square's interactive fountain, which is entertaining and refreshing in the warmer months. ⊠ *Barnard St., between W. Congress and W. Bryan Sts., Historic District.*

Factors Walk. A network of iron crosswalks and steep stone stairways connects Bay Street to Factors Walk below. The congested area of multistory buildings was originally the center of commerce for cotton brokers, who walked between and above the lower cotton warehouses. Ramps lead down to River Street. ■TIP→ **This area is paved in cobblestones, so wear comfortable shoes.** ⊠ *Bay St. to Factors Walk, Historic District.*

FAMILY
Fodor'sChoice
★

Forsyth Park. The heart of the city's outdoor life, Forsyth Park hosts a number of popular cultural events, including film screenings, sports matches, and the annual Savannah Jazz Festival. Built in 1840 and expanded in 1851, the park was part of General Oglethorpe's original city plan and made possible by the donation of land from Georgia Governor John Forsyth. A glorious white fountain dating to 1858, Confederate and Spanish-American War memorials, a rose garden, multiple playgrounds, tennis and basketball courts, and an old fort are spread across this grand park. The fort houses a café, an open-air stage, and lovely fountains. Be sure to stop by Saturday for the bustling farmers' market. The park's 1-mile perimeter is among the prettiest walks in the city and takes you past many beautifully restored historic homes. ⊠ *Gaston St., between Drayton and Whitaker Sts., Historic District.*

10

Isaiah Davenport House. Semicircular stairs with wrought-iron railings lead to the recessed doorway of the redbrick Federal home constructed by master builder Isaiah Davenport for his family between 1815 and 1820. Three dormered windows poke through the sloping roof of the stately house, and the interior has polished hardwood floors and fine woodwork and plasterwork. The proposed demolition of this historic Savannah structure galvanized the city's residents into action to save their treasured buildings. The home endured a history of dilapidation that lingered since the 1920s, when it was divided into tenements. When someone proposed razing it to build a parking lot in 1955, a small group of neighbors raised $22,000 to buy and restore this property. This was the inception of the Historic Savannah Foundation and the first of many successful efforts to preserve the architectural treasure that is the city today. ⊠ *324 E. State St., Historic District* 🕾 *912/236–8097* ⊕ *www. davenporthousemuseum.org* ✉ *$9; $21 includes admission to Andrew Low House and Ships of the Sea Museum* ☺ *Closed early Jan.*

FAMILY
Fodor'sChoice
★
Jepson Center for the Arts. This contemporary building is one of a kind among the characteristic 18th- and 19th-century architecture of historic Savannah. The modern art extension of the Telfair Museum of Art, the Jepson was designed by renowned architect Moshe Safdie. Within the marble-and-glass edifice are rotating exhibits, on loan and from the permanent collection, ranging from European masters to contemporary locals. There's also an outdoor sculpture terrace and an interactive, kid-friendly area on the third level called the ArtZeum. ⊠ *207 W. York St., Historic District* 🕾 *912/790–8800* ⊕ *www.telfair.org/visit/jepson* ✉ *$20, includes admission to the Owens-Thomas House and Museum and the Telfair Museum of Art.*

Johnson Square. The oldest of James Oglethorpe's original squares was laid out in 1733 and named for South Carolina Governor Robert Johnson. A monument marks the grave of Nathanael Greene, a hero of the Revolutionary War. The square has always been a popular gathering place: Savannahians came here to welcome President Monroe in 1819, to greet the Marquis de Lafayette in 1825, and to cheer for Georgia's secession in 1861. ■ **TIP→ Locals call this Bank Square because of the plethora of nearby banks—perfect if you need an ATM.** ⊠ *Bull St., between Bryan and Congress Sts., Historic District.*

FAMILY
Juliette Gordon Low Birthplace. This early-19th-century town house, attributed to William Jay, was designated in 1965 as Savannah's first National Historic Landmark. "Daisy" Low, founder of the Girl Scouts, was born here in 1860, and the house is now owned and operated by the Girl Scouts of America. Mrs. Low's paintings and other artwork are on display in the house, restored to the style of 1886, the year of Mrs. Low's marriage. Droves of Girl Scout troops make the regular pilgrimage to Savannah to see their founder's birthplace and earn merit badges. ⊠ *10 E. Oglethorpe St., Historic District* 🕾 *912/233–4501* ⊕ *www. juliettegordonlowbirthplace.org* ✉ *$15* ☺ *Closed early Jan.*

Lafayette Square. Named for the Marquis de Lafayette, who aided the Americans during the Revolutionary War, the square contains a graceful three-tier fountain donated by the Georgia chapter of the Colonial Dames of America. The Cathedral of St. John the Baptist is located on this square, as are the Andrew Low House and the impressive Hamilton-Turner Inn. The childhood home of celebrated Southern author Flannery O'Connor also sits on this square. ⊠ *Abercorn St., between E. Harris and E. Charlton Sts., Historic District.*

■ NEED A
BREAK

Leopold's. One of the best ice-cream parlors in the area is Leopold's, a Savannah institution since 1919. It's currently owned by Stratton Leopold, grandson of the original owner and the producer of films like *Mission Impossible 3*. Movie posters and paraphernalia make for an entertaining sideline to the selection of ice cream made with the old family recipe. Try the delicious lemon custard or honey, almond, and cream flavors, or unique seasonal inventions like lavender, orange blossom, or rose petal. ⊠ *212 E. Broughton St., Historic District* ☎ *912/234-4442* ⊕ *www.leopoldsicecream.com.*

Madison Square. Laid out in 1839 and named for President James Madison, this square is home to a statue depicting Sergeant William Jasper hoisting a flag, a tribute to his bravery during the Siege of Savannah. Though mortally wounded, Jasper rescued the colors of his regiment in the assault on the British lines. A granite marker denotes the southern line of the British defense during the 1779 battle. The Green-Meldrim House is here. ⊠ *Bull St., between W. Harris and W. Charlton Sts., Historic District.*

Mercer Williams House. A staple on the tourist circuit, this house museum has been the stuff of legend since the release of the longtime bestselling novel *Midnight in the Garden of Good and Evil*. The home was purchased in 1969 by Jim Williams, who purportedly killed his lover in the front den while sitting at the desk where he later died. Scandal aside, Williams was an aficionado of historic preservation, and the Mercer House was one of some 50 properties that he purchased and restored. Designed by New York architect John S. Norris for General Hugh Mercer, great-grandfather of Johnny Mercer, the home was constructed in 1860 and completed after the end of the Civil War in 1868. Inside are fine examples of 18th- and 19th-century furniture and art from Jim Williams's private collection. ■TIP→ **Don't miss a look around the charming gift shop.** ⊠ *429 Bull St., Historic District* ☎ *912/236-6352* ⊕ *mercerhouse.com* ⊠ *$12.50.*

Fodor'sChoice ★ **Owens-Thomas House and Museum.** Designed by William Jay, the Owens-Thomas House is widely considered to be one of the finest examples of English Regency architecture in America. Built in 1816–19, the house was constructed with local materials. Of particular note are the curving walls of the house, Greek-inspired ornamental molding, half-moon arches, stained-glass panels, original Duncan Phyfe furniture, and the hardwood "bridge" on the second floor. The carriage house includes a gift shop and rare urban slave quarters, which have retained the original furnishings and "haint-blue" paint made by the slave occupants. This house had indoor toilets before the White House or Versailles. Owned and administered by the Telfair Museum of Art, this home gives an inside perspective on Savannah's history. ⊠ *124 Abercorn St., Historic District* ☎ *912/790–8889* ⊕ *www.telfair.org/ visit/owens-thomas* ⊠ *$20, includes admission to Jepson Center for the Arts and the Telfair Museum of Art.*

10

Reynolds Square. Anglican cleric and theologian John Wesley is remembered here. He arrived in Savannah in 1736 at the behest of General James Oglethorpe. During his short stay, the future founder of the Methodist Church preached and wrote the first English hymnal in the city. His monument in Reynolds Square is shaded by greenery and surrounded by park benches. The landmark Planters Inn, formerly the John Wesley Hotel, is also located on the square. Ironically, though it was named after a man of the cloth, it was considered the best brothel in town at the turn of the century. ⊠ *Abercorn St., between E. Congress and E. Bryan Sts., Historic District.*

FAMILY
Fodor's Choice
★

Savannah Children's Museum. Adhering to the principle of learning through doing, the Savannah Children's Museum has open green spaces with several stations geared for sensory play, including a water–sand play excavation station, sound station of percussion instruments, and an organic garden. The storybook nook is a partnership with the Savannah public library and encourages visiting youngsters to balance physical and mental recreation. One station includes costumes for stage performances. ⊠ *655 Louisville Rd., Historic District* ☎ *912/651–4292* ⊕ *www.chsgeorgia.org/scm* ✎ *$7.50* ☼ *Closed Sun. in June–Aug.; Closed Mon. and Tues. in Sept.–May.*

Fodor's Choice
★

SCAD Museum of Art. This architectural marvel rose from the ruins of the oldest surviving railroad building in the United States. Appropriately, the architect chosen for the lofty design and remodel project was Christian Sottile, the valedictorian of Savannah College of Art and Design's 1996 graduating class and the current dean of the School of Building Arts. Sottile rose to the hearty challenge of merging the past with the present, preserving key architectural details of the original structure while introducing contemporary design elements. SCAD Museum of Art houses two main galleries with rotating exhibits by some of the most acclaimed figures in contemporary art: the Evans Gallery features works of African American arts and culture, while the André Leon Talley Gallery is devoted to fashion and high style. ⊠ *601 Turner Blvd., Historic District* ☎ *912/525–7191* ⊕ *www.scadmoa.org* ✎ *$10* ☼ *Closed Mon.*

FAMILY
Fodor's Choice
★

Ships of the Sea Maritime Museum. This exuberant Greek Revival mansion was the home of William Scarborough, a wealthy early-19th-century merchant and one of the principal owners of the *Savannah,* the first steamship to cross the Atlantic. The structure, with its portico capped by half-moon windows, is another of architect William Jay's notable contributions to the Historic District. These days, it houses the Ships of the Sea Museum, with displays of model ships and exhibits detailing maritime history. The ambitious North Garden nearly doubled the original walled courtyard's size and provides ample space for naturalist-led walks and outdoor concerts. ⊠ *41 Martin Luther King Jr. Blvd., Historic District* ☎ *912/232–1511* ⊕ *www.shipsofthesea.org* ✎ *$9* ☼ *Closed Mon.*

Telfair Museum of Art. The oldest public art museum in the Southeast was designed by William Jay in 1819 for Alexander Telfair. Within its marble rooms are a variety of paintings from American and European masters, plaster casts of the Elgin Marbles and other classical sculptures, and some of the Telfair family furnishings, including a Duncan Phyfe sideboard and Savannah-made silver. It is the permanent home of the notable Bird Girl statue, made famous on the cover of John Berendt's *Midnight in the Garden of Good and Evil*. The Telfair hosts classical music performances during spring's Savannah Music Festival. ✉ *121 Barnard St., Historic District* ☎ *912/790–8800* ⊕ *www.telfair. org* 🗲 *$20, includes admission to the Jepson Center for the Arts and the Owens-Thomas House and Museum.*

FAMILY **Tricentennial Park and Battlefield.** This 25-acre complex is home to the Savannah History Museum, the Georgia State Railroad Museum, and the Savannah Children's Museum, as well as Battlefield Memorial Park. This site offers an unbeatable introduction to the city and a full day of fun for the whole family. The battlefield was the site of the second bloodiest battle of the Revolutionary War where, on October 9, 1779, 800 of the 8,000 troops who fought lost their lives. ✉ *303 Martin Luther King Jr. Blvd., Historic District* ☎ *912/651–6840* ⊕ *www.savannah.com/tricentennial-park.*

WORTH NOTING

Cathedral of St. John the Baptist. Soaring over the city, this French Gothic–style cathedral, with pointed arches and free-flowing traceries, is the seat of the Catholic diocese of Savannah. It was founded in 1799 by the first French colonists to arrive in Savannah. Fire destroyed the early structures; the present cathedral dates from 1876. Its architecture, gold-leaf adornments, and the entire edifice give testimony to the importance of the Catholic parishioners of the day. The interior spaces are grand and dramatic, including incredible stained glass and an intricately designed altar. ✉ *222 E. Harris St., at Lafayette Sq., Historic District* ☎ *912/233–4709* ⊕ *www.savannahcathedral.org* ⊗ *No tours Sun.*

First African Baptist Church. Slaves constructed this church at night by lamplight after having worked the plantations during the day. It is one of the first organized black Baptist churches on the continent. The basement floor still shows signs of its time as a stop on the Underground Railroad. Designs drilled in the floor are thought to actually have been air holes for slaves hiding underneath, waiting to be transported to the Savannah River for their trip to freedom. It was also an important meeting place during the civil rights era. ✉ *23 Montgomery St., Historic District* ☎ *912/233–6597* ⊕ *www.firstafricanbc.com* 🗲 *$7* ⊗ *Closed Mon.*

Monterey Square. Commemorating the victory of General Zachary Taylor's forces in Monterrey, Mexico, in 1846, this is the southernmost of Bull Street's squares. A monument honors General Casimir Pulaski, the Polish nobleman who lost his life in the Siege of Savannah during the Revolutionary War. On the square sits Temple Mickve Israel (one of the country's oldest Jewish congregations) and some of the city's most beautiful mansions, including the infamous Mercer House. ✉ *Bull St., between Taylor and Gordon Sts., Historic District.*

10

THE SAVANNAH AREA

Fodor's Choice ★   **Bonaventure Cemetery.** The largest of Savannah's municipal cemeteries, Bonaventure spreads over 160 acres and sits on a bluff above the Wilmington River. Once a plantation, the land became a private cemetery in 1846 and the public cemetery was established in 1907. The scenescape is one of lush natural beauty transposed against the elegant and almost eerie backdrop of lavish marble headstones, monuments, and mausoleums. John Muir reportedly camped at Bonaventure in 1867 on his legendary "thousand-mile walk." Local photographer Jack Leigh, novelist and poet Conrad Aiken, and singer-songwriter Johnny Mercer are among those interred here. ☒ *330 Greenwich Rd., Thunderbolt* ☎ *912/651–6843* ⊕ *www.bonaventurehistorical.org.*

FAMILY
Fodor's Choice ★   **Fort Pulaski National Monument.** Named for Casimir Pulaski, a Polish count and Revolutionary War hero, this must-see sight for Civil War buffs was designed by Napoléon's military engineer and built on Cockspur Island between 1829 and 1847. Robert E. Lee's first assignment after graduating from West Point was as an engineer here. The fort was thought to be impervious to attack, but as weapons advanced, it proved penetrable. During the Civil War, the fort fell after bombardment by newfangled rifled cannons. The restored fortification, operated by the National Park Service, has moats, drawbridges, massive ramparts, and towering walls. The park has trails and picnic areas. ☒ *U.S. Hwy. 80, Savannah* ☎ *912/786–5787* ⊕ *www.nps.gov/fopu* 🎟 *$7.*

FAMILY   **Tybee Island.** The Yamacraw Indians originally came to this island in the Atlantic Ocean to hunt and fish, but these days, the island is chockfull of seafood restaurants, chain motels, and souvenir shops—most of which sprang up during the 1950s and haven't changed much since. Fun-loving locals still host big annual parties like fall's Pirate Festival and spring's Beach Bum Parade. Tybee Island's entire expanse of taupe sand is divided into three public beach stretches: North Beach, the Pier and Pavilion, and the South End. Beach activities abound, including swimming, boating, fishing, sea kayaking, and parasailing. Newer water sports have gained popularity, including kiteboarding and stand-up paddleboarding. ☒ *U.S. 80, Tybee Island* ✛ *18 miles east of Savannah* ☎ *912/786–5444* ⊕ *tybeeisland.com.*

Tybee Island Lighthouse and Museum. Considered one of North America's most beautifully renovated lighthouses, the Tybee Light Station has been guiding Savannah River mariners since 1736. It's not the first lighthouse built on this site; the original was built on orders of General James Oglethorpe in 1732. You can walk up 178 steps for amazing views at the top. The lighthouse keeper's cottage houses a small theater showing a video about the lighthouse. The nearby museum is housed in a gun battery constructed for the Spanish-American War. ☒ *30 Meddin Dr., Tybee Island* ☎ *912/786–5801* ⊕ *www.tybeelighthouse.org* 🎟 *$9* ☽ *Closed Tues.*

FAMILY   **Tybee Island Marine Science Center.** Don't miss the Tybee Island Marine Science Center's interesting exhibit on Coastal Georgia, which houses local wildlife ranging from Ogeechee corn snakes to American alligators. Schedule one of two guided walks along the beach and

CLOSE UP

Moss Mystique

Spanish moss—the silky gray garlands that drape over the branches of live oaks—has come to symbolize the languorous sensibilities of the Deep South. A relative of the pineapple, this moisture-loving plant requires an average year-round humidity of 70%, and thus thrives in subtropical climates—including Georgia's coastal regions.

Contrary to popular belief, Spanish moss is not a parasite; it's an epiphyte, or "air plant," taking water and nutrients from the air and photosynthesizing in the same manner as soil-bound plants. It reproduces using tiny flowers. When water is scarce, it turns gray, and when the rains come it takes on a greenish hue. Although it is tempting to grab handfuls of Spanish moss as a souvenir, be careful. It often harbors the biting menaces commonly known as chiggers.

marshes if you're interested in the flora and fauna of the Lowcountry. There is also a "Turtle Talk," which consists of a classroom discussion and hands-on workshop. ■TIP➜ **Arrive early, as parking near the center can be competitive in the busier months.** ✉ *1509 Strand Ave., Tybee Island* ☎ *912/786–5917* ⊕ *www.tybeemarinescience.org* ✺ *$5; tours $10.*

WHERE TO EAT

Southern cuisine is rich in tradition, but the dining scene in Savannah is more than just fried chicken and barbecue. Many of the city's restaurants have been exploring locally sourced ingredients as a way to tweak their usual homespun offerings, a change that is now attracting chefs and foodies alike.

Although the farm-to-table trend was first spotted at upscale spots like Elizabeth on 37th and Local 11ten, more neighborhood restaurants are now getting in on the action. Places like the Green Truck Pub utilize locally raised, grass-fed beef for their burgers, and after-dinner options now even include locally roasted coffee.

10

The arrival of some new kids on the block doesn't mean the old standbys have ridden off into the sunset just yet. For traditional, exquisitely prepared menus, be sure to visit the Olde Pink House, which has been pleasing local palates for decades. Or follow the crowds to the ever-popular Mrs. Wilkes' Dining Room (which even President Obama once visited), where you'll find all the fried chicken, collard greens, and mac 'n' cheese you can handle.

That's just a few ideas to get you started. While exploring Savannah, you're sure to find any number of other exciting options as well, whether you're craving noodle bowls or a simple sandwich.

Live oak allées draped with Spanish moss are a symbol of Savannah.

HOURS, PRICES, AND DRESS

Most popular restaurants serve both lunch and dinner, usually until around 9 pm, later on Friday and Saturday nights. Sunday brunch is a beloved institution, but be prepared to wait for a table at most of the popular spots.

Prices, although on the rise, are less than in most major cities, especially on either coast.

Some locals and restaurant owners have a laid-back attitude about dressing for a night out. If you are hitting a River Street tourist restaurant, a small neighborhood eatery, or a barbecue joint, jeans are just fine. However, if you are going to an upscale restaurant, dress in keeping with the environment, especially on weekend nights.

Restaurant listings have been shortened. For full information, visit Fodors.com.

Use the coordinate (✣ B2) at the end of each listing to locate a site on the Where to Eat and Stay in Savannah map.

WHAT IT COSTS			
$	**$$**	**$$$**	**$$$$**
under $15	$15–$19	$20–$24	over $24

Restaurant prices are for a main course at dinner, or if dinner is not served, at lunch.

HISTORIC DISTRICT

$$ ✕ **Atlantic.** A relative newcomer to the scene, Atlantic brilliantly merges
AMERICAN the fine dining experience with the beloved neighborhood eatery. With
Fodor'sChoice an infusion of locally sourced ingredients and a universal love of the
★ vegetable, Atlantic offers seasonal menus of small plates, sandwiches,
and light bites that are as complex and refined as the best of Savannah's
restaurants. **Known for:** patio dining; exquisite yet affordable wines; no
reservations policy. Ⓢ *Average main: $19* ✉ *102 E Victory Dr., Thomas
Square* ☎ *912/417–8887* ⊕ *www.atlanticsavannah.com* ⊗ *Closed Sun.
No lunch.* ✛ *C6.*

$$ ✕ **B. Matthews Eatery.** The freshly updated and expanded kitchen here
ECLECTIC offers a great menu that ranges from the familiar to the unexpected.
Breakfast is a highlight, while lunch is known for being a great value,
with most of the well-stuffed sandwiches going for around $9. **Known
for:** vibrant brunch and lunch scene; good vegetarian options; unique
twist on Southern classics. Ⓢ *Average main: $19* ✉ *325 E. Bay St.,
Historic District* ☎ *912/233–1319* ⊕ *www.bmatthewseatery.com* ⊗ *No
dinner Sun.* ✛ *D1.*

$$$$ ✕ **Circa 1875.** The closest thing you'll find to a Parisian bistro in Savan-
FRENCH nah, this intimate gastropub offers a menu rich of traditional French
Fodor'sChoice dishes. The escargot and pâté make excellent starters before you move
★ on to main dishes like steak frites or cassoulet. **Known for:** Parisian
atmosphere and authentic French cuisine; intimate, romantic space;
fantastic mussels in broth. Ⓢ *Average main: $31* ✉ *48 Whitaker St.,
Historic District* ☎ *912/443–1875* ⊕ *www.circa1875.com* ⊗ *No lunch.
Closed Sun.* ✛ *B2.*

$$$ ✕ **Cotton & Rye.** In many ways, Cotton and Rye embodies the idea of new
SOUTHERN Savannah, creative and artistic with a strong sense of tradition. The menu
consists of classic, recognizable comfort dishes like fried chicken and beef
stroganoff, but careful intention goes into the preparation and presenta-
tion that result in a delightful sensory surprise. **Known for:** upscale take
on gastropub fare; inventive, homemade desserts; patio dining. Ⓢ *Average
main: $22* ✉ *1801 Habersham St., Downtown* ☎ *912/777–6286* ⊕ *www.
cottonandrye.com* ⊗ *Closed Sun. No lunch* ✛ *C6.*

$$$$ ✕ **Elizabeth on 37th.** Set within the Victorian District, this elegant turn-
SOUTHERN of-the-20th-century mansion has been feeding Savannah's upper crust
Fodor'sChoice for decades. Regional specialties are the hallmark at this acclaimed
★ restaurant, which credits local produce suppliers on its menu. **Known
for:** impressive wine list; top fine-dining experience in town; seven-
course tasting menu option. Ⓢ *Average main: $35* ✉ *105 E. 37th St.,
Thomas Square* ☎ *912/236–5547* ⊕ *www.elizabethon37th.net* ⊗ *No
lunch* ✛ *C6.*

$$$ ✕ **The Florence.** Housed in an old Savannah ice factory, the Florence has
MODERN ITALIAN lots of original architectural details and serves up some of the city's
Fodor'sChoice most innovative flavors. The Italian-influenced menu is crafted by Kyle
★ Jacovino, who has worked in kitchens all over Atlanta and New York.
Known for: seasonal menu inspired by authentic Italian fare; trendy
atmosphere; morning coffee bar. Ⓢ *Average main: $21* ✉ *1B W. Victory
Dr., Historic District* ☎ *912/234–5522* ⊕ *www.theflorencesavannah.
com* ⊗ *Closed Mon. No lunch Tues.–Sat.* ✛ *C6.*

10

$
ASIAN FUSION

✕ **The Flying Monk Noodle Bar.** Noodle, rice, and soup dishes from across Asia come together on the eclectic, flavorful menu at the Flying Monk. The well-appointed space and laid-back atmosphere compliment the savory dishes. **Known for:** authentic Asian fare; quick service; vegetarian-friendly menu. Ⓢ *Average main: $9* ✉ *5 W. Broughton St., Historic District* ☎ *912/232–8888* ⊕ *www.flywiththemonk.com* ✛ *B2.*

$$$$
MODERN ITALIAN
Fodor's Choice
★

✕ **Garibaldi's.** This well-appointed restaurant is well known to locals and travelers alike for its contemporary cuisine. Renowned for well-priced Italian classics, the kitchen also sends out some much more ambitious offerings, albeit at slightly higher prices. **Known for:** elegant and intimate setting; crispy flounder with apricot and shallot sauce. Ⓢ *Average main: $27* ✉ *315 W. Congress, Historic District* ☎ *912/232–7118* ⊕ *www.garibaldisavannah.com* ☾ *No lunch* ✛ *A2.*

$$$$
SOUTHERN
Fodor's Choice
★

✕ **The Grey.** This high-end establishment has made waves in Savannah as a world-class dining experience. Housed in a renovated 1930s Greyhound bus depot, it features a soulful, layered menu designed by a Savannah native who honed her craft in NYC. **Known for:** famed oyster bar; high-end cocktails; cool industrial setting. Ⓢ *Average main: $33* ✉ *109 Martin Luther King Jr. Blvd., Downtown* ☎ *912/662–5999* ⊕ *www.thegreyrestaurant.com* ☾ *Closed Mon. No lunch Sun.* ✛ *A2.*

$$$
SOUTHERN

✕ **The Lady & Sons.** Line up to get a reservation for lunch or dinner because, y'all, this is the place that Paula Deen, high priestess of Southern cooking, made famous. There are plenty of crowds these days, but everyone patiently waits to attack the buffet, which is stocked for both lunch and dinner with crispy fried chicken, mashed potatoes, collard greens, lima beans, and other favorites. **Known for:** celebrity chef Paula Deen; gut-busting Southern eats; homemade dessert classics like banana pudding. Ⓢ *Average main: $24* ✉ *102 W. Congress St., Historic District* ☎ *912/233–2600* ⊕ *www.ladyandsons.com* ✛ *B2.*

$$$$
MODERN
AMERICAN
Fodor's Choice
★

✕ **Local 11ten.** Light-years away from your average neighborhood watering hole, this stark, minimalist place looks like it was transported from a bigger, more sophisticated city. That also goes for the upbeat and contemporary menu, a reason why young chefs head here on their nights off. **Known for:** seasonal menu with farm-sourced ingredients; sea scallops over black rice; open-air rooftop bar. Ⓢ *Average main: $33* ✉ *1110 Bull St., Historic District* ☎ *912/790–9000* ⊕ *www.local11ten.com* ☾ *No lunch* ✛ *B6.*

$$$
SOUTHERN
FAMILY
Fodor's Choice
★

✕ **Mrs. Wilkes' Dining Room.** Everyone knows that this is the city's best Southern cuisine: when former President Barack Obama visited Savannah, he and his entourage had lunch here. Luckily he didn't have to join the rest of the folks lined up outside in order to enjoy the fine Southern fare, which is served family-style at big tables. **Known for:** Southern cooking served family-style; long waits that are well worth it; cash-only policy. Ⓢ *Average main: $22* ✉ *107 W. Jones St., Historic District* ☎ *912/232–5997* ⊕ *www.mrswilkes.com* ▭ *No credit cards* ☾ *Closed weekends and Jan. No dinner* ✛ *B4.*

$$$$
SOUTHERN
Fodor's Choice
★

✕ **Olde Pink House.** This Georgian mansion was built in 1771 for James Habersham, one of the wealthiest Americans of his time, and the historic atmosphere comes through in the original Georgia pine floors of the tavern, the Venetian chandeliers, and the 18th-century English

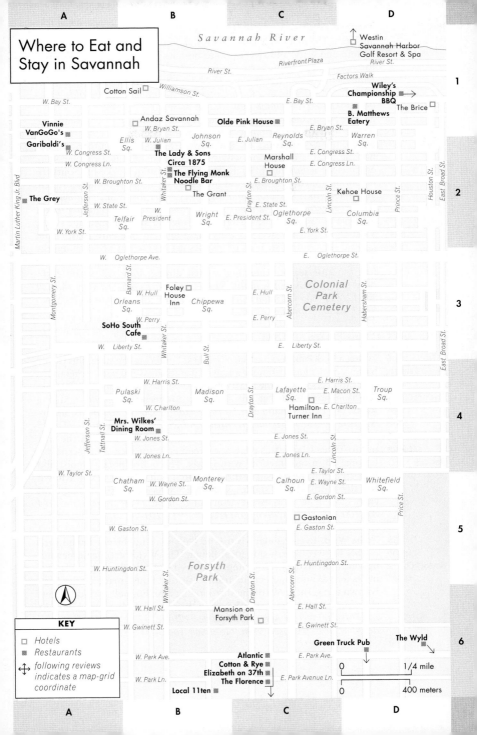

antiques. The menu is just as classic and Southern, with chicken potpie, shrimp and grits, and sweet-potato biscuits gracing the menu. **Known for:** exceptional Southern dining; historical ambience; remarkable wine menu. $ *Average main: $27* ⊠ *23 Abercorn St., Historic District* ☎ *912/232–4286* ⊕ *www.plantersinnsavannah.com/the-olde-pink-house-menu* ☾ *No lunch Sun. and Mon.* ✛ *C1.*

$ ✕ **SoHo South Cafe.** A garage turned art gallery and, finally, a restaurant,
ECLECTIC this spot shares the aesthetic hallmarks of all its previous incarnations. Inside, the gallery roots are still strong thanks to the interesting art, but the food is the reason why people still make this a regular stop, especially for Sunday brunch. **Known for:** unique take on Southern lunch, informed by fresh, local ingredients; awesome Sunday brunch; art gallery vibe. $ *Average main: $12* ⊠ *12 W. Liberty St., Historic District* ☎ *912/233–1633* ⊕ *www.sohosouthcafe.com* ☾ *No dinner* ✛ *B3.*

$ ✕ **Vinnie VanGoGo's.** With a secret dough recipe and a homemade sauce,
PIZZA Vinnie's is critically acclaimed by pizza and calzone enthusiasts from
FAMILY around the Southeast. Lots of visitors get a kick out of watching the cooks throw the dough in the air in the big open kitchen. **Known for:** outdoor seating; bustling, casual dining; long waits and cash-only policy. $ *Average main: $14* ⊠ *317 W. Bryan St., City Market* ☎ *912/233–6394* ⊕ *www.vinnievangogo.com* ▬ *No credit cards* ☾ *No lunch Mon.–Thurs.* ✛ *A1.*

ELSEWHERE IN SAVANNAH

$ ✕ **Green Truck Pub.** Serving one of the best burgers in the state, this casual
BURGER haunt draws diners from far and wide for its grass-fed beef. Vegetarians
FAMILY find satisfaction with the hearty meatless patties. **Known for:** great beer
Fodor'sChoice selection; homemade ketchup and pimento cheese; big crowds and long
★ waits. $ *Average main: $12* ⊠ *2430 Habersham St., Thomas Square* ☎ *912/234–5885* ⊕ *www.greentruckpub.com* ☾ *Closed Sun.* ✛ *D6.*

$ ✕ **Wiley's Championship BBQ.** Tucked away in a strip mall on the way
BARBECUE out to Tybee Island, this relative newcomer to the local BBQ scene has
Fodor'sChoice become an instant favorite with locals. The pulled pork is moist and
★ flavorful, and the brisket is the best you'll find outside Texas. **Known for:** slow-cooked BBQ staples; small space which can mean a long wait; early closing as soon as they run out of meat. $ *Average main: $14* ⊠ *4700 U.S. 80 E, Wilmington Island* ☎ *912/201–3259* ⊕ *www.wileys-championshipbbq.com* ☾ *Closed Sun.* ✛ *D1.*

$$ ✕ **The Wyld.** Even regular visitors to Savannah might not have heard
SEAFOOD of this beloved marsh-side local haunt. The Wyld offers a somewhat
Fodor'sChoice upscale twist to dockside dining, evidenced by the cocktail menu featur-
★ ing lavender bitters, crème de framboise, and house-made ginger beer. **Known for:** great views of the surrounding marsh; small seafood plates; slow but friendly service that's part of the charm. $ *Average main: $15* ⊠ *2740 Livingston Ave., Eastside* ☎ *912/692–1219* ⊕ *www.thewyld-dockbar.com* ☾ *Closed Mon. No lunch Tues.–Fri.* ✛ *D6.*

Victorian homes line the streets in Savannah's Historic District.

WHERE TO STAY

The Hostess City opens its doors every year to millions of visitors who are drawn to its historic and vibrant downtown. Because the majority of attractions are located within the Historic District, most of the city's best hotels are located there, too. Many are within easy walking distance of the city's premier restaurants and historic sites. In terms of accommodations, Savannah is best known for its many inns and B&Bs, which have moved into the stately antebellum mansions, renovated cotton warehouses, and myriad other historic buildings stretching from the river out to the Victorian neighborhoods in the vicinity of Forsyth Park. Most are beautifully restored with the requisite high ceilings, ornate carved millwork, claw-foot tubs, and other quaint touches. A flush of newer boutique hotels has shaken some of the dust out of Savannah's lodging scene and raised the bar for competing properties. Properties like the Brice, Cotton Sail, The Grant, and luxurious Mansion on Forsyth Park would be at home in a much larger city, but all have figured out how to introduce a sleek, cosmopolitan edge without bulldozing over Savannah's charm.

HOTEL PRICES

The central location and relatively high standards of quality in Savannah's Historic District hotels do drive up room rates, especially during peak seasons, holidays, and special events like St. Patrick's Day. The number of hotel rooms continues to increase, and occupancy rates have grown accordingly, even in the former slow season from September through January. October is another relatively busy time thanks to the pleasant temperatures and packed events calendar.

Use the coordinate (⊕ B2) at the end of each listing to locate a site on the Where to Eat and Stay in Savannah map.

Hotel reviews have been shortened. For full information, visit Fodors.com.

WHAT IT COSTS				
	$	$$	$$$	$$$$
Hotels	under $150	$150–$200	$201–$250	over $250

Prices in the hotel reviews are the lowest cost of a standard double room in high season.

THE HISTORIC DISTRICT

$$$$ HOTEL **Andaz Savannah.** The interiors at the Andaz make quite a statement: The exposed-brick walls in the spacious lobby are offset by cozy, nested seating areas. **Pros:** concierge with extensive insider knowledge; excellent location; cosmopolitan rooftop pool. **Cons:** sounds of revelers on Congress Street can sometimes be heard in rooms; no free parking; conference spaces don't match the designer appeal of the rest of the hotel. [$] *Rooms from: $279* ✉ *Ellis Square, 14 Barnard St., Historic District* ☎ *912/233–2116* 🌐 *www.savannah.andaz.hyatt.com* 🛏 *151 rooms* 🍴 *No meals* ⊕ *B1.*

$$$ HOTEL Fodor's Choice ★ **The Brice.** No detail was spared when they made a boutique hotel out of this 1860s warehouse, which later served as a Coca-Cola bottling plant and then a livery stable. **Pros:** staff is genuinely warm and helpful; artistic design mixed with old Southern touches; great view of the secret garden from many of the second floor rooms. **Cons:** neighboring Bay Street can be loud; no free parking. [$] *Rooms from: $224* ✉ *601 E. Bay St., Historic District* ☎ *912/238–1200* 🌐 *www.bricehotel.com* 🛏 *171 rooms* 🍴 *No meals* ⊕ *D1.*

$$$ HOTEL **Cotton Sail.** One of the newer hotels dotting the landscape, this locally owned and operated establishment is perched over River Street and offers expansive views of the Savannah River. **Pros:** hints of period charm; great location; rooftop bar is a great place to meet locals and out-of-towners. **Cons:** bar gets busy on the weekends which can mean noise; not as historic as other properties. [$] *Rooms from: $224* ✉ *126 W. Bay St., Historic District* ☎ *912/200–3700* 🌐 *www.thecottonsailhotel.com* 🛏 *56 rooms* 🍴 *No meals* ⊕ *B1.*

$$$ B&B/INN **Foley House Inn.** In the center of the Historic District, this elegant inn is made up of two town houses built 50 years apart. **Pros:** gorgeous architecture and decor; luxury bath products; complimentary cocktails at night. **Cons:** old pipes can make for slow drainage; fee for parking pass; no elevator. [$] *Rooms from: $219* ✉ *14 W. Hull St., Historic District* ☎ *912/232–6622, 800/647–3708* 🌐 *www.foleyinn.com* 🛏 *19 rooms* 🍴 *Breakfast* ⊕ *B3.*

$$$$ B&B/INN Fodor's Choice ★ **Gastonian.** Guest rooms—many of which are exceptionally spacious—in this atmospheric Italianate inn dating from 1868 all have fireplaces and are decorated with a mix of funky finds and antiques from the Georgian and Regency periods. **Pros:** cordial and caring staff; hot breakfast is hard to beat; afternoon tea and wine and cheese at

night. **Cons:** accommodations on the third floor are a climb; some of the furnishings are less than regal; plumbing is old and sometimes problematic. ⓢ *Rooms from: $279* ✉ *220 E. Gaston St., Historic District* ☎ *912/232–2869, 800/322–6603* ⊕ *www.gastonian.com* ⤴ *17 rooms* ¶⊙ *Breakfast* ⊹ *C5.*

$$
RENTAL
Fodor's Choice
★

▦ **The Grant.** Offering the best of both worlds, the Grant provides a boutique-hotel environment with the freedom of vacation-rental accommodations, the first establishment in Savannah to embrace the so-called "urban suite" trend. **Pros:** quality plus affordability; multiple-room suites great for large parties; overlooks Broughton Street. **Cons:** Broughton Street can be noisy at night; no hotel amenities; parking can be a challenge. ⓢ *Rooms from: $174* ✉ *5 W. Broughton St., Downtown* ☎ *912/257–4050* ⊕ *www. thegrantsavannah.com* ⤴ *17 suites* ¶⊙ *No meals* ⊹ *B2.*

$$$
B&B/INN
Fodor's Choice
★

▦ **Hamilton-Turner Inn.** With bathrooms the size of New York City apartments, this French Empire mansion is celebrated, if not in song, certainly in story, and certainly has a "wow" effect, especially the rooms that front Lafayette Square. **Pros:** wonderfully furnished rooms; breakfast is a treat; long and interesting history. **Cons:** sedate atmosphere won't appeal to everyone; no guest elevator (except for accessible Room 201); street parking only. ⓢ *Rooms from: $229* ✉ *330 Abercorn St., Historic District* ☎ *912/233–1833* ⊕ *www.hamilton-turnerinn.com* ⤴ *18 rooms* ¶⊙ *Breakfast* ⊹ *C4.*

$$$$
B&B/INN
Fodor's Choice
★

▦ **Kehoe House.** Known for its remarkably friendly and attentive staff, this handsomely appointed house, dating from the 1890s, was originally the family manse of William Kehoe. **Pros:** romantic, photo-worthy setting; the two elevators are a rarity in a B&B; great, filling Southern breakfasts. **Cons:** a few rooms have the sink and shower in the room; soundproofing in guest rooms could be better; in-room fireplaces don't work. ⓢ *Rooms from: $251* ✉ *123 Habersham St., Historic District* ☎ *912/232–1020, 800/820–1020* ⊕ *www.kehoehouse.com* ⤴ *13 rooms* ¶⊙ *Breakfast* ⊹ *D2.*

$$$$
HOTEL
Fodor's Choice
★

▦ **Mansion on Forsyth Park.** Sitting on the edge of Forsyth Park, this Marriott Autograph property has dramatic design, opulent interiors with a contemporary edge, and a magnificently diverse collection of some 400 pieces of American and European art, all of which create a one-of-a-kind experience—sophisticated, chic, and artsy only begin to describe it. **Pros:** stimulating environment transports you from the workaday world; full-service spa; complimentary shuttle to River Street. **Cons:** very pricey; some of the art from the early 1970s is not appealing. ⓢ *Rooms from: $251* ✉ *700 Drayton St., Historic District* ☎ *912/238—5158* ⊕ *www.mansiononforsythpark.com* ⤴ *125 rooms* ¶⊙ *No meals* ⊹ *C6.*

$$$$
B&B/INN
Fodor's Choice
★

▦ **Marshall House.** With original pine floors, handsome woodwork, and exposed brick, this is a hotel that provides the charm and intimacy of a B&B. **Pros:** great location near stores and restaurants; exceptional restaurant; balconies offer great bird's-eye views of Broughton Street. **Cons:** no free parking; floors show their age in places; the sounds of bustling Broughton Street can be noisy. ⓢ *Rooms from: $259* ✉ *123 E. Broughton St., Historic District* ☎ *912/644–7896* ⊕ *www.marshallhouse.com* ⤴ *65 rooms, 3 suites* ¶⊙ *No meals* ⊹ *C2.*

10

ELSEWHERE IN SAVANNAH

$$$ RESORT FAMILY Fodor's Choice ★ **Westin Savannah Harbor Golf Resort & Spa.** Within its own fiefdom, this high-rise property with more resort amenities than any other property in the area—including tennis courts, a full-service spa, and a golf course—presides over Hutchinson Island, five minutes by water taxi from River Street and just a short drive over the Talmadge Bridge. **Pros:** heated outdoor pool boasts a great view of River Street; dreamy bedding; great children's program. **Cons:** you are close, but still removed, from downtown; lacks atmosphere; an expensive and annoying resort fee. [$] *Rooms from: $249* ✉ *1 Resort Dr., Hutchinson Island* ☎ *912/201–2000* 🌐 *www.westinsavannah.com* 🛏 *403 rooms* 🍴 *No meals* ⊕ *D1.*

NIGHTLIFE AND PERFORMING ARTS

As the old saying goes, "In Atlanta, they ask you what you do. In Macon, they ask you what church you go to. And in Savannah, they ask you what you drink." Congress Street and River Street have the highest concentrations of bars with live music, especially if you're looking for rock, heavy metal, or the blues. Many of the most popular dance clubs are scattered across the same area. If you're in the mood for something more sedate, there are plenty of chic enclaves known for their creative cocktails and cozy nooks that encourage intimate conversation.

NIGHTLIFE

THE HISTORIC DISTRICT

BARS AND CLUBS

AlleyCat Lounge. A trendy spot in downtown Savannah, AlleyCat Lounge is a backdoor bar with a refined cocktailer attitude. The well-designed subterranean space can only be accessed via the lane south of Broughton Street. The menu resembles a newsprint with entertaining sketches and quotes, and features impressive craft liquors and conceptual beverages. Space is limited, so come early to guarantee your spot. ✉ *207 W. Broughton St., Downtown* ☎ *912/677–0548* 🌐 *www.alleycatsavannah.com.*

Fodor's Choice ★ **Artillery.** A restored landmark, the award-winning Daniel Reed group renovated this unique, intimate space that was once home to the Georgia Hussars pre-Revolutionary cavalry regiment. The end result is one of Savannah's classiest cocktail bars and a resplendent example of contemporary design mixed with historical accuracy. Intricate cocktails feature inspired ingredients like muddled corn, shishito peppers, and smoked pipe tobacco. The wine list is as formidable as the cocktail menu. **TIP→ There is an enforced code of conduct in a classy joint like this; usage of cell phones is highly frowned upon and the dress code is on the border of business-casual and semiformal.** ✉ *307 Bull St., Historic District* 🌐 *www.artillerybar.com.*

Fodor's Choice ★ **Lulu's Chocolate Bar.** This laid-back spot invites you to indulge your sweet tooth. Walking through the door, you're immediately greeted by a dessert case full of freshly baked specialties—try some of the homemade truffles. The menu also includes a spectacular list of specialty drinks, including delectable champagne cocktails, alongside a modest selection of beers and wines. Don't miss the truly divine "drinkable chocolate," an especially fulfilling twist on hot chocolate. ✉ *42 Martin Luther King Jr. Blvd., Historic District* ☎ *912/480–4564* ⊕ *www. luluschocolatebar.com.*

FAMILY **Moon River Brewing Company & Beer Garden.** Savannah's first microbrewery, Moon River occupies a historic building that once served as a hotel, as well as a lumber and coal warehouse. The adjacent outdoor beer garden is known for great people-watching, live music, and breezes off the nearby river. Check out the amazing variety of handcrafted lagers, ales, and wheat beers, compliments of award-winning brewmaster John Pinkerton. Pinkerton monitors the large steel vats of beer, which you can see through the glass partition. Soak up the first few rounds with a good variety of pub food. ✉ *21 W. Bay St., Historic District* ☎ *912/447–0943* ⊕ *www.moonriverbrewing.com.*

The Original. Standing on the site of what was once the most historically significant bar in Savannah (Pinkie Masters), the Original harkens the spirit—and boasts much of the same decor and ambience—of Pinkies, but with a much-needed face-lift. The former dive bar's biggest claim to fame was that Georgia's own Jimmy Carter stood up on the bar to announce his bid for the presidency. The people are friendly, the drinks are cheap, and the vibe is laid-back with zero frills. ✉ *318 Drayton St., Historic District* ☎ *912/999–7106* ⊕ *www.theoriginalsavannah. com* ☾ *Closed Sun.*

Fodor'sChoice **Planters Tavern.** Lighted by flickering candles, this tavern in the basement
★ of the Olde Pink House is one of Savannah's most romantic late-night spots. There's a talented piano player setting the mood, two stone fireplaces, and an array of fox-hunt memorabilia. The upstairs menu is available, with the same quality of service but a slightly less formal approach. ■TIP➜ **The handful of tables fill up fast, but the staff will serve you on your lap anywhere in the place.** ✉ *23 Abercorn St., garden level, Historic District* ☎ *912/232–4286.*

Top Deck Bar. Enjoy the best views of the Savannah River and the cargo ships coming to port from this bar on the rooftop of the Cotton Sail Hotel. During the daytime Top Deck is quite low-key, but gets lively and packed during the evening hours. Enjoy tasty, eclectic light bites, classic mixed drinks, and more inspired signature cocktails. ■TIP➜ **It's the best place in town to catch the sunset while enjoying a drink.** ✉ *125 W. River St., rooftop, Downtown* ☎ *912/436–6828* ⊕ *www.topdeckbar.com.*

GAY AND LESBIAN
Club One. Savannah's mainstay gay bar has also won praise from locals as one of the city's best dance clubs. It's also your destination for entertaining cabaret and drag shows. Although the decor is a little tacky, the scene is wildly fun when the lights go down and the music starts. ✉ *1 Jefferson St., Historic District* ☎ *912/232–0200* ⊕ *www. clubone-online.com.*

10

LIVE MUSIC CLUBS

Casimir Lounge. This sleek nightspot regularly features live jazz and blues—keep an eye out for local favorites like vocalists Trae Gurley and Roger Moss. The decor is luxe, perhaps even a bit over-the-top. There's a great balcony on the side where you can have a drink while enjoying a view of the park. The mussels and burgers are highly recommended. ⊠ *Mansion on Forsyth Park, 700 Drayton St., Historic District* ☎ *912/721–5002* ⊕ *www.mansiononforsythpark.com* ☾ *Closed Sun.–Tues.*

PERFORMING ARTS

FESTIVALS AND SPECIAL EVENTS

Fodor'sChoice **Savannah Music Festival.** Georgia's largest and most acclaimed music festi-
★ val brings together musicians from around the world for more than two weeks of unforgettable performances. The multigenre entertainment ranges from foot-stomping gospel to moody blues to mainstream rock to new takes on classical music. Performances take place in Savannah's premier music venues, as well as nontraditional venues like the rotunda of the Telfair Museum of Art. Festival honcho Rob Gibson spent several years with Jazz at Lincoln Center, so there is no shortage of amazing players. ⊠ *Downtown* ⊕ *www.savannahmusicfestival.org.*

St. Patrick's Day Parade. The city's largest annual festival has evolved over the past two centuries to become one of the largest of its kind in the country. Each March, roughly 700,000 participants tip their hats (and their glasses) to the rolling hills of Ireland. River Street becomes a sea of green: clothes, beer, food, and even the water in city fountains is dyed the color of the clover. ■TIP→ **Hotel rates during this period can be as much as three times the norm, so reserve well in advance.** ⊠ *Downtown* ⊕ *www.savannahsaintpatricksday.com.*

SPORTS AND THE OUTDOORS

The area around Savannah and the barrier islands of the Lowcountry is conducive to nearly all types of water sports. The waters of Savannah are generally warm enough for swimming May through September. For those who would prefer to stay on land, bicycling, jogging, golf, tennis, Ultimate Frisbee, and arena sports dominate.

BEACHES

Tybee Island Pier and Pavilion. This is Tybee's "grand strand," the center of the summer beach action. Anchored by a 700-foot pier that is sometimes host to summer concerts, this stretch of shoreline is your best bet for people-watching and beach activities. Just off the sand at the bustling intersection of Tybrisa Street and Butler Avenue, a cluster of watering holes, souvenir shops, bike shacks, and oyster bars makes up Tybee's main business district. ■TIP→ **There's metered street parking as well as two good-size lots. Both fill up fast during the high season, so arrive early.** There are public restrooms at the Pier and at 15th and Tybrisa Streets. The pier is popular for fishing and is also the gathering

Tybee Island's 700-foot pier plays host to summer concerts.

place for fireworks displays. **Amenities:** food and drink; lifeguard; parking (fee); toilets. **Best for:** partiers; sunrise; surfing; swimming. ✉ *Tybrisa St. at Butler Ave., Tybee Island* ☎ *912/652-6780.*

BIKING

Savannah is table-flat, perfect for biking. Forsyth and Daffin parks are favored by locals. Rails-to-Trails, a 3-mile route, starts 1 mile east of the Bull River Bridge on U.S. 80 and ends at the entrance to Fort Pulaski. Tom Triplett Park, east of town on U.S. 80, offers three bike loops—3.5 miles, 5 miles, and 6.3 miles.

Perry Rubber Bike Shop. At the pulsing corner of Bull and Liberty Streets, Perry Rubber is the go-to shop for repairs and your best bet for rentals. It offers trendy hybrid or city bikes at $20 for a half day or $35 for the full day—helmet, lock, and basket included. ✉ *240 Bull St., Downtown* ☎ *912/236–9929* ⊕ *www.perryrubberbikeshop.com.*

BOATING AND FISHING

FAMILY **Captain Mike's Dolphin Tours.** If boat-bound adventure is what you seek, Fodor's Choice look no further than Captain Mike. Widely popular with tourists and
★ locals alike, Captain Mike's tours have been featured on the Discovery Channel, *Good Morning America,* and in the pages of *Southern Living.* Choose from a 90-minute dolphin tour from $15 per person, or an $18 sunset tour (available May to September). Captain Mike's has a 32-foot cabin cruiser in his fleet and offers inshore and offshore fishing charters. This business is family-owned and operated, and kids are

10

welcome. ⊠ *Lazaretto Creek Marina, 1 Old U.S. Hwy. 80, Tybee Island* ☎ *912/786–5848* ⊕ *tybeedolphins.com.*

Miss Judy Charters. Captain Judy Helmey, a longtime fishing guide and legendary local character, heads up Miss Judy Charters. The company offers packages ranging from 3-hour sightseeing tours to 14-hour deep-sea fishing expeditions. Inshore rates start at around $350 for three to four people for three hours; offshore rates start at $400 for up to six people for three hours. ⊠ *124 Palmetto Dr., Wilmington Island* ☎ *912/897–4921* ⊕ *www.missjudycharters.com.*

Fodor's Choice ★ **Savannah Canoe and Kayak.** Leading you through inlets and tidal creeks, Savannah Canoe and Kayak has highly skilled guides that provide expert instruction for newbies and challenges for seasoned paddlers. You'll also learn about the history of these historic waterways. Half-day tours start at $65 for three hours. ⊠ *414 Bonaventure Rd., Savannah* ☎ *912/341–9502* ⊕ *www.savannahcanoeandkayak.com.*

GOLF

Fodor's Choice ★ **The Club at Savannah Harbor.** The area's only PGA course, this resort property on Hutchinson Island is a free ferry ride from Savannah's riverfront. The lush championship course winds through pristine wetlands and has unparalleled views of the river and downtown. It is also home to the annual Liberty Mutual Legends of Golf tournament, which attracts golfing's finest each spring. A bit pricier than most local clubs, it's packed with beauty and amenities. ⊠ *Westin Savannah Harbor, 2 Resort Dr., Hutchinson Island* ☎ *912/201–2240* ⊕ *www.theclubat-savannahharbor.com* ⊡ *Dynamic pricing $85–$145* ⚐ *18 holes, 7694 yds, par 72* ⚑ *Reservations essential.*

SHOPPING

You would have to make a concerted effort to leave Savannah empty-handed. Whether you're on a quest for designer clothing or handmade candy, Savannah offers up a potent dose of shopping therapy on a silver platter.

SHOPPING DISTRICTS

Broughton Street. Savannah's "main street" has long served as an indicator of the city's changing economic and demographic trends. The first of Savannah's department stores, Adler's and Levy's, emerged on Broughton, followed by the post-WWII introduction of national chains Sears & Roebuck, JCPenney, and Kress. During the 1950s, ladies donning white gloves and heels did their shopping, while kids gathered at the soda counter or caught the matinee. Downtown's decline began in the late 1950s and continued through the '70s, when boarded-up storefronts were the norm rather than the exception. Today, Broughton is again thriving, not only with local boutiques and world-class shops, but with theaters, restaurants, and coffeehouses. ⊠ *Broughton St., between Congress and State Sts., Historic District* ⊕ *www.broughtonstreetcollection.com.*

Downtown Design District. Renowned for its array of fine antiques shops, galleries, lighting showrooms, and interior design boutiques, the Downtown Design District is worth a visit. Stop in some of Savannah's trendier fashion stores, many of them housed in charming historic storefronts. Nearby are the famed Mercer-Williams House and the landmark Mrs. Wilkes' Dining Room, known for some of the area's best family-style Southern food. The picturesque surrounding neighborhoods are also amenable for a nice afternoon stroll. ⊠ *Whitaker St., between Charlton and Gaston Sts., Historic District.*

Fodor'sChoice
★ **Liberty Street Corridor.** With the redevelopment of Broughton Street came an influx of national and high-end retailers that left local shops in search of lower rent. Many set up shop a half-mile south along the oak-lined Liberty Street Corridor. The Crossroads of Liberty and Bull is a particularly thriving shopping neighborhood, with outdoor cafés, pubs, clothing boutiques, art galleries, bookshops, and more. ⊠ *Liberty St. at Bull St., Historic District.*

THE HISTORIC DISTRICT

ANTIQUES

Fodor'sChoice
★ **Alex Raskin Antiques.** This shop is inside the four-story Noble Hardee Mansion, a gilded Italianate home. You can wander through almost all 12,000 square feet of the former grand residence and see how the landed gentry once lived. The building is a bit musty, with peeling wallpaper and patches of leaky ceiling, but the antiques within are in great condition and represent a colorful scrapbook of Savannah's past. They specialize in furniture, rugs, and paintings, but take note of more rare artifacts like tramp art frames and antique doll furniture. Take in the view of Forsyth Park from one of the upper-level porches. ■TIP➜ The **building lacks air-conditioning, so avoid the heat of midday or bring along a fan.** ⊠ *441 Bull St., Historic District* ☎ *912/232–8205* ⊕ *www. alexraskinantiques.com* ☉ *Closed Sun.*

BOOKS

Fodor'sChoice
★ **E. Shaver Booksellers.** Among the city's most beloved bookshops, E. Shaver is the source for 17th- and 18th-century maps and new books on local history, recipes, artists, and authors. This shop occupies 12 rooms of a historic building, which alone is something to see. The whole family can explore the children's book sections. The booksellers are welcoming and knowledgeable about their wares. ⊠ *326 Bull St., Historic District* ☎ *912/234–7257* ⊕ *eshaverbooks.com.*

CLOTHING

James Hogan. Savannah's resident fashion designer and his shop, tucked in a storefront in the Historic District, have brought a touch of glamour to the city. Featured here is apparel designed by Hogan himself, as well as upscale women's fashions from well-regarded American and European designers like Etro, MaxMara, and Ted Baker. ⊠ *412B Whitaker St., Historic District* ☎ *912/234–0374* ⊕ *www.jameshogan. com* ☉ *Closed Sun.*

10

Red Clover. This is the place to be if you want fashionable and affordable apparel, shoes, and handbags. It features sharp looks from up-and-coming designers, all at under $100. It's also a great place to search for unique jewelry. ⊠ *244 Bull St., Historic District* ☎ *912/236–4053* ⊕ *shopredclover.com.*

FOOD

Fodor's Choice
★

Byrd's Famous Cookies. Founded in 1924, this family-owned-and-operated gourmet food company specializes in benne wafers and trademark Savannah cookies (notably key lime) and other house-made crackers. The City Market gift shop sells picture tins of Savannah and gourmet foodstuffs such as condiments and dressings. Free cookie and cracker samples are available. ⊠ *213 West St., at Julian St., Savannah* ☎ *912/233–8816* ⊕ *www.byrdcookiecompany.com.*

FAMILY
Fodor's Choice
★

Savannah Bee Company. Ted Dennard's Savannah Bee Company has been featured in such national magazines as *O*, *Vogue*, *InStyle*, and *Newsweek*, and with good reason—the locally cultivated honey and bath products are simply wonderful. You can sample and buy multiple varieties of honey and even raw honeycombs. Don't miss the delicate mead (honey wine) or the decadent honey lattes. Children enjoy the life-size beehive. ⊠ *104 W. Broughton St., Historic District* ☎ *912/233–7873* ⊕ *www.savannahbee.com.*

GIFTS

Fodor's Choice
★

The Paris Market and Brocante. A Francophile's dream from the time you open the antique front door and take in the intoxicating aroma of lavender, this two-story emporium is a classy reproduction of a Paris flea market. It sells furniture, vintage art, garden planters and accessories, and home fashions like boudoir items and bedding. Although the store will ship to your hometown, there are numerous treasures that can be easily packed away, like soaps, candles, vintage jewelry, kitchen and barware, and dried lavender. ⊠ *36 W. Broughton St., Historic District* ☎ *912/232–1500* ⊕ *www.theparismarket.com.*

Fodor's Choice
★

ShopSCAD. Inside historic Poetter Hall, the Savannah College of Art and Design's shop is filled with handcrafted items guaranteed to be one of a kind. Handmade and hand-dyed silk accessories are cutting-edge, as are original fashion pieces and experimental purses by design students. Just remember that these originals do not come cheap. ⊠ *340 Bull St., Historic District* ☎ *912/525–5180* ⊕ *www.shopscad.com.*

SHOES, HANDBAGS, AND LEATHER GOODS

Fodor's Choice
★

Satchel. This artisanal-leather studio and shop is owned by Elizabeth Seegar, a New Orleans native and graduate of the SCAD. The store specializes in custom leather clutches, handbags, travel bags, and accessories and offers a wide selection of leathers to choose from, including python and alligator. At lower price points are the sharp and handy beverage cozies, cuff bracelets, and wallets. ⊠ *4 E. Liberty St., Historic District* ☎ *912/233–1008* ⊕ *shopsatchel.com* ☾ *Closed Sun.*

GEORGIA'S COASTAL ISLES AND THE OKEFENOKEE

WELCOME TO GEORGIA'S COASTAL ISLES AND THE OKEFENOKEE

TOP REASONS TO GO

★ **Saltwater marshes:** Fringing the coastline, waist-high grasses transform both sunlight and shadow with their lyrical textures and shapes.

★ **Geechee culture:** Vestiges of Georgia's Black Republic, an independent state of freed slaves established on the barrier islands in the mid-19th century, remain at the Sapelo Island settlement of Hog Hammock.

★ **Horses of Cumberland:** Some 200 feral horses, descendants of horses abandoned by the Spanish in the 1500s, roam the wilderness of Cumberland Island.

★ **Jekyll Island:** Originally the exclusive winter retreat of America's exceptionally rich, this village of mansion-size "cottages" is now open to all.

★ **Go for a ride:** Jekyll Island has 25 miles of paved bike paths that traverse salt marshes, maritime forests, beaches, and the island's ever-charming National Historic Landmark District.

1 Sapelo Island. Reachable only by ferry from Meridian, less-developed Sapelo is a protected state wildlife preserve and home to the Geechee, direct descendants of freed African slaves. You must have a reservation for a day tour or to camp or stay at one of the island's small hotels in order to take the ferry over.

2 St. Simons Island. The most developed of the Golden Isles is a well-rounded vacation destination with a variety of hotels and restaurants in varying price ranges.

3 Jekyll Island. Once a playground for the rich and famous, Jekyll is now more widely accessible. Its pristine beaches are not commercialized and are open to all, and the range of resorts and restaurants appeals to a wide range of travelers.

SOUTH
CAROLINA

95

Garden City

16
Savannah · Thunderbolt · ·
Tybee
Windsor Forest · Island
Skidaway Is.

17 Richmond Hill
Keller *Wassaw Is.*
Ossabaw Sound

Midway *Ossabaw
Island*

Riceboro *St. Catherines Sound*
Halfmoon Landing
South Newport · *St. Catherines
Island*
95 Shellman Bluff
Eulonia *Sapelo Sound*
99 **1** Blackbeard Island
Meridian **◆ Sapelo Island**
◆ **Sapelo Island National
Estuarine Sanctuary**
Darien Sapelo Island
Doboy Sound
**Hofwyl-Broadfield
Plantation**
Little St. Simons Island
17 **Fort Frederica
National Monument**
◆ **Sea Island**
Saint Simons
St. Simons Island
2
Brunswick
◆ Jekyll Island
520 **3**
St. Andrews Sound

Incoastal Waterway

4
◆ **Cumberland
Island**

Fernandina Beach
*Amelia
Island*

GETTING ORIENTED

Coastal Georgia is a complex jigsaw wending its way from the ocean and tidal marshes inland along the intricate network of rivers. U.S. 17, the old coastal highway, gives you a taste of the slower, more rural South. But because of the subtropical climate, the lush forests tend to be dense along the mainland, and there are few opportunities to glimpse the broad vistas of salt marsh and islands. To truly appreciate the mystique of Georgia's coastal salt marshes and islands, make the 40-minute ferry crossing from Meridian to Sapelo Island.

4 Cumberland Island.
Reachable only by ferry, this virtually pristine island is a national seashore and has only one accommodation (a former Carnegie family mansion) and a few campgrounds.

5 Okefenokee National Wildlife Range. The Okefenokee is a mysterious world where, as a glance at a map will indicate, all roads disappear. A large, interior wetland navigable only by boat, it can be confusing and intimidating to the uninitiated. None of the individual parks within the area give a sense of the total Okefenokee experience—each has its own distinct natural features. Choose the park that best aligns with your interests and begin there.

GEORGIA'S COASTAL ISLES BEACHES

Remote and largely untouched, the beaches on Georgia's barrier islands sit at the confluence of rich salt marshes and the Atlantic Ocean. Nature-watching on foot or by canoe or kayak is the biggest draw, with dolphins, manatees, nesting sea turtles, more than 300 bird species, and much more found along these shores.

(above) Enjoy a sunset stroll on Georgia's remote beaches. (lower right) Bring your camera to Driftwood Beach—the downed trees make great photo ops. (upper right) Wild horses roam Cumberland Island.

Of all the islands, only two—Jekyll and St. Simons—have undergone significant development. East Beach on St. Simons has the most facilities and is the place to go for sunbathing, swimming, and water sports, while Jekyll's beaches are both accessible and uncrowded. Driftwood Beach, at Jekyll's northern end, is arguably the most picturesque beach on the coast, and dolphins frolic off St. Andrews Beach, at the island's southern tip. Exploring the farther-flung beaches of Sapelo or Cumberland islands requires advance planning and a ferry ride, as both are protected parklands and access is limited. Beachcombing is especially good here.

BEACH CAMPING

Experience the best of Georgia's beaches by pitching a tent shoreside. Cumberland Island has wonderful camping, with standard campgrounds as well as backcountry campsites that can be reached only by hiking trails 5½ to 10½ miles from the ferry dock. There are no stores on the island, so bring all necessary food and supplies. Camping costs $22 per night; reservations are required.

GEORGIA'S COASTAL ISLES BEST BEACHES

NANNY GOAT BEACH (SAPELO ISLAND)

Used as an outdoor classroom by the Sapelo Island National Estuarine Research Reserve, this remote beach, accessible only by boat, offers ample beachcombing and wildlife-watching opportunities. Look for sand dollars and conch shells on its 2 miles of sandy shore while pelicans and osprey fish among the shallows, or bring a seine net to dip for shrimp and crabs. Coastal dunes give way to protected maritime forest, and a ¾-mile trail leads to the historic Reynolds Mansion.

EAST BEACH (ST. SIMONS ISLAND)

The Golden Isles' liveliest stretch of sand occupies the southeastern edge of St. Simons Island, from the Coast Guard station at the end of 1st Street to Massengale Park, both of which offer facilities and access to the hard-packed-sand beach. Here you can swim and sun, boogie board in the mild shore break, or kite surf past the offshore sandbars. This is one of the few beaches in the area with lifeguards, making it a good family destination.

DRIFTWOOD BEACH (JEKYLL ISLAND)

The pristine northern end of Jekyll Island offers beautiful views of St. Simons against a stark and dramatic backdrop. Accessible by trail from the Clam Creek Picnic Area or from North Beachview Drive, near the campground (there's a small parking area on the shoulder) the beach has a graveyard of coastal trees slowly succumbing to the sea, reeling at odd angles as the encroaching tide loosens their roots. Drained of color by the sun and salt-water, they create a maze of craggy limbs, gray against the bright white sand. Come here for the view and the unique scenery, but use caution swimming among the grasping branches.

DUNGENESS BEACH (CUMBERLAND ISLAND)

Nearly 18 miles of unspoiled beach fringe the eastern edge of this national-park island, off the coast of St. Marys. At the southern end, Dungeness Beach is accessible via the *Cumberland Queen II*, a reservations-only, 146-passenger ferry that stops here and at Sea Camp Beach to the north. Beachcombers can potentially find shells and sharks' teeth on the sand here, and Pelican Flats, off the island's southern tip, offers good shore fishing. From the beach it's an easy hike to the ruins of Thomas Carnegie's great estate, Dungeness. Keep an eye out for the wild horses that roam the area.

Updated by
Summer Teal
Simpson Hitch

Georgia's lush barrier islands meander down the Atlantic coast from Savannah to the Florida border. Notable for their subtropical beauty and abundant wildlife, the isles strike a unique balance between some of the country's wealthiest communities and some of its most jealously protected nature preserves. Until recently, large segments of the coast were in private hands, and as a result much of the region remains as it was when the first Europeans set eyes on it 450 years ago. Though the islands have long been a favorite getaway of the rich and famous, they no longer cater only to the well-heeled.

St. Simons, Jekyll, Little St. Simons, and Sea islands constitute Georgia's Golden Isles. And while even today Little St. Simons Island and Sea Island remain privately owned, each with its own exclusive resort catering to the very wealthy, St. Simons and Jekyll islands have morphed into relaxed beach communities. These more developed islands—although by Georgia law, only 35% of Jekyll's land can be developed—have become diverse havens with something for everyone, from beach bums to family vacationers to the suit-and-tie crowd.

Sapelo Island and the Cumberland Island National Seashore are the least developed and, as protected nature preserves, the most ecologically intact of all the islands. With their miles of untouched beaches, forests of gnarly live-oak trees draped with Spanish moss, and rich swamps and marshlands, both islands are ideal camping destinations, with sites ranging from primitive to modern. Noncamping accommodations are available, but limited, and require booking well in advance. Many visitors opt to stay on the mainland and make day trips by ferry, private boat, or kayak.

The Okefenokee National Wildlife Refuge, 60 miles inland from St. Marys, near Folkston, is one of the largest freshwater wetlands in the United States. Spread over 700 square miles of southeastern Georgia and northeastern Florida, the swamp is a trove of flora and fauna that naturalist William Bartram called a "terrestrial paradise" when he visited in the 1770s. From towering cypress swamps to alligator- and snake-infested waters and prairielike wetlands, the Okefenokee is a mosaic of ecosystems, much of which has never been visited by humans.

PLANNING

WHEN TO GO

Early spring and late fall are ideal for visiting the coastal isles and the Okefenokee. By February, temperatures can reach into the 70s, while nights remain cool and even chilly, which keeps the bugs at bay. The high demand to visit these areas before the bugs arrive and after they depart necessitates ferry reservations to Sapelo Island and Cumberland Island National Seashore months in advance for spring and fall; without a reservation, you risk having to wait days at best for a cancellation. If you plan to stay in the immediate vicinity of St. Marys or Meridian, the respective docking points for the Cumberland and Sapelo ferries, or Folkston, the gateway to the Okefenokee, it's advisable to book rooms for these areas well in advance for spring or fall, as accommodations are scarce and the demand is high. The Cumberland Island ferry accepts reservations six months in advance. If you go during the warmer months, always bring water because these areas generally offer minimal services.

By May, sand gnats, deer flies, and mosquitoes swarm the coast and islands in abundance. Don't underestimate their impact: during peak times in some areas they are so thick they sound like hail hitting your car. And though many localities spray, it's imperative to have a good repellent handy, especially when traveling to outlying areas. Despite the subtropical heat and humidity, summer is busy with crowds flocking to the beaches, so you'll want to make reservations at least a couple of months in advance. The season lasts until Labor Day, but you can still expect travelers making weekend getaways until October or late November, when temperatures cool. Hurricane season officially runs from June through the end of November, but August and September are the peak months.

PLANNING YOUR TIME

Although Georgia's coastal islands are along a strip of coastline that is less than 60 miles long, each has a different feel, and a visit requires at least a day. The complications of ferries to Sapelo or Cumberland make it difficult to visit either of those in less than a day, and these visits must generally be planned far in advance. It's possible to base yourself on busy St. Simons Island (or any of the Golden Isles for that matter) and visit much of the region on a series of day trips. The Okefenokee is a bit farther out of the way, but can be visited on a day trip from almost any of the islands; if you have more time, it can be an overnight trip.

GETTING HERE AND AROUND

Visiting the region is easiest by car, because many of the outer reaches of Georgia are remote places with little in the way of alternate transportation. Touring by bicycle is an option for most of the region, but note that the ferries at Sapelo and Cumberland do not allow bicycles on board. Except for Little St. Simons, the Golden Isles are connected to the mainland by bridges around Brunswick and are the only coastal isles accessible by car. Sapelo Island and the Cumberland Island National Seashore can be reached only by ferry from Meridian and St. Marys, respectively.

AIR TRAVEL

The coastal isles are served by the Brunswick Golden Isles Airport, 6 miles north of Brunswick, and the Malcolm McKinnon St. Simons Airport on St. Simons Island. McKinnon accommodates light aircraft and private planes. The closest major airports are in Savannah, Georgia, and Jacksonville, Florida.

Air Contacts Brunswick Golden Isles Airport. ✉ *295 Aviation Pkwy., off I-95, Brunswick* ☎ *912/265–2070* ⊕ *flygcairports.com/brunswick-airport.html.* **McKinnon St. Simons Island Airport.** ✉ *1759 Demere Rd., St. Simons Island* ☎ *912/638–8617* ⊕ *flygcairports.com/st-simons-airport.html.*

BOAT AND FERRY TRAVEL

Cumberland Island and Sapelo Island are accessible only by ferry or private launch. The *Cumberland Queen II* serves Cumberland Island (the National Park Service has a Cumberland Island ferry schedule at ⊕ *www.nps.gov/cuis/reservations.htm*), and the *Katie Underwood* serves Sapelo Island. Advanced reservations are advised for Cumberland, but they are required for passage to Sapelo.

Boat and Ferry Contacts Cumberland Queen II. ✉ *113 St. Marys St., St. Marys* ☎ *877/860–6787* ⊕ *www.cumberlandislandferry.com.* **Katie Underwood.** ✉ *Sapelo Island Visitors Center, Rte. 1, 1766 Landing Rd. SE, Darien* ☎ *912/437–3224* ⊕ *www.sapelonerr.org/visitor-center.*

CAR TRAVEL

From Brunswick take the Jekyll Island Causeway ($6 per car per day) to Jekyll Island and the Torras Causeway to St. Simons. You can get by without a car on Jekyll Island, but you'll need one on St. Simons. You cannot bring a car to Cumberland Island or Sapelo.

TAXI TRAVEL

Island Transport and Taxi Service, as well as on-demand mobile cabs like Uber and Lyft, can shuttle you around St. Simons for fares that range between $7 and $15 depending on your destination.

Taxi Contacts Island Transport and Taxi Service. ✉ *708 E. Islands Sq., St. Simons Island* ☎ *912/634–0113* ⊕ *www.islandtransportandtaxi.com.*

RESTAURANTS

Restaurants range from fish camps—normally rustic dockside affairs—to the more upscale eateries that tend to spawn around the larger towns. And though there's still room for growth, the area now has several menus gaining not only local but nationwide attention. The rising tide of quality has begun to lift all boats. Some restaurants still serve food family-style. *Dining reviews have been shortened. For full information, visit Fodors.com.*

HOTELS

Hotels run the gamut from Victorian mansions to Spanish-style bed-and-breakfasts to some of the most luxurious hotel-spa accommodations found anywhere. Since options are somewhat limited, make your reservations as far in advance as possible. Most hotels offer the full range of guest services, but as a matter of philosophy many B&Bs do not provide televisions or telephones in the rooms. Lodging prices quoted here may be much lower during nonpeak seasons, and specials are often available on weekdays even in high season. *Hotel reviews have been shortened. For full information, visit Fodors.com.*

WHAT IT COSTS			
$	**$$**	**$$$**	**$$$$**
Restaurants	under $15	$15–$20	$21–$24	over $24
Hotels	under $150	$150–$200	$201–$250	over $250

Restaurant reviews are the average cost of a main course at dinner or, if dinner is not served, at lunch. Hotel reviews are the lowest cost of a standard double room in high season.

TOURS

Lighthouse Trolleys Land and Sea Tours offers year-round trolley and boat tours from St. Simons Island and Jekyll Island that explore the surrounding marshes and rivers and get you up close and personal with dolphins, manatees, and other marine life. Kayaks and canoes are also a great way to explore the creeks; Southeast Adventure Outfitters is located on St. Simons Island.

Lighthouse Trolleys Land and Sea Tours. ⊠ *559 Magnolia Ave., St. Simons Island* ☎ *912/638–3333* ⊕ *lighthousetrolleys.com.*

SouthEast Adventure Outfitters. ⊠ *313 Mallory St., St. Simons Island* ☎ *912/638–6732* ⊕ *www.southeastadventure.com.*

SAPELO ISLAND

8 miles northeast of Darien.

The fourth-largest of Georgia's coastal isles—and bigger than Bermuda—Sapelo Island is a unique community in North America. It still bears evidence of the Paleo-Indians who lived here some 4,500 years ago, and is home to the Geechee, direct descendants of African slaves who speak a blend of English and various African languages. This rapidly dwindling community maintains many traditional African practices, including the making of sweetgrass baskets and the use of herbal medicines made from recipes passed down for generations. It's also a nearly pristine barrier island with miles of undeveloped beaches and abundant wildlife. To take the 40-minute ferry ride from Meridian on the mainland through the expanse of salt marshes to Sapelo Island is to enter a world seemingly forgotten by time.

GETTING HERE AND AROUND

You can explore many historical periods and natural environments here, but facilities on the island are limited. Note that you can't simply walk up to the dock and catch the ferry—you need to have a reservation for a tour, a campsite, or one of the island's lodgings (or have prearranged plans to stay with island residents). Bring insect repellent, especially in summer, and leave your pets at home. You can rent a bicycle on the island, but you cannot bring a bicycle on the ferry.

TOURS

FAMILY **Sapelo Sights Tour.** These private, guided tours are led by island native and slave descendant JR Grovner. Grovner highlights island life, culture, and history with visits to Nannygoat beach, tabby ruins of estates and slave quarters, Native American shell mounds, the Sapelo lighthouse, and historic Hog Hammock community. ⊠ *Hog Hammock* ☎ *912/506–6463.*

EXPLORING

Hog Hammock Community. This small settlement near the southern end of Sapelo Island is one of the few remaining Gullah/Geechee communities on the south Atlantic Coast. The Saltwater Geechee people, Georgia's sea-island equivalent to the Gullah of South Carolina, are descendants of slaves who worked the island's plantations during the 19th century. Hog Hammock's roughly 50 residents still maintain their distinct language and customs, which share many characteristics with their West African origins. ⊠ *Sapelo Island.*

Sapelo Cultural Day. This celebration of Geechee folklore, music, food, handcrafts, and art, takes place in Hog Hammock every year on the third weekend in October. Activities include tours of historic attractions on the island and cultural displays such as sweetgrass basket weaving, ring shouts, traditional slave songs, and African heritage dancing. Reservations are required. ⊠ *Sapelo Island* ☎ *912/485–2197* ⊕ *www.sapeloislandga.org* 🖃 *$25.*

Sapelo Island Visitor Center. Start your visit here, on the mainland near the Sapelo Island ferry docks. Check out the exhibits on the island's history, culture, and ecology before purchasing tickets for a round-trip ferry ride and bus tour of the island. The sights that make up the bus tour vary depending on the day of the week, but always included are the old sugar mill, airfield, cemetery, and beach. On Saturday the tour includes the 80-foot-tall **Sapelo Lighthouse**, built in 1820, a symbol of the cotton and lumber industry once based out of Darien, a prominent shipping center of the time. To see the island's **Reynolds Mansion** schedule your tour for Wednesday. To get to the Visitor Center and Meridian Ferry Dock from downtown Darien, go north on Route 99 for 8 miles, following signs for the Sapelo Island National Estuarine Research Reserve. Turn right onto Landing Road at the Elm Grove Baptist Church in Meridian. The visitor center is about ½ mile down the road. ⊠ *1766 Landing Rd. SE, Darien* ☎ *912/437–3224* ⊕ *www.sapelonerr.org* 🖃 *$15* ☉ *Closed Sun. and Mon.* ☞ *Cash or check only.*

A ferry leads to Sapelo Island, one of Georgia's most pristine barrier islands.

WHERE TO EAT

$$$ SEAFOOD 🍴 **The Fish Dock at Pelican Point.** A local staple, Pelican Point has been satisfying locals' hunger for seafood for decades. Fully renovated in 2016, the quintessentially coastal restaurant overlooks the Sapelo River as it runs to the Sapelo Sound. **Known for:** seafood buffet; waterfront dining; deck seating; locally harvested shellfish. [$] *Average main: $23* ✉ *1398 Sapelo Ave., Crescent* ☎ *912/832–4295* 🌐 *www.fishdockrestaurant.com.*

$$ SEAFOOD 🍴 **Mudcat Charlie's.** This tabby-and-wood restaurant on the Altamaha River sits right in the middle of the Two Way Fish Camp and is a favorite haunt of locals from nearby Darien. The restaurant overlooks the boats moored in the marina, and the seafood is local. **Known for:** homemade desserts; local seafood; waterfront dining. [$] *Average main: $15* ✉ *250 Ricefield Way, Brunswick* ✢ *1 mile south of Darien on U.S. 17, just after the fourth bridge. Look for the Two Way Fish Camp sign* ☎ *912/261–0055.*

$$$ SEAFOOD 🍴 **Skipper's Fish Camp.** This upscale take on the fish camp theme lies at the foot of a public dock on the Darien River, where working shrimp boats moor. It has a beautiful courtyard pond and an open-air oyster bar. **Known for:** the views; catching the game; oyster bar; BBQ and seafood. [$] *Average main: $22* ✉ *85 Screven St., Darien* ✢ *At the southern end of Darien, turn right at Broad just before the river bridge, then take the first left down to the waterfront* ☎ *912/437–3474* 🌐 *www.skippersfishcamp.com.*

WHERE TO STAY

$ B&B/INN **The Blue Heron Inn.** Bill and Jan Chamberlain's airy, Lowcountry-style home sits on the edge of the marsh and is only minutes from the ferry at the Sapelo Island Visitor Center. **Pros:** deliciously inventive breakfasts; decks provide great views; friendly ownership and service. **Cons:** the small number of rooms means the place can book up fast; the smaller rooms can feel tight with two people. [$] *Rooms from: $130* ✉ *1346 Blue Heron La., Darien* ☎ *912/437–4304* 🌐 *www.blueheroninngacoast.com* 🛏 *5 rooms* 🍴 *Breakfast.*

$ B&B/INN **Open Gates Bed and Breakfast.** Built by a timber baron in 1876, this two-story, Italianate house on Darien's Vernon Square is filled with antiques that beautifully decorate each room. **Pros:** setting is so lovely that the home's exterior was featured on the cover of Southern Living magazine; easy walking distance to Darien's restaurants and waterfront; the library has an excellent collection of books of local historical interest. **Cons:** not a good choice for singles; some of the baths are shared. [$] *Rooms from: $135* ✉ *301 Franklin St., Box 662, Darien* ☎ *912/437–6985* 🌐 *www.opengatesbnb.com* 🛏 *5 rooms* 🍴 *Breakfast.*

$ B&B/INN **The Wallow Lodge.** A stay at this historic inn at Hog Hammock offers a chance to experience the island's distinct Geechee culture. **Pros:** rowboat is available to guests for exploring the island's creeks; unique decor; next door to the Trough, the town's only bar. **Cons:** the lodge has a communal kitchen, so unless you make prior arrangements for meals, you must bring your own supplies from the mainland; one room doesn't have a bathroom. [$] *Rooms from: $70* ✉ *1 Main Rd., Hog Hammock* ☎ *912/485–2206* 🌐 *www.gacoast.com/geecheetours* 💳 *No credit cards* 🛏 *6 rooms* 🍴 *No meals.*

CAMPING ON SAPELO ISLAND

Comya's Campground. The name of Hog Hammock's only campground comes from the Geechee word meaning "come here." The campground has marsh views and is great for backpackers looking for a more rustic taste of the island life. Campsite reservations are essential and start at $10 per day. ✉ *Not far from Wallow Lodge in Hog Hammock, Sapelo Island* ☎ *912/485–2206* 🌐 *www.gacoast.com/geecheetours.*

NIGHTLIFE

Trough. It seems appropriate that the only watering hole in Hog Hammock is named the Trough. It's a small, bare-bones, belly-up-to-the-bar establishment, but owner Julius Bailey serves his beer ice-cold, and there's usually a good conversation going on. It's next to the Wallow Lodge (operated by Julius's wife, Cornelia), right "downtown." A store on the back side of the bar offers basic supplies and souvenirs. ✉ *1 Main Rd.* ☎ *912/485–2206* 🕒 *Closed Sun.*

CLOSE UP

The Geechee, a Culture Apart

11

Georgia's Geechee, like the Gullah people of South Carolina, are descendants of African slaves who have preserved a distinct culture and language, in large part due to the isolation of the remote coastal areas, such as Sapelo Island, where they live.

The Geechee take their name from the Ogeechee River in north coastal Georgia. Geechee ancestry includes a variety of African tribes, but is particularly marked by the language and traditions of slaves from Sierra Leone, who were brought to work the vast coastal plantations because of their expertise in rice cultivation. Their native tongue, Krio, is still evident in the Geechee language of the region today: *tief/tif* (steal), *ooman/uman* (woman), and *enty/enti* (isn't it so?) are just a few of the easily recognizable words that are similar in Geechee and Krio, respectively. The two languages share similar sentence structures and grammatical elements as well. Geechee, not English, was the first language of Supreme Court Justice Clarence Thomas, who was born and raised in Savannah.

SPORTS AND THE OUTDOORS

BEACHES

Cabretta Beach. Just north of Nanny Goat Beach, Cabretta Beach stretches along Sapelo's eastern shore, with its northern terminus at the outflow of Blackbeard Creek. This remote expanse of hard-packed sand is sometimes visited by fishermen or kayakers on their way to Blackbeard Island, and it's also the site of the Cabretta group campsite, a wilderness camp that can be reserved via Georgia's Department of Natural Resources—there are showers and bathrooms here for campers. **Amenities:** showers; toilets. **Best for:** solitude; sunrise; walking. ⊠ *End of Cabretta Rd.*

Nanny Goat Beach. On the southeastern edge of the island, this beach sits at the heart of the rich ecological zones for which the island is known and protected. Naturalists with the Sapelo Island National Estuarine Research Reserve use this beach as an outdoor classroom, sometimes bringing groups here for beach walks. Visitors can hunt for sand dollars and whelk shells along nearly 2 miles of sandy shore; bird sightings include blue herons, egrets, ospreys, bald eagles, and the occasional plain chachalaca. A 1-mile trail connects this beach with the historic R.J. Reynolds House, crossing five ecological zones along the way. **Amenities:** toilets. **Best for:** solitude; walking. ⊠ *End of Beach Rd.*

CANOEING AND KAYAKING

Altamaha Coastal Tours. The Altamaha River, the largest undammed river on the East Coast, runs inland from near Darien. You can take expeditions along it with Altamaha Coastal Tours, which rents equipment and conducts guided trips from the waterfront in Darien. With them you can explore tidal swamps, marshlands, and Queen and Sapelo islands. Kayak or canoe rentals start at $35 per day. ⊠ *229 Fort King George Dr., Darien* ☎ *912/437–6010* ⊕ *www.altamaha.com.*

Hofwyl-Broadfield Plantation. Rice, not cotton, dominated Georgia's coast in the antebellum years, and the Hofwyl-Broadfield Plantation is the last remaining example of a way of life that fueled an agricultural empire. The main farmhouse, in use since the 1850s when the original house burned, is now a museum with family heirlooms accumulated over five generations, including extensive collections of silver and Canton china. A guide gives an insightful talk on rural plantation life. Though grown over, some of the original dike works and rice fields remain, as do some of the slave quarters. A brief film at the visitor center complements exhibits on rice technology and cultivation, and links to Sierra Leone, from where many slaves were taken because of their expertise in growing rice. ⊠ *5556 U.S. 17 N ⊹ 5 miles south of Darien* ☎ *912/264–7333* ⊕ *www.gastateparks. org/HofwylBroadfield* ▱ *$8* ⊙ *Closed Mon. and Tues.*

ST. SIMONS ISLAND

22 miles south of Darien, 4 miles east of Brunswick.

St. Simons may be the Golden Isles' most developed vacation destination: here you can swim and sun, golf, hike, fish, ride horseback, tour historic sites, and feast on local seafood at more than 50 restaurants. (It's also a great place to bike and jog, particularly on the southern end, where there's an extensive network of trails.) Despite the development, the island has managed to maintain some of the slow-paced Southern atmosphere that made it such a draw in the first place. Upscale resorts and restaurants are here for the asking, but this island the size of Manhattan has only 15,000 year-round residents, so you can still get away from it all without a struggle. Even down in the village, the center of much of St. Simons's activity, there are unpaved roads and quiet back alleys of chalky white sand that seem like something out of the past.

GETTING HERE AND AROUND
Reach the island by car via the causeway from Brunswick.

ESSENTIALS
Visitor Information The Golden Isles Convention and Visitors Bureau. ⊹ *I-95 southbound, between Exits 42 and 38* ☎ *912/264–0202* ⊕ *www.golden-isles.com.* **St. Simons Visitors Center.** ⊠ *529 Beachview Dr.* ☎ *912/638–9014* ⊕ *www.goldenisles.com.*

TOURS
St. Simons Colonial Island Trolley Tours. For more than a decade, this locally owned and operated tour company has been introducing visitors to the history and culture of St. Simons Island. Reaching back 500 hundred years, guides chronicle stories from the days of the island's early Native American inhabitants to modern history. No tour is the same, but the air-conditioned trolley passes by landmark sites of slave-era African American churches, Christ Church Frederica, and the Battle of Bloody Marsh. The tour runs for 1½ hours and costs $20. The trolley departs from near the fishing pier at Pier Village three times daily: 10 am, noon, and 2 pm. ⊠ *St. Simons Pier* ☎ *912/268–0363* ⊕ *www. colonialtrolley.com.*

Stroll along the live oak allées at St. Simons Island.

EXPLORING

Christ Church Frederica. This white-frame, Gothic-style church was built by shipwrights and consecrated in 1886 following an earlier structure's desecration by Union troops. It is surrounded by historic live oaks, dogwoods, and azaleas. The interior has beautiful stained-glass windows and several handmade pews. The cemetery grounds are the final resting place for Golden Isles historical fiction writer Eugenia Price. ✉ *6329 Frederica Rd.* ☎ *912/638–8683* ⊕ *ccfssi.org* ✉ *Donations suggested* ⊘ *Closed Mon.*

Ebo Landing. In May 1803 an Igbo chief and his West African tribesmen became Geechee folk legends when they "walked back to Africa," drowning en masse rather than submitting to a life of slavery. Captured in what is modern-day Nigeria, the tribesmen disembarked their slave ship at Ebo (Igbo) Landing and headed straight into Dunbar Creek, chanting a hymn. Though the site is now private property, it can be seen from the road. ✉ *St. Simons Island* ⊹ *From the F.J. Torras Causeway, turn left on Sea Island Rd. After Hawkins Island Dr., look left (north) just before crossing small bridge at Dunbar Creek. The landing is at a bend in the creek.*

Fort Frederica National Monument. Built by English troops in the mid-1730s, Fort Frederica was constructed to protect the southern flank of the new Georgia colony against a Spanish invasion from Florida. At its peak in the 1740s, it was the most elaborate British fortification in North America. Around the fort today are the foundations of homes and shops and the partial ruins of the tabby barracks and magazine. Start your visit at the National Park Service Visitors Center, which has a film and displays. ✉ *6515 Frederica Rd.* ☎ *912/638-3639* ⊕ *www.nps.gov/fofr.*

FAMILY **Maritime Center at the Historic St. Simons Coast Guard Station.** Set in a restored 1936 coast guard station, this museum—geared as much to kids as adults—features the life of a "Coastie" in the early 1940s, through personal accounts of the military history of St. Simons Island. It also has illustrative displays on the ecology of the islands off the coast of Georgia. **TIP→ Your ticket covers admission to the Lighthouse.** ✉ *4201 1st St.* ☎ *912/638–4666* 🌐 *www.saintsimonslighthouse.org* 🎟 *$12.*

FAMILY **Neptune Park.** Named after St. Simons slave Neptune Small, this newly renovated park is located near Pier Village on the island's south end. The expansive park boasts a picturesque oak canopy and picnic tables amid a sprawling waterfront lawn, beach access, and a large recreation area perfect for families. The Neptune Park Fun Zone has a free playground, a swimming pool ($8 per person) that opens in the warmer months, and a year-round miniature golf course ($8 per round). Also newly renovated, the adjacent pier is good for fishing or watching ships roll in. Public restrooms are outside of the library. ✉ *550 Beachview Dr.* ☎ *912/279–2836* 🌐 *www.glynncounty.org* 🕒 *Golf is closed Mon.–Thurs. during fall and winter months; pools are closed Labor Day–May.*

St. Simons Lighthouse. One of only five surviving lighthouses in Georgia, St. Simons Lighthouse has become a symbol of the island. It's been in use since 1872; a predecessor was blown up to prevent its capture by Union troops in the Civil War. The **St. Simons Lighthouse Museum,** occupying two stories of the lightkeeper's dwelling, tells of the history of the island, the lighthouse, and James Gould, the first lightkeeper of the original lighthouse. The keeper's second-floor quarters contain a parlor, kitchen, and two bedrooms furnished with period pieces, including beds with rope mattress suspension. The last climb of the lighthouse is at 4:30. **TIP→ Your ticket also covers admission to the Maritime Center.** ✉ *610 Beachview Dr.* ☎ *912/638–4666* 🌐 *www.saintsimonslighthouse.org* 🎟 *$12.*

WHERE TO EAT

$$$ SEAFOOD 🍴 **Coastal Kitchen and Raw Bar.** Just off the FJ Torras Causeway on the way to St. Simons, Coastal Kitchen overlooks the Morningstar Marina on the Frederica River, just inside the St. Simons Sound. The fresh, locally sourced seafood is among the best on the island and perfectly complements the sunset views from the outdoor dining patio. **Known for:** waterfront views; great service; live music. [$] *Average main: $20* ✉ *102 Marina Dr.* ☎ *912/638–7790* 🌐 *www.coastalkitchen1.com.*

$ AMERICAN 🍴 **Gnat's Landing.** There's more than a little bit of Margaritaville in this Key West–style bungalow catering to the flip-flop crowd. Seafood is the specialty, with a gumbo that's outta sight. **Known for:** laid-back coastal vibes; locals' hot spot; lively nightlife; tasty low-key fare. [$] *Average main: $13* ✉ *310 Redfern Village* ☎ *912/638–7378* 🌐 *www.gnatslanding.com.*

$
SEAFOOD
FAMILY

✗ **The Half Shell at the Pier.** On an island chock-full of seafood establishments, Half Shell rises above the competition. Established in 2013, it's beloved by locals and visitors alike for the combination of laid-back atmosphere, fresh seafood, and quality preparation and presentation—this is not the stereotypical fried-shrimp shack. **Known for:** fresh oysters—raw, shucked, or steamed; local Georgia shrimp and grits; crab cakes. $ *Average main: $12* ⊠ *504 Beachview Dr.* ☎ *912/268–4241* ⊕ *thehalfshellssi.com* ۞ *No lunch Mon.–Thurs.*

$$$$
AMERICAN
Fodor's Choice
★

✗ **Halyards.** This elegant restaurant with a laid-back attitude makes everything except the ketchup right on the premises. Chef-owner Dave Snyder's devotion to quality has earned a faithful following of discerning locals. **Known for:** quality, made-from-scratch fine dining; seasonal menus; superb wine list. $ *Average main: $28* ⊠ *55 Cinema La.* ☎ *912/638–9100* ⊕ *www.halyardsrestaurant.com* ۞ *Closed Sun. No lunch.*

$
BARBECUE

✗ **Southern Soul BBQ.** This retro-inspired indoor-outdoor establishment occupies a former gas station at a five-points crossroads in the heart of St. Simons Island. Locals claim this as the area's best BBQ and diners flock here for the brisket, pulled pork, and Brunswick stew; it's also a great option for large parties with family-style appetites. **Known for:** retro atmosphere; sizable portions; fried oreos; Brunswick stew. $ *Average main: $9* ⊠ *2020 Demere Rd.* ☎ *912/638–7685* ⊕ *www. southernsoulbbq.com.*

$$
ITALIAN
FAMILY

✗ **Tramici.** This is the Italian offering of David Snyder, owner of the more refined Halyards. Tramici is billed as a neighborhood restaurant, although it's in a shopping center. **Known for:** kid-friendly dining; authentic flatbreads; hearty Italian entrées. $ *Average main: $18* ⊠ *75 Cinema La.* ☎ *912/634–2202* ⊕ *www.tramicirestaurant.com* ۞ *No lunch weekends.*

WHERE TO STAY

$$
HOTEL

⊡ **Holiday Inn Express.** With clean, simple, brightly decorated rooms at great prices, this chain hotel is an attractive option in this price category. **Pros:** good value; nonsmoking. **Cons:** guests have complained that walls are too thin; the breakfast is basic. $ *Rooms from: $169* ⊠ *Plantation Village, 299 Main St.* ☎ *912/634–2175, 888/465–4329* ⊕ *www.ihg. com/holidayinnexpress/hotels/us/en/st-simons-island/ssiga/hoteldetail* ⊷ *60 rooms* ۩ *Breakfast.*

$$$
RESORT

⊡ **King and Prince Beach & Golf Resort.** Your accommodation options at this cushy retreat are spacious guest rooms, two- and three-bedroom apartment-style "villas," and stand-alone guesthouses. **Pros:** sprawling suites; golf-course access; speedy room service. **Cons:** amenities are fairly basic; rooms are relatively small; tide levels can make it difficult to access the beach. $ *Rooms from: $215* ⊠ *201 Arnold Rd.* ☎ *912/638–3631* ⊕ *www.kingandprince.com* ⊷ *147 rooms, 44 villas, 7 guesthouses.*

$$$$
B&B/INN
Fodor's Choice
★

⊡ **The Lodge at Sea Island Golf Club.** This small resort overlooking the sea is one of the top golf and spa destinations in the country. **Pros:** fantastic golfing; elegant, cozy interiors; stately, full marble baths. **Cons:** high price; meals aren't included. $ *Rooms from: $560* ⊠ *100 Retreat Ave.* ☎ *912/634–4300* ⊕ *www.seaisland.com* ⊷ *40 rooms* ۩ *No meals.*

$$ RESORT 🏨 **Sea Palms Resort and Conference Center.** If you're looking for an active getaway, this contemporary complex could be the place for you—it has golf, tennis, a fitness center loaded with state-of-the-art equipment, a beach club, sand-pit volleyball, horseshoes, and bicycling. **Pros:** guests have beach-club privileges; spacious rooms; some rooms have fantastic marsh views. **Cons:** somewhat unimaginative furnishings; the rooms could use updating. [$] *Rooms from: $160* ✉ *5445 Frederica Rd.* ☎ *912/638–3351* 🌐 *www.seapalms.com* 🛏 *132 rooms* 🍴 *No meals.*

$$ B&B/INN 🏨 **St. Simons Inn.** In a prime spot by the lighthouse, and only minutes on foot from the village and the beaches, this European-style inn is made up of privately owned guest rooms—nothing fancy, but they're clean, comfortable, and individually decorated, many with furnishings and art that give off a beachy vibe. **Pros:** excellent location; affordable rates; some pet-friendly rooms. **Cons:** two-night minimum stay on weekends; some rooms are small; individually decorated rooms means some are not as nice as others. [$] *Rooms from: $150* ✉ *609 Beachview Dr.* ☎ *912/638–1101* 🌐 *www.stsimonsinn.com* 🛏 *34 rooms* 🍴 *Breakfast.*

$$ B&B/INN 🏨 **The Village Inn & Pub.** What was once a cinder-block beach house has since won awards for its environmentally friendly design that incorporated the original structure and preserved the surrounding live oaks. **Pros:** great location; courtyard pool and lively on-site pub; owners have taken care to preserve the mossy live oaks. **Cons:** basic rooms; the lively crowd at the pub can be noisy on weekends. [$] *Rooms from: $178* ✉ *500 Mallery St.* ☎ *912/634–6056* 🌐 *www.villageinnandpub.com* 🛏 *28 rooms* 🍴 *Breakfast.*

SPORTS AND THE OUTDOORS

BEACHES

FAMILY **East Beach.** The most expansive stretch of public beach on St. Simons is also one of the most popular in all of the Golden Isles. Entrances sit on either end of the beach: at the Coast Guard Station on 1st Street to the north and Massengale Park on Oak Street to the south. Between the two entrances, this ½-mile stretch of hard-packed white sand is vacation central, with calm, shallow water perfect for swimming, boogie boarding, or windsurfing. Plenty of parking is available, lifeguards watch the waves all summer, and drinking is allowed in plastic containers (no glass bottles). **Amenities:** food and drink; lifeguards; parking; showers; toilets. **Best for:** swimming; windsurfing. ✉ *Ocean Blvd., from 1st to Oak Sts.* 🌐 *www.explorestsimonsisland.com/St_Simons_Beaches.html.*

BIKING

Ocean Motion Surf Co. St. Simons has an extensive network of bicycle trails, and you can ride on the beach as well. Ocean Motion rents bikes for the entire family, from trail bikes to beach bikes to seats for infants. Rates start at $19 per day. ✉ *1300 Ocean Blvd.* ☎ *912/638–5225* 🌐 *www.stsimonskayaking.com.*

CRABBING AND FISHING

FAMILY **St. Simons Island Bait and Tackle.** There's no simpler fun for the kids than to grab a crab basket or fishing pole and head to St. Simons Island Pier next to Neptune Park. This bait shop is near the foot of the pier and is open 364½ days a year. Owners Mike and Trish Wooten have everything from crabbing and fishing gear to snacks and cold drinks. They also sell locally made crab drop nets and fishing rigs. ⊠ *121 Mallory St.* ☎ *912/634–1888.*

GOLF

The top-flight golf facilities at the Lodge at Sea Island are available only to members and guests, but St. Simons has two other high-quality courses open to the general public.

The King and Prince Golf Course. At the north end of St. Simons, on the site of the Hampton Plantation—an 18th-century cotton, rice, and indigo plantation—is a *Golf Digest* "Places to Play" four-star winner. The course, originally designed by Joe Lee, was restored in 2009, and it lies amid towering oaks, salt marshes, and lagoons. ⊠ *100 Tabbystone* ☎ *912/634–0255* ⊕ *www.kingandprince.com* ⊠ *Greens Fee: $79 King and Prince Resort guests, $115 nonguests* ⚐ *18 holes, 6462 yds, par 72* ⊂ *Facilities: Driving range, putting green, pitching area, golf carts, rental clubs, pro shop, golf academy/lessons, restaurant, bar.*

Sea Palms Resort and Conference Center. On a former cotton and indigo plantation, this resort offers 27 holes of golf on a standard 18-hole course and a 9-hole executive course, plus a driving range. Discounts are available through online reservations. ⊠ *5445 Frederica Rd.* ☎ *912/434–4336* ⊕ *www.seapalms.com* ⊠ *Greens Fee: 18-hole course $79; 9-hole course $29* ⚐ *18-hole course: 6477 yds, par 71. 9-hole course: 2460 yds, par 34* ⊂ *Facilities: Driving range, putting green, pitching area, golf carts, rental clubs, pro shop, golf academy/lessons, restaurant, bar.*

KAYAKING AND SAILING

Barry's Beach Service. If sailing is your thing, check out this shop in front of the King and Prince Beach and Golf Resort on Arnold Road for its Hobie Cat rentals and sailing lessons. Barry's also rents kayaks, boogie boards, stand-up paddleboards, beach chairs and umbrellas, and beach funcycles (low, reclining bikes), and conducts guided kayak tours. Locally owned and operated, Barry's has served the Golden Isles since 1977. ⊠ *420 Arnold Rd.* ☎ *912/638–8053* ⊕ *www.stsimonskayaking. com* ⊠ *Sailboat rentals from $85 an hour.*

Ocean Motion. After an instructional clinic, head off to explore the marsh creeks, coastal waters, and beaches with Ocean Motion, which has been giving kayaking tours of St. Simons for more than 30 years. The shop also offers bike rentals and sells all of the necessary gear for a day on the water. ⊠ *1300 Ocean Blvd.* ☎ *912/638–5225* ⊕ *www.stsimons-kayaking.com/ocean-motion.html* ⊠ *Kayak tours from $49 per person.*

SCUBA DIVING

Island Dive Center. Gray's Reef, off Sapelo island, is one of only 14 National Marine Sanctuaries. It's home to loggerhead turtles and part of the northern right whale breeding grounds, all of which makes it an attractive place for diving. Island Dive Center, a five-star PADI center, is the place to go for scuba and snorkeling instruction, equipment rental, and charter trips. Open Sunday and Monday by appointment only. ⊠ *Morningstar Marina, 101 Marina Dr., off F.J. Torras Causeway* ☎ *912/638–6590.*

JEKYLL ISLAND

18 miles south of St. Simons Island; 90 miles south of Savannah.

For 56 winters, between 1886 and 1942, America's rich and famous faithfully came south to Jekyll Island. Through the Gilded Age, World War I, the Roaring '20s, and the Great Depression, Vanderbilts and Rockefellers, Morgans and Astors, Macys, Pulitzers, and Goodyears shuttered their 5th Avenue castles and retreated to elegant "cottages" on their wild coastal island. It's been said that when the island's distinguished winter residents were all "in," a sixth of the world's wealth was represented. Early in World War II the millionaires departed for the last time. In 1947 the state of Georgia purchased the entire island for the bargain price of $675,000.

Jekyll Island is still a 7½-mile playground, but it's no longer restricted to the rich and famous. A water park, picnic grounds, and facilities for golf, tennis, fishing, biking, and jogging are all open to the public. One side of the island is lined by nearly 10 miles of hard-packed Atlantic beaches; the other by the intracoastal waterway and picturesque salt marshes. Deer and wild turkey inhabit interior forests of pine, magnolia, and moss-veiled live oaks. Egrets, pelicans, herons, and sandpipers skim the gentle surf. Jekyll Island's clean, mostly uncommercialized public beaches are free and open year-round. Bathhouses with restrooms, changing areas, and showers are open at regular intervals along the beach.

GETTING HERE AND AROUND

Jekyll Island is connected to the mainland by the Sidney Lanier Bridge. Visitors coming to the island by car must stop at the greeting station to pay a parking fee of $6 per vehicle per day. Once on the island, you'll need a car or a bicycle to get around.

ESSENTIALS

Visitor Information Jekyll Island Welcome Center. ⊠ *901 Downing Musgrove Causeway* ☎ *912/635–3636* ⊕ *www.jekyllisland.com.*

EXPLORING

FAMILY   **Georgia Sea Turtle Center.** A must-see on Jekyll Island, this is one of
Fodor'sChoice   the few sea turtle centers in the country. This center aims to increase
★   awareness of habitat and wildlife conservation challenges for endangered coastal turtles—loggerheads, green, Kemp's ridley, and diamondback terrapin—through turtle rehabilitation, research, and education programs. The center includes educational exhibits and a "hospital," where visitors can view rescued turtles and read their stories. Sea turtles lay their eggs along Jekyll Island beaches from May through August.

Several hundred rehabilitated turtles have been released into the wild since the center opened. ✉ *214 Stable Rd.* ☎ *912/635–4444* 🌐 *gstc.jekyllisland.com* 🎟 *$7.*

Jekyll Island Museum. This quaint museum offers guests a snapshot of Jekyll's rich history, from the life of original natives to the landing of one of the last slave ships at the South end to the golden age of the island, when America's rich and famous wintered at Jekyll. Tram tours ($16) originate at this little museum, departing daily at 11 am, 1 pm, and 3 pm, weather permitting. The 90-minute tour covers the National Historic Landmark District and includes entry into two restored cottages. ✉ *100 Stable Rd.* ☎ *912/635–4036* 🌐 *www.jekyllisland.com/history/museum.*

CAMPING ON JEKYLL ISLAND

Jekyll Island Campground. At the northern end of Jekyll across from the entrance to the fishing pier, this campground lies on 18 wooded acres with more than 175 sites that can accommodate everything from backpackers looking for primitive sites to RVs needing full hookups. Pets are welcome. It's within walking distance to Driftwood Beach but far from the main activity of the island. ✉ *1197 Riverview Dr., Jekyll Island* ☎ *912/635–3021* 🌐 *www.jekyllisland.com/lodging/jekyll-island-campground.*

Fodor's Choice ★ **Jekyll Island National Historic Landmark District.** This 240-acre historic district encapsulates the village that once comprised the winter retreat and seasonal residences for America's wealthiest—Morgan, Pulitzer, Goodyear, Rockefeller, and Vanderbilt among them. Today, the original cottages still stand amidst the historic grounds with the Jekyll Island Club Hotel, founded in 1886, as the crown jewel. Nearby is **Faith Chapel**, built in 1904, which is illuminated by stained-glass windows, including one Tiffany original. The chapel is open daily 8–10 am unless it has been reserved for a wedding. ✉ *Jekyll Island* 🌐 *www.jekyllisland.com.*

FAMILY **Summer Waves.** At this 11-acre park more than a million gallons of water are used in the 18,000-square-foot wave pool, waterslides, children's activity pool with two slides, splash zone, and circular river for tubing and rafting. Inner tubes and life vests are provided at no extra charge. ✉ *210 S. Riverview Dr.* ☎ *912/635–2074* 🌐 *www.summerwaves.com* 🎟 *$19.95* 🕓 *Closed Oct.–Apr. Closed weekdays in Aug. and Sept.*

WHERE TO EAT

$$$$ MEDITERRANEAN Fodor's Choice ★ 🍴 **Courtyard at Crane.** When it was built in 1917, Crane Cottage—actually an elegant Italianate villa—was the most expensive winter home on Jekyll Island. Now, as part of the Jekyll Island Club Hotel, the Courtyard at Crane offers casual alfresco dining in quirky little dining areas. **Known for:** courtyard dining; delicious salads; great service. [$] *Average main: $31* ✉ *Jekyll Island Club Hotel, 375 Riverview Dr.* ☎ *912/635–5200* 🌐 *www.jekyllclub.com* 🕓 *No dinner Fri. and Sat.* ☞ *Closes periodically on the weekends for weddings.*

Learn about Jekyll Island's history as the playground of the rich and famous at the Jekyll Island Museum.

$$ ✕ **Driftwood Bistro.** On-site at Villas by the Sea, Driftwood Bistro is a
SEAFOOD surprisingly tasty off-the-beaten-path find. Here coastal fare meets
Southern classics in a friendly, laid-back environment. **Known for:**
Lowcountry cuisine; vegetarian options; small plates available. $ *Average main: $19* ✉ *1175 N. Beachview Dr.* ☎ *912/635–2521* ⊕ *www.
driftwoodbistro.com* ☽ *No lunch. Closed Sun.*

$$$$ ✕ **Grand Dining Room.** This colonnaded restaurant inside the Jekyll Club
SOUTHERN maintains a tradition of fine dining first established in the 19th cen-
Fodor's Choice tury. The huge fireplace, views of the pool, and sparkling silver and
★ crystal all contribute to the sense of old-style elegance. **Known for:**
grand historical architecture; super Sunday brunch spread; unique
twist on Southern classics; Victorian tea service. $ *Average main: $35*
✉ *Jekyll Island Club, 371 Riverview Dr.* ☎ *912/635–5155* ⊕ *www.
jekyllclub.com* 👔 *Jacket required.*

WHERE TO STAY

$$ 🏨 **Beachview Club.** Grand old oak trees shade the grounds of this luxury
HOTEL lodging. **Pros:** heated pool; relaxing location with beautiful grounds;
property on the beach. **Cons:** not much for kids to do here; rooms
need TLC; no restaurant on-site. $ *Rooms from: $169* ✉ *721 N.
Beachview Dr.* ☎ *912/635–2256* ⊕ *www.beachviewclub.com* ⮑ *38
rooms* ❘◎❘ *No meals.*

$$$ 🏨 **Holiday Inn Resort.** Formerly the Oceanside Inn and Suites, this prop-
HOTEL erty was purchased and extensively renovated in 2014. **Pros:** lovely
FAMILY views; on-site laundry facilities; bike rentals on-site; good value. **Cons:**
best views found on ocean side; rooms near the restaurant are loud

on the weekends. [$] *Rooms from: $205* ✉ *711 N. Beachview Dr.* ☎ *912/635–2211* 🌐 *www.ihg.com* 🛏 *157 rooms* 🍴 *No meals.*

$$$ RESORT Fodor's Choice ★ **Jekyll Island Club Hotel.** This sprawling 1887 resort was once described as "the richest, the most exclusive, the most inaccessible club in the world." The comfortable resort's focal point is a four-story clubhouse, with its wraparound verandas and Queen Anne–style towers and turrets. **Pros:** on the water; old-world charm, with traditional room keys; close proximity to restaurants, shopping, and sea-turtle center. **Cons:** room decor and some appliances could use an update; some rooms are small. [$] *Rooms from: $215* ✉ *371 Riverview Dr.* ☎ *912/635–2600* 🌐 *www.jekyllclub.com* 🛏 *138 rooms, 19 suites* 🍴 *No meals.*

$$$$ RESORT **Westin Jekyll Island.** The introduction of the Westin to Jekyll Island came as a result of the 2014 renovation of much of the island's accommodations and attractions. **Pros:** pet-friendly; eco-friendly; close to convention center and shopping district. **Cons:** landscaping is still maturing; windows don't open to the ocean breeze. [$] *Rooms from: $349* ✉ *110 Ocean Way* ☎ *912/635–4545* 🌐 *www.westinjekyllisland.com* 🛏 *200 rooms* 🍴 *No meals.*

SPORTS AND THE OUTDOORS

BEACHES

Driftwood Beach. For a firsthand look at the stunning effects of erosion on barrier islands, head at low tide to this oceanfront boneyard on North Beach, where live oaks and pines are being consumed by the sea at an alarming rate. The snarl of trunks and limbs and the dramatic, massive root systems of upturned trees are an eerie and intriguing tableau of nature's slow and steady power. It's been estimated that nearly 1,000 feet of Jekyll's beach have been lost since the early 1900s. **■ TIP→ Bring your camera; the photo opportunities are terrific, and this is the best place to shoot St. Simons Lighthouse. The snarling branches of submerged trees can make this a dangerous place to swim, however, so use caution in the water.** Restrooms and other facilities are at the Clam Creek Picnic Area. **Amenities:** parking; showers; toilets. **Best for:** solitude; sunrise. ✉ *Jekyll Island* ✥ *Walk from the trailhead at the east side of the Clam Creek Picnic Area or from the roadside parking area on N. Beachview Dr.*

FAMILY **Great Dunes Beach.** Starting just north of the entrance road on South Beachview Drive, this strand runs from Great Dunes Park, alongside Main Street and the convention center, to South Dunes Beach at Glory Boardwalk (built when the final battle scene of the film *Glory* was shot here) at the soccer complex. This is one of the most accessible beaches on the island, with parking at both ends and good shower-restroom facilities at the park. The white-sand beach is backed by dunes, which are protected wildlife areas, while calm, shallow water, and a mild shore break make this a good spot to swim and play in the surf. **Amenities:** parking; showers; toilets. **Best for:** swimming. ✉ *Jekyll Island* ✥ *S. Beachview Dr. from the beach deck to the Glory Boardwalk* 🌐 *www.jekyllisland.com/activities/great-dunes-beach.*

FAMILY **Great Dunes Park.** A newer addition to Jekyll Island's beach facilities is this centrally located park next to the newly renovated convention center on South Beachview Drive. A beach deck and multiple dune crossovers provide access to the hard-packed beach, and a boardwalk offers beachfront bike parking. Facilities include ample parking, restrooms and changing areas, and a pavilion for local events and festivals. **Amenities:** parking; showers; toilets. **Best for:** swimming. ⌧ *Jekyll Island ⚓ S. Beachview Dr. on the north side of the convention center* ⊕ *www.goldenisles.com/listing/great-dunes-park.*

FAMILY **St. Andrews Beach.** Stretching south of the Glory Boardwalk to the St. Andrews Picnic Area at the very southern end of the island, this narrow beach backs up to dense maritime forest, making it a quiet, secluded bit of coast and a great spot for wildlife viewing or beachcombing. At the picnic area, a short trail leads to a viewing platform overlooking the outflow of Jekyll Creek—keep an eye out for dolphins cruising near the shoreline. A memorial in the picnic area honors the landing of one of the last American slave ships, *The Wanderer.* **Amenities:** parking; toilets. **Best for:** solitude. ⌧ *Jekyll Island ⚓ Take S. Beachview Dr. or S. Riverview Dr. to the southernmost end of the island* ⊕ *www.goldenisles. com/listing/st-andrews-picnic-area.*

BIKING

The best way to see Jekyll is by bicycle: a long, paved trail runs right along the beach, and there's an extensive network of paths throughout the island.

Beachside Bike Rentals. Located near the Days Inn, this one-stop rental shop offers everything from multispeed bikes to double surreys with Bimini tops that look like antique cars and carry up to six adults and two children. The shop also has beach chairs, umbrellas, stand-up paddleboards, and kayaks. ⌧ *60 S. Beachview Dr.* ☎ *912/635–9801* ⊕ *www.beachsidebikerentals.com.*

FAMILY **Jekyll Island Mini-Golf and Bike Rentals.** Play mini-golf or choose from a wide selection of rental bikes (including surrey pedal cars that can hold four people, recumbent bikes, and traditional bikes) at this shop located next to the Red Bug. Rates start at $14 daily for bike rentals and $6.50 for a round of mini-golf. ⌧ *N. Beachview Dr. at Shell Rd.* ☎ *912/635–2648* ⊕ *www.jekyllisland.com/activities/miniature-golf.*

FISHING

Coastal Expeditions. With 40 years of experience in local waters, Captain Eric Moody provides half-day and full-day trips in-shore and offshore for fishing, dolphin-watching, and sightseeing. There's a six person maximum. ⌧ *Jekyll Harbor Marina* ☎ *912/265–3526* ⊕ *www.coast-alcharterfishing.com.*

Jekyll Fishing Center. Larry Crews runs inshore and offshore fishing trips and dolphin-watching and sightseeing tours on four charter boats. He also offers his services as captain to tie the knot for couples with their sea legs. ⌧ *Jekyll Island Fishing Pier, 10 Clam Creek Rd.* ☎ *912/635–3556* ⊕ *www.goldenisles.com/listing/jekyll-island-fishing-center.*

11

GOLF

Jekyll Island Golf Club. A golf destination for nearly 90 years, today this club has four courses: the original 9-hole course called Oceanside Nine (now known as Great Dunes), built in 1926, and three beautifully designed 18-hole courses, plus a clubhouse. ⊠ *322 Capt. Wylly Rd.* ☎ *912/635–2368* ⊕ *www.jekyllisland.com/activities-category/golf-club* ⚑ *Greens Fee: $59 (18 holes), $25 (9 holes)* ⚐ *63 holes, 6469–6701 yds, par 72 (all 18-hole courses)* ⚲ *Facilities: Driving range, putting green, pitching area, golf carts, pull carts, rental clubs, pro shop, golf academy/lessons, restaurant, bar.*

HORSEBACK RIDING

FAMILY **Golden Isles Carriage and Trail.** See Jekyll by horseback with this well-regarded livery company, in business for more than 30 years. Trail rides include visits to the salt marsh and Driftwood Beach, a boneyard of live oaks and pine trees being reclaimed by the sea; narrated carriage tours explore the sights of the historic district. Rides leave from the Clam Creek picnic area across from the Jekyll Island Campground, and the carriages leave from the Island History Center. Perks for families include a petting zoo, horse camp for children, and riding lessons for all ages. The carriage ride is located in a historic building that has been used as a livery for over 100 years. ⊠ *Jekyll Island History Center, 100 Stable Rd.* ☎ *912/635–9500* ⊕ *www.threeoaksfarm.org* ⚑ *Horseback rides from $58 an hour; historic carriage tours from $15 per person* ☾ *Closed weekends.*

CUMBERLAND ISLAND

47 miles south of Jekyll Island; 115 miles south of Savannah to St. Marys via I–95; 45 mins by ferry from St. Marys.

Fodor's Choice ★ Cumberland, the largest of Georgia's coastal isles, is a national treasure. The 18-mile spit of land off the coast of St. Marys is a nearly unspoiled sanctuary of marshes, dunes, beaches, forests, lakes, and ponds. And although it has a long history of human habitation, it remains much as nature created it: a dense, lacework canopy of live oak shades, sand roads, and foot trails through thick undergrowth of palmetto. Wild horses roam freely on pristine beaches. Waterways are homes for gators, sea turtles, otters, snowy egrets, great blue herons, ibises, wood storks, and more than 300 other species of birds. And in its forests are armadillos, wild horses, deer, raccoons, and an assortment of reptiles.

In the 16th century the Spanish established a mission and a garrison, San Pedro de Mocama, on the southern end of the island. But development didn't begin in earnest until the wake of the American Revolution, with timbering operations for shipbuilding, particularly construction of warships for the early U.S. naval fleet. Cotton, rice, and indigo plantations were also established. In 1818 Revolutionary War hero General "Lighthorse" Harry Lee, father of Robert E. Lee, died and was buried near the Dungeness estate of General Nathaniel Greene. Though his body was later moved to Virginia to be interred beside his son, the gravestone remains. During the 1880s, the family of Thomas Carnegie

Wild horses roam freely on Cumberland Island.

(brother of industrialist Andrew) built several lavish homes here. In the 1950s the National Park Service named Cumberland Island and Cape Cod as the most significant natural areas on the Atlantic and Gulf coasts. And in 1972, in response to attempts to develop the island by Hilton Head developer Charles Fraser, Congress passed a bill establishing the island as a national seashore. Today most of the island is part of the national park system.

GETTING HERE AND AROUND

The only access to the island is via the *Cumberland Queen II*, a reservations-only, 146-passenger ferry based near the National Park Service Information Center at St. Marys. The round-trip ticket price is $28. The $7 entry fee to the Cumberland Island National Seashore *(See Exploring)* applies to all island visitors. There are two Park Service docks at the island's south end: the main ferry dock is the Sea Camp Dock, with a secondary stop at Dungeness Dock farther south.

Ferry bookings are heavy in spring and early summer, and then again in early fall. Cancellations and no-shows often make last-minute space available, but don't rely on it. You can make reservations up to six months in advance. The ferry operates twice a day in both directions between St. Marys and Cumberland Island. ■TIP→ Note that the ferry does not transport pets, kayaks, or cars.

Getting around the island is solely by foot or bicycle, which can be rented at the Sea Camp dock.

ESSENTIALS

Ferry Contacts *Cumberland Queen II.* ✉ *113 St. Marys St., St. Marys* ☎ *912/882–4335, 887/860–6787* ⊕ *www.nps.gov/cuis.*

EXPLORING

Fodor's Choice ★ **Cumberland Island National Seashore.** Encompassing the vast majority of Cumberland Island, this 36,347-acre preserve has pristine forests and marshes marbled with wooded nature trails, 18 miles of undeveloped beaches, and opportunities for fishing, bird-watching, and viewing the ruins of Thomas Carnegie's great estate, **Dungeness.** You can also join history and nature walks led by Park Service rangers. Bear in mind that summers are hot and humid and that you must bring everything you need, including your own food, drinks, sunscreen, and insect repellent. The only public access to the island is via the *Cumberland Queen II* ferry. ✉ *101 Wheeler St., St. Marys* ☎ *912/882–4335* 🌐 *www.nps.gov/cuis* 🎟 *Preserve $7, ferry $28.*

OFF THE BEATEN PATH **The First African Baptist Church.** This small, one-room church on the north end of Cumberland Island is where John F. Kennedy Jr. and Carolyn Bessette were married on September 21, 1996. Constructed of whitewashed logs, it's simply adorned with a cross made of sticks tied together with string and 11 handmade pews seating 40 people. It was built in 1937 to replace a cruder 1893 structure used by former slaves from the High Point–Half Moon Bluff community. The Kennedy–Bessette wedding party stayed at the Greyfield Inn, built on the south end of the island in 1900 by the Carnegie family. ✉ *Cumberland Island* ✣ *North end of Cumberland, near Half Moon Bluff, about 12 miles from Sea Camp dock.*

FAMILY **St. Marys Aquatic Center.** If the heat has you, and the kids are itching to get wet, head to this full-service water park on the mainland, where you can get an inner tube and relax floating down the Oasis lazy river, hurtle down Splash Mountain, or corkscrew yourself silly sliding down the Orange Crush. ✉ *301 Herb Bauer Dr., St. Marys* ☎ *912/673–8118* 🌐 *www.stmarysga.gov/department/aquatic_center* 🎟 *$9.95* 🕒 *Closed Oct.–Apr. Closed weekdays Aug. and Sept.*

WHERE TO STAY

ON THE ISLAND

$$$$ B&B/INN 🏨 **Greyfield Inn.** Once described as a "Tara by the sea," this turn-of-the-last-century Carnegie family home is Cumberland Island's only accommodation. **Pros:** air-conditioned in summer; lack of telephone service means complete solitude; social hour with hors d'oeuvres. **Cons:** pricey; no stores on Cumberland; communications to the mainland are limited. [$] *Rooms from: $550* ✉ *Cumberland Island* ✣ *Southern end of the island, accessible by private boat from Fernandina Beach, FL* ☎ *904/261–6408* 🌐 *www.greyfieldinn.com* 🛏 *16 rooms* 🍴 *All meals.*

ON THE MAINLAND

$ HOTEL 🏨 **Cumberland Island Inn & Suites.** Children under 18 stay free at this modern, moderately priced hotel 3½ miles from the St. Marys waterfront. **Pros:** clean, large rooms; affordable rates; kids stay free. **Cons:** not in historic area; not in walking distance to the beach. [$] *Rooms from: $69* ✉ *2710 Osborne Rd., St. Marys* ☎ *912/882–6250, 800/768–6250* 🌐 *www.cumberlandislandinn.com* 🛏 *79 rooms* 🍴 *Breakfast.*

CLOSE UP

Georgia's Black Republic

After capturing Savannah in December 1864, General William Tecumseh Sherman read the Emancipation Proclamation at the Second African Baptist Church and issued his now famous Field Order No. 15, giving freed slaves 40 acres and a mule. The field order set aside a swath of land reaching 30 miles inland from Charleston to northern Florida (roughly the area east of Interstate 95), including the coastal islands, for an independent state of freed slaves.

Under the administration of General Rufus Saxton and his assistant, Tunis G. Campbell, a black New Jersey native who represented McIntosh County as a state senator, a black republic was established with St. Catherines Island as its capital. Hundreds of former slaves were relocated to St. Catherines and Sapelo islands, where they set about

cultivating the land. In 1865 Campbell established himself as virtual king, controlling a legislature, a court, and a 275-man army. Whites called Campbell "the most feared man in Georgia."

Congress repealed Sherman's directive and replaced General Saxton with General Davis Tillison, who was sympathetic to the interests of former plantation owners, and in 1867 federal troops drove Campbell off St. Catherines and into McIntosh County, where he continued to exert his power. In 1876 he was convicted of falsely imprisoning a white citizen and sentenced, at the age of 63, to work on a chain gang. After being freed, he left Georgia for good and settled in Boston, where he died in 1891. Every year on the fourth Saturday in June, the town of Darien holds a festival in Campbell's honor.

$
B&B/INN
Riverview Hotel. The front door to the Riverview could be a time machine transporting you straight to the Old West, circa 1916, the year the hotel was built. **Pros:** old-time touches; excellent location. **Cons:** some rooms seem a little bit shabby; some common areas are not air-conditioned. $ *Rooms from: $84 ⊠ 105 Osborne St., St. Marys* ☎ *912/882–3242* ⊕ *www.riverviewhotelstmarys.com* ↝ *20 rooms* ⦿ *Breakfast.*

$$
B&B/INN
Spencer House Inn. At the heart of St. Mary's historic district, this pink, three-story Victorian inn, built in 1872, is a perfect base for touring the town and Cumberland Island. **Pros:** short walk to the ferry; big balconies with rocking chairs. **Cons:** not recommended for young singles in search of a party; A/C units are near rooms and can be loud. $ *Rooms from: $155 ⊠ 200 Osbourne St., St. Marys* ☎ *912/882–1872, 888/840–1872* ⊕ *www.spencerhouseinn.com* ↝ *14 rooms* ⦿ *Breakfast.*

NIGHTLIFE

Seagle's Saloon and Patio Bar. The closer you get to borders, the more pronounced allegiances become. A case in point is Seagle's Saloon and Patio Bar, a smoky watering hole not far from the Florida state line that's festooned with University of Georgia memorabilia. Bawdy bartender Cindy Deen is a local legend, so expect some Southern sass. ⊠ *105 Osborne St., St. Marys* ☎ *912/882–3242.*

CAMPING ON CUMBERLAND ISLAND

11

Brickhill Bluff Campground. Way off the beaten path, this primitive campsite is a favorite spot to see manatees and dolphins. For those looking for adventure (and not amenities), Brickhill is worth the long hike from the dock. ⊠ *Cumberland Island* ☏ *912/882–4336* ⊕ *www.nps.gov/cuis.*

Hickory Hill Campground. Located in the heart of the island, this primitive camping area is about 1 mile from the beach. Though still in the trees, its canopy is more open than at some of the other sites. ⊠ *5½ miles from Sea Camp ferry dock, Cumberland Island* ☏ *912/882–4336* ⊕ *www. nps.gov/cuis.*

Sea Camp Campground. Close to the ferry dock and with plenty of amenities, this is an ideal spot for first-timers, families, and groups. Expect a fire pit, food cage, and picnic table at each site. ⊠ *½ mile from Sea Camp ferry dock, Cumberland Island* ☏ *912/882–4336* ⊕ *www.nps.gov/cuis.*

Stafford Beach Campground. Located behind the dunes, 3½ miles from the ferry dock, this is the only backcountry site not considered to be in the wilderness. It has more amenities than most of the other, more primitive sites. Expect good tree cover, bathrooms, showers, and a water source. ⊠ *3½ miles from Sea Camp ferry dock, Cumberland Island* ☏ *912/882–4336* ⊕ *www. nps.gov/cuis.*

Yankee Paradise Campground. Surrounded by palmettos, this forested and secluded spot is protected from the wind. It's a long hike back to the ferry dock, but the remoteness could be a big draw for some. ⊠ *7½ miles from Sea Camp ferry dock, Cumberland Island* ☏ *912/882–4336* ⊕ *www. nps.gov/cuis.*

SPORTS AND THE OUTDOORS

BEACHES

Dungeness Beach. From the Dungeness ferry dock to the southern tip of the island, Dungeness Beach covers nearly 2 miles of pristine, remote coast. This wild stretch of sand attracts beachcombers—sharks' teeth are a sought-after find—and fishermen, who cast for redfish and flounder at the southernmost point, called Pelican Flats. Trails lead to Thomas Carnegie's historic estate, Dungeness, and this is also a good area to spot Cumberland's famed wild horses that roam the beach and inland areas here. **Amenities:** none. **Best for:** solitude; sunrise. ⊠ *Cumberland Island* ✛ *Dungeness ferry dock to Pelican Flats.*

Sea Camp Beach. Proximity to the ferry makes this beach fronting the Sea Camp campground the most popular beach among day-trippers, though with only 300 visitors allowed on-island daily, it's never very crowded. Hard-pack trails and a boardwalk allow short nature walks, and the beach has good beachcombing. **Amenities:** showers; toilets. **Best for:** solitude; sunrise. ⊠ *Cumberland Island* ✛ *½ mile north of Sea Camp dock.*

Canoe trips into the Okefenokee Swamp Park reveal its unique ecology.

KAYAKING

Up the Creek Xpeditions. Whether you're a novice or skilled paddler, Up the Creek can guide you on kayak tours through some of Georgia and Florida's most scenic waters. Classes include navigation, tides and currents, and kayak surfing and racing. Trips include Yulee, the St. Marys River, Cumberland Sound, and the Okefenokee Swamp. ✉ *111 Osborne St., St. Marys* ☎ *912/882–0911* ⊕ *jacksonvillekayakcompany.com.*

OKEFENOKEE NATIONAL WILDLIFE REFUGE

Fodor's Choice ★ Larger than all of Georgia's barrier islands combined, the Okefenokee National Wildlife Refuge covers 700 square miles of southeastern Georgia and northeastern Florida. From the air, all roads and almost all traces of human development almost disappear into this vast, seemingly impenetrable landscape, the largest intact freshwater wetlands in the contiguous United States. The rivers, lakes, forests, prairies, and swamps all teem with seen and unseen life: alligators, otters, bobcats, raccoons, opossums, white-tailed deer, turtles, bald eagles, red-tailed hawks, egrets, muskrats, herons, cranes, red-cockaded woodpeckers, and black bears all make their home here. The term "swamp" hardly does the Okefenokee justice. It's the largest peat-producing bog in the United States, with numerous and varied landscapes, including aquatic prairies, towering virgin cypress, sandy pine islands, and lush subtropical hammocks.

None of the parks encompass everything the refuge has to offer; you need to determine what your highest priorities are and choose your gateway on that basis. Day trips and boat rentals can be arranged at any of the parks, and more adventurous visitors can take guided or independent overnight canoe-camping trips into the interior. The refuge offers permits for multiday itineraries along the nearly 120 miles of boat trails. Paddlers camping in the swamp must spend their nights in designated wooden shelters built on stilts over the water.

■**TIP→** Visit between September and April to avoid the biting insects that emerge in May, especially in the dense interior.

GETTING HERE AND AROUND

To get around the Okefenokee swamplands you will need a motorboat, canoe, or kayak, or you'll have to book a tour. Rentals and tours are arranged through individual parks and local outfitters.

Three gateways provide access to the refuge: the eastern (and main) entrance at the Suwannee Canal Recreation Area, near Folkston; a northern entrance at the privately owned Okefenokee Swamp Park near Waycross; and a western entrance at Stephen C. Foster State Park, outside the town of Fargo. There are also two small boat launches (no facilities) at Kingfisher Landing and the Suwannee River Sill on the eastern and western sides, respectively.

The surrounding towns of Folkston, Waycross, and Fargo don't offer much as destinations themselves—they primarily serve as bases from which to visit the swamp.

CAMPING NEAR OKEFENOKEE SWAMP

Laura S. Walker State Park. One of the few state parks named for a woman, this 626-acre park honors a Waycross teacher who championed conservation. The park, 9 miles northeast of the Okefenokee Swamp Park, has campsites with electrical and water hookups. Be sure to pick up food and supplies on the way. Boating, skiing, and fishing are permitted on the 120-acre lake, and there's an 18-hole golf course with a restaurant. ⊠ *5653 Laura Walker Rd., Waycross* ☎ *912/287–4900* ⊕ *www.gastateparks.org/ lauraswalker.*

SUWANNEE CANAL RECREATION AREA

8 miles southwest of Folkston via Rte. 121.

Suwannee Canal Recreation Area, the main entrance to the Okefenokee National Wildlife Refuge, is home to the Chesser Island Boardwalk and the historic Chesser Island Homestead. Vendors offer food service, guided boat tours, and canoe/kayak rentals.

EXPLORING

Suwannee Canal Recreation Area. Extensive open areas at the core of the refuge—like Chesser, Grand, and Mizell prairies—branch off the man-made Suwannee Canal, accessed via the main entrance to the Okefenokee National Wildlife Refuge, and contain small natural lakes and gator holes. The prairies are excellent spots for sportfishing and birding, and it's possible to take guided boat tours of the area leaving from the Okefenokee Adventures concession, near the visitor center. The concession also has equipment rentals, and food is available at the Camp Cornelia Cafe. The visitor center has a film, exhibits, and a mechanized mannequin that tells stories about life in the Okefenokee (it sounds hokey but it's surprisingly informative). A boardwalk takes you over the water to a 50-foot observation tower. Hikers, bicyclists, and private motor vehicles are welcome on the Swamp Island Drive; several interpretive walking trails may be taken along the way. Picnicking is permitted. ✉ *Folkston* ✣ *11 miles southwest of Folkston, GA off Hwy 121/23* ☎ *912/496–7836* 🌐 *www.fws.gov/okefenokee* 🎫 *$5 per car.*

CAMPING IN STEPHEN C. FOSTER STATE PARK

Stephen C. Foster State Park. The park has sites for all types of camping as well as basically equipped, two-bedroom cabins that can sleep up to eight. Be aware that the gates of the park are closed between sunset and sunrise—there's no traffic in or out for campers, so you need to stock up on supplies before the sun goes down. You can book sites and cabins up to 13 months in advance. ✉ *17515 Hwy. 177, Fargo* ☎ *800/864–7275* 🌐 *www.gastateparks.org/StephenCFoster.*

WHERE TO EAT AND STAY

$ SOUTHERN 🍴 **Okefenokee Restaurant.** Everything's home-cooked at this half-century-old, local institution—and from the fried shrimp to the black-eyed peas, it's all good. It opens early for breakfast and has a daily lunch and dinner buffet, which includes tea or coffee, for $10. **Known for:** local hot spot; breakfast buffet; country-style fare; peach cobbler. [$] *Average main: $10* ✉ *1507 3rd St., Folkston* ☎ *912/496–3263* 🕒 *Closed Sun.*

$ B&B/INN 🏨 **The Inn at Folkston.** This Craftsman-style inn with a huge front veranda, porch swings, and rocking chairs is filled with antiques, and each room is uniquely decorated. **Pros:** inn is beautifully restored; owners make you feel like welcome relatives. **Cons:** the many trains that pass by can be noisy; no TVs in rooms. [$] *Rooms from: $120* ✉ *3576 W. Main St., Folkston* ☎ *912/496–6256, 888/509–6246* 🌐 *www.innatfolkston.com* 🛏 *4 rooms* 🍽 *Breakfast.*

SPORTS AND THE OUTDOORS

CANOEING AND CAMPING

Okefenokee Adventures. Guided overnight canoe trips can be arranged by this rental and guiding business. They also do 90-minute interpretive boat tours ($18.50) and have boat, canoe, and kayak rentals (starting at $35 a day). ✉ *4159 Suwannee Canal Rd., Folkston* ☎ *866/843–7926* 🌐 *www.okefenokeeadventures.com.*

Okefenokee Wildlife Refuge. Wilderness camping, by canoe or kayak, in the Okefenokee's interior is allowed by permit only (for which there's a $15 fee per person, per night). Availability is limited and can fill up fast, especially in the cooler seasons. During March and April, the most popular months, trips are limited to two nights. Reservations can be made up to two months in advance. ✉ *2700 Suwannee Canal Rd., Folkston* ☎ *912/496–7836* 🌐 *www.fws.gov/okefenokee* 🎟 *Daily passes $5, good for 7 days.*

OKEFENOKEE SWAMP PARK

8 miles south of Waycross via U.S. 1.

This park sits at the northern entrance to the Okefenokee National Wildlife Refuge and offers unique opportunities for visitors to interact with the abundant wildlife of the swamp via observation areas, water trails, and boat tours.

EXPLORING

Okefenokee Swamp Park. This privately owned and operated park serves as the northern entrance to the Okefenokee National Wildlife Refuge, offering exhibits and orientation programs for the entire family. The park has observation areas, wilderness walkways, an outdoor museum of pioneer life, and boat tours into the swamp that reveal its unique ecology. The 90-foot-tall observation tower is an excellent place to glimpse cruising gators and birds. A 1½-mile train tour (included in the admission price) passes by a Seminole village and stops at Pioneer Island, a re-created pioneer homestead, for a 15-minute walking tour. ✉ *5700 Okefenokee Swamp Park Rd., Waycross* ☎ *912/283–0583* 🌐 *www.okeswamp.com* 🎟 *$17, $27 with 45-min boat tour.*

WHERE TO STAY

$ HOTEL 🏨 **Holiday Inn Express Hotel and Suites.** Among the newer and more updated accommodations in Waycross, the Holiday Inn Express is centrally located to the commercial hub of the city, just down Knight Avenue from the shopping mall. **Pros:** friendly staff; clean rooms. **Cons:** complaints of noise; soft mattresses. [$] *Rooms from: $129* ✉ *1761 Memorial Dr., Waycross* ☎ *912/548–0720* 🌐 *www.ihg.com* 🛏 *78 rooms* 🍴 *Breakfast.*

$ HOTEL 🏨 **Quality Inn and Suites.** The rooms are pretty standard, with green carpets and gold bedspreads, but this is the only full-service hotel in Waycross. **Pros:** affordable rooms; convenient location; good breakfast. **Cons:** older hotel; fairly standard chain experience. [$] *Rooms from: $64* ✉ *1725 Memorial Dr., Waycross* ☎ *912/283–4490* 🌐 *www.choicehotels.com* 🛏 *141 rooms* 🍴 *Breakfast.*

STEPHEN C. FOSTER STATE PARK

Located in Fargo, Georgia, on the banks of the Suwannee River, remote Stephen C. Foster State Park serves as the western entrance for the Okefenokee National Wildlife Refuge. The park offers cottages, campsites, and picnic shelters, plus canoe and bike rentals.

EXPLORING

Stephen C. Foster State Park. Named for the songwriter who penned "Swanee River," this 80-acre island park is the southwestern entrance to the Okefenokee National Wildlife Refuge and offers trips to the headwaters of the Suwannee River, Billy's Island—site of an ancient

Indian village—and a turn-of-the-20th-century town built to support logging efforts in the swamp. The park is home to hundreds of species of birds and a large cypress-and-black-gum forest, a majestic backdrop for one of the thickest growths of vegetation in the southeastern United States. Park naturalists lead boat tours and recount a wealth of Okefenokee lore while you observe alligators, birds, and native trees and plants. You may also take a self-guided excursion in a rental canoe or a motorized flat-bottom boat. ⊠ *17515 Hwy. 177, Fargo* ☎ *912/637–5274* ⊕ *www.gastateparks.org/StephenCFoster* 🎫 *$5 per vehicle.*

SOUTHWEST
GEORGIA

WELCOME TO SOUTHWEST GEORGIA

TOP REASONS TO GO

★ **Callaway Gardens Resort and Preserve:** 14,000 acres of gardens and parkland make this the raison d'être for visiting Pine Mountain. In spring the rhododendrons and wild azaleas take your breath away.

★ **Thomasville:** It's easy to feel transported to Victorian times in and around the mansions and gracious plantation homes of Thomasville. Several are open to the public and feel like living museums.

★ **FDR's Little White House:** The cottage where President Franklin Delano Roosevelt stayed while taking in the healing waters of Warm Springs looks much as it did in his day. You can even see the pools where he was treated for polio.

★ **Jimmy Carter's home town:** President Jimmy Carter and First Lady Rosalynn Carter still live in Plains, Georgia, and still worship at the Maranatha Baptist Church. There are a number of museums and historic sites in Plains dedicated to Carter's legacy.

1 Western Foothills and Farmland. Take a walk through the past with a visit to Franklin Roosevelt's Little White House retreat or tiptoe through the tulips at the 14,000-acre Callaway Gardens. This area also is home to Georgia's largest state park, and massive Fort Benning.

2 The Southwest Corner. Antiques shopping, peach picking, golf courses, and hunting plantations are abundant in this part of the state, particularly in Thomasville, which is celebrated most for its Victorian homes, plantations, and churches.

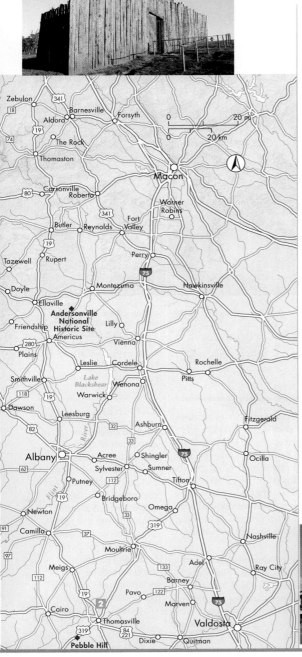

GETTING ORIENTED

Scattered along a vast coastal plain that covers much of the southern part of the state, the small towns of southwest Georgia are best explored by car or by the SAM Shortline. The touring train chugs through the countryside between Cordele and Archery.

SOUTHERN SNACKS

Collards, grits, mac 'n' cheese—the list of dishes originating from the South is long with a storied history that dates back to the plantation days and the Civil War.

(above) Collard greens with bacon (lower right) A bowl of grits isn't complete without a pat of butter. (upper right) Boiled peanuts are at their best piping-hot.

Many of the dishes, which have influences from cuisines as varied as African, Native American, and French, were born of necessity in times of poverty and slavery. Stale bread was turned into bread pudding. Leftover fish became croquettes. Liquid left behind by cooked greens became gravy. The discarded tops of turnips, beets, and dandelions became the stars of a vegetable plate. The unwanted parts of a pig were used to flavor cooked vegetables. Biscuits were used to sop up sauces, so nothing went to waste. And a great emphasis was placed on sharing among family and friends.

Today, you likely won't find boiled peanuts on a mainstream menu in the South. And chitlins, the viscera intestines of a pig, aren't often seen outside of Grandma's country kitchen. But things are starting to change. Thanks to the "local food" movement, many old-fashioned regional snacks are now sold at gourmet markets and sophisticated restaurants.

SAY CHEESE

Pimento cheese, the orange mix of cheddar cheese, mayonnaise, pimiento peppers, and salt and pepper, has long been considered a Southern comfort food. It is traditionally served as a spread on crackers or between two pieces of soft, white bread, and variations on the classic recipe may include ingredients like Worcestershire sauce, jalapeños, and dill pickles.

12

BOILED PEANUTS

Take a drive out of the city and you'll most likely see many a roadside sign advertising this decidedly Southern snack, which—according to legend—has been on the scene since Union General William T. Sherman marched through Georgia. Freshly harvested or raw peanuts are boiled in salted water for four to seven hours, until the shells get soft and the nuts get mushy. They're usually served in a paper bag, which can get soggy, so eat 'em while they're hot.

COLLARD GREENS

Similar to kale and spring greens, collards have thick, large leaves and a slightly bitter taste. Their origins as a Southern food are traced back to the slaves, who would cook them with the scraps from the kitchen: ham hocks, pork neck bones, fatback, and pig's feet. Seasonings typically include onions, salt, pepper, and vinegar. Nowadays it's a Southern tradition to serve collards on New Year's Eve, along with black-eyed peas, for wealth in the new year.

HUSH PUPPIES

Legend has it that this snack got its name from an African cook in Atlanta. She was frying catfish and croquettes when her puppy began to howl. To quiet the dog she gave him a plate of the croquettes, saying, "Hush, puppy." Really, though, a dog's dish is far too lowly a place for these delicious fried

cornmeal dumplings. Today you'll find them on the South's simple country menus and in the breadbaskets of fine-dining establishments.

MAC 'N' CHEESE

In the South, this dish is a vegetable. It's true. Though in these creamy, top-browned bowls of noodles and cheese there's not a veggie in sight, many meat-and-three restaurants list mac 'n' cheese as one of the three vegetables you can get on the side. And who are we to argue? Whether we're talking about traditional mac 'n' cheese or a fancier version with homemade shells, truffle oil, and Gouda, it's a rich and sinful Southern snack.

SWEETS

Southerners have a sweet tooth, bless their hearts. And it's satisfied by a number of indigenous desserts. There's chess pie, a simple pie with just eggs, sugar, butter, and flour that supposedly got its name when a Southern cook said she was making "jes' pie." Then there's pecan pie, created by French settlers in New Orleans. And, of course, there is peach cobbler, a favorite in the South, where the climate allows for early peach harvests and few frosts.

Updated
by Rachel
Quartarone

The rolling agricultural landscapes of a slower, older South, where things remain much the same as they were for generations, can be found within a couple of hours' drive of Atlanta's high-rise bustle. Here small towns evoke a time when the world was a simpler place, where people lived close to the land and life was measured on a personal scale. In southwest Georgia, peanuts, corn, tobacco, and cotton are the lifeblood of the local economies, and you're as likely to see a tractor on a country road as a car.

People in the countryside live far from the hassles of Atlanta's modernity—the daily grind of traffic jams and suburban sprawl. Small towns beckon with their quaint town squares, preserved old homes, and charming bed-and-breakfasts. In southwest Georgia the inclination simply to relax is contagious—it can saturate you slowly but completely, like syrup on a stack of pancakes. Yet, the entire region is not to be dismissed as quiet farmland. Columbus is one of Georgia's largest cities and home to several Fortune 500 company headquarters, as well as acclaimed military, academic, and cultural institutions. Outside of historic downtown Thomasville, you'll find business headquarters and bustling factories.

Southwest Georgia residents are proud of their communities and those they call their own, including such greats as President Jimmy Carter, writers Erskine Caldwell and Carson McCullers, singers Ma Rainey and Otis Redding, and baseball legend Jackie Robinson. For a time even Franklin Delano Roosevelt was drawn here; he returned again and again for the healing mineral waters of Warm Springs.

PLANNING

12

WHEN TO GO

Because many of the towns in the region are off the beaten path, crowds are rarely a problem, though spring (which comes early) and fall (which comes late) are the most popular seasons. If you're not fond of the heat, March to May and September to December are the best times to visit. During this time, book well in advance for the more popular hotels and B&Bs in Pine Mountain, Warm Springs, and Thomasville.

PLANNING YOUR TIME

A traveler could easily get lost on the back roads of southwest Georgia, so perhaps the best way to take in the sites of this region is to park your car and board the SAM Shortline Southwest Georgia Excursion Train in Cordele. The ride will take you to Georgia Veterans State Park, the Rural Telephone Museum, Habitat for Humanity's Global Village, the Rylander Theatre, Windsor Hotel, and Plains. This way you'll get a sense of what spots deserve more time and which are suited for a drive-by.

Many of southwest Georgia's attractions are ideal day trips from Atlanta. Warm Springs, Callaway Gardens, and Pine Mountain are a 90-minute drive from Atlanta. Thomasville is a little more than four hours from Atlanta, so plan on an overnight stay.

GETTING HERE AND AROUND

AIR TRAVEL

Delta Airlines has daily flights into Columbus Metro Airport (CSG) from Atlanta.

Air Contacts Columbus Metro Airport (CSG) *(CSG). ⊠ 3250 W. Britt David Rd., Columbus ☎ 706/324–2449 ⊕ www.flycolumbusga.com.*

CAR TRAVEL

A car is the best way to tour this part of Georgia. Interstate 75 runs north–south through the eastern edge of the region and connects to several U.S. and state highways that traverse the area. Interstate 85 runs southwest through LaGrange and Columbus. Do explore backcountry roads—they offer the landscapes and ambience of the real South. Just be sure to travel with a good road map or GPS—cell phone coverage can be spotty in the countryside.

TRAIN TRAVEL

A great means of seeing the countryside, the Historic SAM Shortline Railroad originates in Cordele and runs west through Georgia Veteran's State Park, Leslie, Americus, Plains, and Archery. It's important to check the schedule, but as a general rule, trains run on Saturday and some Fridays. On select weekends, you can get on or off at any of the stations, stop over for the night, and take the train again the next morning.

Train Contacts Historic SAM Shortline Railroad. *⊠ 105 E. 9th Ave., Cordele ☎ 229/276–0755 ⊕ www.samshortline.com.*

RESTAURANTS

This region of Georgia does lovely things by slow-cooking pork over green oak. Pit-barbecue joints in the area are homey, hands-on, and relatively inexpensive. There's also a growing food scene in the urban areas of the region as talented chefs have set up shop in the quaint downtown storefronts. *Dining reviews have been shortened. For full information, visit Fodors.com*

HOTELS

Lodging in the area runs the gamut from elegant, luxurious properties to low-profile but unique B&Bs to reliable and inexpensive chain hotels. RV parks and campgrounds are also available. *Hotel reviews have been shortened. For full information, visit Fodors.com*

WHAT IT COSTS				
	$	$$	$$$	$$$$
Restaurants	under $15	$15–$19	$20–$24	over $24
Hotels	under $150	$150–$200	$201–$250	over $250

Prices in the restaurant reviews are the average cost of a main course at dinner or, if dinner is not served, at lunch.. Prices for the hotel reviews are for two people in a standard double room in high season.

WESTERN FOOTHILLS AND FARMLAND

You won't be able to visit this slice of Georgia without feeling the influence of two American presidents, Franklin Roosevelt and Jimmy Carter. About 100 miles south of Atlanta, near the Alabama border, Pine Mountain and Warm Springs are the rural retreats they have always been since FDR used to visit, and have retained much of their ambience from yesteryear. The Little White House is among its historical highlights. Plains (Jimmy Carter country) seems cut from the pages of the past.

WARM SPRINGS

97 miles southwest of Atlanta.

Renowned for centuries for the supposed healing properties of its thermal waters, Warm Springs is where the Creek Indians brought their wounded warriors when all other treatments had failed. In the early 1920s news spread that a young Columbus native and polio victim, Louis Joseph, had made a dramatic recovery after extensive therapy in the springs. Word reached Franklin Delano Roosevelt (1882–1945), who had contracted polio, and a 20-year relationship began between him and this remote mountain village, where he built a cottage for his visits that came to be known as the Little White House. Roosevelt's experiences here led to the effort to eradicate polio around the world through the founding of the March of Dimes, and his encounters with his poor rural neighbors fueled ideas for his Depression-era New Deal recovery programs. After Roosevelt's death, the town fell on hard times, but an influx of crafts and antiques shops in the 1980s has revitalized Warm Springs.

GETTING HERE AND AROUND

The best way to visit Warm Springs is to travel from Atlanta on Interstate 85 South to Exit 41. Take a left turn onto U.S. 27A/41, then continue for 35 miles to Warm Springs. Columbus is another good point to embark from; Warm Springs is about 40 miles south on Georgia 85 North. Much of Warm Springs is walkable, but a car is necessary if you want to hit all the high points.

ESSENTIALS

Visitor Information Warm Springs Welcome Center. ✉ *1 Broad St.* ☎ *706/655–3322* 🌐 *www.warmspringsga.us.*

EXPLORING

Fodor's Choice ★ **Little White House Historic Site/FDR Memorial Museum.** Located on the southern end of town, this fascinating historic site contains the modest three-bedroom cottage in which Roosevelt stayed during his visits. The cottage, built in 1932, remains much as it did the day he died here (while having his portrait painted) and includes the wheelchair Roosevelt designed from a kitchen chair. The unfinished portrait is on display, along with the 48-star American flag that flew over the grounds when Roosevelt died. The FDR Memorial Museum includes an interesting short film narrated by Walter Cronkite (last screening at 4 pm), exhibits detailing Roosevelt's life and New Deal programs, and some of Roosevelt's personal effects, such as his 1938 Ford, complete with the full hand controls he designed. Admission here allows you to also visit the nearby pools where Roosevelt took his therapy. The experience is self-guided, but on Saturday mornings at 9:30, there is a special historian-led tour offered; call ahead for reservations. ✉ *401 Little White House Rd.* ☎ *706/655–5870* 🌐 *www.gastateparks.org/LittleWhiteHouse* 🎫 *$12.*

WHERE TO EAT AND STAY

$ SOUTHERN 🍴 **Bulloch House Restaurant.** This long-time local favorite is the place to go for down-home Southern cooking in the area. Although no longer located in the historic Bulloch House, the menu continues to be served buffet style and features Southern classics like buttermilk biscuits, golden fried chicken, and baked ham. **Known for:** fried chicken and other Southern staples; generous buffet dining; sides like fried green tomatoes and turnip greens. [$] *Average main: $12* ✉ *70 Broad St.* ☎ *706/655–9068* 🌐 *www.bullochhouse.com* 🕒 *Closed Mon. No dinner Sun.–Thurs.*

$ B&B/INN 🏨 **Hotel Warm Springs Bed & Breakfast Inn.** In downtown Warm Springs, this historic hotel has plenty of character—the guest rooms have oak furniture and 12-foot ceilings with crown molding. **Pros:** convenient to Warm Springs' sights; storied history; amazing Southern breakfast. **Cons:** no elevator; some say rooms and public spaces could use some refreshing; child-friendly atmosphere not for everyone. [$] *Rooms from: $110* ✉ *47 Broad St.* ☎ *706/655–2114, 800/366–7616* 🌐 *www.hotelwarmspringsbb.org* 🛏 *13 rooms* 🍽 *Breakfast.*

PINE MOUNTAIN

14 miles west of Warm Springs via Rte. 18 and Rte. 194.

Pine Mountain Ridge is the last foothill of the Appalachian chain, and the town of Pine Mountain rests at the same elevation as Atlanta, making it generally cooler than the surrounding communities. The flora and fauna here reflect the town's Appalachian connections. Most visitors are lured by the surrounding area's large-scale attractions—such as Callaway Gardens Resort and Preserve—and are then pleasantly surprised that the small-town burg has a folksy, inviting downtown square. Antiques figure prominently in the area economy, and shops abound in the town center.

GETTING HERE AND AROUND

Pine Mountain can be reached by car from Atlanta via Interstate 85 South and sits 14 miles west of Warm Springs, via Routes 18 and 194. A 90-minute drive from Atlanta, it's a popular destination for day-trippers.

ESSENTIALS

Visitor Information Pine Mountain Welcome Center. ⊠ *101 E. Broad St.* ☎ *706/663–4000, 800/441–3502* ⊕ *www.pinemountain.org.*

EXPLORING

FAMILY

Fodor's Choice

★

Callaway Gardens. South of Pine Mountain Village lies the area's main draw: a 14,000-acre golf and tennis resort with a combination of elaborate, cultivated gardens and natural woodlands. This family-friendly destination was developed in the 1940s by textile magnate Cason J. Callaway and his wife, Virginia, as a way to breathe new life into the area's dormant cotton fields. With more than 1,000 varieties, the Day Butterfly Center is one of the largest free-flight conservatories in North America. **Mountain Creek Lake** is well stocked with largemouth bass and bream. **Ida Cason Callaway Memorial Chapel**—a favorite wedding venue—is a lovely stone chapel nestled in the woods alongside a lake and babbling stream. The **Callaway Discovery Center** is a popular choice for families; especially enjoyable is their daily Birds of Prey show. During the holidays, Callaway lights up with the exciting "Fantasy in Lights." ⊠ *15880 GA Hwy. 18* ☎ *706/663–2281, 800/225–5292* ⊕ *www.callawaygardens.com* ⊠ *$20; free to overnight guests.*

FAMILY

Franklin Delano Roosevelt State Park. At 9,049 acres, F.D. Roosevelt is the largest state park in Georgia. Named for the president who considered this area his second home, it's rich in both history and natural beauty. Several park amenities were built by F.D.R.'s Civilian Conservation Corps during the Great Depression, including multiple cottages and the Liberty Bell Swimming Pool fed by local cool springs. The park contains more than 40 miles of trails, including the popular 23-mile Pine Mountain Trail. Dowdell's Knob, an overlook along the trail, was one of the President's favorite spots to picnic; there's even a statue there now to commemorate him. Within the park are also two lakes and 140 modern campsites, as well as backcountry and pioneer campgrounds. ⊠ *2970 GA Hwy. 190* ☎ *706/663–4858, 800/864–7275* ⊕ *www.georgiastateparks.org/FDRoosevelt* ⊠ *$5 parking fee.*

FAMILY **Wild Animal Safari.** You'll hardly believe you're still in Georgia at this quirky animal preserve northwest of Pine Mountain. Camels, llamas, antelopes, and hundreds of other exotic animals traipse around freely, often coming close to vehicles for a close-up view. You can either drive your own car, rent a Zebra Van, or take a guided bus tour through the 500-acre animal preserve. An added plus is the **Walk-About,** which operates more like a traditional zoo with monkeys, kangaroos, bears, and reptiles on display. **■ TIP→ The park sells special food for you to offer the animals, and some will scamper over your car to get it.** ✉ *1300 Oak Grove Rd.* ☎ *706/663–8744, 800/367–2751* 🌐 *www.animalsafari.com* 🎟 *$24.95.*

WHERE TO EAT AND STAY

$$$$ ECLECTIC 🍴 **Carriage & Horses.** International cuisine is served in this Victorian house north of town and overlooking the horse pastures of Grey Eagle Farm. The eclectic menu includes escargots, crab cakes with lemon sauce, grilled trout (a house specialty), and filet mignon served with garlicky mashed potatoes. **Known for:** traditional fine dining; pastoral setting; great views of the sunset. [$] *Average main: $25* ✉ *607 Butts Mill Rd.* ☎ *706/663–4777* 🌐 *www.cometodagher.com.*

$ RESORT 🏨 **Callaway Gardens Resort.** Stay at this sprawling resort and your room key gains you access to its famous gardens from dawn until dusk. **Pros:** access to famous gardens; wide variety of accommodation types; wonderful full-service spa. **Cons:** some say resort restaurants could use improvement; rooms can vary a lot in terms of size and quality; meals cost extra. [$] *Rooms from: $139* ✉ *17800 U.S. Hwy. 27* ☎ *706/663–2281, 800/225–5292* 🌐 *www.callawaygardens.com* 🛏 *289 rooms,155 cottages, 50 villas* 🍽 *No meals; Breakfast.*

$ B&B/INN 🏨 **Chipley Murrah House B&B.** One mile from Callaway Gardens and near downtown Pine Mountain, this lavish inn occupies a high-style Queen Anne Victorian dating to 1895. **Pros:** welcoming owner; some cottages are pet-friendly; outdoor pool. **Cons:** breakfast is not included with the cottages; decor is a bit dated; kids under 12 allowed only in the cottages. [$] *Rooms from: $110* ✉ *207 W. Harris St.* ☎ *706/663–9801* 🌐 *www.chipleymurrah.com* 🛏 *4 rooms, 3 cottages* 🍽 *Breakfast.*

SPORTS AND THE OUTDOORS

CANOEING AND KAYAKING

Flint River Outdoor Center. About 45 minutes from Pine Mountain (between Thomaston and Columbus) is the Flint River Outdoor Center, which offers up to 20 miles of river courses. Test your skills in everything from a float tube to kayaks running Class II rapids. Some expeditions include an overnight stay at their campsite. ✉ *4429 Woodland Rd., Thomaston* ☎ *706/647–2633.*

HORSEBACK RIDING

Roosevelt Stables. The mountain terrain makes the Pine Mountain area an interesting place for horseback riding. Roosevelt Stables is located in F.D. Roosevelt State Park, although it operates independently. The stables offers 28 miles of trails and offers everything from one-hour rides to overnight trips complete with cowboy breakfasts. ✉ *1063 Group Camp Rd.* ☎ *706/628–7463* 🌐 *www.rooseveltstables.com.*

Azaleas bloom along the lake at Callaway Gardens Resort and Preserve.

COLUMBUS

35 miles south of Pine Mountain.

During the Civil War, Columbus supplied uniforms, weapons, and other goods to the Confederate army, making the city a prime target for Union troops. But it wasn't until April 16, 1865—a week after the war had ended at Appomattox—that the 13,000 cavalrymen known as "Wilson's Raiders" attacked Columbus and burned all the war industries to the ground. The textile mills soon recovered, however, and grew to a prominence that dwarfed their prewar significance. Textiles still play a major role in the Columbus economy.

Today, Columbus is perhaps best known as the home of Fort Benning, the largest infantry-training center in the world; it's also the site of Columbus College's Schwob School of Music, one of the finest music schools in the South. A project to rejuvenate the downtown area has included the renovation of old manufacturing and ironworks buildings and the creation of the 15-mile **Riverwalk** to highlight the city's river origins; this linear park along the Chattahoochee is ideal for jogging, strolling, biking, and rollerblading.

ESSENTIALS
Visitor Information Columbus Convention and Visitors Bureau.
✉ *900 Front Ave.* ☎ *800/999–1613* ⊕ *www.visitcolumbusga.com.*

EXPLORING
Columbus Museum. The state's largest art and history museum focuses heavily on American art ranging from colonial portraiture to provocative contemporary works. Other permanent exhibits showcase

the history and industry of the Chattahoochee Valley. There's always something new and different to see in the temporary exhibit galleries. ✉ *1251 Wynnton Rd.* ☎ *706/748–2562* 🌐 *www.columbusmuseum.com* 🎟 *Free* 🕒 *Closed Mon.*

National Civil War Naval Museum at Port Columbus. Those interested in the nation's Civil War past should make it a point to visit this innovative military museum that focuses on the Confederate navy and its influence on the U.S. Navy's subsequent development. Columbus's riverfront location made it a major player in river transport prior to and throughout the Civil War. Interactive exhibits tell the story of shipbuilding and major Civil War ship battles. You can even walk the decks of partially reconstructed Civil War ships and get a glimpse of what combat was like in a full-scale replica of the CSS *Albermarle*. The museum also boasts the largest collection of Civil War Naval-related flags on display in the country. ✉ *1002 Victory Dr.* ☎ *706/327–9798* 🌐 *www.portcolumbus.org* 🎟 *$7.50.*

FAMILY
Fodor's Choice ★

National Infantry Museum and Soldier Center. Located outside the gates of Fort Benning, this museum examines the role of the U.S. infantry through every war in the nation's history through interactive, technology-rich displays. A must for military buffs, the facility has more than 30,000 artifacts, including weaponry, uniforms, and equipment from the Revolutionary War to the present day. The Family Support Gallery focuses on the sacrifices made by military families and features a children's area where youngsters can try on uniforms and sit in the re-created interior of a Bradley fighting vehicle. The center also features a Giant Screen theater that shows both documentaries and Hollywood blockbusters. ✉ *1775 Legacy Way* ☎ *706/685–5800* 🌐 *www.nationalinfantrymuseum.com* 🎟 *$5 suggested donation* 🕒 *Closed Mon.*

Springer Opera House. Since its opening in 1871, this National Historic Landmark has been known as one of the finest opera houses in the South. In its heyday, its stage boasted legends such as Lillie Langtry and Will Rogers. Today the theater hosts musicals, dramas, and regional talent. It's also the official state theater of Georgia. Tours are offered Monday and Wednesday at 3:30 or by appointment. ✉ *103 10th St.* ☎ *706/327–3688* 🌐 *www.springeroperahouse.org* 🎟 *Tours $5.*

WHERE TO EAT

$$$$
STEAKHOUSE

🍴 **Buckhead Steak and Wine.** At this upscale Southern-style steak house, beef plays a prominent role on the menu with USDA Prime Angus and natural, hormone-free prime rib, N.Y. strip, and rib eye as headliners. Seafood is also done well here, with entrées like cedar-planked Norwegian salmon and shrimp linguine. **Known for:** wide variety of quality steaks; extensive wine list; hearty (and boozy) Sunday brunch. [$] *Average main: $28* ✉ *5010 Armour Rd.* ☎ *706/571–9995* 🌐 *www.buckheadbarandgrill.com* 🕒 *No lunch.*

$
BARBECUE

🍴 **Country's On Broad.** In a land where barbecue reigns supreme, Country's cooks with taste and style. You can eat inside the restaurant, a converted bus terminal decorated with '50s flair, or sit at a table in the 1946 bus turned diner. **Known for:** outstanding barbecue cooked over hickory and oak; unique bus station–turned-diner setting. [$] *Average main: $9* ✉ *1329 Broadway* ☎ *706/596–8910* 🌐 *www.countrysbarbecue.com.*

WHERE TO STAY

$$ HOTEL **Marriott Columbus.** On the site of a vast 1860s complex of warehouses, factories, mills, and a Confederate arsenal, this hotel is a key component of the Columbus Convention and Trade Center just across the street. **Pros:** excellent riverfront location; modern amenities; historic space. **Cons:** large facility may be a turnoff to some; often booked for events; no free breakfast. [$] *Rooms from: $175* ✉ *800 Front Ave.* ☎ *706/324–1800* 🌐 *www.marriott.com* 🛏 *177 rooms* 🍴 *No meals.*

$$ B&B/INN **Rothschild-Pound House Inn & Village.** Listed on the National Register of Historic Places, this B&B includes a main house and separate cottages, and offers a glimpse of old Columbus's elegance—with four-poster mahogany beds, hardwood floors, and period antiques. **Pros:** beautiful architecture; lots of privacy; lovely full breakfast. **Cons:** no pool or spa; upstairs rooms may be difficult to access for some; old-fashioned decor not for everyone. [$] *Rooms from: $175* ✉ *201 7th St.* ☎ *706/322–4075* 🌐 *www.thepoundhouseinn.com* 🛏 *6 rooms, 2 cottages* 🍴 *Breakfast.*

SPORTS AND THE OUTDOORS

Whitewater Express Columbus. Take a thrilling ride down the longest urban white-water rafting course in the world. The Chattahochee Whitewater Park flows right through the heart of downtown Columbus. Thanks to the release of two nearby dams, this 2½-mile, man-made course offers Class I–IV rapids depending on the time of day you hit the water. Morning trips are relatively calm while the late-afternoon high-water trips offer pounding Class IV-plus rapids. Whitewater Express offers guided raft trips daily. The outfitter also offers kayaking, fly-fishing, stand-up paddleboarding, and bike rentals. ✉ *1000 Bay Ave.* ☎ *706/321–4720, 800/676–7238* 🌐 *www.whitewaterexpress.com/chattahoochee.*

PLAINS

85 miles southeast of Pine Mountain via U.S. 27.

This rural farming town—originally named the Plains of Dura after the biblical story of Shadrach, Meshach, and Abednego—is the birthplace and current home of former president Jimmy Carter and his wife, Rosalynn. Although it's the hub of a thriving farming community, the one-street downtown paralleling the railroad tracks resembles a 1930s movie set.

GETTING HERE AND AROUND

From Interstate 85 or Interstate 75, look for the exit to U.S. 280, then exit for Plains.

ESSENTIALS

Visitor Information Plains Welcome Center. ✉ *1763 U.S. 280* ☎ *229/824–7477* 🌐 *plainsgeorgia2.com.*

FESTIVALS

Plains Peanut Festival. Each September the town comes alive with the Plains Peanut Festival, which includes a parade, live entertainment, arts and crafts, food vendors, and races. The Carters are usually active participants in the various events and also conduct book signings. ✉ *Plains.*

King Cotton

Such was Georgia's preeminence in world cotton production at the turn of the 20th century that the international market price was set at the Cotton Exchange in Savannah. And the huge plantations of southwest Georgia were major players in the engine driving the state's economic prosperity. For more than 100 years, from the first time it was planted in Georgia in 1733 until the beginning of the Civil War, cotton was the most commercially successful crop in the state. But because the seeds had to be separated from the lint by hand, production was laborious and output was limited. In 1793 a young Yale graduate named Eli Whitney (1765–1825) came to Savannah's Mulberry Grove Plantation as a tutor to the children of Revolutionary War hero Nathanael Greene. After watching the difficulty workers were having separating the seeds from the cotton,

he invented a simple machine of two cylinders with combs rotating in opposite directions. The "gin," as he called it (short for engine), could do the work of 50 people and revolutionized the cotton industry. So significant was its immediate impact on the U.S. economy that President George Washington personally signed the patent issued to Whitney.

In 1900 the boll weevil insect came to the United States via Mexico and quickly undermined cotton production. The weevil was a major cause of the onset of the economic depression that spread throughout the South. Cotton production was at an all-time low in Georgia by 1978; in 1987 the state began a boll weevil eradication program that has all but wiped out the threat. And the result is that today Georgia is once again one of the top producers in the nation.

EXPLORING

OFF THE BEATEN PATH

Andersonville National Historic Site. About 20 miles northeast of Plains, Andersonville National Historic Site is a solemn reminder of the Civil War's tragic toll. Andersonville, also known as Camp Sumter, was the war's deadliest prisoner-of-war camp. Some 13,000 Union prisoners died here, mostly from disease, neglect, and malnutrition. Photographs, artifacts, and high-tech exhibits detail not just the plight of Civil War prisoners, but also prison life and conditions affecting all of America's 800,000 POWs since the Revolutionary War. ⊠ 496 Cemetery Rd., Andersonville ☎ 229/924–0343 ⊕ www.nps.gov/ande/ index.htm ☜ Free.

Fodor's Choice ★ **Jimmy Carter National Historic Site.** Three different historic sites highlight the life and work of the 39th President of the United States, Jimmy Carter. You can visit the late-1880s **railroad depot** that once housed his 1976 presidential campaign headquarters. Vintage phones play recordings of Carter discussing his grassroots run for the White House. A couple of miles outside town on the Old Plains Highway is the 360-acre **Jimmy Carter Boyhood Farm,** where the Carter family grew cotton, peanuts, and corn; it has been restored to its original appearance before electricity was introduced. Period furniture fills the house, and the battery-powered radio plays Carter's reminiscences of

Andersonville National Cemetery is the final resting place for soldiers who died at Andersonville Prison, the Civil War's deadliest prisoner-of-war camp.

growing up on a Depression-era farm. **Plains High School,** where the Carters attended school, is now a museum and the headquarters of the historic site. Start your visit here with a short orientation film, and pick up a self-guided tour book that explains the sites. ⊠ *Plains High School Visitor Center and Museum, 300 N. Bond St.* ☎ *229/824–4104* ⊕ *www.nps.gov/jica* ✉ *Free.*

Maranatha Baptist Church. The Carters still live in a ranch-style brick house on the edge of town—the only home they have ever owned, and they still worship at the Maranatha Baptist Church. President Carter sometimes teaches Sunday school here Sundays at 10 am; doors open at 8 and the class fills up fast, so arrive early. You will need to go through a security check, but the church volunteers are very efficient at keeping lines moving. Call ahead or check the website for the schedule. The former president and Mrs. Carter always make themselves available to take photos with visitors after the 11 am service, which is a special treat. ⊠ *148 GA 45 N* ☎ *229/824–7896* ⊕ *www.mbcplains.org.*

OFF THE BEATEN PATH
Providence Canyon State Outdoor Recreation Area. Known as "Georgia's Little Grand Canyon," Providence Canyon State Outdoor Recreation Area is actually made up of 16 canyons whose earthen walls display at least 43 different colors of sand. Providence Canyon is a favorite of geologists, photographers, and hikers, who enjoy peering over the canyon's rim and traversing its 10 miles of trails. The park interpretive center is open on weekends seasonally. It's located about 33 miles west of Plains. ⊠ *8930 Canyon Rd., Lumpkin* ☎ *229/838–6870* ⊕ *www. gastateparks.org/ProvidenceCanyon* ✉ *$5 parking.*

WHERE TO EAT AND STAY

$
AMERICAN

✕ **Buffalo Cafe at the Old Bank.** Housed in an old bank in downtown Plains, this café offers soup, salads, burgers, and sandwiches in a cozy hometown setting. Be sure to try their peanut ice cream. **Known for:** quick and casual meals; creamy peanut ice cream; down-to-earth and friendly staff. Ⓢ *Average main: $8* ✉ *118 E. Main St.* ☎ *229/824–4520* ☾ *Closed Sun.*

$
SOUTHERN

✕ **The Cafeteria.** Down-home Southern specialties like fried chicken, barbecued ribs, mashed potatoes, and lima beans are served cafeteria-style in this quaint local spot. You can also order burgers, hot dogs, and basic diner fare off the menu board. **Known for:** soul food served cafeteria style; popular after-church lunch spot. Ⓢ *Average main: $10* ✉ *203 E. Church St.* ☎ *229/824–5458* ☾ *Closed Mon. No dinner Sun.–Thurs.*

$
HOTEL

🏨 **Best Western Plus Windsor Hotel.** Located in nearby Americus, this ornate jewel of a hotel has garnered awards from the National Trust for Historic Preservation. **Pros:** unique historic property; beautiful architectural details; modern amenities. **Cons:** fills up quickly on weekends; no pool; no free breakfast. Ⓢ *Rooms from: $105* ✉ *125 W. Lamar St., Americus* ☎ *229/924–1555* ⊕ *www.windsor-americus.com* ⤣ *53 rooms* ⍥❙ *Breakfast.*

$
B&B/INN

🏨 **Plains Historic Inn.** Each spacious room of this inn, set in a century-old furniture store above an antiques mall, is decorated to reflect the aesthetics of a particular decade between the 1920s and the 1980s. **Pros:** close to tourist attractions; elevator; claw-foot tubs in some bathrooms. **Cons:** breakfast is self-serve; not many eateries nearby; can book up quickly, especially on weekends. Ⓢ *Rooms from: $100* ✉ *106 Main St.* ☎ *229/824–4517* ⊕ *www.plainsinn.net* ⤣ *7 rooms* ⍥❙ *Breakfast.*

THE SOUTHWEST CORNER

Thomasville is the highlight of Georgia's southwest corner. It's among the nation's most appealing small towns, thanks to an inviting town square, shaded glens, historic homes, fine restaurants, and an easygoing air.

THOMASVILLE

236 miles south of Atlanta via I–75 and U.S. 319.

This appealing small town in the Tallahassee Red Hills started out as an agrarian community like its neighbors. Cotton and other cash crops lined its plains and rolling hills, while large plantation homes and simple farmhouses graced the countryside. Unlike its neighbors, Thomasville did not see any battles during the Civil War, so much of the town's antebellum architecture was preserved. After the war—thanks to a local doctor's claim that Thomasville's warm winter climate and balsam breezes had curative effects—Thomasville reinvented itself as a health resort, a popular Victorian concept. Wealthy Northerners fleeing the cold wintered here in large luxury hotels. The wealthiest among them built elegant estates in town and hunting plantations in the farmland along the "Plantation Trace."

You can tour the main house, school, fire station, stable, gardens, and more at Pebble Hill Plantation.

Although Thomasville's resort era has long since ended, the distinct pine-scented air remains, as does the Victorian elegance of the town's heyday. Known as the "City of Roses," it draws thousands of visitors each spring to its annual Rose Festival (the fourth weekend in April). And during the Victorian Christmas, locals turn out in period costumes to enjoy horse-drawn carriage rides, caroling, and street theater.

GETTING HERE AND AROUND

Thomasville, with its rich atmosphere of a bygone era, sits 55 miles south of Tifton and can be reached from Atlanta via Interstate 75 and U.S. 319.

ESSENTIALS

Visitor Information Thomasville Welcome Center. ⌧ *144 E. Jackson St.* ☏ *229/228–7977, 866/577–3600* ⊕ *www.thomasvillega.com.*

TOURS

Taste of Thomasville Food Tour. To explore Thomasville's burgeoning "foodie scene," try a walking food tour that incorporates downtown Thomasville's history with stops and tastings at six celebrated eateries. Tours are offered on Friday and Saturday. They regularly sell out, so it's best to purchase tickets in advance online. ⌧ *Thomasville* ☏ *800/656–0713* ⊕ *www.tasteofthomasvillefoodtour.com.*

EXPLORING

FAMILY **Birdsong Nature Center.** With 565 acres of lush fields, forests, swamps, and butterfly gardens, this nature center is a wondrous haven for birds and scores of other native wildlife. Miles of walking trails meander through the property, and nature programs are offered year-round. ⌧ *2106 Meridian Rd.* ☏ *229/377–4408* ⊕ *www.birdsongnaturecenter. org* ▱ *$5* ☉ *Closed Mon., Tues., and Thurs.*

Lapham–Patterson House. When it was built by Chicago shoe manufacturer Charles W. Lapham in 1884, this three-story Victorian house was state of the art, with gas lighting and indoor plumbing with hot and cold running water. But the most curious feature of this unusual house is that Lapham, who had witnessed the Great Chicago Fire of 1871, had 45 exit doors installed because of his fear of being trapped in a burning house. The house is now a National Historic Landmark because of its unique architectural features. ✉ *626 N. Dawson St.* ☎ *229/226–7664* 🌐 *www.thomascountyhistory.org* 🎟 *$5* 🕒 *Closed Sun.–Thurs.*

Fodor's Choice ★ **Pebble Hill Plantation.** On the National Register of Historic Places, Pebble Hill is the only plantation in the area open to the public. The sprawling home and grounds was last home to sporting enthusiast and philanthropist Elisabeth "Pansy" Ireland Poe who specified that the plantation be open to the public upon her death (in 1978). The property dates to 1825, although most of the original house was destroyed in a fire in the 1930s. Highlights of the current two-story main house include a dramatic horseshoe-shape entryway, a wraparound terrace on the upper floor, and an elegant sunroom decorated with a wildlife motif. The second story now serves as an art gallery displaying the Poe's large sporting art collection. Surrounding the house are 34 acres of immaculately maintained grounds that include gardens, a walking path, a log-cabin school, a fire station, a carriage house, kennels, and a hospital for the plantation's more than 100 dogs (prized dogs were buried with full funerals, including a minister). The sprawling dairy-and-horse-stable complex resembles an English village. ✉ *1251 U.S. 319 S, 5 miles south of Thomasville* ☎ *229/226–2344* 🌐 *www.pebblehill.com* 🎟 *Grounds $5.50, house tour $16* 🕒 *Closed Mon.*

WHERE TO EAT AND STAY

$$$ STEAKHOUSE 🍴 **Chop House on the Bricks.** This upscale steak house is celebrated for its romantic ambience and masterfully prepared meat and seafood dishes. Chef-owner Matt Hagel is passionate about high quality, locally sourced ingredients. **Known for:** artfully prepared steaks and seafood; multiple-course option with wine pairings; date-night hot spot. [$] *Average main: $24* ✉ *123 N. Broad St.* ☎ *229/236–2467* 🌐 *www.chophouseonthebricks.com* 🕒 *Closed Sun. and Mon. No lunch.*

$ SOUTHERN 🍴 **George & Louie's.** The fresh gulf seafood served at this longtime family-owned restaurant is as good as you can find anywhere. Try the broiled shrimp, cooked in olive oil with a smattering of fresh garlic; fresh mullet dinner; or combination platter with homemade deviled crab, shrimp, oysters, scallops, and flounder for one, two, or three people. **Known for:** creatively delicious seafood platters; locally beloved burgers; outdoor dining. [$] *Average main: $13* ✉ *217 Remington Ave.* ☎ *229/226–1218* 🌐 *www.georgeandlouies.com* 🕒 *Closed Sun.*

$$ SEAFOOD FAMILY 🍴 **Jonah's Fish and Grits.** Locals line up for a table at this extremely popular locally owned eatery where seafood is the specialty, of course. Jonah's signature rich and creamy white cheddar grits, Parmesan-crusted rainbow trout, and deep-fried catfish with hush puppies are customer favorites. There are plenty of options for land-lovers, and a kid's menu too. **Known for:** seafood specialties; family-friendly (and Christian) environment; no alcohol. [$] *Average main: $16* ✉ *109 E. Jackson St.* ☎ *229/226–0508* 🌐 *www.jonahsfish.com* 🕒 *Closed Sun.*

$$$$ ECLECTIC 🍴 **Liam's.** With a flair for the unexpected, this bistro turns out a rotating seasonal menu with such updated Southern dishes as pork tenderloin with mashed root vegetable, duck with dumplings, and prime beef tenderloin. Liam's also serves a full cheese cart of various artisanal cheeses from Europe, as well as local selections. **Known for:** eclectic and always changing menu; European brunch on Saturday; outstanding cheese and wine selections. [$] *Average main: $26* ✉ *113 E. Jackson St.* ☎ *229/226–9944* 🌐 *www.liamsthomasville.com* ⏲ *Closed Sun. and Mon.*

$ AMERICAN Fodor's Choice ★ 🍴 **Sweet Grass Dairy Cheese Shop.** This award-winning cheese maker makes its home in Thomasville and operates this shop and café where you can try the farm-fresh cheese along with wines and craft beers. Purchase individual cheeses to go or select an artfully prepared cheese board for a sit-down sampling of the day's offerings. **Known for:** local artisanal cheeses; gourmet desserts and small plates; store selling local food items. [$] *Average main: $12* ✉ *123 S. Broad St.* ☎ *229/228–6704* 🌐 *www.sweetgrassdairy.com/cheeseshop* ⏲ *Closed Sun. and Mon.*

$$$ B&B/INN 🏨 **The Paxton Historic House Hotel.** Each room is unique in this immaculate property, a stately 1884 Victorian mansion with a wraparound veranda. **Pros:** luxurious comfort; friendly innkeepers; old-time charm. **Cons:** no kids allowed; no longer has a pool; not in downtown Thomasville. [$] *Rooms from: $225* ✉ *445 Remington Ave.* ☎ *229/226–5197* 🌐 *www.1884paxtonhouseinn.com* 🛏 *9 rooms* 🍽 *Breakfast.*

ATLANTA, GA

WELCOME TO ATLANTA, GA

TOP REASONS TO GO

★ **The Georgia Aquarium:** The world's largest aquarium draws visitors from all over the globe.

★ **A stroll through the park:** April in Paris has nothing on Atlanta, especially when the azaleas and dogwoods are blooming in the Atlanta Botanical Garden and Piedmont Park.

★ **Following in Dr. King's footsteps:** Home of Martin Luther King Jr., Atlanta was a hub of the civil rights movement. Tour the King Center and his childhood home on Auburn Avenue and see his personal documents at the Center for Civil and Human Rights.

★ **Civil War history:** Artifacts at historic sites throughout the city give you the chance to reflect on those difficult times.

★ **Southern cooking, and then some:** Good Southern food has always been easy to find here, but Atlanta's proliferation of young, talented chefs and its ethnic diversity make it a great place to sample a wide range of cuisines.

1 Downtown. Although tourists flock to sites like the Georgia Aquarium and more residents are moving to the city center, it still has at least a partially earned reputation for being desolate after business hours.

2 Sweet Auburn, the Old Fourth Ward, and East Atlanta. The mile and a half along Auburn Avenue known as Sweet Auburn is considered the epicenter of African American history and achievement in Atlanta. It has undergone restoration since landing on a 1992 list for endangered historic places. Here you can visit Martin Luther King Jr.'s birth home, church, and grave. The neighboring Old Fourth

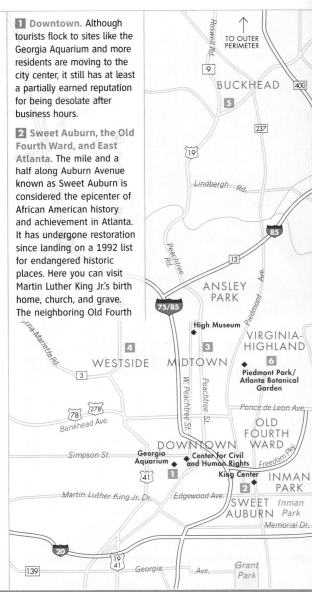

Ward is one of Atlanta's hippest nightlife destinations, and after a wave of revitalization, East Atlanta has some beautiful restored housing stock.

3 Midtown. The picturesque and very walkable Midtown is home to many of Atlanta's major cultural institutions, including the High Museum, and lots of luxurious high-rise condos.

4 Westside. In recent years, chefs, restaurateurs, and designers have flocked to this once-barren industrial expanse opposite the highway from Midtown and transformed it into one of the city's best neighborhoods for shopping and dining.

5 Buckhead. Known for its glamorous condos, majestic homes, and moneyed residents like Elton John, the bars that used to draw crowds here are now largely gone, replaced by ritzy boutiques and stores.

6 Virginia-Highland and the Emory Area. Stroll through the leafy neighborhood at the intersection of Virginia and North Highland Avenues to find trendy stores, patio bars, cozy music venues, and some great food. The area has a sunny disposition, and sits not far from the venerable Emory University.

GETTING ORIENTED

13

Atlanta, the state's capital and seat of Fulton County, was founded in 1837 and sits on the Piedmont Plateau in northern Georgia. Though the metro area spans more than 8,300 square miles, don't let the sprawling size—or all the transplanted Yankees—fool you into thinking Southern hospitality is dead. It's alive and well in Downtown and the surrounding neighborhoods filled with young people and families.

7 Little Five Points and Inman Park. There's a lively mix here, with the majestic old mansions and adorable bungalows of Inman Park just down Euclid Avenue from the gritty bars, restaurants, tattoo parlors, vintage-clothing shops, and street characters of Little Five Points.

8 Decatur. This suburb is about 10 miles east of Downtown. Its charming town square is always buzzing thanks to its many vibrant restaurants, pubs, and stores.

ATLANTA'S CIVIL RIGHTS LEGACY

To some, Atlanta's location in the South may have made it seem an unlikely hotbed for social change, but the city earned an important place in the history of civil rights, particularly through the work and words of Dr. Martin Luther King Jr. Many of the monuments to this rich legacy—including the birth home and church of King—are open to the public.

(above) The tomb of Martin Luther King Jr. and Coretta Scott King (lower right) Martin Luther King Jr. and President Lyndon B. Johnson (upper right) Stained-glass windows at Ebenezer Baptist Church

Tracing back to 1862, when the first African American property owner sold her land for $500 to purchase her enslaved husband's freedom, Atlanta has been a civil rights city. Though many important activists have called this city home, Martin Luther King Jr. stands apart. He was born here, preached here, and raised a family here before he was assassinated in 1968. His legacy is kept alive at the King Center—a living memorial to his work in leading the nation's nonviolent movement for equality and peace.

KING QUOTES

"Freedom is never voluntarily given by the oppressor; it must be demanded by the oppressed."

"I look to a day when people will not be judged by the color of their skin, but by the content of their character."

"All labor that uplifts humanity has dignity and importance and should be undertaken with painstaking excellence."

—Dr. Martin Luther King Jr.

CIVIL RIGHTS WALK

A great way to take a tour of Atlanta's civil rights history is to walk through the Sweet Auburn neighborhood. To get here, take the MARTA train to the Five Points station Downtown and switch to either of the two eastbound lines (the Green/Edgewood/Candler Park or the Blue/Indian Creek line). Get off at the King Memorial stop. All tours are self-guided, and you can download a free audio tour from the Center for Civil & Human Rights Partnership.

Spend time at the Martin Luther King Jr. National Historic Site, also known as **The King Center**, established in 1968 by Coretta Scott King and housing Dr. King's library, a resource center, the Eternal Flame, and the Kings' final resting place. Pause at King's white marble tomb to see its inscription: "Free at last, free at last, thank God almighty I'm free at last."

Stroll along the **International Civil Rights Walk of Fame,** created in 2004 and set up along the National Park Service's Visitor Center to recognize civil rights heroes and cultural icons like Rosa Parks, Stevie Wonder, Hank Aaron, and President Jimmy Carter with 2-foot-square granite markers.

Visit **Ebenezer Baptist Church,** which was founded in 1886 and moved to Auburn Avenue in 1914. King was baptized here and took the pulpit in 1960 as co-pastor with his father. If you're here on a Sunday, you can stop by for a moving service.

Then head to the **Sweet Auburn Curb Market,** which was established in 1918 in a tent before moving in 1924 to its current brick-and-concrete building. The market was segregated, and only white people were permitted to shop inside while black people shopped from stalls lining the curb. That's where the market got its name. Inside are stalls featuring fruits, vegetables, and meats, and small cafés.

ATLANTA IN CIVIL RIGHTS HISTORY

13

1800s: The first African American congressman from Georgia is elected; Booker T. Washington's "Atlanta Compromise" speech is given here.

1900–1940: 25 black people die during the Atlanta Race Riots; Martin Luther King Jr. is born in Atlanta.

1950–1960: Atlanta's segregated bus system is ruled unconstitutional; members of the Student Nonviolent Coordinating Committee stage a sit-in at segregated lunch counters; public pools and parks integrate.

1954: U.S. Supreme Court declares school segregation unconstitutional in *Brown v. Board of Education* ruling.

1973: Maynard Holbrook Jackson Jr. is elected as the city's first African American mayor.

1980s: The King Center is named a national historic site.

2000: Shirley Franklin is Atlanta's first female African American mayor.

Updated by
Chanté LaGon

Originally built as the terminus of the Western & Atlantic Railroad, Atlanta remains a hub for transportation (with the world's busiest airport), industry (with the headquarters for Coca-Cola), art (with treasures on display at the High Museum of Art), and natural wonders (with the world's largest aquarium). The city's half million residents enjoy a mix of old-fashioned Southern charm, offbeat artistic funkiness, chic luxury shopping, superb dining, and major attractions.

In the past, many of the city's big draws—Stone Mountain Park, for example—were outside the city limits. Today there's plenty in town to keep you occupied. The Georgia Aquarium draws visitors who want to get up close and personal with whale sharks. At the Woodruff Arts Center, you can catch a performance by the Atlanta Symphony Orchestra or listen to jazz while strolling the High Museum of Art. The fizzy World of Coca-Cola is dedicated to the hometown beverage. And the Center for Civil and Human Rights is a beacon for justice and equality everywhere.

Atlanta continues to experience explosive growth. A good measure of the city's expansion is the ever-changing skyline; condominium developments appear to spring up overnight, while run-down properties seem to disappear in a flash. In Buckhead—once home to a noisy, raucous bar district—most of the taverns have been razed to bring a Rodeo Drive of the South into being. Office and residential towers have risen throughout Midtown, Downtown, and the outer perimeter (fringing Interstate 285, especially to the north). Residents, however, are less likely to measure the city's growth by skyscrapers than by the increase in the already bad traffic, the crowds, higher prices, and the ever-burgeoning subdivisions that continue to push urban sprawl farther and farther into surrounding rural areas.

Known as "the city too busy to hate," Atlanta has become the best example of the New South, a fast-paced modern city proud of its heritage. Transplanted Northerners and those from elsewhere account for more than half the population, and they have undeniably affected the mood of the city, as well as the mix of accents of its people. Irish immigrants played a major role in the city's early history, along with Germans and Austrians. Since the 1980s, Atlanta has seen spirited growth in its Asian American and Latin American communities. The newcomers' restaurants, shops, and institutions have become part of the city's texture.

13

PLANNING

WHEN TO GO
Atlanta isn't called "Hotlanta" for nothing—in the late spring and summer months the mosquitoes feast, and temperatures can reach a sticky and humid 99°F (thankfully, almost every place in the city is air-conditioned). July 4 weekend can be particularly hectic, due to the influx of runners for the annual 10K Peachtree Road Race. Labor Day weekend also sees major crowds thanks to dozens of popular national festivals, including Dragon*Con and the Decatur Book Festival. The best time to visit is in fall and early winter. When many other cities are beginning to get cold and gray, Atlanta typically maintains a steady level of sunshine and cool breezes. Spring is also a beautiful time to visit with azaleas and dogwoods in bloom. Airfares are fairly reasonable at most times of the year, given that the city is a transportation hub and most Atlanta attractions aren't seasonal.

PLANNING YOUR TIME
Because it would take too long to explore the city end to end in one fell swoop, consider discovering Atlanta one pocket at a time. In Downtown you can stroll through the Georgia Aquarium, tour the CNN Center, and visit the Center for Civil and Human Rights, then finish off the day with dinner and a glass of wine at the historic Ellis Hotel's Terrace Bistro restaurant. Another good pocket includes three adjoining, very walkable neighborhoods, all known for their canopies of trees, cute shops, and fun bistros: Virginia-Highland, Little Five Points, and Inman Park. From there you can drive to East Atlanta and check out its casual bars, tattoo shops, restaurants, and live music. Your third pocket should be Buckhead, a shopper's mecca. Two constants there are Lenox Square and Phipps Plaza, great shopping spots in their own right. Finally, there's the beer-loving, literary hot spot of Decatur, which is increasingly being recognized for its top-notch restaurants.

FESTIVALS
Atlanta Food & Wine Festival. This festival takes place over a four-day weekend in late May or early June in and around Midtown's Loews Hotel. It not only offers incredible food from some of the country's best chefs but also smart seminars on a variety of subjects. ✉ *1065 Peachtree St. NE, Midtown* ☎ *404/474–7330* ⊕ *www.atlfoodandwinefestival.com.*

Atlanta Jazz Festival. The Atlanta Jazz Festival, held Memorial Day weekend, gathers the best local, national, and international musicians for free concerts at Atlanta's Piedmont Park. ⊠ *10th St. and Monroe Dr., Midtown* ☎ *404/546–6826* ⊕ *www.atlantafestivals.com.*

Atlanta Pride. Since 1971, Atlanta has put on one of the most vibrant and popular gay festivals in the country. Thousands of people gather in Piedmont Park every October for Atlanta Pride, which includes a long lineup of entertainers and a market with vendors and organizations from around the area. The main event is the parade, with festive floats and dancers and folks of all stripes marching through the streets of the city. ⊠ *Piedmont Park, 10th St. and Monroe Dr., Midtown* ☎ *404/382–7588* ⊕ *www.atlantapride.org.*

Decatur Book Festival. The Decatur Book Festival is the largest independent book festival in the nation. It takes over Decatur's historic square every Labor Day weekend, with readings, signings, and other literary events. Past keynote speakers have included the novelist Jonathan Franzen and former Decatur resident and current Northwestern University professor Natasha Trethewey, the 19th U.S. Poet Laureate. ⊠ *E. Ponce de Leon and Clairemont Aves., Decatur* ☎ ⊕ *www. decaturbookfestival.com.*

Dragon*Con. Swarms of sci-fi and fantasy fans from around the world descend on Downtown Atlanta every Labor Day weekend to celebrate everything from zombies to *Star Trek.* The popular Saturday morning parade with swarms of Storm Troopers and other movie characters making the route is not to be missed. ⊠ *Downtown* ☎ *404/669–0773* ⊕ *www.dragoncon.org.*

National Black Arts Festival. Celebrating black literature, dance, visual arts, theater, film, and music, this festival is held in venues throughout the city in September and October. Maya Angelou, Cicely Tyson, Harry Belafonte, Spike Lee, Tito Puente, and Wynton Marsalis have all appeared at past events. ⊠ *504 Fair St. SW, West End* ☎ *404/730–7315* ⊕ *www.nbaf.org.*

GETTING HERE AND AROUND

AIR TRAVEL

Hartsfield-Jackson Atlanta International (ATL), the busiest passenger airport in the world, is served by more than 15 airlines, including American, Delta, and Southwest. Although an underground train and moving walkways help you reach your gate more quickly, budget a little extra time for negotiating the massive facility. Because of the airport's size, security lines can be long, especially during peak travel periods. Check ATL's website for Trak-a-Line, which will email you updates about wait times and is surprisingly accurate.

The airport is 13 miles south of Downtown. There are large parking facilities, but they tend to fill up quickly. Check their current capacity on ATL's website. Locals know that MARTA, the regional subway system, is the fastest and cheapest way to and from the airport, but taxis and car-hailing services like Uber and Lyft are also available. The fare by taxi to Downtown is about $35 for one person. From the airport to Buckhead, the fare starts at $40 for one person. Buckhead Safety Cab and Checker Cab offer 24-hour service.

Airport Contacts Hartsfield-Jackson Atlanta International Airport (*ATL*). ⊠ *6000 N. Terminal Pkwy.* ☏ *404/530–7300* ⊕ *www.atlanta-airport.com.*

AIRPORT
SHUTTLES
Airport Metro Shuttle operates shuttles around the clock to destinations around the region. It's recommended that you make reservations 24 hours in advance. Typical shuttle fees range from $45 to $65 for one passenger to Marietta.

Shuttle Contacts Airport Metro Shuttle. ☏ *404/766–6666* ⊕ *airportmetro.com.*

BUS TRAVEL

MARTA operates more than 90 routes covering more than 1,000 miles, but the bus system isn't popular among visitors. The fare is $2.50, and a Breeze card ($2 and reusable) is required. Service is limited outside the perimeter of Interstate 285, except for a few areas in Clayton, DeKalb, and north Fulton counties.

CAR TRAVEL

The city is encircled by Interstate 285. Three interstates also crisscross Atlanta: Interstate 85, running northeast–southwest from Virginia to Alabama; Interstate 75, running north–south from Michigan to Florida; and Interstate 20, running east–west from South Carolina to Texas.

Some refer to Atlanta as the "Los Angeles of the South," because driving is virtually the only way to get around. Atlantans have grown accustomed to frequent delays at rush hour—the morning and late-afternoon commuting periods seem to get longer every year. ■ TIP➔ The South as a whole may be laid-back, but Atlanta drivers are not; they tend to drive faster and more aggressively than drivers in other Southern cities, and they rarely slow down at a yellow light.

If you plan to venture beyond the neighborhoods served by MARTA, you will want to rent a car or use a car-hailing service such as Uber or Lyft. Many national agencies have branch offices all over the city, as well as at Hartsfield-Jackson Atlanta International Airport.

STREETCAR TRAVEL

With 12 stops including Centennial Olympic Park, the Martin Luther King Jr. National Historic Site, and various points in between, residents and visitors alike will appreciate how the line connects neighborhoods, attractions, walk-run-bike paths such as the Beltline, and MARTA. One-way fare is $1 and works in tandem with the city rail system's Breeze card.

Streetcar Contact Atlanta Streetcar. ⊠ *Downtown* ☏ *404/546–0311* ⊕ *streetcar.atlantaga.gov.*

SUBWAY TRAVEL

MARTA has clean and safe subway trains with somewhat limited routes that link Downtown with many major landmarks, like the CNN Center and the Martin Luther King Jr. Memorial. The system's two main lines cross at the Five Points station. MARTA uses a smart-card fare system called Breeze. The cards are available at RideStores and from vending machines at each station by using cash or credit cards. The one-way fare is $2.50, but the cards offer several options, including one-day, seven-day, and 30-day passes.

13

Trains generally run weekdays 5 am to 1 am and weekends and holidays 6 am to 1 am. Most trains operate every 15 to 20 minutes; during weekday rush hours, trains run every 10 minutes.

■ TIP➜ Locals take MARTA to and from Hartsfield-Jackson International Airport, which has the traffic snarls common with larger airports. The $2.50 fare is a fraction of the amount charged by shuttles or taxis. Airport travelers should be careful about catching the right train. One line ends up at North Springs station to the north; the other at Doraville station, to the northeast. Daily parking is free at MARTA parking facilities. Long-term parking rates range from $5 to $8 daily. Not all stations have lots, however.

Subway Contact MARTA. 🕾 *404/848–5000* ⊕ *www.itsmarta.com.*

TAXI TRAVEL

Taxi service in Atlanta can be uneven. Drivers often lack correct change, so bring plenty of small bills. You can also charge your fare, as many accept credit cards. Drivers may be as befuddled as you are by the city's notoriously winding streets, so if your destination is somewhere other than a major hotel or popular sight, it might be best to direct the route from your phone.

In Atlanta taxi fares begin at $2.50, then add $2 for each additional mile. Additional passengers are $2 each, and there's a $2 gas surcharge added to every trip. You generally need to call for a cab, as Atlanta is not a place where you can hail one on the street. Buckhead Safety Cab and Checker Cab offer 24-hour service. Uber and Lyft drivers are also available throughout the city.

Taxi Contacts Buckhead Safety Cab. 🕾 *404/875–3777* ⊕ *www.buckheadsafetycabs.com.* **Checker Cab.** 🕾 *404/351–1111* ⊕ *www.atlantacheckercab.com.*

TRAIN TRAVEL

Amtrak operates daily service from Atlanta's Brookwood Station to New York; Philadelphia; Washington, D.C.; Charlotte, North Carolina; and New Orleans.

Train Contacts Amtrak. ⊠ *Brookwood Station, 1688 Peachtree St., Buckhead* 🕾 *800/872–7245* ⊕ *www.amtrak.com.*

DISCOUNTS AND DEALS

Visitors can take advantage of the deal offered with **Atlanta CityPass**, "the ticket to a New and Old South vacation." An adult pass—which is valid for a nine-day period—costs $76.75 and provides access to five attractions: Georgia Aquarium, World of Coca-Cola, Inside CNN Atlanta Studio Tour, and a choice between the Fernbank Museum of Natural History or the College Football Hall of Fame, and Zoo Atlanta or the Center for Civil and Human Rights. Visit ⊕ *www.citypass.com/atlanta.*

TOURS

Getting to know the many neighborhoods of Atlanta—and increasingly the film sites therein—make guided tours worthwhile. Although historic locations often offer self-guided materials, there's nothing like a local to point out where *The Walking Dead* zombies roamed, or share stories of Atlanta's first suburb and the history of Downtown's most beloved attractions. The best options are given by motor vehicle, whether minicoach, e-car or trolley—all at a slower pace, of course.

ATL-Cruzers. Small tours on small vehicles—whether electric car or Segway—are this tour's hallmark. Atlanta's neighborhoods are the highlight, from Downtown to Midtown to Sweet Auburn. ⊠ *160 Spring St. NW, Downtown* ☎ *404/492–7009* ⊕ *www.atlcruzers.com* ✉ *From $29.*

Atlanta Movie Tours. Get your fill of zombie-trampled sites with tours that visit the filming locations of *The Walking Dead* and *Zombieland.* See the more genteel side of Georgia on the big screen with tours of *Driving Miss Daisy* sites, or landmarks from Margaret Mitchell's heyday. ⊠ *327 Nelson St. SW, Castleberry Hill* ☎ *855/255–3456* ⊕ *atlantamovietours. com* ✉ *From $55.*

Peachtree Trolley. If you're staying Downtown, this tour will familiarize you with the popular destinations there, including the Georgia Aquarium, World of Coca-Cola, and CNN Center. A trip to surrounding areas such as Grant Park and its Oakland Cemetery are also on the route. ⊠ *275 Baker St. NW, at Hilton Garden Inn, Downtown* ☎ *770/425–1006* ⊕ *thepeachtreetrolley.com* ✉ *From $30.*

VISITOR INFORMATION

The Atlanta Convention & Visitors Bureau, which provides information on Atlanta and the outlying area, has information centers at Hartsfield-Jackson Atlanta International Airport, in the Atrium, and Underground Atlanta.

Visitor Information Atlanta Convention & Visitors Bureau. ⊠ *233 Peachtree St., Suite 1400, Downtown* ☎ *404/521–6600* ⊕ *www.atlanta.net.*

EXPLORING ATLANTA

The greater Atlanta area embraces several different counties. The city of Atlanta is primarily in Fulton and DeKalb counties, although its southern end and the airport are in Clayton County. Outside Interstate 285, which encircles the city, Cobb, Gwinnett, and northern Fulton counties are experiencing much of Atlanta's population increase.

Atlanta's lack of a grid system confuses many drivers, even locals. Some streets change names along the same stretch of road, including the city's most famous thoroughfare, Peachtree Street, which follows a mountain ridge from Downtown to suburban Norcross, outside Interstate 285: It becomes Peachtree Road after crossing Interstate 85 and then splits into Peachtree Industrial Boulevard beyond the Buckhead neighborhood and the original Peachtree Road, which heads into Chamblee. Adding to the confusion, dozens of other streets in the metropolitan area use "Peachtree" in their names. ■TIP➜ Before setting out anywhere, get the complete street address of your destination, including landmarks, cross streets, or other guideposts. Street numbers and even street signs are often difficult to find.

Atlanta proper has three major areas—Downtown, Midtown, and Buckhead—as well as many smaller commercial districts and in-town neighborhoods. Atlanta's Downtown is filled with government staffers and office workers by day, but at night the visiting conventioneers—and, as city improvements take hold, residents—come out to play. Midtown, Virginia-Highland, Buckhead, Old Fourth Ward, the Westside, and Decatur are the best places to go for dinner, nightclubs, and shows. Other neighborhoods like East Atlanta, Grant Park, Little Five Points, and Kirkwood have unique characteristics that merit exploration.

DOWNTOWN

Downtown Atlanta clusters around the hub known as Five Points. You'll find the MARTA station that intersects the north–south and east–west transit lines, both of which run underground here. On the surface, Five Points is formed by the intersection of Peachtree Street with Marietta, Broad, and Forsyth Streets. It's a crowded area, particularly when Georgia State is in session, and traffic can be snarled in the early morning and late afternoon. With the Center for Civil and Human Rights joining the Georgia Aquarium, World of Coca-Cola, the Imagine It! Children's Museum and the CNN Center, Downtown has taken on greater interest for travelers. Lush Centennial Olympic Park—built for the 1996 Olympic Games—is a great place to let your children play in the Fountain of Rings or to enjoy a take-out lunch.

TOP ATTRACTIONS

FAMILY
Fodor's Choice
★

Centennial Olympic Park. This 21-acre swath of green was the central venue for the 1996 Summer Olympics. The benches at the Fountain of Rings allow you to enjoy the water and music spectacle—four times a day, tunes are timed to coincide with water displays that shoot sprays 15 feet to 30 feet high. The All Children's Playground is designed to be accessible to kids with disabilities. Nearby is the world's largest aquarium and Imagine It! Children's Museum. The park also has a café, restrooms, and a playground, and typically offers ice-skating in winter. ■TIP→ Don't miss seeing Centennial Olympic Park at night, when eight 65-foot-tall lighting towers set off the beauty of the park. They represent the markers that led ancient Greeks to public events. ⊠ *265 Park Ave. West, Marietta St. and Centennial Olympic Park Dr., Downtown* ☎ *404/222–7275* ⊕ *www.centennialpark.com.*

Fodor's Choice
★

Center for Civil and Human Rights. This three-level, 43,000-square-foot, hands-on museum offers visitors a multisensory immersion into both the U.S. civil rights movement and global human rights efforts. Each exhibit is a force of its own: the quiet and vicarious look at handwritten journals and personal items from Martin Luther King Jr.; the jolting sensation of sitting in at a lunch counter, hearing the threats and slurs that young protesters would have; or the mirrorlike effect of one-on-one stories told by those who've suffered human rights violations—and the workers whose mission it is to triumph over them. The *Rolls Down Like Water* exhibit is superb, bearing the mark of its

The Georgia Aquarium is the world's largest aquarium, with 10 million gallons of water and more than 80,000 animals.

curator, award-winning playwright and film director George C. Wolfe. The center hosts one of the biggest celebrations of the Universal Declaration of Human Rights in the world each December. And the building, itself a work of art reminiscent of folding hands, is steps away from parking and a brief walk to the World of Coca-Cola and Georgia Aquarium. ⊠ *100 Ivan Allen Jr. Blvd., Downtown* ☎ *678/999–8990* ⊕ *www.civilandhumanrights.org* 🎟 *$18.25.*

CNN Center. The home of Cable News Network occupies all 14 floors of this dramatic structure on the edge of Downtown. The 50-minute CNN studio tour is a behind-the-scenes glimpse of the control room, newsrooms, and broadcast studios. Tours depart approximately every 20 minutes. ◾**TIP➜ The tour descends eight flights of stairs, making it difficult for some—a limited number of tours have elevator access.** You can make reservations by telephone or online. ⊠ *1 CNN Center, Downtown* ☎ *404/827–2300* ⊕ *tours.cnn.com* 🎟 *Tour $13–$16.*

FAMILY
Fodor's Choice
★

Georgia Aquarium. With more than 10 million gallons of water, this wildly popular attraction is the world's largest aquarium. The 604,000-square-foot building, an architectural marvel resembling the bow of a ship, has tanks of various sizes filled with more than 80,000 animals, representing 500 species. The aquarium's 6.3-million-gallon Ocean Voyager Gallery is the world's largest indoor marine exhibit, with 4,574 square feet of viewing windows. But not everything has gills: there are also penguins, sea lions, sea otters, river otters, sea turtles, and giant octopuses. The 84,000-square-foot AT&T Dolphin Tales exhibit includes a 25-minute show (reservations required). Hordes of kids—and many adults—can always be found around the touch tanks. Admission includes entry to all

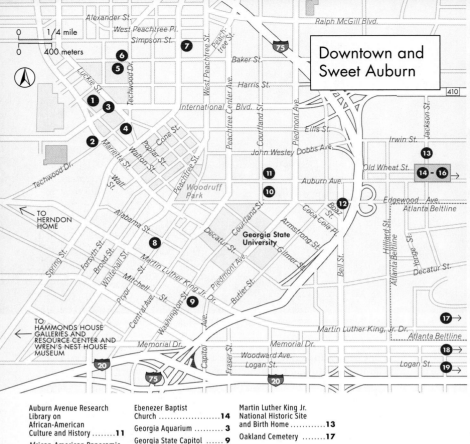

public exhibits, shows, and galleries. Ninety-minute behind-the-scenes tours start at $59.95. There are often huge crowds, so arrive early or late for the best chance of getting a close-up view of the exhibits. ■ TIP➔ Try to buy your tickets at least a week ahead. Online ticketing is best, with discounted rates and emailed tickets you can print out at home. ⊠ *225 Baker St., Downtown* ☎ *404/581–4000* ⊕ *www.georgiaaquarium.org* ✉ *$35.95.*

FAMILY **Imagine It! The Children's Museum of Atlanta** In this colorful and joyfully noisy museum for children ages eight and younger, kids can build sand castles, watch themselves perform on closed-circuit TV, operate a giant ball-moving machine, and get inside an imaginary waterfall (after donning raincoats, of course). Other exhibits rotate every few months. ⊠ *275 Centennial Olympic Park Dr. NW, Downtown* ☎ *404/659–5437* ⊕ *www.childrensmuseumatlanta.org* ✉ *$14.95.*

SkyView Atlanta. Take a seat in one of the Ferris wheel's 42 climate-controlled cars perched 20 stories above Downtown for spectacular views of Centennial Olympic Park and miles beyond. The ride lasts 15 minutes. The wheel comes alive at night with an ever-changing display of colors outlining its rim and spokes powered by the same lighting system as the Eiffel Tower. In true Atlanta fashion, there's a VIP experience that lets you skip long lines and sit privately with your group in a gondola outfitted with Ferrari leather seats and a glass floor for a longer ride. Discount parking is available in nearby lots. ⊠ *168 Luckie St., Downtown* ☎ *678/949–9023* ⊕ *www.skyviewatlanta.com* ✉ *$13.89; $50 VIP.*

FAMILY **World of Coca-Cola.** This shrine to the brown soda's image, products, and marketing is, at 62,000 square feet, twice the size of its previous building and features more than 1,200 artifacts never before displayed to the public. You can sip samples of 100 different Coca-Cola products from around the world and peruse more than a century's worth of memorabilia from the corporate archives. The gift shop sells everything from refrigerator magnets to handbags. ⊠ *121 Baker St. NW, Downtown* ☎ *404/676–5151* ⊕ *www.worldofcoca-cola.com* ✉ *$17.*

WORTH NOTING

Georgia State Capitol. The capitol, a Renaissance-style edifice, was dedicated on July 4, 1889. The gold leaf on its dome was mined in nearby Dahlonega. Inside, the **Georgia Capitol Museum** houses exhibits on its history. On the grounds, state historical markers commemorate the 1864 Battle of Atlanta, which destroyed nearly the entire city. Statues memorialize a 19th-century Georgia governor and his wife (Joseph and Elizabeth Brown), a Confederate general (John B. Gordon), and a former senator (Richard B. Russell). Former governor and president Jimmy Carter is depicted with his sleeves rolled up, a man at work. Visit the website for tour information and group reservations. ⊠ *206 Washington St. SW, Downtown* ☎ *404/656–2846* ⊕ *www.libs.uga.edu/capitolmuseum* ⊙ *Closed weekends and state holidays.*

13

Underground Atlanta. This underground six-block district was created from the web of subterranean brick streets, ornamental facades, and tunnels that fell into disuse in 1929, when the city built viaducts over the train tracks. The Underground opened in 1969 as a retail and entertainment center and remained fairly popular until it was closed in 1980 for the MARTA train project. After a $142 million renovation, it reopened with eateries, retail, and specialty shops. ■TIP➜ AtlanTIX, a half-price ticket outlet theater and cultural attractions, is located in Underground Atlanta. It's open 11 to 6 Tuesday to Saturday, noon to 4 Sunday. ⊠ *50 Upper Alabama St., Downtown* ☎ *404/523–2311* ⊕ *www.underground-atlanta.com.*

SWEET AUBURN, THE OLD FOURTH WARD, AND EAST ATLANTA

Between 1890 and 1930, the Sweet Auburn district was Atlanta's most active and prosperous center of black business, entertainment, and political life. Following the Depression, the area went into an economic decline that lasted until the 1980s, when the residential area where civil rights leader Martin Luther King Jr. (1929–68) was born, raised, and later returned to live was declared a National Historic District. Nearby, the Old Fourth Ward and the East Atlanta area have mostly benefited from slow gentrification. Both are nightlife hot spots and home to some beautifully restored houses. Count Grant Park in that number, too, with its lovingly renovated bungalows and Victorians, many of which edge Grant Park itself, one of the city's green-space gems that houses the Atlanta Zoo.

TOP ATTRACTIONS

African American Panoramic Experience (APEX). The museum's quarterly exhibits chronicle the history of black people in America. Videos illustrate the history of Sweet Auburn, the name bestowed on Auburn Avenue by businessman John Wesley Dobbs, who fostered business development for African Americans on this street. ■TIP➜ Make a day of visiting APEX and the Auburn Avenue Research Library, with lunch at the Sweet Auburn Market. All three are within a short walking distance. ⊠ *135 Auburn Ave., Sweet Auburn* ☎ *404/523–2739* ⊕ *www.apexmuseum.org* ⊠ *$7* ☉ *Closed Sun. and Mon.*

Fodor'sChoice
★
Ebenezer Baptist Church. A Gothic Revival–style building completed in 1922, the church came to be known as the spiritual center of the civil rights movement. Members of the King family, including the slain civil rights leader, preached at the church for three generations. Sitting in the main sanctuary on a quiet day when light is shining through the stained-glass windows can be a powerful experience. The congregation itself now occupies the building across the street. ⊠ *407 Auburn Ave. NE, Sweet Auburn* ☎ *404/331–5190* ⊕ *www.nps.gov/malu* ⊠ *Free.*

Martin Luther King Jr. Center for Nonviolent Social Change. The Martin Luther King Jr. National Historic District occupies several blocks on Auburn Avenue, east of Peachtree Street in the black business and residential community of Sweet Auburn. Martin Luther King Jr. was born here in 1929; after his assassination in 1968, his widow, Coretta Scott

Martin Luther King Jr. was born and raised in this modest Queen Anne–style house.

King, established this center, which exhibits such personal items as King's Nobel Peace Prize, bible, and tape recorder, along with memorabilia and photos chronicling the civil rights movement. In the courtyard in front of Freedom Hall, on a circular brick pad in the middle of the rectangular Meditation Pool, is Dr. King's white-marble tomb; the inscription reads; "Free at last, Free at last, Thank God Almighty I'm Free at last." Nearby, an eternal flame burns. A chapel of all faiths sits at one end of the reflecting pool. Mrs. King, who passed away in 2006, is also entombed at the center. ✉ *449 Auburn Ave. NE, Sweet Auburn* ☎ *404/526–8900* ⊕ *www.thekingcenter.org* ✉ *Free.*

Fodor's Choice
★ **Martin Luther King Jr. National Historic Site and Birth Home.** The modest Queen Anne–style residence is where Martin Luther King Jr. was born and raised. Besides items that belonged to the family, the house contains an outstanding multimedia exhibit focused on the civil rights movement. ■**TIP**➔ **A limited number of visitors are allowed to tour the house each day. Advance reservations are not possible, so sign up early in the day.** ✉ *501 Auburn Ave., Sweet Auburn* ☎ *404/331–5190* ⊕ *www.nps.gov/malu* ✉ *Free.*

FAMILY **Zoo Atlanta.** This zoo has more than 1,500 animals and 200 species from around the world living in naturalistic habitats. The gorillas and tigers are always a hit, as are giant pandas named Yang Yang, Lun Lun, and their four offspring. Children can ride the Nabisco Endangered Species Carousel and meet new friends at the petting zoo while the whole family can take a ride on the Zoo Train. ✉ *800 Cherokee Ave. SE, Grant Park* ☎ *404/624–5600* ⊕ *www.zooatlanta. org* ✉ *$22.99-$25.99.*

WORTH NOTING

Auburn Avenue Research Library on African American Culture and History. An extension of the Atlanta-Fulton Public Library, this unit houses a noncirculating collection of about 60,000 books of African American interest. The archives contain art and artifacts, transcribed oral histories, and rare books, pamphlets, and periodicals. There are three galleries with rotating exhibits, and frequent special events, all of them free. ⊠ *101 Auburn Ave. NE, Sweet Auburn* ☎ *404/730–4001* ⊕ *www.afpls.org/aarl.*

OFF THE BEATEN PATH

East Atlanta Village. This earthy outpost of edgy-cool shops, restaurants, bars, and concert venues started growing, beginning in 1996, thanks to a group of proprietors with dreams much bigger than their bank accounts. Spurning the high rents of fancier parts of town, they set up businesses in this then-blighted but beautiful ruin of a neighborhood 4 miles southeast of Downtown. Soon artists and others came to soak up the creative atmosphere. East Atlanta, which is centered at Flat Shoals and Glenwood Avenues, just southeast of Moreland Avenue at Interstate 20, has had its ups and downs, but has experienced a resurgence. Many of the majestic homes have been renovated, and what remains unrestored seems to romanticize the area's gritty appeal. ⊠ *Flat Shoals and Glenwood Aves., East Atlanta.*

Krog Street Market. This bustling food hall and market draws both residents who live within walking distance and suburbanites driving in from afar. It houses spots like Ticonderoga Club, the latest venture of barmen Greg Best and Paul Calvert, Tex-Mex from Superica, French-inspired dishes from the Luminary, and worth-the-wait ice cream from Jeni's. Plus, you can walk around with your beer from Hop City while you shop at the small outposts hawking everything from chocolate to handmade soaps. ⊠ *99 Krog St., Inman Park* ☎ *770/434–2400* ⊕ *www. krogstreetmarket.com.*

OFF THE BEATEN PATH

Oakland Cemetery. Established in 1850 in the Victorian style, Atlanta's oldest cemetery was designed to serve as a public park as well as a burial ground. Some of the 70,000 permanent residents include six governors, five Confederate generals, and 6,900 Confederate soldiers. Also here are novelist Margaret Mitchell and golfing great Bobby Jones. You can bring a picnic lunch or take a tour conducted by the Historic Oakland Foundation. The King Memorial MARTA station on the east–west line also serves the cemetery. ⊠ *248 Oakland Ave. SE, Grant Park* ☎ *404/688–2107* ⊕ *www.oaklandcemetery.com* ☚ *Tours $12.*

Sweet Auburn Curb Market. The market, an institution on Edgewood Avenue since 1924, sells flowers, fruits, and vegetables, and a variety of meat—everything from fresh catfish to foot-long oxtails. Vendors also include a tasty popcorn stand, an organic coffee shop, and local favorites Bell Street Burritos, Grindhouse Killer Burgers, and Arepa Mia, all of which have opened secondary locations after being incubated here first. Individual stalls are run by a diverse set of owners, making this a true public market—especially significant now, considering that Atlanta's black residents were forced to sell their wares on the curb in the market's early days. ⊠ *209 Edgewood Ave., Sweet Auburn* ☎ *404/659–1665* ⊕ *www.thecurbmarket.com* ☾ *Closed Sun.*

The Atlanta Botanical Garden is a 30-acre oasis inside Piedmont Park.

MIDTOWN AND WESTSIDE

Midtown Atlanta—north of Downtown and south of Buckhead—has a skyline of gleaming office towers that rivals Downtown's. Its renovated mansions and bungalows have made it a city showcase, and so has Piedmont Park and the Atlanta Botanical Garden. It's also the location of the Woodruff Arts Center, one of the largest performing-arts centers in the country, and roughly 20 other arts and cultural venues, including the Museum of Design Atlanta, and the Savannah College of Art and Design (SCAD). The neighborhood is the hub for the city's sizable gay community.

The Westside, once considered a part of Midtown, has earned its own identity. Here you'll find some of the city's best and most sophisticated restaurants, including high-end Bacchanalia, as well as the Atlanta Contemporary Art Center.

TOP ATTRACTIONS

FAMILY
Fodor'sChoice
★
Atlanta Botanical Garden. Occupying 30 acres inside Piedmont Park, the grounds contain acres of display gardens, including a 2-acre interactive children's garden; the Fuqua Conservatory, which has unusual flora from tropical and desert climates; and the award-winning Fuqua Orchid Center. Check out the view from the Canopy Walk, a 600-foot suspension bridge 40 feet above Storza Woods. A variety of special exhibits take place throughout the year. ✉ *1345 Piedmont Ave. NE, Midtown* ☎ *404/876–5859* ⊕ *atlantabg.org* ✑ *$21.95* ⊙ *Closed Mon.*

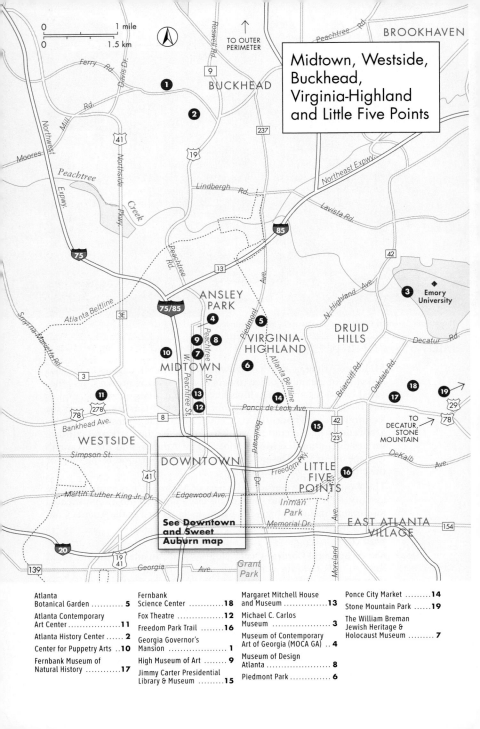

Midtown, Westside, Buckhead, Virginia-Highland and Little Five Points

TO OUTER PERIMETER

BROOKHAVEN

BUCKHEAD

ANSLEY PARK

VIRGINIA-HIGHLAND

DRUID HILLS

Emory University

MIDTOWN

WESTSIDE

DOWNTOWN

LITTLE FIVE POINTS

EAST ATLANTA VILLAGE

See Downtown and Sweet Auburn map

Inman Park

Grant Park

FAMILY
Fodor'sChoice
★

Center for Puppetry Arts. The largest puppetry organization in the country houses a museum where you can see more than 350 puppets from around the world. The elaborate performances include original works and classics adapted for stage. Kids also love the create-a-puppet workshops. The Jim Henson Museum at the Center for Puppetry Arts houses most of the famed puppeteer's collection, and includes rooms that re-create his early days, like his office and workshop. ✉ *1404 Spring St. NW, at 18th St., Midtown* ☎ *404/873–3391* ⊕ *www.puppet.org* 🎫 *$10.50* ⊗ *Closed Mon.*

13

Fodor'sChoice
★

Fox Theatre. One of a dwindling number of vintage movie palaces in the nation, the Fox was built in 1929 in a fabulous Moorish-Egyptian style. The interior's crowning glory is its ceiling, complete with moving clouds and twinkling stars above Alhambra-like minarets. Threatened by demolition in the 1970s, the Fox was saved from the wrecking ball by community activists. Today it hosts musicals, rock concerts, dance performances, and film festivals. ∎TIP➔ **Tours should be scheduled in advance.** ✉ *660 Peachtree St. NE, Midtown* ☎ *404/881–2100 for box office* ⊕ *www.foxtheatre.org* 🎫 *Tour: $18.*

High Museum of Art. This museum's permanent collection includes 19th- and 20-century American works, including many by African American artists. It also has some stellar examples of contemporary and outsider art—don't miss the works by the self-taught artist Rev. Howard Finster. The building itself is a work of art; the American Institute of Architects listed the sleek structure, designed by Richard Meier, among the 10 best works of American architecture of the 1980s. An expansion designed by Renzo Piano doubled the museum's size to 312,000 square feet with three new aluminum-paneled buildings. The roof features a system of 1,000 "light scoops" that filter light into the skyway galleries. The High often partners with other major museums, including the Louvre and New York's Museum of Modern Art. ✉ *Woodruff Arts Center, 1280 Peachtree St. NE, Midtown* ☎ *404/733–4444* ⊕ *www.high.org* 🎫 *$14.50* ⊗ *Closed Mon.*

Margaret Mitchell House and Museum. While she wrote her masterpiece, the author of *Gone With the Wind* lived in an apartment house built in 1899 that she called "the Dump." Volunteers gathered the funds necessary to restore the building in the early 1990s. To many Atlantans, the Margaret Mitchell House symbolizes the conflict between promoting the city's heritage and respecting its roots. The house has been struck by fire twice, in 1994 and 1996. Arson was strongly suspected but no one was ever caught. The visitor center exhibits photographs, archival material, and personal possessions. ∎TIP➔ **Purchase tickets at the Atlanta History Center's Midtown campus at 979 Crescent Avenue.** ✉ *990 Peachtree St. at Peachtree Pl., Midtown* ☎ *404/249–7015* ⊕ *www.atlantahistorycenter.com/mmh* 🎫 *$13.*

Museum of Design Atlanta. The only museum in the Southeast devoted exclusively to design mounts exhibits on fashion, graphics, architecture, furniture, and product design. The eco-friendly building is located just across the street from the High Museum of Art. ✉ *1315 Peachtree St., Midtown* ☎ *404/979–6455* ⊕ *www.museumofdesign.org* 🎫 *$10* ⊗ *Closed Mon.*

FAMILY

Fodor's Choice

★

Piedmont Park. A popular destination since the late 19th century, Piedmont Park is the perfect place to escape the chaos of the city. Tennis courts, a swimming pool, a popular dog park, and paths for walking, jogging, and rollerblading are part of the attraction, but many retreat to the park's great lawn for picnics with a smashing view of the Midtown skyline. ⊠ *10th St. between Piedmont Ave. and Monroe Dr., Midtown* ☎ *404/875–7275* ⊕ *www.piedmontpark.org.*

WORTH NOTING

Atlanta Contemporary Art Center. Established by a group of photographers in the '70s as the arts co-op Nexus, the ACAC exhibits edgy contemporary art. It has the feel of a sophisticated gallery, but the programming is approachable, and its annual Art Party is not to be missed. ⊠ *535 Means St. NW, Downtown* ☎ *404/688–1970* ⊕ *www.atlantacontemporary.org* 🎫 *Free* 🕙 *Closed Mon.*

The William Breman Jewish Heritage & Holocaust Museum. The history of the Jewish community in Atlanta—particularly those who found their way to the burgeoning city after the Holocaust—is told through a permanent exhibit called *Absence of Humanity: The Holocaust Years, 1933–1945.* The facility is the largest archive of Georgia Jewish history and also contains a research library and an education center. ⊠ *1440 Spring St. NW, Midtown* ☎ *678/222–3700* ⊕ *www.thebreman.org* 🎫 *$12* 🕙 *Closed Sat.*

BUCKHEAD

Atlanta's sprawl doesn't lend itself to walking between major neighborhoods, so take a car or MARTA to reach this area, which has some great stores and restaurants. Lenox Square and Phipps Plaza malls are loaded with plenty of upscale shops. Finding a parking spot on the weekends and at night can be a real headache, and long waits are common in the hottest restaurants.

Fodor's Choice

★

Atlanta History Center. Life in Atlanta and the rest of the South during and after the Civil War are a major focus of this fascinating museum. Displays are provocative, juxtaposing *Gone With the Wind* romanticism with the grim reality of Ku Klux Klan racism. Located on 33 acres in the heart of Buckhead, this is one of the Southeast's largest history museums, with a research library and archives that annually serve thousands of patrons. Visit the elegant 1928 **Swan House** mansion, and the plantation house that is part of **Smith Family Farm.** The Kenan Research Center houses an extensive archival collection. Lunch is served at the Swan Coach House, which also has a gallery and a gift shop. ⊠ *130 West Paces Ferry Rd. NW, Buckhead* ☎ *404/814–4000* ⊕ *www.atlantahistorycenter.com* 🎫 *$16.50.*

Georgia Governor's Mansion. This 24,000-square-foot 1967 Greek Revival mansion contains 30 rooms with Federal-period antiques. It sits on 18 acres that originally belonged to the Robert Maddox family (no relation to Georgia governor Lester Maddox, who was its first occupant). ⊠ *391 West Paces Ferry Rd. NW, Buckhead* ☎ *404/261–1776* ⊕ *mansion.georgia.gov* 🎫 *Free.*

From the creation of the cotton gin to the premiere of *Gone With the Wind*, the Civil War to the civil rights movement, you can learn all about it at the Atlanta History Center.

Museum of Contemporary Art of Georgia (MOCA GA). Although the collection here includes artists from around the world, 290 Georgia artists are represented in the space, which is housed in an arts center. More than 1,000 paintings, sculptures, and other works are part of the permanent collection. ⊠ *75 Bennett St., Suite A2, Buckhead* ☎ *404/367–8700* ⊕ *www.mocaga.org* ⌂ *$8* ☉ *Closed Mon.*

VIRGINIA-HIGHLAND AND THE EMORY AREA

Restaurants, bars, and boutiques are sprinkled throughout Virginia-Highland/Morningside, northeast of Midtown. Like Midtown, this residential area was down-at-the-heels in the 1970s. Reclaimed by writers, artists, and a few visionary developers, Virginia-Highland (as well as bordering Morningside) is a great place to explore. To the east, the Emory University area is studded with enviable mansions. Near the Emory campus is Druid Hills, used for film locations for *Driving Miss Daisy,* by local playwright Alfred Uhry. The neighborhood was designed by the firm of Frederick Law Olmsted, which also landscaped Asheville's Biltmore Estate and New York's Central Park.

TOP ATTRACTIONS

FAMILY **Fernbank Museum of Natural History.** One of the largest natural-history museums south of the Smithsonian Institution in Washington, D.C., this museum offers more than 12,000 square feet of gallery space and an on-site IMAX theater. The "Giants of the Mesozoic" exhibit includes an exact replica of the world's largest dinosaur. The café, with an exquisite view of the forest, serves great food. ■TIP→ On the second Friday of each month, the museum hosts Fernbank After Dark, which includes live music and food and cocktails for purchase. ⊠ *767 Clifton Rd., Emory* ☎ *404/929–6300* ⊕ *www.fernbankmuseum.org* ⊠ *$18; Fernbank After Dark $20.*

Jimmy Carter Presidential Library & Museum. This complex occupies the site where Union General William T. Sherman orchestrated the Battle of Atlanta (1864). The museum and archives detail the political career of former president Jimmy Carter. The adjacent Carter Center, which is not open to the public, focuses on conflict resolution and human-rights issues. Outside, the Japanese-style garden is a serene spot to unwind. Both Carter and former First Lady Rosalynn Carter maintain offices here. ⊠ *441 Freedom Pkwy., Virginia-Highland* ☎ *404/865–7100* ⊕ *www.jimmycarterlibrary.gov* ⊠ *$8.*

FAMILY **Michael C. Carlos Museum.** Housing a permanent collection of more than 17,000 objects, this excellent museum, designed by the architect Michael Graves, exhibits artifacts from Egypt, Greece, Rome, the Near East, the Americas, and Africa. European and American prints and drawings cover the Middle Ages through the 20th century. The bookshop sells rare art books, jewelry, and art-focused items for children. ⊠ *Emory University, 571 S. Kilgo Circle, Emory* ☎ *404/727–0519* ⊕ *www.carlos.emory.edu* ⊠ *$8* ⊘ *Closed Mon.*

Fodor'sChoice **Ponce City Market.** The old Sears, Roebuck & Co. building built in 1925 ★ has transformed into Atlanta's hippest place to live, work, shop, and play, especially with the addition of a mini-amusement park on the roof. The historic property is adjacent to the Beltline, with easy access to several neighborhoods. The 2-million-square-foot-development— led by the same group who brought NYC's Chelsea Market to life— is LEED Gold–certified. Eco-friendliness aside, the real draw is the food hall. Walk through the crowds and among industrial-style spiral staircases and original concrete columns to devour coveted burgers from Holeman & Finch; Southern-style fried chicken at Hop's; raw oysters from W.H. Stiles Fish Camp; Korean specialties from Simply Seoul Kitchen; and out-of-this-world cocktails from the Mercury. The Dancing Goats Coffee Bar stays busy, especially when City Winery, a music venue and restaurant in its own right, is hosting events. ⊠ *675 Ponce de Leon Ave., Old Fourth Ward* ☎ *404/692–1670* ⊕ *www.poncecitymarket.com.*

WORTH NOTING

FAMILY **Fernbank Science Center.** The museum, a learning and activity center with connections to the county school system, sits in the 65-acre Fernbank Forest, and focuses on ecology, geology, and space exploration. In addition to the exhibit hall, there's a planetarium as well as an observatory, which is open Thursday and Friday nights 9–10:30, weather permitting. ⊠ *156 Heaton Park Dr., Emory* ☎ *678/874–7102* ⊕ *fsc.fernbank.edu* ⊠ *Free; $7 for planetarium shows* ⊘ *Closed Sun.*

LITTLE FIVE POINTS AND INMAN PARK

About 4 miles east of Downtown, this neighborhood was laid out by famous developer Joel Hurt in 1889. Since then it has faded and flourished a number of times, which explains the vast gaps in opulence evident in much of the architecture here. Huge, ornate Victorian mansions sit next to humble bungalows. But no matter the exact address or style of home—be it modest or massive—Inman Park now commands considerable cachet among many different constituents, including young families, empty nesters, and gays and lesbians. Nearby you'll also find the delightfully countercultural Little Five Points section, with funky boutiques, neighborhood bars, and ethnic eateries.

Freedom Park Trail. One of the neighborhood's best features is the Freedom Park Trail, a particularly pleasant stretch of the PATH Foundation's more-than-250-mile trail system in the metro area. It gives runners, bikers, and dog walkers a peaceful thoroughfare inside the 210-acre Freedom Park. The PATH is the largest public green space in a major metro area developed in the United States in the last century. ⊠ *Moreland Ave. and Freedom Pkwy., Little Five Points* ☎ *404/875–7284* ⊕ *www.pathfoundation.org.*

METRO ATLANTA

FAMILY **Stone Mountain Park.** At this 3,200-acre state park you'll find the largest exposed granite outcropping on Earth. The Confederate Memorial, on the north face of the 825-foot-high mountain, is the world's largest sculpture, measuring 90 feet by 190 feet. There are several ways to see the sculpture, including a cable car that lifts you to the mountaintop and a steam locomotive that chugs around the mountain's base. Summer nights are capped with the **Lasershow Spectacular,** an outdoor light display set to music and projected onto the side of Stone Mountain—attendance is a rite of passage for new Atlantans. There's also 15 miles of nature trails, historical buildings featuring household items from the 18th and 19th century, two golf courses, a campground with a pool, an inn, a resort, several restaurants, and a Civil War museum. Crossroads, an entertainment complex with an 1870s-Southern-town theme, offers costumed interpreters and a movie theater. The SkyHike is a family-friendly ropes course at 12 feet, 24 feet, or 40 feet high. ⊠ *U.S. 78E, Stone Mountain Pkwy., Exit 8, 1000 Robert E. Lee Blvd., Stone Mountain* ☎ *770/498–5690* ⊕ *www.stonemountainpark.com* ⊠ *$15 per car, $38 Adventure Pass.*

13

WHERE TO EAT

This is a city known for its food; many a trip to Atlanta is planned around meals in its barbecue shacks, upscale diners, and chic urban eateries. Traditional Southern fare—including Cajun and creole, country-style and plantation cuisine, coastal and mountain dishes—thrives, as do Asian fusion, traditional Ethiopian, creative vegan, and mouth-scorching Indian food. Catch the flavor of the South at breakfast and lunch in diners and other modest establishments that serve only these meals.

Many restaurants will accept you just as you are; dress codes are extremely rare in this casual city, except in the chicest of spots. Although many restaurants accept reservations, some popular spots operate on a first-come, first-served basis on weekends. Waits at some hot dining locales can exceed an hour, especially if you arrive after 7 pm.

PRICES

Eating in Atlanta is surprisingly affordable, at least when compared with cities like New York and Chicago. Some of the pricier restaurants offer early-bird weeknight specials and prix-fixe menus. Ask when you call to make reservations.

Restaurant reviews have been shortened. For full information, visit Fodors.com. Use the coordinate (✥ 1:B2) at the end of each listing to locate a site on the corresponding map.

WHAT IT COSTS

	$	$$	$$$	$$$$
Restaurants	under $15	$15–$19	$20–$24	over $24

Prices in the reviews are the average cost of a main course at dinner or, if dinner is not served, at lunch.

DOWNTOWN

$$$$ AMERICAN 🍴 **Ted's Montana Grill.** The Ted in question is CNN founder Ted Turner, who has left a significant mark on this city. That's why Atlantans feel a sense of ownership for this chain specializing in bison meat. **Known for:** bison and beef burgers; cozy, clubhouse feel. [$] *Average main: $25* ✉ *133 Luckie St. NW, Downtown* ☎ *404/521–9796* 🌐 *www.tedsmontanagrill.com* ✥ *1:B1.*

SWEET AUBURN, THE OLD FOURTH WARD, AND EAST ATLANTA

$ AMERICAN 🍴 **Argosy.** Dark wood and a welcoming vibe make this cavernous bar with above-average food and a well-curated beer menu feel like a place you can sink into and stay awhile. The staff is knowledgeable and the right kind of attentive. **Known for:** massive beer list; wood-oven pizzas. [$] *Average main: $12* ✉ *470 Flat Shoals Ave., East Atlanta* ☎ *404/577–0407* 🌐 *www.argosy-east.com* ✥ *2:D4.*

$ AMERICAN 🍴 **The Earl.** Scrappy and lots of fun, this bar has a hearty menu of classic pub food. A favorite here is the "Greenie Meanie Chicken," a grilled chicken breast topped with roasted poblano peppers and salsa verde. **Known for:** classic bar food; indie-rock atmosphere thanks to live music. [$] *Average main: $9* ✉ *488 Flat Shoals Ave., East Atlanta* ☎ *404/522–3950* 🌐 *badearl.com* ✥ *2:D4.*

$$ MEXICAN Fodor'sChoice ★ 🍴 **Holy Taco.** Don't fill up on the tortilla chips at this Tex-Mex joint. They are so tasty that you might miss the rest of the inventive menu, which includes surprises like tacos with roasted beef tongue and bacon. **Known for:** inventive takes on Tex-Mex; organic margaritas with fresh ingredients; patio dining on sunny days. [$] *Average main: $15* ✉ *1314 Glenwood Ave., East Atlanta* ☎ *404/230–6177* 🌐 *www.holy-taco.com* ✥ *2:D4.*

$ DINER 🍴 **Home Grown.** Southern comfort food at its finest can be found at this bright, old-school diner. Cheese grits with a good cheddar bite, fluffy biscuits that can be stuffed with anything from sausage and gravy to perfectly fried chicken, and hunks of made-from-scratch cake are just a few of the reasons locals flock to Home Grown. **Known for:** huge Southern breakfasts, lunches, and brunches; in-house thrift store; long waits, especially in the morning. [$] *Average main: $10* ✉ *968 Memorial Dr. SE, Reynoldstown* ☎ *404/222–0455* 🌐 *www.homegrownga.com* 🕒 *No dinner* ✥ *2:D4.*

$ JAPANESE 🍴 **Miso Izakaya.** Chef-owner Guy Wong's *izakaya* (Japanese pub) has gathered a following for his well-executed menu of mostly small plates. Skip the sushi bar for a sampling of crispy duck buns and a noodle bowl with pork belly. **Known for:** refined Japanese small plates; long waits for food. [$] *Average main: $10* ✉ *619 Edgewood Ave. SE, Old Fourth Ward* ☎ *470/225–6252* 🕒 *Closed Sun. No lunch* ✥ *2:D3.*

$$$$ AMERICAN Fodor'sChoice ★ 🍴 **Staplehouse.** The genuine welcome is almost as unexpected as the food at this 2016 James Beard finalist for Best New Restaurant. The dishes from chef Ryan Smith are packed with pedigree, like sorrel foraged from north Georgia and served with supple and smooth sablefish. **Known for:** high-class food in unpretentious setting; unique global wine list; giving back (profits go to local restaurant workers facing unanticipated crisis). [$] *Average main: $25* ✉ *541 Edgewood Ave., Old Fourth Ward* ☎ *404/524–5005* 🌐 *www.staplehouse.com* 🕒 *Closed Mon. and Tues.* ✥ *2:D3.*

$ DINER 🍴 **Thumb's Up Diner.** You haven't really lived, or at least tested the limits of your heart's health, until you've tried "The Heap": a sizzling skillet full of eggs, buttery veggies, and potatoes. Add a fluffy biscuit on the side and this is one of the city's best breakfasts. **Known for:** fluffy and delicious biscuits; long weekend waits. [$] *Average main: $10* ✉ *573 Edgewood Ave. SE, Old Fourth Ward* ☎ *404/223–0690* 🌐 *www.thumbsupdiner.com* 💳 *No credit cards* 🕒 *No dinner* ✥ *2:D3.*

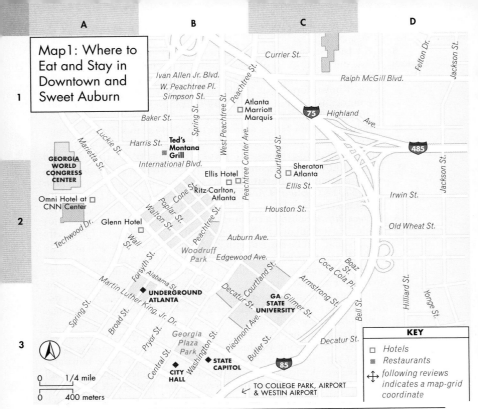

Map1: Where to Eat and Stay in Downtown and Sweet Auburn

1

Currier St.

Ivan Allen Jr. Blvd.
W. Peachtree Pl.
Simpson St.

Ralph McGill Blvd.

Baker St.

Atlanta
□ Marriott
Marquis

75

Highland Ave.

485

GEORGIA
WORLD
CONGRESS
CENTER

Harris St.

Ted's
■ Montana
Grill

International Blvd.

Ellis Hotel
□ □

Sheraton
□ Atlanta

Ellis St.

Omni Hotel at □
CNN Center

Ritz-Carlton,
Atlanta

Houston St.

2

Glenn Hotel
□

Old Wheat St.

Auburn Ave.

Woodruff
Park

Edgewood Ave.

Irwin St.

♦ UNDERGROUND
ATLANTA

GA
STATE
UNIVERSITY

3

Georgia
Plaza
Park

♦ STATE
CAPITOL

Decatur St.

♦
CITY
HALL

85

TO COLLEGE PARK, AIRPORT
& WESTIN AIRPORT

0   1/4 mile
0   400 meters

KEY

□   *Hotels*
■   *Restaurants*
⬦   *following reviews*
     indicates a map-grid
     coordinate

MIDTOWN

$$$$

AMERICAN

✕ **Bar Margot.** This swanky hotel lounge features a seasonal menu made up of small plates meant to be shared such as oysters and crab-fried rice, and more indulgent offerings like a 16-ounce rack of lamb. Don't miss the cocktails dreamed up by one of Atlanta's best mixologists, Paul Calvert. **Known for:** luxurious setting; well-crafted cocktails; upscale small plates. $ *Average main: $30* ⊠ *Four Seasons, 75 14th St., Midtown* ☎ *404/881–5913* ⊕ *www.barmargotatl.com* ⬦ *2:B2.*

$$$$

SOUTHERN

Fodor'sChoice

★

✕ **Empire State South.** Southern ingredients get the fine-dining treatment without the pretension at celebrity chef Hugh Acheson's Midtown favorite, now led by executive chef Josh Hopkins. Empire State South does it all: towering build-your-own breakfast biscuits, beautifully prepared Georgia trout with green beans and pimentos at dinner, and the perfect espresso. **Known for:** diverse wine list; Southern food with flair; extensive coffee bar and coffee menu. $ *Average main: $30* ⊠ *999 Peachtree St., Midtown* ☎ *404/541–1105* ⊕ *empirestatesouth. com* ⬦ *2:B2.*

$$

AMERICAN

✕ **The Lawrence.** The noncorporate upscale pub food at the Lawrence is a welcome addition to the Midtown neighborhood. Dinner options such as king salmon served with spaetzle hash and bacon; oyster po'boys dressed with house tartar sauce; and classic burgers with frites reflect the straightforward menu at this buzzing establishment. **Known for:** creative cocktail menu; one of the best no-fuss burgers in the city; great brunch with patio dining. $ *Average main: $18* ✉ *905 Juniper St. NE, Midtown* ☎ *404/961–7177* ⊘ *No lunch Sat., Sun., and Mon.* ✛ *2:B2.*

$$ ✕ **Mary Mac's Tea Room.** Local celebrities and ordinary folks line up for
SOUTHERN the country-fried steak and fried chicken here. In the Southern tradition, the servers will call you "honey" and pat your arm to assure you that everything's all right. **Known for:** legendary Southern home cooking; friendly waitstaff. $ *Average main: $15* ✉ *224 Ponce de Leon Ave., Midtown* ☎ *404/876–1800* ⊕ *www.marymacs.com* ✛ *2:C3.*

$$$ ✕ **One Midtown Kitchen.** An unassuming warehouse entrance down a side
AMERICAN street near Piedmont Park leads to this seductively lit, industrial-chic restaurant. The wood-roasted pizzas are outstanding, as is the wine list. **Known for:** lively bar scene; great city views from the back porch; constantly changing menu of American cuisine. $ *Average main: $20* ✉ *559 Dutch Valley Rd., Midtown* ☎ *404/892–4111* ⊕ *www.onemidtownkitchen.com* ⊘ *No lunch* ✛ *2:A3.*

$$$ ✕ **South City Kitchen.** The culinary traditions of South Carolina inspire
SOUTHERN the dishes served at this cheerful restaurant. This is the place in the city to try out Southern staples like fried green tomatoes, she-crab soup, and buttermilk fried chicken. **Known for:** creatively prepared catfish; fried green tomatoes with goat cheese; hip, artsy crowd. $ *Average main: $20* ✉ *1144 Crescent Ave., Midtown* ☎ *404/873–7358* ⊕ *www.southcitykitchen.com* ✛ *2:A2.*

$$$ ✕ **Tamarind Seed.** All that is good about Thai flavors—refreshing lime,
THAI spicy basil, hot peppers, cooling coconut, and smoky fish sauces—comes through at this standout known for excellent service. Favorite dishes include chicken with green curry and sea bass with three-flavor sauce. **Known for:** classic Thai flavors; sophisticated setting. $ *Average main: $20* ✉ *1197 Peachtree St. NE, Midtown* ☎ *404/873–4888* ⊕ *www.tamarindseed.com* ⊘ *No lunch Sat.* ✛ *2:A2.*

WESTSIDE

$ ✕ **Amelie's French Bakery.** Georgia Tech students and professionals from
BAKERY nearby downtown flock to this eclectic space for its two counters brimming with an assortment of authentic French pastries. If you don't have a sweet tooth, you can also try the daily changing quiches and soups or recharge with a perfect latte. **Known for:** fresh-baked pastries that seem straight from Paris; unique, welcoming atmosphere. $ *Average main: $8* ✉ *840 Marietta St., Midtown* ☎ *404/921–0276* ⊕ *www.ameliesfrenchbakery.com* ✛ *2:B1.*

$$$ ✕ **Antico Pizza Napoletana.** Antico offers a big slice of cheesy, saucy,
PIZZA chewy, Naples-style heaven. The communal tables, as well as the Ital-
Fodor's Choice ian opera on the stereo, give the place a convivial vibe. **Known for:**
★ authentic Naples-style pizza; communal tables. $ *Average main: $20* ✉ *1093 Hemphill Ave., Midtown* ☎ *404/724–2333* ⊕ *littleitalia.com* ⊘ *Closed Sun.* ✛ *2:B1.*

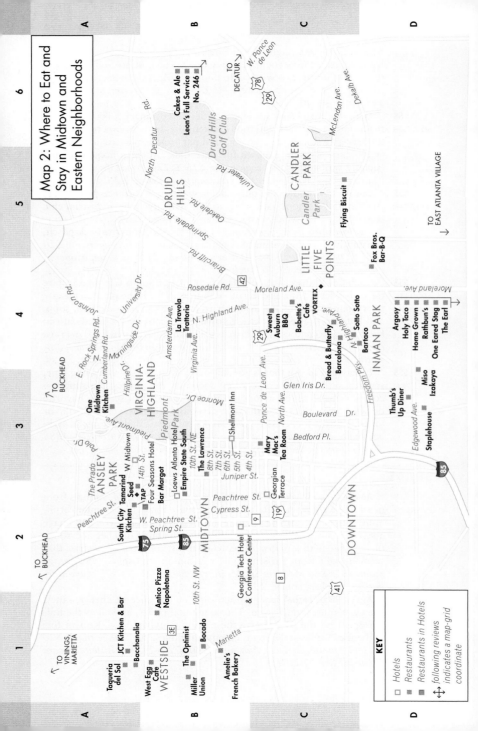

$$$$
AMERICAN
Fodor's Choice
★

✕ **Bacchanalia.** Often called the city's best restaurant, Bacchanalia focuses on locally grown organic produce and seasonal ingredients. The current Westside location, a renovated warehouse with 20-foot ceilings, is decorated in deep, inviting tones. **Known for:** splurge-worthy fine dining; farm-to-table ingredients; excellent wine pairings. $\boxed{S}$ *Average main: $85 ✉ 1460 Ellsworth Industrial Blvd. NW, West End ☎ 404/365–0410* ⊕ *www.starprovisions.com* ☯ *Closed Sun. No lunch.* ✛ *2:A1.*

$$$
MODERN
AMERICAN

✕ **Bocado.** It's rare to see the dining room of this classy Westside staple empty. Local professionals out for casual business lunches dominate the place by day, while at dinnertime friends gather around the bar for cocktails. **Known for:** one of the city's best burgers (with housemade pickles and garlic fries); cozy tables in a fun setting. $\boxed{S}$ *Average main: $20 ✉ 887 Howell Mill Rd., Suite 2, Midtown ☎ 404/815–1399* ⊕ *www.bocadoatlanta.com* ☯ *No lunch weekends. Closed Sun.* ✛ *2:B1.*

$$$$
SOUTHERN

✕ **JCT Kitchen & Bar.** This comfortable, airy restaurant—with pale wood, white, and silver accents—is part of the now-bustling Westside Provisions District. JCT, a "farmstead bistro" with Southern flair, is a great place for a business-casual lunch or a dinner date. The deviled eggs are to die for, as are the perfectly crisp truffle-Parmesan fries. **Known for:** deviled eggs and truffle Parm fries; fancy yet comfortable vibe; outdoor patio with awesome city views. $\boxed{S}$ *Average main: $25 ✉ 1198 Howell Mill Rd., Suite 18, Midtown ☎ 404/355–2252* ⊕ *www.jctkitchen.com* ☯ *No lunch Sun.* ✛ *2:A1.*

$$$$
AMERICAN

✕ **Miller Union.** The Southern-inflected menu here emphasizes locally sourced food. A highlight is the farm egg baked in celery cream with rustic bread; it's one of the best dishes in town. **Known for:** Southern classics, all with local ingredients; sustainable, farm-friendly ethos. $\boxed{S}$ *Average main: $26 ✉ 999 Brady Ave. NW, Midtown ☎ 678/733–8550* ⊕ *www.millerunion.com* ☯ *Closed Sun. No lunch Mon.* ✛ *2:B1.*

$$$
SEAFOOD

✕ **The Optimist.** For top-notch seafood, head to this restaurant in a dazzlingly refurbished warehouse space. You can slurp raw oysters on the half shell from the oyster bar or dive into the seafood gumbo, which has dark, complex gravy and is full of meaty hunks of crab. **Known for:** upscale seafood dishes; cool industrial space; noisy crowds. $\boxed{S}$ *Average main: $23 ✉ 914 Howell Mill Rd., Midtown ☎ 404/477–6260* ⊕ *www. theoptimistrestaurant.com* ☯ *No lunch weekends* ✛ *2:B1.*

$
MEXICAN

✕ **Taquería del Sol.** Don't let the long lines outside this counter-service eatery discourage you. They move quickly, and once you get in you'll be rewarded with a full bar, a wide selection of tacos and enchiladas, and unusual sides like spicy collard greens and jalapeño coleslaw. **Known for:** long lines and cutthroat table-grabbing; fresh salsa and guacamole. $\boxed{S}$ *Average main: $10 ✉ 1200-B Howell Mill Rd., Midtown ☎ 404/352–5811* ⊕ *www.taqueriadelsol.com* ☯ *Closed Sun. No dinner Mon.* ✛ *2:A1.*

$
AMERICAN
Fodor's Choice
★

✕ **West Egg Cafe.** A great place to come for one of the city's best breakfasts, especially if you're staying in Midtown. West Egg serves breakfast all day—locals swear by the blue-plate special and the old-fashioned oatmeal. **Known for:** excellent coffee; huge breakfasts served all day; big crowds. $\boxed{S}$ *Average main: $11 ✉ 1100 Howell Mill Rd., Midtown ☎ 404/872–3973* ⊕ *www.westeggcafe.com* ✛ *2:B1.*

13

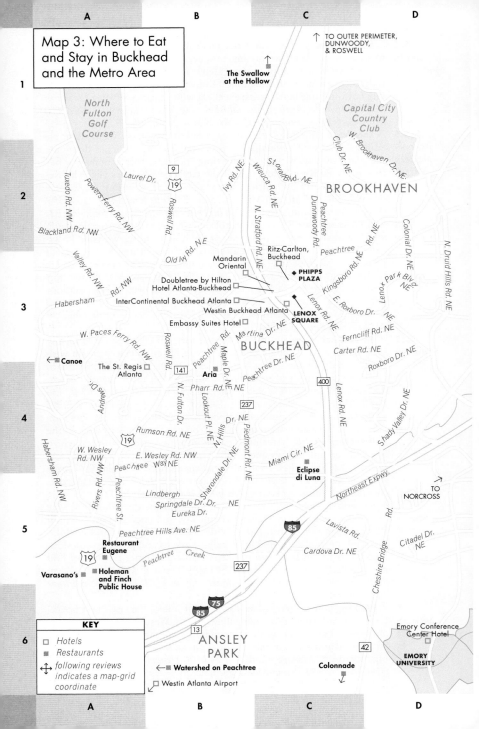

BUCKHEAD

$$$$
AMERICAN

✕ **Aria.** Chef Gerry Klaskala's talent is best captured by his love of rustic and hearty "slow foods"—braises, stews, roasts, and chops cooked over a roll-top French grill. Signature dishes include a lobster cocktail and Zinfandel-braised beef short rib. **Known for:** perfect desserts from renowned pastry chef; slow-cooked classics. Ⓢ *Average main: $30* ✉ *490 E. Paces Ferry Rd., Buckhead* ☎ *404/233–7673* ⊕ *www.aria-atl. com* ⊗ *Closed Sun. No lunch* ✛ *3:B4.*

$$$$
AMERICAN

✕ **Canoe.** This popular spot on the bank of the Chattahoochee River has built a reputation based on such dishes as slow-roasted rabbit with wild mushroom ravioli and Swiss chard. Sunday brunch—with smoked-salmon eggs Benedict, house-made English muffins with citrus hollandaise, and other offerings—is superb. **Known for:** relaxing views of the river; excellent brunch; hard-to-find location. Ⓢ *Average main: $25* ✉ *4199 Paces Ferry Rd. SE, Buckhead* ☎ *770/432–2663* ⊕ *www. canoeatl.com* ⊗ *No lunch weekends* ✛ *3:A3.*

$$
SOUTHERN

✕ **Colonnade.** For traditional Southern food—think fried chicken, ham steak, and turkey with dressing—insiders head to Colonnade, a local institution since 1927 and a magnet for gay men and the elderly. The interior, with patterned carpeting and red banquettes, is a classic version of a 1950s restaurant. **Known for:** vintage atmosphere; huge helpings of traditional Southern cuisine. Ⓢ *Average main: $15* ✉ *1879 Cheshire Bridge Rd., Buckhead* ☎ *404/874–5642* ⊕ *www.colonnadeatlanta.com* ▭ *No credit cards* ⊗ *No lunch weekdays* ✛ *3:C6.*

$$
MEDITERRANEAN

✕ **Eclipse di Luna.** Twentysomethings flock to this bustling place on weekends. The lunch menu includes sandwiches and salads; evening fare consists of tapas such as *patatas bravas con romesco* (potatoes with olive oil and a spicy sauce). **Known for:** traditional tapas menu; danceworthy live Latin music; authentic seafood paella. Ⓢ *Average main: $15* ✉ *764 Miami Circle, Buckhead* ☎ *404/846–0449* ⊕ *www.eclipsediluna. com* ⊗ *No lunch Sun. or Mon.* ✛ *3:C4.*

$$
MODERN
AMERICAN
Fodor's Choice
★

✕ **Holeman and Finch Public House.** Holeman and Finch helped revitalize Atlanta's drink scene with its custom tinctures (alcoholic herbs) and classic cocktails. It also unleashed a local appetite for house-made charcuterie (the city's best might be right here), and had a big hand in the burger craze that swept the city a few years back. **Known for:** limited-time-only cheeseburgers; handcrafted cocktails. Ⓢ *Average main: $15* ✉ *2277 Peachtree Rd., Suite B, Buckhead* ☎ *404/948–1175* ⊕ *www. holeman-finch.com* ⊗ *No lunch weekdays* ✛ *3:A5.*

$$$$
MODERN
AMERICAN

✕ **Restaurant Eugene.** Linton Hopkins (a former James Beard Award winner for best chef in the Southeast) is behind this quiet and sophisticated homage to local ingredients. The "vegetable tasting" is one of the menu's best dishes (and the city's best vegetable plate). **Known for:** impressive vegetable plate; award-winning locally sourced dishes; Southern meats like sweetbreads and pork belly. Ⓢ *Average main: $40* ✉ *2277 Peachtree Rd. NE, Buckhead* ☎ *404/355–0321* ⊕ *www.restauranteugene.com* ✛ *3:A5.*

$$
ITALIAN

✕ **Varasano's.** Software engineer Jeff Varasano was 14 when he set the country's Rubik's Cube record, and he's since changed gears to accomplish the feat of building the perfect pizza. The thin, lightly charred pies

13

Centennial Olympic Park offers great views at night, thanks to the lit-up Ferris wheel and many skyscrapers.

are created by closely following Varasano's intense instructions, including the use of an 800°F oven. **Known for:** one of the city's best pizzas; quirky owner with an interesting backstory; Italian doughnuts for dessert. [$] *Average main: $16* ✉ *2171 Peachtree Rd. NE, Buckhead* ☎ *404/352–8216* 🌐 *www.varasanos.com* ⏲ *No lunch weekdays* ✥ *3:A5.*

$$$$ SOUTHERN 🍴 **Watershed on Peachtree.** Indigo Girl Emily Saliers and three of her friends originally launched this casual restaurant in Decatur, and it eventually became an Atlanta classic renowned for its fried chicken. Chef Zeb Stevenson has maintained the farm-to-table theme and a menu full of updated Southern comfort food in the current Buckhead location. **Known for:** once-weekly fried chicken platter; trendy Southern comfort food; wonderful Sunday brunch. [$] *Average main: $25* ✉ *1820 Peachtree Rd. NW, Buckhead* ☎ *404/809–3561* 🌐 *www.watershed-restaurant.com* ⏲ *No dinner Sun. Closed Mon.* ✥ *3:B6.*

VIRGINIA-HIGHLAND AND THE EMORY AREA

$$$$ ITALIAN 🍴 **La Tavola Trattoria.** This place serves classic Italian dishes in a beautiful setting that still recalls old-school neighborhood dining. Count on regulars like bruschetta and spaghetti with meatballs to be elevated beyond basic but without being too fancy. **Known for:** authentic Italian menu; cozy, romantic atmosphere. [$] *Average main: $25* ✉ *992 Virginia Ave., Virginia-Highland* ☎ *404/873–5430* 🌐 *www.latavolatrattoria.com* ✥ *2:B4.*

$$ BARBECUE 🍴 **Sweet Auburn BBQ.** One of several success stories to come from the Sweet Auburn Curb Market, this offshoot of the market makes classic Southern barbecue available in a part of town where it's lacking.

The meats are slow-smoked, and the sides are delectable. **Known for:** slow-smoked barbecue; laid-back atmosphere; unique offerings like pimento wontons. [$] *Average main: $15* ✉ *656 N. Highland Ave., Virginia-Highland* ☎ *678/515–3550* 🌐 *sweetauburnbbq.com* ✣ *2:C4.*

LITTLE FIVE POINTS AND INMAN PARK

$$$$ EUROPEAN 🍴 **Babette's Cafe.** Sunny yellow walls and back-porch seating add to the homey charm of this renovated bungalow. The restaurant, which describes its cuisine as rustic European, offers such seasonal dishes as New England sole with grilled fennel, and beef tenderloin with Gorgonzola sauce. **Known for:** Sunday brunch popular with locals; dining area full of Southern charm. [$] *Average main: $25* ✉ *573 N. Highland Ave., Inman Park* ☎ *404/523–9121* 🌐 *www.babettescafe.com* 🕑 *Closed Mon. No lunch* ✣ *2:C4.*

$$ TAPAS 🍴 **Barcelona.** The narrow wraparound patio is the draw at this buzzing Spanish-inspired restaurant and wine bar. The must-try paella and weekly wine specials help to keep patrons happy. **Known for:** crowded but must-try patio; low-key but tasty tapas and other Spanish staples; affordable wine list. [$] *Average main: $18* ✉ *240 N. Highland Ave., Inman Park* ☎ *404/589–1010* 🌐 *www.barcelonawinebar.com/atlanta.htm* ✣ *2:C4.*

$ MEXICAN 🍴 **Bartaco.** Take an order card, grab a pencil, and decide what you want in your tacos; Bartaco offers everything from falafel and fish to cauliflower and chorizo. You'll want at least two, even though it's easy to fill up on the unforgettable guacamole. **Known for:** long taco list with unique fillings; breezy patio; delicious and simple margaritas. [$] *Average main: $10* ✉ *299 N. Highland Ave., Inman Park* ☎ *470/400–8226* 🌐 *www.bartaco.com/location/atlanta-inman* ✣ *2:C4.*

$ FRENCH 🍴 **Bread & Butterfly.** Billy Allin, the chef-owner of Cakes & Ale, also helms this bistro that makes you feel like you're hanging on the sidewalks of Paris. The patio is absolutely delightful when the weather is warm, and the pastries, coffee, and wine are just as satisfying. **Known for:** Parisian-style setting; great pastries and full breakfasts; wine-friendly happy hour. [$] *Average main: $10* ✉ *290 Elizabeth St., Inman Park* ☎ *678/515–4536* 🌐 *www.bread-and-butterfly.com* 🕑 *Closed Mon.* ✣ *2:C4.*

$ SOUTHERN 🍴 **Flying Biscuit.** There's a long wait on weekends at this spot, which is famous for its biscuits served with cranberry-apple butter. Dinners may include roasted chicken or turkey meat loaf with pudge (mashed potatoes). **Known for:** biscuits with cranberry-apple butter (also available to go); long waits on weekends. [$] *Average main: $10* ✉ *1655 McLendon Ave., Candler Park* ☎ *404/687–8888* 🌐 *www.flyingbiscuit.com* ✣ *2:C5.*

$$ BARBECUE 🍴 **Fox Bros. Bar-B-Q.** Here's what pays the bills here: brisket, pulled pork, fried pickles, and an artery-cloggin' take on tater tots, served smothered in Brunswick stew and melted cheese. Try to get a seat on the patio, a great place to soak up sun and sip a cold beer. **Known for:** smoked brisket and pulled pork; buzzing patio; fatty but delectable tater tots. [$] *Average main: $15* ✉ *1238 DeKalb Ave., Candler Park* ☎ *404/577–4030* 🌐 *www.foxbrosbbq.com* ✣ *2:D4.*

$$$$ MODERN AMERICAN 🍴 **One Eared Stag.** The adventurous menu at this upscale bistro is changed daily to accommodate the freshest and most interesting ingredients. Chef Robert Phalen loves to play with expectations and flavor combinations, offerings dishes like clams with sofrito and chickpeas or duck with honey and bacon. **Known for:** unexpected but on-point flavor combinations; weekend brunch; communal tables. [$] *Average main: $30* ✉ *1029 Edgewood Ave. NE, Inman Park* ☎ *404/525–4479* 🌐 *www.oneearedstag.com* ⊕ *2:D4.*

$$$$ AMERICAN 🍴 **Rathbun's.** This hot spot is helmed by local super-chef Kevin Rathbun, who once bested Bobby Flay on *Iron Chef*. The space's high ceilings, white tablecloths, exposed brick, and expensive dishes can seem too high-class for some, but Rathbun's maintains a coziness with its fine cuisine. Go for a signature steak or stick to the small-plates menu for a more complete tour of the kitchen. **Known for:** high-quality steaks; fancy small plates; some of the city's best fine dining. [$] *Average main: $30* ✉ *112 Krog St. NE, Suite R, Inman Park* ☎ *404/524–8280* 🌐 *www.rathbunsrestaurant.com* ⏲ *Closed Sun. No lunch* ⊕ *2:D4.*

$$$$ ITALIAN 🍴 **Sotto Sotto.** This hot spot has an adventurous take on Italian cuisine. The former commercial space hops with young, hip patrons dining on seafood risotto, spaghetti with sun-dried mullet roe, and utterly perfect *panna cotta* (custard). **Known for:** inventive Italian dishes; young and hip atmosphere perfect for date night. [$] *Average main: $25* ✉ *313 N. Highland Ave., Inman Park* ☎ *404/523–6678* 🌐 *www.urestaurants.net* ⏲ *No lunch* ⊕ *2:C4.*

DECATUR

$$$$ SOUTHERN Fodor's Choice ★ 🍴 **Cakes & Ale.** Fresh, seasonal veggies frequently take center stage at this crisp, upscale farm-to-table restaurant, and they often come from chef-owner Billy Allin's own garden. There's a large patio with plenty of seating and a view of the sleepy town square for those who like to dine outdoors. **Known for:** farm-to-table dishes like the classic roast chicken; lunch and baked goods at namesake café next door; great outdoor dining. [$] *Average main: $25* ✉ *155 Sycamore St., Decatur* ☎ *404/377–7994* 🌐 *cakesandalerestaurant.com* ⏲ *Closed Sun. and Mon. No lunch* ⊕ *2:B6.*

$$$ MODERN AMERICAN 🍴 **Leon's Full Service.** In a neighborhood flush with craft beer options, Leon's introduced an inventive specialty cocktail menu (as well as its own long list of craft beers). The food menu is full of fun snacks to share while drinking, including fries served with an array of sauces. **Known for:** creative cocktails and craft beers; popular patio with bocce court; standard bar food perfect for sharing. [$] *Average main: $20* ✉ *131 E. Ponce de Leon Ave., Decatur* ☎ *404/687–0500* 🌐 *www.leonsfullservice.com* ⏲ *No lunch Mon.* ⊕ *2:B6.*

$$$$ ITALIAN 🍴 **No. 246.** It's fun to come sit at the oversized bar and sample any number of the smaller plates on this happening Italian eatery's menu. The pastas are delicate and delicious, and the pizzas are thin, charred, and chewy. **Known for:** classic margherita pizza; tasty meatballs, served with a plate of fresh red sauce and basil. [$] *Average main: $25* ✉ *129 E. Ponce de Leon Ave., Decatur* ☎ *678/399–8246* 🌐 *www.no246.com* ⊕ *2:B6.*

METRO ATLANTA

$$ BARBECUE

🍴 **The Swallow at the Hollow.** Bring your biggest appetite when visiting this legendary barbecue restaurant and country-music venue, where everything is homemade, from the sausages to the pickles. Belly up to the long picnic tables for some of the region's best ribs, smoked meats, and cabin bread. **Known for:** down-home barbecue and house-made pickles; live country music; big crowds and long waits. [$] *Average main: $15* ✉ *1072 Green St., Roswell* ☎ *678/352–1975* 🌐 *swallowatthehollow.com* ⏲ *Closed Mon. and Tues.* ✣ *3:C1.*

WHERE TO STAY

One of America's most popular convention destinations, Atlanta offers plenty of variety in terms of lodgings. More than 90,000 rooms are in metro Atlanta, with nearly 12,000 Downtown, close to the Georgia World Congress Center, and Philips Arena. Other clusters are in Buckhead, in the north Interstate 285 perimeter, and around Hartsfield-Jackson Atlanta International Airport.

PRICES

Atlanta lodging facilities basically have two seasons: summer and convention (conventions are generally held year-round, though there are fewer in summer).

Hotel reviews have been shortened. For full information, visit Fodors.com. Use the coordinate (✣ 1:B2) at the end of each listing to locate a site on the corresponding map.

WHAT IT COSTS

	$	$$	$$$	$$$$
Hotels	under $150	$150–$200	$201–$250	over $250

Prices in the reviews are the lowest cost of a standard double room in high season.

DOWNTOWN

$ HOTEL

🏨 **Atlanta Marriott Marquis.** Immense and coolly contemporary, the building seems to go up forever as you stand under the lobby's huge fabric sculpture, which hangs from the skylighted roof 47 stories above. **Pros:** great views; convenient to public transportation. **Cons:** lobby noise can carry to the lower floors; daily parking starts at $35 a day. [$] *Rooms from: $120* ✉ *265 Peachtree Center Ave., Downtown* ☎ *404/521–0000, 888/855–5701* 🌐 *www.marriott.com* 🛏 *1,663 rooms* 🍴 *Breakfast* ✣ *1:B1.*

$$$ HOTEL Fodor's Choice ★

🏨 **Ellis Hotel.** A chic lobby, handpicked modern furnishings, and thoughtful in-room touches are the hallmark of this boutique hotel that provides Southern hospitality in a restored 1913 historic landmark. **Pros:** top-of-the line 24-hour fitness center; farm-to-table dining options; close to MARTA stop. **Cons:** some street noise in rooms; no free breakfast; more expensive than other Downtown hotels. [$] *Rooms from: $239* ✉ *176*

Peachtree St. NE, Downtown ☎ *404/602–0563* 🌐 *www.ellishotel.com* 🛏 *127 rooms* 🍴 *No meals* ✢ *1:B2.*

$ HOTEL 🏨 **Glenn Hotel.** This boutique hotel is a mix of New York sophistication and Miami sex appeal. **Pros:** 24-hour business center; free Wi-Fi; rooftop bar with great city views. **Cons:** parking is $28 per night; lighting might be a bit dim for some guests; small rooms. [$] *Rooms from: $140* ✉ *110 Marietta St. NW, Downtown* ☎ *404/521–2250, 888/717–8851* 🌐 *www.glennhotel.com* 🛏 *119 rooms* 🍴 *Breakfast; No meals* ✢ *1:B2.*

$$ HOTEL 🏨 **Omni Hotel at CNN Center.** An ultramodern marble lobby overlooks Centennial Olympic Park through floor-to-ceiling windows in this sleek two-tower hotel next to CNN's headquarters. **Pros:** convenient location for Downtown tourists; near public transportation; great view of the park from public areas. **Cons:** panhandlers often outside; heavy traffic during rush hour and Philips Arena events; $30 per day for parking. [$] *Rooms from: $170* ✉ *100 CNN Center, Downtown* ☎ *404/659–0000, 800/444–6664* 🌐 *www.omnihotels.com* 🛏 *1,059 rooms* 🍴 *No meals* ✢ *1:A2.*

$$$ HOTEL 🏨 **Ritz-Carlton, Atlanta.** For a luxury experience with useful business amenities, the Ritz can't be beat. **Pros:** top-notch restaurant; ideal for doing business Downtown; impeccable service. **Cons:** the standard rooms can feel small and dated compared to newer options; very expensive; luxury decor not for everyone. [$] *Rooms from: $230* ✉ *181 Peachtree St., Downtown* ☎ *404/659–0400, 800/627–7468* 🌐 *www.ritzcarlton.com/en/hotels/georgia/atlanta* 🛏 *444 rooms* 🍴 *No meals* ✢ *1:B2.*

$$ HOTEL FAMILY 🏨 **Sheraton Atlanta.** In this convention-, family-, and pet-friendly hotel, there's ample meeting and exhibit space, a pool under a retractable roof, and fine dining with delicious takes on Southern fare. **Pros:** convenient location; kid-friendly vibe; large, nicely furnished rooms. **Cons:** can be difficult to navigate towers; not everyone enjoys the family-friendly atmosphere; no free breakfast. [$] *Rooms from: $200* ✉ *165 Courtland St. NE, Downtown* ☎ *404/659–6500* 🌐 *www.sheratonatlantahotel.com* 🛏 *763 rooms* 🍴 *No meals* ✢ *1:C2.*

MIDTOWN

$$$ HOTEL Fodor's Choice ★ 🏨 **Four Seasons Hotel.** Amenities abound throughout this luxury hotel, Atlanta's only five-star property; these touches include marble bathrooms with extra-large soaking tubs, comfy mattresses, and brass chandeliers. **Pros:** great dining options; top-notch service; indoor saline pool. **Cons:** heavily trafficked area during rush hour; small bathrooms; fee for parking. [$] *Rooms from: $250* ✉ *75 14th St. NE, Midtown* ☎ *404/881–9898* 🌐 *www.fourseasons.com* 🛏 *244 rooms* 🍴 *No meals* ✢ *2:B2.*

$$ HOTEL 🏨 **Georgia Tech Hotel & Conference Center.** In the heart of Midtown, this gleaming building gets kudos for its comfortable, contemporary decor, recently renovated rooms, and a staff that understands the needs of business travelers and meeting organizers. **Pros:** pleasant views of the skyline; walking distance to eateries and attractions. **Cons:** short on charm; heavy student traffic when school's in session. [$] *Rooms from: $189* ✉ *800 Spring St. NW, Midtown* ☎ *404/347–9440* 🌐 *www.gatechhotel.com* 🛏 *252 rooms* 🍴 *No meals* ✢ *2:C2.*

$$$ HOTEL 🏨 **Georgian Terrace.** Enrico Caruso and other stars of the Metropolitan Opera once stayed in this fine 1911 hotel that's across the street from the Fox Theatre. **Pros:** the front terrace is a great place for people-watching; proximity to the Fox makes upscale in-house restaurant Livingston a convenient pretheater choice; rooftop pool and penthouse-level fitness room offer incredible city views. **Cons:** smoking is allowed in some rooms and the smoke can drift; postshow and rush-hour traffic is tough to navigate. [$] *Rooms from: $210* ✉ *659 Peachtree St. NE, Midtown* ☎ *404/897–1991, 800/651–2316* 🌐 *www.thegeorgianterrace.com* 🛏 *326 rooms* 🍴 *No meals* ✥ *2:C2.*

$$$ HOTEL Fodor'sChoice ★ 🏨 **Loews Atlanta Hotel.** Georgia's booming film industry brings plenty of celebs to Atlanta, and many of them stay in this sleek glass tower in the heart of bustling Midtown. **Pros:** huge and modern gym and spa; bright, modern rooms; many eateries and bars within walking distance. **Cons:** no pool; large fees for parking. [$] *Rooms from: $250* ✉ *1065 Peachtree St. NE, Midtown* ☎ *404/745–5000* 🌐 *www.loewshotels.com/atlanta* 🛏 *414 rooms* 🍴 *No meals* ✥ *2:B2.*

$$ HOTEL 🏨 **W Midtown.** A trip to this trendy hotel in Midtown feels less like Atlanta and more like New York City, with slick details and more black-suited security guards and velvet ropes than seem necessary. **Pros:** beautiful people; gorgeous views; Manhattan-style chic. **Cons:** self-consciously hip theme can be a bit much; customer service can be spotty; daily fee for Wi-Fi. [$] *Rooms from: $160* ✉ *188 14th St., Midtown* ☎ *404/892–6000* 🌐 *www.watlantamidtown.com* 🛏 *466 rooms* 🍴 *No meals* ✥ *2:A3.*

BUCKHEAD

$$ HOTEL 🏨 **DoubleTree by Hilton Hotel Atlanta - Buckhead.** If the complimentary fresh-baked chocolate-chip cookies that welcome you don't convince you to stay here, maybe the excellent location, spacious rooms, and reasonable rates will. **Pros:** a warm welcome; comfortable beds; next to MARTA. **Cons:** small bar; valet-only parking; no pool. [$] *Rooms from: $180* ✉ *3342 Peachtree Rd. NE, Buckhead* ☎ *404/231–1234* 🌐 *doubletree3.hilton.com* 🛏 *230 rooms* 🍴 *No meals* ✥ *3:B3.*

$$$ HOTEL 🏨 **Embassy Suites Hotel.** Just blocks from the shopping meccas of Lenox Square and Phipps Plaza you'll find this modern suites-only high-rise. **Pros:** convenient to shopping; indoor and outdoor pools; complimentary drinks in the afternoon. **Cons:** Wi-Fi is not free; expensive parking; decor is a bit outdated. [$] *Rooms from: $230* ✉ *3285 Peachtree Rd. NE, Buckhead* ☎ *404/261–7733* 🌐 *embassysuites3.hilton.com* 🛏 *316 suites* 🍴 *Breakfast* ✥ *3:B3.*

$$$ HOTEL 🏨 **InterContinental Buckhead Atlanta.** Marble bathrooms with separate soaking tubs and glass showers, 300-thread-count Egyptian-cotton linens, plush bathrobes and slippers, and twice-daily housekeeping are some of the highlights of the traditionally styled rooms in this hotel, the flagship for the Atlanta-based chain. **Pros:** 24-hour fitness center; convenient to shopping; good on-site restaurant and bar. **Cons:** small spa; complimentary Internet only with rewards program or special room rate; expensive parking. [$] *Rooms from: $215* ✉ *3315 Peachtree Rd. NE, Buckhead* ☎ *404/946–9000, 877/834–3613* 🌐 *www.intercontinentalatlanta.com* 🛏 *422 rooms* 🍴 *No meals* ✥ *3:B3.*

$$$$ ⬚ **Mandarin Oriental.** Sophisticated glamour with a touch of Zen charac-
HOTEL terizes this upscale 42-story Buckhead hotel. **Pros:** attentive staff; quiet
Fodor'sChoice atmosphere; high-end but not stuffy. **Cons:** not much within walking
★ distance besides Buckhead malls and other shopping; very expensive;
Wi-Fi costs extra. Ⓢ *Rooms from: $295* ✉ *3376 Peachtree Rd. NE,
Buckhead* ☎ *404/995–7500* ⊕ *www.mandarinoriental.com/atlanta*
⟿ *127 rooms* ⦾ *No meals* ✛ *3:C3.*

$$$$ ⬚ **Ritz-Carlton, Buckhead.** Decorated with 18th- and 19th-century
HOTEL antiques, this elegant hotel is a regular stopover for visiting celebrities.
Pros: elegant; convenient to shopping; occasional celeb sightings. **Cons:**
drab exterior doesn't seem very ritzy; one of the priciest hotels in the
area; fee for Wi-Fi. Ⓢ *Rooms from: $470* ✉ *3434 Peachtree Rd. NE,
Buckhead* ☎ *404/237–2700* ⊕ *www.ritzcarlton.com/buckhead* ⟿ *510
rooms* ⦾ *No meals* ✛ *3:C3.*

$$$$ ⬚ **The St. Regis Atlanta.** By far Atlanta's most prestigious and regal hotel,
HOTEL the St. Regis is adorned with impressive touches, including the etch-
Fodor'sChoice ing on the elevator doors and the crystals dangling from the hotel's
★ many chandeliers. **Pros:** 40,000-square-foot Pool Piazza with Jacuzzi
and waterfall; lots of spaces for eating, drinking, and relaxing; within
walking distance of high-end shops and galleries. **Cons:** can sometimes
feel overly formal; very expensive; extra fee for Wi-Fi. Ⓢ *Rooms from:
$475* ✉ *88 W. Paces Ferry Rd., Buckhead* ☎ *404/563–7900, 888/627–
7231* ⊕ *www.stregisatlanta.com* ⟿ *151 rooms* ⦾ *No meals* ✛ *3:B4.*

$$$$ ⬚ **Westin Buckhead Atlanta.** What draws guests here is the hotel's location
HOTEL and business-traveler focus. **Pros:** in-room service from the Palm, noted
for its steaks; plenty of restaurants nearby; large fitness center. **Cons:**
expensive for amenities offered; small pool; must pay extra for Wi-Fi.
Ⓢ *Rooms from: $280* ✉ *3391 Peachtree Rd., Buckhead* ☎ *404/365–
0065* ⊕ *www.westin.com/buckhead* ⟿ *365 rooms* ✛ *3:C3.*

VIRGINIA-HIGHLAND AND THE EMORY AREA

$$ ⬚ **Emory Conference Center Hotel.** Done in a modified Prairie Style, this
HOTEL hotel is surrounded by 26 acres of forest preserve near Emory Univer-
Fodor'sChoice sity and about 6 miles from Downtown Atlanta. **Pros:** indoor pool is
★ fun for kids; rooms on higher levels offer pleasant views of wooded
areas; eco-friendly ethos. **Cons:** some small bathrooms; large cam-
pus can make walk to hotel from parking area fairly long; far from
main Atlanta sights. Ⓢ *Rooms from: $190* ✉ *1615 Clifton Rd., Emory*
☎ *404/712–6000* ⊕ *www.emoryconferencecenter.com* ⟿ *325 rooms*
⦾ *No meals* ✛ *3:D6.*

METRO ATLANTA

$$ ⬚ **Westin Atlanta Airport.** The 500 guest rooms feature Westin's signature
HOTEL "heavenly bed" along with a flat-screen TV and Starbucks coffee. **Pros:**
incredibly convenient to the airport and major highways; affordable
room rates; indoor and outdoor pools. **Cons:** not near any restaurants
or attractions; typical airport hotel decor; no free breakfast. Ⓢ *Rooms
from: $150* ✉ *4736 Best Rd.* ☎ *404/762–7676* ⊕ *www.westinatlanta-
airport.com* ⟿ *500 rooms* ⦾ *No meals* ✛ *3:B6.*

NIGHTLIFE AND PERFORMING ARTS

NIGHTLIFE

Atlanta has long been known for having more bars than churches, and in the South that stands out. Atlanta's vibrant nightlife includes everything from cerebral cocktail lounges to dive bars, from country line dancing to high-energy dance clubs.

If you're looking for a gay or lesbian club, you'll find most of them in Midtown, although a few can be found in Buckhead and the suburbs. For up-to-the-minute information on the scene, pick up a free copy of the *GA Voice* (⊕ *www.thegavoice.com*) throughout the city.

SWEET AUBURN, THE OLD FOURTH WARD, AND EAST ATLANTA

BARS

Sister Louisa's Church of the Living Room & Ping Pong Emporium. Folk art meets gay pride meets sangria here. Church, as this popular dive bar is known, has nun mannequins in full habit dangling from the ceiling and choir robes are available for patrons should the spirit move them. There's also an outdoor patio and a spacious second floor with a Ping-Pong table. ⊠ *466 Edgewood Ave. SE, Old Fourth Ward* ☎ *404/522–8275* ⊕ *www.sisterlouisaschurch.com.*

Sound Table. Incredible food and some of the city's best drinks are served at the Sound Table, which turns into a dance club once the kitchen closes. ⊠ *483 Edgewood Ave., Old Fourth Ward* ☎ *404/835–2534* ⊕ *www.thesoundtable.com.*

GAY AND LESBIAN

The Cockpit. This laid-back, smoke-free gay bar has specials or events every night. ⊠ *465 Boulevard, Grant Park* ☎ *404/343–2450* ⊕ *www.thecockpit-atlanta.blogspot.com.*

Mary's. One of the best gay bars in Atlanta, the divey and fun Mary's is known for its "Mary-oke" karaoke night. ⊠ *1287 Glenwood Ave., East Atlanta* ☎ *404/624–4411.*

ROCK

529. A cavelike live music venue with great sound, a full bar, and a patio, 529 hosts local and national emerging indie bands. ⊠ *529 Flat Shoals Ave., East Atlanta* ☎ *404/228–6769* ⊕ *www.529atlanta.com.*

MIDTOWN

BARS

TAP. One of the best features at this pub is the patio—typically populated with after-work execs and trendy Midtowners—which sits out on busy Peachtree Street and provides ample opportunity for people-watching. TAP also serves bar food with an upscale edge, alongside a variety of specialty brews and wine. ⊠ *1180 Peachtree St., Midtown* ☎ *404/347–2220* ⊕ *www.tapat1180.com.*

13

COMEDY

Laughing Skull Lounge. These 73 seats in the back of the Vortex restaurant and bar are Atlanta's most popular destination for local and national touring comedians. Part-time Atlantan Margaret Cho heads here when she's in town to watch and perform. ⊠ *878 Peachtree St., Midtown* ☎ *404/369–1017* ⊕ *laughingskulllounge.com.*

DANCE

El Bar. Behind the El Ponce Mexican restaurant on Ponce de Leon Avenue, El Bar has a tightly packed dance room with live DJs, cold drinks, and a refreshingly unpretentious clientele. ⊠ *939 Ponce de Leon Ave., Midtown* ☎ *404/881–6040* ☉ *Closed Sun.–Wed.*

Opera. Head to this sleek dance club for a theaterlike main lounge, balcony VIP boxes, and banquettes with personal cocktail service. The outdoor area looks like it's straight out of South Beach, with private cabanas and bottle service. Parking in this area can be tricky—street parking often leads to booting or towing—so be prepared to pay garage fees or take a taxi. ⊠ *1150B Crescent Ave. NE, Midtown* ☎ *404/874–0428* ⊕ *www.operaatlanta.com.*

GAY AND LESBIAN

Blake's on the Park. Weekly drag shows, a diverse crowd, and plenty of people-watching all help keep this place near the southwest corner of Piedmont Park popular. ⊠ *227 10th St. NE, Midtown* ☎ *404/892–5786* ⊕ *www.blakesontheparkatlanta.com.*

Bulldogs. A fixture on the gay scene since 1978, Bulldogs is the place to hang out with friends or dance to hip-hop, house, or R&B. ⊠ *893 Peachtree St., Midtown* ☎ *404/872–3025.*

Burkhart's. Gay men come to this neighborhood hangout for pool, karaoke, and drag shows. ⊠ *1492 Piedmont Ave. NE, Midtown* ☎ *404/872–4403* ⊕ *www.burkharts.com.*

My Sister's Room. Billing itself as the city's "most diverse ladies' bar," this lesbian club brings the party with hip-hop, DJs, and karaoke. ⊠ *66 12th St. NE, Midtown* ☎ *678/705–4585* ⊕ *www.mysistersroom.com* ☉ *Closed Mon.–Tues.*

Swinging Richards. A gay male strip club, Swinging Richards draws a fun party crowd. Women are welcome, but bachelor and bachelorette parties are not. ⊠ *1400 Northside Dr. NW, Midtown* ☎ *404/352–0532* ⊕ *www.swingingrichards.com* ☉ *Closed Sun.*

Woofs. Atlanta's first and only gay sports bar has pool and darts as well as 25 TVs. A menu of bar food is also available—perfect for the big game. ⊠ *2425 Piedmont Rd. NE, Midtown* ☎ *404/869–9422* ⊕ *www.woofsatlanta.com.*

ROCK

Drunken Unicorn. Indie bands play in Drunken Unicorn's small performance space. Pull an all-nighter at the neighboring underground dance club MJQ. ⊠ *736 Ponce De Leon Ave. NE, Midtown* ☎ ⊕ *www.thedrunkenunicorn.net.*

Smith's Olde Bar. Smith's Olde Bar schedules different kinds of talent, both local and regional, in its acoustically fine performance space. Food is available in the downstairs restaurant. Covers vary depending on the act, but are usually $5 to $15. ✉ *1578 Piedmont Ave., Midtown* ☎ *404/875–1522* ⊕ *www.smithsoldebar.com.*

Terminal West. Impeccable sound, balcony views, courteous bartenders, and plentiful parking make this Westside venue a top spot to see indie, soul, and EDM shows. ✉ *King Plow Arts Center, 887 W. Marietta St. NW, Midtown* ☎ *404/876–5566* ⊕ *www.terminalwestatl.com.*

VIRGINIA-HIGHLAND AND THE EMORY AREA

BARS

Manuel's Tavern. This local landmark and favorite of left-leaning politicos and media gadflies owes its popularity to its spirit and friendly service. Look for photos of vintage Atlanta sports teams and both local and national politicians, including a younger Bill and Hillary Clinton visiting with the spot's namesake. A crowd gathers around the wide-screen TVs when the Atlanta Braves play. ✉ *602 N. Highland Ave., Virginia-Highland* ☎ *404/525–3447* ⊕ *www.manuelstavern.com.*

JAZZ AND BLUES

Blind Willie's. New Orleans and Chicago blues groups are the main thing here, although Cajun and zydeco are also on the calendar from time to time. The name honors Blind Willie McTell, a native of Thomson, Georgia; his original compositions include "Statesboro Blues," made popular by the Georgia-based Allman Brothers. ✉ *828 N. Highland Ave., Virginia-Highland* ☎ *404/873–2583* ⊕ *www.blindwilliesblues.com.*

LITTLE FIVE POINTS AND INMAN PARK

BARS

Euclid Avenue Yacht Club. If you're looking for a spot at which to become a "regular," here's a great candidate. Euclid Avenue Yacht Club is the kind of place where everybody knows your name. The cans of PBR and friendly staff make everyone feel welcome. ✉ *1136 Euclid Ave. NE, Little Five Points* ☎ *404/688–2582* ⊕ *www.theeayc.com.*

Porter Beer Bar. Try the salt-and-vinegar popcorn or other bar staples such as fries and mac-and-cheese, all with a suggested beer pairing at the Porter Beer Bar. ✉ *1156 Euclid Ave., Little Five Points* ☎ *404/223–0393* ⊕ *www.theporterbeerbar.com.*

Fodor's Choice ★ **Vortex.** Vortex prides itself on being impolite—a look at the "rules" will show you they take no guff—but really it's a friendly bar with great burgers. Ask for the off-menu fried zucchini. Just look for the huge skull, a landmark of Little Five Points, and you've found the door. The bar-restaurant's Midtown location fronts the popular Laughing Skull Comedy Club. ✉ *438 Moreland Ave., Little Five Points* ☎ *404/688–1828* ⊕ *thevortexatl.com.*

ROCK

Star Community Bar. Highly recommended for those who enjoy grunge and rockabilly, and the occasional disco or comedy night. Bands play almost nightly, with covers of $5 to $8, depending on the act. The bar used to be a bank—the Elvis shrine in the vault must be seen to be believed. ✉ *437 Moreland Ave., Little Five Points* ☎ *404/500–4942* ⊕ *www.starbaratlanta.com.*

DECATUR

BARS

Brick Store Pub. You can choose from hundreds of bottled and draft brews—including high-gravity beers—along with some very good burgers, salads, and sandwiches. Upstairs, the popular Belgian beer bar is cavelike and cramped but worth it for the selection. ✉ *125 E. Court Sq., Decatur* ☎ *404/687–0990* ⊕ *www.brickstorepub.com.*

ROCK

Eddie's Attic. Close to the Decatur MARTA station, this bar and restaurant is a good spot for catching local and some national rock, folk, and country-music acts. Cover charges typically range from $5 to $20. ✉ *515B N. McDonough St., Decatur* ☎ *404/377–4976* ⊕ *www.eddiesattic.com.*

METRO ATLANTA

COMEDY

Punchline. The city's oldest comedy club books major national acts. It's ages 21 and up only. ✉ *3652 Roswell Rd.* ☎ *404/252–5233* ⊕ *punchline.com.*

COUNTRY MUSIC

Electric Cowboy. The 44,000-square-foot Electric Cowboy is known for big crowds, bikini contests, and line dancing to country and more mainstream pop and hip-hop. ✉ *1750 N. Roberts Rd., Kennesaw* ☎ *770/420–1565* ⊕ *electriccowboy.com/kennesaw.*

GAY AND LESBIAN

Jungle Atlanta. Located off Atlanta's seedy Cheshire Bridge Road, this nightclub has a popular dance floor and drag stage. ✉ *2115 Faulkner Rd.* ☎ *404/844–8800* ⊕ *www.jungleatl.com.*

KARAOKE

Karaoke Melody. The private room karaoke here is perfect for those who like to hog the mic or prefer to perform in front of smaller crowds. The iPads hold a seemingly endless selection of tunes to sing late into the night. Press the button on the table and full bar service arrives at the door. ■ TIP→ Rooms fill up fast on the weekends, so it's best to reserve ahead of time. ✉ *5979 Buford Hwy., Suite A-11, Doraville* ☎ *770/986–8881* ⊕ *www.karaokemelody.com.*

PERFORMING ARTS

For the most complete schedule of cultural events, check the weekly Access Atlanta section of the *Atlanta Journal-Constitution* (⊕ *www.ajc.com*), the city's lively and free alternative weekly, *Creative Loafing* (⊕ *clatl.com*), or the entertainment monthly, *INsite* (⊕ *www.insiteatlanta.com*). The *Atlanta Daily World* (⊕ *www.atlantadailyworld.com*) and the *Atlanta Voice* (⊕ *www.theatlantavoice.com*), serving the African American community, are also published weekly.

AtlanTIX Ticket Services. Head to the Underground Atlanta mall for half-price same-day tickets for performances as well as half-price same-day and next-day tickets for cultural attractions. ✉ *Underground Atlanta, Visitors Center, 65 Upper Alabama St. SW, Downtown* ☎ *404/588–9890* ⊕ *www.atlantaperforms.com* ☉ *Closed Mon.*

Eventbrite. This ticketing service and app caters to nightclubs and niche events. ⊕ *www.eventbrite.com.*

Ticket Alternative. This website sells tickets to local festivals, events, plays, concerts, and more. ⊠ *Atlanta* ☎ *877/725–8849, 404/897–2388* ⊕ *www.ticketalternative.com.*

Ticketmaster. Ticketmaster sells tickets for the Fox Theatre, the Tabernacle, Philips Arena, and other major venues. ⊠ *Atlanta* ☎ *800/745–3000* ⊕ *www.ticketmaster.com.*

CONCERTS

Atlanta Symphony Orchestra (*ASO*). Under the musical direction of Robert Spano since 2001, the Atlanta Symphony Orchestra has 27 Grammy awards to its credit. It performs the fall–spring subscription series in the nearly 1,800-seat Symphony Hall at Woodruff Arts Center. In summer the orchestra regularly plays with big-name popular and country artists in the outdoor Chastain Park Amphitheatre. ⊠ *Woodruff Arts Center, Symphony Hall, 1280 Peachtree St., Midtown* ☎ *404/733–4900* ⊕ *www.atlantasymphony.org.*

Emory University. On its idyllic campus surrounded by picturesque houses, Emory University has five major venues where internationally renowned artists perform. ⊠ *201 Dowman Dr., Emory* ☎ *404/727–5050* ⊕ *www.emory.edu.*

Florence Kopleff Recital Hall. Georgia State University hosts concerts that are free and open to the public. The hall's entrance is on Gilmer Street, and there's parking in the lot at the corner of Edgewood and Peachtree Center Avenues. ⊠ *10 Peachtree Center Ave., at Gilmer St., Downtown* ☎ *404/413–5900* ⊕ *www.music.gsu.edu.*

DANCE

Atlanta Ballet. The Atlanta Ballet, founded in 1929, is the country's oldest continuously operating ballet company. It has been internationally recognized for its productions of classical and contemporary works. Artistic director Gennadi Nedvigin has aimed to elevate the technical skill of the group since taking the helm in 2016. Most performances, except for the annual *Nutcracker,* are held at the Cobb Energy Performing Arts Centre. ⊠ *Michael C. Carlos Dance Centre, 1695 Marietta Blvd. NW, Midtown* ☎ *404/873–5811* ⊕ *www.atlantaballet.com.*

gloATL. A contemporary dance company helmed by visionary choreographer Lauri Stallings and founded in 2009, gloATL has entranced Atlantans with its site-specific dance performances and collaborations with local artists, which have included Outkast's Big Boi and the Atlanta Ballet. ⊠ *The Goat Farm Arts Center, Goodson Yard, 1200 Foster St. NW, No. 17, Midtown* ☎ ⊕ *gloatl.org.*

OPERA

Atlanta Opera. Major roles at the Atlanta Opera are performed by national and international guest artists; many of the chorus and orchestra members come from the local community. ⊠ *Cobb Energy Performing Arts Centre, 2800 Cobb Galleria Pkwy.* ☎ *404/881–8885* ⊕ *www. atlantaopera.org.*

PERFORMANCE VENUES

Buckhead Theatre. This restored 1931 Spanish baroque theater has sloped floors that make it ideal for the comedy, rock, soul, and country shows hosted here. ⊠ *3110 Roswell Rd., Buckhead* ☎ *404/843–2825* ⊕ *www. thebuckheadtheatre.com.*

Chastain Park Amphitheatre. Home to Atlanta Symphony Orchestra's summer series and other pop concerts, this theater feels more like an outdoor nightclub than a typical performance venue. Pack a picnic, bring a blanket if you've snagged some seats on the lawn, and prepare to listen to your favorite performers over the clink of dishes and the chatter of dinner conversation. ⊠ *4469 Stella Dr. NW, Buckhead* ☎ *404/233–2227* ⊕ *www.classicchastain.com.*

Ferst Center for the Performing Arts. Georgia Institute of Technology's arts center hosts classical, jazz, dance, and theatrical performances. There's ample free parking on weekends. ⊠ *Georgia Tech, 349 Ferst Dr., Midtown* ☎ *404/894–9600* ⊕ *www.ferstcenter.org.*

Fox Theatre. This dramatic faux-Moorish theater is the principal venue for touring Broadway shows, national productions, concerts, and the Coca-Cola Summer Film Festival. ⊠ *660 Peachtree St., Midtown* ☎ *404/881–2100, 855/285–8499* ⊕ *www.foxtheatre.org.*

The Goat Farm Arts Center. A former complex of cotton-factory buildings from the 19th century has been transformed into a 12-acre group of studios and performance and rehearsal spaces for some of Atlanta's most exciting artists and performers. There's a nice on-site coffee shop called the Warhorse, and the Goat Farm also hosts festivals and concerts by local and national touring acts. ⊠ *1200 Foster St. NW, Midtown* ⊕ *www.facebook.com/TheGoatFarmArtsCenter.*

Infinite Energy Center. A 708-seat theater and a 13,000-seat arena as well as a 50,000-square-foot expo center are all here, 30 miles north of Downtown Atlanta. The venue hosts national touring acts and the Atlanta Gladiators hockey team, as well as conventions, sporting events, outlet sales, and jewelry shows. ⊠ *6400 Sugarloaf Pkwy., Duluth* ☎ *770/813–7500* ⊕ *www.infiniteenergycenter.com.*

Lakewood Amphitheater. Four miles south of Downtown Atlanta, this venue draws national popular music acts all summer. There's seating for up to 19,000 in reserved areas and on its sloped lawn. ⊠ *2002 Lakewood Ave. SE* ☎ *404/443–5090* ⊕ *www.thelakewoodamphitheater.com.*

Philips Arena. With a seating capacity of nearly 20,000, Philips Arena is the major venue Downtown. In addition to hosting the biggest musical acts, it's also the home of NBA Atlanta Hawks and WNBA Atlanta Dream. The Philips Arena MARTA station makes getting here a snap. ⊠ *1 Philips Dr., Downtown* ☎ *404/878–3000* ⊕ *www.philipsarena.com.*

Rialto Center for the Performing Arts. Developed by Georgia State University in a beautifully renovated and restructured former movie theater, the Rialto hosts film, theater, and dance, as well as musical performances by local and international performers. ⊠ *Georgia State University, 80 Forsyth St. NW, Downtown* ☎ *404/413–9849* ⊕ *rialto.gsu.edu.*

Spivey Hall. Internationally renowned musicians perform everything from chamber music to jazz at this gleaming, modern, acoustically magnificent performance center 15 miles south of Atlanta. The hall is considered one of the country's finest concert venues. ⊠ *Clayton State University, Simpson Dr., Morrow* ☎ *678/466–4200* ⊕ *www. spiveyhall.org.*

Tabernacle. This former church hosts top acts of all genres in a midsize setting. Seating is limited; the main floor is standing-room only. ⊠ *152 Luckie St., Downtown* ☎ *404/659–9022* ⊕ *www.tabernacleatl.com.*

Variety Playhouse. This 1,000-capacity venue was once a movie theater, and is now one of the cultural anchors of the hip Little Five Points neighborhood. Music lovers come for rock, bluegrass and country, blues, reggae, folk, jazz, and pop. ⊠ *1099 Euclid Ave. NE, Little Five Points* ☎ *404/524–7354* ⊕ *www.variety-playhouse.com.*

Verizon Wireless Amphitheatre at Encore Park. The 12,000-capacity Verizon Wireless Amphitheatre is situated on 45 acres 22 miles north of Downtown Atlanta. The venue hosts a variety of pop, country, and classical acts, including the Atlanta Symphony Orchestra. ⊠ *2200 Encore Pkwy., Alpharetta* ☎ *404/733–5010* ⊕ *www.vzwamp.com.*

Woodruff Arts Center. The Alliance Theatre, the Atlanta Symphony Orchestra, the High Museum of Art, and their combined arts education programs are all housed in this complex. ⊠ *1280 Peachtree St. NE, Midtown* ☎ *404/733–4200* ⊕ *www.woodruffcenter.org.*

THEATER

Actor's Express. This acclaimed theater group presents an eclectic selection of classic and cutting-edge productions in its 150-seat theater at King Plow Arts Center, a stylish artists' complex hailed by local critics as a showplace of industrial design. ⊠ *King Plow Arts Center, 887 W. Marietta St. NW, Suite J-107, Midtown* ☎ *404/607–7469* ⊕ *www. actors-express.com.*

Alliance Theatre. Atlanta's Tony award–winning professional theater presents everything from Shakespeare to the latest Broadway and off-Broadway hits. ⊠ *Woodruff Arts Center, 1280 Peachtree St. NE, Midtown* ☎ *404/733–5000* ⊕ *www.alliancetheatre.org.*

Atlanta Shakespeare Company. The Atlanta Shakespeare Company stages plays by the Bard and his peers, as well as by contemporary dramatists. Performances vary in quality but are always fun. The Elizabethan-style playhouse is a real tavern, so alcohol and pub-style food are available. ⊠ *New American Shakespeare Tavern, 499 Peachtree St. NE, Midtown* ☎ *404/874–5299* ⊕ *www.shakespearetavern.com.*

Dad's Garage Theatre Company. Founded in 1995, this scrappy playhouse with a sense of humor offers a variety of comedy and improv classes and performances as well as original theatrical works. ⊠ *569 Ezzard St., Old Fourth Ward* ☎ *404/523–3141* ⊕ *www.dadsgarage.com.*

Horizon Theatre Co. This professional troupe, established in 1983, debuts provocative and entertaining contemporary plays in its 172-seat theater. ⊠ *1083 Austin Ave., Little Five Points* ☎ *404/584–7450* ⊕ *www. horizontheatre.com.*

13

7 Stages Theatre. Founded in 1979 and in its current location since 1987, 7 Stages is known for an edgy attitude and exciting works. The adjacent bar and coffee house, Java Lords, serves up delicious brews and affordable drinks pre- and postshow. ⊠ *1105 Euclid Ave. NE, Little Five Points* ☎ *404/523–7647* ⊕ *www.7stages.org.*

SPORTS AND THE OUTDOORS

At almost any time of the year, in parks, private clubs, and neighborhoods throughout the city, you'll find Atlantans pursuing everything from tennis to soccer to cycling.

BASEBALL

Atlanta Braves. Atlanta's most beloved team, Major League Baseball's Atlanta Braves, moved to a new, state-of-the-art stadium in 2017. SunTrust Park is in Cobb County, about 15 miles from the Braves' former Downtown home at Turner Field. ⊠ *755 Battery Ave.* ☎ *404/522–7630* ⊕ *www.mlb.com/braves.*

BASKETBALL

Atlanta Hawks. The Hawks play Downtown in Philips Arena. ⊠ *Philips Arena, 1 Philips Dr., Downtown* ☎ *866/715–1500* ⊕ *www.nba.com/hawks.*

BIKING

Silver Comet Trail. Connecting Atlanta with the Alabama state line, the Silver Comet Trail is very popular with bikers. The trail is asphalt and concrete. ⊠ *Highland Station trailhead, South Cobb Dr. and Cumberland Pkwy., Smyrna* ☎ *404/875–7284* ⊕ *www.pathfoundation.org.*

Skate Escape. Bikes and in-line skates are for sale and for rent here. ⊠ *1086 Piedmont Ave., across from Piedmont Park, Midtown* ☎ *404/892–1292* ⊕ *www.skateescape.com.*

Stone Mountain/Atlanta Greenway Trail. Part of the Atlanta–DeKalb trail system, the Stone Mountain/Atlanta Greenway Trail is a mostly off-road paved path that follows Ponce de Leon Avenue east of the city into Stone Mountain Park. The best place to start the 17-mile trek is the Jimmy Carter Presidential Library & Museum. ⊠ *Atlanta* ☎ *404/875–7284* ⊕ *www.pathfoundation.org.*

FOOTBALL

Atlanta Falcons. The Atlanta Falcons have played at the huge Mercedes-Benz Stadium since 2017. Their former stadium, the Georgia Dome, was razed to create a parking deck to accommodate the increasing number of fans and tailgaters. In July and August, training camp is held in Flowery Branch, about 40 miles north of Atlanta. There's no charge to watch an open practice session. ⊠ *35 Northside Dr. NW, Downtown* ☎ *678/686–4400* ⊕ *www.atlantafalcons.com.*

GOLF

Golf is enormously popular here, as the numerous courses attest.

North Fulton Golf Course. This course has one of the best layouts in the area. It's at Chastain Park, within the Interstate 285 perimeter. ⊠ *216 W. Wieuca Rd. NW, Buckhead* ☎ *404/255–0723* ⊕ *www.northfultongc.com* ✉ *$41.50 weekdays, $45.50 weekends* 🏌 *18 holes, 6570 yds, par 71.*

Stone Mountain Golf Club. Stonemont, with several challenging and scenic holes, is the better of the two courses here (the other is Lakemont). ⊠ *Atlanta Evergreen Marriott, 1145 Stonewall Jackson Dr., Stone Mountain* ☎ *770/465–3278* ⊕ *www.stonemountaingolf.com* ✉ *$63 weekdays, $73 weekends* 🏌 *Stonemont: 18 holes, 6129 yds, par 71; Lakemont: 18 holes, 5419 yds, par 71.*

HOCKEY

Gwinnett Gladiators. The Gwinnett Gladiators, a farm team for the NHL's Boston Bruins, play in the ECHL, a nationwide hockey league. Games are played October to April. ⊠ *Infinite Energy Center, 6400 Sugarloaf Pkwy., Duluth* ☎ *770/497–5100* ⊕ *www.gwinnettgladiators.com.*

RUNNING

Check the **Atlanta Track Club's** website (⊕ *www.atlantatrackclub.org*) for weekly Atlanta-area group runs.

Fodor'sChoice
★

Atlanta Beltline. Hit the Beltline however you like: run it, walk it, or bike it. This 22-mile loop of parks, trails, and transit is the perfect way to get an eye-line view of the city and it's the primary way locals take in a bit of the outdoors. There are multiple access points, including the heart of Midtown, the tree-lined West End, and the Freedom Park Trail. There's often art to view as you go, and an official running series to keep things interesting. ⚠ **Be watchful for aggressive cyclists and rollerbladers.** Don't take it personally, just obey the rules of the road: slower traffic should stay to the right. ⊠ *Midtown* ☎ *404/477–3003* ⊕ *www.beltline.org.*

Chattahoochee River National Recreation Area. Crisscrossed by 70 miles of trails, this rec area contains different parcels of land that lie in 16 separate units spread along the banks of the Chattahoochee River. Much of it has been protected from development. ⊠ *Visitor Center, 1978 Island Ford Pkwy., Sandy Springs* ☎ *678/538–1200* ⊕ *www.nps.gov/chat.*

SHOPPING

Atlanta's department stores, specialty shops, malls, and antiques markets draw shoppers from across the Southeast. Most stores are open Monday through Saturday 10 to 9, Sunday noon to 6. The sales tax is 8% in the city of Atlanta and 6% to 7% in Fulton County and the suburbs.

DOWNTOWN

ART GALLERIES

Marcia Wood Gallery. This gallery sells contemporary paintings, sculpture, and photography. ⊠ *263 Walker St., Castleberry Hill* ☎ *404/827–0030* ⊕ *www.marciawoodgallery.com.*

MIDTOWN

ART GALLERIES

Mason Fine Art. Smaller than its original location, the quality of work is not compromised in the three large, open gallery spaces that exhibit contemporary work from regional, national, and international artists. ⊠ *415 Plasters Ave., Midtown* ☎ *404/879–1500* ⊕ *www.masonfineartandevents.com* ۞ *Closed Sun. and Mon.*

WESTSIDE

CLOTHING

Sid Mashburn. This upscale source for classic men's clothing is on the Westside. Next door, Ann Mashburn sells chic ladies' duds. ⊠ *1198 Howell Mill Rd. NW, Midtown* ☎ *404/350–7135* ⊕ *www.sidmashburn. com* ۞ *Closed Sun.*

FOOD

Star Provisions. Fine cookware, gadgets, and tableware, plus top-of-the-line cheeses, meats, and baked goods are what's on offer at this epicurean destination. ⊠ *1198 Howell Mill Rd., Midtown* ☎ *404/365–0410* ⊕ *www.starprovisions.com* ۞ *Closed Sun.*

BUCKHEAD

Anchored by Lenox Square and Phipps Plaza, Buckhead is one of the city's centers for luxury consumption. The Shops Buckhead Atlanta is an impressive entry to the area's high-end retail, with the likes of Tom Ford and Hermès. Boutiques, gift shops, and some fine restaurants line West Paces Ferry Road, Pharr Road, and East Andrews Drive. Cates Center has similar stores. Others are on Paces Ferry Place.

ANTIQUES AND DECORATIVE ARTS

Bennett Street. Home-decor stores, such as John Overton Oriental Rugs-Antiques, and art galleries, including the TULA art center and galleries, join the Stalls on Bennett Street and other antiquing destinations on this street. ⊠ *Bennett St. near 2100 Peachtree Rd., Buckhead* ⊕ *www.buckhead.net/bennettstreet.*

Miami Circle. Upscale antiques and decorative-arts shops are the draw here. ⊠ *Miami Circle and Piedmont Rd., Buckhead* ⊕ *miamicircleshops.com.*

ART GALLERIES

Jackson Fine Art Gallery. The specialty here is fine-art photography. ⊠ *3115 E. Shadowlawn Ave., Buckhead* ☎ *404/233–3739* ⊕ *www. jacksonfineart.com* ☉ *Closed Sun. and Mon.*

MALLS

Lenox Square. One of Atlanta's oldest and most popular shopping centers, Lenox Square has branches of Neiman Marcus, Bloomingdale's, and Macy's next to specialty shops such as Cartier and Mori. Valet parking is available at the front of the mall, but free parking is nearby. You'll do better at one of the several good restaurants in the mall—even for a quick meal—than at the food court. ⊠ *3393 Peachtree Rd., Buckhead* ☎ *404/233–6767* ⊕ *www.simon.com/mall/lenox-square.*

Fodor'sChoice **Phipps Plaza.** Branches of Tiffany & Co., Saks Fifth Avenue, and Gucci
★ are here, as are shops like Lilly Pulitzer and River Street Sweets of Savannah, where the specialty is Southern candies such as pecan pralines. ⊠ *3500 Peachtree Rd. NE, Buckhead* ☎ *404/262–0992* ⊕ *www. simon.com/mall/phipps-plaza.*

Shops Around Lenox. Quite literally around the corner from Lenox Square mall, this collection of Atlanta favorites such as Fab'rik, and specialty shops such as Crate & Barrel and Lululemon Athletica features modern storefronts and green spaces. Stop off at Bhojanic after a day shopping for Indian tapas and traditional thalis. ⊠ *3400 Around Lenox Rd. NE, Buckhead* ☎ *404/237–7710* ⊕ *www.shopsaroundlenox.com.*

VIRGINIA-HIGHLAND AND THE EMORY AREA

The window-shopping's great in Virginia-Highland, thanks to the boutiques, antiques shops, and art galleries. Parking can be tricky in the evening, so be prepared to park down a side street and walk a few blocks.

ART GALLERIES

Young Blood Boutique. Young Blood is an edgy hangout with framed artwork, crafts, and gifts created by indie artists. ⊠ *636 N. Highland Ave., Virginia-Highland* ☎ *404/254–4127* ⊕ *www.youngbloodboutique.com.*

LITTLE FIVE POINTS AND INMAN PARK

Vintage-clothing emporiums, record stores, and some stores that defy description are what draw thrifters and others here.

ART GALLERIES

Whitespace Gallery. An Inman Park staple, Whitespace exhibits contemporary paintings and installations in its renovated carriage house and a smaller satellite gallery, Whitespec. ⊠ *814 Edgewood Ave., Inman Park* ☎ *404/688–1892* ⊕ *whitespace814.com* ☉ *Closed Sun.–Tues.*

BOOKS

A Cappella Books. New and out-of-print titles are sold here; the store hosts regular author appearances. ⊠ *208 Haralson Ave. NE, Inman Park* ☎ *404/681–5128* ⊕ *www.acappellabooks.com.*

Charis Books. This is the South's oldest and largest feminist bookstore. ⊠ *1189 Euclid Ave. NE, Little Five Points* ☎ *404/524–0304* ⊕ *www. charisbooksandmore.com.*

CLOTHING

Clothing Warehouse. The Clothing Warehouse is one of the many colorful vintage-clothing stores in Little Five Points. ⊠ *420 Moreland Ave. NE, Little Five Points* ☎ *404/524–5070* ⊕ *www.theclothingwarehouse.com.*

Junkman's Daughter. Kooky wigs, vinyl corsets, and water pipes are all sold at this funky-junky department store. ⊠ *464 Moreland Ave. NE, Little Five Points* ☎ *404/577–3188* ⊕ *www.thejunkmansdaughter.com.*

DECATUR

Busy downtown Decatur, 8 miles east of Midtown Atlanta, is one of the metro area's favorite spots for dining, sidewalk strolling, and window-shopping. Its town quad, with a sophisticated, artistic vibe, teems with interesting restaurants, specialty shops, and delectable coffeehouses and cafés.

BOOKS

FAMILY **Little Shop of Stories.** With story time three times a week, a wide selection of children's books from board to chapter and beyond, and as frequent host to kids' book authors, this may be the best children's bookstore in Atlanta. ⊠ *133A E. Court Sq., Decatur* ☎ *404/373–6300* ⊕ *www. littleshopofstories.com.*

FOOD

Your DeKalb Farmers Market. It may not be a true farmers' market, but this is truly a market experience to remember. In a sprawling warehouse store 9 miles east of Atlanta, some 142,000 square feet are given over to exotic fruits, cheeses, seafood, sausages, breads, and delicacies from around the world. You'll find root vegetables from Africa, greens from Asia, wines from South America, and cheeses from Europe. The store also has one of the largest seafood departments in the country (with some species still swimming) and sizable meat, deli, and wine sections. The cafeteria-style buffet, with a selection of earthy and delicious hot foods and salads ranging from lasagna to samosas, alone is worth the trip. ■ TIP→ **The market is accessible by MARTA bus from the Avondale rail station.** ⊠ *3000 E. Ponce de Leon Ave., Decatur* ☎ *404/377–6400* ⊕ *www.dekalbfarmersmarket.com.*

METRO ATLANTA

ANTIQUES AND DECORATIVE ARTS

Chamblee Antique Row. You'll find this browser's delight in the suburban town of Chamblee. It's just north of Buckhead and about 10 miles north of Downtown. ⊠ *Peachtree Industrial Blvd. and Broad St., Chamblee* ☎ *770/458–6316* ⊕ *www.antiquerow.com.*

FOOD

Buford Highway Farmers Market. Originally started more than 25 years ago as a specialty Asian grocery, the Buford Highway Farmers Market has grown into a full-blown international marketplace; a turn down each aisle is like a trip to a different country. Make sure to stop at the Eastern European deli counter. ⊠ *5600 Buford Hwy. NE* ☎ *770/455–0770* ⊕ *www.aofwc.com.*

Plaza Fiesta. A 350,000-square-foot Latino shopping mall with more than 280 storefronts, Plaza Fiesta's got everything from cowboy boots to handmade tortillas to quinceañera dresses. ⊠ *4166 Buford Hwy. NE* ☎ *404/982–9138* ⊕ *www.plazafiesta.net.*

13

MALLS

Perimeter Mall. Known for upscale family shopping, Perimeter Mall has Nordstrom, Macy's, Dillard's, Von Maur, and a plentiful food court. Its restaurants include the Cheesecake Factory, and Maggiano's Little Italy. ⊠ *4400 Ashford-Dunwoody Rd., Dunwoody* ☎ *770/394–4270* ⊕ *www.perimetermall.com.*

OUTLETS

The interstate highways leading to Atlanta have discount malls similar to those found throughout the country. About 60 miles north of the city on Interstate 85 at Exit 149 is a huge cluster of outlets in the town of Commerce.

North Georgia Premium Outlets. Here you'll find 140 stores, including Williams-Sonoma, OshKosh B'Gosh, Bose, and numerous designer outlet shops like Coach, Ann Taylor, Banana Republic, and Polo Ralph Lauren. For the true shopper, it's worth the 45 minutes it takes to get here from Atlanta's northern perimeter. ⊠ *800 Hwy. 400 S, at Dawson Forest Rd., Dawsonville* ☎ *706/216–3609* ⊕ *www.premiumoutlets. com/northgeorgia.*

Outlet Shoppes of Atlanta. Head 30 miles northwest of Downtown to get your fill of more than 80 outlet stores including Coach, Kate Spade, Jos. A. Bank, and Nike Factory Store. ⊠ *915 Ridgewalk Pkwy., Woodstock* ☎ *678/540–7040* ⊕ *www.theoutletshoppesatatlanta.com.*

Sugarloaf Mills. Twenty-five miles northeast of Downtown Atlanta, this outlet mall has stores that include Saks Fifth Avenue Off 5th and Last Call by Neiman Marcus. ⊠ *5900 Sugarloaf Pkwy., Lawrenceville* ☎ *678/847–5000* ⊕ *www.simon.com/mall/sugarloaf-mills.*

SHOPPING NEIGHBORHOODS

Atlantic Station. A mixed-use development and outdoor mall, Atlantic Station covers about 10 square blocks, clustered around a green space known as Central Park. Retailers include IKEA, the Dillard's department store, Banana Republic, and H&M. It's easy to reach by car but is also accessible by free shuttle buses from the Arts Center MARTA station. An on-site concierge is happy to help you find your way around or make dinner reservations at the more than a dozen restaurants here. ⊠ *1380 Atlantic Dr.* ☎ *404/410–4010* ⊕ *www. atlanticstation.com.*

Little Five Points. Vintage-clothing emporiums, record stores, and some stores that defy description are what draw thrifters and others here. ✉ *Euclid and Moreland Aves., Little Five Points* ⊕ *www.littlefivepoints.net.*

Virginia-Highland. The window-shopping's great here, thanks to the boutiques, antiques shops, and art galleries. Parking can be tricky in the evening, so be prepared to park down a side street and walk a few blocks. ✉ *Virginia and N. Highland Aves., Virginia-Highland* ⊕ *www.virginiahighland.com.*

Westside. Most of the high-end restaurants and design shops here are located in and around the Westside Provisions District, a complex of former meatpacking warehouses transformed into bustling stores. ✉ *Midtown* ⊕ *www.westsideprovisions.com.*

CENTRAL AND NORTH GEORGIA

WELCOME TO
CENTRAL AND NORTH GEORGIA

TOP REASONS TO GO

★ **The Antebellum Trail:** Traveling this picturesque trail between Macon and Athens will cast you back in time and introduce you to the elegance of the Old South.

★ **Surround yourself in Civil War history:** The second-bloodiest battle of the Civil War was fought for two days at Chickamauga and Chattanooga National Military Park.

★ **Take a hike:** The starting point of the more than 2,100-mile Appalachian Trail is at Springer Mountain, a few miles north of Amicalola Falls, the tallest cascading waterfall east of the Mississippi.

★ **Lovely lakes:** Lake Oconee, Lake Allatoona, Lake Hartwell, and Lake Rabun provide numerous recreational opportunities.

★ **Explore the Native American past:** Visit New Echota, the former capital of the Cherokee Nation, which offers tribute to the proud tribe. Nearby is the historic Vann House, a beautiful three-story residence of Cherokee Chief James Vann.

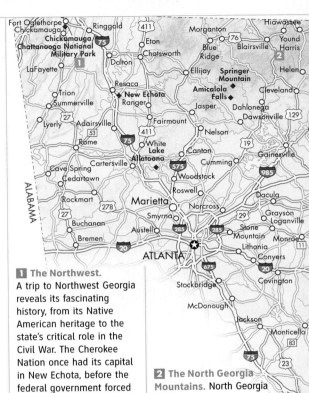

1 The Northwest.

A trip to Northwest Georgia reveals its fascinating history, from its Native American heritage to the state's critical role in the Civil War. The Cherokee Nation once had its capital in New Echota, before the federal government forced members of the tribe on a long, tragic resettlement march to Oklahoma, marking the infamous "Trail of Tears." A few years later, the Civil War's second-bloodiest battle was fought at Chickamauga and Chattanooga National Military Park, which is commemorated by hundreds of monuments and markers in the country's first Civil War battlefield park.

2 The North Georgia Mountains.

North Georgia has become a fascinating meld of the past and the present. Its residents wholeheartedly cherish their Appalachian roots at attractions such as the Foxfire Museum and Heritage Center and the Folk Pottery Museum of Northeast Georgia. They take pride in introducing visitors to their music, as well as their natural surroundings: mountains, hiking trails (including the Appalachian

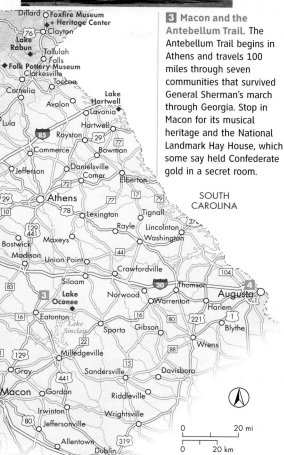

3 **Macon and the Antebellum Trail.** The Antebellum Trail begins in Athens and travels 100 miles through seven communities that survived General Sherman's march through Georgia. Stop in Macon for its musical heritage and the National Landmark Hay House, which some say held Confederate gold in a secret room.

SOUTH CAROLINA

0   20 mi

0   20 km

Trail), and waterfalls. But residents are embracing the mountains' potential for new ventures, as well. Award-winning wineries are springing up across the region, and a passion for fine dining is a natural accompaniment.

4 **Augusta.** Though the Masters Tournament of Golf put this 200,000-person city on the map, Augusta also charms with its antebellum mansions and tree-lined streets dotted with shops.

GETTING ORIENTED

North Georgia's tree-lined mountain roads are a relief from the traffic jams of metro Atlanta. You can spot critters from wild turkeys to deer, stop off for refreshing visits to waterfalls, or savor shopping, lodging, and meals in quaint—and quiet—towns. The area's proximity to metro Atlanta makes it ideal for day trips and overnight stays.

Central Georgia roughly forms a triangle defined by Athens, Macon, and Augusta, which together give you a real flavor of Georgia's elegant past and vibrant future. Madison epitomizes small-town America with its charming antebellum and Victorian architecture. Eatonton, 20 miles down the highway, also has its share of stately historic houses, although your attention will be drawn to the statue of a giant rabbit on the courthouse lawn. It's part of the town's tribute to favorite son Joel Chandler Harris, creator of Br'er Rabbit and Uncle Remus.

14

Updated by
Rachel Roberts
Quartarone

It is often said there are two Georgias: Atlanta and the rest of the state. While Atlanta offers bright lights and big-city action, the regions to the north and southeast are filled with farms, lush forests, sleepy hamlets, and larger towns boasting vibrant arts and cultural scenes. In either direction, there is no shortage of beautiful scenery from the mountains to the north to the rolling hills and rivers to the south.

North Georgia is known for its abundant natural wonders and its cool mountain air. The region is home to the 750,000-acre Chattahoochee National Forest, where several bold rivers, including the Chattahoochee, Oconee, Toccoa, and Chattooga, have their headwaters. Rabun, Burton, Nottley, and Chatuge lakes offer recreational opportunities and camping. To the northwest are quaint river towns like Rome, as well as two important Georgia historic sites: New Echota State Historic Site and the Chickamauga and Chattanooga National Military Park.

Whether planning a day trip from Atlanta or a longer exploration, there is plenty to do and see in Central Georgia. Head down U.S. 441—the Antebellum Trail—from Athens to Macon, and you'll quickly see that the elegance of the Old South is new again, with many historic buildings returned to their original splendor. Athens, home of the University of Georgia, pulses with college life, especially when the Bulldogs are playing. For a taste of old Georgia, Macon's historical architecture is unmatched. Farther east, Augusta is home of the Masters Tournament. Even if you're not drawn to the tees, this city—like so many in Georgia—is undergoing a renaissance of its waterfront and historic districts.

PLANNING

WHEN TO GO

Summer in the South can be unpleasant; temperatures of 90 degrees or higher (plus humidity) cause even the most Southern of Southerners to wilt. The best times to visit Central Georgia are fall and spring, when temperatures are in the 60s and 70s and there are plenty of recreational activities to enjoy. Springtime is particularly lovely in Macon, as the cherry trees are in full bloom.

Spring, summer, and fall are prime times for travel in North Georgia. Weekends are far busier than weekdays, because many visitors drive up from nearby Atlanta for a short getaway. For the mountains, the ideal time is October and early November, when fall color is at its peak. Don't arrive without reservations during spring and early fall festival weekends, when visitors head north to enjoy the spring wildflowers, fall apple and pumpkin harvests, and absolutely blissful weather.

14

PLANNING YOUR TIME

As a transportation hub, Atlanta is the jumping-off point for this region. In fact, many of North and Central Georgia's attractions are little more than an hour's drive from the city, making them perfect for a day trip. Panning for gold in Dahlonega, apple picking in Ellijay, and sampling North Georgia wines are worthy excursions. For a more relaxed pace, plan to stay overnight in the beautiful North Georgia mountains.

The bustling college town of Athens is a great place to start if you are interested in exploring the Antebellum Trail winding through Madison, Milledgeville, and Macon. With so much to do and see, consider breaking up the trip with an overnight stay. These cities also stand alone as day-trip destinations or overnight trips, particularly if history and architecture are of interest.

GETTING HERE AND AROUND

AIR TRAVEL

The gateway airports for North Georgia are Hartsfield-Jackson International Airport in Atlanta and Chattanooga Metropolitan Airport in Chattanooga, Tennessee.

Direct flights are available from Atlanta (ATL) or Charlotte (CLT) to Augusta Regional Airport (AGS) with Delta Airlines or American Airlines. The smaller regional airports mostly serve charters and small private planes. The most economical option to reach most destinations in North and Central Georgia is to fly into Atlanta (ATL) and rent a car.

Airport Contacts Athens Ben Epps Airport. ✉ *1010 Ben Epps Dr., Athens* ☎ *706/613-3420* ⊕ *www.athensairport.net.* **Augusta Regional Airport (AGS)** (*AGS*). ✉ *1501 Aviation Way, Augusta* ☎ *706/798-3236* ⊕ *www. augustaregionalairport.com.* **Chattanooga Metropolitan Airport** (*CHA*). ✉ *1001 Airport Rd., Chattanooga* ☎ *423/855-2200* ⊕ *www.chattairport.com.* **Hartsfield-Jackson Atlanta International Airport** (*ATL*). ✉ *6000 N. Terminal Pkwy., Atlanta* ☎ *404/530-7300, 800/897-1910* ⊕ *www.atl.com.* **Middle Georgia Regional Airport** (*MCN*). ✉ *1000 Terminal Dr., Macon* ☎ *478/788-3760* ⊕ *www.iflymacon.com.*

CAR TRAVEL

U.S. 441, known as the Antebellum Trail, runs north–south, merging with U.S. 129 for a stretch and connecting Athens, Madison, Eatonton, and Milledgeville. Macon is on Route 49, which splits from U.S. 441 at Milledgeville. Washington lies at the intersection of U.S. 78, running east from Athens to Thomson, and Route 44, running south to Eatonton. Interstate 20 runs east from Atlanta to Augusta, which is about 93 miles east of U.S. 441.

Plan on using your car—or renting one—to get around North Georgia. U.S. 19 runs north–south, passing through Dahlonega and up into the North Georgia mountains. U.S. 129 travels northwest from Athens, eventually merging with U.S. 19. GA 75 stems off of U.S. 129 and goes through Helen and up into the mountains. U.S. 23/441 will take you north through Clayton; U.S. 76 runs west from Clayton to Dalton, merging for a stretch with GA 5/515. GA 52 runs along the edge of the Blue Ridge Mountains, passing through Ellijay. Interstate 75 is the major artery in the northwesternmost part of the state and passes near Rome and the Chickamauga and Chattanooga National Military Park.

RESTAURANTS

Central and North Georgia offer an abundance of dining options from hole-in-the-wall barbecue joints to upscale eateries serving sophisticated cuisine. The culinary specialty is Southern food, of course, and a heaping plate of fried chicken washed down with sweet tea is a must. Aside from traditional local fare, plenty of other options are available in larger towns like Athens and Macon. In the North Georgia mountains, you'll find quite a bit of culinary sophistication at many of the charming little bistros on the town squares and near the scenic wineries that dot the Wine Highway. *Dining reviews have been shortened. For full information, visit Fodors.com.*

HOTELS

The most attractive lodging options here tend to have been around for a long time; the structures often date from the 19th century. At such places—most commonly B&Bs but sometimes larger inns—you're likely to find big porches with rocking chairs and bedrooms decorated with antiques. If that's more Southern charm than you're after, you can choose from a smattering of chain hotels. In the North Georgia mountains and near the recreational areas of Central Georgia there is also a large variety of cabins and home rentals. *Hotel reviews have been shortened. For full information, visit Fodors.com.*

WHAT IT COSTS				
	$	**$$**	**$$$**	**$$$$**
Restaurants	under $15	$15–$19	$20–$24	over $24
Hotels	under $150	$150–$200	$201–$250	over $250

Prices in the reviews are the average cost of a main course at dinner or, if dinner is not served, at lunch. Prices in the reviews are the lowest cost of a standard double room in high season.

VISITOR INFORMATION

Georgia Welcome Center. ☎ *706/737–1446* ⊕ *www.exploregeorgia.org.*

THE NORTHWEST

Northwest Georgia is rich in history. Chickamauga and Chattanooga National Military Park reminds visitors of the devastation of the Civil War and the determination of both Southern and Northern soldiers participating in its bloodiest two-day battle. The area also pays homage to Georgia's former Cherokee residents, driven from their verdant homeland in New Echota—once the capital of the Cherokee nation—to dusty Oklahoma on the Trail of Tears. Northwest Georgia lies along the Cumberland Plateau, with its flat-top sandstone mountains.

ROME AND THE CHIEFTAIN'S TRAIL

14

71 miles northwest of Atlanta via I–75 north to U.S. 411/GA 20; 66 miles southwest of Ellijay via GA 53.

Nestled in the countryside of Northwest Georgia is the antebellum town of Rome. Like its Italian namesake, it's built on seven hills with a river running between them. Georgia's Rome sits at the confluence of the Etowah and Oostanaula Rivers and was once a bustling river transportation hub. Cotton was king here, and the city's industry and riverfront location played an important role in the Civil War. With the decline of steamboats and the rise of the automobile, Rome's industry suffered as the interstate highway system reached north to Dalton but did not extend westward to Rome. Nonetheless, Rome reinvented itself as a business and education hub, preserving much of its architecture and green space with scenic river walks and parks. Its central location and historic charm make it a great place to stay and see other points of interest in the Northwest Georgia region.

Rome is also an entry point to Georgia's Chieftain's Trail. Start at Chieftains Museum, the historic home of Major Ridge, one of the signers of the Treaty of New Echota. The treaty was essentially a forced agreement between the Cherokee and the federal government that launched the tragic "Trail of Tears." A significant site on the heritage trail, New Echota returned to farmland after the eviction of the Cherokee, but now serves as a state historic site with re-creations and some original buildings depicting the Cherokee capital as it was in the early 19th century. A bit farther north near Chatsworth, you can also visit the Chief Vann House, the 1804 mansion known as the "Showplace of the Cherokee Nation." For a touch of mystery, head east to Fort Mountain State Park to see a massive rock wall that dates back to AD 500. Many theories abound as to who built it—from unknown Indian tribes to the Cherokee legend of "Moon Eyes"—but, no one knows for sure.

GETTING HERE AND AROUND

This is a good day trip from Atlanta. Take Interstate 75 to Exit 290. Head west on GA 20 until it merges with U.S. 411 S to reach Rome.

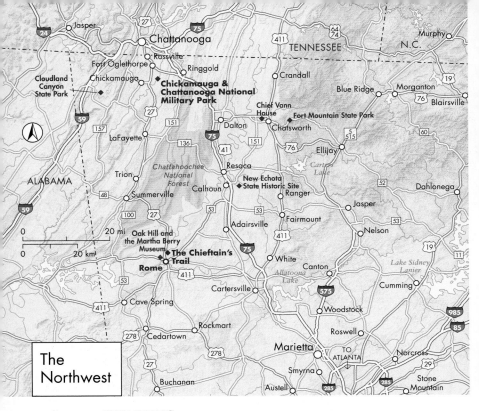

EXPLORING

Fodor's Choice
★

Chief Vann House. This beautiful home with all the trappings of the wealthy planter lifestyle is fascinating because of the intermingling of cultures that took place here. Known as Diamond Hill, this historic site was home to a 1,000-acre plantation—the largest and most prosperous in Cherokee history. In 1804 James Vann, a Cherokee leader of mixed Scottish and Cherokee parentage, built the plantation's stately redbrick mansion with the help of Moravian missionaries and enslaved workers. When Vann was murdered in 1809, his son Joseph took over the property until he was forcefully evicted in 1835. Diamond Hill and surrounding lands were then given away in a land lottery to white settlers, its Cherokee origins wiped away.

Start your visit in the visitor center where you can view a short film and browse exhibits about the site's history. Rangers lead tours of the home, but outdoor exhibits, such as a re-created Cherokee farmstead and plantation kitchen, are self-guided. The kitchen outbuilding also houses an exhibit focused on the daily lives of the 110 enslaved people who resided at Diamond Hill before Vann's departure in 1835. ✉ *82 GA 225, at GA 52A, Chatsworth ✦ 17 miles north of New Echota; 44 miles northeast of Rome* ☎ *706/695–2598* ⊕ *www.gastateparks.org/ ChiefVannHouse* ✇ *$6.50* ⏱ *Closed Mon.–Wed.*

Chieftains Museum. This historic home, now a museum, was built by Cherokee leader Major Ridge and is a part of the Trail of Tears National Historic Trail. The 1828 white clapboard plantation home is built around a two-story log cabin. Visitors can peek behind the plaster walls to see the original wooden foundation. Major Ridge and his family lived here and operated a successful trading post and ferry until 1837 when they were forced out to Oklahoma. Although several other families lived in the home and modified it over the years, it came to be known as "Chieftains" in honor of Ridge. The museum features displays detailing the history of the house, the Ridge family, and artifacts from archaeological digs on the property. ✉ *501 Riverside Pkwy., Rome* ☎ *706/291–9494* ⊕ *www.chieftainsmuseum.org* 🖼 *$5* ☉ *Closed Sun.–Tues.*

FAMILY **Fort Mountain State Park.** This 3,712-acre state park has a 17-acre lake with sandy beach, 14 miles of hiking trails, and 27 miles of mountain-biking trails. The gem of the park is a mysterious wall of rock, 855 feet long, thought to have been built by Native Americans around AD 500. Tent and RV sites ($28–$32) and recently renovated cottages ($175–$200) are available. The park also offers a unique primitive site for camping with horses. ✉ *181 Fort Mountain Park Rd., Chatsworth* ☎ *706/422–1932* ⊕ *www.gastateparks.org/fortmountain* 🖼 *Free; $5 parking.*

FAMILY **New Echota State Historic Site.** Made up of a dozen original and reconstructed buildings, this significant historic site allows visitors to explore the capital of the Cherokee nation on the land where the city once stood. It was here that the Treaty of 1835 was signed by a small group of Cherokee leaders, setting into motion the Trail of Tears. The only original building remaining is the Worcester House, a home and Presbyterian mission station. The Cherokee Council House and Supreme Court are reconstructions, as is the print house, where thousands of books translated in Cherokee and the weekly *Cherokee Phoenix* were published. Other buildings, including the 1805 Vann Tavern, were relocated to the site. A museum and film provide more insight on the rich history of the Cherokee in Georgia. ✉ *1211 Chatsworth Hwy., Calhoun* ✛ *GA 225, 1 mile east of I–75* ☎ *706/624–1321* ⊕ *www.georgiastateparks.org/newechota* 🖼 *$7* ☉ *Closed Sun.–Tues.*

Oak Hill and the Martha Berry Museum. Dedicated to Martha Berry, founder of Berry College, the museum includes exhibits on the history of the college (located just down the street) and a tour of Berry's 1884 Greek Revival family home, Oak Hill. Berry founded the college in 1902 to help impoverished mountain children gain an education and life skills. Today, it is recognized as one of the top small liberal arts colleges in the country. Oak Hill is preserved as it was when Berry died in 1927. Be sure to stroll the picturesque gardens and outbuildings. If time permits, drive through Berry College for a look at the Gothic-style stone Ford Complex built between 1925 and 1931 and donated by Berry's friend, Henry Ford. ✉ *24 Veterans Memorial Hwy., Rome* ☎ *706/368–6789* ⊕ *www.berry.edu/oakhill* 🖼 *$8* ☉ *Closed Sun.*

14

WHERE TO EAT

$$ AMERICAN Fodor's Choice ★ 🍴 **Harvest Moon Cafe.** With its warm exposed brick walls and folk art decor, this local favorite specializes in Southern-inspired, from-scratch cooking. Everything, from the salad dressings to the bread, is made in-house. **Known for:** comfort food; scratch-made bread and desserts. [$] *Average main: $15* ✉ *234 Broad St., Rome* ☎ *706/292–0099* 🌐 *www.myharvestmooncafe.com.*

WHERE TO STAY

$$$$ RESORT 🏨 **Barnsley Resort.** This award-winning resort features luxurious and comfortable accommodations (some brand-new), a championship golf course, spa, restaurant, horseback riding, a sporting club, and miles of nature trails. **Pros:** beautiful grounds; tastefully decorated rooms. **Cons:** pricey; not easy to find at night. [$] *Rooms from: $259* ✉ *597 Barnsley Gardens Rd., Adairsville* ☎ *770/773–7480, 877/773–2447* 🌐 *www.barnsleyresort.com* 🛏 *145 rooms, 36 cottages* 🍽 *No meals.*

$ HOTEL 🏨 **Hawthorn Suites by Wyndham Rome.** Located in Rome's historic downtown district, the Hawthorn Suites is housed in a beautifully renovated 1890s warehouse with original wood floors, brick walls, and a large sky-lit atrium. **Pros:** historical charm; tastefully decorated rooms. **Cons:** no pool; can fill up quickly due to events. [$] *Rooms from: $149* ✉ *100–110 W. 2nd Ave., Rome* ☎ *706/378–4837, 800/337–0246* 🌐 *www.hawthorn.com* 🛏 *65 rooms* 🍽 *Breakfast.*

CHICKAMAUGA AND CHATTANOOGA NATIONAL MILITARY PARK

110 miles northwest of Atlanta via I–75 and GA 2; 42 miles north of New Echota State Historic Site via I–75; 12 miles south of Chattanooga, TN, via U.S. 27.

Fodor's Choice ★ With nearly a million visitors a year, Chickamauga and Chattanooga National Military Park is one of the most popular battlefields in the country. Here you can gain a fuller sense of one of the Confederacy's greatest military victories by touring the battle lines, standing where the soldiers faced the pain and intensity of war, and imagining the cacophony produced by cannons, gunfire, and battle cries. This site, established in 1890 as the nation's first military park, was the scene of some of the Civil War's bloodiest battles. In Chickamauga alone, 34,624 were killed, missing, and wounded in September 1863. Though the Confederates won the battle at Chickamauga, the Union army retained control of Chattanooga. The normally thick cedar groves and foliage covering Chickamauga were trampled and, according to eyewitness accounts, trees were so shot up that a sweet cedar smell mingled with the blood of fallen soldiers.

Some areas around the park now suffer from suburban sprawl, but the 9,000-acre park itself is made up of serene fields and islands of trees. Monuments, battlements, and weapons adorn the roads that traverse the park, with markers explaining the action.

Continued on page 561

A CIVIL WAR TOUR
CHICKAMAUGA BATTLEFIELD

By Rickey Bevington

Chickamauga Battlefield today

A visit to the South isn't complete without an encounter with the history of the "War Between the States." With nearly a million visitors a year, Chickamauga & Chattanooga National Military Park is one of the most popular battlefields in the country. Here you can gain a fuller sense of one of the Confederacy's greatest military victories by touring the battle lines, standing where the soldiers faced the pain and intensity of war, and imagining the cacophony produced by cannons, gunfire, and battle cries.

Lithograph of Battle of Chickamauga, 1890

UNDERSTANDING THE BATTLE

Left and center, commanding generals William S. Rosecrans (Union) and Braxton Bragg (Confederacy). Right, General George H. Thomas (Union), also known as the Rock of Chickamauga

Why was the September 19–20, 1863, Battle of Chickamauga so important? To the war-weary people and soldiers of the Confederacy, it was a morale-boosting victory on the heels of terrible losses at Gettysburg and Vicksburg only months before. To the equally fatigued Union states, it was an important test of their use of Chattanooga, Tennessee, as a supply center from which to launch their advance into the Deep South. Union forces had captured the nearby city less than a month before in a bloodless advance. As they continued their push south into the far northwest corner of Georgia, Atlanta was in their sights. But Confederate soldiers were ready. Over two days of some of the war's fiercest fighting, 16,170 Union and 18,454 Confederate men and boys fell or were injured at the Battle of Chickamauga, named for the nearby creek where hostilities began. On the second day, the Confederates managed to send the Union soldiers into full retreat back to Chattanooga. It would take nine more months of fighting before U.S. General William Tecumseh Sherman was finally able to reach his original objective, Atlanta.

"Stars and Bars" Confederate flag, popular during the beginning of the Civil War.

CIVIL WAR TIMELINE

Civil War Union Flag

President Abraham Lincoln

1861
March 4, Abraham Lincoln is inaugurated.
March 11, Confederate Constitution is signed.
April 12, American Civil War begins.
July 21, First Battle of Bull Run.
1862
September 17, Battle of Antietam.
December 13, Battle of Fredericksburg.
1863
January 1, Lincoln issues the Emancipation Proclamation.
July 1–3, Battle of Gettysburg.

1863: A PIVOTAL YEAR IN THE CIVIL WAR

DECISIVE UNION VICTORIES

On January 1, 1863, President Lincoln issued the Emancipation Proclamation, which declared "that all persons held as slaves" within the seceded states "are, and henceforth shall be free."

Three strategic victories in this year proved crucial to the north's eventual victory over the south. The July 1863 battle of Gettysburg was Confederate General Robert E. Lee's last major offensive; 170,000 men fought over three days with 51,000 casualties, after which Lee retreated to Virginia. The following day, July 4, Vicksburg, MS, surrendered to Union forces laying siege under the command of Union General Ulysses S. Grant. For the north, taking Vicksburg soon meant controlling the Mississippi River south to New Orleans, cutting the Confederacy in half. In early September, Union forces marched into Chattanooga and seized its river, railroads, and a major Confederate supply center. A vital railroad junction, Chattanooga would become the crucial supply center for Union troops advancing south toward Atlanta.

Confederate troops advancing at Chickamauga, drawing by Alfred R. Waud, Civil War correspondant.

BATTLE OF CHICKAMAUGA

In September 1863 Union forces followed Confederates retreating into Georgia after abandoning Chattanooga. Morale was low among southern forces after the summer's defeats, but a chance skirmish launched what would be the largest battle and final Confederate victory in the war's western theater. The two-day clash ended with Union forces rapidly retreating north to safer ground at Chattanooga. Confederates were ecstatic, but this battle did little but buy the south time. One month later, U.S. General William Tecumseh Sherman took command of the Union force at Chattanooga and set his sights on Atlanta.

Sherman's March to Sea

July 4, Confederates surrender Vicksburg.
September 19–20, Battle of Chickamauga.
1864
September 2, Sherman captures Atlanta.
November 15, Sherman begins his "March to the Sea."
1865
April 9, Lee surrenders to Grant at Appomattox Courthouse.
April 14, President Lincoln is shot.
December 6, The Thirteenth Amendment abolishes slavery.

U.S. General William Tecumseh Sherman

14

IN FOCUS A CIVIL WAR TOUR: CHICKAMAUGA BATTLEFIELD

TOURING CHICKAMAUGA BATTLEFIELD

Left, Snodgrass house. Right, replica of Confederate soldier, visitor center

GETTING HERE

From Atlanta, take I–75 north; the 110-mile drive takes about two hours. Take exit 350 (Battlefield Parkway) to Fort Oglethorpe and follow signs to the National Military Park.

PLANNING YOUR TIME

Plan to spend from one hour to an afternoon here. Start with the a visit to the excellent **Chickamauga Battlefield Visitor Center**, which offers a timeline of the battle, a film on the military strategy, a collection of more than 300 antique military rifles, and a well-stocked bookstore. Pack a picnic lunch and go for a hike along one of the park's designated nature trails.

Left, 10th Wisconsin Infantry monument

THE AUTO TOUR

Imagine crawling out of a dense wood into an open field only to see a uniform line of thousands of enemy soldiers marching steadily toward you. That's just one of the battle scenes described in the seven-mile auto tour of the battle's most significant events. Pick up a free map and brochure at the visitor center with information on the sights. From Memorial Day to Labor Day rangers lead artillery demonstrations and free two-hour auto caravan tours.

TOUR HIGHLIGHTS

1 Starting just outside the visitor center heading south from Stop 1 (where the Florida monument now stands), follow the road that on the second day of battle separated a force of 65,000 Confederates firing from your left toward 62,000 Union troops trying to regain position on your right. The tour follows this battle line nearly the length of the battlefield. Unlike most Civil War engagements, this one did not take place in an open field, and the forested landscape has been preserved much as it was on the day of battle.

5 Once you veer west at Viniard Field, you are beginning to follow the steps of the retreating Union forces as they succumbed to Confederates pushing them back toward Chattanooga.

6 The Wilder Brigade Monument is an 85-foot high stone tower honoring Union

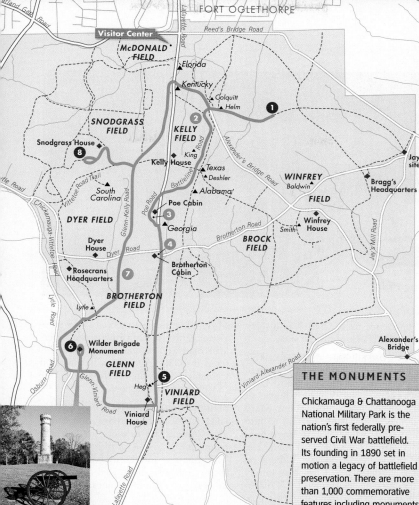

Battlefield and cannon

Map labels:

Visitor Center
Reed's Bridge Road
Lafayette Road
McDONALD FIELD
Florida
Kentucky
Colquitt
Helm
1
2
SNODGRASS FIELD
KELLY FIELD
Snodgrass House
8
King
Kelly House
Texas
Deshler
Alabama
South Carolina
Poe Cabin
3
Georgia
DYER FIELD
Dyer House
Dyer Road
4
Brotherton Cabin
Rosecrans Headquarters
7
BROTHERTON FIELD
Lytle
Wilder Brigade Monument
6
GLENN FIELD
Heg
5
VINIARD FIELD
Viniard House
Lafayette Road
Osburn Road
Glenn-Viniard Road
Lytle Road
Chickamauga-Vittetoe Road
Vittetoe Road Trail
Glenn-Kelly Road
Poe Road
Battleline Road
Alexander's Bridge Road
Brotherton Road
Smith
WINFREY FIELD
Baldwin
Winfrey House
BROCK FIELD
Jay's Mill Road
Jay's Mill site
Bragg's Headquarters
Alexander's Bridge
Viniard-Alexander Road
Battle...

Colonel John Wilder and his "Lightning Brigade," a group of fast-moving cavalrymen known for their rare but deadly Spencer-7 carbine repeating rifles.

8 The tour's final stop is Snodgrass Hill. This is the high ground where U.S. General George H. Thomas stayed behind his retreating army to thwart pursuing Confederates, giving Union forces enough time to reach Chattanooga safely. Many of Thomas' men were killed or captured and taken to the notorious Camp Sumter at Andersonville.

THE MONUMENTS

Chickamauga & Chattanooga National Military Park is the nation's first federally pre-served Civil War battlefield. Its founding in 1890 set in motion a legacy of battlefield preservation. There are more than 1,000 commemorative features including monuments, markers, and tablets placed by veterans whose citizens saw combat here. Take time to admire the monuments' design and inscription, and look for monuments from your home state. Red tablets describe Confederate action and blue mark Union activity. Large pyramids of naval shells indicate where a brigade commander was mortally wounded in combat.

Left, Andersonville Prisoner of War Museum. Right, Kennesaw Battlefield.

To experience more Civil War history in Georgia, check out these sites.

RESACA CONFEDERATE CEMETERY. This intimate, shaded cemetery is the final resting place for more than 450 Confederate soldiers. After the Battle of Resaca in May 1864, resident Mary J. Green returned to her farm to find hundreds of Confederates buried haphazardly where they had fallen. She raised the money to re-inter them on 2 1/2 acres in a corner of the family farm. ⊠ *40 miles southeast of Chickamauga, take I-75 to exit 318 for U.S. 41 to Confederate Cemetery Rd.*

ANDERSONVILLE NATIONAL HISTORIC SITE. The infamous Civil War–era Camp Sumter, commonly called Andersonville, was one of the largest prisons built in the Confederacy. Over 14 months, 45,000 Union soldiers were confined within a 26 1/2-acre open-air stockade; 13,000 died from disease and exposure—a rate of more than 30 a day. You can tour the rebuilt stockade walls and historic prison grounds here. The National Prisoner of War Museum, which also serves as the site's visitor center, is dedicated to the American men and women who have suffered as POWs. Andersonville National Cemetery is the final resting place for those who perished here.

KENNESAW MOUNTAIN NATIONAL BATTLEFIELD PARK. More than 160,000 Union and Confederate soldiers battled here from June 19, 1864, until July 2, 1864. This popular mountain park attracts history enthusiasts as well as runners, hikers, cyclists, and families.

GETTING HERE AND AROUND

Take Interstate 75 north from Atlanta to the exit for Fort Oglethorpe and follow signs through a small but congested area to the National Military Park and to Cloudland Canyon.

EXPLORING

Fodor'sChoice
★

Chickamauga and Chattanooga National Military Park. *See the highlighted feature in this chapter for more information.* ✉ *3370 LaFayette Rd., Fort Oglethorpe* ☎ *706/866–9241* ⊕ *www.nps.gov/chch* 💲 *Free; $5 for Point Park.*

Chickamauga Battlefield Visitor Center. This excellent visitor center and museum offers a time line of the battle, a film on the military strategy that involved 124,000 soldiers, a collection of 346 antique military rifles, and a well-stocked bookstore. There's a 7-mile self-guided auto tour through the park, with numerous spots to stop and view the more than 700 monuments and historical markers in Chickamauga. On weekends during the spring and fall, you can join a free two-hour auto caravan through the park, led by a park ranger. During the summer, rangers offer the tours daily at 10 and 2. Other special programs like guided hikes and demonstrations are offered; check the online calendar or visit the center at the start of your visit. ✉ *3370 LaFayette Rd., Fort Oglethorpe* ✛ *1 mile south of intersection of GA 2 and U.S. 27* ☎ *706/866–9241* ⊕ *www.nps.gov/chch* 💲 *Free.*

**OFF THE
BEATEN
PATH**

Cloudland Canyon State Park. At this 3,448-acre park you can see first-hand the unusual geology of this remote part of northwestern Georgia. Hike down the canyon, which drops 1,100 feet from the rim, and you're literally walking through millions of years of geologic time. If you make it all the way to the bottom—the trail totals 4 miles—you'll be rewarded with sights of two waterfalls. ✉ *122 Cloudland Canyon Park Rd., Rising Fawn* ☎ *706/657–4050* ⊕ *www.georgiastateparks. org/cloudlandcanyon* 💲 *$5 parking.*

THE NORTH GEORGIA MOUNTAINS

To most Georgians, "North Georgia" means the northeast and north central mountains and foothills—from Clayton and Dillard in the east to Hiawassee and Lake Chatuge in the north, and Blue Ridge and Ellijay and the Cohutta Wilderness to the west. Dahlonega, Helen, and several state parks—Black Rock Mountain, Moccasin Creek, Unicoi, Vogel, and Amicalola Falls—are contained within the broad arc of this scenic mountain region.

DAHLONEGA

65 miles northeast of Atlanta via GA 400 and GA 60.

Fodor'sChoice
★

Hoards of fortune seekers stormed the town of Dahlonega (pronounced dah-LON-eh-gah) in the 1820s after the discovery of gold in the nearby hills. The town's name comes from the Cherokee word for "precious yellow metal." But the boom didn't last long; by 1849 miners were starting to seek riches elsewhere. In fact, the famous call, "There's gold in them thar hills!" originated as an enticement to miners in the Georgia mountains to keep their minds away from the lure of the Western gold rush. It worked for a while, but government price-fixing eventually made gold mining unprofitable, and by the early 1920s Dahlonega's mining operations had halted completely.

Many former mining settlements became ghost towns, but not Dahlonega. Today it thrives with an irresistible town square filled with country stores, art galleries, gem shops, old small-town businesses, and several sophisticated restaurants. Gold Rush Days, a festival held the third weekend in October and celebrating the first gold rush in 1828, attracts about 200,000 weekend visitors.

GETTING HERE AND AROUND

It's easy to spend your entire visit in Dahlonega's quaint town square. But a short drive out of town will allow you to climb down into a gold mine, or to taste wine at the local vintners.

ESSENTIALS

Visitor Information Dahlonega-Lumpkin Chamber of Commerce and Visitors Center. ⊠ *13 Park St. S* ☎ *706/864-3513, 800/231-5543* ⊕ *www.dahlonega.org.*

EXPLORING

FAMILY **Consolidated Gold Mine.** Take a guided tour of a real mine, which ceased operations in 1904. With 5 miles of underground tunnels, Consolidated is said to be the largest gold mine east of the Mississippi. Enter the mine (which has been reconstructed for safety), pass through a breathtaking stone passage, and then begin a descent of 120 feet into the mine's geological wonders. Knowledgeable guides expound on historical mining techniques and give demonstrations of tools, such as the "widowmaker," a drill that kicks up mining dust and caused lung disease in many miners. After the tour, guests are invited to pan for gold, prospector-style, from a long wooden sluice. Gemstone mining is also available for an additional fee. ⊠ *185 Consolidated Gold Mine Rd.* ☎ *706/864-8473* ⊕ *www.consolidatedgoldmine.com* 💲 *$16.*

FAMILY **Crisson Gold Mine.** Dahlonega's oldest gold mining establishment open to the public, Crisson's offers the opportunity to get serious about gold prospecting. There's indoor and outdoor gold panning and gem grubbing as well as outdoor exhibits that guide guests through the gold mining process. You can also see mining equipment in action including a 130-year-old stamp mill that's still used to crush gold-bearing quartz. Wagon rides take you by the old tunnels and a functional open pit mine. The gift shop is worth a stop for the gemstone jewelry and unique gold gifts. ⊠ *2736 Morrison Moore Pkwy. E* ☎ *706/864-6363* ⊕ *www.crissongoldmine.com.*

Dahlonega Gold Museum. Located in the center of the town square, this museum has coins, tools, and several large nuggets on display. Built in 1836, this former courthouse is the oldest public building in the state. If you look closely at the bricks that form the building's foundation, you'll notice a sprinkling of gold dust in their formation. Along with two floors of exhibits, the museum features a high-definition film

Dahlonega's town square is worth a stroll with country stores, art galleries, and restaurants.

called *America's First Gold Rush.* Arrive an hour before closing to be sure and catch the film. ✉ *1 Public Sq.* ☎ *706/864–2257* ⊕ *www. gastateparks.org/dahlonega* ⛟ *$7.*

OFF THE
BEATEN
PATH

Amicalola Falls State Park. This is claimed to be the highest cascading waterfall east of the Mississippi, with waters plunging an eye-popping 729 feet through a cluster of seven cascades. The surrounding 829-acre state park contains a visitor center, lodge, and restaurant, and is dotted with scenic campsites and cottages strategically situated near a network of nature trails, picnic sites, and fishing streams. The southern starting point of the more than 2,100-mile Appalachian Trail begins near Amicalola Falls. ✉ *418 Amicalola Falls Lodge Rd., Dawsonville* ⊹ *Off GA 52, 18 miles west of Dahlonega* ☎ *706/265–4703* ⊕ *www. gastateparks.org/AmicalolaFalls* ⛟ *Parking $5.*

VINEYARDS

Grapevines and wineries are popping up all over North Georgia, and burgundy-color signs lead the way to vineyards along the **Georgia Wine Highway.** The Dahlonega area is home to the largest concentration of wineries in Georgia. A listing of current wineries is available at ⊕ *www. georgiawine.com.* ■ TIP➔ **If time doesn't permit individual visits to the wineries, you can try North Georgia wines in the many tasting rooms on the Dahlonega square. Purchase a "Wine Walk" glass at the Dahlonega-Lumpkin County Visitors Center for $5 and get special discounted tastings at Dahlonega's six tasting rooms.**

Frogtown Cellars. This 57-acre vineyard and winery offers picturesque mountain views from its deck as well as a dramatic dining room. Since 2010, Frogtown wines have won more than 200 medals. Winemakers

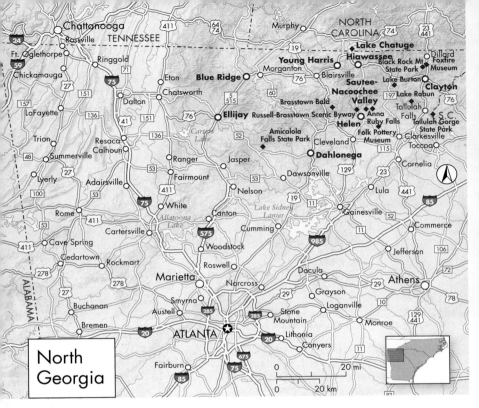

North Georgia

Craig and Sydney Kritzer believe it is one of the most awarded wineries in the country not located in California. Wine tastings are offered daily. Lunch is available Friday to Sunday; Sunday brunch and wine-tasting dinners require reservations. ⊠ *700 Ridge Point Dr., northeast of Dahlonega* ☎ *706/865–0687* ⊕ *www.frogtown.us.*

Montaluce Winery. Reminiscent of a grand Tuscan villa, this 11-acre vineyard features a state-of-the-art, 25,000-square-foot wine-making facility. Montaluce's spacious dining room–restaurant and multilevel terraces provide breathtaking views of mountain scenery. Complimentary winery tours are offered weekdays at 2 and weekends at noon. Wine tastings (for a fee) are offered at Montaluce's Mediterranean-inspired wine bar. Le Vigne, the winery's restaurant, is open for lunch daily with brunch on Sunday. Dinner is offered Wednesday through Sunday. Reservations are recommended. ⊠ *501 Hightower Church Rd.* ☎ *866/991–8466, 706/867–4060* ⊕ *www.montaluce.com.*

Three Sisters Vineyards. Dahlonega's first family-farm winery has 20 acres of plantings including Cabernet Franc, Cabernet Sauvignon, Pinot Blanc, and Chardonnay, along with American varietals such as Cynthiana-Norton. The relaxed winery is named for nearby Three Sisters Mountain, visible from the farm's gazebo. Deli meats and cheeses are available on the weekends, and a deck provides a comfortable spot for a picnic. The tasting room is decorated with folk art and pottery from the area, including a poster that proclaims "Thar's Wine in Them Thar Hills." A favorite from the winery is the robust Fat Boy Red. ✉ *439 Vineyard Way, northeast of Dahlonega* ☎ *706/865–9463* 🌐 *www.threesistersvineyards.com* 🕒 *Closed Mon.–Wed. and Jan.*

Wolf Mountain Vineyards & Winery. This award-winning winery features a 25-acre vineyard with hillside plantings of Cabernet Sauvignon, Syrah, Mourvèdre, and Touriga Nacional. The Craftsman-style lodge housing the winery and café offers tastings for a fee and serves lunch Thursday through Saturday from noon to 3, and a Sunday brunch between 12:30 and 2:30. Reservations are required. Wolf Mountain also offers quarterly gourmet dinners and guided tours of the grounds on weekends at 2. Some of the winery's acclaimed labels include Plenitude, a 70% Chardonnay and 30% Viognier blend, and Instinct, a Rhône-style red blend. ✉ *180 Wolf Mountain Trail, off U.S. 19/60, north of Dahlonega* ☎ *706/867–9862* 🌐 *www.wolfmountainvineyards.com* 🕒 *Closed Mon. Seasonal hours vary; call ahead.*

14

WHERE TO EAT

$$$ SEAFOOD

🍴 **Back Porch Oyster Bar.** Decorated in a breezy Key West style, this authentic seafood restaurant is owned and run by the Creef family, Outer Banks transplants who are serious about seafood. Don't let the landlocked mountain scenery fool you—fresh caught seafood is flown in from around the world daily. **Known for:** fresh oysters and seafood; outdoor dining overlooking the square. [$] *Average main: $24* ✉ *19 N. Chestatee St.* ☎ *706/864–8623* 🌐 *www.backporchoysterbar.net.*

$$$ AMERICAN

🍴 **Corkscrew Café.** This cozy restaurant housed in an old jail offers a martini and tapas bar upstairs and a large covered deck and patio for dining downstairs. Specialties include Mediterranean-inspired tapas that pair well with wine, as well as entrées such as almond-pecan crusted pork chop and rainbow trout. **Known for:** sophisticated comfort food; extensive wine list and creative cocktails. [$] *Average main: $24* ✉ *51 W. Main St.* ☎ *706/867–8551* 🌐 *www.thecorkscrewcafe.com* 🕒 *Closed Mon.*

WHERE TO STAY

$ HOTEL Fodor's Choice ★

🏨 **Amicalola Falls Lodge.** One of the most appealing mountain lodges in Georgia is part of the state park system and features panoramic views over the mountains from the massive glass-windowed lobby. **Pros:** Amicalola Falls and numerous outdoor activities are minutes away; stunning views of the mountains. **Cons:** no swimming pool; buffet-only restaurant is only on-site dining option. [$] *Rooms from: $139* ✉ *418 Amicalola Falls Lodge Rd., Dawsonville* ✥ *20 miles west of Dahlonega* ☎ *706/265–8888, 800/573–9656* 🌐 *www.amicalolafallslodge.com* 🛏 *57 rooms, 14 cottages* 🍽 *No meals.*

$ HOTEL

🏨 **Dahlonega Square Hotel & Villas.** This charming brick-red inn gave new life to the historic McGuire House just off the town square. **Pros:** convenient location walking distance to shops and restaurants; modern rooms and conveniences. **Cons:** often booked well in advance on weekends; no on-site breakfast. [$] *Rooms from: $110* ✉ *135 N. Chestatee St.* ☎ *706/867–1313* 🌐 *www.dahlonegasquarevilla.com* 🛏 *13 rooms, 5 villas* 🍽 *No meals.*

Three Sisters Vineyards has a friendly, down-to-earth tasting room. Be sure to try the Fat Boy Red if it's available.

$ B&B/INN **Lily Creek Lodge.** Tucked away on 9 acres, this eclectic European-styled B&B boasts beautiful grounds with native flower beds, walking trails, a waterfall, swimming pool, and bocce court. **Pros:** lovely grounds; close to Dahlonega, Montaluce, and Wolf Mountain Vineyards. **Cons:** narrow stairs to the uppermost room; rooms need some updating. [$] *Rooms from: $139* ✉ *2608 Auraria Rd.* ☎ *706/864–6848* 🌐 *www.lilycreeklodge.com* 🛏 *13 rooms* 🍴 *Breakfast.*

$ B&B/INN Fodor's Choice ★ **The Smith House.** Just a block from the town square, the family-owned Smith House has been serving guests in their inn and family-style restaurant for generations. **Pros:** comfortable amenities; handicap access on the main floor. **Cons:** no longer has pool; some rooms could use updating. [$] *Rooms from: $139* ✉ *84 S. Chestatee St.* ☎ *706/725–8148* 🌐 *www.smithhouse.com* 🛏 *16 rooms, 4 villas* 🍴 *Breakfast.*

NIGHTLIFE AND PERFORMING ARTS

The Crimson Moon. Set in the historic Parker-Nix Storehouse, a general store built in the 1850s, this intimate venue features local and nationally known live acoustic music, from blues and bluegrass to Celtic, folk rock, and country, five nights a week. It's also a great little café and coffeehouse serving lunch and dinner during the week with breakfast on the weekends. ✉ *24 N. Park St., Suite A* ☎ *706/864–3982* 🌐 *www.thecrimsonmoon.com.*

FAMILY **Historic Holly Theater.** This restored, classic small-town movie theater, built in 1946, stages live theater, movies, children's performances, concerts, and special events. Check out the schedule online for the latest offerings. ✉ *69 W. Main St.* ☎ *706/864–3759* 🌐 *www.hollytheater.com.*

SPORTS AND THE OUTDOORS

Appalachian Outfitters. Stop here to pick up equipment for self-guided canoeing and kayaking trips on the Chestatee and Etowah rivers. Tube rentals and shuttle service are also available for tubing trips on the Chestatee. ⊠ *2084 S. Chestatee, Hwy. 60 S* ☎ *706/864–7117, 800/426–7117* ⊕ *www.canoegeorgia.com.*

HELEN AND SAUTEE-NACOOCHEE VALLEY

32 miles northeast of Dahlonega; 88 miles northeast of Atlanta.

Helen was founded at the turn of the 20th century as a simple lumber outpost. In the 1960s, when logging declined, business leaders came up with a plan to transform the tiny village of 300 into a theme town, and "Alpine Helen" was born. Today many businesses along Helen's central streets sport a distinctive German facade, giving an initial impression that you've stumbled on a Bavarian vista in the middle of Appalachia. ■**TIP→ Don't expect small-town prices for anything from parking to ATM charges.** This is clearly not Bavaria, but the effect can be briefly contagious, making you feel as if you've stepped into a fairy tale. If it's too touristy, visit nearby areas for delightful crafts, shopping, and dining. Sautee and Nacoochee are the homes of the Habersham Winery, the Folk Pottery Museum of North Georgia, and a number of other pottery and craft shops.

GETTING HERE AND AROUND

While the quirky town of Helen may merit a quick stop, other nearby attractions a short drive away are also well worth visiting. Try the Folk Pottery Museum of Northeast Georgia to check out the area's centuries-old pottery tradition and Georgia's famous "face jugs." The Sautee and Nacoochee areas are accessible just south of Helen off GA 75.

ESSENTIALS

Visitor Information Helen Welcome Center. ⊠ *726 Bruckenstrasse, Helen* ☎ *706/878–2181, 800/858–8027* ⊕ *www.helenga.org.*

EXPLORING

Anna Ruby Falls. One of the crown jewels of the vast Chattahoochee National Forest, Anna Ruby Falls is actually the junction of Curtis and York creeks. With a drop of 153 feet, the stunning twin falls are accessible via a paved 0.4-mile footpath from the visitor center to the base of the falls. For more of a challenge, try the 4.6-mile Smith Creek Trail which leads from the base of Anna Ruby Falls to Unicoi State Park. ⊠ *3455 Anna Ruby Falls Rd., Helen* ☎ *706/878–1448* 🖪 *$3.*

FAMILY

Fodor's Choice

★

Folk Pottery Museum of Northeast Georgia. Located 4 miles southeast of Helen in the Sautee Nacoochee Center, this museum showcases a 200-year unbroken tradition of folk pottery in Northeast Georgia (especially in nearby Mossy Creek and the Gillsville-Lula area). Part of the 5,000-square-foot facility outlines how pottery is made and how it was used for essential household purposes. Exhibits showcase a 200-piece collection donated to the museum, including the whimsical face jugs that have become an emblem of Southern folk art. Pottery making demonstrations are frequently offered. Call ahead for dates and times. ⊠ *283 Hwy. 255, Sautee Nacoochee* ☎ *706/878–3300* ⊕ *www.folkpotterymuseum.com* 🖪 *$5.*

14

Habersham Vineyards & Winery. One of the oldest wineries in the state, Habersham Vineyards & Winery started producing in 1983. Stop by the winery's tasting room and gift shop to try one of their signature wines including Chardonnay, Merlot, Cabernet Sauvignon, and popular blends Scarlett, Signet, and Cherokee Rose. ✉ *7025 S. Main St. on GA 75, Helen* ☎ *706/878–9463* 🌐 *www.habershamwinery.com.*

WHERE TO EAT AND STAY

$ GERMAN 🍴 **Hofer's Bakery and Cafe.** Head to Hofer's for authentic, stone hearth, oven-baked breads and pastries, as well as specialties like Wiener schnitzel and bratwurst. On fall weekends, grab a table at their outdoor biergarten and enjoy live music along with your meal. **Known for:** fresh bread and pastries; authentic German cuisine. [$] *Average main: $10* ✉ *8758 N. Main St., Helen* ☎ *706/878–8200* 🌐 *www.hofers.com* 🕒 *No dinner.*

$$ ECLECTIC 🍴 **Mully's Nacoochee Grill.** Hand-cut steaks, fresh seafood, and seasonal vegetables are the focus at this casual restaurant set in a cheerful old house in Nacoochee Village, just outside town. Shrimp and grits, whole fried trout, and slow-cooked ribs are customer favorites. **Known for:** local trout dishes; hand-cut steaks. [$] *Average main: $18* ✉ *7277 S. Main St., Helen* ☎ *706/878–8020* 🌐 *www.mullysnacoocheegrill.com* 🕒 *Closed Mon. and Tues. (winter season only).*

$$$$ RENTAL 🏨 **The Cottages at Smithgall Woods.** As part of a 5,600-acre park run by the state of Georgia, these six cottages, set in old-growth hardwoods, offer a peaceful retreat. **Pros:** a luxurious and secluded retreat; hiking trails nearby. **Cons:** must bring your own fishing equipment; no food service. [$] *Rooms from: $325* ✉ *61 Tsalaki Trail, Helen* ☎ *706/878–3087, 800/318–5248* 🌐 *www.gastateparks.org/SmithgallWoods* 🛏 *6 cottages* 🍽 *No meals.*

$ RESORT 🏨 **The Lodge at Unicoi.** Choose either the comfortable mountain lodge, with 100 renovated lodge rooms, a one-, two-, or three-bedroom cottage (some with a fireplace), or one of the 105 campsites at this state-run accommodation within Unicoi State Park. **Pros:** live bluegrass and gospel music; less than 3 miles from Helen. **Cons:** breakfast isn't included in the rate; can be crowded in peak season. [$] *Rooms from: $125* ✉ *1788 GA 356, Helen* ✥ *3 miles north of Helen* ☎ *706/878–2201, 800/573–9659* 🌐 *www.gastateparks.org/Unicoi* 🛏 *100 rooms, 29 cottages.*

SPORTS AND THE OUTDOORS

FAMILY **Cool River Tubing.** "Tube the Hooch" with Cool River Tubing, which shuttles you on a bus upriver to begin the float back to town. Choose the short (one hour) or long (two hours) float trip. Prices are $8 for a single trip of either length or $12 all day. Cool River also operates a waterslide. A combination all-day ticket for tubing and waterslide is $16. For the land lovers, there's a zipline, climbing wall, and aerial adventure courses at their Headwaters Outpost. You can do it all, plus tubing, for $65. ✉ *590 Edelweiss Strasse, Helen* ☎ *706/878–2665, 706/878–9471 zipline and aerial adventures only* 🌐 *www.coolrivertubing.com.*

SHOPPING

FAMILY **The Gourd Place.** This unique museum and gourd and pottery store is filled with colorful gourd collections from around the world. Owners Priscilla Wilson and Janice Lymburner sell gourds and supplies to preserve dried gourds (a Southern specialty). They also produce attractive natural-glazed stoneware and porcelain dinnerware, vases, bowls, and luminaries using liquid clay poured into gourd molds. ✉ *2319 Duncan Bridge Rd., Sautee* ☎ *706/865–4048* ⊕ *www.gourdplace.com.*

FAMILY **Hickory Flat Pottery.** This working pottery studio in a large 116-year-old roadside farmhouse is filled with lots more than "just" beautiful pottery. Vibrant stained glass, a variety of jewelry, and fiber art are featured, along with the vivid, decorative, and functional stoneware of shop owner Cody Trautner, who enjoys sharing his craft by sending little bags of clay home with children. ✉ *13664 U.S. 197 N, Clarkesville* ✛ *4 miles north of Mark of the Potter* ☎ *706/947–0030* ⊕ *www.hickoryflatpottery.com* ☾ *Closed Tues.–Thurs. Jan.–Mar.*

FAMILY
Fodor'sChoice
★
Mark of the Potter. In an old gristmill with beautiful views of the Soque River, Mark of the Potter offers an outstanding selection of pottery from more than 30 artisans. The emphasis is on functional pieces, with a great variety of clay and firing techniques and glazes in every imaginable color. Items range from coffee scoops to lamps, mugs to elaborate vases and casserole dishes. The shop is legendary among Georgia-pottery lovers. Children and adults alike will enjoy sitting on the porch and feeding the huge pet trout. A potter works on the wheel at the shop on Saturday and Sunday. ✉ *9982 GA 197 N, Clarkesville* ☎ *706/947–3440* ⊕ *www.markofthepotter.com.*

FAMILY **Old Sautee Store.** This unique shop has been operating continuously since 1872. The front part of the store operates more as a museum, with antique farming implements, old-timey tonics and soaps, and even caskets on display. The retail store, influenced by an earlier owner's Scandinavian heritage, continues to sell Swedish farmer's cheese and Norwegian flatbread. Shoppers can also pick up old-time candy and toys. ✉ *2315 GA 17, Sautee* ✛ *5 miles south of Helen* ☎ *706/878–2281* ⊕ *www.oldsauteestore.com.*

EN
ROUTE
Russell-Brasstown Scenic Byway. Beginning and ending in Helen, the Russell-Brasstown Scenic Byway is a 41-mile loop through some of the most dramatic mountain scenery in northeastern Georgia. Start the counterclockwise drive from GA17/74 north of Helen, turn left on GA 180, left again at GA 348, and another left at GA 75 Alternate back to Helen. The loop passes the Raven Cliff Wilderness, wildlife management areas, the headwaters of the Chattahoochee River, a section of the Appalachian Trail, and goes near the state parks of Vogel, Unicoi, Smithgall Woods, and Brasstown Bald Mountain. ✉ *Helen.*

CLAYTON

35 miles northeast of Helen via GA 356, GA 197, and U.S. 76.

The town of Clayton, with a downtown filled with shops, is a gateway to North Georgia's mountains. The beautiful lakeshore and the grandeur of Black Rock Mountain State Park and Tallulah Gorge make a day tour of this area a memorable experience.

The culinary scene in Clayton and surrounding Rabun County has blossomed in recent years. Agriculture has a long tradition in these parts, but the marriage of farmers and chefs working together has yielded spectacular results. In January 2015, the State House of Representatives designated Rabun County as the Farm to Table Capital of Georgia. The local tourism authority, Explore Rabun, offers monthly Grow-Cook-Eat Farm & Food Tours with stops at farms, wineries, and restaurants throughout the region.

GETTING HERE AND AROUND

Clayton makes a good base to explore Tallulah Gorge State Park and its falls and Black Rock Mountain State Park. A short drive northwest on U.S. 76 will take you to several of the region's most appealing lakes, including Rabun and Chatuge.

ESSENTIALS

Visitor Information Explore Rabun—Rabun Tourism Development Authority. ⊠ *184 S. Main St., Suite 136* ☎ *706/212–0241, 706/982–4754 food tours* ⊕ *www.explorerabun.com.* **Rabun County Welcome Center.** ⊠ *232 U.S. 441 N* ☎ *706/782–4812* ⊕ *www.gamountains.com.*

EXPLORING

TOP ATTRACTIONS

FAMILY   **Foxfire Museum and Heritage Center.** Set on the slope of Black Mountain, this outdoor museum re-creates life in Appalachia before the days of electricity and running water. The museum features a collection of authentic and reconstructed log cabins, a gristmill, a blacksmith's shop, an operating weaving workshop, along with tools and displays about life in daily life and mountain culture. The Foxfire organization was born in 1966 when students at the Rabun Gap-Nacoochee School wrote articles for a magazine based on generations-old family stories. Their excitement in chronicling life in the Appalachians has led to more than a dozen Foxfire books, which have sold nearly 9 million copies. ⊠ *200 Foxfire La., off U.S. 441 at Black Rock Mountain Pkwy., Mountain City* ☎ *706/746–5828* ⊕ *www.foxfire.org* ⬚ *$8* ☉ *Closed Sun.*

Fodor'sChoice   **Tallulah Gorge State Park.** The 1,000-foot-deep Tallulah Gorge is one of ★   the most impressive in the country. In the late 1800s this area was one of the most visited destinations in the Southeast, with 17 hotels to house tourists who came to see the roaring falls on the Tallulah River. Then, in 1912, to provide electric power, the "Niagara of the South" was dammed, and the falls and tourism dried up. Today the state of Georgia has designated more than 20 miles of the state park as walking and mountain-biking trails. There's also a 16,000-square-foot interpretive center, a 63-acre lake with a beach, a picnic shelter, and 50 tent and RV sites. ⊠ *U.S. 441, 338 Jane Hurt Yarn Dr., Tallulah Falls* ☎ *706/754–7970* ⊕ *www.gastateparks.org/TallulahGorge* ⬚ *$5 parking.*

WORTH NOTING

FAMILY   **Black Rock Mountain State Park.** At more than 3,600 feet, Black Rock Mountain is the highest state park in Georgia. Named for the black gneiss rock visible on cliffs in the area, the 1,738-acre park has 10 miles of trails, a 17-acre lake, 53 campsites, a pioneer group campsite, and 10 cottages. The park offers majestic overlooks and a trail that leads visitors along the Eastern Continental Divide, from which water flows south and east to eventually reach the Atlantic Ocean, and on the other side, north and west to the mighty Mississippi River. ⊠ *Black*

Hike the rim trails at Tallulah Gorge State Park for spectacular views of the canyon below.

Rock Mountain Pkwy., Mountain City ✛ 3 miles northwest of Clay-
ton ☎ 706/746–2141, 800/864–7275 for camping and cottage reserva-
tions ⊕ www.gastateparks.org/BlackRockMountain ⌸ $5 daily-use fee
⊘ Closed mid-Dec.–mid-Mar.

FAMILY **Lake Burton.** One of the six lakes built by Georgia Railway and Power
Company, this 2,800-acre lake is in the Chattahoochee National Forest.
On the lake, at GA 197, is the **Lake Burton Fish Hatchery,** alongside
Moccasin Creek State Park. It has trout raceways (used to raise trout
from fingerlings) and a kids-only trout-fishing area. In extremely hot
weather, the hatchery is sometimes closed. ■TIP➔ **The state park is**
closed from December to mid-March but the hatchery is open year-
round. ⊠ *3655 Hwy. 197 N, Clarkesville ✛ Off U.S. 76, west of Clayton*
☎ 706/947–3194 ⊕ www.gastateparks.org/MoccasinCreek ⌸ $5 park
parking; free hatchery parking.

Lake Rabun. Built in 1915, the first of six lakes in the state built by
Georgia Railway and Power Company, Lake Rabun covers only 834
acres. Its small size is misleading, as its narrow fingers dart through
mountain valleys. Lightly visited by tourists and populated with weekend homes and old boathouses, it has a low-key charm. The lake offers
boating, fishing, and camping. There's a small beach at **Lake Rabun**
Beach Recreation Area at the east end of the lake available for day use
for a fee. ⊠ *5320 Lake Rabun Rd., Lakemont ✛ West of U.S. 23/441*
via Old Hwy. 441 S and Lake Rabun Rd., 9 miles southwest of Clayton
☎ 706/754–6221 Chattooga River Ranger District Office.

Tiger Mountain Vineyards. Started on a five-generation-old family farm
in 1995 by Dr. John and Martha Ezzard, Tiger Mountain Vineyards

is known for unusual varietals of French and Portuguese grapes such as Touriga Nacional and Tannat, as well as the native Norton grape—grown on the slopes of Tiger Mountain. Tastings are available for a small fee. Lunch and dinner are served on the weekends (April–November) in their lovely restored Red Barn Cafe. The tasting room frequently features live music and events; call ahead for schedule. ⊠ *2592 Old Hwy. 441, Tiger ✈ 8 minutes south of Clayton* ☎ *706/782–4777* ⊕ *www.tigerwine.com.*

WHERE TO EAT

$$$

AMERICAN

✕ **Fortify Kitchen & Bar.** At one of Clayton's designated "farm to table" restaurants, chef Jamie Allred's updated Southern cuisine highlights the region's best produce, meats, and spirits in a relaxed, down-to-earth environment. With exposed brick walls and a small wooden bar you'll want to huddle around, Fortify is simply about good food, fun cocktails, and a wine list that includes a few local selections. **Known for:** focus on local, seasonal ingredients; craft cocktails. $ *Average main: $24* ⊠ *69 N. Main St.* ☎ *706/782–0050* ⊕ *www.fortifyclayton.com* ☉ *Closed Sun. and Mon.*

$

BARBECUE

✕ **The Wicked Pig.** With its ample outdoor patio and live music, this fun little joint in downtown Clayton is a great place to kick back and dig into some fresh-from-the pit hickory-smoked barbecue. There's pulled pork, ribs, and brisket with your choice of seven house-made regional sauces, as well as salads, burgers, and tacos. **Known for:** flavorful smoked 'que; variety of sauces to suit every palate. $ *Average main: $12* ⊠ *151 N. Main St.* ☎ *706/782–4300* ⊕ *www.twpbbq.com* ☉ *Closed Mon. No dinner Sun.*

WHERE TO STAY

$$

B&B/INN

Fodor's Choice

★

▦ **Beechwood Inn.** Operating as an inn for more than 100 years, the Beechwood offers sophisticated yet down-to-earth Southern hospitality in a lovely two-story wood lodge overlooking Clayton. **Pros:** beautiful setting in close proximity to Clayton; food and wine focus. **Cons:** slanted floors in some rooms can be tricky to navigate; most rooms have showers only. $ *Rooms from: $189* ⊠ *220 Beechwood Inn Dr.* ☎ *706/782–5485* ⊕ *www.beechwoodinn.ws* ⇗ *11 rooms, 1 cabin* ❙◉❙ *Breakfast.*

$

HOTEL

▦ **Dillard House.** An inviting cluster of cottages, motel-style rooms, and a popular family-style restaurant, this establishment sits on a plateau near the state border. **Pros:** offers a variety of accommodation styles; fishing and horseback riding available. **Cons:** on-site restaurant relies too much on its past reputation; breakfast not included in rate. $ *Rooms from: $139* ⊠ *768 Franklin St., Dillard* ☎ *706/746–5348, 800/541–0671* ⊕ *www.dillardhouse.com* ⇗ *92 rooms, 25 chalets and cottages* ❙◉❙ *No meals.*

$$

B&B/INN

Fodor's Choice

★

▦ **Glen-Ella Springs Inn & Restaurant.** This restored country inn and restaurant, constructed in 1875 and listed on the National Register of Historic Places, has a rustic but polished charm. **Pros:** eager staff; picturesque perennial and herb gardens. **Cons:** fills up quickly on the weekends; limited number of rooms can accommodate families with children. $ *Rooms from: $185* ⊠ *1789 Bear Gap Rd., Clarkesville*

☎ *706/754–7295, 888/455–8786* 🌐 *www.glenella.com* 🛏 *16 rooms* 🍴 *Breakfast.*

$ B&B/INN 🏨 **Lake Rabun Hotel.** Set in shady hemlocks across the road from Lake Rabun, this romantic hotel, built in 1922, has rough-hewn wood paneling, handmade furniture, and a large working fieldstone fireplace. **Pros:** historic inn rooms as well as recently added contemporary rooms; easy access to Lake Rabun activities; gourmet breakfast included in rate. **Cons:** no room TVs; no elevator; no children under 10. [$] *Rooms from: $149* ✉ *35 Andrea La., Lakemont* ☎ *706/782–4946* 🌐 *www.lakerabunhotel.com* 🛏 *15 rooms, 1 cottage* 🍴 *Breakfast.*

SPORTS AND THE OUTDOORS

WHITE-WATER RAFTING

Chattooga River. The first river in the Southeast to be designated a Wild and Scenic River by Congress, the Chattooga River forms the border between Georgia and South Carolina. With Class II to Class V rapids, the Chattooga is popular for white-water rafting, especially in spring and summer. Movie buffs should note that this was one of the locations for *Deliverance.* ✉ *Clayton* ✣ *From Clayton drive east 7 miles on U.S. 76 to Hwy. 76 Bridge at Georgia–South Carolina state line.*

Nantahala Outdoor Center. The North Carolina–based Nantahala Outdoor Center, the largest rafting company in the region, has an outpost on the Chattooga for Class III and Class IV trips starting at $100 per person. They also offer trips on the Nantahala and Ocoee Rivers. ✉ *NOC Chattooga Outpost, 851A Chattooga Ridge Rd., Mountain Rest* ☎ *888/905–7238* 🌐 *www.noc.com.*

Southeastern Expeditions. This locally owned outfitter offers full-day and overnight guided trips on the Chattooga, starting at $90 per person. ✉ *7350 U.S. 76 E* ☎ *800/868–7238* 🌐 *www.southeastern-expeditions.com.*

Wildwater Rafting. This is the oldest outfitter in the area with a campus that also features ziplining and overnight accommodations. Half-day mini-trips are also offered as well as full-day Section III, IV, and overnight trips on the Chattooga beginning at $74.95 per person. ✉ *1251 Academy Rd., Long Creek* ✣ *1½ miles north of U.S. 76, 12 miles east of Clayton* ☎ *866/319–8870* 🌐 *www.wildwaterrafting.com.*

SHOPPING

FAMILY **Goats on the Roof.** Yes, there really are goats on the roof at this colorful roadside attraction off the main drag near Clayton. While it is kind of a tourist trap, it's a fun one that's down-to-earth and full of charm. The shop features handcrafted items like pottery, goat's milk soaps, Amish furniture, and local jams and jellies, along with toys, T-shirts and goodies. You can also get fresh-made fudge and "nitro" ice cream in the café across the way. There's even gem mining on-site. Of course, the main attraction is the goats, which you can feed via a pulley system. Kids of all ages love this place! ✉ *3026 U.S. 441 S., Tiger* ☎ *706/782–2784* 🌐 *www.goats-on-the-roof.com.*

Main Street Gallery. One of the state's best sources for folk art, Main Street Gallery carries works by more than 75 regional artists. The store also carries jewelry, pottery, paintings, and sculptures. ✉ *51 N. Main St.* ☎ *706/782–2440* 🌐 *www.mainstreetgallery.net* 🕒 *Closed Sun. and Wed.*

HIAWASSEE, YOUNG HARRIS, AND LAKE CHATUGE

26 miles northwest of Clayton, via U.S. 76; 21 miles north of Helen via GA 75/17.

The little town of Hiawassee, population 750, and nearby Young Harris, population 600, are near the largest lake in North Georgia, Lake Chatuge, and the tallest mountain in the state, Brasstown Bald. The lake has excellent boating and other water-themed recreation. Appealing mountain resorts are nearby as well. A half-hour drive leads to Brasstown Bald, where temperatures even on the hottest summer day rarely rise above 80°F. The Georgia Mountain Fairgrounds has a permanent location on the shores of Lake Chatuge. A number of festivals are held at the fairgrounds, including the Fall Festival and State Fiddler's Convention in October, and the Georgia Mountain Fair held in July.

ESSENTIALS

Visitor Information Towns County Chamber of Commerce. ✉ *1411 Jack Dayton Circle, Young Harris* ☎ *706/896–4966, 800/984–1543* 🌐 *www.mountaintopga.com.*

EXPLORING

FAMILY Fodor's Choice ★ **Brasstown Bald.** In the Chattahoochee National Forest, Brasstown Bald reaches 4,784 feet, the highest point in Georgia. Below the Bald is Georgia's only cloud forest, an area of lichen-covered trees often kept wet by clouds and fog. From the observation platform at the top of the Bald on a clear day you can see Georgia, North Carolina, South Carolina, and Tennessee. A paved but steep foot trail leads from the parking lot (where there are restrooms and a picnic area) to the visitor center, which has exhibits and interpretative programs. You also can ride a bus to the visitor center. ✉ *2941 Hwy. 180 Spur, Hiawassee* ✣ *18 miles southwest of Hiawassee via U.S. 76, GA 75, GA 180, and GA 180 Spur* ☎ *706/896–2556* 🌐 *www.fs.fed.us* 🎟 *$5* 🕒 *Closed Jan.–Mar.*

Crane Creek Vineyards. Nestled in the Appalachian foothills, Crane Creek features scenic ponds and 200-year-old oak trees. The winery produces 15 regional artisanal wines based on the 13 grape varieties it grows. The most popular choices are Vidal Blanc, Seyval, and Norton. Tastings are offered for a fee in the tasting room, located in an old farmhouse. Bottles of wine and take-away food are also available to be enjoyed on decks overlooking the vineyards. ✉ *916 Crane Creek Rd., off GA 515, Young Harris* ☎ *706/379–1236* 🌐 *www.cranecreekvineyards.com* 🕒 *Closed Mon.*

WHERE TO STAY

$$ RESORT 🏨 **Brasstown Valley Resort and Spa.** For upscale, lodge-style accommodations in a serene mountain setting, this resort is a great option. **Pros:** elegant but rustic rooms; an abundance of activities on-site. **Cons:** spa is not located in lodge; dining options are limited in off-season. [$] *Rooms from:*

On a clear day, you can see Georgia, North Carolina, South Carolina, and Tennessee from the observation tower at Brasstown Bald.

$190 ✉ 6321 U.S. 76, Young Harris ☎ 706/379–9900, 800/201–3205 🌐 www.brasstownvalley.com 🛏 200 rooms, 8 cottages 🍴 No meals.

$$ RESORT 🏨 **The Ridges Resort on Lake Chatuge.** With new owners and a complete renovation underway in 2017, changes are afoot at this lodge on the shores of gorgeous Lake Chatuge. **Pros:** restaurant on-site; updated rooms. **Cons:** no longer affiliated with adjacent marina which can be confusing; service can be inconsistent. [$] *Rooms from: $151 ✉ 3499 Hwy. 76 W, Young Harris ☎ 706/896–2262 🌐 www.theridgesresort.com 🛏 66 rooms, 13 villas 🍴 No meals.*

BLUE RIDGE AND ELLIJAY

39 miles southwest of Hiawassee via U.S. 76/GA 515; 53 miles northwest of Dahlonega via GA 52 and U.S. 76/GA 515. Ellijay is 15 miles southwest of Blue Ridge via US 76.

Blue Ridge is one of the most pleasant small mountain towns in North Georgia. After you've eaten breakfast or lunch and shopped for antiques, gifts, or crafts at Blue Ridge's many small shops, you can ride the revived Blue Ridge Scenic Railway to McCaysville, a town at the Tennessee line, and then back through the mountains. It's also a paradise for nature lovers. Fannin County (of which Blue Ridge is the county seat) is known as the "Trout Capital of Georgia." The beautiful Toccoa River is a popular destination for fly-fishing, hiking, canoeing, and more.

Just 15 miles southwest is the scenic town of Ellijay. Billed as "Georgia's Apple Capital," Ellijay is also popular among antiques aficionados. The most popular time to visit Ellijay is in fall, when roadside stands brimming with delicious ripe apples dot the landscape. The annual Georgia Apple Festival takes place the second and third weekends of October.

ESSENTIALS

Visitor Information Fannin County Chamber of Commerce and Welcome Center. ✉ *152 Orvin Lance Dr., Blue Ridge* ☎ *706/621–5168, 800/899–6867* ⊕ *www.blueridgemountains.com.* **Gilmer County Chamber of Commerce and Welcome Center.** ✉ *696 First Ave., East Ellijay* ☎ *706/635–7400* ⊕ *www.gilmerchamber.com.*

EXPLORING

FAMILY **Blue Ridge Scenic Railway.** Ride the rails on a four-hour, 26-mile round-trip excursion along the Toccoa River. The trip includes a stop in **McCaysville,** smack on the Georgia–Tennessee state line. Several restaurants, shops, and galleries are open during the two-hour layover. The train, which has open Pullman cars and is pulled by diesel engines, is staffed with friendly volunteer hosts. Premier class is available to those over 18 and includes snacks and a little extra TLC. The ticket office, on the National Register of Historic Places, dates from 1905 and was originally the depot of the L&N Railroad. Children of all ages enjoy the ride. ∎ **TIP➔ In summer you may want to consider the air-conditioned coaches.** ✉ *241 Depot St., Blue Ridge* ☎ *706/632–8724, 877/413–8724* ⊕ *www.brscenic.com* 🎫 *$44–$89, depending on season and ticket type* ⊙ *No train Jan.–Mid-Mar.*

FAMILY **Hillcrest Orchards.** Buy freshly picked apples (usually early September to late November) at this 80-acre farm. Homemade jellies, jams, breads, and doughnuts are available at the farm's market and bakery. On September and October weekends, the Apple Pickin' Jubilee features live music, wagon rides, apple picking, and other activities. There's also a petting zoo and a picnic area. ✉ *9696 GA 52E, Ellijay* ☎ *706/273–3838* ⊕ *www.hillcrestorchards.net* 🎫 *$8–$10 for special events including Apple Pickin' Jubilee* ⊙ *Closed Dec.–Aug.*

Mercier Orchards. This family-owned apple orchard has been producing delicious apples and other fruits for more than 70 years. Apple season is typically from September to November, but even outside the season you can stop in at Mercier's huge farm market and bakery to pick up some of its famous fried apple pies and other homemade goodies. You can also grab lunch in the deli and taste Mercier's own hard-pressed ciders in the farm winery. The orchard is especially buzzing with activity in the fall, when you can take a hayride and pick your own apples, and in the summer when blueberry season arrives. Call ahead to find out what fruits are in season and for the latest details on orchard events. ✉ *8660 Blue Ridge Dr., off Hwy. 5, Blue Ridge* ☎ *706/632–3411* ⊕ *www.mercier-orchards.com.*

FAMILY **Swan Drive-In Theatre.** Originally opened in 1955, this is one of only five drive-in movie theaters operating in Georgia. You can take in a movie under the stars and fill up on corn dogs, onion rings, funnel cakes, and popcorn from the concession stand. ✉ *651 Summit St., Blue Ridge* ☎ *706/632–5235* ⊕ *www.swan-drive-in.com* 🎫 *$8* ⊙ *Closed Mon.–Thurs.; call ahead in winter* ☞ *Cash only.*

WHERE TO EAT

$$$ MODERN AMERICAN 🍴 **Harvest on Main.** Focused on local and seasonal cuisine, this popular Blue Ridge restaurant even harvests its own specialty produce, eggs, and honey. Chef-owner Danny Mellman and his wife, Michelle, who manages the farm, have created a sophisticated yet down-to-earth culinary destination housed in an airy cedar "cabin" downtown. **Known for:** true farm-to-table cuisine; upscale comfort food in an inviting, rustic space; excellent bar program. [$] *Average main: $24* ✉ *576 E. Main St., Blue Ridge* ☎ *706/946–6164* 🌐 *www.harvestonmain.com* 🕒 *Closed Wed.*

$ BARBECUE 🍴 **Poole's Bar-B-Q.** It's hard to miss this East Ellijay barbecue legend. Just look for the roadside "Pig Hill of Fame," a mass of pig-shape signs memorializing the more than 3,000 hogs who have sacrificed their lives for some seriously good 'cue. The owner, Oscar "Colonel" Poole, is quite the colorful character. **Known for:** hole-in-the-wall kitschiness; down-home Southern barbecue. [$] *Average main: $10* ✉ *164 Craig St., East Ellijay* ☎ *706/635–4100* 🌐 *www.poolesbarbq.com* 🕒 *Closed Mon.–Wed.*

WHERE TO STAY

$ HOTEL 🏨 **Best Western Mountain View Inn.** This two-story motel sits high on a hilltop above East Ellijay and half of its rooms have mountain views. **Pros:** close to eating and shopping areas; indoor heated pool. **Cons:** entrance is hard to find; very steep; no elevator. [$] *Rooms from: $109* ✉ *43 Coosawattee Dr., East Ellijay* ☎ *706/515–1500, 866/515–4515* 🌐 *www.bwmountainviewinn.com* 🛏 *52 rooms* 🍽 *Breakfast.*

$$ B&B/INN 🏨 **Blue Ridge Inn Bed & Breakfast.** Housed in an 1890 Victorian just steps from the Blue Ridge Scenic Railway (it was built as the railroad supervisor's home), this lovely B&B blends historic charm with modern creature comforts. **Pros:** easy walking distance to shops and restaurants; historic charm with modern amenities. **Cons:** can't accommodate families with children under 13. [$] *Rooms from: $165* ✉ *477 W 1st St., Blue Ridge* ☎ *706/661–7575* 🌐 *www.blueridgeinnbandb.com* 🛏 *8 rooms* 🍽 *Breakfast.*

MACON AND THE ANTEBELLUM TRAIL

The antebellum South, filtered through the romanticized gauze of *Gone With the Wind,* evokes graciousness, gentility, and a code of honor that saw many a duel between dashing gentlemen. Certainly, the historic architecture along the Antebellum Trail would endorse this picture, and even though many of the white-column mansions were built with the sweat of slaves, there is much to appreciate. Anchored between Macon and Athens, the trail was designated a state trail in 1985, and links the historical communities of Watkinsville, Madison, Eatonton, Milledgeville, and Old Clinton, all of which escaped the rampages of General Sherman's army on his march in 1864 from Atlanta to Savannah.

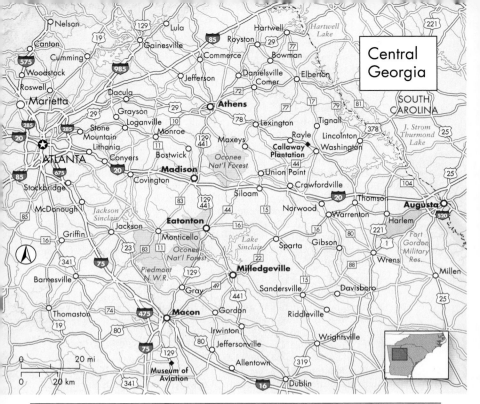

MACON

85 miles southeast of Atlanta via I–75.

At the state's geographic center, Macon, founded in 1823, has more than 100,000 flowering cherry trees, which it celebrates each March with a knockout festival. With 14 historic districts and 6,000 individual structures listed on the National Register of Historic Places, its antebellum and Victorian homes are among the state's best preserved. Everywhere you turn in the downtown business district there are preservation and rehabilitation projects—new lofts, shops, and restaurants now occupy once abandoned buildings. Following a $1.2 million restoration, the Capitol Theatre (originally founded as a bank in 1897) is a popular venue for movies and concerts; after a three-year renovation, St. Joseph's Catholic Church is more impressive than ever; and the old Armory, complete with its first-floor dance hall, is finding new life as a special events space.

Daily news is reported in the *Telegraph*. The *Georgia Informer*, the *11th Hour*, and the upscale *Macon Magazine* are good sources of information on local arts and cultural events.

GETTING HERE AND AROUND

Poet Raymond Farr, in his "Back Roads to Macon," writes of a cozy roadside diner, the sprawling farmland, and a folksy bit of wisdom scrawled on a mailbox in the nearby town of Cordele: "Whatever your destination, thank God you arrive." These kinds of small touches add charm to the back roads to Macon. Or, for a speedier and somewhat less scenic route, jump on U.S. 441.

ESSENTIALS

Visitor Information Macon-Bibb County Convention and Visitors Bureau. ✉ *450 Martin Luther King Jr. Blvd.* ☎ *478/743–1074, 800/768–3401* ⊕ *www.maconga.org.*

EXPLORING

TOP ATTRACTIONS

Fodor's Choice ★

Hay House. Designed by the New York firm T. Thomas & Son in the mid-1800s, Hay House is a study in fine Italianate architecture prior to the Civil War. The marvelous stained-glass windows and many technological advances, including indoor plumbing, make a tour worthwhile. The home's dining room has recently been restored to its 1870s appearance. Tours depart on the hour. For a small upcharge, you can do the "Top of the House" tour, which explores the soaring cupola and widow walk. ✉ *934 Georgia Ave.* ☎ *478/742–8155* ⊕ *www.hayhouse.org* ☞ *$11* ☞ *Last tour begins at 3 daily.*

Ocmulgee National Monument. Located 3 miles east of downtown Macon, Ocmulgee is a significant archaeological site as it's been occupied for more than 17,000 years; at its peak, between AD 900 and AD 1100, it was populated by the Mississippian peoples who were renowned mound builders. There's a reconstructed earth lodge and displays of pottery, effigies, and jewelry of copper and shells discovered in the burial mound. Call or check the park's online schedule for special Lantern Light Tours and other educational opportunities. ✉ *1207 Emery Hwy.* ✛ *Take U.S. 80 E* ☎ *478/752–8257* ⊕ *www.nps.gov/ocmu* ☞ *Free.*

Tubman Museum. This museum honors Harriet Tubman, the former slave who led more than 300 people to freedom as one of the conductors of the Underground Railroad. The museum's signature piece is a large mural depicting several centuries of black culture. Permanent galleries are focused on African American inventors, Middle Georgia history, and folk art. Rotating exhibits showcase African American arts and culture. ✉ *310 Cherry St.* ☎ *478/743–8544* ⊕ *www.tubmanmuseum. com* ☞ *$10* ☉ *Closed Sun. and Mon.*

WORTH NOTING

The Big House - The Allman Brothers Band Museum. Affectionately known as "The Big House," this large Tudor-style building was home to members of the Allman Brothers Band and their families during the early 1970s. It was here that they collaborated and wrote some of the band's early songs, which would eventually bring them stardom and launch a new genre of music—Southern Rock. In 2010, the home was restored and opened as a museum showcasing the band's guitars, clothing, photographs, posters, gold records, and other memorabilia.

✉ *2321 Vineville Ave.* ☎ *478/741–5551* 🌐 *www.thebighousemuseum.com* 🎫 *$10* 🕒 *Closed Mon.–Wed.*

FAMILY **Georgia Sports Hall of Fame.** With its old-style ticket booths, this shrine to Georgia sports with over 300 inductees has the look and feel of an old ballpark; sports buffs will feel right at home. Exhibits, though dated, include a variety of interactive, touch-screen kiosks, and honor sports—including baseball, golf, track and field, and football—at all levels, from prep and college teams to professional. ✉ *301 Cherry St.* ☎ *478/752–1585* 🌐 *www.georgiasportshalloffame.com* 🎫 *$8* 🕒 *Closed Sun. Available for group tours only on Mon.*

FAMILY **Macon Museum of Arts and Sciences.** Displaying everything from a whale skeleton to fine art, this museum appeals to adults and children alike. The Discovery House, an interactive exhibit for children, is modeled after an artist's garret. There's also a mini-zoo and the Mark Smith Planetarium on-site. ✉ *4182 Forsyth Rd.* ☎ *478/477–3232* 🌐 *www.masmacon.org* 🎫 *$10* 🕒 *Closed Mon.*

OFF THE BEATEN PATH **Museum of Aviation.** This museum at Robins Air Force Base has an extraordinary collection of 90 vintage aircraft and missiles, including a MiG, an SR-71 (Blackbird), a U-2, and assorted other flying machines from past campaigns. From Macon take Interstate 75 south to Exit 146 (Centerville/Warner Robins) and turn left onto Watson Boulevard, 7 miles to Route 247/U.S. 129, then right for 2 miles. ✉ *1942 Heritage Blvd., Robins AFB, Warner Robins* ✥ *Off U.S. 129, 20 miles south of Macon* ☎ *478/926–6870* 🌐 *www.museumofaviation.org* 🎫 *Free.*

WHERE TO EAT AND STAY

$$$$ AMERICAN 🍴 **Downtown Grill.** Tucked away in a city block of renovated warehouses, this old-school English steak house and cigar bar is a Macon institution. Old Georgian brick and dark wood accents give a romantic flair to the decor. **Known for:** classic steakhouse options like filet mignon; hard-to-find location; cigar bar on-site. [$] *Average main: $25* ✉ *562 Mulberry St. La.* ☎ *478/742–5999* 🌐 *www.macondowntowngrill.com* 🕒 *Closed Sun.*

$$$ AMERICAN 🍴 **Tic Toc Room.** Upscale and stylish, this downtown restaurant serves new American fare with Asian and Italian influences. Prime steaks are a staple of the menu, which also includes lobster ravioli, osso buco, and seared ahi tuna with crunchy Asian slaw. **Known for:** prime steaks and seafood; former home of Miss Anne's Tic Toc where Macon music legends performed; inventive martinis. [$] *Average main: $23* ✉ *408 Martin Luther King Jr. Blvd.* ☎ *478/744–0123* 🌐 *www.thetictocroom.com* 🕒 *Closed Sun.*

$$ B&B/INN 🏨 **1842 Inn.** With its white-pillar front porch and period antiques, it's easy to see why this place is considered one of the region's top inns. **Pros:** a taste of antebellum grandeur; friendly, attentive service. **Cons:** no suites available; often booked up. [$] *Rooms from: $189* ✉ *353 College St.* ☎ *478/741–1842, 800/336–1842* 🌐 *www.1842inn.com* 🛏 *19 rooms* 🍽 *Breakfast.*

$ HOTEL 🏨 **Hilton Garden Inn Macon/Mercer University.** There aren't many hotels in downtown Macon, but this trusted chain is just 2 miles from the city center on the campus of Mercer University, making it a safe bet.

Ocmulgee National Monument, just outside Macon, includes a reconstructed meeting place, the Earth Lodge, and artifacts of the Mississippian peoples who lived here 1,000 years ago.

Pros: easy access to downtown and the interstates; suites with sitting areas available. **Cons:** a bit pricey for the area; can be busy with college groups. $ *Rooms from: $129* ✉ *1220 Stadium Dr.* ☎ *478/741–5527* ⊕ *www.hiltongardeninn.com* ⇆ *101 rooms* ⧉ *No meals.*

MILLEDGEVILLE

32 miles northeast of Macon on GA 49.

Novelist and short-story writer Flannery O'Connor is one of Milledgeville's most famous residents. The author of novels *Wise Blood* and *The Violent Bear It Away* spent the last 13 years of her life at her family farm just north of town.

Locals believe ghosts haunt what remains of the antebellum homes in Milledgeville. Laid out as the state capital of Georgia in 1803 (a title it held until Atlanta assumed the role in 1868), the town was not as fortunate as Madison in escaping Union torches during the Civil War. Sherman's troops stormed through here with a vengeance after the general heard hardship stories from Union soldiers who had escaped from a prisoner-of-war camp in nearby Andersonville. Quite a few antebellum buildings remain, including the Old Governor's Mansion and the old statehouse.

GETTING HERE AND AROUND

Travel by car to Milledgeville, then park and hop aboard the Milledgeville Trolley Tour. This red coach will take you through the city's landmark historic district, with stops at such spots as the Old Governor's Mansion and the Stetson-Sanford House. The tour leaves from

Spend an afternoon strolling through Eatonton's historic district, which is full of antebellum homes.

the Convention & Visitors Bureau and is available weekdays at 10 and Saturday at 2 for $12.

ESSENTIALS

Visitor Information Milledgeville Convention & Visitors Bureau. ✉ *200 W. Hancock St.* ☎ *478/452–4687, 800/653–1804* ⊕ *www.milledgevillecvb.com.*

EXPLORING
TOP ATTRACTIONS

Andalusia Farm. A picturesque farm with peacocks, a pond, and a lofty barn, Andalusia inspired much of Flannery O'Connor's work. The 1850s farmhouse, untouched since her death in 1964, provides incredible insight into the life of this prolific writer. The home and grounds are open for self-guided tours, and the gift shop sells her books and other memorabilia. ✉ *2628 N. Columbia St.* ☎ *478/454–4029* ⊕ *www. andalusiafarm.org* 💲 *$10 (suggested donation)* ⊘ *Closed Mon.–Wed.*

Old Governor's Mansion. This grand 1838 Greek Revival mansion became Sherman's headquarters during the war. His soldiers are said to have tossed government documents out of the windows and fueled their fires with Confederate money. Home to eight Georgian governors, and the founding building of Georgia College and State University, the mansion underwent a painstaking $10 million restoration in the early 2000s. Guided tours of the building are given daily, on the hour. Specialty tours can be arranged in advance for an additional fee. ✉ *120 S. Clark St.* ☎ *478/445–4545* ⊕ *www.gcsu.edu/mansion* 💲 *$10* ⊘ *Closed Mon.*

WORTH NOTING

Flannery O'Connor Room. Fans of Southern literature will want to visit the Flannery O'Connor Room at Georgia College and State University's Russell Library. Many of the author's handwritten manuscripts and a few furniture items are on display. A highlight is viewing the typewriter where she wrote many of her famous tales. ⊠ *221 N. Clarke St.* ☎ *478/445–4391* ⊕ *www.gcsu.edu/library* ⌕ *Free* ☾ *Closed Sun. and university breaks.*

Memory Hill Cemetery. Flannery O'Connor, who suffered from lupus and died at age 39, is buried at historic Memory Hill Cemetery. Literary scholars from around the world come here to pay their respects. ⊠ *300 W. Franklin St., Macon.*

14

WHERE TO EAT AND STAY

$

PIZZA

✕ **The Brick.** This eatery has a comfortable, worn-at-the-elbows appeal, the perfect backdrop for munching on massive pizzas with names like the Hogzilla and Hawaii Five-Oh. Vegetarians will appreciate the Environmentally Correct pie with its all-veggie toppings. **Known for:** homemade pizza, pasta, and "pub grub"; good beer selection. Ⓢ *Average main: $9* ⊠ *136 W. Hancock St.* ☎ *478/452–0089* ⊕ *www.thebrick93.com.*

$$

B&B/INN

☖ **Antebellum Inn.** This classic Southern mansion, converted to an inn, features two parlors, a wraparound porch, a guest cottage, and five unique guest suites. **Pros:** excellent home-cooked breakfasts; lovely grounds with pool. **Cons:** books up quickly; wine and cheese reception not offered consistently. Ⓢ *Rooms from: $159* ⊠ *200 N. Columbia St.* ☎ *478/453–3993* ⊕ *www.antebelluminn.com* ⇘ *5 rooms, 1 cottage* ⧀ *Breakfast.*

EATONTON

20 miles northwest of Milledgeville on U.S. 129/441.

Right in the middle of the Antebellum Trail, Eatonton is a historic trove of houses that still retains the rare Southern architecture that survived Sherman's torches. But this isn't the only source of pride for this idyllic town. Take a look at the courthouse lawn; it's not your imagination—that really is a giant statue of a rabbit.

The **Eatonton-Putnam Chamber of Commerce** provides printed maps detailing landmarks related to Eatonton native Alice Walker, who won the Pulitzer Prize for her novel *The Color Purple*. It also has information on the many fine examples of antebellum architecture in Eatonton, including descriptions and photographs of the town's prize antebellum mansions, and a walking tour of Victorian homes.

GETTING HERE AND AROUND

As with most cities along the Antebellum Trail, Eatonton is best reached by car. As you travel there via U.S. 441, check out the scenic views of pastures, mountain valleys, and rivers.

ESSENTIALS

Visitor Information Eatonton-Putnam Chamber of Commerce. ⊠ *Plaza Arts Center, 305 N. Madison Ave.* ☎ *706/485–7701* ⊕ *www.eatonton.com.*

EXPLORING

FAMILY **Uncle Remus Museum.** Eatonton is the birthplace of celebrated novelist Joel Chandler Harris, of Br'er Rabbit and Uncle Remus fame. This museum, built from authentic slave cabins, houses countless carvings, paintings, first-edition books, and other artwork depicting the characters made famous by the imaginative author. It's on the grounds of a park. Note the museum closes for lunch from noon until 1 daily, so plan your visit accordingly. ✉ *Turner Park, U.S. 441, 214 Oak St.* ☎ *706/485–6856* ⊕ *www.uncleremusmuseum.org* 💲 *$5.*

SPORTS AND THE OUTDOORS

Eatonton sits in the center of Georgia's Lake Country. Lake Oconee and Lake Sinclair, both created and maintained by Georgia Power, are nearby.

Lake Sinclair Recreation Area. Lake Sinclair is a favorite of anglers and is the site of a fishing tournament each year. Georgia Power maintains several parks with boat ramps, fishing piers, and campgrounds. About 11 miles from Eatonton, Lake Sinclair Recreation Area, maintained by the U.S. Forestry Service, has a beach, boat ramp, and campsites. ✉ *Twin Bridges Rd.* ☎ *770/297–3000* ⊕ *www.fs.fed.us.*

Lawrence Shoals Park. On the shores of Lake Oconee, the second-largest body of water in Georgia, Lawrence Shoals Park offers a boat ramp, beach area, picnic shelter, and camping facilities. ✉ *123 Wallace Dam Rd.* ☎ *706/485–5494* ⊕ *www.georgiapower.com/lakes.*

MADISON

22 miles north of Eatonton on U.S. 129/144.

In 1809 Madison was described as "the most cultured and aristocratic town on the stagecoach route from Charleston to New Orleans," and today that charm still prevails, in large part because General Sherman's Union Army deliberately bypassed the town, thus saving it for posterity. From the picturesque town square, with its specialty shops and businesses, you can walk to any number of antebellum and other residences that make up one of the largest designated historic areas in Georgia.

ESSENTIALS

Visitor Information Madison-Morgan County Convention & Visitors Bureau. ✉ *115 E. Jefferson St.* ☎ *706/342-4454* ⊕ *www.visitmadisonga.com.*

EXPLORING

Heritage Hall. Madison is the historic heart of Georgia, and although many of the lovely homes are privately owned, this Greek Revival mansion, circa 1811, is open to the public. Rooms are furnished in the 19th-century style and offer insight into the elegant lifestyle of an average well-to-do family. Combo tickets are available to tour Heritage Hall along with two other historic homes within walking distance. ✉ *277 S. Main St.* ☎ *706/342-9627* ⊕ *www.friendsofheritagehall.org* 💲 *$10.*

Madison-Morgan Cultural Center. This 1895 Romanesque Revival building was one of the first brick schools in the area. A museum features a restored 1895 classroom and a replica of an antebellum-era parlor.

There are also art galleries and other exhibits. Check the online calendar for performances and events. ✉ *434 S. Main St.* ☎ *706/342–4743* 🌐 *www.mmcc-arts.org* 🎟 *$5* 🕓 *Closed Mon.*

WHERE TO EAT AND STAY

$$ AMERICAN 🍴 **Madison ChopHouse Grille.** Popular with locals, this casual eatery in the heart of the downtown shopping district offers bar-and-grill classics like sandwiches (called "sammies" here), burgers, steaks, and such Southern specialties as fried pork chops and ribs. While the bar is a focal point, it's a family-friendly joint. **Known for:** fresh-from-the-grill steaks and burgers; casual bar setting. [$] *Average main: $15* ✉ *202 S. Main St.* ☎ *706/342–9009* 🌐 *www.madisonchophouse.com.*

$$$ MODERN AMERICAN 🍴 **Town 220.** Next door to the James Madison Inn, this upscale bistro offers lunch and dinner Tuesday through Saturday. Owner and executive chef Fransisco De La Torre is passionate about fresh, quality ingredients. **Known for:** attentive, knowledgeable service; French cuisine standards. [$] *Average main: $22* ✉ *220 W. Washington St.* ☎ *706/752–1445* 🌐 *www.town220.com* 🕓 *Closed Sun. and Mon.*

$ B&B/INN 🏨 **The Farmhouse Inn.** On a sprawling plot, this country inn offers 5 miles of wooded trails to explore, well-stocked ponds to fish, goats and chickens to feed, and a grassy picnic area to enjoy beside the Apalachee River. **Pros:** a great family destination; room options for individuals and groups. **Cons:** fills up often for weddings and events; remote, farm location not for everyone. [$] *Rooms from: $125* ✉ *1051 Meadow La.* ☎ *706/342–7933* 🌐 *www.thefarmhouseinn.com* 🛏 *5 rooms, 1 house, 1 cottage* 🍽 *Breakfast.*

$$ B&B/INN 🏨 **The James Madison Inn.** In the heart of the historic district, this new building across from Town Park has rooms named for Madison's historic homes. **Pros:** luxurious touches; spa services available. **Cons:** expensive for the size of the rooms. [$] *Rooms from: $199* ✉ *260 W. Washington St.* ☎ *706/342–7040* 🌐 *www.jamesmadisoninn.com* 🛏 *19 rooms* 🍽 *Breakfast.*

SPORTS AND THE OUTDOORS

Southern Cross Guest Ranch. A short drive from Madison you'll see miles upon miles of rolling pastures—an ideal landscape for horses. There are numerous horseback-riding outfits in the area, but one of the best is Southern Cross Guest Ranch. Located 7 miles outside Madison, it offers horseback-riding excursions for $45 to $80 per person. For the horse lovers who can't bear to leave, there are comfy bed-and-breakfast-style accommodations. The ranch offers all-inclusive packages, which include lodging, horseback riding, and meals. ✉ *1670 Bethany Church Rd.* ☎ *706/342–8027* 🌐 *www.southcross.com.*

ATHENS

30 miles northeast of Madison via U.S. 129/441; 70 miles east of Atlanta via I–85 north to Rte. 316.

Athens, an artistic jewel of the American South, is known as a breeding ground for famed rock groups such as the B-52s and R.E.M. Because of this distinction, creative types from all over the country flock to its trendy streets in hopes of becoming, or catching a glimpse of, the next big act to take the world by storm. At the center of this artistic melee is the University of Georgia (UGA). With more than 30,000 students, UGA is an influential ingredient in the Athens mix, giving the quaint but compact city a distinct flavor that falls somewhere between a misty Southern enclave, a rollicking college town, and a smoky, jazz club–studded alleyway. Of course, this all goes "to the Dawgs" if the home team is playing on home turf; although, even then, Athens remains a truly fascinating blend of Mayberry R.F.D. and MTV. The effect is as irresistible as it is authentic.

To find out what's on in Athens, check out the *Athens Banner-Herald* (daily) and the weekly *Flagpole*.

GETTING HERE AND AROUND
Parking can be scarce on the city streets. Leave yourself extra time to find a spot, then take in the city and its shopping, nightlife, campus, and culture on foot. Ride share services like Uber and Lyft are also an option.

The Athens Welcome Center runs historic tours of downtown and surrounding neighborhoods daily at 1 pm. Tours are 90 minutes long and $15 per person.

ESSENTIALS
Visitor Information Athens Convention & Visitors Bureau. ⊠ *300 N. Thomas St.* ☎ *706/357–4430* ⊕ *www.visitathensga.com.*

EXPLORING
TOP ATTRACTIONS
Church-Waddel-Brumby House. The streets of Athens are lined with many gorgeous old homes, some of which are open to the public. Most prominent among them is the Federal-style Church-Waddel-Brumby House. Built in 1820, it is the town's oldest surviving residence. The museum is home to the Athens Welcome Center, where you can pick up information and arrange for tours. ⊠ *280 E. Dougherty St.* ☎ *706/353–1820* ⊕ *www.athenswelcomecenter.com.*

Georgia Museum of Art. On the campus of the University of Georgia, the museum serves a dual purpose as an academic institution and the official public art museum of the state of Georgia. The permanent collection contains a wealth of 19th- and 20th-century paintings—some from noted American artists like Georgia O'Keeffe and Winslow Homer. It also houses the Samuel H. Kress Study Collection of Italian Renaissance art. Special exhibitions display cherished works of art from around the world. ⊠ *90 Carlton St., University of Georgia* ☎ *706/542–4662* ⊕ *www.georgiamuseum.org* ▣ *Free* ☉ *Closed Mon.*

Fodor's Choice ★ **State Botanical Gardens of Georgia.** Just outside the Athens city limits, you'll find this tranquil, 313-acre wonderland of aromatic gardens and woodland paths. It has a massive conservatory overlooking the **International Garden** that functions as a welcome foyer and houses an art gallery, gift shop, and café. ⊠ *2450 S. Milledge Ave., off U.S. 129/441* ☎ *706/542–1244* ⊕ *www.uga.edu/botgarden* ▣ *Free.*

University of Georgia. Athens has several splendid Greek Revival buildings, including two on campus: the **university chapel** built in 1832, just off North Herty Drive, and the **university president's house** that was built in the late 1850s. Easiest access to the campus in downtown Athens is off Broad Street onto either Jackson or Thomas Street, both of which run through the heart of the university. Maps are available at the visitor center. ✉ *570 Prince Ave.* ⊕ *www.uga.edu.*

WORTH NOTING

Taylor-Grady House. Constructed in 1844, the Taylor-Grady House gives a fine sense of history. It has been restored to its 1860s appearance to accurately represent the time when Henry Grady resided here. Grady, a famed newspaper man and booster of the "New South," lived here while he attended the University of Georgia. ✉ *634 Prince Ave.* ☎ *706/549–8688* ⊕ *www.taylorgradyhouse.com* 💵 *$3* ⊗ *Closed weekends.*

T.R.R. Cobb House. Once home to a key author of the Confederate Constitution, T.R.R. Cobb, this historic home has had quite a journey. The Greek Revival structure, with its signature octagonal wings, stands about two blocks from its original location. The house was moved in the 1980s to Stone Mountain, where it sat untouched for 20 years. In 2005, the house was moved back to Athens and meticulously restored. Now open to the public, it details 19th-century Southern life. ✉ *175 Hill St.* ☎ *706/369–3513* ⊕ *www.trrcobbhouse.org* 💵 *$2 suggested donation* ⊗ *Closed Sun. and Mon.*

WHERE TO EAT

$$$$
ECLECTIC
Fodor's Choice
★

✕ **Five & Ten.** This cozy yet sophisticated restaurant put the Athens culinary scene on the map almost two decades ago with chef Hugh Acheson's inventive cuisine that blends European technique with down-home Southern cooking. Acheson, an Ottawa native, honed his culinary skills in classical French kitchens in Ontario and San Francisco before settling in Athens. **Known for:** chef-driven menu focused on local, seasonal ingredients; romantic old-house setting. 💲 *Average main: $28* ✉ *1073 S. Milledge Ave.* ☎ *706/546–7300* ⊕ *www.fiveandten.com.*

$
VEGETARIAN

✕ **The Grit.** This vegetarian paradise has been a favorite in Athens for more than two decades, serving freshly made non-meat food even carnivores adore in the casual comfort of a historic building. A popular dish of browned tofu cubes and brown rice may sound bland, but it's far from it—even the tofu-fearful say it's yummy. **Known for:** vegetarian fare; tasty breakfasts and weekend brunch. 💲 *Average main: $7* ✉ *199 Prince Ave.* ☎ *706/543–6592* ⊕ *www.thegrit.com.*

$$
AMERICAN

✕ **Last Resort Grill.** A favorite of locals and tourists alike, the Last Resort is a popular spot for lunch, dinner, and Sunday brunch. For brunch, entrées like shrimp and grits, stuffed French toast, and breakfast enchiladas please a variety of palates. **Known for:** Sunday brunch; outstanding desserts; inventive Southern cuisine. 💲 *Average main: $17* ✉ *174–184 W. Clayton St.* ☎ *706/549–0810* ⊕ *www.lastresortgrill.com.*

$$$
AMERICAN

✕ **The National.** Little sister to widely acclaimed Five & Ten, the National is more casual, evoking the atmosphere of a European café, with its Mediterranean-inspired dishes that make creative use of local ingredients. Prosciutto-wrapped grilled figs, hummus with lamb, and slow-roasted beef hanger steak are a few favorites. **Known for:** Mediterranean-inspired fare; creative use of local and seasonal ingredients;

14

laid-back, wine-sipping environment. $ *Average main: $24* ✉ *232 W. Hancock Ave.* ☎ *706/549–3450* ⊕ *www.thenationalrestaurant.com.*

$ ✗ **White Tiger Gourmet.** Local foodies flock here for chef Ken Manring's
AMERICAN   delicious smoked meats and burgers at this hip but homey order-at-the-counter restaurant. Housed in an old storefront in the Boulevard Historic District just outside downtown, there aren't many indoor tables, but there's plenty of space to spread out in the picnic area outside. **Known for:** flavorful meats smoked daily; inventive vegetarian dishes; Southern-style Sunday brunch. $ *Average main: $8* ✉ *217 Hiawassee Ave.* ☎ *706/353–6847* ⊕ *www.whitetigergourmet.com* ☽ *No dinner Sun.–Wed.*

WHERE TO STAY

$ 🛏 **Graduate Athens.** This upscale boutique hotel, which underwent a
HOTEL   complete renovation in 2015, offers a full-service spa, restaurant, coffee shop, and a lively nightclub in a villagelike setting. **Pros:** spa, pool, and easy access to amenities; great restaurant and club. **Cons:** live music at on-site restaurant and bar can bring a late crowd; room rates are pricey for university event weekends. $ *Rooms from: $129* ✉ *295 E. Dougherty St.* ☎ *706/549–7020* ⊕ *www.graduateathens.com* ⤢ *122 rooms* ¶O¶ *No meals.*

$$ 🛏 **Hotel Indigo Athens.** Sleek and modern, Hotel Indigo is one of down-
HOTEL   town Athen's newer accommodations. **Pros:** spacious guest rooms; large bathrooms; pet-friendly. **Cons:** fee for parking; pet-friendly aspect may not appeal to all. $ *Rooms from: $179* ✉ *500 College Ave.* ☎ *706/546–0430* ⊕ *www.indigoathens.com* ⤢ *130 rooms* ¶O¶ *No meals.*

NIGHTLIFE

40 Watt Club. This famed indie-rock club is known for helping to launch the careers of R.E.M., the B-52s, and other local bands that grew out of the college scene. Nirvana, the Flaming Lips, and Sonic Youth all played here back in the day. Today, you'll find a mix of local and national acts gracing the stage—from country to punk to pop. ✉ *285 W. Washington St.* ☎ *706/549–7871* ⊕ *www.40watt.com.*

Georgia Theatre. A legendary Athens live music venue, Georgia Theatre continues to host many well-known national and local acts. The historic building once served as a movie theater and Masonic lodge. Catch a show in the theater or head up to the rooftop bar for drinks and snacks. ✉ *215 N. Lumpkin St.* ☎ *706/850–7670* ⊕ *www.georgiatheatre.com.*

▮ EN
ROUTE   Along U.S. 78 you'll find **Washington,** a picturesque community that exudes a bustling turn-of-the-last-century charm and is a great stopover en route to Augusta. The first city chartered in honor of the country's first president, Washington is a living museum of Southern culture. Brick buildings, some of which date to the American Revolution, line the lively downtown area, which bustles with people visiting cafés and antiques shops. The Confederate treasury was moved here from Richmond in 1865, and soon afterward the half-million dollars in gold vanished. This mysterious event has been the inspiration for

numerous treasure hunts, as many like to believe the gold is still buried somewhere in Wilkes County.

Callaway Plantation. Be sure to stop by historic Callaway Plantation, 4 miles west of downtown. Here, at a site dating to 1785, you can experience the closest thing to an operating plantation. Among a cluster of buildings on the estate you can find a blacksmith's house, schoolhouse, and weaving house. An ancient family cemetery is also fun to explore. During the second week of both April and October the estate comes alive with Civil War reenactments and activities such as butter-churning and quilting demonstrations. ⊠ *U.S. 78, 2160 Lexington Rd., Washington* ☎ *706/678–7060* ⌂ *$7* ⏱ *Closed Sun. and Mon.*

AUGUSTA

97 miles southeast of Athens via GA 10 and I–20; 150 miles east of Atlanta via I–20.

Although Augusta escaped the ravages of Union troops during the Civil War, nature itself was not so kind. On a crossing of the Savannah River, the town was flooded many times before modern-day city planning redirected the water into a collection of small lakes and creeks. Now the current is so mild that citizens gather to send bathtub toys downstream every year in the annual Rubber Duck Race.

Check out the *Augusta Daily Chronicle* and the *Metro Spirit* for up-to-the-minute information of what's going on in town.

GETTING HERE AND AROUND

Explore this part of the classic South via car, then park to wander the streets full of shops and restaurants. You can also canoe on the river or along the 1845 tree-lined Augusta Canal, a natural habitat for herons and other birds.

The Augusta Convention & Visitors Bureau, housed in the Augusta Museum of History, conducts Saturday trolley tours throughout the historic district of Augusta ($15). It's a great introduction to the historic city.

ESSENTIALS

Visitor Information Augusta Convention & Visitors Bureau. ⊠ *560 Reynolds St.* ☎ *706/724–4067* ⊕ *www.visitaugusta.com.*

EXPLORING

TOP ATTRACTIONS

FAMILY **Augusta Canal Discovery Center.** Housed in a converted mill in the Augusta Canal National Heritage Area, this museum traces Augusta's important role in developing Georgia's textile industry. The looms are still powered by the building's original turbines; they also provide the power to juice up the museum's Petersburg canal boats. Tours of the **canal,** usually one hour long, start here and are a fascinating trip through history. Guides are well versed in the passing sights, which include assorted wildlife, a working 19th-century textile mill, and two of Georgia's only remaining 18th-century houses. ⊠ *1450 Greene St.* ☎ *706/823–0440* ⊕ *www.augustacanal.com* 🎫 *$6 admission only, $14 with boat tour* 🕐 *Closed Sun. and Mon. in the summer and winter.*

Augusta Museum of History. This museum, in the same building as the Augusta Welcome Center, is a great first stop in understanding Augusta's rich history. Begin your visit by taking a 12,000 year journey through the region's past by touring the permanent exhibition, "Augusta's Story." Other exhibits explore the history of health care in Augusta, the role of the railroads, and, of course, the Masters Tournament. Adults and kids alike will enjoy exploring the Transportation Corridor's 1920s trolley car, a 1914 locomotive, and a reconstructed 1930s gas station. Another favorite is an exhibit devoted to native son, James Brown. ⊠ *560 Reynolds St.* ☎ *706/722–8454* ⊕ *www.augustamuseum.org* 🎫 *$4* 🕐 *Closed Mon.–Wed.*

Augusta Riverwalk. The well-maintained pathways of the Riverwalk (between 5th and 10th Streets) curve along the Savannah River and are the perfect place for a leisurely stroll. The upper brick portion connects downtown attractions like St. Paul's Church and the Morris Museum of Art. There are a few shops and restaurants along the way, but not as many as you might expect. On Saturday mornings between April and November, look out for the Saturday River Market at the 8th Street Plaza. The lower paths offer a close-up view of wildlife and a peek at the graceful homes of North Augusta, South Carolina. ⊠ *5th to 10th Sts.*

Morris Museum of Southern Art. This is a splendid collection of Southern art, from early landscapes, antebellum portraits, and the Civil War period through neo-impressionism and modern contemporary art. The first institution dedicated to Southern art and artists, the museum also holds up to 10 special exhibitions each year bringing important, though sometimes little-known, artists to the forefront. ⊠ *Riverfront Center, 1 10th St., 2nd fl.* ☎ *706/724–7501* ⊕ *www.themorris.org* 🎫 *$5* 🕐 *Closed Mon.*

WORTH NOTING

Meadow Garden. Augusta's oldest residence, Meadow Garden was the home of George Walton, one of Georgia's three signers of the Declaration of Independence. At age 26, he was its youngest signer. ⊠ *1320 Independence Dr.* ☎ *706/724–4174* ⊕ *www.historicmeadowgarden.org* 🎫 *$5* 🕐 *Closed Sun. and Mon.* ↪ *Last tour of the day begins at 3:15.*

Olde Town. Along Telfair and Greene Streets, Olde Town is a restored neighborhood of Victorian homes, although many are still very much works in progress. A drive along Olde Town's streets provides a glimpse of many popular 19th-century architectural styles. ⊠ *Telfair and Greene Sts.*

WHERE TO EAT AND STAY

$ | ✕ **Boll Weevil Cafe and Sweetery.** Named for the insect that ruined the
AMERICAN | cotton industry, this quirky little café on the Riverwalk offers some of the best desserts in Augusta, not to mention soups, sandwiches, and

Southern specialties like fried green tomatoes. Step inside the former warehouse and you'll find a pastry case filled with at least 30 decadent desserts, all made on the premises. **Known for:** decadent desserts; sandwiches on fresh-baked bread. $ *Average main: $13 ⊠ 10 James Brown Blvd.* ☎ *706/722–7772* ⊕ *www.thebollweevil.com.*

$$$$ ✕**Frog Hollow Tavern.** Reservations are recommended at this stylish
AMERICAN downtown restaurant born out of chef-owner Sean Wight's desire to create a sophisticated yet comfortable dining and social club that highlights the freshest local and regional ingredients. Wild-caught shrimp and grits with house-made andouille and local tomatoes, and pan-roasted duck breast are just some of the menu items. **Known for:** attentive service; focus on local and regional ingredients. $ *Average main: $25 ⊠ 1282 Broad St.* ☎ *706/364–6906* ⊕ *www.froghollowtavern.com* ☽ *Closed Sun.–Tues.*

$$ ⊡ **Augusta Marriott at the Convention Center.** Just off the Riverwalk, the
HOTEL Marriott is the city's only full-service downtown hotel. **Pros:** excellent location; indoor and outdoor pool. **Cons:** large and confusing layout. $ *Rooms from: $179 ⊠ 2 10th St.* ☎ *706/722–8900* ⊕ *www.marriott. com* ⤶ *372 rooms* ⦿*No meals.*

$$ ⊡ **The Partridge Inn Augusta, Curio Collection by Hilton.** Perched on top of a
HOTEL hill overlooking Augusta, this National Trust Historic Hotel underwent a multimillion-dollar renovation in 2015 to become part of Hilton's Curio Collection. **Pros:** on-site restaurant known for its outstanding Sunday brunch; complimentary valet parking; relaxing atmosphere. **Cons:** lots of stairs and occasionally uneven floors. $ *Rooms from: $151 ⊠ 2110 Walton Way* ☎ *706/737–8888* ⊕ *www.curiocollection. com* ⤶ *143 rooms* ⦿*No meals.*

SPORTS AND THE OUTDOORS

GOLF

Forest Hills Golf Club. Founded in 1926, Bobby Jones made his "grand slam of golf" here in 1930. The well-kept public course offers tee times seven days a week. *Augusta Magazine* continually names it the "Best Public Golf Course" in the area. Reservations are suggested. ⊠ *1500 Comfort Rd.* ☎ *706/733–0001* ⊕ *www.theforesthillsgolfcourse.com* ⚑ *18 holes. 7231 yds. Par 72. Green Fee: $40/$50. Facilities: Driving range, putting green, pitching area, golf carts, pull carts, rental clubs, pro shop, lessons, restaurant.*

Masters Tournament. In early April, Augusta hosts the much-celebrated annual Masters Tournament, one of pro golf's most distinguished events. It's broadcast in 180 countries. Tickets for actual tournament play are extremely limited for the general public, but you can try to get tickets for one of the practice rounds earlier in the week—which, for golf addicts, is still hugely entertaining.

The Augusta National Golf Club, home of the Masters Tournament, is known for its exclusivity. Membership is handed down through families, so unless you know someone, you aren't going to get to play there, much less get a glimpse of the grounds. However, there are plenty of other golf courses in this golfer's town.

TRAVEL SMART
THE CAROLINAS
AND GEORGIA

Visit Fodors.com for advice, updates, and bookings

GETTING HERE AND AROUND

▌ AIR TRAVEL

Flying time to Atlanta is 4 hours from Los Angeles, 2 hours from New York, 2 hours from Chicago, 2 hours from Dallas, and 9 hours from London. By plane, Charlotte is an hour northeast of Atlanta, Raleigh 75 minutes northeast, Wilmington 1½ hours east, Asheville 1 hour north, and Charleston, Hilton Head, and Savannah an hour east–southeast.

Travelers flying into the Carolinas or Georgia are likely to pass through Hartsfield·Jackson Atlanta International Airport. It's by far the most popular airport in the region, and is the busiest in the world, at least in terms of number of passengers—more than 101 million annually.

AIRPORTS

The sheer number of flights at Hartsfield-Jackson Atlanta International Airport (ATL)—more than 2,600 arriving and departing flights daily—makes it an obvious, if sometimes hectic, choice. With some 308 concessionaires at the airport, it's easy to find a bite to eat or something to read, and Wi-Fi is available throughout, as are laptop plug-in stations. Hartsfield-Jackson has three interfaith chapels; the chapel in the atrium is open from 9 am to 5 pm daily, and the chapels on Concourses E and F are open 24 hours a day. A customer-service office and staffed customer-service desks answer questions. Waiting passengers can also check out museum exhibits throughout the airport, including a display of Martin Luther King Jr. memorabilia on International Concourse E. The international terminal, Concourse F, has several art installations to explore. Smoking areas are located on Concourses B, C, E, F, and T. Overnight visitors can choose from 70 hotels and motels near the airport, most with free shuttle service. Give yourself extra time, as you'll have to tackle crowds whether waiting to buy a burger, getting through

security, or boarding the underground train to other concourses. The airport's website regularly updates estimates of waits at security areas and on-site parking areas. Arrive 90 minutes before a flight in the United States and allow two hours for international flights. Allow enough time to be at the gate 30 minutes before boarding. Those returning rental cars need to allow time for that process and a short ride on the ATL SkyTrain (to the domestic terminal) or a shuttle bus (to the international terminal) from the rental car center. Keep track of laptops and be ready to collect suitcases as soon as they arrive at the carousels for security's sake.

North Carolina's Charlotte Douglas International Airport (CLT), near the border of North Carolina and South Carolina, is a US Airways hub. Although not as vast as Hartsfield-Jackson, Charlotte Douglas is quite large, and its people-moving systems work well. Tired travelers can plop down in one of the trademark, handcrafted white rocking chairs in the Atrium, a tree-lined indoor crossroads between airport concourses that also offers a food court with mostly fast-food outlets. Within a few miles are more than a dozen hotels, most with free airport shuttles. In the center of the state, right off Interstate 40, is Raleigh-Durham International Airport (RDU), a prime gateway into central and eastern North Carolina. Its two terminals serve 11 million passengers annually. Triangle Transit provides bus transportation from the airport to the surrounding communities of Raleigh, Durham, and Chapel Hill. Those who live in the western reaches of the Triangle are just as likely to use the Piedmont Triad International Airport (GSO), at the convergence of four interstates in North Carolina. It primarily serves the Triad area—Greensboro, Winston-Salem, and High Point—as well as some cities in southwestern Virginia.

The portal to western North Carolina is Asheville Regional Airport (AVL), which expanded in 2009 to include amenities like boarding ramps, a gallery featuring regional art, and a guest-services center. It provides nonstop flights to Atlanta, Charlotte, Chicago, New York, Newark, and, in Florida, Fort Lauderdale, Fort Myers, Punta Gorda, Sanford (Orlando), and St. Petersburg.

For visits to the North Carolina coast, fly into Wilmington International Airport (ILM), a small facility with service by two carriers. Upstate South Carolina has the small but user-friendly Greenville–Spartanburg International Airport (GSP), which sometimes has lower fares than either the Charlotte or Asheville airport.

Airport Information Asheville Regional Airport. ✉ *61 Terminal Dr., Fletcher* ☎ *828/684-2226* ⊕ *www.flyavl.com.* **Charlotte Douglas International Airport.** ✉ *5501 Josh Birmingham Pkwy., Charlotte* ☎ *704/359-4000* ⊕ *www.charlotteairport. com.* **Greenville–Spartanburg International Airport.** ✉ *2000 GSP Dr., Suite 1, Greer* ☎ *864/877-7426* ⊕ *www.gspairport.com.* **Hartsfield-Jackson Atlanta International Airport.** ✉ *6000 N. Terminal Pkwy., Atlanta* ☎ *404/530-7300* ⊕ *www.atl.com.* **Piedmont Triad International Airport.** ✉ *1000 A Ted Johnson Pkwy., Greensboro* ☎ *336/665-5600* ⊕ *www.flyfrompti.com.* **Raleigh-Durham International Airport.** ✉ *2400 John Brantley Blvd., Morrisville* ☎ *919/840-7700* ⊕ *www. rdu.com.* **Wilmington International Airport.** ✉ *1740 Airport Blvd., Wilmington* ☎ *910/341-4125* ⊕ *www.flyilm.com.*

GROUND TRANSPORTATION

Of all the airports in the region, only Hartsfield-Jackson Atlanta International is well served by public transportation. The Metropolitan Atlanta Rapid Transit Authority, better known as MARTA, has frequent service to and from the airport. It's the quickest, cheapest, and most hassle-free way into the city. MARTA's north–south line will get you downtown in 15 to 20 minutes for just $2.50. MARTA riders can also travel to Midtown, Buckhead, Sandy Springs, and Doraville—reaching into north suburban Atlanta. MARTA's Airport Station is located inside the terminal and can be accessed from the north and south sides of the terminal near the baggage claim area. Trains run weekdays 4:45 am to 1:15 am, and weekends and holidays 6 am to 1:15 am. Most trains operate every 15 to 20 minutes; during weekday rush hours, trains run every 10 to 15 minutes. You can print out a copy of the rail map from the MARTA website or pick one up at any station.

Charlotte's Area Transit System (CATS) connects passengers to several city center locations with its "Sprinter" express bus service. The Sprinter operates every 20 minutes weekdays 5:29 am to 11:54 pm, and every 30 minutes weekends 6 am to 12:55 am.

Triangle Transit (TT) has an airport bus-shuttle service that connects to Raleigh-Durham International Airport, but the shuttle does not operate on Sunday. The airport shuttle meets TT regional buses at the TT Bus Center in Research Triangle Park.

Most of the airports in the region are served by Uber, taxi, limo, and shuttle services. Private limousine or van services also serve the major airports. In Atlanta, use only approved vehicles with the airport decal on the bumper, which ensure the drivers are charging legal fares and have knowledge of local destinations.

TRANSFERS BETWEEN AIRPORTS

Contacts Charlotte Area Transit System. ☎ *704/336-7433* ⊕ *www.ridetransit.org.* **Metropolitan Atlanta Rapid Transit Authority.** ☎ *404/848-5000* ⊕ *www.itsmarta.com.* **Triangle Transit.** ☎ *919/485-7433* ⊕ *www. triangletransit.org.*

FLIGHTS

Hartsfield-Jackson Atlanta International Airport is the primary hub of Delta Airlines and a focus city for Frontier, Spirit, and Southwest Airlines. Altogether, 21 domestic and international passenger airlines, including their regional carriers, fly into Atlanta. American Airlines has a hub at North Carolina's Charlotte Douglas International Airport, which is also served by more than a dozen other airlines. Raleigh-Durham International is not a hub for any carrier but is serviced by nine airlines. Commuter airlines, including Delta Connection, American Eagle, and United Express have service between many smaller North Carolina airports as well as those in South Carolina. United Express also serves Georgia, New York, Washington, D.C., Chicago, and major Florida airports. Allegiant offers low-fare options to Savannah and Myrtle Beach.

■ BIKE TRAVEL

Throughout coastal Georgia and the Carolinas, hills are few and the scenery is remarkable. Many bike routes are marked on North Carolina's Outer Banks, around Savannah's and Georgia's coastal islands, and in greater Charleston and coastal South Carolina's Lowcountry. Mountain biking trails have popped up all over the Carolinas and North Georgia. The Pisgah National Forest and the Great Smoky Mountains are both national hotbeds for premier mountain biking. Cycling in larger cities in the region, especially Atlanta, can prove difficult. Although bike paths are available, riding on streets is often necessary and can prove daunting.

DeLorme's *Atlas & Gazetteer* state maps, available in bike shops and drugstores, contain useful topographic detail. Many tourist boards and local bike clubs also distribute bike maps.

Websites can also be helpful. Southeastern Cycling (⊕ *www.sadlebred.com*) has information on road and trail riding throughout the Southeast and has free ride maps. Mountain Biking in Western North Carolina (⊕ *www.mtbikewnc. com*) has information on mountain trails. Trails.com (⊕ *www.trails.com*) offers information on more than 30,000 bike trails, including many in Georgia and the Carolinas. A year's subscription costs $49.95; a trial subscription is free.

Bike Maps DeLorme. ⊠ *2 DeLorme Dr., Yarmouth* ☎ *800/561-5105* ⊕ *www.delorme. com.* **Georgia Bikes.** ☎ *706/740-2453* ⊕ *www.georgiabikes.org.* **North Carolina Division of Bicycle and Pedestrian Transportation.** ⊠ *1552 Mail Service Center, Raleigh* ☎ *919/707-2600, 877/368-4968* ⊕ *www.ncdot.gov/bikeped.* **South Carolina Trails Program.** ⊠ *1205 Pendleton St., Columbia* ☎ *803/734-0173* ⊕ *www.sctrails.net.*

■ BOAT TRAVEL

Ferries are a common, and often necessary, way to get around coastal areas, and especially to visit North Carolina's Outer Banks and Georgia's Sea Islands.

The Ferry Division of the North Carolina Department of Transportation operates seven ferry routes over five separate bodies of water: the Currituck and Pamlico sounds and the Cape Fear, Neuse, and Pamlico rivers. Travelers use the three routes between Ocracoke and Hatteras Island, Swan Quarter, and Cedar Island; between Southport and Fort Fisher; and between Cherry Branch and Minnesott Beach. Ferries can accommodate any car, trailer, or recreational vehicle. Pets are permitted if they stay in the vehicle or are on a leash. Telephone and online reservations for vehicles are available for the Cedar Island–Ocracoke and Swan Quarter–Ocracoke routes; on other routes space is on a first-come, first-served basis. Schedules generally vary by season, with the largest number of departures May through October.

Ferries are the only form of public transportation to Sapelo and Cumberland islands in Georgia. The Georgia

Department of Natural Resources operates a ferry between Meridian and Sapelo. Advance reservations are required, and can be made by phone or at the Sapelo Island Visitor Center in Meridian. From March to November a privately run passenger ferry runs daily between St. Marys and Cumberland Island. The rest of the year the ferry does not operate on Tuesday and Wednesday. Reservations are essential, especially in March and April.

In North Carolina the Cedar Island–Ocracoke and Swan Quarter–Ocracoke ferries cost $1 for pedestrians, $3 for bicycles, $10 for motorcycles, and $15 for cars, and up to $45 for other vehicles (trailers, boats, motor homes). The Southport–Fort Fisher ferry costs $1 for pedestrians, $2 for bicycles, $3 for motorcycles, and $5 to $15 for vehicles. Tickets can be purchased with cash or traveler's checks. Personal checks are not accepted. The other North Carolina ferries are free.

In Georgia the pedestrian round-trip ferry to Sapelo Island costs $15 for adults and $10 for children and includes a guided tour of island historical sites. Advanced reservations are required. The pedestrian ferry to Cumberland Island costs $20 round-trip, plus a $4 national park fee.

Boat Information Cumberland Island National Seashore. ⊠ *101 Wheeler St., St. Marys* ☎ *912/882–4336, 877/860–6787,* ⊕ *www.nps.gov/cuis.* **North Carolina Department of Transportation Ferry Division.** ⊠ *8550 Shipyard Rd.* ☎ *800/293–3779* ⊕ *www.ncdot.gov/ferry.* **Sapelo Island Visitor Center.** ⊠ *1766 Landing Rd. SE, Darien* ☎ *912/437–3224* ⊕ *www.sapelonerr.org.*

▮ CAR TRAVEL

A car is the most practical and economical means of traveling around the Carolinas and Georgia. Atlanta, Savannah, Charleston, Myrtle Beach, and Asheville can also be explored fairly easily on foot or by using public transit and cabs, but a car is helpful to reach many of the most intriguing attractions, which are not always downtown. ▮TIP➔ **When returning rental cars to airports, always allow extra time to check in vehicles.**

Although drivers make the best time traveling along the South's extensive network of interstate highways, keep in mind that U.S. and state highways offer some delightful scenery and the opportunity to stumble on funky roadside diners, leafy state parks, and historic town squares. Although the area is rural, it's still densely populated, so travelers rarely drive for more than 20 or 30 miles without passing roadside services, such as gas stations, restaurants, and ATMs.

Among the most scenic highways in the Carolinas and Georgia are U.S. 78, running east–west across Georgia; U.S. 25, 19, 74, and 64, traveling through the Great Smoky Mountains of western North Carolina; U.S. 17 from Brunswick, Georgia, along the coast through South Carolina and North Carolina; and the **Blue Ridge Parkway** from the eastern fringes of the Great Smoky Mountains through western North Carolina into Virginia.

Unlike some other areas of the United States, the Carolinas and Georgia have very few toll roads. Currently, only Georgia State Route 400 in Atlanta, the Cross Island Parkway on Hilton Head, South Carolina, the Southern Connector in Greenville, South Carolina, and the Triangle Expressway in Wake and Durham counties, North Carolina, are toll roads.

RENTAL CARS

It's important to reserve a car well in advance of your expected arrival. Rental rates vary from city to city, but are generally lowest in larger cities where there's a lot of competition. Economy cars cost between $27 and $61 per day, and luxury cars go for $70 to $198. Weekend rates are generally much lower than those on weekdays, and weekly rates usually offer

TRAVEL TIMES AROUND THE CAROLINAS AND GEORGIA BY CAR

From	To	Time/Distance
Atlanta, GA	Savannah, GA	4 hours / 248 miles
Asheville, NC	Great Smoky Mountains National Park, Cherokee entrance	1 hour / 50 miles
Charlotte, NC	Atlanta, GA	4 hours / 244 miles
Charleston, SC	Raleigh, NC	4 hours / 279 miles
Durham, NC	Asheville, NC	3½ hours / 224 miles
Hilton Head, SC	Columbia, SC	2½ hours / 152 miles
Winston-Salem, NC	Charlotte, NC	1½ hours / 84 miles

big discounts. Rates are also seasonal, with the highest rates coming during peak travel times, including Thanksgiving and Christmas holiday seasons. Local factors can also affect rates; for example, a big convention can absorb most of the rental-car inventory and boost rates for those remaining.

Don't forget to factor in the taxes and other add-ons when figuring up how much a car will cost. At Atlanta's Hartsfield-Jackson International Airport, add the 7% sales tax, 11.11% airport concession-recovery fee, 3% city rental car tax, $5 daily customer facility charge, and $0.80 to $1.30 vehicle license-recovery charge. These "miscellaneous charges" mean that a weekly rental can jump in price far higher than the rental agency cost.

Some off-airport locations offer lower rates, and their lots are only minutes from the terminal via complimentary shuttle. Also ask whether certain frequent-flyer, American Automobile Association (AAA), corporate, or other such promotions are accepted and whether the rates might be lower for other arrival and departure dates. National agencies include Alamo, Avis, Dollar, Enterprise, and National Car Rental.

ROADSIDE EMERGENCIES

Travelers in Georgia and the Carolinas have help as close as their cell phones in case of emergencies on roadways. The Georgia Department of Transportation's Intelligent Transportation System works on three levels. First, drivers statewide can call 511 to report problems, get directions, information on traffic, MARTA, and Hartsfield airport. Next, on the 300 miles of metro Atlanta interstate highways, Highway Emergency Response Operators (HEROs) help motorists with everything from empty gas tanks to medical emergencies. Finally, the Georgia Navigator system provides statewide information on the Internet on roadway conditions and, in Atlanta, everything from drive times to incident locations to roadway conditions. Welcome centers statewide can also access that information.

In an emergency, drivers in North Carolina should call 911. In metro areas such as Raleigh, Durham, Burlington, Greensboro, Winston-Salem, Charlotte, and Asheville, and in the Pigeon River Gorge area, drivers on major U.S. highways and interstates receive roadside assistance through the Department of Transportation's Incident Management Assistance Patrols (IMAPs). The IMAP staff remove road debris, change tires, clear stalled vehicles, and can call a private tow truck. Motorists should dial *HP to reach the highway patrol and have an IMAP truck dispatched. In North Carolina's congested metro and construction areas, use the NCDOT Traveler Information Management System (TIMS) on the Internet or via cell phone. Go to ⊕ *www.*

ncdot.org and click the link for "Travel Information." Search for travel updates by region, roadway, or county. Both the Great Smoky Mountains National Park and the Blue Ridge Parkway lure travelers to the state. The state's western area has many narrow, steep, and winding roads near such towns as Asheville, Boone, Sylva, and Waynesville. Use extra caution there, and pay extra attention to winter weather reports for snow and ice when roads may be closed.

South Carolina's Incident Response Program operates on interstate highways in urban areas including Charleston, Columbia, Florence, and the constantly busy Myrtle Beach area (specifically the Highway 17 bypass and U.S. 501). Stranded motorists can call *HP for help and reach the local highway patrol dispatch system. The state operates hundreds of traffic cameras to monitor traffic flow and identify accident sites on all five interstates and in the Myrtle Beach area. They also have a camera at the intersection of Interstate 95 and Interstate 26, in case of hurricane evacuations.

Roadside Assistance Contacts Department of Transportation's Incident Management Assistance Patrols (IMAPs). ☎ *HP ⊕ www.ncdot.org/traffictravel. **Georgia Department of Transportation's Intelligent Transportation System.** ☎ 511, 877/694-2511 ⊕ www.itsga.org/intelligent-transportation-systems-in-georgia. **South Carolina Incident Response Program.** ☎ 855/467-2368, *HP ⊕ www.scdot.org/getting/shep.aspx.

RULES OF THE ROAD

Both of the Carolinas and Georgia prohibit all drivers from texting while driving. Georgia law prohibits drivers under 18 from using cell phones for any purposes. North Carolina allows drivers under 18 to answer phone calls from their parents and to report emergencies. Unless otherwise indicated, motorists may turn right at a red light after stopping if there's no oncoming traffic.

When in doubt, wait for the green. In Atlanta, Asheville, Charleston, Columbia, Charlotte, Savannah, and the Triangle and Triad cities of North Carolina, be alert for one-way streets, "no left turn" intersections, and blocks closed to vehicle traffic.

In Georgia, always strap children under age eight or under 40 pounds (regardless of age) into approved child-safety seats or booster seats appropriate for their height and weight in the back seat. Children younger than age eight and weighing less than 80 pounds must be properly secured in child restraints or booster seats in North Carolina. Child-safety seats or booster seats are required for children younger than six and weighing less than 80 pounds in South Carolina.

Watch your speed, as police are more than happy to write tickets to speedy out-of-towners. In Georgia, a "Super Speeder Law" allows the state to issue an additional $200 fine to drivers exceeding 75 mph on a two-lane road or 85 mph on any roadway.

▌CRUISE SHIP TRAVEL

Carnival has ships to Bermuda, the Bahamas, and the Caribbean that depart from Charleston primarily in spring and fall. Princess Cruises, Holland America, Regent Seven Seas Cruises, and Crystal Cruises occasionally call at Charleston. American Cruise Lines offers intracoastal tours that wind through historic Savannah, Charleston, and Beaufort. Blount Small Ship Adventures hosts an intimate eight-day cruise that begins in Charleston and ends in Jacksonville, Florida.

▌TRAIN TRAVEL

Several Amtrak routes pass through the Carolinas and Georgia; however, many areas are not served by train, and those cities that do have service usually only have one or two arrivals and departures each day. The *Crescent* runs daily through Greensboro, Charlotte, and Atlanta as it travels between New York and New Orleans. Three trains, the *Palmetto,* the *Silver Meteor,* and the *Silver Star* make the daily run between New York and Miami via Raleigh, Charleston, Columbia, and Savannah. The *Carolinian* runs daily from New York to Charlotte, via Raleigh.

Amtrak offers rail passes that allow for travel within certain regions, which can save a lot over the posted fare. Amtrak has several kinds of USA Rail Passes, offering unlimited travel for 15, 30, or 45 days, with rates of $459 to $899, depending on the area traveled, the time of year, and the number of days. Amtrak has discounts for students, seniors, military personnel, and people with disabilities.

ESSENTIALS

■ ACCOMMODATIONS

With the exception of Atlanta, Savannah, Charleston, Asheville, and Charlotte, most lodging rates in the region fall at or below the national average. They do vary a great deal seasonally; however, coastal resorts and mountainous areas tend to have significantly higher rates in summer. Fall color creates demand for lodging in the mountains; expect high-season rates. All major chains are well represented in this part of the country, both in cities and suburbs, and interstates are lined with inexpensive to moderate chains.

In many places, consider forgoing a modern hotel in favor of a historic property. There are dozens of fine old hotels and mansions that have been converted into inns, many of them lovingly restored. Some may offer better rates than chain hotels. Bed-and-breakfasts are big in some cities, notably Charleston, Savannah, and Asheville. Each of these cities has two dozen or more B&Bs. There also are loads of B&Bs in many small towns along the coast and in the North Georgia and western North Carolina mountains.

In many coastal resort areas, vacation-home and condo rentals dominate the lodging scene. The North Carolina Outer Banks, Myrtle Beach, and Hilton Head are major rental areas, each with several thousand rental properties. Rental prices vary by season, with peak summer rental rates that can double or more over off-season rates.

In the North Carolina and Georgia mountains, cabins are popular. These are usually owner-operated businesses with only a few cabins. In Georgia many state parks rent cabins, and they're often excellent values. In the mountains a number of lodges are available. These vary from simple accommodations to deluxe properties with spas, golf courses, and tennis courts. Many attract families that come back year after year. Mountain lodges are closed for several months in winter.

Thousands of families camp in the Carolinas and Georgia. The North Carolina Outer Banks, the Sea Islands of Georgia, and the Great Smoky Mountains National Park and Pisgah and Nantahala national forests in western North Carolina are especially popular with campers.

The lodgings listed are the cream of the crop in each price category.

APARTMENT AND HOUSE RENTALS

The far-flung resort areas of the Carolinas and Georgia are filled with rental properties—everything from cabins to luxury homes. Most often these properties, whether part of a huge corporation or individually owned, are professionally managed; such businesses have become an industry unto themselves.

Carolina Mornings and Carolina Mountain Vacations rent cabins in the high country of North Carolina. Homestead Log Homes has properties in the Pine Mountain area of Georgia. Intracoastal Vacation Rentals has long-term as well as off-season rentals on the coast of Cape Fear. Hatteras Realty, Midgett Realty, and Sun Realty handle properties on North Carolina's Outer Banks. Island Realty focuses on the Charleston and Isle of Palms area in South Carolina. Hilton Head Rentals and Resort Rentals of Hilton Head Island offer rentals on Hilton Head. StayTybee handles properties on Georgia's tiny Tybee Island.

Apartment and House Contacts Carolina Mornings. ☎ *855/398–0712* ⊕ *www.carolinamornings.com.* **Carolina Mountain Vacations.** ☎ *877/488–8500, 877/488–7501* ⊕ *www.carolinamountainvacations.com.*

Hatteras Realty. ☎ 800/428-8372 ⊕ www.hatterasrealty.com. **Hilton Head Rentals.** ⊕ www.hiltonheadrentals.com. **Homestead Log Homes.** ☎ 706/663-4951 ⊕ www.homesteadloghomes.com. **Intracoastal Vacation Rentals.** ☎ 855/346-2463 ⊕ www.intracoastalrentals.com. **Island Realty.** ☎ 843/886-8144, 866/380-3983 ⊕ www.islandrealty.com. **Midgett Realty.** ☎ 252/986-2841, 866/348-8819 ⊕ www.midgettrealty.com. **Resort Rentals of Hilton Head Island.** ☎ 800/845-7017, 843/686-6008 ⊕ www.hhivacations.com. **StayTybee.** ☎ 866/512-0531, 912/786-0531 ⊕ www.staytybee.com. **Sun Realty, Outer Banks.** ☎ 888/853-7770 ⊕ www.sunrealtync.com.

BED-AND-BREAKFASTS

Historic B&Bs and inns are found in just about every region in the Carolinas and Georgia and include quite a few former plantation houses and lavish Southern estates. In many rural or less touristy areas, B&Bs offer an affordable and homey alternative to chain properties. In tourism-dependent destinations, expect to pay about the same as for a full-service hotel. Many of the South's finest restaurants are also found in country inns.

Reservation Services Asheville Bed & Breakfast Association. ☎ 828/250-0200 ⊕ www.ashevillebba.com. **Association of Historic Inns of Savannah.** ☎ 912/232-5678 ⊕ www.historicinnsofsavannah.com. **Romantic Inns of Savannah.** ⊕ www.romanticinnsofsavannah.com. **South Carolina Bed & Breakfast Association.** ⊕ www.southcarolinabedandbreakfast.com.

CAMPING

The Carolinas and Georgia are popular for trailer and tent camping, especially in state and national parks. Georgia offers camping sites at more than 40 state parks, including four along its Atlantic coastline: River's End on Tybee Island, Jekyll Island, Cumberland Island, and Sapelo Island. In South Carolina a similar number of state parks offer campsites. North Carolina's unique coastline offers primitive campsites on beachfronts and among southern swamp forests and sounds, including Hammocks Beach State Park on Bear Island. There are 29 other state parks that offer campsites across the state. For detailed information on the state parks and to reserve a site, visit the state parks' websites.

A variety of camping experiences are available at Great Smoky Mountains National Park, including backcountry and horse camping. Reservations for Elkmont, Smokemont, Cades Cove, and Cosby, the park's most popular developed campgrounds (with flush toilets and running water), are required from May 15 to October 31. Camping outside those dates or at the parks' other campgrounds is first-come, first-served.

Camping Contacts Georgia State Parks. ☎ 800/864-7275 ⊕ www.gastateparks.org. **Great Smoky Mountains National Park.** ☎ 865/436-1200 ⊕ www.nps.gov/grsm. **North Carolina State Parks.** ☎ 877/722-6762 ⊕ www.ncparks.gov. **South Carolina State Parks.** ☎ 866/345-7275 ⊕ www.southcarolinaparks.com.

HOME EXCHANGES

With a direct home exchange you stay in someone else's home while they stay in yours. Some outfits also deal with vacation homes, so you're not actually staying in someone's full-time residence, just their vacant weekend place.

HOTELS

In summer, especially July and August, hotel rooms in coastal areas and the mountains can be hard to come by unless you book well in advance. In the mountains, the autumn leaf-peeping season, typically early October to early November, is the busiest time of the year, and on weekends nearly every room is booked. Lodging in North Carolina's Triad area is difficult during the twice-yearly international furniture shows: in April and October all rooms are booked within a 30-mile radius of the show's location in High Point. Lodging in downtown

Atlanta, despite its density of hotels, can be problematic during trade shows at the Georgia World Congress Center and the AmericasMart complex.

Some of the most interesting hotels in the region are housed in historic buildings, particularly in well-preserved old cities like Charleston and Savannah. To find notable historic hotels throughout the region, visit the National Trust for Historic Preservation's Historic Hotels of America website (⊕ *www.historichotels.org*).

▌ EATING OUT

The increase of international flavors in the region reflects the tastes and backgrounds of the people who have flooded into the Carolinas and Georgia over the past couple of decades. Bagels are as common nowadays as biscuits, and, especially in urban areas, it can be harder to find country cooking than a plate of hummus. For the most part, though, plenty of traditional Southern staples—barbecue, fried chicken, greens, and the like—are available.

Atlanta now has a big-city mix of neighborhood bistros, ethnic eateries, and expense-account restaurants. A new wave of restaurants in Charleston and Savannah serves innovative versions of Lowcountry cooking, with lighter takes on traditional dishes. In North Carolina, you can find some nationally recognized restaurants in Charlotte, Asheville, and Durham. Outside the many resort areas along the coast and in the mountains, dining costs in the region are often lower than those in the North.

Vegetarians will have no trouble finding attractive places to eat in any of the larger metropolitan areas, although in small towns they may have to stick with pizza. Asheville is a haven for vegetarians; it has been named in many lists of the top vegetarian cities, including being named the most vegetarian-friendly city in the United States by People for the Ethical Treatment of Animals (PETA).

The food truck scene has made its way to most major cities in the Carolinas and Georgia, providing a quick way to grab decently priced cross-cultural eats at all hours. Websites like Roaming Hunger (⊕ *www.roaminghunger.com*) provide details on local food truck whereabouts.

For some of the best food in the region, seek out restaurants that specialize in "farm to table" cuisine and frequently change their menus to feature the season's best produce. In the coastal regions, try the seafood shacks by the docks where fresh seafood is virtually guaranteed.

MEALS AND MEALTIMES

The Southern tradition of Sunday dinner—usually a midday meal—has morphed to some degree, at least in urban areas, to Sunday brunch. For many people this meal follows mid-morning church services, so be advised that restaurants will often be very busy through the middle of the day. In smaller towns many restaurants are closed Sunday. On weekdays in larger cities, restaurants will be packed with nearby workers from before noon until well after 1:30 pm. On Saturday, eateries in cities can be packed from morning through night. In small towns and big cities, weekday nights—when crowds are less likely and the staff can offer diners more time—can be the most pleasant for fine dining.

Southerners tend to eat on the early side, with lunch crowds beginning to appear before noon. The peak time for dinner is around 7. However, late-evening dining is not unusual in big cities, college towns, and tourist destinations.

RESERVATIONS AND DRESS

For the most part, restaurants in the Carolinas and Georgia tend to be informal. A coat and tie are rarely required, except in a few of the fanciest places. Business-casual clothes are safe almost anywhere.

WINES, BEER, AND SPIRITS

Blue laws—legislation forbidding sales on Sunday—have a history in this region dating to the 1600s. These bans are still observed in many rural areas, particularly with regard to alcohol sales. Liquor stores are closed Sunday in the Carolinas. Beer and wine can't be sold anywhere before noon in North Carolina and South Carolina on Sunday. There are entire counties in the Carolinas and Georgia that prohibit the sale of alcoholic beverages in restaurants. Some cities and towns allow the sale of beer and wine in restaurants, but not mixed drinks. In North Carolina, bottled distilled spirits are sold only through "ABC" (Alcoholic Beverage Control) outlets; beer and wine are available in most grocery and convenience stores.

Although the Carolinas and Georgia will never be the Napa Valley, the last decade has seen a huge increase in the number of vineyards. North Carolina now has more than 150 wineries, and the Yadkin Valley is the state's first federally recognized American Viticultural Area, with more than 400 acres of vineyards in production. Asheville Biltmore Estate Wine Company is the most popular winery in the United States, with about 1 million visitors each year. Georgia's Wine Highway, which guides visitors to a number of wineries, runs from just north of Atlanta up through the North Georgia mountains. Muscadine and scuppernong grapes are native to warmer parts of the region; the sweetish wine from these grapes is gaining more respect. Traditional wine grapes are also widely grown.

Microbreweries are common all over the region, with hot spots being Atlanta, Asheville, Wilmington, Charlotte, and Charleston, as well as the Triangle of Raleigh, Durham, and Chapel Hill. There are more than 170 microbreweries in North Carolina, some two dozen in South Carolina, and more than 50 in Georgia, despite state laws on alcohol distribution that have crimped their growth.

▌HEALTH

With the exception of the mountains of North Georgia and western North Carolina, in the Carolinas and Georgia, it's hot and humid for at least six months of the year. Away from the coast, midsummer temperatures can reach the high 90s, making heat exhaustion and heatstroke real possibilities. Heat exhaustion is marked by muscle cramps, dizziness, nausea, and profuse sweating. To counter its effects, lie down in a cool place with your head slightly lower than the rest of the body. Sip cool, not cold, fluids. Life-threatening heatstroke is caused by a failure of the body to effectively regulate its temperature. In the early stages, heatstroke causes fatigue, dizziness, and headache. Later the skin becomes hot, red, and dry (due to lack of sweating), and body temperatures rise to as high as 106°F. Heatstroke requires immediate medical care.

At the beach or anywhere in the sun, slather on sunscreen. Reapply it every two hours, or more frequently after swimming or perspiring. Remember that many sunscreens block only the ultraviolet light called UVB, but not UVA, which may be a big factor in skin cancer. Even with sunscreen it's important to wear a hat and protective clothing and to avoid prolonged exposure to the sun.

The coastal areas of the Carolinas and Georgia, especially the swamps and marshes of the Lowcountry, are home to a variety of noxious bugs: mosquitoes, sand flies, biting midges, black flies, chiggers, and no-see-ums. Most are not a problem when the wind is blowing, but when the breezes die down—watch out! Experts agree that DEET is the most effective mosquito repellent, but this chemical is so powerful that strong concentrations can melt plastic. Repellents with 100% DEET are available, but those containing 30% or less should work fine for adults; children should not use products with more than 10%.

Products containing the chemical picaridin are effective against many insects, and don't have the strong odor or skin-irritating qualities of those with DEET. The plant-based oil of lemon eucalyptus, used in some natural repellents, performed well in some studies. Mosquito coils and citronella candles also help ward off mosquitoes.

For sand flies or other tiny biting bugs, repellents with DEET alone are often not effective. What may help is dousing feet, ankles, and other exposed areas with an oily lotion, such as baby oil, which effectively drowns them.

The mountains of western North Carolina and North Georgia generally have few mosquitoes or other biting bugs, but in warm weather hikers may pick up chiggers or ticks. Use repellents with DEET on exposed skin. Wasps, bees, and small but ferocious yellow jackets are common throughout the region.

Feel free to drink tap water everywhere in the region, although in coastal areas it may have a sulfur smell. Many visitors to the beaches prefer to buy bottled water.

▌ MONEY

Although the cost of living remains fairly low in most parts of the South, travel-related costs (such as dining, lodging, and transportation) have become increasingly steep in Atlanta. Tourist attractions are pricey, too. For example, a tour of CNN Center is $16, admission to the High Museum of Art in Atlanta is $14.50, and getting into Georgia Aquarium is a steep $35.95. Costs can also be dear in resort communities throughout the Carolinas and Georgia.

If you plan on seeing multiple attractions in a city, look for money-saving passes sold at local visitor centers. Atlanta, for instance, participates in the national CityPASS program. The pass includes admission to six key attractions for $75, which is half of what you'd pay if buying individual admissions. Check out ⊕ *www. citypass.com* for more information.

Prices throughout this guide are given for adults. Substantially reduced fees are almost always available for children, students, military personnel, and senior citizens.

▌ PACKING

Smart but casual attire works fine almost everywhere. A few chic restaurants in the cities prefer more elegant dress, and tradition-minded lodges in the mountains and resorts along the coast still require jackets and ties for men at dinner. For colder months pack a lightweight coat, slacks, and sweaters; bring along heavier clothing in some mountainous areas, where cold, damp weather prevails and snow is not unusual. Keeping summer's humidity in mind, pack absorbent natural fabrics that breathe; bring an umbrella, but leave the plastic raincoat at home. A jacket or sweater is useful for summer evenings and for too-cool air-conditioning. And don't forget insect repellent and sunscreen.

▌ SAFETY

In general, the Carolinas and Georgia are safe destinations for travelers. Most rural and suburban areas have low crime rates. However, some of the region's larger cities, such as Atlanta, have high crime rates.

In urban areas, follow proven traveler's precautions: don't wander onto deserted streets after dark, avoid flashing large sums of money or fancy jewelry, and keep an eye on purses and backpacks. If walking, even around the historic district, ask about areas to avoid at a hotel or a tourist information center; if in doubt, take a taxi.

In the Smoky Mountains the greatest concerns are driving on some of the curving and narrow roads—sometimes in heavy traffic—and theft of property and credit cards from vehicles in parking lots. Sometimes thieves will watch for motorists locking valuables in their trunks before leaving their cars. Single-car collisions, with motorists hitting trees or rocky outcroppings, are the cause of most accidents. Stolen property is rare in campsites. Drivers should also keep in mind that cell phones don't often work in the park. If visitors encounter bears, they are advised not to move suddenly, but to back away slowly.

▮ TAXES

Sales taxes are: Georgia 4%, North Carolina 4.75%, and South Carolina 6%. Some counties or cities may impose an additional sales tax of 1% to 3%. Most municipalities also levy a lodging tax (usually exempting small inns) and sometimes a restaurant tax. The hotel taxes in the South can be rather steep—as much as 8% in some places in Georgia and many counties in North Carolina. Taxes and fees on car rentals, especially if rented from an airport, can easily add 30% or more to the bill.

▮ TIME

Georgia and the Carolinas fall in the Eastern Standard Time (EST) zone, which is the same as New York and Florida, making it three hours ahead of California.

▮ TIPPING

Tipping in the Carolinas and Georgia is essentially the same as tipping anywhere else in the United States. A bartender typically receives from $1 to $5 per round of drinks, depending on the number of drinks. Tipping at hotels varies with the level of the hotel, but here are some general guidelines: bellhops should be tipped $1 to $5 per bag; if doormen help to hail a cab, tip $1 to $2; maids should receive $1 to $3 in cash daily; room-service waiters get $1 to $2 even if a service charge has been added;

and tip concierges $5 or more, depending on what service they perform.

Taxi drivers should be tipped 15% to 20% of the fare, rounded up to the next dollar amount. Tour guides receive 10% of the cost of the tour. Valet parking attendants receive $1 to $2 when you get your car back. Tipping at restaurants varies from 15% to 20% by level of service and level of restaurant, with 20% being the norm at high-end restaurants.

▮ TOURS

The Carolinas and Georgia predominantly attract visitors traveling independently, usually by car. But some areas—notably Savannah, Charleston, Asheville, and the Great Smoky Mountains—get a number of escorted bus tours. Collette Vacations offers a seven-day "Southern Charm" tour featuring stops in Charleston, Savannah, and Jekyll Island. The escorted tour prices start at $1,799 per person. You stay at first-class hotels, such as the Jekyll Island Club, and the price includes most breakfasts and some dinners. Tauck has an eight-day tour of Charleston, Savannah, Jekyll Island, and Hilton Head, staying at such high-end hotels as the Omni Oceanfront Resort on Hilton Head. The cost is $3,190 per person. For one-stop-shopping, check with specialty travel agencies like Affordable Tours, which offers a variety of tour operators and discounted prices.

▮ VISITOR INFORMATION

Going online is the fastest way to get visitor information, and all of the state tourism offices listed below have excellent websites, with maps and other travel information. However, if you'd like to visit an actual visitor information center, Georgia Travel and Tourism has 12 official centers around the state, including a location at Hartsfield-Jackson Atlanta International Airport.

Contacts Georgia Travel and Tourism. ⊠ *Buckhead* ☎ *800/847–4842* ⊕ *www. exploregeorgia.org.* **North Carolina Travel & Tourism Division.** ⊠ *301 N. Wilmington St., Raleigh* ☎ *800/847–4862* ⊕ *www.visitnc. com.* **South Carolina Department of Parks, Recreation, and Tourism.** ⊠ *1205 Pendleton St., Room 248, Columbia* ☎ *803/734–1700, 866/224–9339* ⊕ *www.discoversouthcaro-lina.com.*

ONLINE TRAVEL TOOLS
ALL ABOUT THE CAROLINAS AND GEORGIA
Civil War Traveler. This website has information about Civil War sites in the Carolinas and Georgia, as well as in other states. ⊕ *www.civilwartraveler.com.*

Doc South. At this website you'll find a vast collection of historical documents and archives on Southern history, culture, and literature. ⊕ *docsouth.unc.edu.*

Dr. Beach. Dr. Stephen Leatherman offers his take on the best beaches nationwide. In 2016, two Carolina beaches made his top 10 beaches list: Ocracoke, on the Outer Banks in North Carolina, was No. 4; in South Carolina, Kiawah Island's Beachwalker Park was No. 10. ⊕ *www. drbeach.org.*

Garden & Gun. The online version of this popular magazine focused on Southern culture features travel and food articles on many Georgia and Carolinas destinations. ⊕ *www.gardenandgun.com.*

Southern Living. The online edition of Southern Living has many articles on travel, attractions, gardens, and people in the region. ⊕ *www.southernliving.com.*

ART AND CULTURE
Gullah Culture. From the PBS program with Bill Moyers, this is a good introduction to Gullah life and culture. ⊕ *www.pbs.org/now/arts/gullah.html.*

Handmade in America. The goal of this community organization is to establish western North Carolina as the nation's center of handmade objects. ⊕ *www. handmadeinamerica.org.*

FODORS.COM CONNECTION

Before your trip, be sure to check out what other travelers are saying in the Forums on ⊕ www.fodors.com.

Penland School of Crafts. This website is devoted to the famous crafts school in the North Carolina Mountains, but it also has a wealth of information on crafts in the region. ⊕ *www.penland.org.*

Southern Highland Craft Guild. The guild represents more than 900 craftspeople in the Southeast. ⊕ *www.southernhighland-guild.org.*

GOLF
Georgia State Park Golf Courses. Search this website for detailed information on Georgia's public golf courses. ⊕ *www. georgiagolf.com.*

Golf Guide. This online guide has links to most golf courses in the Carolinas and Georgia. ⊕ *www.golfguideweb.com.*

Golf Link. This website offers information on nearly all the golf courses in the region. ⊕ *www.golflink.com.*

Golf North Carolina. Search a database of North Carolina's 400 golf courses on this website. In addition to the usual course information, this site has sections on golf tips and area information. ⊕ *www.golf-northcarolina.com.*

OUTDOORS
Appalachian Trail Conservancy. The conservancy is dedicated to preserving the nation's longest footpath, which runs from Georgia all the way to Maine. ⊕ *www.appalachiantrail.org.*

Blue Ridge Parkway. Log on to this site for detailed information on one of the most beautiful roads in America. ☎ *828/298–0398* ⊕ *www.blueridgeparkway.org.*

Georgia State Parks. The parks' website covers accommodations, recreational activities, and special activities at one of the best state park systems in the United States. ⊕ *www.gastateparks.org.*

National Forests in North Carolina. A comprehensive guide to the state's national forests. ☎ *828/257–4200* ⊕ *www.fs.usda. gov/nfsnc.*

National Park Service. The website offers information on all of the national parks in the region, including the Great Smoky Mountains, the country's most popular national park. ☎ *865/436–1200* ⊕ *www. nps.gov/grsm.*

North Carolina State Parks. Basic information on state parks is available on the website. ⊕ *www.ncparks.gov.*

South Carolina State Parks. This colorful site features information on accommodations, outdoor activities, and even discounts offered at the parks. ☎ *803/734–0156* ⊕ *www.southcarolinaparks.com.*

WINE

Georgia Wine Country. The excellent site for Georgia Wine Country has information on almost 75 wineries in Georgia. ⊕ *www.georgiawinecountry.com.*

North Carolina Wines. This comprehensive site offers facts on more than 150 wineries in North Carolina. ⊕ *www.visitncwine.com.*

Winegrowers Association of Georgia. A guide to touring and tasting at Georgia's wineries. ⊕ *www.georgiawine.com.*

INDEX

PHOTO CREDITS

Front cover: Ricksause I Dreamstime.com [Description: Sunrise at the Outer Banks, North Carolina]. 1, Robb Helfrick. 2-3, Jeff Greenberg / age fotostock. 5, Pat & Chuck Blackley /Alamy. **Chapter 1: Experience the Carolinas and Georgia.** 8-9, Bill Russ/NC Tourism. 18 (all), Bill Russ/NC Tourism. 19 (left, top center and right), Bill Russ/NC Tourism. 19 (bottom center), John Barreiros/Flickr. 20 (left), William Struhs. 20 (top center), wjarrettc/Flickr. 20 (bottom center), Michael G Smith/Shutterstock. 20 (right), Brian Stansberry/Wikimedia Commons. 21 (left), Middleton Place. 21 (top center), Tim Brown Architects/Flickr. 21 (bottom center), Riverbanks Zoo and Garden. 21 (right), Lorie McGraw/iStockphoto. 22 (left), Robb Helfrick. 22 (top center), Rickey Bevington. 22 (bottom center), Georgia Department of Economic Development. 22 (right), Brittany Somerset. 23 (left), Georgia Department of Economic Development. 23 (top right), Georgia Department of Economic Development 23 (bottom right), Georgia Department of Economic Development. **Chapter 2: The North Carolina Coast.** 39, MarkVanDykePhotography / Shutterstock, 41 (both), Bill Russ/NC Tourism. 42, Brian Leon/ Flickr. 43 (top and bottom), Bill Russ/NC Tourism. 44, Bill Russ/NC Tourism. 55 and 57, Bill Russ/NC Tourism. 62, Robb Helfrick. 70, Pat & Chuck Blackley / Alamy. 80, Gianna Stadelmyer/Shutterstock. 86, Bill Russ/NC Tourism. **Chapter 3: Central North Carolina.** 95, SeanPavonePhoto/iStockphoto, 97 (bottom), Bill Russ/NC Tourism. 98, Coralimages2020 I Dreamstime.com. 106, Bill Russ/NC Tourism. 114, Bill Russ/NC Tourism. 128, Old Salem Museums & Gardens. 135, Johnny Stockshooter / age fotostock. 141, nickledford/Flickr. 144, Historic Latta Plantation. **Chapter 4: Asheville and the North Carolina Mountains.** 149, Awakenedeye I Dreamstime.com. 151, Bill Russ/NC Tourism. 152, Bill Russ/NC Tourism. 161, Fotoluminate LLC / Shutterstock. 185 and 188, Bill Russ/NC Tourism. 192-193 and 198, Robb Helfrick. **Chapter 5: Great Smoky Mountains National Park.** 201, jo Crebbin / Shutterstock. 203 (top), National Park Service photo. 203 (bottom), cwwycoff1/Flickr. 204, keith011764/Flickr. 224-25, Bill Russ/NC Tourism. 226 (left), Jlaessle/Wikimedia Commons. 226 (top center), Bernard B. ILarde/Wikimedia Commons. 226 (bottom center), Mary Terriberry/Shutterstock. 226 (bottom right), rjones0856/Flickr. 226 (top right), pellaea/Flickr. 227 (left), Jean-Pol GRANDMONT/WIkimedia Commons. 227 (top center), Steffen Foerster Photography/Shutterstock. 227 (bottom center), WiZZiK/Wikimedia Commons. 227 (bottom right), Derek Ramsey/Wikimedia Commons. 227 (top right), John Seiler/iStockphoto. 228, Kord.com / age fotostock. 229 (left), Thomas Takacs/iStockphoto. 229 (right), Jeff Greenberg / age fotostock. 230, Pat & Chuck Blackley / Alamy. 233, Paul Tessier / Shutterstock. 235, Heeb Christian / age fotostock. 241, M Blankenship/Shutterstock. **Chapter 6: Myrtle Beach, SC, and the Grand Strand.** 251, Myrtle Beach Area CVB. 253 (top), Stacie Stauff Smith Photography/Shutterstock. 253 (bottom) and 254, Myrtle Beach Area CVB. 255 (top), Stacie Stauff Smith Photography/Shutterstock. 255 (bottom), Myrtle Beach Area CVB. 256, Brookgreen Gardens. 262, Bob Pardue - SC / Alamy. 282, StacieStauffSmith Photos / Shutterstock. **Chapter 7: Charleston, SC.** 289, f11photo/Shutterstock. 291 (top), William Struhs. 291 (bottom), Charleston Area CVB for / www.Explorecharleston.com. 292, Charleston Area CVB. 296, Richard Cummins /age fotostock. 300, Muffet/Flickr, [CC BY 2.0]. 302, Gabrielle Hovey/Shutterstock. 304, Richard Cummins / age fotosock. 306, Rainer Kiedrowski / age fotostock. 308, Pgiam/iStockphoto. 319, Richard Cummins/age fotostock. 333, Robb Helfrick. **Chapter 8: Hilton Head, SC, and the Lowcountry.** 339-343 (top), Hilton Head Island Visitor & Convention Bureau. 343 (bottom), Alison Lloyd, Fodors.com member. 344, Hilton Head Island Visitor & Convention Bureau. 345 (bottom), Otokimus/Shutterstock. 345 (top), Ron Diggity/Flickr. 346, Kendra Natter, Fodors.com member. 353, Eric Horan/age fotostock. 362, Hilton Head Island Visitor & Convention Bureau. 365, Courtesy of the Hilton Head Island Visitor & Convention Bureau. **Chapter 9: The Midlands and the Upstate, SC.** 379, SuperStock/age fotostock. 381 (top and bottom), L Barnwell/Shutterstock. 382, Richard Cummins / age fotostock. 387, Gabrielle Hovey/Shutterstock. 393, Tashka I Dreamstime.com. 401, Robert D. Howell / Shutterstock. **Chapter 10: Savannah, GA.** 405, Sepavo I Dreamstime.com. 407 (top), Georgia Department of Economic Development. 407 (bottom), William Britten/iStockphoto. 408, Katherine Welles/iStockphoto. 412-413, Robb Helfrick. 422, trinum/iStockphoto. 427, Georgia Department of Economic Development. 433, Clicksy/Flickr. **Chapter 11: Georgia's Coastal Isles and the Okefenokee.** 437, Robb Helfrick. 439, Barbara Kraus/iStockphoto. 440, Georgia Department of Economic Development. 441 (bottom), Jo Jakeman/Flickr. 441 (top), Brandon Laufenberg/iStockphoto. 442, Robb Helfrick. 447 and 451, Georgia Department of Economic Development. 458, Jekyll Island Museum and Jekyll Island Club Hotel. 462, dougandme/Flickr. 466, Robb Helfrick. **Chapter 12: Southwest Georgia.** 471, Cyrille Gibot / age fotostock. 473 (top), Jeffrey M. Frank/Shutterstock. 473 (bottom), Georgia Department of Economic Development. 474, Mona Makela/Shutterstock. 475 (bottom), Jaimie Duplass/Shutterstock. 475 (top), Yuan Tian/iStockphoto. 476, Oberstark I Dreamstime.com. 482, Durden Images / Shutterstock. 486, Georgia Department of Economic Development. 488, Robb Helfrick. **Chapter 13: Atlanta, GA.** 491, Walter Bibikow / age fotostock. 492 (left), Georgia Department of Economic Development. 492 (right), Kevin Rose/AtlantaPhotos.com. 494, Ian Dagnall / Alamy. 495 (top), Georgia Department of Economic Development. 495 (bottom), Wikimedia Commons. 496, Georgia Department of Economic Development. 503, Kevin Rose/AtlantaPhotos.com. 507, Mondan80 I Dreamstime.com. 509, John E Davidson / age fotostock. 513, Atlanta History Center. 524, Appalachianviews I Dreamstime.com. **Chapter 14: Central and North Georgia.** 545 and 547, Georgia Department of Economic Development. 548, Robb Helfrick. 555 (top), divemaster-king2000/Flickr. 555 (bottom), Library of Congress Prints and Photographs Division. 556 (top left and top center), Wikimedia Commons. 556 (top right, center, bottom left, and bottom right) and 557 (top and bottom left), Library of Congress Prints and Photographs division. 557 (bottom right), Wikimedia Commons. 558 (top left), Blair Howard/iStockphoto. 558 (bottom), Legacy Images by Violet Clark/Flickr. 558 (top right), divemasterking2000/Flickr. 559, Jeffrey M. Frank/Shutterstock. 560 (left) Georgia Department of Economic Development. 560 (right), Mikephotos I Dreamstime.com. 563, Ian Dagnall / Alamy. 566, Three Sisters Vineyards. 571 and 575, Georgia Department of Economic Development. 581, Robb Helfrick. 582, Georgia Department of Economic Development. **Back cover, from left to right:** Artazum and Iriana Shiyan / Shutterstock; Appalachianviews I Dreamstime.com; StacieStauffSmith Photos / Shutterstock. **Spine:** Jill Lang/iStockphoto.

NOTES

ABOUT OUR WRITERS

A midwestern native, Michele Foust has learned what keeps Georgia on people's minds. She spent years editing business, metro, and feature stories for the *Atlanta Journal-Constitution* and ajc.com before becoming a freelance writer fulltime. She lives with her husband, Scott, and two rescue dogs, and savors the colorful fall foliage in North Georgia's mountains. She updated the Experience chapter this edition.

Oak Park, Illinois, native Chanté LaGon has nearly two decades' experience in all things word-related, from news features to poetry. She moved to Atlanta in the late '90s to join the *Atlanta Journal-Constitution,* and later served as Managing Editor for the weekly *Creative Loafing.* She combined her love of music and words as founding editor of a hip-hop magazine while in North Carolina, where she attended college, and has been an integral part of that scene in Atlanta, along with the electronic music, nightlife, arts and culture scenes there. She edited the Atlanta chapter for this edition.

Stratton Lawrence settled in Charleston after graduating from Davidson College, preceded by the rambling childhood of a Navy brat. A former staff writer at *Charleston City Paper,* he's a frequent contributor to *Charleston Magazine* and the Post and Courier's *Charleston Scene.* He lives with his wife, photographer Hunter McRae, on Folly Beach, where he drew inspiration for his first book, *Images of America: Folly Beach,* released in 2013 by Arcadia Publishing. For this edition he updated the Charleston, Myrtle Beach, and Midlands and the Upstate, SC chapters.

Sally Mahan is originally from Detroit. She fell in love with the Lowcountry several years ago when she moved to Savannah to work at the *Savannah Morning News.* She left the Lowcountry to work as an editor in Key West, and then went back to Michigan to work at the *Detroit Free Press.* However, her heart remained in the Lowcountry. In 2004, she settled in her adopted hometown of Bluffton, SC, just minutes from Hilton Head Island. She updated the Hilton Head and Travel Smart chapters for this edition.

Rachel Roberts Quartarone is a Georgia native with deep Southern roots. Her family has been firmly planted in North Georgia for more than five generations. She resides in Atlanta with her husband and two sons. As a journalist and museum consultant, she enjoys writing about her passions—history, food, travel, and Southern culture. For this guide, she updated the North and Central Georgia and Southwest Georgia chapters.

A product of the Deep South, Summer Teal Simpson Hitch began her writing career after a happenstance move to Savannah, Georgia, led her to follow her passion and pursue a livelihood in writing and journalism. She is highly food (and wine) motivated, dive certified, and collects vintage Eva Zeisel, deer antlers, and local contemporary art. She is a contributor to *Savannah Magazine, South Magazine,* and *Connect Savannah,* as well as local blogs. She has been a Fodor's contributor since 2011 and updated the Savannah and Georgia's Coastal Isles and the Okefenokee chapters.

Asheville native and former New Orleans newspaper editor and publisher Lan Sluder has written more than a dozen books on travel and retirement subjects. That includes *Fodor's Belize*, *Easy Belize*, *Amazing Asheville*, and *Moving to the Mountains*. His articles have appeared in publications worldwide including *Caribbean Travel & Life*, the *New York Times*, Canada's *Globe & Mail*, the Travel Channel website, *Bangkok Post*, the *Tico Times*, *Where to Retire*, and the *Chicago Tribune*. Lan's home base in North Carolina is a 250-acre mountain farm near Asheville, settled by his ancestors in the mid-1800s. His hobbies include restoring vintage Airstream trailers and Rolls-Royce motor cars, bridge (he wrote a book on learning to play this card game), following the Yankees, and he is an avid beekeeper. Lan has for many years authored the Asheville and the North Carolina Mountains and Great Smoky Mountains National Park chapters as well as the "Great Smoky Mountains Through the Seasons" feature for this guide. He also worked on the North Carolina Coast chapter this edition.

Kristen Wile is an editor at the city magazine of Charlotte, North Carolina, where she focuses on dining. She loves learning about cities through food, and her husband Jon is always a willing sidekick—as are their two rescue pitbulls (although they're not always invited). She updated the Central North Carolina chapter this edition.